Rereading the Bible

Rereading the Bible

An Introduction
to the
Biblical Story

J. Bradley Chance
Milton P. Horne

Department of Religion
William Jewell College

Prentice Hall   Upper Saddle River, NJ 07458

Library of Congress Cataloging-in-Publication Data

Chance, J. Bradley.
   Rereading the Bible : an introduction to the biblical story /
  J. Bradley Chance and Milton P. Horne.
     p.   cm.
  Includes bibliographical references and index.
  ISBN 0-13-674276-9
  1. Bible Introduction.   I. Horne, Milton P.   II. Title.
  BS475.2 .C43 2000
  220.6'1—dc21

                      99-21603
                      CIP

Editor-in-Chief: Charlyce Jones Owen
Acquisitions Editor: Karita France
Assistant Editor: Emsal Hasan
Production Editor: Joe Scordato
Copy Editor: Stephen Hopkins
Cover Designer: Bruce Kenselaar
Editorial Assistant: Jennifer Ackerman

This book was set in 10/12 Times Roman by Stratford Publishing Services and was printed and bound by R. R. Donnelley & Sons Company. The cover was printed by Phoenix Color Corp.

Unless otherwise indicated, the Scripture quotations contained herein are
from the New Revised Standard Version Bible, copyright © 1989 by the Division
of Christian Education of the National Council of the Churches of Christ in the
USA. Used by permission. All rights reserved.

Translations of the Dead Sea Scrolls contained herein are from García Martínez, F.,
The Dead Sea Scrolls Translated, co-published by Brill, Leiden, and Eerdmans,
Grand Rapids, MI, 1996. Used by permission. All rights reserved.

ISBN 0-13-674276-9

PRENTICE-HALL INTERNATIONAL (UK) LIMITED, *London*
PRENTICE-HALL OF AUSTRALIA PTY. LIMITED, *Sydney*
PRENTICE-HALL CANADA INC., *Toronto*
PRENTICE-HALL HISPANOAMERICANA. S.A., *Mexico*
PRENTICE-HALL OF INDIA PRIVATE LIMITED, *New Delhi*
PRENTICE-HALL OF JAPAN, INC., *Tokyo*
PEARSON EDUCATION ASIA PTE. LTD., *Singapare*
EDITORA PRENTICE-HALL DO BRASIL, LTDA., *Rio de Janeiro*

To Mary and Karen
for their love and inspiration

List of Abbreviations

Biblical Texts

The Old Testament/Hebrew Bible

Abbreviation	Book	Abbreviation	Book
Gen	Genesis	Isa	Isaiah
Exod	Exodus	Jer	Jeremiah
Lev	Leviticus	Lam	Lamentations
Num	Numbers	Ezek	Ezekiel
Deut	Deuteronomy	Dan	Daniel
Josh	Joshua	Hos	Hosea
Judg	Judges	Joel	Joel
Ruth	Ruth	Amos	Amos
1/2 Sam	1/2 Samuel	Obad	Obadiah
1/2 Kgs	1/2 Kings	Jon	Jonah
1/2 Chron	1/2 Chronicles	Mic	Micah
Ezra	Ezra	Nah	Nahum
Neh	Nehemiah	Hab	Habakkuk
Esth	Esther	Zeph	Zephaniah
Job	Job	Hag	Haggai
Ps (*pl.* Pss)	Psalms	Zech	Zechariah
Prov	Proverbs	Mal	Malachi
Eccl	Ecclesiastes		
Song	Song of Solomon		

The Apocrypha/Deuterocanonicals

Abbreviations	Book	Abbreviations	Book
Tob	Tobit	Song of Thr	Prayer of Azariah and the Song of the Three Jews
Jdt	Judith		
Add Esth	Additions to Esther		
Wis	Wisdom of Solomon	Sus	Susanna
Sir	Sirach	Bel	Bel and the Dragon

Bar	Baruch	1/2/3/4 Macc	1/2/3/4 Maccabees
1 Esdr	1 Esdras	Pr Man	Prayer of Manasseh
2 Esdr	2 Esdras		
Let Jer	Letter of Jeremiah		

The New Testament

Abbreviations	*Book*	*Abbreviations*	*Book*
Matt	Matthew	1/2 Thess	1/2 Thessalonians
Mk	Mark	1/2 Tim	1/2 Timothy
Lk	Luke	Titus	Titus
Jn	John	Philem	Philemon
Acts	Acts	Heb	Hebrews
Rom	Romans	Jas	James
1/2 Cor	1/2 Corinthians	1/2 Pet	1/2 Peter
Gal	Galatians	1/2/3 Jn	1/2/3 John
Eph	Ephesians	Jude	Jude
Phil	Philippians	Rev	Revelation
Col	Colossians		

Secondary Works

AASOR	Annual of the American Schools of Oriental Research
AB	Anchor Bible
ABD	*The Anchor Bible Dictionary.* Edited by D. N. Freedman. 6 Volumes. New York: Doubleday, 1992
AnBib	Anelecta biblica
ANET	*Ancient Near Eastern Texts Relating to the Old Testament.* 3d Ed. Edited by J. B. Pritchard. Princeton, NJ: Princeton University Press, 1969.
ANRW	*Aufstieg und Niedergang der römischen Welt*
ANTC	Abingdon New Testament Commentary
ASR	*American Sociological Review*
BA	*Biblical Archaeologist*
BAR	*Biblical Archaeology Review*
Bib	*Biblica*
BibRev	*Bible Review*
BJRL	*Bulletin of the John Rylands University Library of Manchester*
BSac	*Bibliotheca Sacra*
CANE	*Civilizations of the Ancient Near East.* Edited by J. M. Sasson. New York: Scribner's, 1995.
CBQ	*Catholic Biblical Quarterly*
CHJ	*The Cambridge History of Judaism.* Edited by W. D. Davies and L. Finkelstien. Cambridge: Cambridge University Press, 1984.
EncJud	*Encyclopedia Judaica.* Jerusalem and New York: Macmillan, 1972.
HNTC	Harper's New Testament Commentaries
HSM	Harvard Semitic Monographs
HTR	*Harvard Theological Review*
HUCA	*Hebrew Union College Annual*

IBC	Interpretation: A Bible Commentary for Teaching and Preaching
ICC	International Critical Commentary
IDB	*Interpreter's Dictionary of the Bible*. Edited by G. A. Buttrick. 4 Volumes. Nashville, TN: Abingdon, 1962.
IDBSup	*Interpreter's Dictionary of the Bible. Supplementary Volume*. Edited by K. Crim. Nashville, TN: Abingdon, 1976.
IEJ	*Israel Exploration Journal*
Int	*Interpretation*
IRT	Issues in Religion and Theology
JAOS	*Journal of the American Oriental Society*
JBL	*Journal of Biblical Literature*
JNES	*Journal of Near Eastern Studies*
JNSL	*Journal of Northwest Semitic Languages*
JSJ	*Journal for the Study of Judaism in the Persian, Hellenistic and Roman Period*
JSNTSup	Journal for the Study of the New Testament—Supplement Series
JSOT	*Journal for the Study of the Old Testament*
JSOTSup	Journal for the Study of the Old Testament—Supplement Series
Martínez	Martínez, F. G. *The Dead Sea Scrolls Translated*. Grand Rapids, MI: Eerdmans, 1996.
MDB	*Mercer Dictionary of the Bible*. Edited by W. Mills. Macon, GA: Mercer University Press, 1990.
NAC	New American Commentary
NCB	New Century Bible
NEA	*Near Eastern Archaeology*
NovTSup	Novem Testamentum, Supplements
NRSV	The New Revised Standard Version of the Bible
NTS	*New Testament Studies*
OTG	Old Testament Guides
OTL	Old Testament Library
PRS	*Perspectives in Religious Studies*
RR	*Review of Religion*
SacPag	Sacrina Pagina
SBLDS	Society of Biblical Literature Dissertation Series
SBLSP	*Society of Biblical Literature Seminar Papers*
SBLSS	*Society of Biblical Literature Semeia Studies*
SBT	Studies in Biblical Theology
ScanJOT	*Scandinavian Journal of the Old Testament*
SNTSMS	Society of New Testament Studies Monograph Series
TD	*Theology Today*
Vermes	G. Vermes, ed. and trans. *The Complete Dead Sea Scrolls in English*. New York: Allen Lane/Penguin, 1997.
VT	*Vetus Testamentum*
VTSup	Vetus Testamentum, Supplement
WBC	World Bible Commentary
ZAW	*Zeitschrift für die alttestamentliche Wissenschaft*

Contents

Professorial Preface

Employing this Text to Teach Students to Read the Bible

Who Are this Text's Implied Readers?

We claim that the implied reader of this text is the student and that the implied author is the teacher. But such terms are hardly without ambiguity, for there exist different types of students and teachers. We do not mean by students the ones who spread out on their beds around the time most of us are going to sleep and browse over this secondary text with one eye on the book and the other eye and both ears on late-night syndicated reruns of *Seinfeld*. Immediately, the readers of this professorial preface may conclude that we obviously do not have real student readers in mind. We would contend that any text that attempts to address the student reader described above has given up the cause of trying to teach careful and critical reading.

We are not ready to give up. Our implied reader, therefore, is the student who is willing to read the primary text of the Bible with care, employing this secondary text as a guide to his or her reading. Professors who are looking for a text that does not require that the student read the Bible, follow a sustained argument, or actually prepare for class can stop reading here and continue their search for their ideal text.

The implied authors of this text *are* teachers who want to teach students to read the Bible critically, not simply to tell them in the simplest terms what critical scholars think about the Bible. That is a very important feature of this text. We believe it far more important that students learn to read the Bible with a critical perspective than that they simply memorize key critical hypotheses or significant moments in the history of biblical interpretation.

Our rationale for this is twofold. First, if this is the only course in biblical studies that students have, we think it more important that they learn a way of reading the Bible than that they memorize the influence of, say, the Tübigen school on nineteenth-century New Testament scholarship or even the main contenders in today's historical Jesus debate (though we do not ignore the issue of contemporary Jesus research). The former (a way of reading) may have a lasting impact on the student; the latter may not. And yet the former can also provide a perspective from which to make sense of those occasional news stories on the latest debates in biblical studies (such as the Jesus Seminar). Second, if the reader majors in religious studies, both she or he and the professor will benefit from learning and adopting a critical way of reading. Such a way of reading lays a valuable foundation for subsequent courses and makes exposure to various critical theories and movements in the history of biblical scholarship more meaningful, for now the student sees himself or herself in conversation with other critical readers and not just learning what some authoritative "they" have said about the Bible.

The Genre of this Text

This text does not follow the traditional genre of biblical introductions. We do not, as is obvious even from a review of the table of contents, simply lay out the Bible in canonical order and proceed. Professors who are quite satisfied with traditional introductory genres, may not find this text useful. In our own teaching, however, we have found traditional genres of introduction to be inadequate for at least two reasons. First, it is virtually impossible to survey the sixty-six books of the Bible in a typical fifteen-week semester, a problem compounded when one also wants to explore the Deuterocanonicals/Apocrypha. Inevitably, professors must be selective. Conversations that we have heard, especially at the Academic Teaching and Biblical Studies Group of the SBL, have asked why the textbooks themselves do not assist professors in the selection process, rather than trying to cover everything. We have assisted in the selection process in this text, making no pretense to cover everything. Note that the subtitle to our text is "An Introduction to the Biblical Story," not "A Survey of the Bible."

Second, and stemming from the issue of trying to cover everything, texts that attempt to survey the whole Bible must do one of two things. If they are to be thorough, the texts must be very long, requiring that students read copious amounts of secondary material, not to mention volumes of primary material. We envy professors who have students who will do all of this reading. Regrettably, few such students attend the college where we teach. Consequently, professors are forced to cull reading assignments from the secondary and primary texts. While this does have a certain advantage, allowing the professor to focus in on texts she or he wishes to explore, it can create confusion for the students who are required to read selected pages from the secondary texts and perhaps even skip whole chapters. If assigned reading material assumes that the student has read (and mastered) material that the professor has had to cut from the required reading, frustration can ensue. We believe that it is better to prepare a textbook that students can read in its entirety, rather than to create a book designed to be read as a whole but which students must read selectively due to constraints of time.

To address this problem of length, other textbooks may take a different approach and reduce discussions to a more manageable length. But this can result in a very cursory *descriptive* presentation of introductory issues, which may not go much beyond what one would find in a good study Bible, such as the *Harper-Collins Study Bible.* Trying, for example, to cover Genesis through Deuteronomy in one chapter may be necessary if one follows traditional introductory genres. But we have found that it does not allow for much in the way of close and careful reading of primary texts. We have chosen to focus on selected primary texts, which we read closely and carefully. When the semester is finished, we believe our student readers will have a good grasp of the biblical story as a whole, as well as having developed skills of critical reading of the primary texts. Both of these learning processes together lay a good foundation for future study of the Bible in whatever contexts students may find themselves.

Why "Intertextuality"?

Some professors may find this approach too daunting for the beginning student. We find this approach very useful pedagogically. Professorial readers should consult our more detailed discussion of intertextuality in the second part of Chapter 1; we offer here but a very brief summary. We employ the term *text* in a broad sense, speaking of *literary texts* (actual preserved texts, such as "the Bible"), *social texts,* by which we mean the texts of culture (e.g., language, ideology, theology, and history), and *interpretive texts,* by which we mean the interpretations that emerge from the intersection of various texts, including the *self-text* of the interpreter.

We also employ the language of story, adopting this language to the various texts—literary, social, and interpretive. We speak of a "story in the Bible" that corresponds to the literary text. We speak of numerous stories "behind the text" of the Bible—the various social texts of culture and history that inform the story in the text. And we speak of stories "in front of the text" of the Bible, by which we mean the various self-texts of the readers that are quite influential in the formation of interpretive texts.

Pedagogically, we find this approach useful for a number of reasons. First and foremost, intertextual reading requires close, comparative reading of different literary texts. We speak in this text of specific quotations or near quotations of an earlier text in a later text (what we call "micro-level intertextuality") or allusive echoes, be they faint or strong, which reverberate between a focal literary text and other texts (be they literary or social—what we call "macro-level intertextuality"). Regardless of whether we are speaking of specific quotations (or near quotations) embedded in later texts or echoes that exist between two texts, they can be discerned only with close and careful reading of the primary text. Recall that critical reading is our goal and, thus, intertextuality is a good approach, for it fosters such reading.

Second, due attention to *literary* texts allows us to give careful scrutiny to the story *in* the Bible. Although we do not claim that we offer students a literary introduction to the Bible, students will learn that there exists a literary world within the Bible that one cannot simply assume matches up with a historical world that exists outside the Bible. They learn that one cannot always read the Bible referentially. The conclusion of critical scholars that there regularly exists a chasm, whether it be wide or narrow, between narrative worlds and various social and/or historical worlds, which exist outside the narrative world, is a crucial distinction for novice readers to learn. The persistent use of the terms *literary text* and *social text* regularly keeps before students the concept that we are talking about two different kinds of texts, even if they are interrelated.

Third, and flowing directly from our second point, by defining text as broadly as we have, including not only literary texts but social texts, we facilitate the interconnections between the "story in the text" and the various "stories behind the text." Though we do, in Chapters 2 and 9 especially, offer an overview of the broader historical and social contexts of the biblical world, we reserve detailed analysis of the various social texts to the chapters where such information is immediately relevant. We employ the language of social texts to denote the various texts that lay behind the literary text—social texts such as culture and history. More important, we regularly connect the literary text of the Bible with these various social texts by offering suggestions to the student readers how this or that social text has shaped the biblical (literary) text. Students regularly see, therefore, the connections between the many social texts that lay behind the literary text and literary text of the Bible itself. This allows students to recognize the historically and culturally conditioned character of the story in the Bible. We believe that any professor of Bible will acknowledge with us that critical reading truly begins when students cease to read the Bible as though it were produced (to use the divine passive!!) in a vacuum, independent of the complexities of history and the various competing ideologies that surround the literary text.

Finally, the attention given to self-texts and interpretive texts that emerge from the intersection of various texts allows us to keep before students the fact that "readers make sense." Biblical scholarship stands in something of a transitional state these days. Post-modernism affects many of us enough so that we no longer speak about cold, objective interpretation that simply lays bare "*the* meaning" of a given text, such as the Bible. "Readers *do* make sense" and create meaning. The explicit acknowledgment that self-texts do inform and shape interpretive texts benefits student readers in at least two ways.

First, each knows that she or he has a self-text (once they understand the term). They begin to understand that they bring something with them to the interpretive enterprise and that their own self-texts shape how they read the text. Second, this awareness opens the door to the recognition that other readers, *including creators of biblical literary texts, who themselves were interpreters of earlier texts,* also bring to the text their own distinctive self-texts. Ancient, as well as modern, readers make sense. Keeping this before the student allows the professor to make great strides in creating a critical awareness that meanings are not simply deposited in the Bible, but emerge from the act of reading the text.

Using the Argument of this Text

The argument pressed in this text is consistent and persistent: the Bible came to be as a result of interpretive readings of earlier texts and traditions. We call such interpretive readings "rereadings." Of course, this approach touches bases with common features of traditional critical scholarship, such as source, tradition, and redaction criticisms. Readers will note, however, that we employ these classic criticisms as means to an end: helping students come to understand how the Bible came to be.

In summary fashion, we lay forth here the way the argument develops as the text unfolds. Professors who employ this textbook as a tool to help students read the Bible should revisit (reread!) this section frequently throughout the teaching term. We divide the text into four parts. Part One consists of two chapters that serve to introduce students to the whole concept of rereading.

Chapter 1 introduces students to the Christian and Hebrew Bibles. Even here students begin to see that the communities who shaped these texts into their present canonical form were inviting subsequent readers to read this collection of texts in a certain way. For example, the placing of the Law and Prophets together in the Hebrew Bible implies a close relationship between these two collections of texts. On the other hand, the Christian Old Testament separates the Law and the Prophets, implying something of a distance between the two collections of texts. In the second part of Chapter 1, we introduce students to the whole issue of intertextuality, summarized in the preceding section of this preface. We employ examples from American history to show students that intertextuality is a common phenomenon, even if the term is not so common. We also use some biblical examples to introduce students to intertextual reading and to allow them to see how later biblical texts can interpret and reread earlier texts.

Chapter 2 moves students fully into intertextual reading. We have two basic goals in this chapter. First, we want to introduce novice readers to a very basic outline of the story of Israel. Experience has taught us that they do not know it. To accomplish this, we offer a summary of the great historical narratives of the Bible: the Tetrateuch (and Deuteronomy), the Deuteronomistic History, the Chronicler and 1 Maccabees. We then employ some historical recitals, or summaries, from the Bible itself (from Nehemiah and Sirach) to review this basic outline and to introduce students to a thorough and more careful intertextual comparison of the two summaries. With this, students begin to see that the same story can be told in very different ways. These differences offer us an opportunity to show students the way varying social texts could impact the way one tells the story of Israel. The Deuteronomic theological pattern influences Nehemiah; a priestly perspective shapes Sirach's telling of the story. Hence, students begin to learn how the social text shapes the self-text of the ancient reader and, thus, the literary text that the ancient reader produced.

Part Two moves our study more directly into a reading of the Hebrew Bible. Chapter 3 examines the literary text of Ezra-Nehemiah, a text to which we shall return often in Part Two of the text. The exploration of this narrative introduces students to the world of post-Exilic Judaism and various issues that emerged as significant in Judaism during this period: the Temple, the Torah, and an ideology of self-exclusion endorsed by many Jewish people of this era. Yet we also explore the problems that arise when we attempt to read Ezra-Nehemiah as a straightforward referential narrative of history. Students learn a crucial issue necessary for critical readers, specifically that the narrative world (the literary text of Ezra-Nehemiah) does not simply reflect the historical world (or historical social text) that lies behind that narrative. This distinction will prove invaluable in subsequent chapters, for we will regularly explore how the presentation of the stories of the law, prophets, Temple, kingship, and the people *in the literary text* does not simply jibe with the critical historical reconstructions of these same stories.

We then devote a chapter each to five significant stories that shape the larger biblical story: the law, the prophets, the Temple and priesthood, kingship, and the people (Chaps. 5–8). Chapter 4, the story of the law, employs Ezra-Nehemiah to introduce students to the important role that law played in post-Exilic Jewish life. While learning of the importance of law, students also see reasons why critical scholars do not think the law was yet in the final form in which we now find it in the Pentateuch. This raises the question of how the law developed. Through study of both the form and content of the Covenant Code, we show that ancient Israelite law emerged from social contexts different from the narrative setting of Mt. Sinai. The principle learned in Chapter 3 regarding the distinction between the literary text and the historical social text is now applied to the issue of law: Israelite law, while emerging gradually in the life of Israelite society, has been reread and associated with the foundational event of the Exodus and wilderness period. We conclude by showing how the historian of Ezra-Nehemiah, writing in that formative period of sacred scripture, also rein-terprets the importance of the story of the land. Drawing from the Abrahamic tradition—wherein land is a grant—and the Deuteronomic tradition—wherein land is contingent upon the keeping of the law—students see both the parallels and conflicts between the setting of the post-Exilic historian and the story of the book of Deuteronomy, and thus the historian's attraction to the two different traditions regarding the land.

Chapter 5 examines the story of the prophets. Again, students learn that the faith community of post-Exilic Judaism reread the prophets. We remind students that Nehemiah 9 (studied in Chap. 2) closely con-nected the law and the prophets, interpreting the prophets as calling Israel back to the law. But we show how traditions available to the author of Ezra-Nehemiah pertaining to two central prophetic figures, Haggai and Zechariah, do not portray these prophets as concerned about the law at all, thus reinforcing the claim that the complete formulation of law only came late. We then explore the prophetic books of Haggai and Zechariah where, again, we show students the law was not of concern to these prophets. Rather, they were concerned to address the critical issues of their time, such as rebuilding of the Temple and the roles of such important leaders as Zerubbabel and Joshua, claiming authority not from any written (or oral) law, but from Yahweh. Through careful reading of the primary texts, students recognize why we must acknowledge that the prophetic books are the products of later compilers and editors, and that these later editors were themselves rereading the prophetic traditions they inherited, creating literary text that spoke directly to their contempo-rary readers. We close this chapter by introducing students to a significant legacy of prophecy, apocalypti-cism and its literature. Here students learn that many in the faith community of Judaism came to read prophets as long-range foretellers of Israel's destiny, a way of reading the prophets that would profoundly impact the early Christian community.

Chapter 6 devotes attention to the story of the Temple and the priesthood. It is in this chapter that we begin to devote much more attention to the two great histories of the Deuteronomist and the Chronicler. We begin with a consideration of the Temple story of Ezra-Nehemiah, tracking the sources this historian used to construct his Temple story. Students are able to see that the post-Exilic setting had a vested interest in reinter-preting its inherited traditions due to the absence of any traditional political definition. We then turn to consider the Deuteronomistic historian's understanding of the centralization of worship in the story of Josiah's reforms. Students see the conventional reading of the passage in 2 Kings 23, especially through its intertextuality with the book of Deuteronomy. Students also consider the social text of the Dueteronomic legists as they radically reinterpret the legitimacy of Israel's traditional worship of Yahweh at multiple local shrines. Finally, we revisit the role of the Temple in post-Exilic and Hellenistic apocalyptic speculation. Students see that much of apoca-lyptic thought (introduced in Chap. 5) has the Temple and its eventual restoration as the main focus because of the contemporary sense that the restoration had not yet occurred as fully as had been expected.

Chapter 7 follows the exploration of the Temple with a convenient counterpart, the exploration of kingship. We again return to the great histories, the Deuteronomistic History and the Chronicler, to examine how the post-Exilic historian reinterprets the post-Exilic Davidic promise. Through a close comparison of 2 Samuel 7 and 1 Chronicles 17 students see clearly the effects of the Chronicler's social text. At a time when there could be no king, the strategy of the Chronicler was one of abandoning the concept of kingship as an autocracy, and replacing it with the concept of theocracy. Offering these as the most important boundaries for Israel's understanding of kingship, we then turn to consider the possibility of the divinity of kingship. Students explore several examples of the metaphorical elevation of the king to the status of near deity within the framework of cultic literature (Psalms). We show that this elevated status emerges in a context where the sonship of the king functions to legitimize monarchy, which was initially an unpopular form of political or-ganization. The elevation of the status of the king from mortal to son of God lays the foundation for explor-ing the final messianic horizon of Israelite kingship. Here we revisit the concept of eschatology and its role in shaping the Jewish-Hellenistic understanding of God's activity in a world that had grown totally evil. We trace the Davidic and royal images from the Deuteronomist and the Chronicler through the Psalms well into the Hellenistic and Qumranic literature in order to illustrate how failed hopes and religious visions call for their postponement until a near future.

Chapter 8 concludes the investigation by focusing upon the people of God. Again we begin by rereading Ezra-Nehemiah and its very narrow criteria for defining who was and was not a member of God's community. The post-Exilic social text, we recall, is very concerned about intermarriage with foreigners. But even more important in this setting is the assumption that the true people of God are those who went through the Exile. This is born out in examinations of oracles from the pre-Exilic and Exilic prophets Jeremiah, Ezekiel, and Isaiah, who understood the true Israel no longer in a political sense, but in the sense of having passed through the Exile. We then examine the idea of covenant as it occurs in narrative traditions about Abraham. Both Genesis 15 and 17 (even though chapter 17 assumes the existence of chapter 15) convey the idea of covenant as promise. We explore differing explanations of the social text, one Davidic, the other post-Exilic. We conclude by examining the Deuteronomistic understanding of covenant as a relationship in which the deity lays obligations upon his people. While no attempt is made to suggest that Deuteronomist is directly rereading the old Abrahamic traditions, students see that this Deuteronomistic view becomes popular only *after* the fall of the Northern kingdom, when Judah and its theologians realize the possibility that Judah could also fall. The true people of God are those who keep his covenant by observing the law.

Part Three moves us into our study of the New Testament. In Chapter 9 we examine the historical, political, and religious world of early Christianity—the social text of Palestine and the larger Roman Empire. The discussion employs selected texts from Luke-Acts that make reference to political religious leaders and philosophical and religious groups, pointing out how the narrator rarely provides any specific information about these leaders or groups. This allows students to see that biblical writers regularly assumed on the part of their readers knowledge about the various social texts of their time, knowledge that contemporary readers typically do not posses. This chapter fills that void.

Chapter 10 surveys the whole of Luke-Acts. Students explore issues of critical introduction to these narrative, such as the Synoptic problem and the issues surrounding the employment of the gospels as historical sources for learning about Jesus of Nazareth. Following this introduction section, the chapter offers an overview of the narrative of Luke-Acts. The purpose of this is to provide students with a broad introduction to the story of Jesus and his earliest followers, at least as told by one New Testament author. The chapter concludes with an analysis of a selected historical problem, similar to the analysis of Ezra-Nehemiah in Chapter 3. This serves to remind readers that the literary text cannot simply be read referentially; that is, one cannot simply assume that the world of the literary text always reflects the historical social text that stands behind the narrative.

Part Four devotes each chapter to separate detailed studies of New Testament rereadings of the five stories we studied in Part Two, addressing these stories in an order most conducive to a study of the New Testament: kingship, the Temple and priesthood, the law, the prophets, and the people. Chapter 11 (kingship) introduces students to the parables of Jesus, focusing attention on how Jesus reread Jewish scriptures and traditions of kingship and how his subsequent followers reread Jesus' rereadings. Thus, we reinforce for students that the Bible is the result of subsequent layers of reinterpretation of earlier traditions. We then move to a study of Mark's passion narrative. We offer a concise comparison of Mark's literary text with that of John to show students that there exists confusion between the two regarding the date of Jesus' crucifixion. This allows us to reiterate to students that in the New Testament, as well as in the Hebrew Bible, one cannot simply read the literary text referentially. We then examine how Mark's passion narrative rereads significant features of the story of kingship from the scriptures, interpreting kingship (messiahship) in light of the fact of Jesus' crucifixion, rereading the relationship between the king and the Temple, and identifying Jesus not only with the Messiah, but the son of God and son of man. Finally, we explore Paul's rereading of the story of kingship through a study of 1 Corinthians 15, showing students how Paul reread various scriptural texts through the lens of his theological social texts to redefine the enemies whom God's king is to conquer. We also show students how Paul's identification of Jesus with the "second Adam" shaped the way he combined various scriptural texts and applied them to Jesus.

Chapter 12 moves our study to rereading the story of the Temple. First, we compare Luke with 4 Ezra, showing how these two texts made sense of the destruction of Jerusalem and the Temple in 70 CE. While both viewed the Temple's destruction as divine judgment, the cause of such judgment is quite distinct. Further, while 4 Ezra looked forward to a literal restoration of Jerusalem and the Temple, Luke is virtually silent with regard to such a hope. This raises the question of how Christians made sense of the tradition, deeply embedded in Jewish scripture, that the era of restoration would bring with it a restoration of Jerusalem and the Temple. We explore Ephesians next to show that this text redefined the Temple to be the Christian community. We also use our study of Ephesians to examine how a subsequent Christian author has reread Paul and *why* such a rereading of Paul was necessary in light of changing social texts. Our study of Hebrews allows us to show students specifically how Christians reread the story of the priesthood, redefining the priesthood in the person of Jesus. Finally, we study Revelation, offering numerous intertexts with Jewish scriptures in order to show that the final book of the Christian canon reread various scriptural texts about the glorified Jerusalem, identifying the new Jerusalem with the people of God, the church.

Chapter 13 studies Christian rereadings of the story of the law. We begin with a study of Galatians and argue that Paul's conviction that gentiles, as gentiles, were welcome into the ranks of God's people required that he challenge the tenets of "another gospel" that insisted that gentiles undergo circumcision in order to be considered descendants of Abraham. Paul's argument that the law was a temporary measure, distinct from the promise God made to Abraham and his "seed," is very much grounded in a specific polemical context. This polemical context drives his reading of the scriptures, going so far as to claim that followers of the law are actually descendants of Hagar, whereas only those who claim the "promise" are descendants of Sarah. We use this chapter as an opportunity to study the Sermon on the Mount, paying careful attention to the social text of conflict between Matthew's community and the Jewish synagogue. For Matthew, the law is still valid, offering a distinct contrast with Paul's understanding of the law. The different social texts of Paul and Matthew, in part, explain their different approaches to the law. Yet, for Matthew the law is valid as it is interpreted by Jesus, the Messiah, not as interpreted by the emerging rabbinic leadership. Students see that the Sermon on the Mount is not an abstract and timeless ethical treatise, but a literary construction designed to address a specific social text of conflict. We conclude our study of the Sermon on the Mount by arguing that Jewish scriptural traditions of a new covenant informed Matthew's rereading of the law.

Chapter 14 explores Christian rereadings of the story of the prophets and prophecy. Employing Matthew 1–2 as a point of departure, we study how Christians reread prophetic texts and applied them specifically to Jesus. We also examine how, in many first century Jewish and Christian circles, the interpretation of the scriptures was itself considered an inspired activity. Matthew, we argue, did not consider scriptural interpretation itself as inspired, a stance that he took because of the specific social text he was attempting to address. This again allows students to see how social text shapes the construction of the literary text. We move then to Paul's debate with the Corinthian congregation on the issue of prophecy and tongues. This debate allows students to see that serious disagreements could exist within the early Christian community over spiritual phenomena and, most especially, over the role of women as practitioners of such phenomena. We argue that Paul's concern to address what he perceived as a divided community drove the way he reread scriptural texts about the relationship between men and women, all with an aim to silence the women prophets. This allows students to see, once again, how social texts shape the reading of literary texts. We conclude with a brief study of the Pastoral Epistles, arguing that a social text of severe conflict within the church drove the author of these epistles to reread both Paul and pertinent scriptural texts to silence women prophets (indeed, virtually all prophets) and substitute for the voice of the prophet the authoritative voice of the male bishop. Again, students see that the literary texts emerge in response to specific social texts.

Chapter 15 visits the story of the people. We begin with a study of Romans, arguing that Paul is facing a very different social situation than he faced in Galatians. In Romans, Paul is addressing a Christian community divided between Jewish and gentile Christians—a community that he wants to be reconciled. We focus attention on Romans 9–11, showing that Paul has reread the Deuteronomic theological perspective in order to explain the fact that most Jews of his time had not recognized Jesus to be the Messiah. Paul's use of the Deuteronomistic pattern allows him to conclude that, in the end, all Israel will be saved. Paul argues that God has not given up on Israel. We relate Paul's argument quite specifically to the issue of division facing the Roman church in order to show students how the specific social text can shape the reading of the literary text.

When we move to John's gospel, the story of the people turns in a different direction. A social text of conflict between Jewish and Christian communities shapes the fourth gospel's understanding of the Jewish people. We argue that in the Gospel of John, Jesus and his followers totally supplant "the Jews" as the people of God. This perspective reveals itself in the way that John rereads various scriptural texts, applying texts and images that originally dealt with Israel to Jesus and his followers. We conclude by making clear to students that the New Testament, represented here by Paul and John, presents two very different readings of the relationship between the Jewish people and God.

As a whole, this text tries to show how and why the various literary texts we explore came to be as a process of rereading. Such rereading was necessary, given that social texts were in a constant state of flux, requiring subsequent interpreters of received traditions and texts to reinterpret these traditions and texts in ways that would address meaningfully these ever-mutating social texts. Students convinced by the argument of this textbook can come to recognize that when, even today, people read these scriptural texts, we do much the same thing as ancient readers: We reread these literary texts in the context of our own social and self-texts, giving new meaning to them, as necessary, that they might speak to our worlds. Readers, both ancient and modern, make sense and create meaning.

Using this Text

As the previous discussion has attempted to show, this book presents an argument. Professors unsympathetic with the gist of the argument, for whatever reason, would probably not profit from the use of this text (unless one wants to use it as point of departure for debate, in which case one will need to decide whether she or he is teaching an audience that would benefit from class presentations that offer a resistant reading to the whole of this text's argument). We have used the text successfully in a "desk-top" version for a number of semesters during the text's production. Of course, we wrote the text and are sympathetic with its approach, and, therefore, we employ this text to press our argument.

In order to facilitate the use of this text to guide student reading of the biblical text, we have placed at the beginning of each subsection a list of "Learning Goals." These goals can provide focus both for the professor and the students. They give guidance to the students in what they are to look for as they read the primary text and the secondary text. We have also included sections entitled "Guiding Study Exercises." Careful reading of these study exercises will reveal that they are tied to the learning goals. Students who address these questions (in whatever manner the professor requires) will have a means of self-assessment as to whether they are mastering the stated learning goals.

Professors can also use the guiding study exercises to aid in the assessment of student learning. We are fortunate enough to teach small classes, allowing us to require submission of homework or to begin the class period with a writing exercise based on the homework that the students submit for our review. Professors who must teach in larger classes might divide the class into groups and require random and periodic submission of the homework from a particular group. We have found this very valuable, for it allows for on-going assessment of student learning. After reviewing the homework or in-class writings, we can immediately identify the goals that the students are not clear about, and we can address, by way of review, these goals quite specifically in the next class period before moving on to the assignment for that day. Learning goals and guiding study exercises can also serve as points of departure for classroom discussion and presentations. Professors can also encourage students to master the goals by making clear that test questions will spring from the learning goals and guiding study exercises.

Professors will also find numerous tables of intertexts in the book. We have found it useful to make photocopies of these tables (using the enlargement feature of the copy machine, if necessary) to prepare transparencies of the tables. This allows for focused investigation of the intertexts, with the professor referring to the overhead visual projection of the table and the students being able to follow his or her discussions with the table printed in their textbooks.

Finally, numerous "Closer Look" boxes are placed throughout the textbook. These boxes are intended to offer supplementary or illustrative information that can enrich the students' understanding of what they are reading in the main text. For example, a "Closer Look" box in Chapter 10, "Finding the Real Words of Jesus," introduces students to the various criteria employed by many scholars to locate within the gospel traditions the teachings of Jesus of Nazareth. The boxes also regularly raise questions or briefly introduce an issue pertaining to critical biblical studies. For example, Chapter 2 offers a brief box entitled "Histories and Critical Methods." Here students are introduced very generally to the hypothesis of JEDP. While the box does not explain the hypothesis in detail, it does provide professors who want to spend more time on this issue a point of departure for further exploration.

The method and approach of this text are different from textbooks with which we are familiar. We are confident, based on our own experience, however, that the approach works. We welcome constructive criticisms and comments from professors for future editions. We would like to thank Ralph J. Brabban II of Palm Beach Atlantic College for his review of the manuscript and for his helpful suggestions.

J. Bradley Chance
chanceb@william.jewell.edu
Milton P. Horne
hornem@william.jewell.edu

PART ONE

Introduction

CHAPTER ONE

Learning to
Reread the Bible

What Is the Bible?

Learning Goals

- To learn essential information about the structure and general content of the Bible.
- To learn the distinctions between the Christian Old Testament and the Hebrew Bible.

Guiding Study Exercises

1) What are the two major divisions of the Bible? Describe succinctly their relationship to each other.
2) List the major divisions of the Hebrew Bible and the Christian Old Testament. Why might they be structured differently?
3) What do we mean by the Apocrypha and Deuterocanonicals? Why does the essentially same material have two different names?
4) What is the LXX and what does it have to do with existence of the Deuterocanonicals and Apocrypha?

An appropriate first step for rereading the Bible would be to offer a clear definition of what the Bible is. That may seem for many like a needless exercise, for surely everyone knows what the Bible is: "The inspired word of God"; "The sacred writings of a major world religion"; "A collection of ancient religious stories." Yet, there is no one, simple definition of the Bible.

This textbook will focus its study on the **Christian** Bible, the ancient and authoritative writings of the Christian religion. The texts that make up the Christian Bible do have much in common with the Bible of Judaism, though the Christian Bible and the Jewish Scriptures are not at all identical to one another. Furthermore, it is somewhat simplistic to speak of *the* Christian Bible, for there is not agreement even among Christians as to what texts should make up the Bible.

The Old Testament/Hebrew Bible

The **Old Testament** (OT) of the Christian Bible is quite similar, though not identical, to the **Hebrew Bible**, the scriptures of the Jewish faith. As the term *Hebrew Bible* implies, the Jewish scriptures were originally written, for the most part, in the Hebrew language during the first millennium BCE. Eventually, beginning around the year 250 BCE, Jewish students of the Hebrew Bible translated these texts into the Greek language. Scholars call this translation the **Septuagint**, abbreviated as LXX. When the Jews translated their scriptures into Greek, they not only translated the books that now appear in the Hebrew Bible, but also they translated *additional books* as well. That the additional books are not found today in the Hebrew Bible (but were included in the Septuagint) implies that at the time of the translation the Jewish community had not yet firmly decided exactly what was to be included in their scriptures. In the days of Jesus and his followers, Jews, many of whom were bilingual, would read from either the Hebrew Bible or the Septuagint, viewing both of them as scripture (much in the same way that a modern person might read from more than one version of the Bible and view all the versions as scripture.)

The Jewish faith community divides the Hebrew Bible into three major sections (see Table 1.1). The **Torah** (meaning "law," "instruction," or "teaching") consists of five books or scrolls. The *Nebi'im* (or "prophets") consists of two subsections, the "former prophets," consisting of four scrolls, and the "latter prophets," also consisting of four scrolls. The third section, the *Kethubim* (or "writings"), consists of eleven scrolls.

In the OT of the Bible, these texts from the Hebrew Bible form the core of the material. Note that the OT (Table 1.2), does not arrange the books in the same way as does the Hebrew Bible. The OT divides the books into *four* major sections (not *three* as in the Hebrew Bible): the **Pentateuch** (or the Law), the historical books, the books of poetry and wisdom, and the prophetic books. Furthermore, in some versions of the OT, there are several books that do not appear in the Hebrew Bible. Before proceeding with this discussion, it might help students to observe that Christianity consists of three main branches: Roman Catholic, Orthodox, and Protestant. For the most part, the Roman Catholic and Orthodox Christians agree with respect to the content of the OT (see Table 1.3 to note the minor variations). The Protestant version of the OT consists of fewer books than the OTs of Catholic and Orthodox Christians.

As one studies the Tables 1.1 through 1.3, the following observations may prove helpful. First, notice how differently the Christian and Jewish faith communities arrange the material (compare Tables 1.1 and 1.2). In the Jewish tradition, "the Law and the Prophets" were the foundation of the sacred writings of Judaism.[1] The structure of the Hebrew Bible seems to reflect this central importance with the Torah and the Nebi'im making up the first two major sections of the Bible. On the other hand, the early Christians often tended to want to divorce the law (God's commandments to his people of old) from the gospel (God's gracious offering of salvation through Jesus Christ).[2] Furthermore, early Christians tended to emphasize the prophetic portions of the

---

[1]This is a phrase used often, even in the NT; it demonstrates the NT writers' familiarity with Jewish ways of thinking. More on this will be said in the next section of this chapter.

[2]E.g., Jn 1:17 reads, "The law indeed was given by Moses; grace and truth came through Jesus Christ." See also Gal 3:23: "Now before faith came, we were imprisoned and guarded under the law until faith would be revealed."

Books of the Hebrew Bible

Table 1.1

Books of the Hebrew Bible

Torah (Law)	Nebi'im (Prophets)	Kethubim (Writings)
Genesis Exodus Leviticus Numbers Deuteronomy	FORMER PROPHETS[1] Joshua Judges Samuel Kings LATTER PROPHETS[2] *Major Prophets:* Isaiah Jeremiah Ezekiel *Minor Prophets* (Book of the Twelve): Hosea Joel Amos Obadiah Jonah Micah Nahum Habakkuk Zephaniah Haggai Zechariah Malachi	Psalms Job Proverbs Ruth Song of Songs Ecclesiastes Lamentations Esther Daniel Ezra/Nehemiah[3] Chronicles[3]
	[1]Four books make up the "Former Prophets." Samuel and Kings are one book in the Hebrew Bible. They are two books in the Old Testament. Note that Daniel is not included in the collection of prophets. [2]There are also four books that make up the "Latter Prophets," with "the Twelve" representing one book.	[3]Originally Ezra/Nehemiah and Chronicles were *two* books in the Hebrew Bible. From the medieval period onwards (as well as in the Christian Old Testament), however, Ezra and Nehemiah became two separate books, and Chronicles was also divided between 1 and 2 Chronicles.

A Closer Look: The Apocrypha/Deuterocanonicals. These books that are part of the Roman Catholic and Orthodox OTs, but not part of either the Hebrew Bible or Protestant OT, have an interesting history. Because these books were translated into Greek and were part of the Septuagint, some have argued that the Greek-speaking Jews considered these "extra" books to be canonical scripture. It is hasty, however, to conclude that because these books were translated into Greek the translators viewed them as scripture in some formal sense. More likely, the fact of their translation offers evidence that the Jewish community had not yet decided formally on what was scripture and what was not. Ultimately, however, the Jewish religious community did not accept these books as canonical (see below, "A Closer Look: When Did the Books of the Hebrew Bible become 'Bible'?").

Christians from the end of the first century onward, however, did make use of these additional books, since they were found within the Greek translations of the Jewish scriptures. In 382 CE Jerome was commissioned to translate the Bible into Latin. He did not choose to include these additional books, arguing that only those books of the *Hebrew* Bible were scripture. Nonetheless, the larger church, both the Roman Catholic and, eventually, the Orthodox churches, accepted as deuterocanonical these other books. Protestant reformers of the sixteenth century CE agreed with Jerome that only books of the Hebrew Bible should be considered canonical. Thus, these additional books were taken out of the OT and placed in a separate section called the Apocrypha. The Roman Catholic Church responded, formally declaring that the Deuterocanonical books were fully authoritative and inspired (Council of Trent, 1546). It was common until the early nineteenth century for Protestant Bibles to include the Apocrypha in a separate section of the Bible. Eventually, however, Protestant groups began to produce Bibles without the Apocrypha.

For further study, J. H. Charlesworth. "Apocrypha (Old Testament Apocrypha)." *ABD* 1.292–294; R. C. Dentan. "Apocrypha (Jewish Apocrypha)." *The Oxford Companion to the Bible.* Edited by B. M. Metzger and M D. Coogan. New York: Oxford University Press, 1993. Pp. 37–39; J. L. Trafton. "Apocryphal Literature." *MDB.* Pp. 41–46.

For more advanced study, B. M. Metzger. *An Introduction to the Apocrypha.* New York: Oxford University Press, 1957; G. W. E. Nickelsburg. *Jewish Literature Between the Bible and the Mishnah.* Philadelphia: Fortress, 1981.

Jewish scriptures, arguing that these books paved the way for the coming of Jesus by prophesying (or predicting) his life, death, and resurrection. Given this, it is not surprising that the OT literally separates the law from the prophets, putting between the law (representing God's old relationship or **covenant** with his people of old) and the prophets (pointing ahead to God's new relationship or covenant with his new people, saved by Christ) the historical and poetic books.[3]

Second, Table 1.2 notes that the Catholic and Orthodox OTs contain longer versions of Esther (of the historical books section) and Daniel than are found in the Protestant version. The

[3]See J. A. Sanders, " 'Spinning' the Bible," *BibRev* 14.3 (1998) 22–29, 44–45.

Table 1.2

The Old Testament

Table 1.2 presents OT books that appear in both Roman Catholic and Orthodox Bibles. Orthodox OTs contain some books in addition to those listed below (see Table 1.3). The Protestant OT does not include the italicized books; one may find these books in Protestant Bibles that include the Apocrypha.

Law	History	Poetry/Wisdom	Prophets
Genesis	Joshua	Job	Isaiah
Exodus	Judges	Psalms	Jeremiah
Leviticus	Ruth	Proverbs	Lamentations
Numbers	1 and 2 Samuel	Ecclesiastes	*Baruch*[2]
Deuteronomy	1 and 2 Kings	Song of Solomon	Ezekiel
	1 and 2 Chronicles	*Wisdom of Solomon*	Daniel[3]
	Ezra	*Ecclesiasticus (Ben Sirach)*	Hosea
	Nehemiah		Joel
	Tobit		Amos
	Judith		Obadiah
	Esther[1]		Jonah
	1 Maccabees		Micah
	2 Maccabees		Nahum
			Habakkuk
			Zephaniah
			Haggai
			Zechariah
			Malachi
	[1]Roman Catholic and Orthodox Bibles contain a longer version of Esther. This longer version is found in the Protestant Apocrypha.		[2]Baruch is one chapter longer in the Orthodox Bible. This additional chapter is a separate book in the Apocrypha, entitled The Letter of Jeremiah. [3]Roman Catholic and Orthodox Bibles contain a longer version of Daniel. This material is found in the Apocrypha as three separate books. See the discussion in text.

Table 1.3

The Protestant Apocrypha

The list below contains all of the books found in the Apocrypha of the Protestant Bible, in the order their appearance. Pay careful attention to the headings of each column, noting that Roman Catholic and Orthodox Bibles do not contain exactly the same Old Testament books.

Books in the Roman Catholic and Orthodox Old Testaments.	Books found in the Orthodox Old Testament only	Book found in appendix to the Vulgate Bible	Book found as an appendix to the Orthodox Old Testament

Tobit
Judith
Esther
  (long version)
Wisdom of
  Solomon
Ecclesiasticus
  (Ben Sirach)
Baruch
The Letter of
  Jeremiah
  (= chap. 6 of
  Orthodox version
  of Baruch)
Additions to Daniel
  Prayer of Azariah
  and the Song of
  the Three Jews
  Susanna
  Bel and the
  Dragon
1 Maccabees
2 Maccabees
	1 Esdras (found in appendix of the Latin Vulgate [Roman Catholic] Bible under the title 3 Esdras)
	
	Prayer of Manessah (found in appendix of Vulgate Bible)
	Psalm 151
	3 Maccabees
		2 Esdras (entitled 4 Esdras in Vulgate)	4 Maccabees

books of Daniel and Esther are shorter in the Protestant version, as well as in the Hebrew Bible. The "additions to Daniel" appear in the **Apocrypha** as three separate and additional books: *The Prayer of Azariah* (found in chap. 3 of the Catholic and Orthodox version of Daniel), *Bel and the Dragon,* and *Susanna* (found at the end of chap. 12 of the Catholic and Orthodox versions of Daniel). Similarly, the version of Esther found in the Catholic and Orthodox OTs is considerably longer than the Protestant or Hebrew versions. One may find this longer edition of Esther in the Protestant Apocrypha.

A Closer Look: When Did the Books of the Hebrew Bible become "Bible"?

Among the books of the Apocrypha is a text entitled Sirach. Originally composed in Hebrew ca. 180 BCE, it was translated into Greek by Sirach's grandson approximately 50 years later. The grandson added a prologue to his translation, in the context of which he speaks three times of "the Law and the Prophets and the other books." This would imply that the threefold division of the current Hebrew Bible was in place by this time. Most scholars believe that the Jewish community viewed the Torah as authoritative scripture by the fifth century BCE, and the Prophets as scripture by the third century BCE, though it was sometime later before the current *order* of books within the Prophets was agreed upon. Scholars are not in agreement as to when the Jewish community came to consensus on the precise contents or order of the Writings (what Sirach's prologue calls "the others"). Some scholars argue that the issue of the content of the books of the Hebrew Bible was settled as early as the second century BCE. Others argue that it was not until the end of the first century CE.

For further study, N. M. Sarna. "Order of Books in the Hebrew Bible"; and R. T. Beckwith. "Canon of the Hebrew Bible and the Old Testament." *The Oxford Companion to the Bible.* Editied by B. M. Metzger and M D. Coogan. New York: Oxford University Press, 1993. Pp. 98–102; J. A. Sanders. "Canon, Hebrew Bible." *ABD* 1.837–52.

For more advanced study, J. W. Miller. *The Origins of the Bible: Rethinking Canon History.* New York: Paulist Press, 1994; J. A. Sanders. *Canon and Community: A Guide to Canonical Criticism.* Philadelphia: Fortress, 1984.

The New Testament

The **New Testament** (NT), the second half of the Bible, consists of twenty-seven books (see Table 1.4). They were composed in the Greek language sometime between the years 50–150 CE. One finds three different types of literature among these NT books. The first five books of the NT consist of narrative material. The first four narratives are called **gospels**, meaning "good news." The titles of these gospels are Matthew, Mark, Luke, and John. Each offers a narrative of Jesus' life, telling of the "good news" of God's salvation through the life, death, and resurrection of his son, Jesus. The fifth narrative, The Acts of the Apostles, tells of the history of some of the more influential of the earliest followers of Jesus. Modern readers will observe that these narratives are not like modern biographies or histories. Still, most readers would recognize at least the broad similarity between these narratives and their modern counterparts.

The second major section of the NT consists of letters or epistles. There are twenty-one such books. Again, to moderns these documents appear very different from a contemporary letter. First, many of them are much longer than a typical modern letter. Second, many of these letters are not very personal. The recipients of many of these letters are whole congregations of people. Finally, some of these letters, such as the ones entitled Hebrews or 1 John, actually read more like a reflective treatise on some aspect of the early Christian religion and its life.

Table 1.4

The New Testament

All major Christian denominations agree on both the content and order of the NT books

Gospels and Acts (Narrative Books)	Letters	Apocalypse

Matthew
Mark
Luke
John
Acts of the Apostles
	Letters of Paul
	Romans
	1 Corinthians
	2 Corinthians
	Galatians
	Ephesians
	Philippians
	Colossians
	1 Thessalonians
	2 Thessalonians
	1 Timothy
	2 Timothy
	Titus
	Philemon
	Hebrews (traditionally
	    ascribed to Paul)
	General or
	    Catholic Letters
	James
	1 Peter
	2 Peter
	1 John
	2 John
	3 John
	Jude
		Revelation

Careful observers will notice something of an ordered arrangement to these letters. First they will notice that a man named Paul is the stated author of thirteen of these texts. The first nine of these letters are addressed to churches and appear in the NT from the longest to the shortest of letters. Individuals are the recipients of the last four letters: two to Timothy, one to Titus, and one to Philemon. James, Peter (two letters), John (three letters), and Jude are the stated authors of the last seven of these twenty-one letters. Traditionally, biblical scholars have called these seven missives "general" or "catholic epistles" because they are addressed to the **church** in general, not to specific churches or individuals, as are Paul's letters. In Gal 3:9, one of Paul's letters, Paul refers to James, Cephas (an alternative name for Peter), and John as "pillars" of the church. Note that the order in which Paul refers to these pillars is the precise order in which the letters bearing their names appear in the NT. Is this coincidental? Jude, the brother of Jesus, rounds out the final seven letters.

Hebrews now stands between the thirteen letters of Paul and the seven catholic letters. This letter is anonymous, making no explicit claims of authorship. From a relatively early time, ancient readers associated this letter with Paul (an association that most modern interpreters do not accept, simply because there is no evidence that Paul wrote the letter). But granting for the sake of this discussion the early Christian tradition of Pauline authorship for Hebrews, this results in a total of fourteen letters that Paul wrote. The following arrangement results for the epistle section of the NT: twenty-one letters total; fourteen (or 7×2) by Paul, and seven (7×1) by the pillars and Jesus' brother. Many believe that this numerical arrangement revolving around the number seven is not a coincidence, but shows some type of purposeful arrangement of the NT.

Revelation, or the **Apocalypse** (the Greek word for "Revelation") is the last book of the NT. Revelation 2–3 presents *seven* letters to *seven* churches. Note the similarity here to the structure of the epistle section of the NT, also structured around the number seven. Many modern read-

---

A Closer Look: When Did the Books of the New Testament become "Bible"? The early Christians who composed the books that are now found in the second section of the Bible did not write these texts intending that they be added to the scriptures as "the New Testament." Yet by the mid-second century CE, Christians had begun to gather Christian texts together, such as the four gospels, the letters of Paul, and other texts that were considered useful in the life of the church. They are, today, included in the NT. They even began to read these texts in worship, along with passages from the scriptures. By the end of the second century, a leading church bishop named Irenaeus appeals to what he calls "apostolic writings" as distinctively authoritative texts that one can use to argue against teachings that conflict with the emerging church standards of true doctrine. By around the year 400 CE, the twenty-seven books that compose the current NT were acknowledged by the church as distinctively authoritative writings among the scores of other gospels, letters, and apocalypses that Christians had composed to express their faith.

For further study, R. B. Brown. *An Introduction to the New Testament.* New York: Doubleday, 1997. Pp. 3–19; A. B. du Toit. "Canon, New Testament." *The Oxford Companion to the Bible.* Edited by B. M. Metzger and M D. Coogan. New York: Oxford University Press, 1993. Pp. 102–104.

For more advanced study, H. K. Gamble. *The New Testament Canon: Its Making and Meaning.* Philadelphia: Fortress, 1985; B. M. Metzger. *The Canon of the New Testament.* Oxford: Clarendon, 1987; L. M. McDonald. *The Formation of the Christian Biblical Canon.* Peabody, MA: Hendrickson, 1995.

ers will find the content of the book of Revelation quite curious. Unlike the narrative books and the letters, which are at least broadly familiar to moderns in terms of the genre of literature they represent, the Apocalypse has quite a distinctive style when compared to contemporary literature. Moderns forced to categorize it by today's comparisons might recognize similarities to fantasy or science fiction. However, this type of literature, called "apocalyptic literature," consisting of dramatic visions of the cataclysmic end of the world and God's victory over evil, was a very popular genre in the ancient world. Early Christian readers would have had no problem knowing how to interpret and make sense of this final book of the Bible.

Terminology

Given all the terminology that one can employ to talk about the Bible, readers need to understand how this textbook will employ specific terminology.

- Hebrew Bible. This text will employ *Hebrew Bible* when referring to the books of this collection in their ancient, pre-Christian, settings. Part Two of this book will employ this terminology.
- Scriptures or Jewish scriptures. New Testament writers often referred in their writings to the books found in the Hebrew Bible. However, they tended to use the word *scripture(s)* to denote these books. Parts Three and Four of this text, therefore, will follow this practice.
- Septuagint or LXX. This text will employ these terms when it discusses specifically this Greek translation of the Hebrew Bible.
- Apocrypha or Deuterocanonicals. This textbook will employ the terms *Apocrypha* and **Deuterocanonical** interchangeably, intentionally choosing to make no judgment regarding the **canonical** status of these documents. To be sure, for many readers of this text, this collection of documents is not considered part of the Bible. Yet inclusion of these texts in this introductory textbook on the Bible is warranted for two reasons. First, the Deuterocanonicals are considered part of the Bible for the majority of Christians around the world. Furthermore, the Apocrypha was regularly included in Protestant Bibles until recent times. Thus, it is fitting that students acquire at least a basic familiarity with these texts. Second, the books of the Apocrypha contain a wealth of valuable information about Jewish history and religious thought in the two centuries prior to the birth of Jesus. Readers' understandings of the Jewish world during these crucial centuries are enriched by study of these texts.
- Other Jewish writings. Readers will discover that, in addition to the Hebrew Bible and the Deuterocanonicals, many other Jewish religious texts exist that can enrich one's knowledge of the biblical world. Students will learn about these texts as they become relevant for biblical materials being studied.

What Is Intertextuality and Rereading?

Learning Goals

- To understand the meaning of intertextuality and rereading and their relationship to one another.
- To understand key terms, such as literary text, social text, interpretive text, and self-text.
- To understand the terms micro- and macro-level intertextuality.
- To understand at a basic level typology as a kind of intertextual reading.

Guiding Study Exercises

1) Offer two to three sentence definition of *intertextuality*. What does it have to do with *rereading*?
2) List and briefly define the three different types of texts discussed in this chapter.
3) What are micro- and macro-level intertextuality? Offer an example of each *that does not come from the material of this chapter.*
4) Define typology. Read the following biblical texts. Which one(s) offer an example of typology and why? 1 Cor 15:42–49; Rom 5:7–13; Jn 15:1–11.
5) Write a paragraph summarizing what is essential about your own self-text in relationship to your understanding of the origins of the Bible.
6) How does this new information about the Bible potentially influence your approaches to interpreting the Bible?

Understanding intertextuality and rereading is a crucial matter of introduction. Both terms may seem foreign and even intimidating to introductory readers. Yet folk engage in intertextual rereading all the time, even if they do not use this term to describe what they are doing. Essentially intertextuality occurs when a reader of a text or a set of texts intersects this text or set of texts with one or more other texts. It is in the intersection of one text or set of texts with another text or set of texts that interpretation emerges. This textbook refers to such interpretation as "rereading." The process of rereading provides a plausible model for understanding the origins of the Bible. Each successive generation receives from its predecessors a body of texts, in this case, sacred texts. These texts become a means of making life meaningful. But each generation also rereads the texts, that is, reinterprets them for their own use and the use of future generations to which such texts will be passed. The Bible, according to this model, is therefore a collection of received and reinterpreted sacred texts passed on and successively reinterpreted by members of their respective worshipping communities. To understand this concept more thoroughly, one must understand what the word *text* means and the process of interpretation.[4]

---

[4]See D. Penchansky, "Staying the Night: Intertexuality in Genesis and Judges," *Reading Between Texts: Intertextuality and the Hebrew Bible* (ed., D. N. Fewell; Louisville, KY: Westminster/John Knox, 1992) 77–88.

Literary Text

A **literary text** likely comes first to readers' minds when they hear "text." A literary text refers to "written and preserved material." "Intertextuality" in this context denotes "the relationship between juxtaposed literary texts."[5] This kind of literary intertextual juxtaposition can occur on at least two levels, a micro-level and a macro-level.[6]

Micro-level intertextuality refers to intertexts where there exists a high degree of verbal correspondence. For example, when one text incorporates into itself a quotation or near quotation of another text, one finds micro-level intertextuality. A couple of examples from the world of American history and politics can illustrate this type of intertextuality.

One of the most famous lines from America's significant texts is found in the *Declaration of Independence*: "We hold these truths to be self-evident, that all men are created equal." Given that the quotation is from such an important literary text in the American experience, interpreters of the American story have often quoted, or offered near-quotations, of this line. For example, Abraham Lincoln began his famous Gettysburg Address with these words: "Fourscore and seven years ago our fathers brought forth on this continent a new nation, conceived in Liberty, and dedicated to the proposition that all men are created equal." Note at the end of this sentence the micro-level intertext to the *Declaration*. This intertext compels readers (and original listeners) to interpret Lincoln's address in connection with the foundational literary text of the American story. One interprets the meaning of the address at Gettysburg not simply *in* the text of Lincoln's words, but *between* the text of Lincoln's address and the *Declaration*. This is significant, for contemporaries of Lincoln had generally interpreted "The War between the States" as a war concerning states' rights. Yet through his quotation of the *Declaration,* Lincoln is suggesting that the Civil War is not about *states'* rights, but about *human* rights, most especially the rights of slaves to be free people.[7] While Lincoln could have made this point without quoting from the literary text of the *Declaration,* the appeal to this revered literary text of American beginnings invites listeners and readers to understand his words in conversation with the high principles of America as expressed in its own significant literary texts.

Martin Luther King, Jr. also offers two examples of a micro-level intertext in his "I Have a Dream" speech.[8] The introduction to his speech offers the first intertext: "Fivescore years ago, a great American, in whose symbolic shadow we stand today, signed the Emancipation Proclamation. This momentous decree came as a great beacon light of hope to millions of Negro slaves who had been seared in the flames of withering injustice." The phrase, "fivescore years ago," is an intertext with the opening line of Lincoln's "Gettysburg Address," which begins, "Fourscore and seven years ago. . . ." One can understand the phrase "fivescore years ago" even if one does not recognize the intertextual allusion, but the meaning of the phrase "fivescore years" is richer if one recognizes the intertextual allusion. This intertext encourages listeners and readers to inter-

---

[5]*Ibid.,* 77.

[6]See I. N. Rashkow, "Intertextuality, Transference, and the Reader in/of Genesis 12 and 20," *Reading between Texts,* 57–59. See below under "Social Text" for a discussion of macro-level intertextuality.

[7] See, G. Wills, *Lincoln at Gettysburg* (New York: Simon & Schuster, 1992).

[8]*I Have a Dream: Writings and Speeches which Changed the World* (ed. J. M. Washington; San Francisco: Harper-SanFrancisco, 1986/1992) 101–106.

sect King's speech with that of Lincoln's address, inviting them to compare the important principles laid forth in Lincoln's speech with those King would articulate. The meaning of the words
"fivescore years ago" is found not only *in* King's speech, but *between* King's speech and Lincoln's speech (that is, King is saying more than 100 years ago). This speech, King is implying,
continues the great struggle for freedom to which Lincoln referred in his speech a century earlier.

King's speech preserves a second micro-level intertext: "So I say to you, my friends, that
even though we must face the difficulties of today and tomorrow, I still have a dream. It is a dream
deeply rooted in the American dream that one day this nation will rise up and live out the true
meaning of its creed—we hold these truths to be self-evident, that all men are created equal." Obviously, King is quoting from the literary text of the *Declaration* to give sanction to his appeal.
By quoting from this text, he was encouraging listeners and readers to intersect the ideal of American principles with the failure of America to live up to its own principles. He could have made
his point simply by saying that he had a dream that one day black America would have the same
rights and freedoms as white America. But through this micro-level intertext, one finds meaning
not simply *in* King's words, but *between* his words and the words from America's own foundational text—words with which any American would have a difficult time disagreeing. These examples show that intertextual interpretation takes place even in the world of political debate and
rhetoric. While the word may sound intimidating, intertextual interpretation actually comes quite
naturally. People do it all the time.

Social Text

Social texts constitute another type of text worthy of exploration. David Penchansky defines this
as "the text of culture," which he further describes as "the environment in which a literary text is
produced."[9] In short, literary texts do not exist in a vacuum, but within the larger (con)texts of society and culture. This social/cultural text can also intersect, just as other literary texts can, with
the literary text that one is trying to interpret.

Texts and Social Texts. In the context of life there exist many kinds of social texts. *Language* is one very familiar example. It is an indispensable tool of communication within a group,
society, and culture. Literary texts, of course, offer one example of the social text of language.
But there are other kinds of language texts. There are *oral texts,* texts that exist in the world of
face-to-face conversation, speeches, and even professorial lectures. There are *somatic texts,* texts
that people generate when they say something through their body language (the Greek word for
"body" is *soma*). There are *ritualistic texts,* symbolic actions that speak and communicate (e.g., a
wedding ceremony or a funeral). Language, in its various forms, is part of a people's social text.

Something as simple as "the wink" can offer a specific example of a somatic type of social
text.[10] A quick wink at another person can communicate flirtation (or harassment—depending on
the [con]text!). But how does one know that the wink is communicating sexual flirtation? Does
not the larger cultural context—the social text—in which one lives teach one that this particular
action means flirtation?

---

[9]"Staying the Night," 78.

[10] The example of the wink is drawn from C. Geertz's seminal essay, "Thick Description: Toward an Interpretive
Theory of Culture," *The Interpretation of Cultures* (New York: Basic Books, 1973) 3–30.

Ideology represents another type of social text. Ideology is a shorthand way of referring to a group's or society's shared set of values, assumptions, and **worldviews**. A group's ideology provides for members of a group a grid or lens through which or by which the group, and individuals within the group, can make sense of things. Like other cultural systems (religion, philosophy, and science), ideology too plays an important role, "provid[ing] a template or blueprint for the organization of social and psychological processes."[11] For example, the ideology that came out of the intellectual movement known as the Enlightenment has greatly influenced Western culture. Many Enlightenment thinkers wanted to throw off what they considered to be oppressive controls placed on people's lives by superstition and irrationality. These thinkers believed that powerful institutions, such as the monarchical state and the church, undergirded and oversaw this oppression. Out of this context such values as individual liberty of thought and religion emerged. Liberal democratic thinking was born, with the United States' own revolution against the king of England serving as the first great experiment of Enlightenment thought. The culture of the United States highly values individual rights and liberties, the freedom of religion, the freedom of thought and speech and academic and scientific inquiry, and even the *free* market of capitalism. Such values find their roots in this ideology of the Enlightenment. This ideology forms for those reared under its tutelage a framework, lens, and grid through which and by which to interpret and make sense of things in the world, including the texts that are written and read. Intertextual interpretation that takes into account the social text is concerned with exploring how one's ideology shapes one's interpretation of texts.

Another social text that makes up the fabric of a culture is religious thought or **theology**. Theology is quite similar to ideology in that it, too, provides for a group or even a whole culture a framework, lens, or grid, through which and by which the group or culture can interpret and make sense of experiences. *Functionally,* therefore, religion, like politics or economics, could justifiably be discussed as a certain kind of ideology. On a practical level, however, religious thought is worthy of separate discussion, particularly in a text about the Bible, which most people would likely consider to be a theological book rather than an ideological book.

Like ideology, religious thought offers "a template or blueprint for the organization of social and psychological processes" (Geertz). But religion includes an implicit, and often explicit, claim to provide a template or blueprint that comes from beyond this world—a blueprint for life that comes from the gods or God. Religion offers to its adherents understandings of the world that claim to be rooted in divine, suprahuman, authority. Ideological systems generally admit to being human creations; religious systems of thought claim to be revealed from the deity (or deities). As to whether the templates and blueprints offered by the Bible are human constructions (ideology) or transcendent truths (theology), each reader must decide for herself or himself. However, since writers of the Bible would surely think that they were presenting transcendant truths, and not humanly constructed ideologies, it is appropriate to refer to the religious social texts to which the Bible gives expression as *theological* social texts.

History is another type of social text. History tells a people's story and certainly the story a people tells about itself contributes to that larger environment of culture that produces and interprets texts. For example, one who knew nothing about American history could make some sense

---

[11]Geertz, "Ideology as a Cultural System," *ibid.,* 216.

of Lee Harper's novel *To Kill a Mockingbird.* Yet one who knows those chapters of America's story that have to do with slavery, segregation, and racism cannot help but intersect Harper's literary text with the social text of the American story. Such a reader would also recognize *Mockingbird's* agenda to challenge this feature of American life and to subvert and offer a rereading of these chapters of this nation's experience. Furthermore, the authors of many texts, and this is most especially true of the Bible, simply assume that the reader knows the story of the people being talked about in the text. Beginning readers often find the Bible inaccessible to them because the various authors of the Bible assume that readers know the history of Israel, including key figures and events. Familiarity with this part of Israel's social text will undoubtedly make the Bible more understandable.

A social text, therefore, is that web of interrelated texts that one may identify minimally as language, ideology, theology, and history. These various types of social texts are closely interrelated, for culture, ideology, and history mutually support and reinforce one another. A people's ideology, for example, will shape the way a people writes its history.

Macro-level intertextuality. Texts can offer allusions to or quotations from other specifically defined texts, as the above discussion of micro-level intertextuality showed. But there also exists **macro-level intertextuality**. Here a text intersects with a larger event, theme, or story, with such intersection having a low degree of verbal correspondence between the texts. These larger events, themes, or stories are part of the fabric of the social text in which folk originally produced and read texts. *To Kill a Mockingbird* is a literary text whose meaning is richer if the reader knows the social text of American history. Meaning emerges for the reader in the context of the dialogue taking placed between *Mockingbird* and the larger social text of American culture. This would be an example of a macro-level intertext.

A biblical illustration can make this clearer. A particular literary text found in the Bible reads as follows:

> [1]When Israel was a child, I loved him, and out of Egypt I called my son. [2]The more I called them, the more they went from me; they kept sacrificing to the Baals, and offering incense to idols. [3]Yet it was I who taught Ephraim to walk, I took them up in my arms; but they did not know that I healed them. [4]I led them with cords of human kindness, with bands of love. I was to them like those who lift infants to their cheeks. I bent down to them and fed them. [5]They shall return to the land of Egypt, and Assyria shall be their king, because they have refused to return to me. [6]The sword rages in their cities, it consumes their oracle-priests, and devours because of their schemes. [7]My people are bent on turning away from me. To the Most High they call, but he does not raise them up at all. [8]How can I give you up, Ephraim? How can I hand you over, O Israel? How can I make you like Admah? How can I treat you like Zeboiim? My heart recoils within me; my compassion grows warm and tender. [9]I will not execute my fierce anger; I will not again destroy Ephraim; for I am God and no mortal, the Holy One in your midst, and I will not come in wrath. [10]They shall go after the LORD, who roars like a lion; when he roars, his children shall come trembling from the west. [11]They shall come trembling like birds from Egypt, and like doves from the land of Assyria; and I will return them to their homes, says the LORD (Hos 11:1–11).

As one reads through the text, one eventually recognizes that the speaker is God (see v. 9), who is depicted as telling something of a story. God speaks of how he called his son Israel out of

Egypt and attempted to rear this child to walk in a proper way. Yet the son was a rebellious child and followed after other gods. God, therefore, will punish this son: God will return this people to Egypt and a foreign power (Assyria) will rule over them. But God cannot give up on his child. God will not destroy his child Israel (also named Ephraim in v. 9). God's people shall return to their Lord, and then they will return from Egypt and Assyria and God will return them to their homes.

The story, in and of itself, makes sense. Yet this little story is alluding to a number of other events and stories that were operative in the world of ancient Israel, even though the specific text of Hosea does not refer to any *specific* literary text. Hosea, without referring to any specific literary text, is referring to a significant feature of Israel's social text: its history, and, specifically, its story of the escape from Egypt. While Hosea is alluding to the story of the escape from Egypt, he is not quoting from or alluding to any *specific* literary text that tells this story. The story of escape from Egypt served in ancient Israel as a bedrock social text to which many biblical writers again and again referred. When readers are familiar with this particular story, as well as the larger story of Israel's ongoing rebellion against God, they can more easily make sense of literary texts, such as Hos 11:1–11, that allude to such stories.

This short literary text from Hosea also alludes to a theological social text. The reader can easily detect a plot of sorts in this literary text: God calls Israel to be his people; the people rebel against God; God threatens punishment of the people; the people return to their God; God restores the people to their land. This particular plot line virtually saturates the whole of the Hebrew Bible.[12] This story line of call, rebellion, punishment, repentance (returning to God), and restoration lay at the core and center of Israel's assumptions about its identity and how it was to relate to its god[13] and to other cultures and peoples. It provided, as theological and ideological texts do, the lens and grid, the template and blueprint, through which Israel made sense of the experiences of the nation.

Matthew 2:13–15, which students should now read, illustrates further the idea of intertextual reading.

Matthew's narrative about the birth of Jesus was composed several centuries later than the text from Hosea. Matthew's text can illustrate *both* micro- and macro-level intertextuality. One finds a micro-level intertext in vv. 14–15: "Then Joseph got up, took the child and his mother by night, and went to Egypt, and remained there until the death of Herod. This was to fulfill what had been spoken by the Lord through the prophet, *'Out of Egypt I have called my son.'*" The italicized portion of v. 15 is a direct quotation of Hos 11:1b, a clear example of a micro-level intertext. However, in the context of Matthew's larger narrative of the birth of Jesus, the text has a meaning different from that of Hosea. In Hosea, *Israel* is the "son" whom God called out of Egypt; in Matthew the same words clearly denote Jesus as God's son. In Matthew the calling out of Egypt is not a reference to Israel's escape from Egypt, but the flight of Jesus and his family to Egypt to escape the plot by King Herod to kill all the babies in Bethelehem in an effort to destroy Jesus. Later Matthew's story says that after Herod died and the danger was past, Joseph brought his family back out of Egypt to the land of Judea. By placing the ancient prophet's words into the

---

[12] This "social text" we refer to as "the Deuteronomistic pattern." More will be said of this later.

[13] This text uses "god" (lower case) to refer to the various deities who inhabit the story of the Bible, including the god of Israel. "God" (upper case) is used as a proper name to denote this god of Israel.

context of a new story—the story about the birth of the Jesus whom he believed to be the son of God—Matthew has given new meaning to the words of Hosea.

The initial examination of micro-level intertextual interpretation discussed how allusions to earlier texts can invite readers of these earlier texts to reinterpret, or reread, these earlier texts (recall Lincoln's appeal to the *Declaration,* inviting people to understand the Civil War as being about human rights, not states' rights). Matthew appears to be doing much the same thing. The center of attention in Hosea's text is Israel and its relationship with God, a relationship that began when God called his son (Israel) out of Egypt. Yet Matthew is shifting the center of attention away from Israel and focusing on Jesus. He appears to be inviting readers to reread, to understand in a new way, this classic text from the ancient prophet: the central character in God's action is not Israel, but Jesus of Nazareth, the son of God and the **Messiah**. What accounts for this shift of focus, from Israel to Jesus?

The idea of social text can help one to understand what Matthew is doing. The earliest followers of Jesus, most of whom were folk reared as Jews and steeped in the Jewish traditions and scriptures, came to embrace a new social text. This social text was a new theological story, template, or blueprint, by which and through which these followers of Jesus made sense of their experiences *and* the Jewish scriptures. One can sum up this new social text with the statement, "Jesus, the Messiah and son of God, is the fulfillment of the story of Israel." Matthew, who believed Jesus to be *the* son of God, read the reference to God's son in Hos 11:1b as being, therefore, ultimately about Jesus. Even a quick review of the larger text from Hosea will show that *in the context* of Hosea, there is nothing in the text of Hosea itself to indicate that Hos 11:1 is about Jesus who was to be born centuries after Hosea lived. But Matthew reads, or rereads, the literary text of Hosea 11:1 through the lens of a new social text: *Jesus* is the son of God. Thus he finds in the text a meaning that another reader who did not share Matthew's Christian social text would not see. Matthew has intersected his Christian social text (Jesus is the son of God) with the ancient literary text of Hosea and presented to his readers a new understanding, or rereading, of Hos 11:1. The meaning of Hos 11:1, for Matthew, emerges not from the text of Hosea alone, but in the dialogue that takes place *between* the literary text of Hosea and the social text of Matthew's Christian (theological/ideological) beliefs.

The text from Matthew can also illustrate macro-level intertextual reading. Recall that macro-level intertextual reading takes place when a literary text appeals not so much to a particular literary text, but to a larger story, or even larger social text. (Recall how Hos 11:1 in its ancient context appealed to the larger story of Israel's escape from Egypt.) Matthew could have seen that Hos 11:1b, when read in the larger literary context of Hos 11:1–11, was *literally* about Israel. Might Matthew be suggesting in this allusion to Hos 11:1 that one should compare Jesus' story to the larger story of Israel? Just as Israel, God's son, was called out of Egypt by God in the days of its beginnings, so Jesus, God's son, was also called out of Egypt in the days of his beginnings. Might Matthew be inviting readers to compare, and even contrast, the story of Israel as God's son to the story of Jesus as God's son? God's son Israel was a rebellious child, running after other gods. Will Jesus be such a son, or will he be the kind of son God wanted Israel to be—obedient and faithful? These are the kinds of interpretive questions that readers who engage in intertextual reading can ask.

The comparison of the Jesus story with the story of Israel illustrates a specific type of macro-level intertextual reading that biblical interpreters call **typology**. Typology is a way of reading that assumes that "characters and scenes prefigure later events."[14] In this instance, Israel's story prefigures Jesus' story. This type of intertextual reading offers readers a rich method by which to intersect various stories and themes found within the Bible. To understand typology better, read carefully 1 Cor 10:1–6 and the following comments.

Paul, the author of this text, *specifically* states in v. 6 that events from the story of ancient Israel ("our ancestors," as he calls Israel in v. 1) serve as "examples," or "types," for his readers. Paul is writing this letter several centuries after the events to which he is referring took place. But it is obvious that he wants to apply features of the ancient story to the lives of his readers. Readers of *this* textbook who may be unfamiliar with the story of ancient Israel may not understand the macro-level intertextual allusions (as indeed some of Paul's first-century CE readers might not have understood the allusions). But when one does understand these intertexts and can then read Paul's text in conversation with them, one can construct out of this text richer meaning.

In the story of Israel's escape from Egypt, the Jewish scriptures speak of the people being led during the day by a cloud, as they trekked through the wilderness on the way to their ultimate destination (a land called Canaan, which they believed God had promised to their ancestors). They also passed miraculously through the sea, escaping their Egyptian pursuers. God miraculously fed the people during their pilgrimage and supplied water for them through a rock that Moses, their leader, struck with his rod, releasing the water. Paul is intersecting this ancient story of God's people with the current story of God's people.

Baptism was a ritual of initiation into the Christian church. Note how Paul understands ancient Israel's passing through the cloud and sea as a kind of baptism (vv. 1–2). Another significant part of early Christian worship was a sacred meal. It consisted of bread and wine, symbols of the body and blood of Jesus, who, the Christians believed, died a sacrificial death to ensure the forgiveness of their sins. Paul interprets the food and drink miraculously provided by God to the ancient Israelites as "types" for the spiritual meal that first-century Christians shared (vv. 3–4). He even states that the rock from which this water came was Christ (v. 4b), alluding to the early Christian idea that Jesus was the source of the bread and wine that Christians shared in their sacred meal. Paul offers such rereadings of the Jewish scriptures to make the point that God provided a kind of baptism and sacred meal to the ancient Israelites, even as later God provided baptism and a sacred meal to the Christian who worshipped in Corinth. God expected obedience from the ancient Israelites. Paul says in v. 5 that they were not obedient and, therefore, God struck them down. Paul then applies this ancient event as a warning to his readers, encouraging them not to "desire evil as they [the ancient Israelites] did" (v. 6).

Note how Paul is intertextually connecting two social texts. One cannot adequately understand the way Paul is interpreting the story drawn from Jewish scriptures unless one understands something about early Christian worship practices (the ritualistic texts of baptism and the sacred meal). Likewise, one cannot adequately understand what Paul is saying about early Christian worship practices unless one is familiar with the specific allusions that Paul is drawing from the story of Israel in the Jewish scriptures (the cloud, the sea, the miraculous food and drink, and the rock). Paul's words in 1 Cor 10:1–6 find meaning not only *in* the text but in the dialogue taking place *between* this literary text, the social text of early Christian worship practices—ritualistic

---

[14]Rashkow, "Intertextuality," 58.

Paul speaks of the "supernatural rock" from which water came forth for the Israelites in the wilderness (1 Cor 10:4), offering a rereading of Exod 17:6 and Num 20:8. One can see the water trails coming forth from the rocks of the Wilderness of Zin. People, such as Moses, who knew the ways of the wilderness would know how to find water flowing beneath the rocks. (Chance and Horne)

texts—and the historical social text of ancient Israel's story. It is in this intertextual dialogue between texts, both literary and social, that the typological interpretation emerges.

Social text, therefore, adds a complex and rich feature to intertextuality. Intertextual reading takes place not only between literary texts, but between literary texts and social texts (and even between social texts and other social texts). Social/cultural texts, consisting of language, ideology, theology, and history form a complex web of interlacing and intersecting concepts, values, worldviews, and assumptions. People produce and interpret literary texts within the fabric of these interlacing and intersecting concepts. Awareness of the various social texts with which biblical literary texts are in dialogue enriches the meaning one can find in these texts.

Interpretive Text

What happens when one engages in the act of interpretation? When people read a text, be it a literary text or even some kind of social text (such as a somatic text or a ritualistic text), just what are they doing when they attempt to make sense of, or interpret, this text? The end result of this interpretive enterprise, the sense one makes of a text that she or he is trying to interpret, is an **interpretive text**. But how does one get there?

David Penchansky introduces his discussion of the interpretive text this way: "The third understanding of intertextuality requires us to take into account *our own participation in the act of interpretation* as we produce a new text every time we process old information."[15] It is imperative to keep in mind that people do not interpret texts in a vacuum. People exist in the context of a social text; people live in that web of interlacing and intersecting features of culture, such as language, ideology, theology (if they are religious), and history. People carry to the text they wish to interpret their own distinctive sets of values, worldviews, ideologies, theologies, and histories. It would not be far-fetched to say that in a very real sense each person, or each self, who engages in the act of interpretation carries within himself his own distinctive "text." Each self, in other words, is a kind of text. As James Voelz says, *"The reader must be seen as a text.* Or perhaps more accurately, the states, actions, hopes, fears, and knowledge of a reader's life experience comprise a 'text.'"[16] In the end, it is in the context of this self-as-text that the actual act of interpretation takes place.

This textbook argues that persons who wrote the Bible were themselves readers of texts. Hosea was a reader of the story of ancient Israel and its relationship with God. The particular text that he created (Hos 11:1–11) was his particular reading of that story. Matthew was a (re)reader of Hosea, reading Hosea's ancient text through the lens of his own self-as-text, a self very much fashioned by the Christian social text that viewed Jesus of Nazareth as the fulfillment of Israel's story. Paul was also a (re)reader of the ancient story of Israel. He intersected this ancient story of Israel's wilderness wandering with the Christian ritualistic social texts of baptism and the sacred meal. Matthew and Paul have each produced interpretive texts of the earlier literary and social texts of their heritage.

---

[15]"Staying the Night," 85 (emphasis added).

[16]J. W. Voelz, "Multiple Signs, Levels of Meaning and Self as Text: Elements of Intertextuality," *Intertexuality and the Bible, SBLSS* 69/70 (eds., G. Aichele and G. A. Phillips; Atlanta, GA: Scholars Press, 1995) 149–164; quotation is from p. 154 (emphasis original).

St. Luke Displaying a Painting of the Virgin (1652–1653), by Giovanni Francesco Barbieri (Il Guercino [1591–1666]), illustrates visually the idea of rereading. In ancient times, artists and doctors belonged to the same guild, leading people to conclude that Luke the physician and author of the Gospel of Luke was also an artist. That gave rise to the tradition that the portrait of Jesus and Mary found in the Church of Bologna was actually painted by Luke. Il Guercino's painting depicts Luke, apparently inspired by angelic guidance, preparing this painting. Note how a number of features contribute to this visual "rereading" of Luke's role by Il Guercino: the ancient practice of physicians and artists sharing the same guild, the existence of an actual painting supposedly painted by Luke, and the belief of the artist that Luke, the gospel writer and artist, was inspired. (Oil on canvas; 87″ × 71″ (220.9 × 180.3 cm). Nelson-Atkins Museum of Art, Kansas City, Missouri [Purchase: Nelson Trust])

This text offers its own (re)readings of Matthew's and Paul's (re)readings. Hence, this text is also an interpretive text. And the process does not end there. Real readers of this interpretive text will bring with them their own selves-as-texts. In the context of their own **self-texts**, they will read the interpretive texts offered herein and may agree or disagree with these readings. They may reread Hosea's text differently than Matthew did, or reread the experience of Israel's wanderings in the wilderness differently than Paul did, or disagree with this text's interpretive texts of Hosea, Matthew, and Paul. In the context of the dialogue that takes place between the intersections of various texts—the literary text of the Bible, the intertextual allusions to other literary and social texts within the Bible, the interpretive texts presented by this textbook, and the self-texts that each reader of this text and the biblical text brings to these texts—each individual reader creates a distinctive interpretive text. Thus real readers should not view this text's rereadings of the biblical texts as definitive, but rather as suggestive. This text's readings may or may not inform student readers' own interpretive texts. Yet by engaging this text's readings of the biblical text, readers will be able to formulate readings that are truly their own.

Conclusion: Readers and Stories

The literary text of the Bible presents a story. Recall that Hosea's text alluded to the story of God's leading Israel out of Egypt; recall how Paul's text alluded to the story of Israel's wandering in the wilderness. There is a story *in* the text of the Bible. Understanding the Bible requires that one understand at least the basic contours of this story found *within* the text.

There is also a complex story *behind* the text of the Bible. Much of that story behind the literary text lives in the world of the social text. The story behind the text involves the culture out of which the literary texts that now make up the Bible came; it involves the history, the ideology, and the theology that stands behind the literary text. This story behind the text also includes the story of *how* the many people who produced the literary text of the Bible did so. This story of how and why folk wrote the Bible is, itself, a kind of historical social text. In other words, the Bible not only talks about historical events, such as Israel's escape from Egypt, but the *telling* of the Bible's story of Israel's escape from Egypt itself has its own history. And the eventual writing down of that story into a literary form also has a history. Thus, this text will devote attention to "the story behind the text." This phrase denotes not only the story of historical events to which the Bible refers but also the story of how the ancient community of faith handed down and eventually wrote down this story.

Finally, there exists a story *in front of* the text. This is the story that each reader brings to the reading of the biblical story. Think of "the story in front of the text" as another way of referring to the self-text that every reader brings with her or him to the reading experience.

Thus, throughout this text, readers need to understand that there is a close relationship between the three interlocking and interrelated sets of stories and texts. The story *in* the text corresponds to the *literary text*. The story *behind* the text corresponds to the *social text* in all of its rich complexity. And the story *in front of* the text corresponds to the *self-text,* the text/story of the interpreter that informs his or her reading of the literary and social texts and out of which emerges his or her *interpretive text.* Finally, since every act of reading and interpretation takes place in the context of the complex intersection of literary text, social text, and self-text, every act of reading is a "rereading." Each reader's self-text is an ever-mutating and ever-evolving text, as the reader grows in knowledge and experiences. Thus, with each reading experience the reader is a slightly different person than he or she was the last time. As the reader changes, readings will change. Hence, the Bible will never run out of meanings. Rereading the Bible will continuously take place.

For Further Reading

Suggestions for further reading, located at the end of each chapter, will generally not duplicate bibliography cited in the footnotes or "Closer Look" boxes.

What Is the Bible?

Basic introductions:

Harris, S. L. *Understanding the Bible.* 4th ed. Mountain View, CA: Mayfield, 1997. Pp. 1–23.

Hauer, C. E. and Young, W. A. *An Introduction to the Bible: A Journey into Three Worlds.* 4th ed. Upper Saddle River, NJ: Prentice-Hall, 1998. Pp. 3–19.

More advanced introductions:

Beasley, J. R., et. al. *An Introduction to the Bible.* Nashville, TN: Abingdon, 1991. Pp. 15–67.

Hayes, J. H. *Introduction to the Bible.* Philadelphia: Westminster, 1971. Pp. 3–29.

Critical Study Bibles.

There are several excellent study Bibles. Below are some of the best.

The HarperCollins Study Bible (New Revised Standard Version with the Apocrypha). Edited by W. A. Meeks. New York: HarperCollins, 1993.

The New Oxford Annotated Bible (New Revised Standard Version with the Apocrypha). Edited by B. M. Metzger and R. E. Murphey. New York: Oxford University Press, 1991.

The Oxford Study Bible (Revised English Bible with the Apocrypha). Edited by M. J. Suggs, K. D. Sakenfeld, and J. R. Mueller. New York: Oxford University Press, 1992.

What Is Intertextuality and Rereading?

(All the following are relatively advanced.)

Eslinger, L. "Inner-biblical Exegesis and Inner-biblical Allusion: The Question of Category." *VT* 42 (1992) 47–58.

Fishbane, M. *Biblical Interpretation in Ancient Israel.* Oxford: Clarendon Press 1985.

———. "Inner-Biblical Exegesis: Types and Strategies of Interpretation in Ancient Israel." *The Garments of Torah.* Bloomington and Indianapolis, IN: Indiana University Press, 1992. Pp. 3–18.

Hays, R. B. *Echoes of Scripture in the Letters of Paul.* New Haven, CT: Yale University Press, 1993.

Kugel, James. "How Should the Bible Be Taught?" *The Bible and the Liberal Arts: Papers from a Conference October 16–17, 1986.* Crawfordsville, IN: Wabash College, 1986. Pp. 1–20.

————. "The 'Bible as Literature' in Late Antiquity and the Middle Ages." *Hebrew University Studies in Literature and the Arts* 11 (1983) 20–70.

Nielsen, K. "Intertextuality and Biblical Scholarship." *ScanJOT* 2 (1990) 89–95.

Sipke, D, ed. *Intertextuality in Biblical Writings: Essays in Honor of Bas van Iersel.* Kampen: Uitgevers-maatschappij J. H. Kok, 1989.

CHAPTER TWO

Israel's Developing Story

Introduction

Review

Chapter 1 argued that the Bible is complex in both its origins and final form. Both aspects of its complexity stem from the different groups that have reread and added to its stories. Successive generations of readers have interpreted its literary text from the perspectives of continually changing social texts. The Bible's story, embraced as a sacred literary text, has therefore merged with the stories of its readers—their self-texts—to create a rich interpretive framework explaining everything from origins to destinies.

Preview

This chapter examines Israel's story intertextually. It offers a summary of the narrative within the Hebrew Bible and then examines two summaries of that narrative that are within the larger confines of the story itself (including the Apocrypha). The purpose is to offer readers a method to begin learning the biblical story while reflecting upon those theological perspectives that have invited the many reinterpretations, or rereadings, of that story. The two summaries invite readers to put the overall biblical story into two different historical and theological frameworks. Those theological perspectives are called Deuteronomic[1] and priestly and are set in the Exilic and post-Exilic periods.

---

[1]In this text the following distinction between Deuteronomic and Deuteronomistic is made: the term *Deuteronomic* refers to the school of thought or theological perspective that produced the core of book of Deuteronomy (chaps. 12–26) and influenced the production of other literature in the Hebrew Bible, including the later additions to the book of Deuteronomy. *Deuteronomistic* describes that wider literature, e.g. the Deuteronomistic History, produced under the influence of the Deuteronomic theology or school. See glossary.

A Survey of the Biblical Historical Narratives

Learning Goals

- To learn a basic outline of events, characters, and varying theological perspectives of the narrative in the Hebrew Bible.
- To learn and begin using some of the key terminology of critical biblical studies.
- To learn enough of the story of ancient Israel as presented in the Hebrew Bible to begin laying a foundation for reflection on biblical origins.

Guiding Study Exercises

1) Write three- to five-sentence definitions (in your own words) of the following terms: theology; Deuteronomistic History; Hellenistic; self-text; Tetrateuch; Chronicler's History.
2) Write a paragraph explaining the function of the so-called Deuteronomistic pattern within the Deuteronomistic History.
3) Explain some of the key differences in theological outlook between the Tetrateuch and the Deuteronomistic History.
4) Reflection: How might one's assumptions regarding biblical origins affect one's understanding of the meaning of the Bible?

Introduction to the Biblical Survey

The biblical story consists of three ancient histories. The **Tetrateuch** comprises the first four books of the Bible: Genesis, Exodus, Leviticus, and Numbers. The final form of these books is late, but scholars believe that the traditions they pass on are quite ancient and that earlier literary settings of the material may go back to ninth and tenth centuries BCE. The **Deuteronomistic History** comprises the books of Deuteronomy, Joshua, Judges, 1–2 Samuel, and 1–2 Kings. These function as a unity in their depiction of Israel's settlement and flourishment in the land of Canaan. The historians ascribe these events as extending from the late second millennium to the middle of the sixth century BCE. The final composition of the Deuteronomistic History dates from the Exilic period (ca. 550 BCE), even though a first edition dates to the reign and religious reforms of King Josiah (ca. 622 BCE).[2] The books of Chronicles, Ezra, and Nehemiah compose what is called the Chronicler. The setting of these books, as well as their historical and theological perspectives are

---

[2]See S. L. McKenzie, "Deuteronomistic History," *ABD* 2.160–68, for a survey of the various alternative dates of composition proposed by scholars.

very similar. Still, some scholars doubt that the books originate from the same hand.[3] Scholars date the composition of these books at around 400 BCE.[4] The books of this very late history narrate virtually the same story as that in the Deuteronomistic History except for two significant features. First, Chronicles does not tell the story of the Northern kingdom that split off from the Southern kingdom. Second, Ezra and Nehemiah extend the history much further than the Deuteronomistic History to include the release of Judean exiles from Babylon.

It is common to speak of the narrative in the Bible as a story, although readers will very quickly discover that it is not written and transmitted for entertainment alone. There is a normative aspect to it. The readers of the story whose interpretations are preserved within its pages regard it as authoritative, even as inspired. Reading the Bible *as* a story, then, only provides an avenue to become engaged in its purposes, its conflicts, its characters, and finally with its deity.

Tetrateuch (and Deuteronomy)

The Tetrateuch narrates the story of creation to the period of Israel's wandering in the wilderness of Zin in their escape from slavery in Egypt. The episodes about Abraham (changed from Abram) and his family, their migration to Egypt and their eventual escape are ascribed by the writers to the mid-second millennium BCE. Though the traditions are quite ancient, the present form of the biblical text reveals some careful editorial arranging of the material, beginning with the stories of the origins of the universe in Genesis 1–11.

A Closer Look: Histories and Critical Methods. The claims of the presence of distinct histories such as the Tetrateuch and the Deuteronomistic History within the Hebrew Bible is an outcome of the application of critical modes of investigating the Bible. These critical methods rely on readers' attempts to explain narrative inconsistencies, repetitions, and stylistic variations within the biblical narratives through hypotheses of multiple authors and composite literary origins over an extended period of time. The acronym *JEDP* reflects the view that there are at least four narrative sources, with their various authors, editors, and traditions, behind the present form of the Pentateuch: J stands for the Yahwistic source; E, the Elohistic source; D, the Deuteronomic source; and P, the priestly source.

For further study, R. Friedman. *Who Wrote the Bible?* Princeton, NJ: Prentice Hall, 1987.

For more advanced study, S. J. DeVries. "Review of Recent Research in the Tradition History of the Pentateuch." *1987 SBLSP.* Edited by K. Richards. Atlanta, GA: Scholars Press, 1987. Pp. 459–502.

---

[3]See R. L. Braun, "Chronicles, Ezra, and Nehemiah: Theology and Literary History," *Studies in the Historical Books of the Old Testament* (VTSup 30; Leiden: E. J. Brill, 1979) 52–64.

[4]See J. Blenkinsopp, *Ezra Nehemiah* (OTL; Philadelphia: Westminster, 1988) and H. G. M. Williamson, *Ezra, Nehemiah* (WBC; Waco, TX: Word, 1985).

Genesis 1–11. The book is called Genesis, which in Greek means "beginning." The opening eleven chapters of the Bible do more than narrate the creation story and ensuing primeval history, however. They offer a sweeping perspective on the nature of *all* humankind as well as on the nature of the deity. God is known to his creation both as one who speaks all things into existence (Gen 1:3, 6, 9) and as one who shapes creation with his own hands (Gen 2:7). Humans are created in the "image and likeness" of God (Gen 1:26) and yet they strive to be "like God, knowing good and evil" (Gen 3:5). Ultimately, being like God leads to human disobedience toward God (Gen 3:1–7) and this behavior gets the man and his wife removed from the garden paradise of Eden (Gen 3:22–24). The story that follows is one of humankind's wandering farther and farther away from God and that garden.

Symbolically, these stories explore the implications of the human capacities for both good and evil. The universal perspective is maintained throughout by the concern for genealogy, "the generations," or *toledot,* of particular families and of creation: heaven and earth (2:4a), Adam (5:1–32), Noah (6:9), Noah's three sons (10:1), and Shem (11:10).[5] Moreover, humans are shown to be capable of murder (Gen 4:1–16) as well as righteousness (Gen 6:9). The creator responds to human rebellion both by destroying the human race and by beginning again (Genesis 6–9), and then by relenting, forming a universal covenant, and conceding that humans are "evil from youth" (Gen 8:21). The first eleven chapters conclude by making clear the all-consuming alienation of humanity. Yet, in retrospect, the genealogies within these chapters both structure the narrative and telescope the deity's process of selecting a family through whom God will seek to dwell with his creation.

Genesis 12–50. These chapters are significant in that they introduce readers to Israel's patriarchal ancestors and depict the deity's initiative to overcome the alienation that plagues humanity. Like the narratives of Genesis 1–11, these chapters are also arranged by genealogies: Terah and Abraham (11:27–25:11), Ishmael (25:12–18), Isaac and Jacob (25:19–35:29), Esau-Edom (36:1–37:1), and finally, Jacob with Joseph and his brothers (37:2–50:26).[6] Keeping with the book's theme of beginnings, God sets aside one man, Abraham, through whose family he will overcome the separation that has scattered all creation. God promises, asking virtually nothing in return, to make Abraham a great family (Gen 12:1–3; 15:5; 17:4), to bless his family with a special relationship (Gen 15:15–16), and to give him and his descendants a special land (Gen 15:16; 17:7–8).[7] Readers can only wonder, however, whether such promises are truly realizable given human nature as elaborated in Genesis 1–11. Abraham himself is shown to be capable of great faith as he leaves his homeland of Mesopotamia (Gen 12:1), trusts God for offspring (15:6), enters into a special covenant with God (17:23), and risks sacrificing his only son, Isaac, for the sake of his commitment to God (Gen 22:1–24). But he is also shown to be a person capable of equally wretched behavior in his lying to the Egyptian Pharaoh about his wife (Gen 12:10–20) and in his failure to intervene on behalf of his wife's maid, his own concubine, Hagar (Gen 16:1–15). The inability of the family of Abraham to live worthily of God's promises functions as

---

[5] J. Blenkinsopp, *The Pentateuch* (New York: Doubleday, 1992) 59.

[6] *Ibid.,* 99.

[7] D. Clines' book *The Theme of the Pentateuch* (Sheffield: JSOT Press, 1978) is an especially readable and helpful book as students seek to make sense of the narrative and thematic lines in the first four (five) books of the Hebrew Bible.

a foil to emphasize God's commitment to go to nearly any length to keep his promise despite the behavior of his chosen family.

Abraham's descendants, Isaac (Genesis 24–26) and Isaac's son Jacob (Genesis 26–37), reveal similar aspects of the human predicament. Isaac attempts the same deception as his father by lying to a foreign king that his wife is his sister (Gen 26:1–11). Ironically, Isaac comes to life's end as an old blind man deceived by his younger son Jacob into giving up the blessing reserved for Jacob's elder twin, the first born, Esau (Gen 27:1–45). Jacob's story dominates the remainder of the book in the exposition of both the heights and depths he and his children experience in their wanderings between the Canaan land, Mesopotamia, and their final destination, Egypt.

Jacob is an especially important figure in Israel's story, as he is the father of the twelve tribal heads (Gen 35:22b-26; Josh 4:8). It is his other name, Israel, that is given to the nation (Gen 32:22–32; 35:9–15). But his original name, Jacob, means "the supplanter," or one who trips people up. He lives up to his name as he steals from his brother the blessing reserved for the first born (Gen 27:1–45), as he tricks his father-in-law in order to enrich his own flocks of sheep (Gen 30:37–31:9), and as he attempts to deceive his brother Esau yet again while feigning a repentant heart (Gen 33:1–20). But his name is changed to Israel in the confrontation with the deity at Peniel (Gen 32:22–32; cf. 35:9–15), a name that commemorates and signifies struggle with God (Gen 32:27–32). Still, God is true to his promise and blesses Jacob with descendants, twelve sons and a daughter (Gen 34:1–24; 35:22–26), who themselves come to be the powerful families that eventually occupy the Canaan land. It is through Joseph, one of Israel's sons by his wife Rachel,

Tel es Seba', or biblical Beer-Sheba, is the site of numerous patriarchal episodes, not the least of which is the episode where Yahweh reveals himself to Isaac and reiterates the promise made to Abraham (Gen 26:23–25). Here archaeologists have reconstructed the ruins of the Iron Age II city that served as one of the traditional boundaries of the state of Israel (e.g., Amos 8:14; 1 Sam 3:20 1 Chron 21:2). (Chance and Horne)

that Israel and his children migrate into Egypt during a severe famine in the Canaan land (Genesis 27–50).

Exodus-Deuteronomy. These books tell the story of the escape from Egypt to Canaan under the leadership of Moses and Aaron. It is through the events of this journey that the deity forges a special relationship with the now great family of Israel. Although the book of Exodus begins with a summary of the people's genealogy (Exod 1:1–7), such genealogies no longer play as vital a role as before in reiterating the theme of the narratives. Readers could more easily recognize a structure in the itinerary of places at which the children of Israel stop on their way out of Egypt (Exod 12:37; Num 22:1; see also Numbers 33 for a list). Perhaps a more significant macrostructure is a three-part itinerary: Israel's persecution in and escape from Egypt (Exod 1:1–15:21), Israel's two-year stay at Sinai (Exod 19:1–Num 10:10), and Israel's wandering in the wilderness on either side of the Sinai experience (Exod 15:22–18:27; and Num 10:11–26:13). Clearly, the most formidable part of this narrative is the Sinai material: The brunt of its contents is the cultic regulations of the book of Leviticus, the central and shortest book of the **Pentateuch**.[8] The narratives in these books are only secondary to the much larger structural concern of worship, priestly regulation, and cultic service—the means by which the special relationship is established. Table 2.1 illustrates the thematic centrality of worship and priestly service by showing the parallels in language between the construction of the sanctuary in the wilderness (Exod 39:42; 40:33) and the very creation of the cosmos (Gen 2:1–2).

Table 2.1

The Sanctuary and Creation

Creation of the World	Construction of the sanctuary
And God saw everything that he had made, and behold, it was very good (Gen 1:31).	And Moses saw all the work, and behold, they had done it (Exod 39:43).
Thus the heavens and the earth were finished (Gen 2:1).	Thus all the work of the tabernacle of the tent of meeting was finished (Exod 39:32).
God finished his work which he had done (Gen 2:2).	So Moses finished the work (Exod 40:33).
So God blessed the seventh day (Gen 2:3).	So Moses blessed them (Exod 39:43).[9]

[8]Blenkinsopp, *The Pentateuch,* 138.
[9]*Ibid.,* 218.

When Moses and Aaron lead the people out of Egypt to God's mountain, Yahweh meets his people there, appearing to them in thunder, lightning, and a thick cloud (Exod 19:16). Through Moses the people receive the book of the covenant, a collection of laws that forms the basis for the people's relationship to Yahweh as his priests (Exod 19:6; 24:7). The people affirm that they will keep all of Yahweh's laws (Exod 24:3b), and Moses offers burnt offerings and sacrifices to Yahweh there on the mountain. It is within this narrative setting, Exodus 25–31, that the laws concerning the construction of the Ark of the covenant, and the tabernacle (or tent), and the sacred vestments of the priests are given. Also, within this context of lawgiving, the people rebel against Yahweh, oddly under Aaron's leadership, by making an idol and worshipping it (Exod 32:1–19). This act provokes Yahweh's wrath (Exod 32:11); Moses breaks the tablets on which the law has been written (Exod 32:19) and a slaughter of the idolatrous people in the camp breaks out (Exod 32:25–29). Here the Levites are first set apart for cultic service, due to their zeal for Yahweh (Exod 32:28). The book concludes with Yahweh's appearance to Moses (Exod 33:7–23), a reiteration of the law that had been on the broken tablets (Exod 34:1–35), and a completion of the construction of the Ark, the tabernacle, and the priestly vestments (Exodus 35–40).

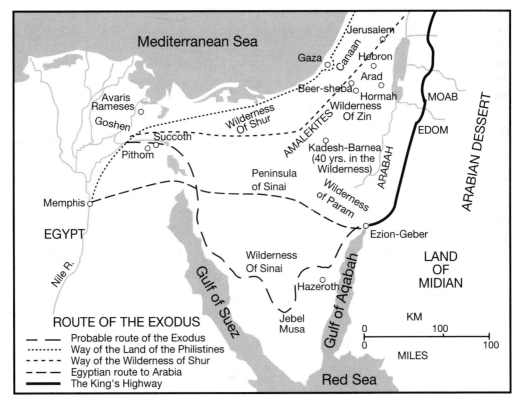

Various hypothetical models of the Exodus. (Adapted from John Tullock, *The Old Testament Story,* © 1981, p. 30. Used by permission of Prentice Hall, Upper Saddle River, NJ)

From Leviticus 1 to Numbers 10 the setting of the narrative remains Sinai. The people camped there continue to receive laws. While these laws most likely reflect the accumulated traditions of Israel's entire history, they have been selectively placed within the narrative of the people's wilderness wanderings and revelation at Sinai. When they leave Sinai after two years (Num 10:11; Deut 1:6) to go to the land of Canaan (Num 10:33), an important motif of complaining and rebellion resumes (Exod 16:1–21; cf. Num 11:1–9; Exod 17:1–7; cf. Num 20:1–13; and 13:30–33; 14:2–4; 16:1–17:13).

The rebellious and fractious band of people makes its way to Kadesh-barnea from which it launches a reconnaissance mission from the south into the Canaan land. The majority of the spies who go, representatives from each tribal family, bring back a negative report about the land (Num 13:25–29). Only one tribal representative, Caleb, of the tribe of Judah, speaks favorably of going in to the land (Num 13:30). Yahweh's wrath burns against these people, and Moses has to intercede for them yet again. But Yahweh does not relent. He punishes the people by making them return to the wilderness to purge their present generation of its faithless members (Num 14:26–35). Here, in this period of forty-year wandering, Moses continues to settle disputes of conflict between priestly families (Num 16:1–17:11), to receive laws (Num 19:1–22), and to lead in military battle (Num 21:1–35). The concluding chapters of Numbers (22–36) are set in the plains of Moab, across the Jordan River from Jericho, the place from which the later generation launches its entry into the Canaan land. There Miriam dies (Num 20:1); Aaron dies (Num 20:25–29); and Moses himself dies (Num 27:12–23; Deut 34:1–12), but not before offering his people, the children of Israel, one last reminder to keep the law. This farewell speech, which reiterates the law, is the book of Deuteronomy. The rebellious generation has died off (Deut 2:16); the people are now ready to enter the new land of Canaan.

Deuteronomistic History

The story is about the settlement of the Canaan land and the emergence of a monarchy, around 1000 BCE, that establishes a political empire. The empire eventually falls as it splits into Northern and Southern kingdoms around 922 BCE, and then succumbs to more powerful nations. After a period of about 200 years the Northern kingdom falls to **Assyria**, around 722/721 BCE, and its population is deported and scattered. Within another 150 years, around 587 BCE, the Southern kingdom falls to Babylon and its upper class citizens, priests, and nobles are deported to Babylon.

Deuteronomy. The second great history, the Deuteronomistic History, begins with the story of the entry into the land. Scholarly consensus holds that the book of Deuteronomy, containing a law code in chapters 12–26, originally introduced the Deuteronomistic History. Although the book of Deuteronomy concludes the Pentateuch in the present, completed form of the Bible, it is not originally a part of the Tetrateuch. The Deuteronomistic historians used the periods in ancient Israel's history of the settlement in Canaan (Joshua)—the period of the Judges (Judges–1 Samuel 7), the period of the united monarchy (1 Samuel 8–1 Kings 11), and the period of the divided monarchy (1 Kings 12–2 Kings 25)—to develop a theology that is distinct from that of the Tetrateuch.[10] The rationale for the **Deuteronomic theology** is set out in the sermons and laws in-

---

[10]See, for instance, H. W. Wolff, "The Kerygma of the Deuteronomical Historical Work," *The Vitality of the Old Testament Traditions* (ed. W. Brueggemann and H. W. Wolff; Atlanta, GA: John Knox, 1974) 83–100.

cluded in the book of Deuteronomy. The key feature of the book is its law code, arranged as the central part of the book (Deuteronomy 12–26).

Defining theological features of the Deuteronomic perspective would include its concern for worship of Yahweh alone (Deut 13:1–5; cf. Exod 20:2–6), its worship in one central place (ostensibly Jerusalem: Deuteronomy 12; cf. Exod 20:24), its insistence that possession of the Canaan land (one of God's promises in the Tetrateuch) is contingent on keeping the commandments (Deut 7:12–16; 8:19–20; 11:8–11), and its affirmation that Yahweh's word comes to his people through his messengers, the prophets (Deut 13:1–11; 18:15–22). This central collection of laws, understood to have come from Sinai (or Horeb: Deut 1:6), is balanced on both sides by a historical prologue (Deut 1:1–4:43), a series of introductory sermons and admonitions (Deut 4:44–11:32), a concluding admonition (Deuteronomy 27–32), and a farewell blessing and narrative of the ordination of Joshua (Deuteronomy 33–34).

Joshua. The book of Joshua outlines a story of military invasion and tribal allotment under the leadership of Joshua, Moses' successor. The opening chapters portray the children of Israel making preparation for invasion (Josh 1:1–5:12), part of which preparation is the proper observation of the laws in Deuteronomy (Josh 1:7–9). The story of this invasion spells out the importance to the Deuteronomistic historians of obedience to Yahweh as a contingency of successful occupation of the land. Failure to obey means failure to occupy the land fully (Josh 7:1–26; 9:3–21). The instructions for holy war set out in Deuteronomy 20 are the background for the warfare conducted in the invasion. Similarly, the laws that abide after the captured lands have been apportioned to tribes (e.g., Josh 12:1–19:51) are based upon the book of Deuteronomy (cf. Josh

A Closer Look: Did It Happen? One perplexing question that arises upon reading a book such as Joshua is, "Did it really happen?" That is, does Joshua narrate events that are historical? One cannot help but wonder whether there is any evidence that the walls of Jericho, for instance, came falling down on the seventh day of the siege at the seventh blast of the trumpet (Josh 6:15–17). To answer the question, readers must differentiate the story in the text (literary text) and the story behind the text (historical social text). Part of that process begins by identifying the genre, or type of text, one is reading. It may well be that the ancient writer was not intending to be historical in the same sense that modern readers understand the term. In that case, readers must learn that there are other ways for texts to have meaning without their being historical.

For further study, T. E. Fretheim. *Deuteronomistic History.* Nashville, TN: Abingdon. 1983. Pp. 27–35; V. H. Matthews, and J. C. Moyer. *The Old Testament: Text and Context.* Peabody, MA: Hendrickson Press, 1997. Pp.11–15.

For more advanced study, P. R. Ackroyd. "The Historical Literature." *The Hebrew Bible and Its Modern Interpreters.* Edited by D. A. Knight and G. M. Tucker. Philadelphia: Fortress Press, 1985. Pp. 297–303; R. Alter. *The Art of Biblical Narrative.* New York: Basic Books, 1981; G. W. Coats. *Saga, Legend, Tale, Novella, Fable.* Sheffield: JSOT Press, 1985. Pp. 7–15.

20:1–22:34; and Deuteronomy 19). In its conclusion Joshua offers a testament (Josh 23:1–24:33) just as Moses did (Deuteronomy 31).

Judges. The book of Judges actually opens with the theme of settlement from the preceding book of Joshua (Judges 1–2).[11] In the main, the book of Judges concerns the next major era of Israel's history focusing upon the move from rule by judges to rule by a king. The Deuteronomistic historians continue to emphasize Deuteronomic theology by setting out in the opening three chapters a kind of literary pattern that reminds the reader of the implications of failing to keep the law (Judg 1:1–3:6). Judges 2:11–19 sets out this pattern as sin (Judg 2:11–13), punishment due to Yahweh's anger (Judg 2:14–15), Yahweh's seeing their distress (perhaps because they "cry out" or because they repent [Judg 2:15b, 19]), Yahweh's delivering the people by raising up a judge (Judg 2:16), and the prosperity of the people, who then begin the cycle of sin again (Judg 2:18–23).[12] The episodes are loosely structured and concern individual charismatic leaders, who deliver their particular tribes or tribal coalitions (Judg 3:7–16:31). Throughout the series of episodes and especially in the final episodes (Judg 17:1–21:25), the narrative makes clear the constant threat the peoples are under due to anarchy and the lack of civil unity. The concluding verse (Judg 21:25) is an ominous foreshadowing of the debate that will ensue in the remainder of the history: do these loosely organized tribes need a king to govern them?

1 and 2 Samuel–1 and 2 Kings. The books of 1 and 2 Samuel and 1 and 2 Kings concern the rise and fall of the monarchy among the children of Israel. The divine promise to the patriarchs, Abraham, Isaac, and Jacob, had been one of *unconditional* possession of the land of Canaan (Gen 15:17–21; 17:7–14; 28:10–16; 35:9–15). The Deuteronomistic historians, however, represent this promise as contingent upon obedience to the law of Moses (Deut 8:18–20; 11:8–12; 32:44–47; Josh 1:8; 24:26–28). Obedience to Yahweh through worship of him alone gives way in Samuel to the new challenge of such religious commitment while offering obeisance to a monarch. The character Samuel functions as a priest (1 Sam 7:7–14) and as a judge (1 Sam 7:15–8:3), and also serves as a mediator in the people's request to have a monarch. The reasons the people want a king include their wanting to be like other nations (1 Sam 8:5) and the legitimate need for military leadership (1 Sam 8:20). The costs of kingship asserted by Samuel consist of heavy tax levies (1 Sam 8:12–17) and an implicit rejection of Yahweh as king (1 Sam 8:8–9).

The remainder of 1 and 2 Samuel narrates the careers of Saul (1 Samuel 9–14), and his shaky reign as ruler over a few of the tribes, and his rival, the young David, who exceeds Saul in popularity largely because of his extraordinary victory over the Philistine Goliath (1 Samuel 17). The real challenge for one who would be king, however, lies in the unification of the independent tribes. Thus while Saul is busy being king, David lives as a mercenary soldier and outlaw. He wins notoriety and secures alliances through marriages that would eventually help him unify the tribes scattered across Canaan (1 Sam 25:39–43; 22:9–23). When the showdown comes between the house of Saul and the house of David, David has the upper hand through greater political sup-

---

[11]With the exception of Joshua, each book actually finishes its story in the first few chapters of the following book: Judges continues into Samuel; Davidic succession continues into Kings.

[12]Readers should take note that this so-called pattern is an oversimplification. One scholar, T. E. Fretheim, *Deuteronomistic History* (Nashville, TN: Abingdon, 1983) 42, believes that the nation's apostasy takes far more complex forms.

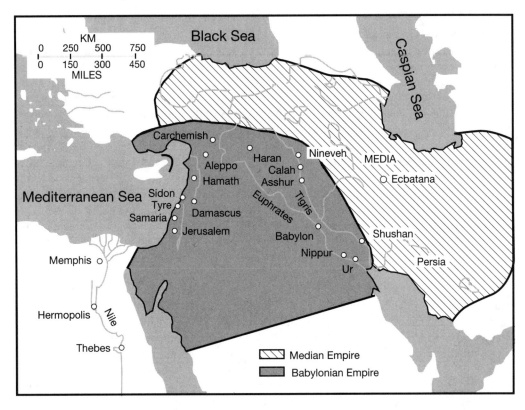

Babylon conquered Judah in 587 BCE. (From John Rogerson and Philip Davies, *The Old Testament World*, © 1989, p. 103. Reprinted by permission of Prentice Hall, Upper Saddle River, NJ)

port (2 Sam 5:1–5). The new king quickly captures the centrally located Jebusite city of Jerusalem, makes it his capital, and shrewdly has the Ark of the covenant brought there to symbolize Yahweh's blessing upon David's reign (1 Sam 6:1–23). Yahweh promises David and his family an eternal place on the throne of Jerusalem (2 Samuel 7).

The story of David's son Solomon and his succession to his father's throne dominates the remainder of 2 Samuel and extends to the opening chapters of 1 Kings (2 Samuel 11–1 Kings 2). It is Solomon who builds the Temple in Jerusalem (1 Kgs 5:5–6; 8:1–9:5), but also establishes the pattern of international alliances (1 Kgs 3:1; 5:1; 11:1) that officially legitimates the worship of foreign deities in Jerusalem (1 Kgs 11:1–8). This pattern of international relations and the subsequent worship of foreign deities recurs in the historian's assessment of nearly every king who follows Solomon, both northern and southern. As judgment for this, adversaries rise up against Solomon, one of whom had been in his labor force (1 Kgs 11:14–40). When Solomon dies, these adversaries, especially Jeroboam, son of Nebat, are waiting to negotiate their relationships to the throne. The heir, Rehoboam, refuses to negotiate and the kingdom splits (1 Kgs 12:6–20).

The remainder of the books of 1 and 2 Kings traces the fates of these two kingdoms and their kings. The theological cast is created by the required obedience to the command to worship

Yahweh alone and by the stresses created by the international political conflict in which the two nations find themselves. It is in this context that prophets play an important role in the story. They

---

A Closer Look: Who Were the Kings? For convenience's sake the kings of Israel (the northern kingdom) and Judah (the southern kingdom) are listed here along with the dates of their reigns. As scholarly opinion differs, the following dates must remain only an approximation. Readers should consult other sources (listed below) to make comparative judgments on dates and methods of dating.

United Monarchy

Saul	1020–1000 BCE
David	1000–961 BCE
Solomon	961–922 BCE

The Divided Monarchy

Judah		Israel	
Rehoboam	922 (1 Kgs 12:1–14:31)	Jeroboam	922 (1 Kgs 11:26–14:20)
Abijam	915 (1 Kgs 15:1–8)	Nadab	901 (1 Kgs 15:25–26)
Asa	913 (1 Kgs 15:9–24)	Baasha	900 (1 Kgs 15:27–16:7)
Jehoshaphat	873 (1 Kgs 22:41–50)	Elah	877 (1 Kgs 16:8–10)
Jehoram	849 (2 Kgs 8:16–24)	Zimri	876 (1 Kgs 16:11–20)
Ahaziah	842 (2 Kgs 8:25–29; 9:29)	Omri	876 (1 Kgs 16:21–28)
Athaliah	842 (2 Kgs 11:1–3)	Ahab	869 (1 Kgs 16:31–22:40)
Jehoash	837 (2 Kgs 12:1–21)	Ahaziah	850 (1 Kgs 22:51–2 Kgs 1:18)
Amaziah	800 (2 Kgs 14:1–22)	Jehoram	849 (2 Kgs 3:1–3; 9:14–26)
Uzziah	783 (2 Kgs 15:1–7)	Jehu	842 (2 Kgs 9:1–10:31)
Jotham	742 (2 Kgs 15:32–38)	Jehoahaz	815 (2 Kgs 13:1–9)
Ahaz	735 (2 Kgs 16:1–20)	Jehoash	801 (2 Kgs 13:10–13)
Hezekiah	715 (2 Kgs 18:1–20:21)	Jeroboam II	786 (2 Kgs 14:23–29)
Manasseh	687 (2 Kgs 21:1–18)	Zechariah	746 (2 Kgs 15:8–12)
Amon	642 (2 Kgs 21:19–26)	Shallum	745 (2 Kgs 15:13–16)
Josiah	640 (2 Kgs 22:1–23:30)	Menahem	745 (2 Kgs 15:17–22)
Jehoahaz	609 (2 Kgs 23:31–34)	Pekahiah	738 (2 Kgs 15:23–26)
Jehoiakim	609 (2 Kgs 23:34–24:7)	Pekah	737 (2 Kgs 15:27–28)
Jehoiachin	598 (2 Kgs 24:8–17)	Hoshea	732 (2 Kgs 17:1–18)
Zedekiah	597 (2 Kgs 24:18–25:7)		
FALL	587	FALL	722/721

For a comparison of dates see H. G. May. *Oxford Bible Atlas.* London: Oxford University Press, 1974. Pp. 18–19. For still broader comparison of scholarly views, see J. H. Hayes and J. M. Miller, eds. *Israelite and Judaean History.* London: SCM Press, 1977. Pp. 678–683.

function as mediators between Yahweh, the kings, and their people. The historians are careful to indicate that history turns upon the word of Yahweh, as delivered through his servants, the prophets (1 Kgs 17:1–19:21; 20:1–25; 22:1–40; 2 Kgs 19:1–7; 22:14–20). Actual reference to the law of Moses, however, is nonexistent in most of the history of the kings. The ostensible reason for such silence is provided when, during the reign of one of the late kings, Josiah, the book of the law is discovered, having been lost in the Temple (2 Kgs 22:1–23:35). This discovery not only explains in the narrative the failure of the kingdoms, but casts judgment upon the kings and their priests for allowing the law of Moses to become lost. The united kingdom of David and Solomon came to an end around 922 BCE, having existed only some eighty years. The divided monarchy lasts for different durations. The northern kingdom of Israel, whose capital city was Samaria, fell to Assyria in 722/21 BCE. The southern kingdom of Judah, whose capital city was Jerusalem, fell to **Babylon** in 587 BCE. The leading citizens of Judah are then carried into **Exile** in Babylon. The Deuteronomistic historian's judgment is that both kingdoms and their kings failed to keep Yahweh's commandments (2 Kgs 17:7–20).

The Chronicler

Aside from a few references to the Exile in letters (Jer 29:1–14) and hymns (Ps 137:1–9), there is a large gap in biblical information about the Exile. The histories and prophetic texts begin again with the period of restoration following the Exile. As mentioned previously, the Chronicler does extend the story beyond the period of Babylonian Exile (ca. 587–538 BCE) to the period of the restoration of Judah and Jerusalem under the aegis of the Persian empire. This extension of the Chronicler's story implies that the history is written much later than the Deuteronomistic History, obviously when there is more story to tell. But this extension further aids in the dating of the history. It is a story that begins with Cyrus' release of Judean captives in the "first year" of his reign (Ezra 1:1). The challenge of the restoration is to retain connections with the traditions and lifestyles prior to the Exile in Babylon, while living under the political domination of a foreign power, Persia. The Temple is rebuilt (Ezra 4:1–6:22) and thus the sacrificial religion is restored. Some years afterwards Ezra is commissioned to go to Jerusalem to establish the rule of law regulating both social and religious behavior (Ezra 7:1–10:43; Neh 8:1–10:39). Still a few years after this Nehemiah also returns to Jerusalem. There only remains yet to build the protective wall around the restored city (Neh 1:1–7:73), which he oversees as the Persian governor of the city and surrounding villages.

The restored Jerusalem looks much different from the Jerusalem in the time of the kings, however. The city is a part of a Persian province and there can be no Judean, Davidic monarch. There is only a governor who rules under the authority of the Persian court. The priests who officiate in the Temple take on a new role of authority in this case. In this restoration period both Levites and Priests officiate jointly in the Temple. With the absence of a king, the role of a written law code takes on a more vital significance as well.

Maccabees

There is yet another gap in the biblical coverage of its own national history; namely, in the time that passes between the restoration of Jerusalem in the Persian period to the threat posed by the

The Ishtar Gate leading into the city of ancient Babylon was devoted to Ishtar, goddess of love and war. Bulls and serpent-headed dragons, built in relief upon the city wall, symbolize the importance of the city and its king. (Courtesy of Larry McKinney/William H. Morton)

Hellenistic culture. The book of Macabbees, written in the late second century BCE, therefore assumes readers know that around 333 BCE Alexander the Great conquered the Persian empire and established his own empire (1 Macc 1:1–4). This began a cultural war, so to speak, between Athens and Jerusalem, that came to a violent climax in the Maccabean revolt of 167 BCE.

Antiochus IV Epiphanes, a member of the Syrian Seleucid family and ruler of Syria and Palestine, sought to impose Hellenistic culture upon the Jews of Palestine by force. Some Jews were open to compromise with the ruling powers, but the book of 1 Maccabees is not sympathetic with this conciliatory spirit (1 Macc 1:11–14). Thus, when Antiochus raids Jerusalem's Temple to support his wars (1 Macc 1:20–28) and issues an edict that "all [his subjects] should be one people and . . . give up their particular customs" on the threat of death (1 Macc 1:41–42; cf. v. 50), a priest named Mattathias and his sons rebel (1 Macc 2:15–28) and go to war, resisting Hellenistic domination. The remainder of the story recounts the war led by Judas, his brother Jonathan, and their brother Simon to resist the kings of Syria and their Hellenizing influence. The revolt and ensuing battles establish one final period of political independence, about 100 years, in Jerusalem and the surrounding regions, but then General Pompey of Rome takes Jerusalem in 63 BCE, thus beginning the Roman domination of the region.

Outlining Israel's Story:
Nehemiah 9:6–37; Sirach 44–50

Learning Goals

- To learn the major themes of the biblical narrative.
- To locate those major themes and subthemes within the Bible and its own narrative framework.
- To understand the basic features of Deuteronomic and Priestly theology.

Guiding Study Exercises

1) Make an outline of the main elements and central characters of Israel's story. To the best of your ability, find the location in the Bible of the larger biblical episodes to which the summaries allude.
2) Write out some of the defining features of Deuteronomic theology based upon your understanding of its distinctive aspects at this point.
3) Describe how Deuteronomic theology shapes the way the prayer of Nehemiah interprets the story of Israel.
4) Describe how Priestly ideology shapes the way Sirach summarizes Israel's story.

The first text for comparison with the biblical narrative is Neh 9:6–37. This summary, or **historical recital**, allows readers to draw inferences about the status of the biblical narrative itself because of the dating of the summary's composition and what is included within it or excluded from it. The summary of Nehemiah 9 is not the only example of the historical recital in the Bible. Readers find passages very similar to such a recital in the Psalms (e.g., Psalms 78, 105, 106, 135, 136),[13] indicating that such summaries were used in the context of worship. The point is that retelling, and necessarily summarizing, the national story is not simply an isolated event in the book of Nehemiah. It was a part of the official religion of the nation, providing multiple perspectives on the nation's history. Careful reading of such summaries, therefore, allows subsequent readers to compare the different ways that ancient Israelites and Judeans thought of their own story.

As readers think of this post-Exilic summary against the longer overview summary at the beginning of this chapter (or of one's own knowledge of the Hebrew Bible's story), two things should become evident. First, there is a very similar outline between the Nehemiah summary and the biblical narrative. It treats the same characters and key events that shape the biblical narrative. Second, the writer of Nehemiah has nevertheless read (or remembered) the story selectively.

---

[13]Other summaries, or historical recitals, included in the biblical narrative would include Ezek 20:4–44; Deuteronomy 1–4; Jdt 5:5–21; Wis 10:1–12:27; Heb 11:2–39, Jas 5:10–11

What has been selected for emphasis gives readers an indication of the writer's **theological** and **ideological** convictions.

Nehemiah 9:6–37: Ezra's Prayer

The summary is couched within the context of a prayer offered by Ezra.[14] The opening verses of the chapter provide crucial information as to the time (twenty-fourth day of the month, v. 1), the characters (the people of Israel were assembled, v. 1), and the activities in which they were involved (they were fasting and in sackcloth [v. 1] and had separated themselves "from all foreigners, and stood and confessed their sins" [v. 2]). The prayer offered by Ezra begs for a reading of its larger context, but this must wait until Chapter 3. For the present it is sufficient to focus upon the story that is within this prayer. Readers should immediately recognize six major periods outlining Israel's story paralleling the larger biblical narrative (summarized previously): creation (9:6), patriarchal ancestors (9:7–8), Exodus from Egypt (9:9–11), wandering in the wilderness (9:12–21), settlement of the Canaan land (9:22–25), and rebellion (9:26–31). Brief comments are offered to call attention to the distinctives of the Nehemiah summary.

Creation: Nehemiah 9:6. Ezra's prayer begins with the affirmation that the Lord, Yahweh, is maker of heaven and earth. The biblical story begins with the familiar episode of creation: "In the beginning, when God created the heavens and the earth" (Gen 1:1). It is not clear whether the writer of Ezra-Nehemiah, and in particular this summary, had Genesis 1–3 in mind, however. It is rather a fact that the language used in Nehemiah more nearly resembles that in 2 Kgs 19:15 and Jer 32:17, the former a part of the Deuteronomistic History. The fact that there are other references to creation throughout the Bible nevertheless suggests that the affirmation of Yahweh as creator came to play an important role in the larger biblical narrative (e.g., Psalms 104 and 136; Job 38–39; Prov 8:22–31).

Patriarchal ancestors: Nehemiah 9:7–8. Next comes the reference to Abram, who came from Ur of the Chaldeans (Mesopotamia), and whose name was changed to Abraham. The historian's perspective reveals two features: first, the emphasis on Abraham and his family as "chosen." Because God chose Abraham and found him faithful, he made a covenant with him to give him a special land. That grant of land was the promise of that covenant. Abraham's descendants would dispossess the inhabitants of that land, and claim it for their own. This motif of chosenness figures prominently in Ezra's insistence upon keeping the lineage pure (Ezra 9:2, 10). Second, the historian is here compelled to affirm the Lord's faithfulness: "and you have fulfilled your promise, for you are righteous" (v. 8). The theological argument here is that, even though Yahweh made a promise to Abraham regarding the land, it cannot be argued that the deity has not been faithful. There must be another explanation for the people's present distress under Persian rule.

Exodus: Nehemiah 9:9–11. Reference to the most centrally important part of Israel's story follows in these verses. The summary mentions God's miraculous leadership in the wilderness, his miraculous feeding of his people, and his meeting with his people at Mt. Sinai. It is interesting in this summary that Moses is not mentioned in reference to the leadership out of Egypt. Nor is his performance of signs and wonders mentioned, as it is in the larger biblical narrative. Moses

---

[14]Relying here on the NRSV translation. In the Hebrew text, Ezra's name is not mentioned. Ezra's name occurs in the LXX, which the NRSV chooses here.

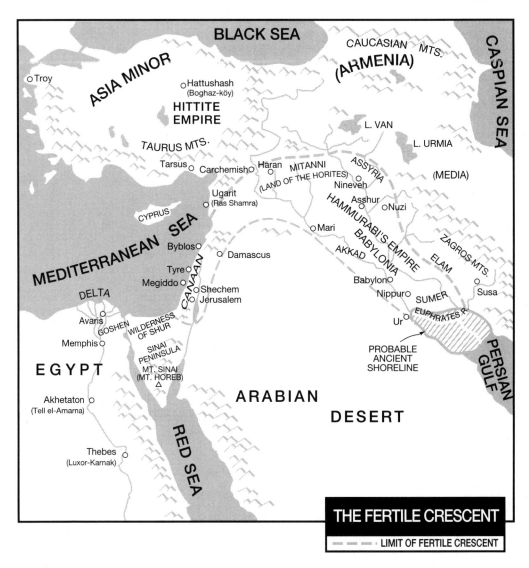

The Fertile Crescent. This map of the ancient Near Eastern world, the Fertile Crescent, indicates the geographical scope against which the Bible's story is told. Adapted from B. W. Anderson, *Understanding the Old Testament,* 4th ed., © 1998, p. 28. Used by permission of Prentice Hall, Upper Saddle River, NJ. Adapted from *The Westminster Historical Atlas to the Bible* (rev. ed.), George Ernest Wright and Floyd Vivian Filson, eds. Copyright 1956, by W. L. Jenkins. Adapted and used by permission of the Westminster Press, Philadelphia, PA)

here is seen primarily as a lawgiver, although the book of Deuteronomy does remember his performance of "signs and wonders" as a prophet (Deut 34:10–12). Nevertheless, in this summary Yahweh seems to manage everything else on his own.

Wandering in the Wilderness: Nehemiah 9:12–25. The most lengthy section of this summary concerns Israel's experiences in the wilderness. These materials reflect the author's awareness of materials mainly in the Tetrateuch. For instance, the reference to the deity's leadership through the pillars of cloud and fire (Neh 9:2) occurs both in Exod 13:21 and Num 14:14. In both instances the people are about to set out on a journey through the desert lands between Egypt and Canaan. The next episode is Israel's experience at Mt. Sinai, where the people worship Yahweh. It is here that the deity gives the people the laws and ordinances through Moses, making them aware of the importance of keeping the Sabbath (vv. 13–14). Notice that Neh 9:13 and 14 twice state the fact that the Lord gave the people laws.

There continue references to Yahweh's miraculous provisions of "bread from heaven" and "water from the rock" (v. 15), references to episodes in Exod 16:4 and Num 10:8. The language concerning Israel's inheritance of the land of Canaan (v. 15) sounds the same as that in Deut 11:31 or Josh 1:11. Similarly, the language concerning the people's "hardness of hearing" and their "rebellion" are features that are mentioned again in Nehemiah's summary. It resembles the language in Deut 10:16; 2 Kgs 17:14; and Jer 7:26, the first two a part of the Deuteronomistic History. One of the most interesting inclusions in this summary is the reference to Israel's apostasy with the molten calf (v. 18), though Aaron is *not* named. The section on the wilderness concludes with a reference to God's gracious care of the people for forty years in the wilderness, despite their rebellion. This reference to forty years of wandering may be found both in Num 14:26–35 and in Deut 1:34–40 and 2:1–7. Interestingly, in these texts the wilderness wandering is depicted primarily as a *punishment* laid upon the faithless people. This offers an informative contrast with Nehemiah 9, which emphasizes the wilderness as a demonstration of God's merciful sustenance of his people.

Settlement: Nehemiah 9:22–25. The verses in Neh 9:22–25 summarize the events of the people's settlement of the Canaan land, the land they would occupy as a promise from Yahweh. The stories of conquest are contained in the Deuteronomistic History, in the books of Joshua and Judges 1–2. In Nehemiah's summary there are allusions to conflicts with nations prior to Israel's entry into Canaan. These are references to Sihon, king of Heshbon, and Og, king of Bashan, whose stories can be found prior to Joshua or Judges in the book of Numbers, especially chapters 21 and 32. The language regarding Israel's conquering fortresses and fortified cities sounds like Deut 3:5, while the references to cities, filled houses, and the best orchards and vineyards sound like Deut 6:11. The era of settlement is here remembered as a time of victory, success, and prosperity. But it is this very prosperity that leads the people to rebel against Yahweh's covenant.

Rebellion: Nehemiah 9:26–31. These verses recall the rebellion ("murmuring") motif of the wilderness narratives. Additionally, the familiar Deuteronomistic pattern of rebellion, oppression, repentance, and restoration is clear in vv. 26–27. The people forget God's Torah and kill the prophets. God gives them into the power of their enemies who oppress them; the people cry out to God for deliverance and he responds by sending a savior who delivers them. The pattern occurs two more times in vv. 28–31. Within this repeating pattern in Nehemiah readers must take note of the repetition of the cause of the people's oppression: failure to keep the commandments of Yahweh—those same commandments that were given to Israel, through Moses, on Mt. Sinai so many years before (vv. 26, 29).

The final prayer of vv. 32–37, though no longer strictly summarizing the ancestors' story, nevertheless is an informative connection with the section on rebellion. It represents the final cry of the people who are portrayed as living in the time of Ezra-Nehemiah and are under the political domination of the Persian empire.[15] The previous three cycles of rebellion, oppression, repentance, and deliverance only present the people as crying out twice (vv. 27 and 28). The concluding prayer, no longer a prayer from the past, though very much like the prayers of the past, asks God, who because of his great mercy has not given up on his people, not to consider their present distress a small thing (v. 32). Within this prayer, the remainder of the biblical history is compressed. The summary simply refers to kings, princes, priests, and fathers, none of whom kept Yahweh's Torah. It is clear that within the confines of this summary the writer connects the present day's slavery with the sin of the past (see Table 2.2). In this way there is the implicit foundation to admonish the new community to keep the law.

Influence of Deuteronomic Theology

Comparison of Nehemiah's summary with the larger Tetrateuchal and Deuteronomistic Histories shows that there is clear macro-level intertextuality between the two. Nehemiah's summary, while drawing material from both histories, shows a preference for the Deuteronomic themes. While any general conclusions would be premature, readers necessarily wonder why the summary

Table 2.2

**Outline of Israel's History:
Ezra's Prayer and the Biblical Narrative**

Nehemiah 9	Event	Biblical Text	Date (BCE)
v. 6	Creation	Genesis 1–3	??
vv. 7–8	Patriarchs	Genesis 12–50	2000–1300
vv. 9–11	Exodus	Exodus 1–15	1250
vv. 12–21	Wilderness (and Sinai)	Exodus 16–18; Num 10:11–36:13	1250–1200
vv. 22–25	Settlement	(Deuteronomy, prep for) Joshua and Judges 1–2	1200–1020
vv. 26–31	Rebellion	Judges 3ff.; Samuel and Kings	1020–539
vv. 32–37	Moment of Decision	Ezra-Nehemiah	465–420

[15]H. G. M. Williamson, *Ezra, Nehemiah,* 316–318.

says so little about those theological themes of the tabernacle, the priestly service, and Yahweh's presence that are so central to the Tetrateuch.

Readers should recall the Deuteronomistic pattern of sin, oppression, repentance, and restoration encountered in the book of Judges, throughout the books of Samuel and Kings, and used as a structuring motif here in Nehemiah's summary. Readers will also recall that Deuteronomic theology, as set forward in the book of Deuteronomy, insists upon the centrality of Mosaic law. The Deuteronomistic History frequently offers narratives that illustrate or test the laws of the Deuteronomic Code. While the precise formulation "the law of Moses" is largely absent in the narratives until the law code is ostensibly recovered in the days of Josiah, there is nevertheless the insistence through Samuel and Kings that the people and their leaders are to obey Yahweh's commandments. Consistent with the Deuteronomistic pattern, punishment follows disobedience. Hence, in Nehemiah's summary the people suffer as a result of their failure to keep Yahweh's commandments as given through the law of Moses. Consistent yet again with Deuteronomic thought, prophets make the commandments of Yahweh known to the people. The Deuteronomistic historian makes his history turn on this word from Yahweh. Nehemiah's frequent reiteration of the work of prophets (9:26, 30) is further attributable to the influence of Deuteronomic thought.

Sirach 44–50: Sirach's Hymn

An investigation of yet a later retelling of Israel's story is equally revealing of variations stemming from the author's different theological commitments (self-text) and social setting (social text). Sirach 44–50, a short selection from a much longer book in the Apocrypha, contains this "hymn to ancestors."[16] It is not a historical recital in the same sense as that in Nehemiah. However, the hymn clearly presupposes the biblical narratives, reflecting its present sequence and enumerating its featured leaders. The book of Sirach was written in the Hellenistic period, ca. 185 BCE, not long before the time of the Maccabees, by one who calls himself "Jesus son of Eleazar." Most of the contents resemble the kinds of materials contained in the biblical books of Proverbs and Job, for which reason Sirach is considered an example of wisdom literature.

The different purpose of Sirach's hymn leads to a focus upon characters rather than events. Thus, Sirach's hymn is far more extensive than the summary in Nehemiah.[17] Despite these generic differences, readers benefit by comparing Sirach with both Nehemiah and with the broader biblical narratives.

Abraham (Patriarchal ancestors): Sirach 44:19–21; Nehemiah 9:7–8. After introducing the hymn by treating Enoch (44:16) and Noah (44:17), both of whom come from the primordial history (Genesis 1–11), Sirach turns to Abraham and his descendants Isaac and Jacob (44:19–23). There appear to be minor differences in the treatments of the figure of Abraham. The most interesting departure from the biblical narrative as well as from Neh 9:7–8 is that Sirach has Abraham

---

[16]The editorial heading in the NRSV translation is actually in the LXX version of Sirach: *pateron humnos.*

[17]Notice the characters Sirach includes that Nehemiah does not: Enoch (44:16); Noah (44:17); Isaac, Jacob (44:22–23); Aaron (45:6–26); Joshua, Caleb, Samuel (46:1–20); Nathan, David, Solomon, Jeshua, Nehemiah (48:1–49:13).

keeping the law "of the Most High" even before there was a law of Moses. The effect is to clarify that Abraham's worthiness through his righteousness is the basis for God's selection of Abraham and his descendants. It is on this basis that Abraham enters into a covenant with the Lord (v. 20). Only then does the deity make any kind of promise of blessing, either of progeny or of an inheritance of land (v. 21). This seems a clear departure from the way Gen 12:1–3; 15:1–6; and even Genesis 17 read, which have Yahweh extending promises without any prior display of obedience from Abraham.

Moses (Exodus): Sirach 45:1–5. References to this theme come in Sirach's treatment of the character Moses (45:1–5), though the specific allusions to the nation's Exodus from Egypt are very general in comparison to Nehemiah's. In v. 3 there is the reference to "miracles," presumably an allusion to the signs and wonders in Egypt. However, the following reference to Moses being glorified "in the presence of kings" need not refer only to the experience of the escape from Egypt. Moses has other encounters with kings in the wilderness experience of Israel's story (e.g., Numbers 21). In the treatment of Moses, Sirach hastens on to the events that, in Nehemiah, fall in the wilderness period of Israel's story.

Moses and Aaron (Wandering in the Wilderness). Sirach 45:1–5 continues the story of Moses with references to his reception of the commandments from God for the people. It is interesting that Sirach agrees with Nehemiah by doubling references to Moses' reception of the commandments. Sirach 45:3c reads, "He gave him commandments for his people," and "[he] gave him the commandments face to face" (v. 5b). There is a similar duplication in Neh 9:13 and 14.

The lengthiest theme in both versions of the story is the wilderness theme. Perhaps the most noticeable difference is that Sirach devotes more space to Aaron, Moses' brother, than to any other biblical event or character (Sir 45:6–26). Moses gets only five verses (Sir 45:1–5). That alone is curious, given the importance of Moses and the law in the Deuteronomistic History. Nehemiah, however, says nothing about Aaron directly, the priesthood, nor those cultic matters so predominant in the Tetrateuch. Further, Sirach has no references to God's miraculous guidance, the forty years of wandering, the provisions of food, the nation's rebellion, and it has no references to God's mercy in the face of such rebellion, all of which are essential parts of Nehemiah's version. For Sirach, every event concerning the wilderness is about Aaron and all of his high priestly glory. Nehemiah does mention one incident in the wilderness that concerns Aaron, but Nehemiah does not mention Aaron's name. This is the incident with the molten calf (Neh 9:18). Comparing this reference to the story as found in Exod 32:1–35, readers see that it was Aaron who facilitates the apostasy of the people, while Moses is on the mountain in the presence of Yahweh. While Nehemiah is silent about *Aaron's* involvement in the incident, Sirach *leaves the incident out* all together.[18] Clearly there is a serious rereading going on in Sirach's version. Two further observations elaborate the focus.

First, it is quite apparent that Sirach presents Aaron in such a way as to highlight his importance. He does this by devoting more space to Aaron, heaping extensive praise on him, and even leaving out the parts of the story that might detract from that purpose. Sirach's level of praise for Aaron rivals not only that given to Moses, but that given to the great king David as well. Sirach

---

[18]Notice Sirach's reference to the Dathan and Abiram incident, which is narrated in full in Numbers 16. In the story in Numbers, Moses is one of the central figures against whose leadership the various parties rebel. Moses' name does not even occur in this context in Sirach.

argues that just as God promised kingship to David's heirs, so he promised the priesthood to Aaron's heirs (Sir 45:25). There might even be significance in the fact that Sirach mentions that David was sinful (Sir 47:11). Of course, God takes David's sins away, but he is sinful nevertheless. The notation of David's sinfulness allows the silence of Sirach about Aaron's involvement in the molten calf to stand out even more sharply. Sirach seems to manufacture an incredible silence about the whole affair.

Second, the positive emphasis given to Aaron helps to explain why such attention is given to the Temple and the priesthood (the Temple personnel) at the end of the summary. Note, for example, that Sirach is careful to state that David was closely involved with the sanctuary of Israel, as well as the various festivals and altar singers who complemented Temple worship (Sir 47:9–10). Sirach is careful to explain that Solomon actually built the sanctuary (47:13). Interestingly, Sirach even reports that Aaron was encircled with many golden bells "to make their ringing heard in the Temple" (Sir 45:9). What is most curious about this statement is that Aaron lived centuries *before* Solomon built the house for God that was to be called "the Temple." Sirach's desire to associate the Temple, which did not yet even exist, with Aaron clearly indicates an interest on Sirach's part in highlighting and reinforcing this religious institution. Finally, it is not insignificant that Sirach ends his survey of Israel's heroes by offering praise to a certain Simon, son of Onias, the high priest during the time that Sirach was writing his book (Sir 50:1–29). Note, once again, the explicit association of the priest Simon with the Temple (Sir 50:1). Clearly, Sirach believes that the history of Israel's heroes culminates in the ruling priest of his time. This indicates that Sirach highly valued the priests and the institution of public worship with which they were associated, the Temple.

Sirach's Priestly Perspective

Again, readers must pause both to acknowledge that in retelling Israel's story, the story of the Hebrew Bible, Sirach has chosen to emphasize different aspects of the story from Nehemiah's summary. No doubt elements both of Sirach's own self and the social texts of his time provide the basis for this. But for readers, it is yet more evidence of how ancient readers both *read* and *wrote* history. Clearly, in the face of such diversity in the versions of Israel's story, modern readers may not lose sight of those influences upon an ancient historian's use of his sources. Sirach interprets the story of ancient Israel differently, choosing both to delete from and to add to the story for the sake, ostensibly, of his contemporary audience.

The emphasis upon the Temple service in Sirach 50 seems to suggest the writer's strong sympathies with the service of the priests. But the emphasis upon Aaron, the high priest of antiquity and founder of the Israelite cult, over the importance of even Moses or David, makes this hypothesis of priestly ideology much firmer and convincing. Sirach even revises the wilderness story to leave out the golden calf incident, so that there could be no doubt about Aaron's faithfulness. Comparing this with Exodus 32 reveals what a remarkable revision this is. To be sure, keeping the law of Moses is of key importance to Sirach as a whole (Sir 1:26; 2:16; especially 24:19–24), but the law only points to the glory of the presence of the Lord in the Temple under the leadership of the sons of Aaron and the high priest Simon. This writer seems to be giving more weight to those materials in the Tetrateuch, which emphasize God's presence through the sanctuary and his priestly servants, rather than those materials that follow in the Deuteronomistic History (remember that Nehemiah's summary weights more heavily the Deuteronomistic History).

A Closer Look: Dating Events in the Bible

Since the biblical literature represents a collection of writings from multiple perspectives, historical settings, sociological contexts, and ideological intentions, the dates stated or implied within the stories themselves invite corroboration from external sources. Archaeologists provide the possibility of such corroboration indirectly through their reconstruction of the ancient world, in this case the ancient Near East, apart from biblical sources. Using material culture (e.g., site surveys, geography, stratigraphy, pottery typology, etc.) archaeologists provide summaries of the ethnological, cultural, and social changes within a region over a period of time. The task for biblical readers is to understand how the material culture then corresponds to the literary witness of the Bible.

The following chart sets out the broad cultural eras of Palestine, based upon the different material culture and technology available at a given time. The columns that follow are hypothetical correlations of the biblical story with those material cultures.

CULTURAL PERIOD	BIBLICAL EVENT	HYPOTHETICAL DATES
Middle Bronze (2000–1550 BCE)	*Patriarchs* Abraham Isaac Jacob Joseph	(Within the Middle Bronze Period)
Late Bronze (1550–1200 BCE)	*Exodus* Wilderness Sinai (Torah)	1250 BCE
Iron Age I (1200–900 BCE)	*Settlement* Period of Judges	1200 BCE 1200–1000 BCE
	Monarchy Divided monarchy (Old traditions used to justify monarchy)	1000–587 BCE 922 BCE
Iron Age II (900–600 BCE)	(Earliest biblical documents) Fall of Northern kingdom (Samaria) to Assyria	850 BCE (?) 722/21 BCE
Iron Age III (600–539 BCE Babylonia)	Fall of Southern kingdom (Judah) to Babylon	587 BCE

CULTURAL PERIOD	BIBLICAL EVENT	HYPOTHETICAL DATES
	Exile of Judah and Jerusalem in Babylon	587–539 BCE
	(Deuteronomistic History)	550 BCE
(539–333 BCE Persia)	Restoration of Jerusalem under Persia	539–450 BCE
	Temple rebuilt	515 BCE
	Ezra comes to Jerusalem	458 BCE
	Nehemiah comes to Jerusalem	445 BCE
	(Chronicles, Ezra-Nehemiah written 400 BCE)	400 BCE
Hellenistic Culture (333–64 BCE)	(Jesus ben Sirach)	185 BCE
	Maccabean revolt	167 BCE
	Qumran community	150 BCE
Roman Culture (64 BCE–324 CE)	Herod the Great	40 BCE

For further study, W. G. Dever. "What Archaeology Can Contribute to an Understanding of the Bible," *BAR* 7.5 (1981) 40–41; W. G. Dever. "The Emergence of Early Israel," *Archaeology and Biblical Interpretation.* Edited by J. R. Bartlett. London and New York: Routledge, 1997. Pp. 20–50; J. M. Miller. "Old Testament History and Archaeology," *BA* 50 (Mar, 1987) 55–63; P. R. S. Moorey. *A Century of Biblical Archaeology.* Louisville, KY: Westminster/John Knox Press, 1991; G. E. Wright, "The New Archaeology," *BA* 38 (Sept–Dec, 1975) 104–115.

Conclusion

The comparison of these two summaries of Israel's story, one written in the early post-Exilic period, the other in the later Hellenistic period, forms the grounds for the claim that Israel's story, the biblical story, comes into being through the process of ongoing reinterpretation. Of course, this statement can and should be refined a great deal further. Nevertheless, readers can isolate both micro- and macro-level intertextuality within the various books of the scriptures that reveals this reinterpretation and the theological and sociological influences motivating its various stages. Two points of still greater significance follow. First, it would be very difficult in light of this study to think of Israel's story holistically. Rather, the story in the Bible is really a complex of stories, each one growing from and reinterpreting other parts of that story. Reading knowledgeably requires understanding those individual parts and the discrete contexts that produced them. Second, it is also clear that there is a strong human element to the production of this story made up of many stories. Individuals served in varying leadership roles to help their audiences understand the changing significances of religious traditions in the face of changing times. Whatever else inspiration might mean, it does not exclude human participation in the transmission and reinterpretation of stories the community regarded as sacred.

For Further Reading

A Survey of the Biblical Historical Narratives

Clines, D. J. A. *The Theme of the Pentateuch.* Sheffield: JSOT Press, 1978.

Freedman, D. N. "Pentateuch." *IDB* 3.711–727. (*Recommended for beginning students.*)

Brueggemann, W. "The Kerygma of the Deuteronomistic Historian." *Int* 22 (1968) 387–402. (*Recommended for beginning students.*)

———. "The Kerygma of the Priestly Writers." *ZAW* 84 (1972) 397–414.

Davies, G. I. "The Wilderness Itineraries and the Composition of the Pentateuch." *VT* 33 (1983) 1–13.

Outlining Israel's Story

Conrad, E. W. "Heard But Not Seen: The Representation of 'Books' in the Old Testament." *JSOT* 54 (1992) 45–59. (*Recommended for beginning students.*)

Whybray, R. N. *Introduction to the Pentateuch.* Grand Rapids, MI: Eerdmans, 1995. (*Recommended for beginning students.*)

Mullen, E. T., Jr. *Ethnic Myths and Pentateuchal Foundations.* Atlanta, GA: Scholars Press, 1997.

PART TWO

The
Hebrew
Bible

CHAPTER THREE

The Story Behind Israel's Story in Ezra-Nehemiah

Introduction

Review

Chapter 2 presented textual evidence as grounds for the claim that biblical origins stem from a process of ongoing reinterpretation, or rereading. The extensive story within the Bible has been summarized repeatedly in contexts of worship and narrative. But each retelling of the story bears remarkable changes. These changes provide suggestive evidence that readers rewrite the story from their own unique points of view, defined both by their historical settings and theological commitments.

Preview

This chapter explores the social text pertaining to post-Exilic Judah. The social text concerns the social, cultural, and historical events that both stand behind the story and the story's author. Methodologically, history affects readers at both the micro- and the macro-levels of intertextuality. At the micro- level of intertextuality a literary text may relate to specific historical events. At the macro-level, literary texts may make only very broad allusions to historical events, taking great liberties with what is actually known of these events. Readers must determine how nearly a literary text intersects with known historical events.

The discussion that follows examines selected intertexts between the literary text of Ezra-Nehemiah and the social text of the restoration of Jerusalem. This period of Judean history warrants attention because much evidence, both internal and external to the Bible, suggests that this period is determinative in shaping the religious experience that gives rise both to the story in Ezra-Nehemiah and to the later use of that story as scripture. The claim that rereading stands behind biblical origins therefore receives further grounding in a fuller understanding of the historical period that demanded such rereading. That historical period is the Persian period (538–333 BCE).

The Story of the Restoration: Ezra-Nehemiah

Learning Goals

- To understand how Israel's story (as a historical recital) functions in one literary context.
- To understand the importance of Ezra-Nehemiah as a historical reference point for the origins of scripture.
- To learn one post-Exilic version of the restoration of Jerusalem.

Guiding Study Exercises

1) Write a 250-word (approximately one double-spaced page) summary of the highlights of the narrative in Ezra-Nehemiah. How does the plot hold the two books together into one single story?
2) Where in the overall narrative do the immediate events surrounding Ezra's confessional prayer (the retelling Israel's story) fit in? Why might one say that Ezra's prayer functions as a climax to the narrative?
3) How do the events in Ezra-Nehemiah relate to the prophecy of Jeremiah that is mentioned in Ezra 1?
4) What is it about the context in which Ezra reads from the law of Moses that makes the reader think that he (Ezra) is reading scripture?

One of the fundamental assumptions behind the work of reconstructing biblical history is that context shapes meaning. Readers of texts are therefore also asked to reconstruct the social, cultural, intellectual, political, and other scenarios that were in effect at the time the literary text was originally written and first read.

A strict historical critic therefore believes that a text has no meaning apart from the meaning it had for the first audience for whom it was written.[1] One implication is that the full meaning of a text may be limited by the interpreters' inability to reconstruct the initial context. Reading therefore is an exercise in compromise between text and context.

The Day They Told the Story

In order to reconstruct the socio-historical context in which Ezra-Nehemiah tells Israel's story, readers have to look more carefully at the larger literary context in which the summary is found. The literary text gives the reader clues about the historical text that produced it.

In Neh 9:1 readers encounter language that still requires more information. The verse specifies the twenty-fourth day of *this* month, betraying the narrator's assumption that the reader al-

---

[1]See, for instance, E. Krentz, *The Historical-Critical Method* (G. M. Tucker, ed.; Philadelphia: Fortress Press, 1975) 2; quoting A. Richardson and W. Schweitzer, eds., *Biblical Authority for Today* (Philadelphia: Westminster, 1951) 241–244.

This cut into the earth at Lachish, the famous fortified city in Judah, allows a view of the strata of dirt, debris deposits, and artifacts. Through careful attention to relative position within a series of strata, archaeologists may begin to hypothesize the relative dates of artifacts found within and their correspondence with other aspects of antiquity. (Chance and Horne)

ready has in mind which particular month he is talking about. The only reference to which month, however, comes in the last half of 7:73. The events of chapters 8, 9, and 10 all take place in the seventh month. On the first day of the seventh month the people assemble before the "Water Gate" (8:1) of the city of Jerusalem to hear Ezra the scribe read from the "book of the law of Moses" (8:1). The governor Nehemiah, Ezra, and the Levites are all present, and they encourage the people not to mourn or weep since the day is holy to the Lord (8:9). On the second day of this month (8:13), the "heads of ancestral houses" along with priests and Levites come again to Ezra the scribe to "study the words of the law" (8:13). On this day the people discover that the law speaks of a religious festival that is to be observed during the seventh month, the feast of **Succoth**.[2] But it is not until the twenty-fourth day of the seventh month that the people mourn and make public confession. As the text now stands, the day of mourning and confession of sins climaxes a month of reading and studying the law of Moses and of celebrating the feast of Succoth.

Nehemiah 10 culminates in the signing of a formal commitment within the community to keep the law of God. This singular act follows logically upon the many references to Israel's

---

[2]While there can be no certainty on the status of the books now called the Pentateuch, there can be no doubt that the people were reading something like that preserved in Lev 23:33–36. This festival corresponds to the feast of ingathering, which comes at the end of the agricultural year. See Exod 23:14–17; 34:18–24; Deut 16:1–17. Notice that the passage in Deuteronomy calls this third festival "Succoth," or "booths."

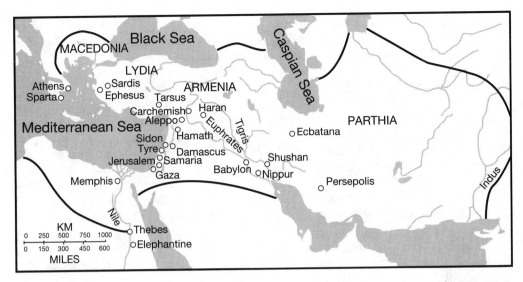

The Persian Empire. The capital of Darius I was Persepolis. The remoteness of Jerusalem gives some indication of both the Persian king's administrative abilities and the crucial location of Jerusalem on the western border of the empire. (From John Rogerson and Philip Davies, *The Old Testament World,* © 1989, p. 110. Reprinted by permission of Prentice Hall, Upper Saddle River, NJ)

apostasies in the summary of Israel's story (9:6–37), voiced within Ezra's prayer. The people and their ancestors have failed up until this time to keep the law and the commandments. This failure explains the many unfortunate circumstances that plague the people and the city (e.g., 9:16, 26, 29). The political leaders, the Levites, and the priests all affix their names to the document first (10:1–27). They then are followed by the rest of the people and all who "have separated them- selves from the peoples of the lands to adhere to the law of God, their wives, their sons, their daughters . . ." (10:28). The reference to the people's separation from foreigners is similar to that encountered in 9:2. Readers may therefore begin to be suspicious that this element of separation is an important part of the story.

These actions seem to be leading up to some kind of a climax. There is celebration and read- ing of the law of Moses, mourning and confession of sins, separation from non-Israelite persons, and finally the signing of a formal commitment to observe the law of Moses by all who agree to be separate from foreigners. At the heart of the confession of sin is the summary of Israel's story, which is itself a story of rebellion and failure to keep the commandments of God, even though God was gracious and merciful. But for what larger sequence of events do these episodes serve as the climax? What events lead up to this dramatic moment of commitment on the part of the refugees of Jerusalem? Only a look at the broader context of the story can answer that question.

The Celebration in Its Larger Context

The celebration of the seventh month takes place within the context of the people's return to **Judah** and Jerusalem from captivity in **Babylon**. The story of the book of Ezra-Nehemiah por- trays a general time frame spanning from the days of Cyrus' decree, which liberated the Israelites

(539 BCE), to the latter days of Artaxerxes I (465 BCE–424 BCE), nearly 120 years later. The narrative develops around the accomplishments of a governor, Sheshbazzar, a crown prince, Zerubbabel, a priestly scribe, Ezra, and another governor, Nehemiah.[3]

The accomplishments of these characters, respectively, include the rebuilding of the Temple, the establishment of Mosaic law within the community of repatriated Jews, and the rebuilding of the defensive wall around the city of Jerusalem. It is helpful to think of these three major activities as segments outlining the story of Ezra-Nehemiah. Ezra 1–6 concerns the rebuilding of the Temple and depicts events that take place before Ezra and Nehemiah returned to Jerusalem. Ezra 7–10 concerns the establishment of the law of Moses as the guide by which the community is to govern itself. One of the chief concerns of the community during Ezra's days is the problem of intermarriage between Jews and non-Jews in light of the strictures imposed by the law of Moses. Finally, Nehemiah 1–13 tells the story of the rebuilding of the defensive wall around the city, including the episode of the great month of celebration and recommitment (Neh 8–10), after the restorative work is completed.

The Rebuilding of the Temple: Ezra 1–6. The plot is tied very closely to the need to rebuild the Temple. Ezra 1:1–5 begins with the fulfillment of a promise made by Jeremiah the prophet

---

A Closer Look: Were Sheshbazzar and Zerubbabel both Davidic Heirs? While it is clear that the character Zerubbabel is of royal ancestry (e.g., Neh 12:1; 1 Chron 3:10–19), one could get the same idea about another character, Sheshbazzar, since in Ezra1:8 he is referred to as "prince of Judah." The implications would be that the restoration of Jerusalem would also amount to a restoration of the Davidic throne. Several hints in the text mitigate against such an interpretation of Sheshbazzar's title. First, the title "prince" (*nasi'*) need not mean only royal "prince," but rather can designate a tribal head or head of ancestral house (e.g., 1 Chron 2:10; 4:38; 5:6; 2 Chron 1:2; 5:2). Second, another reference to Sheshbazzar from an Aramaic source (Ezra 5:14) refers to him as a "governor" (*pehah*), not "prince." The implication is that the broad term *prince* is more of a generic term for leader. As to whether Sheshbazzar was actually a governor, scholars are divided. One scholar treats both Sheshbazzar and Zerubbabel as governors appointed by the Persian court.[4] Another scholar argues this to be impossible since Palestine was not an independent province until the time of Nehemiah, thus making the appointment of a separate governor during those years unnecessary.[5]

For more advanced study, S. Japhet. "Sheshbazzar and Zerubbabel Against the Background of the Historical and Religious Tendencies of Ezra-Nehemiah." *ZAW* 94 (1982) 66–98.

---

[3]Both internal and external evidence cause scholars to read the "books" of Ezra and Nehemiah as one, Ezra-Nehemiah. The internal evidence includes the overlapping of their two missions in the present form of the text. The external evidence includes the treatment of the "book" by ancient readers as a single text.

[4] See E. M. Meyers, "The Persian Period and the Judean Restoration: From Zerubbabel to Nehemiah," *Ancient Israelite Religion* (Philadelphia: Fortress, 1987) 21, n. 8.

[5]S. E. McEvenue, "The Political Structure in Judah from Cyrus to Nehemiah," *CBQ* 43 (1981) 353–364.

concerning the Jews' return to their homeland after the **Exile**. Ezra 6:16–22, the final verses of this section on Temple restoration, has the people dedicating the completed house of God and celebrating the feast of the **Passover**. On first reading it appears to be a success story in nearly every way. The people have successfully rebuilt the Temple and the vessels that had been used in the Temple of Solomon, some seventy years prior to the setting of this story, are in the proper hands (1:7–11). Families of former exiles who had retained their genealogical heritage return to Jerusalem, including Levites and other Temple servants (2:1–67), so that the city of Jerusalem and the surrounding countryside of Judah may be repopulated with people who claim legitimate ownership of the land. The proper clergy could now serve in the Temple as tradition required.

Kings and officials. It is Cyrus, the Persian king (550–530 BCE), who issues the edict that allows the Jews to return to Jerusalem. While the text implies that the return was inevitable since it was predicted by a Hebrew prophet decades before (Ezra 1:2–4), Cyrus seems to be more than a willing participant. He takes personal charge of the rebuilding of the Temple (1:4) and sees that the original Temple vessels are returned (1:7–8). This same spirit of Persian enthusiasm is carried on some twenty years later by Darius (522–486 BCE), the king in whose sixth year of reign (Ezra 6:15) the Temple is actually completed (Ezra 6:1–15). Finding the original decree of Cyrus concerning the rebuilding of the Temple, Darius reestablishes the intent of his predecessor so that the Temple might be completed (6:1–5).

Prophets and priests. After years of delay (before Darius comes to the throne), the intervention of the prophetic figures Haggai and Zechariah—both of whom have biblical books named after them—and the priest Jeshua, along with Zerubbabel, finally gets the work on the Temple rolling again. This is not to suggest that the conflict has ended. The work on the Temple no sooner resumes (Ezra 5:1–2), when Tattenai, the governor of the province Beyond the River, and others begin to harass the refugees about their authority to rebuild. Yet even in the face of more opposition, the people do not stop work this time (5:5). After an exchange of official letters, Darius issues his own decree reestablishing the official legitimacy of the work (5:1–15). Thus the people of Jerusalem are successful in completing the Temple around the year 515 BCE. The episode concludes on a high emotional level. The Temple is complete and the community leaders have restored Temple worship. Worship had not taken place in the Temple since the Babylonian king Nebuchadnezzar had destroyed it in 587 BCE.

On reflection and further reading, however, it is an uneasy restoration. Readers suspect that Jerusalem will continue to succeed only as long as it retains the favor of the Persian kings. But what then? The story has already illustrated the results of the absence of Persian support. Further, readers also wonder about conflicts between the peoples of the land and the repatriated city and region. Such questions form the backdrop for the second major episode concerning Ezra and the law of Moses.

Ezra and the Establishment of Moses' Law: Ezra 7–10. The story of Ezra's mission begins, as in the previous Temple episode, with a commission from a Persian king. Here it is Artaxerxes[6] who commissions Ezra to return to Jerusalem with any of the people of Israel who wish to accompany him (7:12–13). Ezra's commission involves four tasks. First, he is "to make inquiries about Judah and Jerusalem according to the law of your God" (7:14). Second, Ezra is "to convey the silver and gold that the king and his counselors have freely offered to the God of Israel" to "buy bulls, rams, and lambs . . . [to] offer them on the altar of the house of your God in

---

[6]If Artaxerxes I, 465–424 BCE; if Artaxerxes II, 404–358 BCE. See discussion below.

Jerusalem" (7:15–16). Third, he is to deliver the vessels "that have been given you for the service of the house of your God" (7:19). Ezra's fourth task, which consists of two parts, is to "appoint magistrates and judges who may judge all the people in the province . . . who know the laws of your God" (7:25), and, to "teach those who do not know [the laws]" (7:25). These four tasks, two concerning the law of Moses and two concerning the worship in the Temple, provide an outline so that the reader may anticipate the immediately ensuing plot of the story.

Ezra's return: Ezra 7–8. The opening two chapters deal with the commissioning by King Artaxerxes and the various details of Ezra's return. Since Artaxerxes has been so generous in his support of the Temple and has sympathy for the establishment of the law, Ezra is reluctant to request protection while en route to Jerusalem. He therefore appeals to God for help. The text reads, "he [God] listened to our entreaty" (8:21–23). Readers cannot lose sight of the fact that, even though it is Artaxerxes who commissions the activity of Ezra, it is "the God of heaven" who stands behind the king to "put such a thing as this into the heart of the king to glorify the house of the LORD in Jerusalem" (7:27).

Ezra's journey begins in the first month (7:9). He discovers that there are no descendants of Levi among the group, and it takes extra time for Levites to come and join the group. The Levites come from Casiphia, a place that had evidently come to be a Jewish religious center of importance in Babylon. The king entrusts the Levites with the offering and the vessels from the Temple (8:24–30). Upon their arrival in Jerusalem some five months later (7:9), they deliver both the offering and the Temple vessels from King Artaxerxes into the hands of the priests and Levites already in Jerusalem (8:33–34). The journey to Jerusalem concludes with burnt offerings, according to the commission of the Persian king, thus completing two of the four tasks for which Ezra was commissioned at the very beginning (8:35–36).

Ezra and the law: Ezra 9–10. The narrative then turns from external threat to the internal threat of intermarriage with non-Jewish peoples. The earlier notice in 4:1–3 foreshadowed this as it speaks of Israel's relationships with the peoples of the land. When Ezra hears the news of the intermarriages, he tears his garments and pulls his hair out, symbolic acts of denigration and desolation (9:3–4). He offers a prayer of confession on behalf of the people of the community for this sin. His prayer also anticipates some of the themes and subthemes of the prayer in Neh 9:6–37. For comparison's sake, examine the references to the sinfulness of the people since the days of their ancestors (9:7), the present state of slavery (9:9), the mercifulness of God (9:9), and the forsaking of God's commandments given through the prophets (9:10–11).

Ezra's prayer of confession stirs the response of some of the people who gather to him as he prays (10:1–2), and who then encourage him to take action. These pledge their support in the form of a covenant with God "to send away all these wives and their children" (10:3). First the Levites and priests enter into this covenant (10:5). Then the word is spread throughout Judah and Benjamin, traditional tribal regions surrounding the city of Jerusalem, that all of the returned exiles should gather to Jerusalem under threat of losing their property. The people assemble in the ninth month, the winter season, and under Ezra's direction confess that they have indeed done as accused. Since there are so many persons assembled who have intermarried with non-Jews, and since it is winter and the matter cannot therefore be investigated properly, the proposal is made that Ezra appoint heads of families to look into the matter. He does, and they do, completing their assignment on the first day of the first month (10:17), exactly one year from the beginning of their journey to Jerusalem (7:9). The episode concludes with a lengthy list of priests, Levites, and laypersons who have been involved in a mixed marriage.

At this juncture in the story Ezra has almost completed all the assignments given to him by Artaxerxes. He has returned the Temple vessels to the Temple, brought the king's offering for support of sacrifices, inquired about the law, and appointed heads of families to look into one legal infraction, namely, mixed marriages. But he has not yet taught those persons the laws of God that will govern the city and surrounding Jewish communities. Moreover, even though the people and the clergy stand in agreement with Ezra and have even sworn to keep the law, there is only a very abrupt notice that they have sent their wives away (10:44). In short, reading the book of Ezra alone leaves one feeling like the story stands somehow incomplete. Ezra has yet to complete his task.

Nehemiah's Mission and the Climax of the Story. Nehemiah, Ezra's counterpart, is a Jew who rises to an important secular position within the Persian government (Neh 2:1). It is from this privileged position that he hears of news of Jerusalem from a repatriated exile and obtains permission from King Artaxerxes to rebuild the city (2:5–8). Nehemiah is appointed governor of Judah (5:14) and is granted extensive leave to accomplish this task. His first term of service lasts twelve years, that is, from the twentieth year of King Artaxerxes (2:1) until the thirty-second year (13:6). After a relatively brief hiatus, during which time he returns to Persia, Nehemiah comes back to Jerusalem for a second term of office (13:7). The book of Nehemiah may be conveniently divided into three parts: first, Nehemiah's rebuilding of the wall and reforms (chaps. 1–7); second, the continuation of Ezra's story with the reading and teaching from the law of Moses (chaps. 8–9); and third, the response of the community of Jerusalem and Judah, which foreshadows the future of the Jerusalem community (chaps. 10–13).

Nehemiah's wall and reforms. Nehemiah's story describes the successful completion of a difficult task against almost insurmountable opposition. The city wall, providing protection and defensive capability, further symbolizes a measure of independence and autonomy for the people who live inside. But the wall lays in ruins at the beginning of the story. The opposition from Sanballat, Persian governor of the province of Samaria to the north, and from Tobiah, Persian governor of the province of Ammon to the southeast, is unrelenting (2:10; 4:1–5, 7–9; 6:1–9, 10–14). Although there is no reference to an actual military attack by any of these peoples, the story makes it clear that those working to rebuild the wall perceive such a threat to be a reality (4:21–23).

Internal factors pose no less a threat than these external ones. While engaging in this enormous building project, the struggling economy of Jerusalem and Judah places the people in severe distress (5:1–13). A famine requires the mortgaging of fields and vineyards in order to pay taxes. Pledges on those mortgages require payments, oftentimes of the workers' last articles of clothing, or even through their enslavement. Impoverished citizens can hardly be expected to work on a city building project while going hungry, lacking clothing, and having lost their land to creditors. Nehemiah intervenes by urging these creditors to return mortgaged lands and to forgive debts. The work on the wall is completed in fifty-two days; the people of the land stand in awe. After Nehemiah enrolls the population genealogically, there comes the seventh month of celebration, confession, and commitment to keep the law, especially by being separate from peoples of other nations (Nehemiah 8–10).

The conclusion: a return to Nehemiah 8–13. The story moves toward its conclusion with various glimpses of the community of Jerusalem. First, there is a summary of persons living in Jerusalem and in the surrounding villages, including the clergy (11:3–36). Then there is a list of priests and Levites who served from the days of Zerubbabel (520 BCE) to the days of Nehemiah (445 BCE [12:1–27]). Then, after great suspense, there comes the dedication of the wall of Jerusalem (12:27–43). Readers are not surprised by this since the work of rebuilding the wall seems to have been Nehemiah's greatest contribution. However, the dedication of the wall does not come until *after* the community devotes itself wholly to the law by separating itself from the other nations. Only then is the wall of Jerusalem dedicated. The story concludes with "the shutting in of the Jewish people."[7] Then, in the final chapter of the story, the people begin to fail in each area of the book's major concerns: "the temple and its services (e.g., v. 11), the separation from foreigners (vv. 23–28), and the use of the wall (vv. 15–22)."[8] This conclusion recalls for readers the questions and doubts that lingered from the opening episode before Ezra came to establish reform.

The promise of Jeremiah (Ezra 1) is now put into an interesting light. The promise might be fulfilled through devotion to the law, the separation from non-Jewish peoples, and the ensuring of that separation by the building of a wall. But the wall is only as strong as those persons within, and with the conclusion in Nehemiah 13, readers begin to hear the echo of the summary in Nehemiah 9. The rebelliousness of the ancestors portrayed in that historical recital live on in the lives of their children. In the face of such possibility, the existence of the Jerusalem community, newly restored, seems to be teetering on the same issues that had confronted the ancestors of this community.

Ezra in the Persian Period

Learning Goals

- To understand how literary texts are influenced by the specific social texts that lie behind them.
- To understand the major rulers of Persia, who played a vital role in determining the fate of the post-Exilic Jewish community in Jerusalem.
- To understand the meaning of macro-level intertextuality as illustrated by the relationships between the Persian setting and the composition of Ezra-Nehemiah

Guiding Study Exercises

1) Prepare a brief synopsis of the history of the Persian empire from 539–423 BCE, including references to the various kings.[9]
2) In what ways could one argue that the Persian empire had influence upon the writing of biblical documents?
3) Explain the meaning of *macro-level intertextuality* and offer examples from the intertexts between Ezra-Nehemiah and the Persian social text.
4) How specifically does an awareness of the social text broaden a reader's understanding of the story in Ezra-Nehemiah?

[7]D. J. Clines, *Ezra, Nehemiah, Esther* (Grand Rapids, MI: Eerdmans, 1984) 228.

[8]H. G. M. Williamson, *Ezra, Nehemiah* (WBC; Waco, TX: Word, 1985) lii.

[9]Resources might include E. M. Yamauchi, *Persia and the Bible* (Grand Rapids, MI: Baker Book House, 1990); H. Hayes and J. M. Miller, eds., *Israelite and Judean History* (London: SCM Press, 1977).

Chapter 1 claims that history is one of the most important social texts of the Bible. Having now completed a brief review of the literary text of Ezra-Nehemiah, readers may consider the social text behind the literary text. By examining the social text behind the literary text, the story *behind* the story, the function of the story becomes more readily apparent. Historical and sociological background informs specific aspects and episodes of that story. One aspect of the Ezra-Nehemiah story particularly germain to the concerns of this book is Ezra's reading of the "book of the law of Moses." Even though it is only mentioned in the narrative, such activity betrays the author's assumptions that this law book functions in ways not unrelated to those of scripture. Whatever the law book of Moses actually was—and it is not entirely clear what it was—the summary in Neh 9:6–37 takes for granted key elements of those parts of Israel's story that now make up the **Pentateuch** (Genesis–Deuteronomy) and the **Deuteronomistic History** (Deuteronomy, Joshua, Judges, Samuel, Kings). The key question has to do both with the historicity of the events that are contained in Nehemiah 8–10, as well as the existence of the biblical story in some completed and authoritative form at the time when Ezra-Nehemiah was written. Did Ezra really read from a scroll that had come to be authoritative in the community? What readers are going to find, however, is that modern historians do not deal in the realm of absolute answers. Rather, they weigh the evidence, seeking to find what is more or less probable. First, it is important to get a sense of the historicity of the story that is narrated in Ezra-Nehemiah. Certain conclusions about when the narrative was written may be drawn from inferences about the story in relationship to knowledge of historical events of the **Persian period**. Other conclusions, such as the ancient existence of scripture in the same sense that moderns understand scripture, are far less certain.

The Era of Babylon and Persia

The setting of the story makes clear the political domination by the Persian empire. The significance of Persian domination is not fully appreciated unless readers also understand what preceded Persia. Judah and its capital city, Jerusalem, fell under the political power of Persia because Babylon had fallen to the Persians in 539 BCE. Fewer than 150 years after Israel fell to Assyria, Jerusalem fell to the Babylonians (587 BCE). According to the Bible, in the first deportation to Babylon, some ten years prior to this date, the upper class citizenry—the religious, political, and economic leaders—were taken away (2 Kgs 24:13–14), and only the poorest were left behind in Jerusalem and in the surrounding countryside.

The biblical story itself could lead readers to think that life in captivity was not necessarily so bad. Obviously, Jews like Nehemiah were able to excel to positions of authority under the Babylonian and Persian regimes. The episode in Ezra 8:15–20, regarding the Levites who lived at Casiphia, portrays a group of persons who were apparently able to retain their identities as priests in this community. There is no real evidence that Jews were oppressed during this time. Ezekiel 33:30–33 implies that the people in the Babylonian setting had a great deal of independence. The letter that Jeremiah sent to the captives in Babylon presupposes the people's ability to plant gardens, build houses, marry, and give daughters in marriage (Jer 29:5–7). In other words, the picture is one of a relatively autonomous lifestyle.

But there is also testimony in the Bible that life in captivity was the ultimate disaster. It represented loss of the land that Yahweh had given to his people. The promise that a Davidic king would always have a throne in Jerusalem was now seriously called into question (Ps 89:35–37;

46–52). The Temple lay in ruins, and this surely raised the question in the hearts and minds of many as to whether Yahweh was still with his people (Ezek 11:22–25). The picture of desolation, pain, and suffering intensifies through the portrait of fallen Jerusalem painted by the author of the biblical book of Lamentations. For such people, the destruction of Jerusalem could only mean one thing: Yahweh had punished his people. Or, even worse, Yahweh was no more; he had been overpowered by the Babylonian deities. That is why, in the midst of such darkness and despair, a word of hope could be so powerful. Those Jews living in Babylon who saw the advance of the Persian king toward Babylon had reason to think about a new beginning. Those who still believed that Yahweh reigned in the heavens explained Babylon's captivity by Persia in 539 BCE as Yahweh's doing. He indeed was more powerful than the Babylonian deities. Cyrus the Persian was Yahweh's servant (Isa 45:1–8). Of course, there were those who were less inclined to interpret the events theologically and actually ridiculed such explanations (Isa 49:14). Still, it is in such a social and historical context that the events narrated in Ezra-Nehemiah take place. There was a mix of persons and perspectives. Some believed that Yahweh was going to restore Jerusalem to its erstwhile grandeur, while others believed that those days were completely over.

The Persian Setting

Persia came to dominate the ancient Near Eastern world after the fall of Babylon. As mentioned previously, the story in Ezra-Nehemiah turns on the participation, even wholehearted cooperation, of Persian kings and officials in rebuiding the Jerusalem Temple and the city walls. The time period spans the reigns of five Persian kings, from 539 BCE to 423 BCE (see Table 3.1), nearly 120 years. The narrative mentions the lavishing of many gifts upon the Jewish refugees and implies the support of the Persian court for the official religion of Jerusalem. It states that there was even documentation of these events within the chronicles of Cyrus' scribes, and it includes letters that purport to be the actual documents that came from the Persian capital. This is certainly a series of extraordinary claims; the question is, can they be corroborated? The answer is, in varying degrees of completeness, and with differing degrees of micro- and macro-levels of intertextuality, yes. The artifactual and textual evidence outside the Bible reveals the same context to be sure. However, it does not alone reflect the theological interpretation of events that overlays the biblical story.

As a general rule, the further back in time one's investigation, the less artifactual evidence there is. This is certainly the case in reconstructing the Jewish community in Palestine during the reign of Persia. Scholarly knowledge of ancient Persia itself, however, is quite extensive due to several ancient sources, as well as texts and artifacts. Herodotus was a fifth century BCE Greek who authored *Persian Wars,* a history of the war between Greece and Persia. While his history mainly concerns Greece, it is useful in its insight about Persia, due to Herodotus' own travels across the Persian empire. **Josephus'** *Antiquities,* Book 11, narrates the events of the Jews from the time of Cyrus until the end of the Persian empire under Darius III. Josephus was a Jewish historian who wrote in the first century CE, and, while he was certainly far removed from the events and his work is of varying degrees of usefulness, he is an excellent example of Greco-Roman historiography in his self-conscious use of sources and his attempt to posit natural causes behind

Table 3.1

Persian Kings (539–423 BCE)

King	Dates (BCE)
Cyrus	539–530
Cambyses	530–522
Darius I	522–486
Xerxes	486–465
Artaxerxes I	465–423

events.[10] Such sources offer at least macro-level intertexts between Ezra-Nehemiah and the historical events behind the text.

In addition to such histories, texts that come from ancient Babylon and Persia also help readers to reconstruct macro-level intertexts between the era and the story in Ezra-Nehemiah. One of the most important extant texts is that of the so-called Cyrus Cylinder. This was a cylindrical object on which Cyrus had inscribed his famous decree regarding the Persian policy of tolerance toward the nations within the empire. One passage reads," I returned to (these) sacred cities on the other side of the Tigris, the sanctuaries of which have been in ruins for a long time, the images which (used) to live therein and established for them permanent sanctuaries. I (also) gathered all their (former) inhabitants and returned (to them) their habitations."[11] This text would seem to reinforce the claim, at a macro-level, of the opening text of Ezra 1:1–2. Likewise, texts found in Egypt, written in Aramaic, the official language of the Persian empire, allow readers to understand more about how the Persian administration worked on the western frontier. Some of the texts come from Elephantine, an island in the Nile river that was the home of a Jewish military colony during the fifth century. Still other **papyri**, discovered at Wadi Daliyeh, just north of Jericho in Palestine, make reference to an important family in the area of Samaria, which is also mentioned in the story of Nehemiah (e.g., Neh 4:1; 6:1). This is the family of Sanballat, and at least three generations of that family are mentioned in the papyri.[12]

Clearly there is a helpful array of nonbiblical materials, Jewish and non-Jewish, against which to compare the biblical text. These provide information that facilitates some reconstruction of the economic, political, and social circumstances in which those early, idealistic refugees returned to restore Jerusalem to the glory of an era gone by. There may not be corroborating evidence for

---

[10]Josephus deserves a fuller discussion than space affords here. See the remarks of J. H. Hayes and J. M. Miller in *Israelite and Judean History* (London: SCM Press, 1977) 6–13

[11]Quoted in J. L. Berquist, *Judaism in Persia's Shadow* (Minneapolis, MN: Fortress, 1995) 24.

[12]See F. M. Cross, "Papyri of the Fourth Century BC from Daliyeh: A Preliminary Report on Their Discovery and Significance," *New Directions* (1969) 45–69.

every element of Ezra-Nehemiah's story, but there is enough evidence to indicate the general authenticity of the story narrated in that book.

Cyrus, 539–530 BCE. There is macro-level intertextuality between the biblical story and Cyrus' actual reign. The policies of Cyrus toward non-Persian populations in Babylon, noted previously, are well known. Yet while the biblical narrative interprets Cyrus' liberal policies as sympathetic to religious freedom, it is possible to understand these actions another way. Cyrus was an able administrator. He sought to control his empires by moving persons to the margins of the empire. He expanded the borders by annexing and colonizing, thus making the far reaches of his domain more productive. His willingness to establish religious shrines for the people living in those outlying areas might easily be interpreted as his recognition that his policies would thereby be made more attractive. This made it still more likely that these far-reaching parts of the empire would then pay tribute, contributing thereby to the economic prosperity of his empire.[13]

In other words, it was in the very best political interest of Persian hegemony to allow conquered peoples living in Babylon to go home—just as long as they remained loyal to Persia. From a Persian perspective, then, it was not Yahweh who sent the people back to Jerusalem, but Cyrus, the great king. Cyrus was not a worshipper of Yahweh (see Isa 45:4); that viewpoint derives from the Jewish interpretation of the benefits Persian policy brought to those who wished to return to Jerusalem. Neither was the state religion of Persia monotheistic. Rather Cyrus, like his successors, worshipped all of the state deities of Persia and other nations. It made good political sense to gain the favor of the all of the gods. Thus, it would follow that Cyrus had no special predisposition toward the Jews. Through his political policies the Phoenicians and the Elamites, as well as the Jews, returned to their homelands.[14]

Cambyses, 530–522 BCE. There is little macro-level intertextuality between the biblical story and the reign of this Persian king. Cyrus' son, Cambyses, was in charge of Babylonian affairs during the reign of his father, and thus he knew Cyrus' policies and chose to continue them. In 530 he performed the ritual duties of the king at the new year festival in place of Cyrus, and he

---

A Closer Look: The Cyrus Cylinder. The clay cylinder, known as The Cyrus Cylinder and inscribed in Akkadian cuneiform, was discovered in Babylon in 1879 by Rassam. In addition to making a public statement about his policies toward Babylonians and other non-Persian peoples, the text contains the various titles by which Cyrus was known, including "King of the World" and "King of the Four Quarters (of the Earth)." The text indicates that the Persian army entered Babylon and took the city "without fighting or battle."[15]

For more advanced study, A. Kuhrt. "The Cyrus Cylinder and Achaemenid Imperial Policy." *JSOT* 25 (1983) 83–94.

---

[13]See Berquist, *Judaism in Persia's Shadow,* 25–26.

[14]*Ibid.,* 25.

[15]See Yamauchi, *Persia and the Bible,* 87–89

The Cyrus Cylinder. See "A Closer Look: The Cyrus Cylinder." (© Copyright The British Museum)

was appointed regent in Babylon before his father set out on his last military campaign. Perhaps his main accomplishment was the invasion and conquest of Egypt in 525 BCE. In this military action, Cambyses continues the expansionist policies of his father.

It is probably fair to say that Cambyses does not really make enough of a change in the policies of Cyrus to warrant any close consideration of how Jerusalem might have been affected. Even in his invasion of Egypt, his armies did not pass through Palestine. Direct intervention in the affairs of Judah and Jerusalem was therefore not necessary. Thus, the struggling young Jewish community is left alone to continue to develop. What may be even more significant, in retrospect, is that during this period of relative calm, the Jerusalem residents did *not* attempt to rebuild the Temple.

Darius I, 522–486 BCE. There is at least macro-level intertextuality between the biblical story and actual events of this period. It was during the reign of Darius I that the people of Jerusalem completed the rebuilding of the Temple, according to Ezra 6. Persian records indicate that Darius had taken the throne as a usurper,[16] asserting that he was not a direct heir of Cyrus and Cambyses. He found an empire in disarray due to the abandonment of a strong system of taxation, yet it still had a strong military base with which to maintain order across their vast territory. Restoration of centralized power and the reestablishment of submission and tribute from nations on the outskirts of the empire required immediate military action.[17] One of Darius' strategies for maintaining control of the empire, especially in the locales where there had been revolt, was the

---

[16]Darius overthrew Gaumata, who himsef usurped the son of Cyrus, Cambyses.

[17]Within the first few years of his reign Darius campaigned against Elam, Babylon, Parsa, Media, Assyria, Egypt, Parthia, Margiana, Sattigydia, and Saka. See Berquist, *Judaism in Persia's Shadow,* 53.

building of temples. This created popular support for his administration. From a Persian point of view, then, Darius' support of the Jerusalem Temple was, again, a matter of good foreign policy.

Along a similar line of thought, Darius had equally strategic approaches for maintaining this power. He is remembered as an administrator as much as he is a militarist. Darius reorganized the empire into twenty provinces, or *satrapies,* providing each with its own governmental structure.[18] The governor of each province was, of course, answerable to the king, but had the independence to regulate local government and, more important, levy taxes as was necessary in the particular locale. Darius' control was extended even more effectively by the publication of laws. Each governor, such as Zerubbabel in Jerusalem, utilized traditional local laws to form the royal law code, so that local people had input in the development of the law codes. In Judah, the official interest of the king in promoting the instruction in the law was in keeping with official Persian policy. Ezra's promulgation of the traditional law of Moses, as portrayed in the biblical story, would have been effective, therefore, largely because it had the official sanction of the Persian court. Without implying that the Persian policy was the only motivating force to publish the traditions and laws of Israel as an authoritative document—like scripture—it is clear that this was very likely an important factor.

Xerxes, 486–465 BCE. The story in Ezra-Nehemiah skips from the period of Darius and the Temple to the reign of Artaxerxes I and Ezra's promulgation of the law of Moses. However, the changes in policy toward the outlying territories of the empire under the reign of Xerxes, the fourth Persian king, are worth noting as they very likely contributed to the economic crises that Nehemiah and Ezra inherited. His policies toward the nationalistic religions of the kingdoms throughout the empire changed to antipathy, when compared with the policies of his predecessors. Xerxes promoted a policy that both withdrew support for non-Persian temples, and in some cases, enforced the destruction of them.[19] Growing economic troubles brought on by a stagnant economy and expensive military campaigns sought remedy mainly through raising taxes. An exclusivistic pro-Persian nationalism contributed to a policy of taxing non-Persians. Despite this increase in revenue, the government's assets were nevertheless depleted and interest was high.

Judah's status had already changed somewhat with Darius' successful conquest of Egypt. Judah became a vital link to another part of the empire. With Xerxes' armies passing through Palestine on their ways to war with Greece, the Temple in Jerusalem played a vital role as a center for Persian government ministers. But the exorbitant taxation left the community of Judah lacking adequate resources.

Artaxerxes I, 465–423 BCE. When Artaxerxes I came to the throne, the western borders of the empire were increasingly difficult to rule. Artaxerxes sought to reverse his father's policies toward foreign religions. Nevertheless, the economic woes went unaddressed. During this king's reign, Egypt and Greece united forces in opposition to Persia. With the increasing difficulties concerning the maintenance of the borders of the empire, Judah fell under the influence of opposition parties. When the Persian army made its way through Palestine on the way to Egypt, Judah found itself in the midst of struggle. It is therefore possible to interpret the rebuilding of the walls of Jerusalem during this king's reign as a Persian move to fortify important imperial cities on the

---

[18]*Ibid.,* 54
[19]*Ibid.,* 88–89.

western front.[20] Similarly, readers can understand the appointment of strong governors, such as Nehemiah, as a Persian attempt to maintain control in a region that was falling under the economic influence of Egypt and Greece.

Reflecting upon the reigns of these five kings, clearly there are intertexts between the story in Ezra-Nehemiah and the social text behind the story. The crucial elements of the biblical story seem to correspond at a macro-level to some particular policy promoted by a particular Persian king. Is the biblical story the same as the story derived from sources external to the Bible? Obviously, it is not. But the two stories are related intertextually, and many of the claims of the biblical story are plausible given the socio-historical context of the story. One key difference, however, is that the Jewish point of view gives expression to the conviction that Yahweh was behind all of it. The Jewish perspective reckons that the Persian kings were not acting of their own accord. They were merely servants of the Jewish god. And yet it is not difficult to see how a return to Jerusalem could be interpreted as Yahweh's intervention. Remember, to some in Babylon the destruction of the Temple in Jerusalem had indicated the worst of all possible tragedies. For those persons and their heirs who survived them, a return to Jerusalem must surely have been beyond hope. The impossible had surely happened when Cyrus overthrew Babylon and proclaimed that captives could return home.

Theology and History in Ezra-Nehemiah

Learning Goals

- To understand that literary conventions are also a part of the social text behind the literary texts.
- To understand the impact that theological and ideological perspectives can have upon a writer's interpretation of his own social text.
- To begin mapping the boundaries of the implications of the terms *history* and *theology*.
- To reflect upon the possible impact that one's own theological and ideological assumptions have upon day-to-day existence.

Guiding Study Exercises

1) Summarize in a paragraph the evidence that contemporary literary genres influenced the writing of the story of Ezra-Nehemiah.
2) Describe the chronological difficulties in Ezra-Nehemiah and summarize the possible solutions.
3) Summarize how the author of Ezra-Nehemiah tells his story of restoration so as to emphasize key theological issues.
4) How has your reading about the influence theology might have had on the Bible's narration of history helped you to reflect upon your own religious self-text?

---

[20]*Ibid.,* 108.

Introduction

The summary of the Persian context helps readers understand the social and historical forces at work in fifth century BCE Judah. The people in Judah, trying to eke out their existence under the domination of the political superpower, interpreted the events of their day in the most familiar terms at hand: the religious significance of the story of their ancestors. Clearly there is an intertextual relationship between the story in the text and the story behind the text. Cyrus had legitimate political reasons for releasing captives, yet "the LORD stirred up the spirit of King Cyrus" (Ezra 1:1). Although it was Darius' policy to seek favor of the foreign nations within his empire by building temples for their deities, the Jewish view was, "they finished their building by command of the God of Israel and by decree of Cyrus, Darius, and King Artaxerxes of Persia" (Ezra 6:14b). Even though it was Artaxerxes' attempt to maintain tighter control on the frontier nations by promulgating laws, Ezra affirms, "Blessed be the LORD, the God of our ancestors, who put such a thing as this into the heart of the king to glorify the house of the LORD in Jerusalem" (Ezra 7:27). It is clear that a significant measure of religious interpretation of the historical events is going on in these intertextually related episodes. Isolating such distinctions between the literary texts and the social text provides a basis from which to draw inferences about the historian and the characteristics of his point of view. It is his point of view that not only allows later readers to hypothesize his setting but also to understand how he is controlling the intertextuality between the literary text and the larger social text.

To a certain extent, the question about the book of the law of Moses turns on one's understanding of ancient history writing. It is therefore necessary to examine how the biblical historian controls that intersection between what he knows happened in the social text of Israel's story and what his faith affirms through his representation of the literary text of Israel's story. This intersection of different texts becomes clear in Ezra-Nehemiah's use of ancient literary genres. Especially significant is the recognition that the writer of this post-Exilic history relies upon multiple sources and feels free to rearrange the chronology of events to serve his theological purposes.

Ancient Literary Genres

Understanding the ancient historian's craft begins with identifying and recognizing the **genre** or type of literature one is reading. Such recognition plays a vital role in interpreting that literature. For instance, reading a short story is different than reading a full-length novel. In the former, the author immediately and quite deliberately begins developing the contours of character. In the latter, character development may proceed at a much more leisurely pace. The uninformed reader probably suffers through the early chapters of a novel and perhaps feels somewhat rushed and cheated in a short story. By analogy, similar challenges of genre recognition confront biblical readers. One would not want to read a proverb, for instance, the same way one reads a narrative or a psalm. Neither would one read sacred history as though it were secular history. Informed readers know in advance the distinctions between these literary genres and make the necessary adjustments in how they read. This seems elementary, of course, but for many readers it is seldom a factor in reading the Bible or reflecting upon its origins. Grasping the genre of Ezra-Nehemiah is no less significant for the present consideration.

Ezra-Nehemiah is a narrative, or story, and this story concerns a most important series of events in the history of Israel's life as a nation. At a number of points the story intersects successfully, if broadly, with the historical context it attempts to portray, so readers may conclude that the narrative has a certain degree of factuality about it. A closer look, however, will also reveal some remarkable points at which Ezra-Nehemiah departs from history, suggesting that there may be other matters at stake than merely the historian's reporting of the events of antiquity.

Historical Genres Consisting of Multiple Sources. Modern readers generally understand that historians draw on multiple sources of information as they reconstruct their histories. Suspicions are aroused when there is a narrative that claims to be historical yet only offers one source as the basis of its claims. Historians do research, assemble many sources of information, arrange the differing points of view that characterize those sources, and then write something that incorporates those sources and respective points of view. Another close look at Ezra-Nehemiah with this point in mind calls forward the hypothesis that the story contained within this narrative also incorporates several sources.

This is not terribly difficult to see when readers heed the language that is used throughout the story. For instance, one readily encounters numerous instances of first person narration, language that suggests the narration is being told autobiographically. Practically all of the last part of Ezra (chaps. 8–10) is narrated in the first grammatical person, as are large parts of Nehemiah (1:1–7:73; 12:31–43; 13:4–31). These kinds of materials form a rather striking narrative contrast with materials that utilize the third grammatical person, such as Ezra 1–6 and Nehemiah 8–10. While an author is certainly free to use varying narrative strategies, the use of an autobiographical, first person narrator is virtually nonexistent in the historiographical narrative literature of the Hebrew Bible. This leads many to suspect that the historian actually utilized the memoirs of these characters to construct his story, and did not merely create these autobiographical sections for dramatic effect.

Upon careful examination, other possible sources also come to light. While the reader of the English text cannot appreciate this, Ezra 4:7–6:8 is written in **Aramaic**, not Hebrew. The existence of an entire section of narrative in another language suggests yet another source preserved by the historian. Further, this Aramaic section contains materials that are in the form of official, government correspondence between Persian ministers of state and provincial governors. One can discern references to several letters: one in 4:6 to Ahasuerus (Xerxes?), one in 4:7–16 by Rehum written to Artaxerxes, one sent as a reply from Artaxerxes in 4:17–22, one from the satrap Tattenai to Darius in 5:7–17, and a reply from Darius to Tattenai in 6:2–12, in which there is reference to the earlier decree of Cyrus (6:2–5). To be sure, historians can create such details as letters all in an attempt to make the story they are writing feel authentic. They may create such aspects, as in this case, to heighten and suspend the tension of the plot of the story—a most effective narrative strategy. The letters within Ezra-Nehemiah, however, match in rhetorical style and language so well with other official (and nonbiblical) correspondences dating from the same time period that scholars believe these letters to be based on the real things. Once again, there is a convincing intersection, even if at a macro-level only, between the social text—in the form of these letters within the narrative—and the literary text itself.

Finally, the numerous lists the writer incorporates into the narrative cannot be overlooked as examples of extra-biblical genres. There are lists of Temple vessels (Ezra 1:7–11), returnees (Ezra 2:1–70; 8:1–14; Neh 7:6–65), persons who had participated in mixed marriages (Ezra 10:18–43), persons who had built the wall (Neh 3:1–32), family heads in Jerusalem (Neh 11:3–19), persons in the villages (Neh 11:25–36), priests and Levites from the time of Zerubbabel (Neh 12:1–9),

> ***A Closer Look: Aramaic Letters from Elephantine.*** As is evident in the book of Ezra-Nehemiah, the genre of letter-writing was preserved within the narrative. Outside of the narrative some remarkable Aramaic letters have been recovered by archaeologists. These particular letters are from a Jewish military outpost at Elephantine, Egypt, dating from the reign of Darius II, the successor of Artaxerxes I. One letter is written from Yahwistic priests at Elephantine to the governor of Judah, and it is a second appeal for support in rebuilding a Yahwistic temple at that outpost. On the occasion of this letter, support is sought from the political leaders, since the preceding letter, addressed to Jerusalem priests, had not yet been answered. The letter makes it unambiguously clear that there had been a temple at Elephantine, and that it was destroyed by Egyptians. The entire community wishes it to be rebuilt so that the worship of Yahweh in Egypt might proceed. One excerpt reads: "If it please our lord, take thought of this temple to rebuild it, since they do not let us rebuild it. Look to your well-wishers and friends here in Egypt. Let a letter be sent from you to them concerning the temple of the god Yaho to build it in the fortress of Elephantine as it was built before; and the meal-offering, incense, and burnt offering will be offered in your name."[21]
>
> ***For more advanced study,*** Walter Beyerlin. *Ancient Near Eastern Texts Pertaining to the Bible.* London: SCM Press, 1965.

and others. Again, all of these lists function in the story to contribute a sense of authenticity and factuality about the story, but very likely these—especially these—derive from the hands of other people who had charge, not of telling stories, but of keeping records.

In order to define the nature of the genre of Ezra-Nehemiah, readers must begin by describing what they see. This narrative clearly contains several sources made up of different subgenres: narratives, memoirs, official documents, and lists of records, all of which are clearly distinguished by their particular rhetorical styles. The story of Ezra-Nehemiah and the restoration of Jerusalem appears, therefore, to be a composite piece of work, woven together out of many sources of information. The historian has given careful consideration to the arrangement of those sources within his story and then has preserved those sources within his narrative.

Historical Genres and Rearranging Chronology. Even though the historian is interested in including his sources, in ancient historiography writing this does not hinder the historian from manipulating those sources. In the book of Ezra-Nehemiah one of the most compelling cases for this kind of manipulation lies within the detail of the relative chronologies of the two main characters, Ezra and Nehemiah. *Recall that the story in its present form leaves the impression that Ezra and Nehemiah were contemporaries whose ministries overlapped* (see Neh 8:9). But upon closer reading of the plot of the story it seems highly likely that the two missions of Ezra and Nehemiah to Jerusalem did not coincide at all. Such a circumstance makes it rather difficult to conclude that the story of the restoration of Jerusalem actually corresponds as an accurate "snap shot" of the social text behind the story. Look more closely at the problem.

---

[21]*ANET,* 492.

The question of the relative time frame for these two characters is a crux in the academic study of the two biblical books. Readers first encounter an important notice in Ezra 7:7 that Ezra's journey to Jerusalem takes place "in the seventh year of King Artaxerxes" (458 BCE). Nehemiah's dates in Neh 1:1 and 2:1, however, indicate that his journey to Jerusalem begins "in the twentieth year of King Artaxerxes" (445 BCE).[22] A simple operation of subtraction shows that there is a thirteen-year difference in the two characters' journeys. Yet the reading in Neh 7:73–9:37 leaves the distinct impression that Ezra is in Jerusalem for that great celebration during the seventh month of Nehemiah's first year (see especially 8:9). This implies that thirteen years have passed before Ezra finally reads the law before the people. But Ezra brings back the law with him in 458 BCE. Recall that teaching the people the law was one of his assignments from King Artaxerxes. Is it reasonable to think he would wait some thirteen years before completing the assignment given to him by the king? This complication therefore calls for a reexamination of the amount of time that passes in the narrative.

In fact, there is a series of time references in Ezra that, in the absence of other indications, give readers the impression Ezra's mission, except for the reading of the law, was completed in one year. Both Ezra 7:9 and 8:31 have the party leaving Babylon in the first month of Artaxerxes' seventh year (458 BCE). Ezra 7:8 has them arriving in Jerusalem in the fifth month. By the ninth month the people are well into the midst of their crisis of intermarriage (10:9). In the tenth month Ezra appoints heads of families to investigate the matter (10:16). By the first day of the first month of the succeeding year (457 BCE), the investigators have presumably interviewed every person who has taken a foreign wife (10:17). In other words, Ezra's mission appears to be winding down around the year 457 BCE, about one year after he leaves Babylon. Strangely, in the book of Nehemiah Ezra is not even mentioned for the first seven chapters and, aside from Neh 1:7–9, neither is the law. Then both Ezra and the law mysteriously reappear together in Nehemiah 8, thirteen years later. These ambiguities within the story spark the curiosity of many readers. Consequently, scholars have for some time sought to solve this crux.

There is yet more information that suggests Ezra's visit to Jerusalem came not before Nehemiah's, but after. For instance, when Ezra offers his prayer of repentance he makes reference to events that only come *later* in the story about Nehemiah. He thanks God for giving the people "a *wall* in Judea and Jerusalem" (Ezra 9:9). Admittedly, one single reference such as this does not necessarily mean that Ezra actually came after Nehemiah. Perhaps Ezra is referring to a metaphorical, not literal, "wall." But it certainly does not dissuade readers from their suspicions about the general chronological ambiguities. Further, the portrait in Ezra is that the marriage reforms were a sweeping success (Ezra 10:1–5, 16–17, 44). Indeed, Nehemiah's story would seem to confirm this, especially as one reads Nehemiah 10. Why then are the reforms reenacted in Neh 13:1–3 and 23–30? Are readers to assume that the reforms of Ezra, if indeed they came first, were a failure? Not necessarily. It is possible that Ezra's reforms worked for a while. The story may well be acknowledging the reality that for reforms to remain in effect there must be ongoing commitment and recommitment to them. One final point illustrates a further difficulty. Ezra is said to serve

---

[22]Also, the month of Chislev of v. 1 actually comes after the month of Nisan, the former being the ninth month, the latter being the first month of the year. Hence, the book apparently has the sequence of Nehemiah's memoirs slightly out of order.

alongside the high priest Jehohanan, "son of Eliashib" (Ezra 10:6 and Neh 12:23).[23] But reading farther into the story, Nehemiah is said to serve alongside the high priest Eliashib (3:1, 20). If one assumes this to be the same Eliashib, as one might on first reading, then Ezra serves with the son of Eliashib, or perhaps even his grandson.[24] The implication is that Ezra actually followed Nehemiah rather than preceded him.

How do modern readers deal with such ambiguities and chronological difficulties? Scholars have offered at least three different proposals as guidelines for this difficult task. The first proposal, call it proposal A, retains the text as it stands on the grounds of such explanations as offered above: the possibility that the wall in Ezra 9:9 is to be read metaphorically and that Ezra's reforms were indeed successful, albeit only for a while. Proposal A, in other words, offers a series of counterproposals, or alternative readings, to the plain interpretation of such **anachronisms**. This approach maintains that Ezra visited Jerusalem in 458 BCE, some years before the return of Nehemiah. The second proposal, proposal B, grows from the recognition that there was indeed a second Persian king with the royal name of Artaxerxes (Artaxerxes II), whose period of rule (404–359 BCE) corresponds to the need to date Ezra's visit later than Nehemiah's. Placing Ezra's return to Jerusalem in the seventh year of Artaxerxes II means that Ezra arrived in Jerusalem around 398/97 BCE. Obviously, this solution requires that readers also accept the placing of Ezra's arrival and work *before* that of Nehemiah to be due to the chronological rearrangment of the final author (or authors) of the story of Ezra-Nehemiah. In other words, Ezra's precedence over Nehemiah only exists in the literary text and not in the social text that can be discerned through historical reconstruction. A third proposal, proposal C, cuts a path down the middle of these two previous alternatives. Some have suggested that if the text of Ezra 7:7, which speaks of the seventh year of Artaxerxes, were emended to read "the thirty-seventh year of Artaxerxes," assuming that the text speaks of Artaxerxes I and not Artaxerxes II, then that would place Ezra's visit to Jerusalem in the year 428 BCE. Nehemiah returns to Babylon after twelve years, sometime around 433 BCE, and then returns for a second term as governor a short while later (Neh 13:6). This proposal would place Ezra in Jerusalem with Nehemiah, though only *after* Nehemiah's first term of office. Proposal C indeed satisfies some of the chronological difficulties. Nevertheless, its main weakness is that the emendation of the text in Ezra 7:7 is quite speculative. How therefore does a reader decide between these proposals? Generally, in the absence of any compelling evidence for proposals B and C, scholars tend to retain the text—with all of its chronological difficulties—as it stands.[25] But this does not remove the reality that the text itself gives evidence of having been rearranged chronologically by a secondary hand.

Theology through History

The argument is pressed toward the conclusion that theological reflection involves both literary and historical sensitivities. On the one hand, readers must keep in mind the reality of the events

[23]One may infer that he is the high priest because of his chambers in the Temple, "the house of God," and because it seems unlikely that someone of Ezra's stature would have lodged with a person who did not hold some significant office in Jerusalem during the period of reform.

[24]Since the Hebrew/Aramaic word for "son" could denote either. This would implicitly suggest that Ezra served in Jerusalem a whole generation later than the time of Nehemiah.

[25]The solutions to this crux are many and complicated. One can read them in H. G. M. Williamson, *Ezra, Nehemiah*, xxxix–xliv; or in J. Blenkinsopp, *Ezra-Nehemiah* (OTL; Philadelphia: Westminster, 1988) 140–144.

that stand behind the biblical narratives. On the other hand, readers must remember that those events take on ever new significances as time passes and as later audiences reflect upon those events. It is helpful at this point to recall the discussion in the conclusion to section one of this chapter. There readers saw that as the story of Ezra-Nehemiah stands presently, there is, first, the rebuilding of the Temple (Ezra 1–6), then the recommitment to the law (Ezra 7–10 and Nehemiah 8–10), and only then, is there the dedication of the wall (Nehemiah 12). Furthermore, readers should recall that the day of reading and later the recommitment to the law comes as a kind of climax to the entire celebration of the seventh month, not to mention the story of Ezra-Nehemiah. Common sense, of course, would convince readers that the building of the wall was historically one of the most essential components to the survival of the refugees in Jerusalem. Yet, in the story world, that event is placed *after* Ezra calls the people to separate from foreigners (Ezra 9); the dedication of the wall comes only *after* the people recommit themselves to keep the law. While this makes for anachronistic history, it makes for compelling theology. The people are shut into Jerusalem, foreigners are shut out of Jerusalem, and the people must keep their commitments to the law. The story ends in Nehemiah 13, however, with the people's commitments already being broken.

The ancient historian has to maintain a balance between his interest in antiquity, his knowledge of actual events, and his own personal convictions. He is committed to his theology, his community's struggle to reinvent itself, and his own role in that immediate struggle. But these convictions, regardless of where they come from, cause him to reread the story of Jerusalem's restoration in a certain way. The historian interprets the history of the period to assert his conviction that keeping the law of Moses is vital to the community's survival. It was the law that would legitimize the rigorous observance of the rituals of Temple service, as well as the avoidance of mixing with other nations.

Put another way, historical events become the vehicles for theological affirmation. One biblical scholar seeks to explain the relationship between literature and historical event by offering a contemporary parallel in the debate surrounding the construction of the Holocaust museum in Washington, D.C. One critic of the museum argued that by building such a shrine there was the potential for it to become "a universal symbol of suffering," thus losing its tie to the historical event of World War II and the Jewish persecution that ensued in that specific setting and context. In a sense, by giving the Holocaust greater significance in society's collective memory, it also has lost some of its historicity.[26] While this argument did not prevent the building of the museum, the point is well taken. Readers must therefore remember that as ancient writers reflected upon the meanings of the historical events of their ancestors, in obtaining larger significance through the community's memory, they necessarily lost some of their ties to specific history. In contrast, in reconstructing some of those historical contexts in which biblical events occurred, those events necessarily relinquish some of their power to capture the theological imagination.

Conclusion

The problem of reading ancient history is complicated by understanding the intertexts between the text and the social text. In reconstructing the social text, as in the case of Ezra-Nehemiah, clearly there is broad agreement between the social text and the literary text. But it is also clear

[26]B. W. Anderson, "Historical Criticism and Beyond, " *BibRev* 9 (1993) 9, 17.

that the writer controls that intertextuality of history and his story by the use of certain literary genres. Ancient historiography of the sort encountered in Ezra-Nehemiah seems to have genuine antiquarian interests, indicated in the use and inclusion of many sources. The conventions of ancient historiography, furthermore, allow the writer to insert his own theological views by interpreting and even rearranging the chronology of his sources.

It would be incautious to generalize about all the books in the Bible from a reading of Ezra-Nehemiah, yet it is fair to say that history as modern readers know it and practice it is not the governing factor in the meaning of biblical texts. Ancient historians felt free to perpetuate an imaginative interplay between theological confession and historical event. This permitted them to rearrange chronology, heighten the significance of character, and above all, to create a narrative world where God reigned supreme.

For Further Reading

The Story of the Restoration: Ezra-Nehemiah

Ackroyd, P. R. "Faith and Its Reformulation in the post-Exilic Period," *Theology Digest* 27 (1979) 323–346.

Fensham, F. C. "Some Theological and Religious Aspects in Ezra and Nehemiah." *JNSL* 11(1983) 59–68. (*Recommended for beginning students.*)

Ezra in the Persian Period

Balentine, S. "The Politics of Religion in the Persian Period." *After the Exile.* Edited by J. Barton and D. Reimer. Macon, GA: Mercer University Press, 1996. Pp. 129–146.

Smith, M. "Jewish Religious Life in the Persian Period." *CHJ* I, 219–278. (*Recommended for beginning students.*)

Stern, E. "The Persian Empire and the Political and Social History of Palestine in the Persian Period." *CHJ* I, 70–87.

Theology and History in Ezra-Nehemiah

Cross, F. M. "A Reconstruction of the Judean Restoration." *JBL* 94 (1975) 4–18.

Reynolds, C. "Is History a Thing of the Past?" *RR* 47 (1994) 197–206. (*Recommended for beginning students.*)

CHAPTER FOUR

The Story of the Law

Introduction

Review

The previous three chapters have introduced readers to the intertextual method of this text, a brief overview of the biblical story, and some historical-critical methods for investigating the origins of the Bible. Readers should understand that interpreting the Bible demands attention to both the literary text—the story *in* the Bible—and the social text—the story *behind* the Bible. It was the social and historical circumstances behind the story of Ezra-Nehemiah, many of which were retold in the story, that shaped the production of the story. The book of Ezra-Nehemiah, which was written during the Persian period, both reflects the social text of that time period and tells the story of ancient Israel (in the prayer of Ezra in Neh 9:6–37) from the vantage point of that social text.

Preview

Chapter 4 focuses upon the law of Moses, one of the most important themes of the biblical story. Readers have already seen that Ezra-Nehemiah portrays the law of Moses functioning as though it were scripture. One would hypothesize, therefore, that there should be a strong correspondence between the laws mentioned in Ezra-Nehemiah and those in the present form of the Pentateuch. Lacking such strong correspondence, the chapter will press toward the hypothesis that the Pentateuch might rather have been quite undefined at the time of the Persian period, making it even less likely that *modern* notions of scripture were in existence in the fifth century BCE.[1] Given the uncertainty of the date of Pentateuchal origins, the second part of the chapter will examine some of the intertexts between the three major law codes within the Pentateuch. Form critical and redaction critical methodologies will illustrate the further complexities of determining their origins. The third and final part of the chapter will examine one singularly important theological theme that functions alongside the law and possibly provides another means of dating the origins of the law.

---

[1]See H. G. M. Williamson, *Ezra, Nehemiah* (WBC; Waco, TX: Word, 1985) xxxvii for a brief survey of scholarly views. There is a strong consensus among scholars that Ezra's so-called law was not the Pentateuch as we now know it.

Ezra-Nehemiah Interpreting Law Codes
Nehemiah 7–10

Learning Goals

- To understand the nature of the evidence that the law codes were not finalized until the post-Exilic period.
- To understand the evidence that legal traditions needed to be reread (reinterpreted) in both the pre- and post-Exilic periods.

Guiding Study Exercises

1) In a paragraph summarize the way Neh 8:13–16 rereads the festival of booths.
2) Outline succinctly the stages of rereading of the various legal traditions regarding intermarriage.
3) Outline succinctly the stages of rereading of the various legal traditions regarding the Sabbath.

Readers already know that the historian writing Ezra-Nehemiah is reinterpreting Israel's story (see Chap. 2). It makes sense to assume that he is also reinterpreting the smaller components of that story, such as the law. In fact, one cannot read the book of Ezra-Nehemiah without realizing what a vital role the law plays in the narrative. For instance, in the episode of the rebuilding of the Temple, Zerubbabel builds the altar in order to offer burnt offerings, "as prescribed in the law of Moses the man of God" (Ezra 3:2). Ezra himself, who traces his own priestly lineage back to Aaron through Zadok, is also "a scribe skilled in the law of Moses" (Ezra 7:6). It is his commission from King Artaxerxes I to teach the "laws of your God" to "those who do not know them" (Ezra 7:25). The task of teaching the law was a special task of the **Levites**, as indicated in Nehemiah 8, and also in the Chronicler's history (2 Chron 17:8–9), as well as in the Deuteronomic law itself (Deut 31:9–13).

What is so extraordinary about Nehemiah 8 is the detailed description of the activity accompanying the reading of the law, as well as the particular epithets that are used to identify the law. Being a very late portrait of the law and its function within the community, readers have a touchstone for intertextual comparison within the Hebrew scriptures against other, probably much earlier, portrayals of the law's function.

Awareness of the Laws in the Pentateuch

The many references to the law in the narrative of Nehemiah 8–10 invite comparison with other biblical passages that speak of the law. In Exod 24:12–14, for instance, the Lord calls Moses atop the mountain in order to give him the stone tablets "with the law and the commandments." A cursory reading of Exodus 24 reveals what a difficult and convoluted narrative it is. But it suffices at this point simply to know that this episode serves in the larger narrative as a climax to Moses' receipt of the law atop Mt. Sinai. Moses' first trip to the summit comes in Exod 19:3, after which he faithfully reports God's words to the people at the foot of the mountain. The reader is to understand that the chapter contains the actual words the Lord delivers to Moses (chaps. 20–23). The materials in 21:1–23:33 are known as the **Covenant Code**. Since Ezra 3:2 mentions the law of Moses, it is natural to suppose that these are the materials the historian of Ezra-Nehemiah assumes his characters to be reading.

Nehemiah 7:73b presents the people gathered to hear the law read in "the seventh month." As they continue reading and studying the law on the next day they discover that they are to live in "booths" during "the festival of the seventh month" (8:13–14). According to Nehemiah, Moses has commanded the observance of this great religious festival of **Succoth** during this seventh month. However, examining the Covenant Code (Exod 21:1–23:33), it is impossible to find the festival of the seventh month, nor, for that matter is there any command that the people should live in booths during this month. There are references to three festivals in the Covenant Code, only they have different names: the "festival of unleavened bread" (Exod 23:15), the "festival of harvest of the first fruits" (Exod 23:16), and the "festival of ingathering" (Exod 23:16b). It therefore seems unlikely that the historian behind the Ezra-Nehemiah story could have had the law code that is contained in Exodus in mind as he described the events of the seventh month during Nehemiah's day. At the very least, the late historian was referring to a different way of depicting Israel's cultic calendar.

There are two other major codes of law contained in the Hebrew Bible, however. Reading through the **Pentateuch** eventually leads to the **Holiness Code**, contained in Leviticus 17–26. This code of law is parallel somewhat to the Covenant Code in that it is concerned also with the social life of the community. It gets its name from the repetitive phrases that express the Lord's concern that his people be holy (e.g., Lev 19:2; 20:26). In contrast to the Covenant Code, there is a provocative intertext with the story in Nehemiah 8. In Lev 23:4–43 there are the three yearly festivals that the people are to observe. Indeed, these three coincide with Exodus' assertion of three yearly festivals. But it is interesting to see that in vv. 5–8 the first festival is a **Passover** offering followed by the festival of unleavened bread. This Passover offering has an added dimension in distinction to the passage in Exodus. Verses 23–32 refer to the "seventh month," an allusion that is quite similar to the narrative in Nehemiah (cf. Nehemiah 8). But in Leviticus there are still more extensive connections with Nehemiah. In Lev 23:33 there is a reference to the fifteenth day of the month as the beginning of the seven-day festival of "booths." According to the Holiness Code the people are, indeed, to live in the booths (v. 42) for the duration of the seven-day festival. What is more, there is also a correspondence between Leviticus and Nehemiah regarding the gathering of "palm branches." They are not an exact match, but readers can certainly agree that there is macro-level intertextuality between these two passages (see Table 4.1).

One could certainly surmise that the writer of Ezra-Nehemiah knew of this code of law in Leviticus. Not only is the festival called the feast of booths, unlike that in Exodus, but the people are "to live in booths." What is more, both passages have references to the gathering of leafy branches, especially palm branches. In Leviticus there is no reference to using the branches for the booths, while in Nehemiah, this is the ostensible purpose of the branches. In Lev 23:39 there is a reference to harvest at the end of the year; however, that agrees with the statement in Exod

Table 4.1

The Festival of Booths

Leviticus 23:39–42	Nehemiah 8:13–16
39Now, on the fifteenth day of the *seventh month,* when you have gathered in the produce of the land, you shall keep the festival of the Lord, lasting seven days; a complete rest on the first day, and a complete rest on the eighth day.	13On the second day the heads of ancestral houses of all the people, with the priests and the Levites, came together to the scribe Ezra in order to study the words of the law.
40On the first day you shall take the fruit of majestic trees, *branches of palm trees,* boughs of leafy trees, and willows of the brook; and you shall rejoice before the Lord your God for seven days	14And they found it written in the law, which the LORD had commanded by Moses, that the people of Israel should *live in booths* during the festival of the *seventh month,*
41You shall keep it as a festival to the LORD seven days in the year; you shall keep it in the *seventh month* as a statute forever throughout your generations.	15and that they should publish and proclaim in all their towns and in Jerusalem as follows, "Go out to the hills and bring branches of olive, wild olive, myrtle, *palm,* and other leafy trees to make *booths,* as it is written."
42You shall live in *booths* for seven days; all that are citizens in Israel shall live in *booths,*	16So the people went out and brought them, and made *booths* for themselves, each on the roofs of their houses, and in their courts and in the courts of the house of God, and in the square at the Water Gate and in the square at the Gate of Ephraim.

23:16. In the summary of the celebration in Nehemiah there is no reference to the agricultural significance of the feast. In this latter passage, the feast is much more completely devoted to the celebration of booths and, especially, to the reading of the law. Nevertheless the passage in Leviticus tends to intersect much more specifically with the narrative in Ezra-Nehemiah than with the passage in Exodus.

Of course, the reference to the agricultural significance in Leviticus is absent from Nehemiah. Continuing to read through the Pentateuch leads to the third major law code, the **Deuteronomic Code**, which is contained within the book of Deuteronomy (chaps. 12–26), the final book in the Pentateuch. As already stated, the book of Deuteronomy is a final set of instructions or a sermon of Moses, before the people cross over the Jordan River into the land that they are to inherit. Within the law code itself (Deut 16:13–15) there is a reference to the observance of the festival of booths. There is no explicit reference to the seventh month, however. Rather, as in Exodus, the festival of booths is associated with the agricultural season, specifically, with the gathering in of "the produce from your threshing floor and your wine press" (Deut 16:13). Neither is there any reference to the gathering of palm branches or other leafy plants as in Leviticus and in Nehemiah. Thus, one could easily surmise that the historian who wrote Ezra-Nehemiah was very likely drawing on Leviticus' understanding of the festival rather than Deuteronomy's interpretation, since Nehemiah seems to have more in common with the book of Leviticus than with either Deuteronomy or Exodus.

Looking beyond the law code to the appendix of the book of Deuteronomy,[2] there is a most remarkable provision for the reading of the law that seems to create a macro-level intertext with Nehemiah 8. Deuteronomy 31:10–13 commands that in every seventh year the law should be read in a public convocation. Most remarkable, however, is the fact that this reading is to take place during the feast of booths. Now this is a very near approximation to the depiction in Nehemiah 8. For, while there is no reference in Nehemiah to the seventh *year* relative to the period of time Ezra had already been in Jerusalem, it is clear that Ezra gathers the people in the seventh *month* for the purpose of reading the book of the law of Moses (Neh 8:1). Moreover, as in Deuteronomy 31, the law is read to those "who have not known it" so that "they may hear and learn to fear the LORD your God" (Deut 31:13).

Clearly, the historian writing Ezra-Nehemiah knows of at least the Deuteronomic Code and the Holiness Code. He preserves the palm branches and designation of the festival in the seventh month from Leviticus. He also associates the reading of the law with the festival as in Deuteronomy. It would be very difficult, therefore, to conclude that the writer of Ezra-Nehemiah did not know of the materials that were contained within the Pentateuch. That which the historian portrays Ezra to be reading in Nehemiah 8 seems to have a lot in common with some of the materials within the Pentateuch[3]

The Law Calls for Reinterpretation

The book that Ezra is portrayed as reading, which is presented as the law, would appear to have a great deal of authority within the community. Nehemiah 8:8 reads, "So they read from the book, from the law of God, with interpretation. They gave the sense, so that the people understood the reading." Not only does the narrative present the book as "the law of God," but the officials are very careful to help the people to understand it. It is clearly given a central place in the course of the celebration, and furthermore, the people make significant life changes on the basis of its

---

[2]It is so-called because many scholars believe that 31:1–34:12 is not an original conclusion to the book. Rather, these chapters contain several later additions and assume historical circumstances that could only exist after the Exile was over. See A. D. H. Mayes, *Deuteronomy* (NCB; Grand Rapids, MI: Eerdmans, 1981) 45–47; 371–72.

[3]In fact, F. Crüsemann, *The Torah,* (Minneapolis, MN: Fortress, 1996) 342, concludes that "The Book of the Covenant, Deuteronomy and the priestly law, all three great law codes form the basis of Nehemiah 10; the legal aspect of the entire Pentateuch is fully present."

words. The people separate themselves from "all foreigners" (9:2), and they, along with their priests, Levites, and officials, are willing to affix their names to a written promise that they would, unlike their ancestors of the past, observe diligently the words of the law in the future (9:38 10:31).

But what is the nature of this law that the people are committing themselves to keep? Recall that the law codes themselves are not necessarily in agreement on any particular point, and the historian feels free to mix the law codes together. Is the historian merely combining the law codes, reinterpreting those laws according to a kind of logic that grows from the particular socio-historical context in which he himself is living? If this is so, then it cannot be concluded that the law of Moses, even though it had central authority in this community, was necessarily beyond the reach of further rereading of the post-Exilic community. Rather, readers must consider the idea of rereading ancient texts to be a part of a process of creating and passing on authoritative texts.

The Law of Intermarriage. The laws of intermarriage and Sabbath will suffice at this point as further examples. An examination of Nehemiah 10 reveals that they are but two of the laws that the people commit to through the signing of the document.[4] One of the intriguing ironies of the very strict law prohibiting intermarriage with non-Jewish peoples is that Israel's story bears witness to a rich tradition of intermarriage. Although there are traditions that oppose the practice (e.g., Gen 34:8–17), some of the patriarchs themselves married non-Israelite women (e.g., Moses and Zipporah, Exod 2:21–22; see also Num 12:1–6; and Abraham and Hagar, Gen 16:1–6). Perhaps even more curiously, the Deuteronomic Code itself—which so strongly opposes intermarriage (see below)—actually retains an apparently older legal tradition that *assumes* the legitimacy of intermarriage (see Deut 21:10–14). This is an interesting fact in light of what is in Nehemiah 10. In Neh 10:30, the people pledge not to "give our daughters to the peoples of the land or take their daughters for our sons." This comes in a context that states explicitly that the people in Jerusalem represent the "holy seed" of God's people, and that intermarriage threatens the **purity** of this seed. From a nonreligious perspective, there are simply some very sound social reasons for forbidding it, even though one of the most consistent concerns seems to be its threat to the practice of Yahwism.

In antiquity, marriage was much more an economic arrangement among and within communities than it was an arrangement for the mutual bliss of two individuals. An unwise marriage outside of one's ethnic group could have far-reaching economic implications. The bride price paid by the groom's family and the dowry offered by the bride's family were terms of economic exchange, providing a compensation for loss of a family member, on the one hand, and a pledge for future inheritance, on the other. In the setting of Nehemiah, where the refugees were relatively poor and the resident inhabitants were more wealthy, the community prohibited any economic exchange that served to benefit outsiders, whether immediately or eventually. The only way that the struggling young community could prosper was to keep its internal economy, especially its land, to itself.[5]

Against such a social background, a community's interest in strictly controlling marriage is at least understandable. What is perhaps even more intriguing, however, is that this economic mo-

---

[4]Others included temple tax (vv. 33–34), contribution of wood for temple (v. 35), firstfruits (v. 36), firstborn (v. 37), contribution of dough, fruit, wine, and oil (v. 38), tithe (38–40), regular care for temple (v. 40).

[5]J. Blenkinsopp's article, "The Social Context of the 'Outsider Woman' in Proverbs 1–9," *Bib* 72.4 (1991) 457–73, offers some basic insight into the correlations between the symbolic expression within these narratives and the biblical wisdom literature and this fundamental economic dilemma.

tive is probably a tacit concern that lies behind quite a different kind of legitimization for such prohibitions of intermarriage. The marriage laws considered here seek legitimization by appeal to the potential threat of religious corruption. However, in the most ancient passage, Exod 34:11–16, the concern for religious **apostasy** seems not to fit too smoothly with the specific law against intermarriage. Read and consider Exod 34:11–16, regarded by many scholars to be a very ancient collection of laws.

Before looking at these verses in greater detail, one may wonder why there is yet another law code at this point in the narrative, so close to a similar law code in Exodus 20–23. While it would be a great help to the student to have already read the entire biblical narrative, it must suffice for now to rely on the following description of the narrative context that surrounds this second law code in Exodus. Exodus 32 narrates an episode in which the people sin against Yahweh by making a golden calf (see Neh 9:18). While this is happening, Moses is atop Mt. Sinai receiving the law. When Yahweh alerts Moses to his peoples' sin, Moses' anger causes him to throw down the tablets of law, thus breaking them (Exod 32:19). After the people are punished, Moses returns to the top of the mountain to receive a second law. That is what is contained in Exod 34:11–16. It is within *this* replacement law code that readers find a most intriguing marriage law.[6]

This very ancient literary context prohibits intermarriage because of the threat of religious **syncretism**, the joining together of two different religious belief systems. Notice especially the list of Canaanite nations that the people are to drive out of Canaan. Among the intriguing aspects of this passage is that the opening verse (v. 11) is a promise that Yahweh will drive out these inhabitants. What follows in v. 12, however, is an admonition not to make a covenant with the inhabitants of the land. One can only ponder how such could be possible if they were in fact driven out! One possible explanation for this conflicting logic is that originally the idea had a different function. At one time the statement in v. 11 may rather have served to legitimate the idea of **holy war** with no thought of prohibiting intermarriage. Readers might hypothesize that the ensuing legal stipulation about intermarriage reflects a different and possibly later situation for which the text was reread: Israel was trying to establish its identity in a land occupied by many different nations, and it uses an old holy war formula to reinforce its admonitions to be distinctive.[7] Only, Israel's distinctiveness must now be achieved in terms of religious purity through the avoidance of intermarriages, rather than through political and ethnic purity achieved by holy war. The concept of ethnic purity, which was achieved at an earlier time through holy war, is reread through the imposition of stricter marriage laws.

A second passage concerning mixed marriage is informative along these same lines. It likely dates from a time later than that in Exodus 34, especially since it is associated with the Deuteronomic legal corpus. Yet it formulates the same law in a way that clears up some ambiguity inherent in the older law in Exodus 34. Read now Deut 7:1–6.

Readers observe in this instance that it is not the deity alone who clears the nations away but the people themselves with God's help; he "gives them over to you and you defeat them" (v. 2). Notice also, however, the passage includes virtually the same list of Canaanite nations as in the more ancient formulation of Exodus 34, with Deuteronomy adding the "Girgashites" to the

---

[6]The reader should compare these commandments with those in Exod 20:1–17, however. Shouldn't they agree?

[7]D. J. A. Clines, "Nehemiah 10 as an Example of Early Jewish Biblical Exegesis," *JSOT* 21 (1981) 116. The authors rely on this article extensively for the explanation of this point.

A Closer Look: Canaanite Religion. Ancient Israel was not different from any political entity in that her culture and institutions were forged in conversation, sometimes in conflict, with those of the neighboring nation-states. Canaanite polytheism grew from agriculturalism. It offered a formidable challenge to the developing transcendent monotheism of strict Yahwism. The development of pantheons of deities and myths about their acitivites, relationships, and exploits were all conceived as symbolic reflections of the annual agricultural cycle and the ever-present threat to society from the natural world. For example, the autumn festival celebrated the storm god Baal's victory over Yamm, the sea, thus reestablishing order out of Chaos. Another myth that functioned at the new year festival was that of Baal's victory over Mot, death and sterility. The long hot and dry Canaanite summer was depicted as Baal's death. The change of seasons bringing autumn's rains was understood as Baal's resurrection, which came thanks to the victory of his sister, Anat, over Mot. The myth of the marriage of the moon god and goddess not only perpetuates the fertility motifs of agricultural religion, but provides a cosmic basis for marriage. It is no wonder that marriage with its attending significance for fertility formed an easy connection with Canaanite myths and religion.

For further study, J. Gray. *Near Eastern Mythology.* New York: Peter Bedrick Books, 1988. Pp. 68–102; M. Smith. "Myth and Mythmaking in Canaan and Ancient Israel. In *CANE* 3.2031–41.

For more advanced study, J. Day. "Canaanite, Religion of." *ABD* 1.831–37; H. Ginsburg. "Ugaritic Myths, Epics, and Legends." *ANET* 3rd ed. Pp. 129–155.

list. More intriguing is that at the time when scholars believe the ancient legal specialists composed this law code, these nations were long gone! The writer of this text includes **anachronistically** a list of foreign nations with only formulaic significance. The question is, "why"? Obviously, the passage in the older tradition associates the still older holy war formula with the problem of intermarriage. But the audience contemporary with the Deuteronomist's rereading must surely wonder who these peoples are since they are no longer a physical reality, nor, therefore, a real political or religious threat. For the Deuteronomic interpreter these nations can therefore only have *symbolic* meaning; that is, they symbolize the threat of religious corruption. There is no chance of these ancient and nonexistent nations really posing a threat of intermarriage to readers contemporary with the Deuteronomic lawgiver. But by setting the law on intermarriage in the context of holy war, as in Exodus 34, the later lawgiver is rhetorically reinvoking a call to extreme commitment. In his day, however, this extreme commitment will be practiced in terms of religious devotion only, since there is no physical threat of intermarriage with these specific peoples.[8]

[8]*Ibid.,* 116.

The still much later formulation of this same law prohibiting intermarriage, in Neh 10:30, would seem to reformulate both of these laws. Look again at the text: "We will not give our daughters to the peoples of the land or take their daughters for our sons." This verse suggests a culmination of the interpretation of both of the two older laws in Exodus and Deuteronomy. In Exod 34:16 the prohibition is against the marriage with the "daughters" of those nations; in Deuteronomy the law contains the material in Exod 34:16 but is further expanded to prohibit the giving of Israelite women to their "sons." In Nehemiah there is the Deuteronomic formulation, but also a different description of the people with whom the post-Exilic community may not make such exchanges. Remember that in Deuteronomy and Exodus there is a list of *specific* nations against whom Israel, originally, had at one time been engaged in holy war. In Nehemiah they are simply "the people of the land," a phrase that makes the anachronistic list of nations in Deuteronomy much more relevant for the contemporary **Palestinian** audience of the writer of Ezra-Nehemiah. This stands in contrast to the appeal to an older formulation in the days of Ezra. In Ezra 9:1 the officials come to Ezra and say, "The people of Israel, the priests, and the Levites have not separated themselves from the peoples of the lands with their abominations, from the Canaanites, the Hittites, the Perizzites, the Jebusites, the Ammonites, the Moabites, the Egyptians, and the Amorites." The apposition within Ezra-Nehemiah of the older list of nations with the much less specific but more current phrase "peoples of the lands," provides definition of the less specific phrase. In addition, the use of the old formula, even though anachronistic, brings the situation of contemporary marriage practices within the purview of the forgotten law, something Ezra was charged to do.

The Laws of the Sabbath. Similar kinds of variations exist between the several **Sabbath** laws also. Recall that in Neh 10:31 the writer depicts the people, priests, and Levites pledging to observe the Sabbath by refusing to buy grain or merchandise from "the people of the land" who bring it to Jerusalem on the Sabbath. During his second term as governor, Nehemiah actually has the city gates shut to prevent these merchants from having access to the city on the Sabbath (Neh 13:19–20). So what is the Sabbath?

The word derives from a Hebrew verb, *sabat,* which means "to cease, desist, or rest." In its noun form Sabbath denotes that day on which an individual ceases from labor and other activities. It is not merely the cessation from work that defines the significance of this day in the Bible, however. The word also carries with it the connotation of religious celebration. Cessation from work on the Sabbath came to be an act of religious celebration devoted to the Lord. Thus the term implies both cessation from activities and deliberate devotion to the deity.[9] Yet the different law codes vary in their understanding of the nature of that devotion. In Table 4.2 consider the two different treatments of Sabbath devotion in Exodus and Deuteronomy (the italicized text indicates the variances between the two texts).

The Exodus version is very likely the version of the Sabbath law with which readers are most familiar, if they have ever heard of it at all. Notice that a strong appeal is made to God's work in creating the universe as a legitimization for keeping the law (v. 11; see the story in Gen 1:1–2:3). That is, by observing the Sabbath, one imitates the deity. Such imitation of the deity fills the keeping of the day with religious significance. In other words, the cessation from work is not

[9] See Gerhard F. Hasel, "Sabbath," *ABD* 5.849–56.

Table 4.2

The Sabbath Laws

Exodus 20:8–11	Deuteronomy 5:12–15
8*Remember* the Sabbath day, and keep it holy. 9Six days you shall labor and do all your work. 10But the seventh day is a Sabbath to the LORD your God; you shall not do any work—you, your son or your daughter, your male or female slave, your livestock, or the alien resident in your towns.	12*Observe* the Sabbath day and keep it holy, as the LORD your God commanded you. 13Six days you shall labor and do all your work. 14But the seventh day is a Sabbath to the Lord your God; you shall not do any work— you, or your son or your daughter, or your male or female slave, *or your ox or your donkey,* or any of your livestock, or the resident alien in your towns, *so that your male and female slave may rest as well as you.*
11For in six days the LORD made heaven and earth, the sea, and all that is in them, but rested the seventh day; therefore the Lord blessed the sabbath day and consecrated it.	15*Remember that you were a slave in the land of Egypt, and the Lord your God brought you out from there with a mighty hand and an outstretched arm; therefore the LORD your God commanded you to keep the Sabbath day.*

simply a matter of rest because humanity needs to recover from the stress of work. Rather, it has significance beyond the realm of human existence.

The version of this law in Deuteronomy reveals some differences. Deuteronomy 5:6–18, and vv. 12–15 especially, offer a slightly different rationale for observing the special day of rest. It is not difficult to recognize the variations in language. For example, Deuteronomy uses "observe" in v. 12, whereas Exodus uses "remember" in v. 8. The most striking difference, however, is the rationale put forward for the actual observance of the day. In Exodus the appeal is to "remember" that the Lord rested after his work, and thus one should so imitate the deity (Exod 20:11). In Deuteronomy the appeal is not nearly so full of spiritual significance. Rather, the reasons for Sabbath rest are humanitarian: If one needs rest from work, so does one's family, slaves, and livestock. Clearly the code appeals for one to remember the national story of Israel's slavery in Egypt (see the story in Exodus 1–2) in order to legitimize the appeal to provide humane treatment of all (Deut 5:15). The Sabbath is a day of humanitarianism. It is no less of a command from Yahweh in the Deuteronomic version of it, yet it is simply not given the level of spiritual significance as the version in Exodus.

Why these differences? Do these two versions come from different schools of thought? Yes, very likely, although this does not necessarily imply that there was not awareness of the other version by each author. Clearly, there is an influence shared between them. Do they come from different time periods in Israel's history? That is a still more difficult question to determine for certain. Many think so, although the arguments often are quite subjective and therefore lack conviction. It may be enough for now simply to note that the same Sabbath laws are preserved within the pages of the Pentateuch with quite different rationales of motivation and legitimization. Quite possibly they come from different stages of development in ancient Israel's religion, although there is no conclusive evidence to offer as definitive proof. What this allows readers to realize, rather, is that the writer of Ezra-Nehemiah may not simply have had any single code of law in mind when he was writing his history.

From another perspective, however, surely a process of development and interpretation similar to the marriage laws stands behind them. Look again at the two Sabbath law formulations above and notice that both specify that no "work" should be done on the day. That may seem clear enough, but what constitutes "work"? Examination of different references to this Sabbath prohibition of labor suggests at the very least that the law is rather undefined. So, for instance, Exod 34:21 states the Sabbath law as follows: "Six days you shall work, but on the seventh day you shall rest; even in plowing time and in harvest time you shall rest." The qualification that the law applies even in plowing and in harvest time—the two most important times of the farmer's season—suggests that "work" here refers to occupational work, that is, work one does for a livelihood. Such an understanding might be behind the prophet Amos' (eighth century BCE) interpretation of Sabbath law when he mocks and condemns the rich by saying: "Hear this, you that trample on the needy, and bring to ruin the poor of the land, by saying, 'When will the new moon be over so that we may sell grain; and the sabbath, so that we may offer wheat for sale?'" (Amos 8:4–5). One finds further definition of work in Exod 35:2–3, which states: "Six days shall work be done, but on the seventh day you shall have a holy sabbath of solemn rest to the LORD; whoever does any work on it shall be put to death." "You shall kindle no fire in all your dwellings on the sabbath day." With the material in Exod 35:3 there is now a concern for domestic work in addition to occupational work. Numbers 15:32–36 provides a parallel qualification. It concerns a man gathering sticks on the Sabbath who is subsequently stoned to death. In a similar fashion another prophetic passage, Jer 17:19–27, prohibits the carrying of burdens on the Sabbath.

Now, if one were able to date these passages and list them in sequence, one might be able to suggest a model of reinterpretation. One scholar argues, in fact, that the oldest passage is that in Exodus 34, which only prohibits occupational work. Next is the prohibition of domestic work in Exod 35:3, that is, work in the home. Jeremiah 17 focuses the prohibition still further by prohibiting the carrying of any kind of burden on the Sabbath. And, although Amos 8:5 assumes the prohibition of selling merchandise on the Sabbath, the passage in Nehemiah 10:31, the most recent of the set, qualifies this further by prohibiting buying on the Sabbath.[10] At each successive stage of development, the prohibition is more tightly focused. The law increasingly excludes activities that people may perform on the Sabbath.

The point is that even though there was some form of an authoritative collection of law codes—such as Ezra reads in Neh 8:8—those codes, or even that code, was not beyond the need

---

[10]D. J. A., Clines, "Nehemiah 10," 111–117.

for interpretation and later reinterpretation by successive communities of readers. The intertextuality of these marriage laws and Sabbath laws therefore provides stark evidence of the process of interpretation behind the biblical text. The prohibition of mixed marriages with the "people of the land" is a rereading of the lists of foreign nations originally included in the older laws. The phrase "people of the land" speaks more to the contemporaneous situation under which the historian wrote the story of Ezra-Nehemiah. Likewise, the very strict prohibition of activities on the Sabbath also reflects the circumstances contemporaneous with the writer of these books.

The Story behind the Law Codes of the Pentateuch
Exodus 21:1–23:33

Learning Goals

- To understand that the law codes contained within the Hebrew Bible are themselves products of a process of rereading and interpretation.
- To understand that little of the materials contained in these law codes actually originate in judicial settings.
- To understand and recognize different forms of so-called law through form criticism of the Hebrew Bible.
- To understand and recognize the principles behind so-called redaction criticism.

Guiding Study Exercises

1) Locate and identify the various decalogues in the Hebrew Bible.
2) Explain in a 250-word essay why it is significant that the narrative context of these law codes differs from the sociological setting envisioned by the laws themselves.
3) Summarize the main steps a form critic might take to identify the social context of a passage of scripture.
4) Summarize the fundamental assumptions and conclusions of redaction critics as they investigate various stages of redaction of the Covenant Code.

Granting that the historian of Ezra-Nehemiah is interpreting laws with which he had some familiarity raises the question of the origins of those law codes themselves. Readers should keep in mind that these three codes of law (the Covenant Code, the Holiness Code, and the Deuteronomic Code) are not the only collections of law in the Hebrew Bible. Others include smaller collections of instruction such as the decalogue(s) of Exod 20:1–17, 34:17–26 (see above), and Deut 5:6–21. Other collections take the form of curses, such as those contained in Deut 27:15–26. The materials within Leviticus 18 and 19 seem to have strong affinities with these. Often scholars refer to yet other legal materials in the Hebrew Bible as the **Priestly Code**, though this designation does not refer to a collection of materials nearly so discernible as those mentioned previously. Rather, these so-called priestly materials generally include all of the remaining legal prescriptions, deriving from priestly sources, scattered throughout the Pentateuch (e.g., Exod 12:1–27; 13:1–16; 25–31; 35–40; Leviticus 1–16; 27; Num 1:1–10:10; 15:1–31; 18–19; 27:1–11; 28–30; 35–36). It is not a very neat picture. The materials are not set out as systematic collections of law. Rather, as with the book of Ezra-Nehemiah, they are incorporated into broad narrative contexts. To appreciate the laws in the Pentateuch fully one must master the narratives as well.

The narrative context of the Covenant Code suggests that these laws came from God to Moses while Moses was atop Mt. Sinai (see Chap. 2). The second law code (the Holiness Code of Leviticus 17–26) is given presumably while the people are still at the foot of Mt. Sinai. Of course, the narrative does not treat this material as a second law code per se. Rather, it is still a part of Yahweh's instruction at Sinai. Numbers 10 is a decisive point in the narrative as the people finally leave Sinai to make their way to the land of Canaan. After a failed attempt to enter the land from the south (Num 14:39–45), the people remain in the wilderness forty years, until the entire generation dies off and a new generation arises (Num 14: 26–35; Deut 1:1–5). The third code of law (the Deuteronomic Code of Deuteronomy 12–26) occurs in a narrative context forty years later, when a new generation with new opportunities stands on the east side of the Jordan River preparing to go into the land of Canaan. Here Moses speaks to them one last time. The book of Deuteronomy is that final **testament** of law before Moses dies.

Focusing upon the law codes within this narrative context gives the reader pause for reflection. One would expect the law of God, even if it was merely repeated three times, to be the same. Put another way, there should be a high degree of **micro-level intertextuality** among the laws. To be sure, at the macro-level there are indeed broad structural and thematic similarities in the arrangements of these codes. Note the following parallels: (See Table 4.3) each code begins with altar regulations (Exod 20:24ff; Deut 12:1–27; Lev 17:1–7); they each conclude with blessings and cursings (Exod 23:20–33; Deuteronomy 27; Leviticus 26). There is overlap in their thematic concerns. They share stipulations in slave laws (Exod 21:2–11; Deut 15:12–18; Lev 25:39). All three codes have calendars for annual cycles of worship (Exod 23:15–19; Deuteronomy 16; Leviticus 23), regulations for sacrifice (Exod 22:30, 23:18; Deut 15:19–23; Leviticus 22), and prohibitions against charging interest (Exod 22:25; Deut 23:20; Lev 25:36–38).[11]

Searching for micro-level intertextuality, however, reveals many differences. The treatment of Nehemiah 8–10 showed how differently the law codes understand the annual cycles of worship (Exod 23:15–19; Deuteronomy 16; Leviticus 23). Exodus treats these three as the agricultural festivals of Unleavened Bread, First Fruits, and Ingathering. Leviticus follows basically the same sequence but has different names: Passover and Unleavened Bread, First Fruits, and Booths, during which is the Day of Atonement. Deuteronomy contains the references to Passover, but offers a different rationale for the use of Unleavened Bread. Leviticus refers to the feast of Unleavened Bread separately from the Passover. Deuteronomy simply rationalizes the Unleavened Bread as a reminder of the expeditious haste of the Exodus from Egypt (Lev 23:4–8; Deut 16:1–8). Leviticus adds an eighth day to the celebration of the feast of Booths in the seventh month, while Deuteronomy speaks only of a seven-day festival (Lev 23:39; Deut 16:13–15). Deuteronomy

---

[11]See Crüsemann's, *The Torah,* and his more succinct statement of these similarities, 8.

Table 4.3

Structural and Thematic Similarities in the Law Codes

Common Feature	Exodus 21:1–23:33	Leviticus 17–26	Deuteronomy 12–26
1. Altar regulations	Exod 20:24–26	Lev 17:1–7	Deut 12:1–27
2. Blessings & Cursings	Exod 23:20–33	Leviticus 26	Deuteronomy 27–28
3. Common themes: • slave laws	Exod 21:2–11	Lev 25:39–55	Deut 15:12–18
• worship calendar	Exod 23:15–19	Leviticus 23	Deuteronomy 16
• sacrifice regulations	Exod 22:30; 23:18	Lev 27:26–28	Deut 15:19–23
• interest prohibitions	Exod 22:25	Lev 25:36–38	Deut 23:20

later incorporates the reading of the law during this same feast (Deut 31:9–13), while nothing is said of this in Leviticus. In other words, even though the narrative context implies these law codes to be the same, they are quite different. Ultimately it is this kind of comparison that leads scholars to regard them as originally different law codes that have only secondarily been incorporated into a narrative framework. The next question is then how one gets behind the narrative context to the social context in which the laws originally functioned.

Form and Socio-Historical Context of Law

Readers who wish to understand what lies behind the narrative framing of these law codes must appreciate the fundamental assumptions of **form criticism**. This method draws inferences about the social setting, or social text, of a literary text based upon the patterns of speech reflected within the text. To be sure, one need not think that such methods apply only to law codes. Scholars commonly apply form criticism to other parts of the Bible as well (see Chap. 5 on prophets). The driving assumption of form criticism is that speech may achieve distinctive patterns, or forms, depending upon the social situation in which speech functions. One would expect, for instance, that the set phrases, language, style of delivery, and even the various messages would vary strikingly between a Christian worship service and a rock concert. Assuming that one knew something about both of those settings, it would not be too difficult to recognize, on the basis of the language alone, from which settings the appropriate speech samples came.

   Casuistic and Apodictic Law. The Covenant Code is a classic literary text for the study of the various forms of law, and thus for hypothesizing the different social settings behind the laws within. It becomes one of the linch pins of the argument that these two different kinds of law, **casuistic** and **apodictic**, were not originally joined together, nor originally framed by the present narrative context. In the 1920s and 1930s, the German scholar Albrecht Alt set out a framework for the form-critical study of the laws in the Bible.[12] He differentiated between two broad categories of law, apodictic and casuistic. Casuistic law dominates Exod 21:1–23:22. The term casuistic comes from the Latin *casus* meaning "fall," "chance," or "case." It designates law that is formulated on the basis of specific cases or instances that require some kind of judicial process; case law is another way of thinking of it. It has a very distinctive and easily recognizable pattern. It opens with some kind of conditional clause, most typically introduced with the conditional particle "if." The clause introduced by "if" is called the *protasis*. It sets out the specific circumstance that the law addresses. This second clause is called the *apodosis*. It sets out the remediation or the judgment. For instance, consider Exod 22:2: "If a thief is found breaking in, and is beaten to death, no bloodguilt is incurred." The protasis puts forward the case of a thief who is caught in the act of breaking and entering and who is killed. The question is then, presumably, what happens to the person who kills him. The ensuing stipulation provides further definition of the seriousness of the crime: "but if it happens after sunrise, bloodguilt is incurred." This final qualification suggests that one is not culpable for killing a thief in one's house if it is nighttime. Notice also how impersonal this law is. It is set out in the third grammatical person. There is no language of direct address. It has the effect of communicating objective law to which the community is to submit.

   As nineteenth- and twentieth-century archaeological digs began to unearth the civilizations contemporaneous with ancient Israel,[13] the world soon discovered that there was nothing particularly unique about this kind of legal formulation in Israel's scripture. There are well known examples of this type of law in law codes that come from **Mesopotamia**. One of the most famous ancient law codes is that of Hammurabi, king of the Old **Babylonian** Dynasty (1728–1626 BCE).[14] Notice the micro-level intertextuality between the biblical version of Exod 22:2 (above) and the old Babylonian version: "If a seignior made a breach in a house, they shall put him to death in front of that breach and wall him in." The following law is also related: "If a seignior committed robbery and has been caught, that seignior shall be put to death."[15] As far as the particular pattern, or form, of speech is concerned, there is indeed a micro-level intertext. Both reflect the third person impersonal style and both utilize the conditional clause, or the protasis, followed by the apodosis. Both laws reflect a similar ethos, although they are addressing different specific situations or "cases." In the biblical example, the law addresses the case of the person who beats a thief to death in his house. The Babylonian law is only concerned about the dispensation of

---

[12]See the more recent translation, A. Alt, "The Origins of Israelite Law," *Essays on Old Testament History and Religion* (Oxford: Basil Blackwell, 1966) 79–132.

[13]P. R. S. Moorey, *A Century of Biblical Archaeology* (Louisville, KY: Westminster/John Knox Press, 1991).

[14]The dates are from T. Meek, *ANET,* 163.

[15]*Ibid.,* 167, col. I.

justice to the thief. In this latter case the punishment is death—whether the thief is caught in the daytime or not. Even though they are related laws, each one reflects a different concern that grows from its function within a different setting. The key point is, on the basis of form critical analysis, Israel's casuistic law appears to have come from within a legal setting that was shared by civilizations beyond Israel's borders.

Apodictic law reflects a much different pattern of speech and is itself easily recognizable. The word itself comes from a Greek root that means "to demonstrate" or "to show," and can even bear the sense of "to instruct." The key feature of this instructional law is the mode of direct address, as it is typically formulated in the second person. Most usually it also is framed as a form of negative address: "You shall not oppress a resident alien" (Exod 23:9). "You shall not delay to make offering from the fullness of your harvest and from the outflow of your presses" (Exod 22:29). Notice that the mode of direct address creates a much more personal sounding statement. Further, there is no statement of any punishment as in the casuistic form of law. Rather, there is simply a direct statement of right and wrong. These seem to be assertions of moral laws or general principles far more than specific matters that might be enforced in a judicial context.

Unlike the casuistic law, the origins of this kind of instructional law are far less clear. Albrecht Alt himself believed that this kind of law was unique to Israel's expression of its relationship to Yahweh. Again, archaeological discoveries have provided compelling parallel patterns outside of the sphere of Israelite scripture. Two possible backgrounds are suggested by similarities with other kinds of literature. Some scholars believe that the ancient treaty form stands behind the direct address.[16] For example, in one ancient Mesopotamian treaty, there is an exchange

---

A Closer Look: Hammurabi's Code. The publication of Hammurabi's code toward the end of the eighteenth century BCE is not to imply that other civilizations in the region and era had no laws themselves. Rather, the establishment of this stele in at least two locations (Babylon and Sippur) says more about the king's use of law (all kings were in principle committed to the maintenance of justice) to establish his renown as one who had a policy of justice, than it does about jurisprudence itself. The laws were written in a highly stylized form, making it difficult, if not impossible, to read for the ordinary citizen. Further, although there were clay copies, the laws were only publicly available in two places.

For further study, S. Grengus. "Legal and Social Institutions of Ancient Mesopotamia." *CANE* 1.469–84; J. Sasson. "King Hammurabi of Babylon." *CANE* 2.901–15.

For more advanced study, T. Jakobsen. "An Ancient Mesopotamian Trial for Homicide." *AnBib* 12 (1959) 130–150; T. Meek. "The Code of Hammurabi." *ANET* 3rd ed. Pp. 163–180.

---

[16]E.g., G. Mendenhall, *Law and Covenant in Israel and the Ancient Near East* (Pittsburgh, PA: The Biblical Colloquium, 1955); D. McCarthy, *Treaty and Covenant* (AnBib 21; Rome: Pontifical Biblical Institute, 1963).

The stele of Hammurabi, located in the Louvre in Paris, on which is published Hammurabi's law code. A stele is simply a huge, cylindrical pillar of stone. In antiquity such were used in architecture, serving a public purpose as a document. (Courtesy of Larry McKinney/William H. Morton)

of language between Niqmepa of Alalakh and Ir-dim of Tunip that provides a striking intertext with apodictic law. One stipulation concerns the extradition of runaway slaves. It reads:

> If a fugitive slave, male or female, of my land flees to your land, you must seize and return him to me, (or), if someone else seizes him and takes him to you, [you must keep him] in your prison, and whenever his owner comes forward, you must hand him over to [him]. If (the slave) is not to be found, you must give him (the owner) an escort, and he may seize him in whatever town he (the slave) is found.[17]

One may easily see the second person mode of address here. However, it is clear that in this example there is also an accompanying conditional form, representing a variation of the strict characteristics of the pattern. Readers should take caution, though. Just because there is a macro-level intertext between the biblical apodictic law and the language of the ancient treaty, the evidence is only suggestive and requires a great deal more evidence.

The second possible social text behind the apodictic, or instructional, law comes from within the biblical **wisdom literature**.[18] This canonical corpus of literature includes the books of Job, Proverbs, and Ecclesiastes; within the Deuterocanonicals there are Sirach and The Wisdom of Solomon. This literature gives expression to a movement within Yahwistic circles that emphasized human observation rather than the revelation of God. There is an interest in an intellectual tradition more than a sacred tradition. Instruction is one of its defining features, especially in Proverbs 1–9. Some of the most distinctive features include a father's admonition to a child formulated in imperatives and negative admonitions. Actually, this instruction sounds similar to the laws in Exodus 21 and intensifies the possibility of a connection between law and Wisdom instruction. Consider the following proverb: "My child, be attentive to my words; incline your ear to my sayings. Do not let them escape from your sight; keep them within your heart" (Prov 4:20–21).

Obviously, there are similar kinds of imperatives in the proverbial material as in the Covenant Code. But again, caution is warranted as it is not clear whether there actually is a connection between apodictic law and Wisdom. It should suffice, however, simply to recognize that so-called apodictic law bears greater resemblance to moral instruction in Wisdom literature or with the stipulations in ancient international treaties than it does with case law that functioned in ancient judicial settings.

The form critical categories set out above actually make the picture too neat, whatever the social settings of the laws are. Readers soon discover that there are forms of law that do not fit exactly the criteria for either casuistic or apodictic law. Exodus 23:4, for example, states, "When you come upon your enemy's ox or donkey going astray, you shall bring it back." The legal stipulation stems from a very specific case, complete with the spelling out of specific remediation. This is a characteristic of casuistic law. But notice also the language of the direct second person address: the law addresses "you." This is a feature of apodictic law. Exodus 22:25 is also couched in the form of casuistic law, yet it also utilizes the second person mode of address: "If you lend

---

[17]*ANET*, 531.

[18]E.g. M. Weinfeld, *Deuteronomy and the Deuteronomic School* (Oxford: Oxford University Press, 1972).

money to my people, to the poor among you, you shall not deal with them as a creditor; you shall not exact interest from them." This mixed type of law, which has features of both casuistic and apodictic law, lends credence to the hypothesis that one type of law has influenced the other in an evolutionary process. The hypothesis takes on even greater significance for dating the law codes in view of the fact that casuistic law occurs only in the Covenant Code. The Holiness Code and the Deuteronomic Code contain only the apodictic type.[19]

Further, it is not just formal structure alone that suggests an evolution in both the law codes and their narrative contexts. The point made at the very outset of this section is now quite significant: according to the story, the people are in the Sinai desert when they receive the laws. Their lifestyle for forty years is one of being constantly on the move. However, the laws themselves reflect a settled agricultural community. For instance, Exod 23:10 offers a regulation about agricultural land use. Notice the laws concerning liability for destruction of one's agricultural produce in Exod 22:6. Further, note that there are laws concerning property, especially livestock (Exod 22:9–10), laws that assume class distinctions (Exod 21:2–6 and 23:3), as well as various other laws that reflect a developing community along with its economic and judicial systems (Exod 23:1–2, 6, 9). What is more, the religious festivals connect with the cycles of the agricultural season (Exod 23:14–17). It simply would make no sense for people wandering around in the desert to organize their great religious festivals around *agricultural* seasons. In short, these laws simply do not reflect life in the desert. They reflect life in the Canaan land. The narrative context in which the law codes are placed look secondary to the laws themselves. To put a finer point on things, if these law codes functioned in real social contexts—treaties, instruction, judiciary—and if their social contexts produced them, then it was long *after* the Sinai and Wilderness periods that these laws would have emerged in Israelite life. Thus, even though in their final literary form the laws are presented as though offered by Moses during Israel's encampment at Sinai, form criticism allows readers to see that many of these laws could have emerged only *after* Israel had settled in the land of Canaan.

Redaction and the Literary Context

Form criticism helps readers understand how the legal materials in the Pentateuch had a life of their own apart from a literary context. **Redaction criticism** allows readers to understand that these once independent materials did not come into such elaborate narrative contexts haphazardly. The term *redaction* is an Anglicization of the German word *Redakteur,* meaning "editor." Once scholars recognize the seams separating the varying component parts of the legal materials (through form criticism), it is then necessary to hypothesize the process by which these texts were joined together. While an editor is not responsible for writing the component parts, he is responsible for arranging them in some sequence that was meaningful to him and his audience. The redaction critic attempts to reconstruct the aims of this editor or redactor by drawing inferences from the sequence, repetition, formal patterns, connecting language, and framing devices that connect the laws into a unity.

---

[19]A fourth type of law concerns capital crimes: "You shall not permit a female sorcerer to live" (Exod 22:18); "Whoever sacrifices to any god, other than the LORD alone, shall be devoted to destruction" (Exod 22:20). See a helpful introduction to law in Dale Patrick, *Old Testament Law* (Atlanta, GA: John Knox, 1985) 23–25.

A few initial observations help readers to see a kind of overarching symmetry in the forms used within the Covenant Code (see Table 4.4). Notice that the casuistic laws are contained in the first half of the code, 21:1–22:16. After a brief collection of capital laws (22:18–20), suddenly the formal characteristics shift to apodictic law, the kind of law characterized by direct address. This formal characteristic extends from 22:21 to 23:19. Looking still more closely, there appears to be a symmetry that exists at a thematic level also. Beginning from the extremities of the code there are two different sets of altar and sacrifice laws in 20:22–26 and 23:13–19 (items A and A′). Within these frames there are slave laws in 21:2–11 (B) and a Sabbath law in 23:10–12 (B′), both having parallel emphases on the numbers *six* and *seven*. Then there are two large blocks of material in 21:12–22:19 (C) and 22:21–23:9 (C′), each of which opens and closes with parallel short collections. Both 21:12–17 (Ca) and 22:17–19 (Ca′) contain capital crimes. Likewise 22:21 (C′a) is a law forbidding the oppression of foreigners and it is balanced by 23:9 (C′a′), which addresses the same topic. The central law of the entire code, finally, is 22:20 (D), which is a prohibition of sacrificing to any other god beside Yahweh.

Readers must exercise caution in adopting such structural hypotheses. There is no way to prove that the redactor intended any of this. Yet scholars spend a great deal of time seeking to uncover such plausible structural arrangements because they provide a point for comparing other such collections of materials. Exodus 34:11–26, a text considered in part one of this chapter, seems to reflect a structure similar enough to the Covenant Code to suggest to one scholar some interdependence between the two (see below). Canonically this decalogue follows the Covenant Code. In the logic of the narrative the materials contained within it *replace* the tablets that Moses breaks upon his descent from the mountain (Exod 32:15–20). To reiterate an earlier point, readers would expect to find very similar laws if, in fact, the decalogue of Exodus 34 serves to replace the

Table 4.4

Symmetry of the Covenant Code

A. 20:22–26 Altar and sacrifice laws
   B. 21:2–11 Slave laws (on six and seven years)
      C. 21:12–22:19 Various casuistic laws
         a. 21:12–17 Capital crimes
            b. 21:18–22:16 Other casuistic laws
         a′ 22:17–19 Capital crimes
            D. 22:20 Sacrifice to other gods
      C′. 22:21–23:9 Various apodictic laws
         a 22:21 Foreigners
            b. 22:22–23:8 Other apodictic laws
         a′ 23:9 Foreigners
   B′. 23:10–12 Sabbath (on six and seven days)
A′ 23:13–19 Altar and sacrifice laws

material that was on the tablets Moses broke, presumably the decalogue found in Exod 20:1–17. Indeed, Exod 34:1 specifically depicts Yahweh as saying that he "will write on the [new] tablets the words that were on the former tablets, which [Moses] broke." Yet, if readers compare the two decalogues,[20] they see that there is not much in common at all. Even near parallels (Exod 20:4 and 34:17; 20:8–11 and 34:21) are formulated with strikingly different language. The decalogue in Exod 20:1–17 is far more concerned about social relationships than cultic relationships (see especially vv. 12–18). By contrast, the decalogue in 34:11–16 is concerned almost exclusively with guidelines for the proper worship of Yahweh. What is more, if the editor who placed the decalogue in Exodus 34 intended it as a kind of summary of what goes before, it certainly leaves much out.

Crüsemann nevertheless observes several macro-level intertexts between Exod 34:11–26 and Exod 21:1–23:19 that are of interest (see Exod 23:23–26 and 34:11–16; 23:12–19 and 34:18–26).[21] What is of further importance is that the strictly casuistic form of legal materials contained in the first half of the Covenant Code (21:1–22:16) occurs in no other law code but the Covenant Code. The Holiness Code as well as the Deuteronomic Code only utilize the apodictic formula in their law codes. Notice further that the decalogue in 34:11–26 seems to be halved by an introductory concern with the land (vv. 11–16) and then with instructions about proper worship. In a larger way, the Covenant Code is also halved, having casuistic law concerning social relationships *in the land* followed by apodictic law concerned with religious instruction. The center points of both the Covenant Code as well as the decalogue in Exodus 34 is a prohibition to worship any other deity (cf. Exod 22:20 and 34:17). It may well be, Crüsemann supposes, that the Covenant Code is based on this much older decalogue, which it both incorporated and expanded by adding new material.[22]

Such hypotheses carry with them other implications about the relative antiquity of the decalogues and the relative dating of the law codes in their final redactions, none of which go undisputed by other scholars.[23] They further call for more elaboration of the theological implications of such rereadings of more ancient material. But for the present purposes, the hypothesis above illustrates the process that might well lie behind the composition of much of the legal material that readers encounter within the Pentateuch. It is clearly related to the process of reinterpretation of legal materials readers encountered in the treatment of Ezra-Nehemiah. Recollection of that ancient narrative requires moving to yet another level of redaction.

Redaction of Law and Narrative. The redaction of these laws and narratives works on a yet larger level. Remember the three law codes mentioned at the beginning of this section: the Covenant Code, the Holiness Code, and the Deuteronomic Code. All three are woven into Israel's story even though it is likely that, at one time, they were quite independent from any overall narrative context. The structural similarities between them suggest that they were not originally intended to complement each other. More likely, they existed to replace each other. What is more, the strict casuistic form of the law (Exod 21:1–22:16) is absent in the Holiness Code and the Deuteronomic Code. That form is replaced with the more instructive kinds of apodictic forms. However, within the narrative context of the Hebrew Bible, these law codes now stand side by side.

---

[20] So called because of Exod 34:28, and the apparent parallels created by the narrative framework.

[21] See Crüsemann's complex treatment, *The Torah,* 115–169

[22] *Ibid.,* 115–169.

[23] See alternative views set out in E. W. Nicholson, *God and His People* (Oxford: Basil Blackwell, 1985).

The narrative provides the rationale for the several law codes. The Covenant Code is set in that context of the first encounter with Yahweh at the mountain of God, Mt. Sinai (Exodus 19–24). There the people see the fire and hear his voice. There Moses first makes a covenant between Yahweh and the people. The people seal the covenant with Yahweh in Exodus 24, and they remain in the camp at the foot of the mountain. In the ensuing chapters, the people receive instructions on building the Ark and the tent (Exodus 25–26), as well as other laws regulating worship (Exod 27:1–31:18). These laws God wrote on stone tablets (Exod 31:18). Next is the tragic incident of the golden calf (Exodus 32–34), as a result of which Moses breaks the tablets. There is now a logical reason *within the narrative* for a second version of the decalogue to be presented (Exod 34:1, 11–28). The narrative continues, having the people situated at the foot of the mountain until Num 10:32. Prior to leaving this mountain, the people continue to receive laws from Yahweh, including the Holiness Code (Leviticus 17–26). Finally, Num 10: 33 states, "So they set out from the mount of the LORD three days' journey with the Ark of the covenant of the LORD going before them three days' journey, to seek out a resting place for them." The people travel through the wilderness, attempt to move into the promised land (Numbers 14), and are repulsed because of their doubt. As punishment they wander in the wilderness for thirty-eight years, until the doubting generation dies off. Then the book of Deuteronomy begins with the people camped on the east side of the Jordan River. The Deuteronomic law follows within this narrative setting, presented as Moses' final sermon to a new generation that must go in to claim their inheritance. This third code of law, the Deuteronomic Code, asserts that the inheritance of land may only be claimed if the people commit themselves to keeping the laws and commandments. The book of Deuteronomy, and thus the final book of the Pentateuch, ends with the people on the east side of Jordan, having not yet claimed their inheritance of land. The Pentateuch therefore ends with God's promise, contingent upon his people keeping the law, yet to be fulfilled.

Just as readers compared the laws within the Pentateuch with those in Ezra-Nehemiah, they can compare the narrative outline of the Pentateuch with that in Ezra's prayer (Neh 9:6–37). Ezra's prayer in Nehemiah 9 (see Chap. 2 of this text), presents a summary of Israel's narrative that follows the basic outline of the Pentateuch as it now exists. This allows the firm conclusion that by the time of the writing of Ezra-Nehemiah, there existed at least a basic outline of the story of Israel's origins. The study of Ezra-Nehemiah also allows readers to conclude that the law of Moses was *beginning* to emerge in post-Exilic Jewish society as an authoritative collection of laws. Readers recall that Ezra had to teach the people this law. Further, the story in Ezra-Nehemiah assumes that many leading religious leaders (the priests and Levites) were ignorant of some key features of this law, especially laws against intermarriage. This allows the inference that this law of Moses was actually something new to many in this post-Exilic society. Might it have been new because the very idea that the Mosaic origins of the Jewish legal traditions was itself an idea in its relative infancy?

The Pentateuch brings together two features of post-Exilic Jewish life: an extended narrative that tells the story of Israel's origins (the story told in abbreviated form by Ezra in his prayer of Nehemiah 9), and the great law codes along with other laws and instructions that had developed over Israel's history. By connecting the laws of Jewish life with the story of Israel's origins, that is, by incorporating the "story of the law" into the story of Israel's beginnings, the final redactors of the Pentateuch were saying something quite specific: We are a people of the law. The law was becoming central to the identity of God's people, and the late redactors of the narrative and legal materials wanted their readers to believe that it had been so since the days of Moses.

The Law and the Inheritance of Land
Genesis 12:1–3; 15:1–11; 17:1–8; Deuteronomy 6:10–25

Learning Goals

- To understand the importance of the image of "land" in Israel's story of relationship with Yahweh.
- To understand the competing visions of land as promise and land as contingency within Israel's story.

Guiding Study Exercises

1) Reflect in two paragraphs (or more, if desired) on the implications of a promise that comes without obligations, and then with obligations, of law. How, for instance, might this inform one's notion of grace?
2) How might the tradition of God's promise of land require later rereading in a period when the people cannot possess the land? Discuss specifically how Deuteronomy provides this rereading.
3) Considering the theory of biblical origins put forward in this book, how might this influence one's own way of understanding the origins of the Bible?

There are some interesting parallels between Ezra-Nehemiah's struggling community in Jerusalem and Deuteronomy's wanderers camped on the east side of the Jordan, waiting to enter the land. Neither of them has control of the land of their inheritance, both of them have been admonished to keep the law, and for both of them the future claim to the land with its prosperity depends upon their faithfulness in keeping the law. The prayer in Nehemiah 9 has many references to the people's failure to keep the law. There the land also plays a prominent role in Israel's story. From the very beginning of the story, God's promise to Abraham is that of land: "and you found his heart faithful before you, and made with him a covenant to give to his descendants the land of the Canaanite, the Hittite, the Amorite, the Perizzite, the Jebusite, and the Girgashite" (Neh 9:8). Yahweh's miraculous deliverance and provision in the wilderness was for the purpose of leading his people into the land: "and you told them to go in to possess the land that you swore to give them" (9:15). Even when the people stiffened their necks and rebelled, Yahweh was faithful to his promise: "So the descendants went in and possessed the land, and you subdued before them the inhabitants of the land, the Canaanites, and gave them into their hands" (9:24).

The prayer ends with related statements about the people's abuse and misuse of the land. Verse 35 observes that "Even in their own kingdom, and in the great goodness you bestowed on them, and in the large and rich land that you set before them, they did not serve you and did not turn from their wicked works." The people who possessed the land did not keep the law. Thus, the following verse describes the present circumstances of Nehemiah's setting: "Here we are, slaves to this day—slaves in the land that you gave to our ancestors to enjoy its fruit and its good gifts"

(9:36). The admonition of Moses to the people camped on the east side of Jordan, having not yet possessed the land of their inheritance, is relevant to the people who are enslaved within their own land many years later. In order to claim their inheritance, they, too, must keep the law.

Readers will recall that Chapter 2 treats Deuteronomy as both an introduction to the Deuteronomistic History and as connected with the Tetrateuch. An explanation is now necessary for how it could be both. Scholars believe that the post-Exilic setting is reflected in making Deuteronomy the conclusion to the Pentateuch rather than the introduction to the history of the settlement of the land. Scholars speculate that this is because the post-Exilic community, coming off its experience of having *lost* the land and only recently having been permitted to return to it, could identify to a far greater extent with a people who had yet to realize the promise of their inheritance than with people who had already realized it.[24] Deuteronomy is a kind of pivotal book, therefore, in that it not only asserts the centrality of obedience to the commandments as a means of relationship to Yahweh, but it makes possession of the land of inheritance contingent upon such diligence. Reading the patriarchal stories of the Tetrateuch carefully, however, makes readers aware that this Deuteronomic understanding of an explicit connection between possession of the land and obedience to the law seems itself to be a major rereading.

Land as Promise (Genesis 12:1–3; 15:1–6; 17:1–8)

Abraham's (Abram's) story begins in Genesis 12 with Yahweh's call for him to leave the land of his father's heritage (Gen 11:31–32) and to go to a land Yahweh promises as an inheritance. Nor is this the only promise. Yahweh promises Abraham to make him a great nation (especially significant foreshadowing of the episode about Abraham's inability to father children), and to bless all the nations of the earth through Abraham's offspring.

This idea of Yahweh's promise to Abraham and his descendants may function for the reader as a kind of device for creating suspense in each episode. There is uncertainty as to how or whether Yahweh's promise will be fulfilled. For instance, in the episode about the conflict between Abraham and Lot (Genesis 13), Abraham gives Lot his own choice as to what part of the land he will take. The reader cannot help but wonder whether this will thwart Yahweh's promise for Abraham to receive the land. Similarly, when Abraham takes the Egyptian woman Hagar for his concubine, and even fathers a child by her, the reader cannot help but wonder whether, again, Yahweh's promise of inheritance must be fulfilled through a person from a country that would someday be a mortal enemy of Israel.

What is perhaps most striking is the silence concerning what Abraham and his family are to do in order to possess this land. *There is no conditional statement, no "if clause," that precedes the promise.* Yahweh simply says "I will," and "you go." What a contrast from the picture in Nehemiah's summary, where possession of the land is a matter of keeping the law.

Genesis 15:1–16. Twice Yahweh then appears to Abraham and seals these promises. In Gen 15:1–11 there is reference both to Yahweh's promise of heirs (vv. 2–6), and of land (vv. 7–11). Yahweh promises that Abraham shall have children through his hitherto infertile wife Sarai. Abraham believes Yahweh and "the Lord reckoned it to him as righteousness" (v. 6). Abraham

---

[24]See D. J. Clines, *The Theme of the Pentateuch* (JSOTSup 10; Sheffield: JSOT, 1978).

The Sacrifice of Isaac (ca. 1612–1613), by Peter Paul Rubens (1577–1640). Rubens' representation of the episode known as the "binding of Isaac" (Gen 22:1–19) captures the pathos of both the threat of the deity's broken promise to Abraham as well as the suffering of an innocent. (Oil on wood panel; 55–1/2″ × 43–1/2″ (141.0 × 110.5 cm). Nelson-Atkins Museum of Art, Kansas City, Missouri [Purchase: Nelson Trust])

then asks about possession of the land and Yahweh makes a promise. Here the promise acknowledges that Abraham's heirs will be slaves in Egypt before inheriting the land, but what is significant, again, is that the promise of land stands *without any obligations* laid on Abraham or his heirs.

Genesis 17:1–8. After the episode with Abraham's concubine, Hagar (Genesis 16), Yahweh appears again (as "God Almighty") and announces his covenant with Abraham. He promises that Abraham will have numerous offspring (v. 6), and, again, promises him that he shall possess the land of Canaan "for a perpetual holding" (v. 8). The only obligation God lays upon Abraham and his descendants is that he and all his male descendants shall be circumcised as a sign of the covenant (the promise!) between Yahweh and Abraham.

As readers follow the Pentateuchal narrative, allusions to this promise of land to Abraham frequently recur. For instance, when Jacob, Abraham's grandson, is heading back east to take a wife, Yahweh, "God of Abraham your father" (Gen 28:13), appears to him in a dream and says, "the land on which you lie I will give to you and to your offspring" (Gen 28:13). Again, when Yahweh appears to Moses to commission him for the task of leading the people out of Egypt, the Lord says, "I have come down to deliver them from the Egyptians, and to bring them up out of the land to a good and broad land, a land flowing with milk and honey, to the country of the Canaanites, the Hittites, the Amorites, the Perizzites, the Hivites, and the Jebusites" (Exod 3:8; cf. 6:4). In fact, the rather open-ended promise of land to the **patriarchs**, reiterated to Moses, is strikingly similar to the unconditional promise that was made to King David. As the Deuteronomistic History records, Yahweh promises David that there will always be a Davidic heir on the throne in Jerusalem, and this promise is made also without obligation: "Your house and your kingdom shall be made sure forever before me; your throne shall be established forever" (2 Sam 7:16).

Land as Contingency (Deut 6:10–25)

Yahweh promises the land to his people, the descendants of Abraham, without the obligation of keeping the law. According to these Abrahamic traditions, the land is a gift from Yahweh. However, when Moses presents the law again to the people as they prepare to cross into the land of Canaan, *then, suddenly, the inheritance of the land is made contingent upon the people's keeping of the law.* The sermonlike instructions (Deuteronomy 1–11) that precede the law code itself (Deuteronomy 12–26) make the same point: "So now, Israel, give heed to the statutes and ordinances that I am teaching you to observe, so that you may live to enter and occupy the land that the LORD, the God of your ancestors, is giving you" (4:1). Notice that this verse refers to the promise that Yahweh has made to the ancestors. So the book of Deuteronomy is aware of the promises made to Abraham. The Deuteronomist presents, however, quite a different perspective on the matter of land.

Deuteronomy 6:10–15. The Deuteronomist includes references to the patriarchs and the promise of the land elsewhere as well. The land is to be a place of bounty and fullness, indeed, but the emphasis in these verses is on the fact that it is a gift. The emphasis upon the gift of the land certainly maintains the intertextual relationship with the unconditional promise to the patriarchs. In the hands of the Deuteronomist, however, this idea of gift implies all the more deeply the presence of an obligation. The people of Israel have not worked for the land, nor caused it to yield its bounty. Rather, it is the Lord who has given it. By emphasizing the land as gift, the Deuteronomist lays the groundwork, so to speak, to make explicit what he thinks is implied: *God gives the gift of land for the very purpose of drawing his people into a relationship, a relationship that has obligations.* Notice that v. 15 makes clear, however, that failure to remain loyal to Yahweh alone will mean that the people will lose the land.

Deuteronomy 6:20–25. In these verses, the connection between law and land is even more explicit. The Deuteronomist envisions the importance of teaching each generation about the meaning of the law. Readers encounter here the instruction of how to explain to children the connection between land and law. Here the law is unambiguously connected with the inheritance of the land; it finds its meaning in the realization of the promise of land, a promise, readers are reminded, that God made to the patriarchal ancestors.

Unfortunately, there is no scholarly consensus about which of these traditions is rereading the other. The older view argued that the Abraham traditions reflected a very old literary source (the Yahwistic source) that achieved its literary formation in the monarchic period. This view had great confidence in the form critic's ability to reconstruct oral stages of the ancient tradition.[25] It further relied upon the archaeologist's spade to reconstruct the world in which the ancient patriarchs flourished.[26] Since the patriarchal stories achieved a sanctioned literary status before the work of the Deuteronomist and the later Deuteronmistic Historian, then these latter works were clearly rereading the more ancient literary source in light of the historical setting of the seventh and sixth centuries BCE. In this case, the older promise tradition gave way, in light of the people's unfaithfulness (as indicated in the Exile), to a belief that the land was contingent upon obedience to law.

A more recent view reverses the sequence of literary origins. With the growing lack of confidence in the reconstruction of the oral stages of traditional materials,[27] an increasing number of scholars have resorted to more methodologically strict literary analyses of the Pentateuchal and Deuteronomistic materials as literature. They tend to emphasize that there is no reference to Abraham in any pre-Exilic literature (within the prophets, for instance) in the Bible,[28] and they conclude the lateness of the literary formation of these patriarchal traditions. They further note the ambiguity and misinterpretation of archaeological reconstructions of the second millenium BCE, the hypothesized era in which Abraham would have lived.[29] In this case, the final editor of the Pentateuch produces at a much later date the stories of the patriarchs and is rereading the Deuteronomist's work in doing so. The patriarchal narratives, composed in the post-Exilic setting in the shadow of the great Deuteronomistic History, would not change in any way the contingency of the land based upon law, however. Rather, the patriarchal narratives would stress ethnic boundaries for their contemporary audience, struggling to find their own identity. Without detracting from the force of obligation to the law, the patriarchal narratives would emphasize *to whom* the promise was given more than the nature of the promise itself.[30]

---

[25]See, for instance, O. Eissfeldt's *The Old Testament: An Introduction* (3rd ed.; Oxford, 1966); R. E. Clements, *Abraham and David* (SBT 5; London: SCM Press, 1967); H. W. Wolff, "The Kerygma of the Yahwist," *Int* 20 (1966) 131–158.

[26]For example, see J. Bright's *A History of Israel* (Philadelphia: Fortress, 1959, 1980).

[27]Thus R. N. Whybray, *The Making of the Pentateuch* (Sheffield: JSOT Press, 1987).

[28]See Blenkinsopp's summary in *The Pentateuch* (New York: Doubleday, 1992) 118–129; also, see the brief summary article of J. Van Seters, "Tradition and Social Change in Ancient Israel," *PRS* 7 (1980) 96–113.

[29]T. L. Thompson, *The Historicity of the Patriarchal Narratives* (Berlin: De Gruyter, 1974).

[30]See, for instance, E. T. Mullen, Jr., *Ethnic Myths and Pentateuchal Foundations* (Atlanta, GA: Scholars Press, 1997) 57–86.

Conclusion

The narrative of Ezra Nehemiah suggests that the law of Moses comes to play an increasingly vital role in the post-Exilic community of Jerusalem and Judah. The many suppositions that this law of Moses represented the Pentateuch in its final form, or some authoritative document that functioned as moderns think of scripture, cannot be demonstrated, however. The intertexts between the present Pentateuch and the laws in Ezra-Nehemiah reveal that there was still a process of development concurrent with the writing of Ezra-Nehemiah. That process of development is made even more recognizable through the work of form and redaction critics. The complexities of multiple legal sources, an evolution of legal forms, and the importance of inserting legal collections into larger narrative frameworks seem to stand behind the production of works like Ezra-Nehemiah and the Pentateuch itself. Though the ancient historians were guided by their own theological commitments, even so important a theological belief as the land receives different emphases depending upon the critical assumptions readers hold about the relative dating of the literary documents themselves.

For Further Reading

Ezra-Nehemiah Interpreting Law Codes

Briant, P. "Social and Legal Institutions in Achaemenid Iran." In *CANE* I. Pp. 517–528. (*Recommended for beginning students.*)

Jacobs, L. "Torah, Reading of." *EncJud* 15.1246–55. (*Recommended for beginning students.*)

The Story Behind the Law Codes of the Pentateuch

Carmichael, C. *Law and Narrative in the Bible: The Evidence of Deuteronomic Laws and the Decalogue.* Ithaca, NY: Cornell University Press, 1985.

Levenson, J. L. "The Theologies of Commandment in Biblical Israel." *HTR* 78 (1980) 17–33.

Patrick, D. "The Covenant Code Source." *VT* 27 (1977) 145–157. (*Recommended for beginning students.*)

The Law and the Inheritance of Land

Long, B. O. "Recent Field Studies in Oral Literature and their Bearing on Old Testament Criticism." *VT* 26 (1976) 187–198.

Loewenstamm, S. E. "The Divine Grants of Land to the Patriarchs." *JAOS* 91 (1971) 509–510.

Shanks, H. "Scholars Face Off Over Age of Biblical Stories: Friedman vs. Van Seters." *BibRev* 10 (August 1994) 40–44, 54. (*Recommended for beginning students.*)

Wagner, N. E. "Abraham and David?" *Studies on the Ancient Palestinian World.* Edited by J. W. Wevers and D. B. Redford. Toronto: University of Toronto Press, 1972. Pp. 117–140.

CHAPTER FIVE

The Story of the Prophets

Introduction

Review

Chapter 4 investigated several intertexts between specific laws, biblical narratives, and law codes in order to reflect upon the origins of the book of law that Ezra reads in Ezra-Nehemiah. There is no way to be certain whether the author of Ezra-Nehemiah knew of any book exactly like the present Pentateuch. However, the study surfaced enough intertextual correspondence for readers to infer that the period of Ezra-Nehemiah was possibly a formative time for the Pentateuch, and thus for the authority of the Pentateuch and its laws. If the redaction process that stands behind the law codes, which is exemplified in the Covenant Code, parallels the production of the Pentateuch to any extent, then readers have some idea of what a complex process of composition was involved in producing the Pentateuch.

Preview

In this chapter the law leads to an investigation of prophets. Nehemiah 9 portrays prophets playing a major part in Israel's story through their exhorting the people to keep the law. This is intriguing since the law, in its authoritative Pentateuchal form, had not achieved any final or unified form until the Second Temple period, when Ezra-Nehemiah was written. There seems to be warrant, therefore, to compare the roles of prophets in Ezra-Nehemiah with what can be seen of their work prior to the Second Temple period. Readers will see significant rereading of prophets first in reference to Ezra-Nehemiah's understanding of two key **post-Exilic** prophets, Haggai and Zechariah. Then, a comparison between Haggai and Zechariah and three classical prophets in their comparative views of the Temple demonstrates both continuity as well as variation. Finally, the post-Exilic prophets Haggai and Zechariah lay the groundwork for a new rereading of prophetic activity that profoundly influences later interpretations of prophecy as apocalypticism.

Haggai and Zechariah: Temple and Not Law
Haggai and Zechariah 1–8; Review Ezra 1–6

Learning Goals

- To understand that the post-Exilic prophets Haggai and Zechariah do not appear to know anything about Mosaic law.
- To understand some of the forms of speech that characterize prophetic oracles.
- To understand that biblical prophets addressed contemporary audiences (such as political leaders) and contemporary issues (such as the Temple).
- To develop skills in reading the prophetic literature, while recognizing the complex history of this literature's composition.

Guiding Study Exercises

1) What does Nehemiah 9 understand the primary role of the prophets to be? How does this portrayal compare and contrast with the primary role of the prophets Haggai and Zechariah as they are portrayed in Ezra 1–6? As they are portrayed in the books that bear their names?

2) What are some of the speech patterns of the prophets that help readers begin to form hypotheses about possible prophetic social texts?

3) Review the relevant texts from Haggai and Zechariah concerning the Temple and Zerubbabel. Do these prophets foretell the distant future or offer exhortation and encouragement for their own situation? Justify your response with textual evidence.

4) Read carefully Zech 6:9–15. Why might critical scholars think that *originally* the prophetic oracle spoke of crowning Zerubbabel rather than Joshua? What might have prompted a later editor to reread (and rewrite) this prophetic oracle?

Prophets in Ezra-Nehemiah

There are two problems in comparing the pictures of prophets in both Ezra and Nehemiah. The first concerns how the words of the prophets relate to history; the second, how (or whether) their words reflect any concern for Mosaic law. The summary of Israel's story in Neh 9:6–37 is of interest because, even in the sketchiest outlines of Israel's story, the prophets are not absent. The summary mentions them three times. All three times Nehemiah says that their message comes from the law of Moses. The first reference appears in 9:26, where, with refrainlike consistency, the narrator recalls the sinfulness of the Israelite people: "Nevertheless they were disobedient and rebelled against you and cast your law behind their backs and killed your prophets, who had warned them in order to turn them back to you, and they committed great blasphemies." The summary portrays the rebellion of the people as a disregard for the law. The prophets speak out against this behavior. Such service, portrayed again in v. 30, is costly and Israel is indicted for killing those prophets who came to call the people back to keeping the law.

However, Ezra 1–6 portrays the prophets Haggai and Zechariah quite differently. Here the two prophets play a vital role in motivating Zerubbabel, the second governor of the province, and Jeshua, the high priest, to commit to the continuance of the rebuilding of the Temple. Ezra 5:1–2 is a good example. Of course, it is difficult to know whether the reference in v. 2 to "the prophets of God" refers to Haggai and Zechariah alone or whether there were in Jerusalem others who together constituted a guild of prophets and encouraged the rebuilding of the Temple. In any event, there is a second reference to the crucial efforts of Haggai and Zechariah in Ezra 6:14–15.

In both places the writer says that the prophets "prophesied" or were "prophesying." Readers wonder whether this is what is meant in Nehemiah 9 when the writer says the prophets "warned them." Indeed, one who is even slightly familiar with the New Testament story has very likely heard the word "to prophesy" used in reference to the foretelling of Jesus of Nazareth. This use of the word most likely shapes modern readers' understandings of what prophecy is. For example, Matthew's birth narrative of Jesus—as many other of his narratives—appeals to the authority of a prophet in the Hebrew scriptures to reinforce the validity and significance of his own story. "All this took place to fulfill what had been spoken by the Lord through the prophet . . ." is a typical phrase in Matthew's gospel, followed frequently by a citation from a particular prophetic book (see Chap. 14). Reading the Hebrew Bible's prophets through the lens of the New Testament's understanding of what they do leaves one with the impression that prophets are mainly foretellers. Their words relate to future historical events, not to the events of their own generations.

But notice in the narrative in Ezra 1–6 that the prophetic characters do not seem to do much foretelling at all. Neither do they make reference to God's laws or commandments as in Nehemiah 9. Rather, they seem to be speaking to an audience in the historical present about the contemporary challenge of rebuilding the Temple. On the other hand, readers should note that there stands at the opening of the book of Ezra a reference to the prophetic activity of Jeremiah, a seventh-century prophet, that looks a lot like foretelling (Ezra 1:1). This opening looks more like what one might encounter in the New Testament, and is a very crucial allusion in later literary texts. The writer of Ezra also seems to be sympathetic with the view that prophecy is a kind of revelation about future events, in this case the events contemporaneous with the story the author is telling. His understanding of the events of the return to Jerusalem are based upon his own insight into the significance of the words of Jeremiah the prophet, who lived a century prior to the events depicted in this narrative. Thus the modern reader of the prophets must struggle with the idea that prophets are remembered as offering two kinds of messages. The first is a message that speaks to the present and, at most, immediate future of the prophet's own time. The second message seems to address the distant future from the prophet's own time, which later readers then understood to have a bearing on their own time.

A second question concerns the prophets' relationship to the law of Moses, and readers approach this question by inquiring about prophetic **theology**. Recalling the observations in the preceding paragraphs, one would suspect that the law of Moses shaped and guided the perspective of prophetic preaching. Now, it may well be that the references to the prophets are simply too brief in Ezra 5 and 6, but there is certainly no reference to their preaching being concerned in any way with the law of Moses. Rather, they are concerned with the Temple. Admittedly, the lack of any reference to the law of Moses may not seem so significant to a first time reader. Such silence regarding the Mosaic law is worth remembering, however, especially as the investigation reveals that even earlier prophets made no specific appeal for authority to the law of Moses. These are the two guiding questions, then: the first concerns the prophet's orientation to history, and the second, his theological and **ideological** outlook. These questions will serve as a platform from which to begin the present inquiries into the prophetic books bearing the names of the prophetic characters in Ezra 1–6, that is, Haggai and Zechariah.

The Prophetic Books of Haggai and Zechariah

Reading the actual books that bear the names of Haggai and Zechariah provides a basis for comparing how the writer of Ezra-Nehemiah reread their prophetic careers. Their message seems to be of the immediate type, not the foretelling type. They also seem to be far more concerned with the Temple and its role in the community than with the law of Moses. Readers should note that it is not necessary for the present purposes to read the latter parts of Zechariah (9–14). These materials, which scholars often refer to as the Second Zechariah, assume a much different setting: the reference in 9:13 to "Greece" suggests a rereading of Zechariah from yet a still later time period. Only the ten short chapters made up of Haggai 1–2 and Zechariah 1–8, materials deriving from the early **Persian period**, especially during the early reign of Darius I, are the focus of the present investigation.

The Literary Text. A first reading of these chapters must surely seem difficult, but careful reading raises questions about what lies behind this literary text. Prophetic speech is some of the most difficult reading in the Bible due to its compactness and general absence of defining contextual material. The chapters in Haggai are introduced by references to the year and month relative to the reign of King Darius I. There are two chapters in the book of Haggai, eight in the book of Zechariah. But upon closer examination, it is much more logical to organize the structure of the message along the lines of the chronological notices. The two chapter markings in Haggai actually mislead the reader. The book of Haggai is better organized into four sections: 1:1–15 (1–11 and 12–15); 2:1–9; 2:10–19; 2:20–23. Notice five chronological headings arranged sequentially, suggesting five sections instead of four: 1:1; 1:15; 2:1; 2:10; and 2:20. Each of these sections can be dated to a particular month and year. These sections also suggest a progression of prophetic speech and audience response relative to the overall mission of the prophet: the rebuilding of the Temple.[1]

The same kinds of arrangements are evident in Zechariah. Chronological headings arrange the sections of prophetic oracles. So 1:1 places the beginning of Zechariah's work in the eighth month of the second year of Darius's reign. Note 1:7 and 7:1 with this in mind. One would infer from these entries that there was an overlap in the two prophetic ministries and that Zechariah's extended beyond that of Haggai, into the "fourth year of King Darius" (7:1). However, one should also observe that in the case of Zechariah there are collections of prophetic oracles that are not so dated, for example, 1:18–6:15, leaving readers to search for other criteria by which to fit

---

[1]This information is available in the standard commentaries: C. L. Meyers and E. M. Meyers, *Haggai, Zechariah 1–8* (AB 25B; Garden City, NY: Doubleday, 1987) xxix - lxxii; or D. L. Petersen, *Haggai and Zechariah 1–8* (Philadelphia: Westminster, 1984) 17–39 and 109–125.

these into the context provided by the chronological notations. Such other criteria could include narrative statements, chronological notices, and summaries, all of which give the reader insight into the origins of the prophetic book. Such notices typically are not in the prophet's voice, however, making clear that more than a single point of view shapes the collection of prophetic oracles. The voice of the narrator stands against the voice of the prophet and presumably reflects the editor's interpretation. It is the editor of the prophet's oracles, for instance, who places the oracles in chronological order. Readers may infer from these two voices that there are at least two stages of tradition, more likely three, in the development of prophetic books: an oral stage (the preaching of the prophet), a written stage (the writing down of the oracles, which may have come partly from the prophet himself), and an editorial stage (the collection and arranging of the written prophetic oracles). These two or three voices lead readers to begin examining the various social texts that stand behind the literary text.

The Social Text(s). As with the law codes, the next step is to move behind the literary text by focusing upon both the form and the content of the prophet's speech. Compare Hag 1:1 with 1:2, or 1:13a with 13b. There is an obvious distinction between prophetic speech and the editor's framing statements. This distinction, however, is not nearly so pronounced in Haggai as it is in Zechariah. In fact, scholars debate the **genre** of Haggai precisely because of this ambiguity: Is it a collection of poetic prophetic sayings or mainly a prose narrative that in some respects imitates books of prophetic collections?[2] Zechariah provides much clearer distinctions between prophetic speech and editorial narration, due mainly to the kind of prophetic speech that is included.

A Closer Look: Prophecy. Prophecy in the Hebrew Bible is consistently understood as that social role of speaking for God. Prophets, in other words, were messengers. They could have various defining social characteristics. Some were from the north, Israel (Hosea, Jeremiah), others from the south, Judah (Isaiah of Jerusalem, Micah, Amos). They could have other occupations, such as shepherd (Amos) or priest (Ezekiel, Jeremiah), along with the role they enacted as prophets. As time passed, their messages seem to change. The prophets who spoke before the Exile, for instance, regularly announced inevitable doom to come upon the states of Israel and Judah (see especially Amos, Micah, Hosea, and Jeremiah). The prophets after the Exile generally announced the Lord's forgiveness and encouraged rebuilding of post-Exilic Jerusalem. Before the Exile their messages consisted of explanations of what Yahweh was going to do in the immediate future. After the Exile, prophets seem to have a broader perspective on all of history in general, pushing the fulfillment of more ancient prophecies off into the extended future.

For further study, J. Barton. "Prophecy (Postexilic Hebrew)." *ABD* 5. 489–94; J. Blenkinsopp. *A History of Prophecy in Israel.* London, SPCK: 1984.

For more advanced study, J. Barton. *Oracles of God: Perceptions of Prophecy in Israel after the Exile.* London: Darton, Longman & Todd, 1986; R. R. Wilson. *Prophecy and Society in Ancient Israel.* Philadelphia: Fortress, 1980.

---

[2]Meyers and Meyers, *ibid.,* lxxiii; Petersen, *ibid.,* 31–32.

Artist's conception of the prophet Isaiah. (Fra Bartolommeo, Florentine, c. 1472–1517. Il Profeta Isaia. Firenze, R. Galleria Uffizi. Alinari/Art Resource)

Prophetic rhetoric. **Form critics** are interested in patterns of speech because such patterns help to establish the rhetorical characteristics behind the literary context of a prophetic announcement (see Chap. 4 on the law). Rhetoric simply refers to the relationships between the speaker, the audience, and the medium of communication. One of the most distinctive recurring patterns of speech in the words of the prophets is the **messenger formula**. It occurs frequently throughout both the books of Haggai and Zechariah. Look carefully at Hag 1:2–11. Scattered throughout the passage are several occurrences of formulaic sayings concerning "the word of the Lord." The narrator's words, "Then the word of the Lord came by the prophet Haggai" (1:1, 3; cf. also 2:1 and 10), introduce the speeches of the prophet, while the prophet's own charge from the Lord is to announce, "Thus says the Lord" (1:2, 7) or "a saying of the Lord" (2:7, 9). The prophet spoke in the first person voice of Yahweh; the prophetic "I" becomes the deity's person. In Hag 1:7–8, for instance, the instruction voiced by the prophet, "Go up to the hills and bring wood and build the house, so that *I* may take pleasure in it and be honored, says the Lord" (*italics* ours), is understood to be a saying of Yahweh that Yahweh's messenger, the prophet, merely repeats.

A second crucial dimension to appreciating prophetic rhetoric is understanding the prophetic role as one of offering both judgment and salvation. In Hag 1:4 there is **diatribe**, language that reflects disputation with an audience, preceding the announcement of Yahweh's word of reproach in 1:5. In 2:4, by contrast, the messenger formula introduces an exhortation for the people, their governor, and their high priest to have courage. An announcement of the Lord's presence and imminent salvation follows the exhortation. In offering their messages of salvation or judgment, prophets felt free to couch their words from the Lord in varying forms. They might even imitate the language forms of worship **liturgy**, of jurisprudence, of **priestly** instruction, or of the wise man posing a riddle. Indeed, the recurring speech forms suggest to scholars social settings in which the prophet functioned. Consider the following examples.

In Hag 2:10–14, the prophet has a word from the Lord to request a ***torah***, or "instruction," from the priests concerning a point of ritual law. The oracle entails a brief description of the priestly decision-making process to answer the question whether **holiness** is as contagious as uncleanness?[3] Such **macro-level intertexts** with priestly forms of speech—which certainly suggest the speaker's familiarity with priestly social texts—might be a basis for hypothesizing that Haggai was himself a priest, or closely affiliated with priestly circles. In this case, the prophet's message, formulated as an attack, is motivated by a priest's perspective on what the people of Jerusalem are saying: "These people say the time has not yet come to rebuild the Lord's house" (v. 2). As in other prophetic books, prophets took advantage of their audience's assumptions about their roles. At an earlier point in Israelite history, the prophetic office had as its task the announcement of the Lord's judgment against the enemies of Israel, especially in instances where the nation was preparing for war (see e.g., 1 Kgs 22:1–12). It was an innovation of ninth- and especially eighth-century prophecy for prophets to turn the tables, as it were, and utilize such assumptions about the prophet's role to announce the Lord's judgment *against* his own people as well (see e.g., Amos' use of the **"oracles against the nations"** as a means of condemning Israel, Amos 1–2).[4]

---

[3]Petersen, *ibid.*, 73–76. Notice here Petersen's helpful appeal to distinctions between Aaronic priestly concerns (distinguishing clean vs. unclean) and Levitical concerns (juridical matters), suggesting that Haggai's appeal is to Aaronic priests and their sympathies.

[4]See J. Barton, *Amos' Oracles Against the Nations* (Cambridge: Cambridge University Press, 1977).

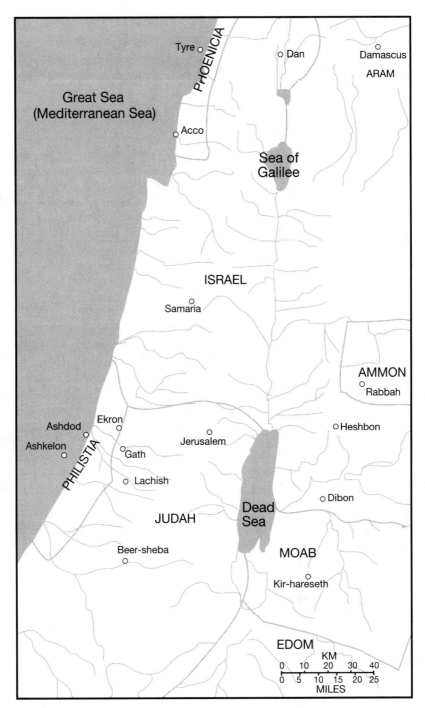

Israel and Judah. The traditional boundaries of the kingdoms of ancient Israel and Judah are Dan in the north and Beer-Sheba in the south. (From John Royerson and Philip Davies, *The Old Testament World,* © 1989, p. 69. Reprinted by permission of Prentice Hall, Upper Saddle River, NJ)

On the other hand, notice that in 2:1–9 the prophet announces a word of encouragement to the leader of the people, Zerubbabel. Acknowledging the desperate situation of the day ("Is it [the Temple ruins] not in your sight as nothing?"), the prophet announces the Lord's presence, "I am with you" (v. 4). The announcement of the Lord's presence, an oracle of salvation, forms a **micro-level intertext** with a similar announcement to Moses at his commissioning to lead the captives from slavery in Egypt (Exod 3:12, 13–15). It reinforces the conclusion that this prophet sees the rebuilding of the Temple as a saving event to be ranked with the highest moments in Israelite history. In v. 5 the prophet elaborates on this story of deliverance from Egypt as the basis upon which Zerubbabel and the people may press ahead confidently and fearlessly with the rebuilding of the Temple. Of course, Haggai was not the only sixth-century prophet to make use of Israel's story. His predecessor, Deutero-Isaiah (Isa 40–55 [see below]), also appealed to the Exodus story to provide a conceptual model for encouraging the exiles to return home (Isa 48:20–23; 52:3–6).

An additional detail in Hag 2:1–9 is that the word of encouragement achieves a remarkable metaphorical height in its vision of the historical scope of the events and its association with "the day of Yahweh." Haggai portrays the Lord's presence as having cosmic significance, not just local significance: God will shake the heavens and the earth and the sea and dry land. This is related to a similar portrayal of Yahweh's presence at Sinai, again, when he appeared to Moses and Israel to establish a covenant with them. Only in Haggai the scope of the Lord's activities reach much further, for the rebuilding of the Temple will affect *all* nations. By using language such as "On that day" (2:23) and "in a little while" (2:6), the prophet reapplies the much older tradition that envisioned Yahweh as a warrior who intervened for his people (see Exod 17:14–16). Yahweh's intervention through the rebuilding of the Temple would establish a new day that was beyond the ordinary workings of society and history.

In the book of Zechariah readers encounter another distinctive kind of prophetic oracle. This is the vision oracle. It is somewhat difficult to explain since modern readers usually consider visions and dreams to be the result of ordinary psychological activity rather than a unique medium by which God communicates with humanity. Still, images that come to the prophet in visions offer a contrast with those images that come to the prophet in words. Visions are significant images that the prophet *sees* in people or events, rather than *hears* from Yahweh. In Zechariah there is one interpreting the vision for the prophet. That one, usually a heavenly being, must translate/interpret the visual image into words. The images are enigmatic in nature, requiring interpretation, and have behind them the specific events that the prophet's community finds itself facing.

The characteristic language accompanying such a vision depicts the act of seeing. Zechariah says, "In the night *I saw* a man riding on a red horse" (1:8); or, "then *he showed* me the high priest Joshua standing before the angel of the Lord" (3:1). Such a form of speech is certainly not new with Zechariah in the sixth century BCE. More ancient prophets also had visions: Amos, an eighth-century Judean prophet (who preached to the Northern kingdom of Israel), has a very important series of visions that help him to understand the nature of his call to prophesy on behalf of the Lord (Amos 7:1–9 and 8:1–9:4). Likewise, Isaiah of Jerusalem, another eighth-century prophet, has a vision that enigmatically defines the nature of his call to preach to Jerusalem, Isa 6:1–13 (see also Ezek 1:1–3:11). Zechariah 1–8 consists of eight vision oracles coming to the prophet in the night (1:8), and at such time that the prophet had to be awakened in order to see them (4:1).

In a way analogous to Haggai's expansion of the significance of the "day of the Lord," Zechariah expands the significance of visions such as those of Amos. The macro-level intertextuality between the visions of Amos and Zechariah allow readers to see new development in the later vision oracles. In Zech 1:7–17 there is a vision of several horsemen who, the prophet is told, patrol the earth. Their report to the Lord that the whole earth "remains at peace" provokes a crisis for the prophet, a crisis that rests in the fact that if the whole earth is at peace, then judgment against the enemies of this new Jerusalem community cannot be taking place. The prophet immediately asks the Lord a question (v. 12). The Lord replies through an angelic intermediary with a promise of his presence implying that his anger against the other nations will be consummated when his people rebuild the Temple (vv. 14–16). There is a sense of immediacy about the Lord's promise; judgment of the nations is not far away and the Lord's action in history hinges upon the completion of his house, the Temple.

For the sake of comparison, the same kind of imminence is clear in the opening series of three oracles in Amos 7:1–9. In Amos' case, however, the vision shows Yahweh's intervention bringing harm to his people and not good. The opening vision (vv. 1–3) pictures a locust swarm eating the crops that went to the people who worked the land after the king and landowners received their share of the harvest. Amos, like Zechariah, is provoked by what he sees and he intervenes. In this vision Yahweh relents. Note, however, that there is no angelic intermediary. The prophet receives the word on his own. A similar pattern follows in the second vision (vv. 4–6). The prophet's direct intervention dissuades Yahweh from destroying the land with fire. But the third vision is an announcement of inescapable doom. Yahweh will hold the plumb line of justice in Israel and he will execute inevitable judgment. It is but a matter of time before Yahweh acts. Thus the prophet's audience finds itself living in anticipation of the Lord's cataclysmic intervention.

Macro-level intertextuality is evident between the visions of Zechariah and Amos in that both announce Yahweh's imminent presence and judgment. They differ, however, in that Amos' language indicates the Lord confines his action to a rather limited set of historical parameters. In Zechariah, the scope of the Lord's actions suggest a much larger, universal stage. In Zechariah, Yahweh's intervention seems to transcend the mere social, historical, and political boundaries that constrain the human realm of reality. It takes on a more utopian aspect than a historical one. Where once prophets like Amos could pinpoint evil by referring to specific sociological abuses— the oppression of the poor, the failure of the people to offer pure worship, the abuse of justice— the tendency in Zechariah's day was to elevate that reflection on evil to a much broader, symbolic realm that transcends history. A woman confined to a basket personifies evil (5:6–7); a flying scroll symbolizes the judgment and curse upon those who steal and swear falsely (5:1–4). This symbolic imagery, joined with a meta-historical perspective and communicated to the prophet through angelic intermediaries, forms the basis for what will develop into full blown apocalyptic thinking (see below).

The content of prophetic speech. The content of prophetic speech is equally vital in reconstructing the social texts behind the prophetic literature. In the cases of Haggai and Zechariah there is a phenomenon unparalleled in the entire corpus of prophetic literature. These prophets both have as the main thrust of their prophetic ministries the reestablishment of the Temple and its services. According to these prophets, the Lord's imminent breaking into history to establish a new age can only happen through the rebuilding of the Temple. The opening oracle of Haggai argues that it is not right for the people of Jerusalem to be living in their finished houses while the house of the Lord lies in ruins (1:4). The irony in this speech is that the people have settled for less in so doing. They sow much but harvest little; they eat but never to satisfaction (2:6). Yahweh simply cannot bless the people until they reestablish his house and its service—the Temple and its sacrificial service.

Haggai's oracles on the Temple develop still further that distinctive priestly perspective implied by his use of a priestly *torah* (see the previous discussion). Haggai believes that there is a strict principle of retribution that governs society and history. Retribution implies an understanding that life is organized and governed by a force where every action has a consequence. Proper action is rewarded with good, improper action is punished. This supposed relationship between action and its consequences is characteristic of Deuteronomic theology also, so readers should not infer that it is only an Aaronic, or priestly, perspective. In Haggai, the rebuilding of the Temple is understood as an act that could secure the consequence of Yahweh's blessing. In Hag 2:10–19 note the theology behind the diatribe: "Before a stone was placed upon a stone in the Lord's Temple, how did you fare? When one came to a heap of twenty measures, there were but ten; when one came to the wine vat to draw fifty measures, there were but twenty." The prophet's pro-Temple leanings are clear. Without the Temple there will only be hard times. If Haggai is not a priest, then he certainly operates within priestly circles and promotes priestly perspectives.

Zechariah also greatly emphasizes the rebuilding of the Temple, but not in the same way as Haggai. Even a first reading of the two books reveals the overlap between the two prophets both chronologically and thematically (the rebuilding of the Temple; see 1:16, 4:6–10; 6:12). A most distinctive feature of both these prophets is that each speaks of two leaders within the community: a high priest, Joshua, and a governor, Zerubbabel (Hag 1:12; 2:2; Zech 3:8–10 and 4:1–14). Two of the visions in Zechariah are of special interest, for they shed light upon political developments in the post-Exilic political situation in Jerusalem. These two visions embed within themselves oracles that are *nonvisionary*. Consider, as an example, the vision beginning in Zech 4:1. Verse 6, a nonvisionary oracle, interrupts the vision of the lampstand. The different introductory language makes this apparent. In Zech 4:1 there is typical visionary language (see above), and in 4:6 and 8 there is typical messenger language. Further, close reading shows that the words in vv. 6–7 do not actually answer the question that the prophet asks of the angel in v. 4. Rather, the oracle of vv. 6–7 asserts the preeminence of Zerubbabel's—the Davidic heir's—authority in the governance of Jerusalem. The oracle that follows (vv. 8–10) asserts Zerubbabel's extensive involvement in rebuilding the Temple. The answer to the question raised in v. 4, which the two oracles on Zerubbabel interrupted, comes in vv. 10b-11, which explains that the two olive trees are the two anointed ones, or two rulers. This latter response in the vision suggests that, as in Haggai, there are two rulers instead of one in post-Exilic Jerusalem. The oracles in vv. 6–7 and 8–10, which an editor has most surely inserted between vv. 5 and 11, assert that the Davidic ruler Zerubbabel has preeminence over Joshua, the priestly ruler.[5] The *final* form of the literary text, however, diminishes the strength of that assertion. The second oracle, Zech 6:9–15, functions similarly.

The overall text implies that the final editor had before him specific oracles from Zechariah (and Haggai) that emphasized the importance of the restoration of the Davidic king who, in the

---

[5]*Ibid.,* 120–121. Petersen interprets these visions as meta-historical and not necessarily a reflection of actual historical circumstance; K. Koch, *The Prophets II* (Philadelphia: Fortress, 1986) 163–164, sees them as a present-day proclamation of the future eschatological reign of the two.

early post-Exilic period, *shared* the rule with a priestly leader. Yet by the time the final editor is completing his work, the Davidic ruler has passed from the stage. Readers are reminded that in Ezra 1–6 the emphasis upon a Davidic heir in Jerusalem completely vanishes in Ezra 7–10. The priestly aristocracy eventually rules in Judah (recall that Ezra was an Aaronic priest). The final editor retains these oracles about the supremacy of Zerubbabel, but inserts them into other oracles that focus either on Joshua the priest (6:11) or on *two* leaders (4:3, 11–14). By recontextualizing the oracles, the text in its final form diminishes the authority of Zerubbabel (the Davidic ruler) and elevates the authority of Joshua (the priestly ruler). The editor has reread the traditions so that they might speak more clearly to the social (con)text of the editor's own time when the priests ruled Judah (see Chap. 6).

Clearly, Haggai and Zechariah are not remembered for their emphasis upon the Mosaic law. Neither do they talk much about the distant future. Their message is far more situated to the immediate circumstances of the Jerusalem community in the reign of Darius I. The speech forms and themes within their books suggest that their social texts are shaped by priestly concerns and especially the reinterpretation of the significance of the Davidic heir. Their understanding of Yahweh's intervention in the life of their community is characterized by the centrality of the Temple.

Prophets and the Temple:
The Heritage of Haggai and Zechariah
Isaiah 56; 66; Jeremiah 7; 26; Ezekiel 40:1–4; 44:1–14

Learning Goals

- To understand that within the Bible there are competing theological perspectives on the Temple.
- To understand that different prophets who spoke in the name of Yahweh did not necessarily agree with each other in their visions of restoration.
- To understand that the post-Exilic prophets inherited a prophetic tradition as a part of their social text.

Guiding Study Exercises

1) State the evidence for the conclusion that prophets contemporary with Haggai and Zechariah had differing views of the Temple.
2) In what sense are readers to understand the criticisms of the Temple that are voiced by the prophets Jeremiah (seventh century BCE) and Isaiah of Jerusalem (eighth century BCE)?
3) Write two paragraphs setting out the similarities and differences one sees between views of the Temple as expressed by Zechariah, Third Isaiah, and Ezekiel.
4) To what extent are the views of Haggai and Zechariah merely putting forward the views of earlier prophets on the Temple?

Readers should take caution not to think that Israel's prophetic tradition only concerned Temple matters. On the contrary, prophets have the reputation for being far more concerned with questions of social justice, championing the causes of society's oppressed and powerless. For present purposes, however, the Temple is a helpful thematic touchstone to seek connections between post-Exilic prophets and three **pre-Exilic** prophets: Isaiah, Jeremiah, and Ezekiel. The purpose of this section is to show that even though post-Exilic prophets spoke for Yahweh, as did pre-Exilic prophets, they did not necessarily share a single message or theology.

Readers should also keep in mind that the books of Isaiah, Jeremiah, and Ezekiel are more collections of sayings than they are books in a contemporary sense. They are heavily edited, and in the case of Isaiah contain oracles that span 200 to 300 years. Through the centuries the disciples of prophets had written down their masters' words, making them available for succeeding generations to study, interpret, and arrange.[6] The book of Ezekiel is much more tightly arranged and incorporates chronological information, as in Haggai and Zechariah. The final edited forms of these books, with the deliberate arrangements of sayings, inhibit contemporary readers from getting a clear view of the prophet himself. Rather, readers encounter the editor's impression of the prophet.

Isaiah and the Temple: Isaiah 66:1–5

This heading makes several critical assumptions. One of the most important is that there are at least three distinct stages of prophetic tradition within the book of Isaiah. The first, associated chiefly with Isaiah 1–39, is thought to grow from the preaching of a prophet called Isaiah of Jerusalem. His work was accomplished in Jerusalem mainly in the eighth century BCE (737–701), during the reigns of kings Ahaz, Jotham, and Hezekiah (see Isaiah 7–8; 36–39). He was generally sympathetic with the Jerusalem court and Temple institutions, but he condemned the abuses that had grown up within them. Chapters 40–55 of the book derive from later prophetic tradition that scholars refer to as "Deutero-Isaiah," or "Second Isaiah." This prophet, the Second Isaiah, accomplished his work largely in Babylon toward the end of the **Babylonian** empire (550–539 BCE). Still sympathetic with Jerusalem and her traditions, his is the voice that encourages persons to return and rebuild the old city when Cyrus the Persian liberated the nations held captive by Babylon (see Isa 45:1–7). Finally, there is a third prophetic tradition in Isaiah 56–66, which scholars refer to as "Trito-Isaiah," or "Third Isaiah." He is very likely a near contemporary of Haggai and Zechariah.[7] The views of the Temple in this tradition are of special interest here because they contain at least two perspectives: one is critical of the views of Haggai and Zechariah (as in 66:1–5); the other, which forms the framing oracles for the collection, assumes the existence of the Temple and is much more open about who may be admitted (as in 56:1–8 and 66:18–24).[8]

Isaiah 66:1–5 reflects a slightly polemical tone regarding the appropriateness of Temple worship. It is different from the strong admonitions of Zechariah and Haggai who not only insisted that the people rebuild the Temple and properly maintain its service, but also that the day of

---

[6]G. von Rad's *The Message of the Prophets* (New York: Harper & Row, 1967) is still one of the standard introductory works. On this topic see pp. 2–29.

[7]Compare J. Berquist, *Judaism in Persian's Shadow* (Minneapolis, MN: Fortress, 1995) 73–86; and J. Blenkinsopp, *A History of Prophecy in Israel* (London: SPCK, 1984) 232–251.

[8] See C. Westermann, *Isaiah 40–66* (OTL; Philadelphia: Fortress, 1969) 296–306.

A Closer Look: Key Evidence of Three Prophetic Stages in Isaiah. Scholars who believe there are three distinct prophetic voices within the book of Isaiah do so for historical, literary, and theological reasons. Isaiah 40–55 frequently refers to circumstances that are dated in the Babylonian period. References to Cyrus (Isa 44:28; 45:1), to Babylon (Isa 43:14; 47:1, 5; 48:14, 20), and to Babylonian deities (Isa 46:1) indicate the speaker has firsthand knowledge of the Babylonian history and religion in the years ca. 539 BCE. While the materials in Isaiah 1–39 have a much more complex literary history and reflect origins from both pre- and post-Exilic periods, they generally either originate from or reflect upon the period of Assyrian conflict with Judah. References to the Judean King Uzziah and his death in 736 BCE (Isa 6:1), Ahaz and the Syro-Ephraimite conflict in 734 BCE (Isa 7:1–17), the attempt at a political coalition with Egypt in 705 BCE (30:1–5; 31:1–5), and the Assyrian siege of Jerusalem in 701 BCE (Isaiah 36–37) all point to a much earlier setting than chapters 40–55. The oracles in Isaiah 56–66 seem to reflect the struggles within the community after the return to Jerusalem. There is a framing vision of a rebuilt Temple (Isa 56:1–8; 66:18–23) that reflects a much different cultus in that foreigners are welcomed. The oracles within these two outer boundaries (e.g., Isa 56:9–57:13) reflect the kinds of social and theological struggles readers see in Ezra-Nehemiah .

For further study, R. E. Clements. "The Unity of the Book of Isaiah." *Interpreting the Prophets.* Edited by J. L. Mays and P. J. Achtemeier. Philadelphia: Fortress, 1987. Pp. 50–61; J. F. A. Sawyer. *Prophecy and the Biblical Prophets.* Oxford: Oxford University Press, 1993. Pp. 83–95.

For more advanced study, R. N. Whybray. *Isaiah 40–66.* Grand Rapids, MI: Eerdmans, 1981, Pp. 38–43.

salvation would be ushered in thereby. The passage in Third Isaiah expresses a perspective that is critical of such an exclusive understanding of the role of the Temple.[9] The strong criticism of sacrifice in v. 3 challenges not simply the Temple building, but the ritual within the Temple as well. But who would take such a critical stance toward the Temple in the post-Exilic community? The reference to those who "tremble at my word" (vv. 2 and 5) is the same term that is used for those who supported Ezra against the practice of intermarriage in Jerusalem (Ezra 9:4; 10:3, 9). It is possible that the term "those who tremble at my word" designates a specific party of persons who advocated priority of the observance of the law of Moses.[10] A still broader question is whether this polemical perspective represents an isolated post-Exilic point of view, or is part of a more ancient tradition.

---

[9]R. N. Whybray, *Isaiah 40–66* (Grand Rapids, MI: Eerdmans, 1975), 280, points out that, rather than a criticism of Temple worship per se, it is more in line with pre-Exilic prophecy that insisted on humility and morality to accompany Temple worship.

[10]J. Blenkinsopp, *Prophecy in Israel,* 249–250.

One of the major finds at Qumran among the so-called Dead Sea Scrolls is a complete roll containing the book of Isaiah. The roll is presently kept in the Shrine of the Book, Jerusalem. (Israel Museum/David Harris)

An examination of the biblical tradition shows that there is a long history of anti-Temple sentiment, beginning with the Isaianic tradition itself. It may be important that in Second Isaiah's vision of restoration there is only scant attention to the rebuilding of the Temple (e.g., Isa 44:28). Of course, he is concerned about the rebuilding of Jerusalem, and offers his generation an extraordinary vision of God's presence with his people (e.g., Isa 54:11–17). But it is intriguing that this prophet does not emphasize the Temple as a central feature of that restoration. The older tradition of Isaiah of Jerusalem condemns improper Temple worship (Isa 1:10–11). He proclaims, "Hear the word of the Lord, you rulers of Sodom! Listen to the teaching of our God, you people of Gomorrah! What to me is the multitude of your sacrifices? says the Lord; I have had enough of burnt offerings of rams and the fat of fed beasts; I do not delight in the blood of bulls, or of lambs, or of goats." The opening chapter of the book in which this passage stands is a general summary of the message of the eighth-century prophet.[11] By addressing his audience as people of Sodom (a macro-level intertext with the story in Genesis 18–19), the prophet implies a shocking level of immoral activity in the city of Jerusalem. One may not argue from this that the prophet saw no place for Temple worship in the religious practice of his day. Rather, the prophet believed that cultic ritual without a moral purity was empty. Third Isaiah, then, simply rereads a very old

---

[11]See R. E Clements, "The Unity of the Book of Isaiah," *Old Testament Prophecy* (Louisville, KY: Westminster/John Knox Press, 1996) 93, who attributes this observation to G. Fohrer, "Jesaja 1 als Zusammenfassung der Verkündigung Jesajas," *ZAW* 74 (1962) 251–280.

message that had been preached by many prophets, including Isaiah of Jerusalem (see also Amos 5:21–24; Mic 6:6–8; Ps 50:7–11).

Clearly, some of the oracles contained in the Third Isaiah, the contemporary of Haggai and Zechariah, present a contrasting prophetic point of view on the Temple. Because this perspective appears to be so deeply rooted in the prophetic traditions of ancient Israel, readers may be hearing in Third Isaiah the voice of another religio-political party offering opposition to prophets such as Haggai and Zechariah. That opposition party may have been claiming authority for their view in the old oracles of Isaiah of Jerusalem. This party may well have had another vision of restoration not so closely tied to Temple religion and its ruling priestly families (see Chap. 6). Based upon the Ezra-Nehemiah story, readers may too conveniently conclude that such opposition was an external threat only. Clearly, there were different visions of the restoration that emerged within Jerusalem as well.

Jeremiah and the Temple: Jeremiah 7:1–7

Similar to the book of Isaiah, Jeremiah offers an editor's portrait of the prophet; unlike Isaiah, the materials are more homogeneous in form and span a shorter period of history. Many readers believe that the narratives were composed by a Deuteronomistic editor wishing to portray Jeremiah as a supporter of the Josianic reforms (see Chap. 2).[12] Thus 1:1–3 has Jeremiah beginning his preaching in the thirteenth year of Josiah, the king who is remembered as bringing religious reform to Jerusalem. The problem with such dating is that Jeremiah's oracles themselves seem to condemn royal apostasy as much as the people's (2:8, 26; 4:9; 5:1–6). The passages that express Deuteronomic theology (remember, Josiah's men discover what became Deuteronomy, 2 Kgs 22: 1–13) could just as easily have come from the hands of the Deuteronomistic editor (see 11:1–17; 22:15–16).

Jeremiah's Temple sermon, 7:1–26, is repeated in the opening chapter of the second half of the book, 26:1–15, and thereby plays a central role in defining the shape of the book's message.[13] While both passages are recollections of the prophet's preaching against the Temple, note that the version in Jeremiah 26 is concerned more about the setting and the official response to the sermon ("beginning of the reign of Jehoiakim," 26:1). That the Deuteronomistic editor should be interested in this sermon comes as no surprise since Deuteronomic theology places great emphasis upon the Temple as central to proper worship of Yahweh (Deuteronomy 12; 13:1–5; see Chap. 2 of this text). The more detailed presentation of the sermon in Jer 7:1–26, however, makes the explicit connections between righteous living as the basis for pure Temple worship. Anything short of this is regarded as idolatry.[14]

The opening verses of Jeremiah 7 accuse the people of Jerusalem of being deceived into believing that the Temple alone was enough to assure the deity's presence (vv. 3–4). The people are

[12]Blenkinsopp, *Prophecy in Israel,* 162; J. F. A. Sawyer, *Prophecy and the Biblical Prophets* (rev. ed.; Oxford: Oxford University Press, 1993) 95–97

[13]O'Connor, K. "Do not Trim a Word: The Contributions of Chapter 26 to the Book of Jeremiah," *CBQ* 51(1989) 617–630.

[14]Thus R. E. Clements, "Jeremiah 1–25 and the Deuteronomistic History," *Old Testament Prophecy,* 111–112.

called to amend their ways, to "act justly one with another" (v. 5), not to oppress the alien, the orphan, and the widow, and not to "go after other gods." Note especially vv. 8–12 where the sermon makes micro-level intertexts with two other biblical traditions. The first intertext is with the legal tradition and especially with the decalogue. Verse 9 lists stealing, murder, adultery, swearing falsely, making offerings to Baal, and going after other gods as crimes perpetrated within the community despite devotion to the Temple. Compare these crimes with those listed in the decalogue in Deut 5:6–21. The list in Jeremiah is not in the same sequence; the concern for other gods comes first in the decalogue. The second intertext is with the tradition of the destruction of **Shiloh**. Shiloh was one of the old **levitical** Yahwistic shrines destroyed by the **Philistines** (1 Sam 4:1–11). The story of Shiloh's fall and the punishment of the Levite Eli and his sons, as well as the entire levitical priesthood (see Chap. 6), functions in the sermon to illustrate the outcome of the failure to incorporate righteous behavior with right worship.

This blend of ethical purity with Temple worship provides the theological social text for later prophets. Zechariah argued strongly in favor of the immediate rebuilding of the Temple in his setting, but he did not advocate that the people avoid other matters of righteousness. Note the oracle in Zech 7:8–14. The pronouncement answers a question about the observance of a fast in memory of the fall of Jerusalem (7:1–7). Proper piety would make such a fast mandatory. The prophet accuses the inquisitors of false piety (vv. 5–7) and then reminds them that true piety consists of more than ritual observance. In vv. 9–10 he says, "Render true judgments, show kindness and mercy to one another; do not oppress the widow, the orphan, the alien, or the poor; and do not devise evil in your hearts against one another." This admonition in Zechariah has a decided ring of the concerns of the Deuteronomist about it, just as occurs in the much earlier oracle of Jeremiah. But it further illustrates the possibility that the admonitions to rebuild the Temple in Zechariah's preaching need not have been admonitions to forsake the obligations of morality and ethical behavior prescribed by individual Yahwistic righteousness.

Ezekiel and the Temple: Ezekiel 44:9–14

Like Isaiah and Jeremiah the book of Ezekiel is in its final form a heavily edited book. The school devoted to Ezekiel's preaching and teaching shaped the preserved sermons to create their image of the prophetic character. Ezekiel is portrayed as a near contemporary of Jeremiah, having suffered deportation to Babylon himself in 598 BCE. Unlike Isaiah and Jeremiah, there is hardly any biographical information on the prophet. The prophet is known mainly through his words, not unlike Haggai and Zechariah. Whereas Isaiah and Jeremiah have a great deal of poetry within them, Ezekiel does not. His oracles are mainly prose and give the impression that his preaching was conceived to fit into a book from the beginning. Isaiah and Jeremiah are portrayed as having kings and governmental officials as their audience. This is not so for Ezekiel. He addresses his oracles to Babylonian captives who lack power.[15]

The book is organized into four sections: Ezekiel 1–24 concern judgment, 25–32 present oracles against the nations, 33–39 offer hope for restoration, and 40–48 present a vision of the Temple. Ezekiel 44:9–14 comes from the final and climactic section of the book that gives voice

---

[15]See J. Wevers, for instance, *Ezekiel* (NCB; Grand Rapids, MI: Eerdmans, 1969).

to its high hopes for the restoration of the Temple. The text (see Ezek 40:1) dates the vision to the twenty-fifth year of the Exile (or 573 BCE, dating from the deportation of King Jehoaichin [598 BCE]). By this time the Babylonian king Nebuchadnezzar was dead and the ruler of the day, Nabonidus, was absent from his throne. It may well be that the exiles contemporary with this vision had begun to entertain hopes of restoration to their homeland. The Temple vision may be subdivided into three parts. Ezekiel 40:1–43:12 concern the physical layout of the future Temple, 44:1–46:24 deal with rules governing access to the Temple and its ceremonies, and 47:13–48:35 divide the land among the people.[16] There are further provisions that betray Ezekiel's biases. The opening chapters picture the return of the Lord's "glory" into the Temple, symbolizing Yahweh's restored presence with his people. The second section (Ezekiel 44–46) specifies three classes of rulers: priests, Levites, and princes (see Chap. 6). The priests are the sons of Zadok, an earlier Jerusalemite family of priests. The Levites are from the family of Levi (see Ezek 44:9–14). More significant than this is that Ezekiel assigns to the Davidic king, the civic ruler, a minimal role. The king, or prince as Ezekiel calls him, is consigned to a role relatively insignificant next to that of the Zadokite priest (45:7–8). Attend carefully to 44:9–14 to see the strongly pro-Temple sentiment of this prophet.

The passage seems certainly to have contributed to the social text of the post-Exilic prophets Haggai and Zechariah. While it is difficult to know to what extent the late sixth-century prophet Zechariah knew of Ezekiel's vision of the Temple, it is clear that Zechariah's Temple vision differs in several respects. For one thing, Ezekiel's vision has a wall around the Temple (40:5); Zechariah pictures the Lord's presence as a ring of fire around the Temple (Zech 2:1–5). More significantly, Zechariah knows nothing of the division between the two classes of priests, Zadokites and Levites. On the other hand, Ezekiel does not envision there being a high priest as does Zechariah (3:1). Perhaps even more significantly, Zechariah does not seem to have as much difficulty with the assertion of the Davidic heir, Zerubbabel, as the civic leader alongside the high priest, Joshua (Zech 4:1–10). It may well be that Zechariah simply has a much different agenda for the Temple and finds it necessary to offer a different depiction for the people of his day, while providing an interpretation that could look toward a messianic future.[17] Whatever the case, Zechariah's main differences with Ezekiel are at the point of political and religious rule within the restoration community.[18]

Readers find greater agreement between Zechariah and Ezekiel on the matter of foreigners within the Temple community. Ezekiel was very concerned that no foreigners "uncircumcised in heart and flesh, of all the foreigners who are among the people of Israel, shall enter my sanctuary" (44:9). Zechariah's vision of the uncleanness of the high priest, Joshua, an uncleanness that un-

---

[16]M. Greenberg, "Ezekiel's Program of Restoration," *Interpreting the Prophets* (eds. J. L. Mays and P. J. Achtemeyer; Philadelphia: Fortress, 1987) 215–236, believes that there is a striking similarity to these three thematic sections and the Tetrateuchal material that deals with the building of the sanctuary (Exodus 35–40), who has access to the activities in the sanctuary (Leviticus), and the assignment of tribes around the sanctuary (Numbers 1–11).

[17]See Petersen, *Haggai and Zechariah*, 116–119.

[18]These differences notwithstanding, Paul Hanson, *The Dawn of Apocalyptic* (Philadelphia: Fortress, 1979) believes that Zechariah and Haggai are reinterpreting the Temple visions of Ezekiel.

doubtedly comes from having lived among the unclean foreigners of Babylon,[19] gives expression to the prophet's awareness of the same problem of intermingling. This may also further the reader's understanding of Zechariah's own sense of priestly purity. Curiously, however, Zechariah's vision of the new age does envision the people of the foreign nations coming and joining themselves to Yahweh (2:11). Haggai's request for a priestly teaching on the transferability of uncleanness seems also to assume the importance of cultic purity in the mix of Jews and peoples of the land (2:11–15). Indeed, one cannot but recall the later concern of Ezra's with the intermarrying be- tween Jews and non-Jews within the Jerusalem community (Ezra 9:1–2).

These concerns about the uncleanness of foreigners offer an intriguing intertext with the preaching of another contemporary of Third Isaiah. Recall from the discussion above one of the Isaianic prophets who was not particularly sympathetic to the priestly agenda of Temple restora- tion in the post-Exilic community. By contrast, the oracle in Isa 56:6–8 sees the Temple as a gathering place for *all* the nations. Foreigners and eunuchs—this latter in *opposition* to the Deutero- nomic law! (see Deut 23:1)—shall come to the Lord's holy mountain! The prophet claims in the name of Yahweh that "their burnt offerings and their sacrifices will be accepted on my altar; for my house shall be called a house of prayer for all peoples. Thus says the Lord God, who gathers the out- casts of Israel, I will gather others to them besides those already gathered" (56:7).

This pro-Temple, post-Exilic Isaianic prophet does stipulate that these foreigners shall "join themselves to the Lord," and shall keep the Sabbath and not profane it. Compare also Isa 66:18–23, another convincing affirmation of the Temple's accessibility to foreigners. Both state- ments open and close the collection of post-Exilic Isaianic oracles, functioning as a kind of edito- rial framework in which the reader is to interpret the prophet's words.[20] Readers cannot overlook how much broader the vision in this prophetic framework is than Haggai's or even Zechariah's. Compared with Ezekiel, who refused to admit foreigners into the Temple at all, Third Isaiah's pro-Temple framing vision is *much* broader.

It is clear that the preaching of their prophetic predecessors shaped the social texts of the prophets Haggai and Zechariah. These later prophets preserved through their rereading the words of their predecessors. Yet, it is also clear that the prophetic preaching of Haggai and Zechariah was not the full expression of the sentiment of the post-Exilic community. If one were only to read their preaching as representative of the attitudes of the repatriated exiles, one would not have all of the information. Within Third Isaiah there are conflicting voices on the Temple. The view that asserted righteousness over ritual was not unique to its time period. That voice surely drew upon prophetic ancestors who expressed concern about the potential hollowness of the rituals of sacrificial religion. Isaiah of Jerusalem and Jeremiah both give expression to that perspective.

It is even more important to recognize that theological disagreement issued into divisive ac- tions. More often than not, political power, rather than the efficacious word or the absolute truth of a prophet's preaching, decided the validity of a prophetic assertion. In the end, history records that the Temple was rebuilt and that the Zadokite priestly family presided over it. What happened to those voices of opposition who counseled caution in assuming that the carefully wrought ser- vices of the Temple contained the fullness of the worship of Yahweh?

[19]See Meyers and Meyers, *Haggai and Zechariah,* 218.
[20]See C. Westermann here, *Isaiah 40–66* (Philadelphia: Westminster Press, 1969) 295–308.

Prophecy and the Origins of Apocalypticism
Isaiah 59; 65; Daniel 7–12

Learning Goals

- To understand the meaning of the theological, social, and literary features of emerging apocalyptic literature in the Hebrew Bible.
- To understand that apocalypticists share some common assumptions and practices of biblical prophets.
- To understand that there are alternative ways of reading biblical apocalyptic literature.

Guiding Study Exercises

1) What does the word *apocalyptic* mean? How is apocalyptic eschatology different from prophetic eschatology?
2) What threats were Jewish people facing in Jerusalem and Judah during the Hellenistic period? What is the connection between these threats and the rise of apocalypticism?
3) How does the problem of internal Jewish conflict lead to the Maccabean revolt?
4) What is meant by *ex eventu* prophecy? Explain how it functions to communicate to the reader the eschatological views of the writer.
5) Write a paragraph explaining how your views of biblical prophets are challenged or reinforced by this presentation.

The work of the Israelite prophet was to provide vision. Such vision initially gave meaning to events in the immediate future rather than the distant future. The prophet's task was to interpret his vision of God's presence into real socio-historical reality. Thus, Second Isaiah interpreted Cyrus' overthrow of Babylon as God's salvation for the Jews. Haggai and Zechariah understood it to be God's will that the returning exiles rebuild the Temple. Ezekiel's painstaking measurements of the Temple indicate his own understanding that the Temple denoted God's *real* presence in history. As Moses' law became central to religion in this period, that also became a way of translating Yahweh's presence with his people. What is more, these visions of Temple and law reflect a kind of optimism that God can live with his people and have a purpose for the present world.

Apocalyptic literature reflects some drastic changes. The optimism about the possibilities for God's presence in the immediate world, as well as Israel's nationalistic hopes, disappears. Apocalyptic texts abandon the view that the immediate world can harbor justice and righteousness. These texts do not offer visions about God's activity through political figures and structures in the present. Visionaries who project God's presence into the future by abandoning confidence in the present reality replace the classical biblical prophet. In order to begin thinking about this new way of articulating God's will, readers must consider at least three different features of apocalyptic literature: its worldview, the social circumstances behind it, and its literary peculiarities. The new worldview is illustrated in the relationship between prophetic eschatology and apocalyptic eschatology. The social circumstances may be described in terms of conflict between the powerful and the disenfranchised. The literary peculiarities grow from the new religious worldview and, in particular, reflect an imaginative assertion of the cosmic and transcendent over the mundane and historical worlds.[21]

Apocalyptic Eschatology vs. Prophetic Eschatology

One of the defining characteristics of apocalyptic is its **eschatology**. Eschatology has to do with final things, the end of the world, or the consummation of time and space as it is known. This notion forms an interesting macro-level intertext with earlier prophets. Jeremiah, for instance, announced that Yahweh was about to destroy Jerusalem through the armies of Babylon. The prophet was interpreting his sense of Yahweh's justice into present social and political realities. However, apocalypticists abandon the idea of God's working in and through present political structures to accomplish his tasks. Thus, P. Hanson states, "Prophetic eschatology is transformed into apocalyptic at the point where the task of translating the cosmic vision into the categories of mundane reality is abdicated."[22] The abandonment of history is the result of the belief that the present time has grown too evil. An example of one such visionary who paints the present circumstances in the darkest of hues is found in Third Isaiah. The oracle in Isa 59:9–14 is a forerunner of later apocalyptic visionaries: "Therefore justice is far from us, and righteousness does not reach us; we wait for light, and lo! there is darkness; and for brightness, but we walk in gloom" (Isa 59:9). The ensuing judgment in vv. 16–19 is one of utter destruction. Ultimately, the apocalypticist announces that the end shall come upon the enemies of the Lord (who happen also to be the enemies of the visionary). But the Lord will do this himself rather than rely upon any mediating political power as in the earlier prophets.

This eschatological perspective is perhaps seen more clearly in yet another passage from Third Isaiah where again the prophet's community is described in the most dismal of terms. Perhaps Isa 65:1–7, the opening of a larger oracle contained in vv. 1–16, sounds like the usual prophetic denunciation that is associated with the classical prophets. Indeed, there is within these verses the assertion of the sins of the people. But there is no clear political identity of these people. Unlike Amos for instance, who directs his judgment at the city of Samaria, or Isaiah of Jerusalem who aims his words against all the inhabitants of Judah, this prophetic oracle of Third Isaiah distinguishes only between the righteous and the unrighteous. Thus, the vision pronounces judgment and salvation simultaneously. There will be judgment upon those within the group who deserve judgment, and salvation for those who deserve salvation. In other words, the boundaries

---

[21]J. Berquist's discussion of apocalyptic is especially approachable for students, *Judaism in Persia's Shadow,* 177–192.

[22]Hanson, *Dawn of Apocalyptic,* 49. Note Berquist's criticisms of Hanson, *ibid.,* 184–185, and his own much different view of the origins of apocalyptic. See also D. S. Russell, *Divine Disclosure* (Minneapolis, MN: Fortress, 1992) 28.

between good and evil are no longer *political* boundaries. The visionaries deliberately blur the lines that mark Yahweh's punishment within history and outside of history.

The abandonment of the present world for a new world is most clearly seen in the conclusion of this chapter in Isaiah. To be sure, Second Isaiah used similar language of new creation (41:20), and spoke of the restoration of Jerusalem (54:11–17). In this latter instance, the metaphorical language elevated to a new height what the prophet saw happening in his day through Cyrus: "O afflicted one, storm-tossed, and not comforted, I am about to set your stones in antimony, and lay your foundations with sapphires." The difference between Second Isaiah and these visions from Third Isaiah, therefore, is the relative confidence the former has in his contemporary historical circumstances. In Second Isaiah Yahweh is still working through the present historical and political circumstances to bring salvation to his nation and Jerusalem (Isa 40:1). In Isaiah 65 the visionary has given up on the possibility of redeeming the present circumstances. The only avenue remaining is to start over anew. Thus Isa 65:17–20 continues with a vision of radical departure from the present to a new world. It will inspire the young Christian movement that undergoes persecution in the first century CE. That is because such vision frees the community from having to work within the framework and confines of what they regard as evil social circumstances.

Apocalypticism Expresses Social Conflict, Special Knowledge

In the previous discussion of the social text of Haggai and Zechariah, readers observed diverging prophetic views of the Temple. These differing views allow the hypothesis of differing theological and ideological groups existing within the post-Exilic community. The narrative in Ezra-Nehemiah would imply that there was a pro-Temple, priestly group that dominated the post-Exilic Jerusalem community. Consequently, the Jewish community preserved this dominant group's story. Evidently, those persons espousing a religion that was more cautious about the role of the Temple live on only as the opponents of the dominant group. One asks, naturally, what happens to the groups whose beliefs and practices are not represented by the official, majority religion?

There were other kinds of groups within the post-Exilic community besides those interested in prophetic eschatology or the Temple particularly. The Hebrew Bible contains a significant portion of literature, for instance, that is ascribed to the sages. The literature of the sages, called **wisdom literature**, testifies to yet another group within the post-Exilic community, which existed during the time when this literature was most likely assembled. While they may not have constituted a political group per se, they were "a class of learned men" within the community who believed they had special insight.[23] The Book of Daniel, dating from the Hellenistic period (see below), identifies "those who are wise" in several places in the second half of the book. They are called the *maskilim* (11:33, 35; 12:3, 10), and they could be the ones who authored the book, and thus the apocalyptic thrust of the book.[24] Minority groups such as these, though not necessarily the *maskilim* in particular, conceivably began to view themselves as disenfranchised from the

[23]*Divine Disclosure,* 31. Though it has not been a convincing view, G. Von Rad believed that apocalyptic had its roots in the wisdom movement, *Theology* (2 vols.; London: SCM Press, 1965) 1.441–59.

[24]See J. J. Collins, "Daniel and His Social World," *Interpreting the Prophets,* 249–260.

authoritative groups. As such they lacked an adequate voice within the overall community. Their interpretations of the prophets differed from that of the socially empowered religious elite. Moreover, they began to see themselves as suffering on behalf of the truth. They reacted to the majority view as evil and outside of God's will. They then gradually pulled away from mainstream religious society.

One of the best examples of such a break comes from a period later than the Persian period. Many scholars believe that the residents of Qumran, the village in the Judean wilderness near the caves in which the Dead Sea Scrolls were found, were **Essenes**.[25] After the Maccabean revolt in 164 BCE and the establishment of the Hasmonean control of the Jerusalem Temple, the members of this group grew dissatisfied with religious leadership and fled to the wilderness. It was there they practiced their faith on their own terms, feeling they had little or nothing in common with the dominant religious party in Jerusalem. Many scholars further believe that it was the residents of Qumran who produced the scrolls found in the caves, many of which were apocalyptic documents.

Thus under this hypothetical view, the groups that opposed the religious interpretation of the political circumstances in the post-Exilic period might well have become marginal groups that gradually came to believe that they had no voice in defining the official religion of the day. They may well have asserted their views of the darkness of the time period against the views of the dominant religious and political leaders of the day—persons like Ezra and Nehemiah. Having lost any political power, any hope of control, any semblance of representation, the group envisions a new day, initiated by Yahweh, in which the deity would sweep away their enemies, hear their voice, and restore the truth. Who were these groups of persons? Perhaps they were rival priests, from rival priestly families, who had been given little or no place in the Temple service.[26] Priests and Levites have already been mentioned, and Chapter 6 will consider their roles in the Temple as a basis for the sociological background calling for ever-new theological expansions and explanations of their circumstances. For now it must suffice simply to say that there is ample evidence of different religio-political groups within post-Exilic society to warrant this hypothesis that social conflict is at least part of the social text of apocalyptic movements. This formulaic mix of social conflict and a heightened sense of prophetic eschatology will be the basis of fully formed apocalyptic expression in the still later Maccabean period, to which the closing section turns to conclude this discussion of prophecy.

Apocalypticism and the Emergence of a Literary Genre

The passages in Isaiah 59 and 65 are only forerunners of apocalyptic literature. They have features of apocalypticism in that they begin to express interest in an age beyond their contemporary historical and political realities. Further, they emerge possibly from disenfranchised and marginalized

---

[25]H. Shanks, "Essene Origin—Palestine or Babylonia," *Understanding the Dead Sea Scrolls* (New York: Random House, 1992) 79–84. For an opposing view see A. Crown and L. Cansdale, "Qumran: Was it an Essene Settlement?" *BAR* 20.5 (1994) 25–35; 73–55.

[26]This would be J. Miller's view, *The Origins of the Bible* (Minneapolis, MN: Paulist Press, 1994), who is clearly influenced by Hanson's thesis, *The Dawn of Apocalyptic*. J. Berquist, *Judaism in Persia's Shadow,* argues that apocalypticists need not have been marginalized groups. Rather, they were highly educated, middle-management bureaucrats dissatisfied with Persian policy.

social groups. The final criterion by which one might recognize apocalypticism is literary in nature. Not only is it represented by a distinctive worldview, behind which is a reality of social groups engaged in conflict, but it comes to have its own very distinctive literary characteristics as well.

An examination of an excerpt from the book of Daniel moves from the Persian period to the Hellenistic period (see the historical survey in Chap. 2). Not only is Daniel an apocalyptic book, but it bears great influence upon later first-century CE perspectives concerning the Christ. There are macro-level intertexts between Daniel 7, Ezekiel, and Zechariah that suggest apocalypticists themselves were rereading the prophets, perhaps searching for some contemporary significance for an older oracle. Daniel, however, moves well beyond the visions of these older prophets in the esoteric nature of his imagery.

The Hellenistic Period (333–63 BCE). Generally speaking, the period begins with Alexander the Great and his conquest of the world. The term *Hellenism,* which derives from the Greek word for Greece—*Hellen*—denotes the phenomenon of Greek culture that, through Greek political hegemony, came to have a profound influence on the world. Alexander conquered Persia in 333 BCE, ending approximately 200 years of Persian world domination. Roughly ten years later, in 323 BCE, Alexander himself died, leaving his vast world conquests to be governed by his generals. The area of Palestine, which had been under Persian rule, now came under the authority and influence of Greek culture and politics. Because of its geographical location, Palestine was situated between two major kingdoms: Egypt, ruled by Ptolemy, and Syria, ruled by Seleucus, both rulers having formerly been generals of Alexander. These two ruling families competed for the control of Palestine. During the first century after Alexander's death, Egypt, under the rule of the Ptolemies, controlled Palestine. There was little change from Persian rule. The high priest continued as both the religious and civil head of Judah and Jerusalem. This arrangement continued for a while after the Seleucids of Syria defeated the Ptolemies, wresting control of Palestine from their hands in 198 BCE.

The problem in Jerusalem was Hellenism. Greek culture, communicated most powerfully through its religion and educational institutions, posed a daunting opponent to the traditional Jewish perspectives on the world. The **gymnasium**, with its emphasis upon the importance and beauty of the body, was antithetical to the more modest views of Jewish tradition. Under the peaceful reigns of the Ptolemies and the early Seleucid leaders, it was convenient for Jews, especially wealthy and educated Jews, to incorporate Hellenistic perspectives into Judaism. However, more traditional Jews came to regard such groups of people as traitors. Jason, for instance, a high priest during this Hellenistic period (171–168 BCE), authorized the construction of a gymnasium in Jerusalem devoted to the Greek gods Hermes and Hercules. Such actions illustrate the openness on the part of some to non-Jewish perspectives. On the other hand, there were the rural classes of Jews who resisted such an assimilation of Judaism into Greek culture. These groups of persons argued for Jewish distinctiveness on every point. It was imperative to keep the law of Moses strictly. There could be no relaxation in the observance of proper Temple worship. Put briefly, the cries of purity from the leadership of Ezra and Nehemiah, could be heard yet again. The difference at this later period was that this cry was not heard from the lips of nobles and officials. Only the country folk were so concerned.

Under the Seleucid ruler Antiochus Epiphanes IV (175–163 BCE) there arose a strong antagonism toward Jews who refused to embrace Hellenism openly and freely. Antiochus stationed his troops in Jerusalem, symbolizing foreign rule. He erected a citadel, known as the Akkra, in which to garrison his troops. He desecrated the Jewish Temple by erecting an altar to Zeus on the

Temple grounds. Such provocative behaviors surely aggravated the Jews who were trying to maintain their Judaism through the assimilated Greek cultural forms. But for the strict separatists, these actions were intolerable and led to revolt. The revolt in 167 BCE was led by another family of priests, the Maccabees, headed by the patriarch, Mattathias. (Maccabees are also called **Hasmoneans**, after their ancestor Hasmoneus.) Judas Maccabeus followed his father, Mattathias, in revolt when Antiochus tried to force Jews to offer sacrifices to pagan deities. In Chapter 6 we will return to the Maccabeans and continue our discussion on the Temple in the Hellenistic period.

Literary Opposition to Persecution. As an example of literary opposition to the persecution of the period, consider the book of Daniel. It is the only example of fully formed apocalyptic literature within the Hebrew Bible. It dates from the Maccabean period and thus reflects the social and cultural conflicts within the Jewish and Hellenistic world of its day. The book is in two parts. Chapters 1–6 consist of narratives about Daniel and his friends at service within the Babylonian and Persian courts in the sixth-century BCE. In that setting there is not the kind of wide-reaching persecution assumed in the second half of the book, chapters 7–12. In Daniel 1–6 persecution is limited to specific instances. Yet the latter part of the book reflects the time of sweeping Jewish persecution during the reign of Antiochus IV.

The narratives in the first half of the book consist mainly of tales of Daniel's heroic exploits over foreign kings and courts. Clearly these narratives, in part one, serve to elevate the ethos of remaining faithful to one's heritage, even in the context of a foreign community and its foreign influences. The parallels between Daniel and his friends in the Babylonian and Persian court and the Jews in a Hellenistic setting are not difficult to imagine. But God is portrayed as faithful to Daniel, who is himself faithful to a strict understanding of Jewish law. The second half of the book is narrated autobiographically, in the first grammatical person. Whereas in the first part of the book there are dreams, in Daniel 7–12 there are esoteric visions. The dreams that are given by God for Daniel to interpret reveal Daniel's wisdom. He successfully interprets the dreams and thereby provides instruction for the kings under whom Daniel and his friends serve. In chapter 7, the opening chapter of the book's second half, the dreams change to visions that Daniel by himself is unable to understand. They require the interpretation of a heavenly intermediary. These visions provide the interpretation of the contemporary times and events for the Hellenistic audience. But they do so by using symbolic language and imagery to represent the mundane situation. Notice the allusions both to the political situations as well as to the internal conflicts within the community in Daniel 7:13–18.

This is only a very small portion of the ending of Daniel's vision. The thrust of this portion of the much lengthier vision is that a "human being" (the phrase translates the more familiar "son of man") appears before the throne of the Ancient One. The Ancient One gives this son of man kingship over all nations of the world. Daniel asks for a heavenly interpreter and such is granted. Then the explanation of the vision (of four beasts rising out of the water—see 7:1–12) interprets the vision's significance for world politics. It also explains that the holy ones (undoubtedly these are the oppressed persons in the apocalyptic community waiting for God's justification of their cause) would receive the kingdom and possess the kingdom forever. The vision gives expression to the future hopes of those who are being persecuted.[27]

Two literary peculiarities of this passage are of special interest for their intertextuality with earlier prophets. First, as an example of macro-level intertextuality, consider the convention of

---

[27]See S. Towner, *Daniel* (IBC; Atlanta, GA: John Knox Press, 1984) 91–115.

using *symbolic language* and *imagery*. The vision of Daniel is of four beasts coming out of the sea (7:1–8), each of which devours its successor. Readers have seen symbolic language in the classical prophets before, of course. Ezekiel is known for such symbolism in his well-known vision of dry bones (Ezekiel 37). Readers have read the visions of Zechariah that also require the interpretation of a heavenly figure (Zech 1:7–17). The main difference is that, as apocalyptic literature progresses, the symbols become more esoteric. The connections between the reality behind the symbols are increasingly remote. For instance, in Zechariah's vision the symbols stand for situations and circumstances that exist on earth. In Daniel's vision, not only does he see symbols of earthly realities, he sees images that stand for heavenly realities. With apocalypticists there seems to be a movement toward more "heavenly visions" as opposed to mere "symbolic visions."[28] This would reinforce the inclination that apocalypticism tends to be more concerned with the world beyond than with present social and historical reality.

A second peculiarity is the nature of the prophet's *ex eventu* (or "from the event") relationship to the intended audience. Recall that pre-Exilic prophecy is very much grounded in the immediate events of the prophet's day. Any concern with the future is only in the very immediate future. However, apocalypticists give this a twist in that they often relate history as prophecy. As an analogous example, one may see how the Chronicler retells the Deuteronomistic History from his knowledge of how the future turns out (Chaps. 6 and 7). This seems to be the perspective of the apocalypticist, too. In this, there is a break with classical prophets such as Ezekiel and Zechariah.

Reading through Daniel 7 readers see that the story is set in Babylon and Persia during and shortly after the time of the Exile (the sixth century BCE), but the vision concerns events that lie in the future, events up to the time of the second century BCE. The vision itself speaks of a succession of four kings (7:17), most likely referring to the kings and kingdoms of Babylon, Media, Persia, and Greece. The fourth king is the most dreaded. The vision describes in the greatest detail the fourth king (vv. 19–27). More significantly, it is also the king about whom there is the least error in historical detail. This suggests the likelihood that the book and the visions were actually written during the period of the fourth king, referring, more specifically, to one of the horns in verse 7, which most likely refers to Antiochus IV. The actual author of the text placed the visions on the lips of a prophet (Daniel) who lived long before the time of the actual author. To the readers contemporary with this second-century author, this has the effect of creating an imminent time frame. The readers are living in the days foreseen by the ancient seer Daniel. Not only does this legitimize the prophet's words, but it means to the readers that the day of justification is very near. Ultimately, the time frame becomes a basis for the seer to encourage the audience to endure persecution just a bit longer because salvation is near. *Ex eventu* prophecy only serves to reinforce the eschatological outlook already noted previously.

Thus, to investigate apocalyptic as a literary genre readers must keep in mind the intertextual relationships with earlier prophecy. Apocalypticists describe visions about the future. Heavenly mediators interpret these visions. The visions often consist of some heavenly scene, far beyond the realm of the earthly setting. Such visions are expressed in symbolic language. The symbols grow to be increasingly esoteric. And finally, the eschatological purview of the seer comes to its sharpest expression in the *ex eventu* relationship of the apocalypticist to the intended audience.

---

[28]This distinction is made by C. Rowland, "Apocalyptic Literature," *It is Written: Scripture Citing Scripture* (eds., D. A. Carson and H. G. M. Williamson; Cambridge: Cambridge University Press, 1988), 177.

Conclusion

This overview of the story of prophets and prophecy has been limited, but from the post-Exilic perspective the process of rereading is clear. The historian writing Ezra-Nehemiah rereads Haggai and Zechariah as these two prophets reread the prophecies of earlier prophetic messengers. In the Ezra-Nehemiah narrative the two prophets looked fairly similar. As depicted in the biblical books with their names, there were some striking differences. Indeed, they both spoke in favor of the Temple, but not in the same way. Both were deeply involved in the political matters of the day: the relationship of the Jews to Persia and, especially, the role of the high priest relative to the Davidic heir. In other words, these prophets did not just speak about religious matters, they related these religious matters to the political situation of the day. In this, Haggai and Zechariah were very much like their predecessors, Isaiah of Jerusalem, Jeremiah, and Ezekiel. Their rhetoric indicated their perspective: They were messengers of Yahweh, they were visionaries, they brought words of compassion and salvation, of judgment and doom. The prophetic voice was not necessarily the majority voice. Eventually, some prophetic visions gave expression to the concerns of a community that felt excluded and in conflict with another part of the community. Such conflict gave expression to different political and religious points of view, all of which sought their justification in appeals to Yahweh's word as revealed to earlier prophets. Even prophets did not always agree. Apocalyptic thought and rhetoric finds its roots in prophetic preaching. The belief in direct revelation, the experience of ecstatic visions, and the belief in Yahweh's eventual entrance into history to save his people gave rise to the prophetic preoccupation with a salvation that was experienced in another world and given expression in a kind of esoteric imagery of heavenly symbols. With the rise of apocalyptic thinking, in which the prophets of old (like Daniel) came to be read as offering detailed visions of the future, many within the Jewish community came to read *all* the prophets as predictors of the distant future. Jesus ben Sirach captures well this way of *rereading* the prophets: He says of Isaiah, "By his dauntless spirit he saw the future, and comforted the mourners in Zion. He revealed what was to occur to the end of time, and the hidden things before they happened" (Sir 48:24–25). There will be more to say about this futuristic way of reading the prophets in Chapter 14.

For Further Reading

Haggai and Zechariah: Temple and Not Law

Berger, P. "Charisma and Religious Innovation: The Social Location of Israelite Prophecy." *ASR* 28 (1963) 940–950. (*Recommended for beginning students.*)

Steck, O. "Theological Streams of Tradition." In *Tradition and Theology in the Old Testament.* Edited by D. A. Knight. Philadelphia: Fortress, 1977. (*Recommended for beginning students.*)

Wilson, R. R. "Prophecy and Ecstasy: A Reexamination." *JBL* 98 (1979) 321–337.

Prophets and the Temple: The Heritage of Haggai and Zechariah

Clements, R. E. "The Ezekiel Tradition: Prophecy in a Time of Crisis." *Israel's Prophetic Heritage: Essays in Honour of Peter Ackroyd.* Edited by R. Coggins, A. Phillips, and M. Knibb. Cambridge: Cambridge University Press, 1982.

Dutcher-Walls, P. "The Social Location of the Deuteronomists: A Sociological Study of Factional Politics." *JSOT* 52 (1991) 77–94.

Levenson, J. D. *Theology of the Program of Restoration of Ezekiel 40–48.* Missoula, MT: Scholars Press, 1976.

Long, B. O. "Social Dimensions of Prophetic Conflict." *SBLSS* 21 (1982) 31–53.

Prophecy and the Origins of Apocalypticism

Collins, J. J. *The Apocalyptic Imagination.* New York: Crossroads, 1984.

LaCocque, A. *Daniel in His Time.* Columbia: University of South Carolina Press, 1988.

Smith, J. Z. "Wisdom and Apocalyptic." *Visionaries and Their Apocalypses.* Edited by P. D. Hanson. IRT 4. Philadelphia: Fortress, 1983. Pp. 101–120.

Stone, M. "Revealed Things in Apocalyptical Literature." *Magnalia Dei: The Mighty Acts of God.* Edited by F. M. Cross, W. E. Lemke, and P. D. Miller, Jr. New York: Schocken Books, 1976.

Appendix to Chapter Five

The central concern of the discussion in Chapter 5 is to trace Haggai and Zechariah to a few of their prophetic ancestors and prophetic heirs. The table below sets out the historical relationships of the other biblical prophets. Included are only those prophetic books that are so considered from the perspective of the Christian biblical tradition (see Chapter 1). The dates given are approximate and attempt to place the date of the prophet's ministry, not the book that grew up around the prophet's tradition.[29] All dates are Before the Common Era (BCE).

Prophet	*Date(s)*	*Contemporaneous Events*
Elijah	9th century	Ahab (ca. 869–850)
Elisha	9th century	Syrian wars
Amos	ca. 760–755	Jeroboam II (786–746)
Hosea	ca. 745–733	Invasion of Tiglath-Pileser
Isaiah of Jerusalem	ca. 734–701	Salvation of Jerusalem
Micah	ca. 734–701	Ahaz, Hezekiah
Nahum	ca. 615	Sack of Ninevah
Habakkuk	ca. 609–598	Vassalage to Babylon
Zephaniah	ca. 615–609	Josianic revival
Jeremiah	ca. 609–587	Fall of Jerusalem
Ezekiel	ca. 593–563	Exile
Obadiah	ca. after 586	Exile in Palestine
Second Isaiah	ca. 556–539	Decline of Babylon
Haggai	ca. 520	Darius I/Restore Temple
Zechariah (1–8)	ca. 520–518	Darius I/Restore Temple
Third Isaiah	ca. 522–486	Darius I/Temple
Malachi	ca. 486–465	Xerxes' reign/Jerusalem
Joel	ca. 433–333 (?)	Decline of Persia
Jonah	ca. 433–333 (?)	Decline of Persia/Greek

[29]For these dates refer to J. Blenkinsopp, *A History of Prophecy in Israel*; and J. M. Ward, *Thus Says the Lord* (Nashville, TN: Abingdon, 1991); J. Berquist, *Judaism in Persia's Shadow.*

CHAPTER SIX

The Story of the Temple

Introduction

Review

While prophets did call the people of Judah and Israel back to moral purity, the references within their oracles to the Mosaic law, as such, are few. Prophets do not appear to be either referring to the codes of law or appealing to the authority of Moses. Thus, the summary in Nehemiah is likely an idealistic view of prophets, composed after the official promulgation of the Mosaic law. Nevertheless, the prophetic assertion of Yahweh's righteousness in society is evident in various attitudes toward the Temple. In Isaiah of Jerusalem and Jeremiah, Temple worship is incomplete apart from commitment to a moral lifestyle. As social and political situations changed, and Yahweh's blessing could no longer be realized through traditional social and political institutions, a new prophetic movement rooted in an apocalyptic perspective put off that promise of blessing to a distant future time and a celestial place.

Preview

Since the Temple dominates both post-Exilic narrative and prophetic literature, it is logical to turn next to the Temple's role in the larger story. As with the prophets and the law, the post-Exilic period is a seminal time of rereading older Temple traditions. The book of Ezra-Nehemiah offers an interesting interpretation of the Temple in view of the Chronicler, a near contemporary. But the Chronicler is also rereading the Deuteronomistic perspective on the Temple since the Deuteronomistic History is one of the Chronicler's sources. One of the key points of rereading concerns the problem of legitimizing the Temple. The Chronicler must establish the Temple's legitimacy against other competing Yahwistic Temples in a similar way as the Deuteronomist had done some 150 to 200 years prior. The Temple achieves an even more heightened apocalyptic significance in the hands of the covenanters at Qumran, but it remains for the first-century CE Christian communities to explain how an institution so vital to the Jewish life and story could be abandoned altogether.

David and the Temple: Ezra-Nehemiah and the Chronicler
1 Chronicles 17; 22–29; 2 Chronicles 1–7;
Review Ezra 1–6

Learning Goals

- To understand the relationship between the Davidic king and the institution of the Temple in the post-Exilic setting.
- To understand the socio-historical reasons for the Chronicler's rereading of the Temple.

Guiding Study Exercises

1) List at least three contradictions *within* the Chronicler's story of David's involvement in building the Temple.

2) Write a paragraph explaining the rationale of David's involvement in building the Temple according to 1 Chronicles 17.

3) How do the chapters that follow 1 Chronicles 17 reread this chapter's more ancient understanding of David's role in building the Temple? *Why* might the Chronicler have reread so radically this earlier tradition?

4) In a short essay explain the social text behind 1 Chron 17:14: "but I will confirm him in my house and in my kingdom forever, and his throne shall be established forever."

5) How has the Chronicler's intention to legitimate the enhanced status of the Levites shaped the way he tells the story of David's involvement in the reorganization of the Levites in 1 Chron 23:27–32?

Introduction

Readers recall that the first part of Ezra-Nehemiah's story makes a strong connection between King David and the Temple. It is such a strong connection that one cannot tell the story of the Temple without also attending to the king. King David, who reigned around 1000 BCE (some 550 years before Ezra-Nehemiah), was the ruler who united the northern and southern tribes under one government (2 Samuel 3–4). He also chose Jerusalem as the capital city (2 Sam 5:6–10). He established the city as the religious center by bringing the Ark of the covenant with its tent to reside within the city (2 Sam 6:1–19). He wanted to build a Temple, but it remained for his son Solomon to carry out that dream (2 Sam 7:1–17; 1 Chron 17:1–15). Throughout Ezra-Nehemiah there are references to David's involvement with the Temple, most of which concern that king's establishment of the service of the Temple. Looking back on an isolated verse such as Ezra 3:10 shows us that the priests, Levites, and sons of Asaph (the musicians) serve according to a plan that was established by King David: "When the builders laid the foundation of the temple of the Lord, the priests in their vestments were stationed to praise the Lord with trumpets, and the Levites, the sons of Asaph, with cymbals, according to the directions of King David of Israel" (see also Ezra 8:20, as well as Neh 11:23; 12:24, 36, and 45–46). This particular episode of the story of David's involvement in the Temple, however, only occurs in the later history of 1 and 2 Chronicles. It does not occur in the earlier Deuteronomistic History (Joshua, Judges, Samuel, and Kings). As with Ezra-Nehemiah, 1 and 2 Chronicles were originally one book, having only been separated in the process of translation into Greek and by subsequent use within various communities of faith. Scholars date the book of Chronicles in the same general historical period as Ezra-Nehemiah (c. 400 BCE). So the writer of Ezra-Nehemiah, whether drawing on this later history or not, would nevertheless have had access to the Chronicler's sources and traditions, and he would very likely see things from a similar perspective in that they both shared a common social text.[1]

Summary of the Chronicler's Story of the Temple

Briefly, the materials from 1 Chronicles 17 and 22–29 tell the story of David's initial request to build a permanent Temple for Yahweh through the completion and dedication of that Temple by David's son Solomon. The scope of the Chronicler's History is much larger than that of the Deuteronomistic historian in that it begins with a chronology of Adam (cf. Gen 2:4–24) and stretches through the beginning of kingship in Jerusalem, focusing upon its three great kings, Saul, David, and Solomon. The narrative extends to the period of Cyrus' decree that all Babylonian captives should return to their homelands (see 2 Chron 36:22–23 and Ezra 1:1–3). The reigns of David and Solomon in particular represent a single period in the Chronicler's history. Because of their devotion to matters of proper worship of Yahweh in contrast to their predecessor, Saul, the Chronicler presents David and Solomon as presiding over the period of Israel's national "climax of virtue and achievement."[2] It is in this emphasis upon the close relationship between the Davidic house and the Temple that readers see the Chronicler's deepest theological convictions.

Outline of the Story. The literary text of the Chronicler's story challenges readers in two ways: first, there are apparent contradictions regarding David's involvement in building the Temple; second, acknowledging different sources behind these contradictions, readers must then explain how these later sources are rereading the earlier. 1 Chronicles 17 falls right into the middle of an episode in which the narrative has already depicted David as sympathetic to proper worship. Chapters 13–16 portray David as being largely responsible for setting the building of the Temple into motion. No sooner does he come to the throne in Jerusalem than he brings the Ark of the covenant into the city (13:1–14; 15:1–29). In chapter 17 David requests to build a permanent dwelling place—a Temple—for the portable Ark (17:1). Shortly after Nathan the prophet offers his own blessing on the project, the prophet receives word from Yahweh that, in fact, David is *not* to build a Temple after all. The Temple project must wait for one of David's heirs to accomplish this feat (17:11–15). Two points in this episode are worth noting for future reference.

---

[1]Compare H. G. M. Williamson, *I and II Chronicles* (NCB; Grand Rapids, MI: Eerdmans, 1982)15–17; S. Japhet, *I & II Chronicles* (Louisville, KY: Westminster/ John Knox, 1993) 23–28; P. Ackroyd, *The Chronicler in His Age* (JSOTSS 101; Sheffield: JSOT Press, 1991) 8–86.

[2]S. Japhet, *ibid.,* 10. Japhet further observes that these two characters' lives and reigns parallel and complement each other: "David is the founder and initiator, while Solomon is the executor and culminator of their shared period."

First, note the rationale for preventing David's Temple building. 1 Chronicles 17:5 has Yahweh insisting that he does not want such a house, that he has always lived in a tent, a tabernacle, having always moved about as his people moved about. The contrast between a permanent Temple and a portable tent suggests interesting alternative theologies: in the former case the deity remains in one place; in the latter, the deity moves about to many places. Second, note that this narrative reproduces nearly exactly the version of the story as it stands in the earlier Deuteronomistic History (2 Sam 7:1–17). Chapter 7 of this textbook will revisit this passage concerning kingship. It suffices here simply to observe that one of the Chronicler's sources is surely the much older Deuteronomistic History. On the basis of this older source, David is prevented by the deity from building the Temple.

There is, however, more than one source at work in the Chronicler's history of David's building the Temple: one that favors his involvement, and one that does not. Readers see this in the various explanations for why David does not build the Temple. The chapters between 1 Chronicles 17 and 22 portray David's involvement in wars with surrounding nations. He subdues all of his enemies (18:1–20:8), and as the result of his need to appease Yahweh's anger over his prideful census of the people, he secures Ornan's threshing floor and erects an altar (21:1–22:1). This location on which he erects the altar will become the site on which the Temple eventually will be built. Chapter 22 then portrays David's involvement in the preparations for the Temple his son is to build. It is here the reader discovers that the heir who will build the Temple is, in fact, Solomon. David not only gathers great stores of materials with which to build the Temple, seeing that his son is "young and inexperienced" (v. 5), but charges his son to build the house for Yahweh.

The words of the king's charge to his son in chapter 22 seem to be an expansion of the detail in chapter 17. The words in 22:10 about "building a house for my name," and "He shall be a son to me . . ." parallel 17:12. But notice that the rationale for why David himself is not building the Temple has changed (see Table 6.1). As the king recounts his experience to his son Solomon, he is prevented from building a Temple because the Lord says to him, "You have shed much blood and have waged great wars" (v. 8). How different this is from the rationale in 1 Chronicles 17, drawn from the Deuteronomistic source.

Reading in 2 Chron 2:1–2 brings further surprise in that Solomon is presented here as not only deciding himself to build a Temple, but also gathering the materials for the Temple, despite the work his father has already done on his own initiative. "Solomon decided to build a temple for the name of the Lord, and a royal palace for himself. Solomon conscripted seventy thousand laborers and eighty thousand stonecutters in the hill country, with three thousand six hundred to oversee them." There are only the briefest references to the work of gathering that David has already done (2 Chron 2:7, 14). Clearly, this episode on Solomon seems to assume that David did not actually have much to do with the Temple, just as 1 Chronicles 17 suggests. The Chronicler appears to have drawn upon and included two views regarding David's association with the building of the Temple. The one minimizes David's involvement in the Temple-building process, corresponding to the Deuteronomistic History, the other maximizes David's involvement and is distinctive to the Chronicler.

The passages of 1 Chronicles 23–27 are of singular interest, therefore, for answering questions regarding David's advance preparation for the Temple service. These chapters of the Chronicler's narrative portray David as the organizer of the Jerusalem clergy (23–26), as well as organizer of the people of Israel themselves (27:1–34). Chapter 23:1 begins with the notices that

Table 6.1

David and the Temple

1 Chronicles 17:6	1 Chronicles 22:8
Wherever I have moved about among all Israel, did I ever speak a word with any of the judges of Israel, whom I commanded to shepherd my people, saying, "Why have you not built me a house of cedar?"	But the word of the Lord came to me, saying, "You have shed much blood and have waged great wars; you shall not build a house to my name, because you have shed so much blood in my sight on the earth."

"David was old and full of days" and he "made his son Solomon king over Israel." Observe also that David orders the roles of the Levites (23:3–32, 24:20–30), the priests, (24:1–19), the singers (25:1–31), the gatekeepers (26:1–19), the treasurers (26:20–28), and the judges and officers (26:29–32). He then goes on to organize the people themselves by divisions (27:1–15), according to the leaders of the tribes (27:16–24), and he then appoints stewards and counselors (27:25–34). Reading this section against 1 Chronicles 17 must surely cause readers to wonder how one who was directed *not* to build the Temple could be so extensively involved in administratively building and organizing the Temple and its service despite the Lord's command. But further, at Solomon's coronation and then at the completion of the Temple, there is the greater curiosity that Solomon says that *he* planned much of this project *on his own*.

1 Chronicles 28–29 depicts a climax to David's life. Here he publicly commences the building of the Temple by retelling his story in a public address (28:1–10) and by transferring to his son his *written* plan of the Temple, which came from Yahweh (28:11–21). David's reign concludes with the listing of his many contributions to the Temple, his blessing of the Lord, and, finally, his making Solomon his successor as king. Readers simply cannot conclude these passages without knowing that David played the key role in conceptualizing, planning, and underwriting the entire project. And yet readers know that at least one version of the Temple story, 1 Chronicles 17, understands that David is absolutely *not* to build the Temple at all. Chapter 7 of this textbook investigates the absence of these details in the Deuteronomistic historian's version (2 Sam 7:1–17). The later version that is incorporated into the Chronicler's History is clearly *rereading* David's involvement in Temple building. How can the pious historian do this? Two important dimensions of the Chronicler's social text provide insight.

King and Temple. Several social texts coalesce to shape the literary text just encountered. First is the belief that kings were responsible for building national temples. This notion taps deeply into one of the most common ancient understandings of the role of kingship.[3] The implication is that kings were deeply involved in the founding and maintenance of national worship.

---

[3]William Riley, *King and Cultus in Chronicles* (Sheffield: JSOT Press, 1993) 60. Riley's study explores the role of cult upon the Chronicler's desire to retell the story of Israelite kingship.

The Chronicler's story therefore reflects a much broader socio-historical **ideology** in portraying David as the virtual founder of Israelite worship, even though his son Solomon is the one who actually builds the first Temple in Jerusalem. What is more, David is blessed with the promise that through his lineage there will continue this connection between kingship and worship. A closer look at 1 Chron 17:10–15 reveals the priorities given to the Temple above the king, a priority made more significant by the fact that at the time when the Chronicler is actually writing (post-Exilic, late Persian period) the Davidic dynasty had longed passed from the stage.

When Yahweh rejects David's request to build a Temple, he promises that, "The LORD will build you [David] a house. I will raise up your offspring after you, one of your own sons, and I will establish his kingdom" (17:11). The establishment of David's "house" is given new and different significance by Yahweh. The following verse (v. 12) claims that this son will build a house for Yahweh and further declares that Yahweh will establish this son's throne. The promise continues with an image of the relationship between king and deity as that between father and son—the king is the son of the deity!—and the deity's love shall never be taken away from his son. But notice that in this promise the kingdom is understood more broadly than as a mere political kingdom. Verse 14 portrays Yahweh as saying that this Davidic kingdom is actually Yahweh's kingdom and Yahweh's house: "But I will confirm him in *my* house [the Temple] and in *my* kingdom forever, and his throne shall be established forever." Again, Chapter 7 of this textbook will consider this passage in greater detail.

For now, observe how the promise to establish the throne of David's lineage forever finds fulfillment in the context of references to *God's* house and *God's* kingdom. With these as the concluding words of the promise, it begins to look as though Yahweh's house, the Temple, has pre-eminence over the Davidic political kingdom. The political kingdom of David and his lineage ("house") exists forever only in the context of the Temple's existence. In other words, Yahweh's promise to David not only has political significance, but deeply abiding religious and spiritual significance as well. According to the Chronicler, the Davidic kings were to preside over a religious and spiritual kingdom as well as a political kingdom. David's extensive involvement in the establishment of the **cult** (1 Chronicles 23–27) fits in well with the Chronicler's view of what is really important. Worship and the ongoing service of the Temple is at least as important as the king himself.

David and Moses. A second connection between king and Temple is sought by the Chronicler in his association of David with Moses. In this late history there are frequent appeals to Moses' law as a source of authority. Even in the materials preceding chapter 17—materials that depict David bringing the Ark to Jerusalem—David's activities are in concert with the law of Moses, from the Levites carrying the Ark (15:15) to the offering of proper sacrifice by the priests (16:39–40). The very plan of the Temple that David hands over to Solomon is said to be "in writing at the Lord's direction" (28:19), a phrase that may allude to the Mosaic authority of these kingly actions.[4] The story in Ezra-Nehemiah, despite its various references to Davidic involvement in the establishment of the Temple service, also cites Moses as an authority for these actions. Zerubbabel, for instance, offers up burnt offerings "as prescribed in the law of Moses the man of God" (Ezra 3:2; see also Neh 10:28–30). What is more, the summary of Israel's story in

---

[4]Certainly this is the way the verse is read by S. J. De Vries, "Moses and David as Cult Founders in Chronicles," *JBL* 107/4 (1988) 622; S. Japhet, *I & II Chronicles*, 497–498, goes into greater detail regarding the ambiguities of the language.

Nehemiah gives significant weight to the ordinances, laws, statutes, and commandments that Moses receives upon Mt. Sinai (Neh 9:13–14, 16, 26, 29). Clearly, in both Ezra-Nehemiah as well as Chronicles, there is a cultic tradition that has already been laid down, and David is acting within and upon this tradition. To put it another way, the texts portray *both* Moses and David as having some role in the founding of Israelite national worship. The question is why? Why give so much cultic authority to a political figure like David when, according to our stories, Moses has already laid down proper cultic guidelines?

The answer may lie in what one scholar sees as the Chronicler's greatest theological innovation: that of telling ancient Israel's story by validating *both* of the two great biblical theological traditions, the Davidic-Zion tradition and the Mosaic-Sinai tradition, without presenting one over the other.[5] Chapter 2 of this text has already indicated that Deuteronomic theology emphasizes the centrality of the law of Moses that was given by Yahweh at Mt. Sinai. Scholars refer to this theological emphasis as the *Moses-Sinai tradition*. By contrast, there is a tradition, also in the Deuteronomistic History, the prophet Isaiah of Jerusalem, and some of the Psalms, that seems not to know anything about Moses and the law of Sinai. Rather, it emphasizes Jerusalem (Zion), Yahweh's choice of this city as his dwelling place, and the king as Yahweh's son and vice-regent (see chap. 7). Scholars refer to this tradition as the *Davidic-Zion tradition*. While there are reasons in the Chronicler's social text for idealizing this Davidic-Solomonic period (see below), at the very least it accounts for the Davidic-Zion theology that permeates the Chronicler's story. Readers might be surprised at the Chronicler's combination, however, in view of the diminishment of kings and kingship in the Deuteronomistic History, the Chronicler's central source. Kings (including David and his heirs) are treated in that source as any other member of the nation of Israel, that is, as bound by the Mosaic law (see Deut 17:14–20). The phrase "law of Moses" only occurs six times in the entire Deuteronomistic History (Josh 8:31, 32; 23:6; 1 Kgs 2:3; 2 Kgs 14:6; 23:5). Four of those occurrences are spoken by the Deuteronomistic narrator, who makes judgments on the kings; only twice does the phrase occur on the lips of a character, one of whom is indeed David (Josh 8:31; 1 Kgs 2:3). At the literary level this absence implies for the Deuteronomistic historian a poetic explanation for the fall of Jerusalem: The people did not keep the law of Moses. On the other hand, since it is David who admonishes Solomon to keep the law of Moses, this constitutes justification for the Chronicler's bringing together the Mosaic and Davidic traditions around the character of David.

The Chronicler's Social Text

If it is accurate to think of the Chronicler as bringing two great theologies together in retelling Israel's story, readers must ask what precipitates such theological harmonizing. The following discussion will argue that three specific aspects of the Chronicler's social text provide the warrants for this late historian's theological commitments. First, there is a need to reemphasize the legitimacy of the Jerusalem Temple. Even though Jerusalem's Temple had been rebuilt under the aegis of the Persian court, it is clear that for the Jews of the **Diaspora**, Jerusalem was not the exclusive Jewish shrine. Chapter 3 has already noted that the Jewish military colony at Elephantine, in Egypt, had its own temple in the fifth century BCE. When it was destroyed by the Egyptians, the

[5]P. R. Ackroyd, "The Theology of the Chronicler," in *The Chronicler in His Age* (JSOTSup 101; Sheffield: JSOT Press, 1991).

community of Elephantine sought permission from Jerusalem to rebuild it. No such permission was granted. It is difficult to speculate on the meaning of the absence of any response to the requests. It suffices here simply to say that the question of Jerusalem's exclusive right to function as Judaism's central shrine was open for debate as a result of Jews being scattered all over the world.

Readers know that such questions of authority plagued the restoration process from the very beginning. While it is not clear who the groups referred to in Ezra 4:1–4 were, it is clear that the question of religious exclusivism reached beyond the immediate family of returned exiles. The question of the legitimacy of those who had remained in the land of Palestine was not settled. Archeological discoveries indicate that another temple was built on Mt. Gerizim sometime in the fourth century BCE, and ancient sources indicate that this was the **Samaritan** temple.[6] Many scholars believe that this temple was the outcome of conflict between the exiles returning to Judah and those residents of **Samaria** who had been excluded from the restoration process by Zerubbabel. While it is unlikely that the actual building of this temple to the north of Jerusalem was a factor in the polemic behind the Chronicler's emphasis upon the legitimacy of Jerusalem, such conflict is certainly in its formative period during the days of the Chronicler's writing.[7] Thus, it makes sense from a polemical standpoint to marshal all of the traditional material possible in favor of the Jerusalem Temple. If both David and Moses indicate that Jerusalem is the exclusive place of worship, then the Chronicler's case is made more convincingly.

The real challenge for the Chronicler was to legitimize the Jerusalem Temple as the central and unique place of worship without, however, making it unnecessarily exclusive. By reinvoking the old traditions of David and Solomon to redefine the meaning of the Chronicler's present existence, he called to mind the last day when the Northern and Southern kingdoms were united. Although the Temple was in Jerusalem of Judah, it was nevertheless to be the Temple for all Israel. This was important since there was more at stake than competition from other temples.

The second aspect of the Chronicler's social text concerns the problem of social and political fragmentation. The Babylonian Exile had redistributed both population and social classes. The first deportation of 597 BCE saw the king, Jehoiachin, deported along with the upper classes of Jerusalem and the vessels of the Temple. Only the "poorest people of the land" remained (2 Kgs 24:14). The second deportation, some nine years later (2 Kgs 25:1), accompanied the burning of the Temple and palaces (2 Kgs 25:9) and the removal of the people who remained in the city. Again, the text notes that "the captain of the guard left some of the poorest people of the land to be vinedressers and tillers of the soil" (2 Kgs 25:12). In both instances of deportation, the text mentions that the poorest strata of the population, the farmers who lived around Jerusalem, were left behind. Indeed little is said about these people who were not deported. But, there were enough of these people to warrant the Babylonian king's appointment of a governor, Gedaliah (2 Kgs 25:22). And even though some of that population fled to Egypt after assassinating the appointed governor (2 Kgs 25:22–26), there was a continuing presence of people who survived in the region.

There is no way to be certain about the fates of these people. One scholar believes that this population continued to survive, albeit in a fashion radically different from the days prior to the

[6]Josephus, *Jewish Antiquities,* 11.346–47.

[7]G. Widengren, "The Samaritan schism and the construction of the Samaritan temple," in *Israelite and Judean History* (eds., J. H. Hayes, J. M. Miller; London: SCM Press, 1977) 511–514.

A Closer Look: The Samaritan Temple. It was in the early Hellenistic period that residents of Samaria were displaced to Shechem. On a sight nearby, Mt. Gerizim, these residents built a temple. The site, Mt. Gerizim, is mentioned in Deuteronomy 27:11 as the location where a Mosiac covenant ceremony had once taken place, thus providing scriptural authority for this temple. This group also produced a version of the Pentateuch (called "The Samaritan Pentateuch"), appropriately interpreted so as to justify the existence of their temple. Were these Jews? Most likely their alternative temple would imply their dissociation with Jerusalem, and may indicate their attempt to identify with the "true Israel." However, it is probably appropriate to regard them as simply one expression of the several Judaisms that existed in the Hellenistic period.

For further reading, J. Rogerson and P. Davies. *The Old Testament World.* Englewood Cliffs, NJ: Prentice Hall, 1989. Pp. 343; F. Murphy. *The Religious World of Jesus.* Nashville, TN: Abingdon, 1991. Pp. 278–80.

For more advanced study, R. J. Coggins. *The Samaritans and Jews.* Oxford/Atlanta, GA: Basil Blackwell/John Knox Press, 1975; H. H. Rowley. "Sanballet and the Samaritan Temple." *BJRL* 38 (1955–56) 166–198.

deportation. It is likely that these survivors continued a meager economic subsistence and even continued their religious practice, although without a Temple. Over the period of decades before the exiles began to return to Judah and Jerusalem, new patterns of government, worship, economy, and even land ownership would surely have been established by these people. Thus, when exiles began to return to Judah, they did not return to an unpopulated and pristine situation. Rather, there were people there, who had established life in a new way. These new ways and new patterns of living would have been quite different from the memories preserved by the people—the upper classes of people—who survived in exile. Upon their return to Judah, the clash between memories and the real lives of survivors surely contributed to the conflicts described in the memoirs of Ezra and Nehemiah.[8] Further, after the deportations of 597 and 587 BCE, it is not clear what the relationship between the appointed governor in Jerusalem and the province of Samaria was. If Judah fell under the government of Samaria, as it might well have, then the Persian establishment of Judah as an independent province created further conflict and division.[9]

In any event, vestiges of the division between the northern and southern regions (Samaria and Jerusalem), and divisions between nobility and commoner, rich and poor, remained even after the restoration of Jerusalem had begun. The Temple became for the Chronicler a religious symbol of unity. In the process of asserting its uniqueness and centrality, it also was a means of bringing all people together. It reasserted the idea of "all Israel" gathered before the deity.

The third aspect of the Chronicler's social text concerns the conciliation between Levite and Zadokite. Nothing symbolizes the Chronicler's emphasis on reunification more than his urgent rereading of the history of these two priestly families that served in David's court. Recall

[8]J. Berquist, *Judaism in Persia's Shadow* (Minneapolis, MN: Fortress Press, 1995) 26–27.

[9]B. Oded, "Judah During the Exilic Period," in *Israelite and Judean History* , 476–480.

that the Chronicler has David assigning roles of Temple service to *both* Levites and Zadokites (1 Chron 23:2–24:31). The Chronicler's main literary source, the Deuteronomistic History, has only one of the two families serving in the Temple, the Zadokites. Even though David appointed both priestly families to serve (2 Sam 8:15–17), the Levites, under the leadership of Abiathar at that time, were expelled from service when Solomon came to the throne (1 Kgs 2:26–27). Thus, the Levites have no place in the official story of the monarchy, according to the Deuteronomistic historian. The problem of their absence goes beyond blood to geography, though. It may well be that the Levitical families of priests have their origins in the shrines to the North, while the Zadokites are tied to the South.[10] In this case, David's rationale for having two families of priests, each representing the political regions the king was trying to represent, is clear. The two families provide ownership of the Temple for the different parts of the land. By expelling one family, Solomon was excluding the northern priests, their traditions, and their people from full ownership in the Temple.[11]

The extent of the conflict between the two priestly families, which the Chronicler sought to address through his history, is further evident within the Tetrateuch. Some of the **double traditions** within the Tetrateuch differ with each other in relationship to these two different priestly perspectives. For instance, a comparison of Numbers 16 and Lev 10:1–7 reveals similar stories that favor one or the other of the priestly families. Readers are cautioned at the outset, however, since the passage in Num 16:1–40 is itself a conflation of two different narrative episodes of rebellion. In 16:1 there are both Levites and Reubenites identified; in v. 2 they "confront" Moses while in v. 3 they assemble against Moses and Aaron. The confrontation initiated by Korah and the Levites takes place in front of the tabernacle; the confrontation with Dathan and Abiram, the Reubenites, takes place at their dwellings (vv. 12; 25–27). Korah's controversy with Moses is over the question of relative cultic authority between priest (Aaron's family, Zadokite ancestry) and Levite, v. 8. With the Reubenites, the holy offering is not an issue, vv. 12–14. All of this is simply to explain that readers must compare the appropriate parts of the story in Numbers 16 with similar parts in Lev 10:1–7.

In this case, readers see that the two passages address the same topic, but resolve it with two different results. In both there is a test to see who might bring an offering of fire to Yahweh (Num 16:6–9; 15–19; Lev 10:1–3). In Numbers 16 it is the Levites who are rebuked; in Lev 10:1–7 it is two families of **Aaronides** who are rebuked. It is not difficult to suppose that each family would preserve the version of its history that favored itself the most. This hypothesis in itself is a firm reminder of the role the self-text plays in reading sacred traditions. That both stories are included in the Tetrateuch implies that it too was composed at a time when conciliation between the two families of priests was mandated.

The Chronicler's history, quite apart from the Tetrateuchal sources, addresses the controversies between these priestly families by writing the Levites back into the story and having David assign them a viable role in the service of the Temple. Again, by appealing to David, the king whose reputation the Chronicler restores, the historian achieves the necessary legitimization of the Temple in the context of fragmenting social and political stress.[12]

---

[10]Thus, F. M. Cross, "The Priestly Houses of Early Israel," in *Canaanite Myth and Hebrew Epic* (Cambridge: Harvard University Press, 1973) 195–215.

[11]*Ibid.,* 207–208.

[12]See also R. Braun, *1 Chronicles* (WBC 14; Waco, TX: Word Books, 1986) xxv–xxxviii.

The City of David. Archaeological reconstructions of the various layers of civilization in the vicinity of Ophel, the old City of David, located today about 300 yards south of medieval Jerusalem. (Chance and Horne)

The Temple in the Deuteronomistic Historian's View
2 Kings 22–23; 2 Chronicles 34–35; Deuteronomy 12

Learning Goals

• To understand that the Deuteronomic perspective on the centralization of Temple worship is a radical rereading of still more ancient traditions.

• To understand the distinction between cult purification and cult centralization.

• To understand some of the divergencies between Priestly perspectives on the Temple and those of the Deuteronomist.

Guiding Study Exercises

1) Write two paragraphs identifying and explaining the relationship between the Chronicler's and the Deuteronomistic historian's accounts of Josiah's reforms.

2) List the specific reforms carried out by Josiah in 2 Kings 23 and identify the specific commandments from Deuteronomy that these reforms reflect.

3) What relative significance does the book of the law have in the two accounts of Josiah's reforms?

4) Explain and illustrate from the book of Deuteronomy the idea of desacralization. Reflect upon some possible implications such a movement might have for modern readers.

In rereading the past for his post-Exilic community, the Chronicler elevates the significance of the age of David and Solomon, attempting to revitalize the importance of the Jerusalem Temple in order to reestablish the identity of the people. It is not that the Temple is the only means for the Chronicler of defining official faith in Yahweh. He, too, knows that ritual alone is empty unless there is some engagement of the individual's own faith and heart-felt religion (e.g. 2 Chron 15:1–7; 16:7–10). Still, the Temple is a central symbol of God's presence with his people, and of who may belong to the community in the Second Temple period.

The question of the Temple's centrality and uniqueness becomes less clear if readers compare some of the Chronicler's material with that of the Deuteronomistic historian. For while the Chronicler's social text was one in which the Temple was of necessity both central and unique in the absence of both king and state, the pre-Exilic age in which the Deuteronomic movement begins produces a literature where the Temple's centrality and uniqueness is being defined on quite different grounds. A comparison of the two historians' different treatments of Josiah's reforms raises the questions that connect with the larger and more ancient Deuteronomic movement in pre-Exilic Israel.

Josiah and his Reforms: 2 Kings 22–23

The parallel text in the Chronicler's history, 2 Chronicles 34–35, should be read simultaneously with the focal passage in 2 Kings. The Chronicler begins the story with introductory material (vv. 1–2), then moves to the eighth and twelfth years of Josiah's reign as the time when the king begins to "seek Yahweh" (v. 3) and purge Jerusalem of foreign cults (vv. 3–7). The purge of foreign cults extends well beyond the boundaries of Judah to land that would have been taken over from Assyrian domination in the North (see below). Then the narrative moves to the eighteenth year when, in the course of repairing the Jerusalem Temple (34:8–13), the king's servants discover "the book of the law of the Lord given through Moses" (34:14). The discovery of the law code provokes repentance in the king (34:19–21), inquiry of the Lord through the prophetess Huldah (34: 22–28), reading of the book before all the people of Judah and Jerusalem (34: 29–30), and a renewal of covenant to keep the law (34:31–33). The activities of Josiah's eighteenth year (35:18) conclude with a celebration of the Passover of the sort that had not been seen, according to the Chronicler, since the days of Samuel (35:16–19). However, readers should notice the extensive involvement of the Levites (35:3–6, 8, 14–15) in keeping with the Chronicler's own understanding of their role in the Temple (1 Chronicles 23).

The version in 2 Kings 22–23, the Chronicler's main source, provides a similar, but in some respects quite different, account of the events. Reading the two versions in comparison, the most immediate major difference is that the Deuteronomistic historian jumps immediately to king Josiah's eighteenth year, the year of the discovery of the law code in the Temple (22:3–20). Further, in the Deuteronomistic account, the reforms, which take place in the Chronicler's twelfth year, are *all* enacted in the Deuteronomistic eighteenth year. The latter part of the narrative, 2 Kings 23, is devoted to the summary of these reforms, with but the briefest reference to the keeping of Passover (23:21–23). Interestingly, the Deuteronomistic account attributes the keeping of the Passover to the lawbook discovered in the Temple with the formula, "as prescribed in this book of the covenant" (23:21–22). No such attribution is made in the Chronicler's version.

While these brief comparisons do not nearly exhaust the variations and more nuanced differences between the two accounts, readers see enough at the level of the literary text to suspect that the social text of the Deuteronomistic historian is quite different from that of the Chronicler. Clearly, the Deuteronomistic narrative structures the story so that the reforms are unambiguously related to the law book. The king hears the words of the book of the law, repents, renews the covenant, and only then begins the reforms. The narrative makes this connection to law explicit in two places. In 2 Kgs 23:21 the Passover is observed because of the words of the law book. The implication in the Deuteronomistic History is that the Passover has not been kept because the law has been lost. The historian is even more directive in the summary passage in 23:24, where he says, "so that he established the words of the law that were written in the book that the priest Hilkiah had found in the house of the Lord." This statement seems to sum up the Deuteronomistic slant on Josiah's reforms: they came about as a result of the discovery of the law book, a recommitment to covenant, and the king's devotion. By contrast, the Chronicler does not base the reforms on the law. The reforms begin *before* the law code is discovered. The Passover, though significant, is no more significant from that observed in Hezekiah's day (2 Chronicles 30). For the Chronicler the law code is discovered as a *result* of the purification of the Temple, almost as a reward.

It is important that readers first make a very important distinction between certain of King Josiah's activities, whether reading the Chronicler or the Deuteronomist. There is a difference between his purifying of the Temple and the policies he established that made it the central and unique place of worship for the nation. Several of Josiah's royal predecessors had on previous occasions taken measures to purify Jerusalem and the Temple of foreign cults. For instance, Asa (913–873 BCE) is said to have done "what was right in the sight of the Lord" by the Deuteronomistic historian (2 Kgs 15:11). He purified the Temple by removing male cultic prostitutes, idols, and images. However, the historian concludes by saying, "The high places were not taken away." Similarly, King Jehoash (837–800 BCE) is also regarded as one who "did what was right in the sight of the Lord all his days" (2 Kgs 12:2). Nevertheless, the Deuteronomist says, "the high places were not taken away; the people continued to sacrifice and make offerings on the high places" (2 Kgs 12:3). Josiah's reforms are singularly important because, in addition to purging the Temple of foreign cults, he also removes the high places. Josiah was not the only king who sought to attempt to remove the high places, however. His grandfather, Hezekiah, also purified the Temple and took away the high places (2 Kgs 18:1–8). Hezekiah's reform failed, though, because his son Manasseh "rebuilt the high places that his father Hezekiah had destroyed" (2 Kgs 21:4). But Josiah's purification is associated with both a removal of high places and the discovery of the book of the law in the Temple.

Centralization and Religion in Israel until Josiah. This perspective that values the principle of centralization, that is, that Yahweh is to be worshipped at one unique location, is itself a rather remarkable rereading of more ancient religious traditions. The Deuteronomistic History itself preserves traditions of *lawful* Yahwistic worship at multiple local shrines, many of which are also designated "high places." The occurrence and narrative treatment of the religion at these places imply that worship at such shrines was at one time acceptable.

It is difficult to summarize briefly all of the worship practices of ancient Israelites, but a few textual excerpts illustrate the diversity of Yahwistic worship that flourished long before Josiah's reforms and centralization. Readers will observe that one of the most revered prophets of ancient Israel, Samuel, offered sacrifice in his home town in "the land of Zuph" (1 Sam 9:5). The text (NRSV) refers to this as a "shrine," but the Hebrew word is *bama* (1 Sam 9:13), which is also translated "high place." It is the same word used in 2 Kgs 23:5, 8, and 15 as the object of Josiah's destruction. There the word is translated "high place." However, readers encountering the narrative in 1 Samuel 9 for the first time would not get any indication that there was something unlawful about Samuel's offering of sacrifice on behalf of his village. Likewise, David's son Solomon, who built the Temple, made offerings at a high place. Gibeon was the site at which Solomon offered "a thousand burnt offerings on that altar" (1 Kgs 3:4). And then, the narrative relates that Yahweh appeared to Solomon in a dream by night to invite Solomon to make a request of Yahweh.[13] Of course, the narrative makes clear in 3:2 that, while the people in Solomon's day were themselves "sacrificing at the high places," it was because no house had yet been built for the name of the Lord. Nevertheless, it is evident that these local shrines, of which there were many, were legitimate at one time.

Even after the Temple was built by Solomon in Jerusalem, there were legitimate shrines at which to worship Yahweh. They were not high places to be sure, but their existence and legitimacy gives expression to the legitimacy of worshipping Yahweh at sites other than Jerusalem. For instance, in the story of Elijah's contest with prophets of the pagan Baal cult (1 Kgs 18:1–40), the prophet Elijah himself builds an altar at which to make sacrifice to Yahweh. Elijah's deity, Yahweh, consumes the sacrifice in the presence of both Baal worshippers and Yahweh worshippers and thus legitimizes Elijah as prophet and his message of the exclusive worship of Yahweh. There is no hint, however, that Elijah has made an illegal altar.

A Closer Look: Cultic Sites and the Sacred. Worship sites were chosen in antiquity because of their association with the sacred. The term *sacred* implies the idea of separateness or the state of being set apart from the ordinary or profane. Thus, both in space and in time, worship appropriates the idea of the sacred. Space becomes sacred by virtue of a deity's self revelation. In the Bible individuals establish altars because they have had some experience with the deity in a certain place. In religions where deities were associated with the heavens, heights logically put worshippers in closer proximity to their deities. In religions where the deity could manifest him or herself in natural phenomena such as trees (e.g., Gen 35:4; Josh 24:26), waters (e.g., Gen 16:13–14; 24:62; 25:11), volcanic mountains (Exod 3:1–6), etc., such places also could be identified as sacred. Thus, the impulse to build altars on sacred spaces should come as no surprise. In view of this understanding of the sacred and this practice of establishing altars where individuals experience the sacred, what is even more surprising is the attempt to curtail and confine the experience of the sacred to only one space.

For further study, R. DeVaux. *Ancient Israel.* London: Darton, Longman & Todd, 1961. Pp. 274–288.

For more advanced study, F. M. Cross, "The Religion of Canaan and the God of Israel." *Canaanite Myth and Hebrew Epic.* Cambridge, MA: Harvard University Press, 1974. Pp. 1–76; D. N. Freedman, " 'Who is Like Thee Among the Gods?' The Religion of Early Israel." *Ancient Israelite Religion.* Edited by P. Miller, P. Hanson, and S. McBride. Philadelphia: Fortress, 1987. Pp. 315–335.

---

[13]See R. DeVaux, *Ancient Israel* (London: Darton, Longman & Todd, 1961) 287–288.

The ancient city of Arad, some 15 miles south of Hebron, was an important fortification in the south (Josh 12:14; Jdg 1:16). The existence of an altar within the city, depicted in this photo, is evidence that Jerusalem was not always the sole location for the worship of Yawheh. (Chance and Horne)

Even the stories of the patriarchs in the Tetrateuch include episodes that take place at important cultic sites. Abraham, as well as his sons Isaac and Jacob, is frequently erecting shrines where God was manifested through some natural sign. In Gen 12:6–7, Abraham stops at Shechem to erect a shrine at the "Oak of Moreh." This shrine continues to play a significant role as a worship center for several generations in several episodes of the patriarchal narratives. Jacob also builds a shrine at Shechem (Gen 33:18–20), as well as at Bethel (Gen 35:5–8; see 28:18–22). Still later, in the episode of Israel's conquering of the land of Canaan, Joshua requires at Shechem that the people who are inheriting the land put aside all of their idols to other deities (Josh 24:21–24). What is more, he buries the bones of Joseph at that very cultic site (Josh 24:32).

These are only a few of the many shrines devoted to Yahweh across Palestine and throughout the biblical story. Space prevents references to other significant shrines. The point is that the Deuteronomistic historian begins to place a value on centralization of worship in Jerusalem in the wake of an extensive tradition of Yahwistic worship at many local shrines.

The Archaeological Evidence of Multiple Shrines. Various archaeological digs in Israel have helped to illuminate the social text behind these biblical references to multiple shrines. While archaeologists are not able to reconstruct every aspect of the religion practiced in antiquity, that there are religious artifacts at all provides further evidence that the worship of Yahweh at sites other than Jerusalem was understood as the norm. For instance, inscriptions at Kuntillet 'Ajrud, a small Judean village between Gaza and Elath occupied during the period of the Israelite and

Judean monarchies, indicate that Yahweh was worshipped in this local setting. In one inscription dating from the eighth century BCE, the divine name *Yahweh* occurs in a formula that implies the local understanding of Yahweh as a manifestation of the national deity. The specific formula, a blessing formula, includes the deity name (DN) plus a geographical name (GN) in a genitive relationship (indicating possession). Thus, one inscription reads, "Yahweh of Samaria;" another, "Yahweh of Teman."[14] Though these may have been manifestations of one national deity, it is not difficult to see how the various geographical designations could lead to the belief that they were independent deities because of the deity's association with that place.

The references to Yahweh at Kuntillet 'Ajrud do not necessarily imply that Yahweh was the only deity worshipped. The association of the deity names with the term *'asherah* in the inscriptions at least raises the question about the possibility that, as with the Canaanite **pantheon**, Yahweh had a consort. The meaning of the term is the deciding factor and is open for debate, to be sure. Some scholars note that 'asherah was a goddess in Canaanite texts, and was the consort of 'El, the chief god of the Canaanite pantheon. Since the formulas at 'Ajrud offer blessing to the deity "and to his/its 'asherah," it is not difficult to infer that the blessing is directed to both the deity, in this case Yahweh, and the consort. However, other scholars argue that the possessive form implies that the 'asherah is a thing and not a deity. Thus, an alternate view is that the 'asherah is some kind of cultic object associated with the deity of the shrine.[15]

The biblical story attests to both an understanding of 'asherah as a deity as well as some kind of cultic object at the shrine. King Asa, who purified the Jerusalem cult (see above), also deposed the queen mother because "she had made an abominable image for 'asherah" (1 Kgs 15:13). It is not clear what the image was. Since 'asherah was a fertility goddess, there is speculation that the image may have been a phallus or a figurine with exaggerated female genitalia.[16] Nevertheless, it is clear that the reference to 'asherah is to more than an object. Likewise, in the story of Elijah and the pagan prophets there is a reference to "400 prophets of 'asherah" (1 Kgs 18:19). Here again, the context makes clear that these prophets are servants to a deity, not to a sacred object.

On the other hand, looking to the reforms of Hezekiah, the only king preceding Josiah who removed the high places, there is a reference to the king's cutting down the 'asherah ("the sacred pole," 2 Kgs 18:4). In this context these are objects that have some function in the context of the shrine. Likewise, Manasseh, Josiah's father, rebuilds the high places and makes an 'asherah (2 Kgs 21:3). The passage is not referring to a deity as such, but, again, some kind of object.

The Deuteronomic Law and Centralization: Deuteronomy 12:1–32

Part of the social text of the pre-Exilic Deuteronomistic History (Dtr[1])[17] includes the legislation contained in the book of Deuteronomy. The narrative in 2 Kings 22–23, indeed, implies that there

---

[14]See P. K. McCarter, Jr., "The Religion of the Israelite Monarchy," in *Ancient Israelite Religion* (eds., P. Miller, P. Hanson, S. D. McBride; Philadelphia: Fortress, 1987) 137–156.

[15]*Ibid.,* 143–144.

[16]G. H. Jones, *1 & 2 Kings* (2 vols.; NCB; Grand Rapids, MI: Eerdmans, 1984) 1. 283–284.

[17]The broad scholarly consensus continues to be that the Deuteronomistic History was composed in at least two stages: the first was pre-Exilic and dated from the reforms of Josiah around 622 BCE; the second was Exilic and dates from after the destruction of Jerusalem and the release of King Jehoiachin in 561 BCE (2 Kgs 25:27). See F. M. Cross, "The Themes of the Book of Kings and the Structure of the Deuteronomistic History," in *Canaanite Myth and Hebrew Epic,* 274–289.

was a recently discovered law code upon which the reforms of the king were based. Contemporary scholarship has hypothesized that the book that was found was itself part of the law code that is contained in the present Deuteronomy 12–26.

This hypothesis derives chiefly from the strong intertextual relationship between the instructions in Deuteronomy and the reforms of Josiah recorded in the 2 Kings 23 narrative. For instance, Josiah abolishes the 'asherim (2 Kgs 23:4, 6, 7 and 14) as instructed in Deut 7:5; 12:3; 16:21; he removes the vessels made for the host of heaven (2 Kgs 23:4 and 5), which corresponds to Deut 17:3; he eliminates sacred prostitution (2 Kgs 23:7), corresponding to Deut 23:17–18; he defiled the cult devoted to Molech (2 Kgs 23:10), as instructed in Deut 12:31 and 18:10; and, while this list is not exhaustive, one further significant act is his observation of Passover in Jerusalem (2 Kgs 23:22–23), in accordance with Deut 16:1–8.[18] The observation of Passover is especially significant in relationship to the question of centralization since the feast had originally been one that was observed in local family groups (Exod 12:1–13, 21–27).

The emphasis on centralization of worship, thus localizing Yahwistic worship to the confines of the Jerusalem Temple, is actually a ***desacralizing*** move rather than the opposite.[19] In other words, the effect of dismantling the high places and deposing the local priests who served at local shrines around the countryside was one of *withdrawing* religious significance from those shrines and all of the activities associated with them, including some that pertained to the Temple itself. Several examples serve to illustrate this point. Note the statement in Deut 12:5 that the "place" at which people should worship is made sacred because Yahweh's "name" dwells there. This notion, referred to frequently as *name theology,* stands out in contrast to the belief that the deity himself lives in a Temple. For Deuteronomic theology, Yahweh does not live in a house, but in the heavens. The purpose of the Temple is not so much to meet God there, but to offer prayer.

In light of this desacralizing perspective, several traditional aspects of Israelite religion are reread by the Deuteronomic school. For instance, in the Priestly traditions the Ark of the covenant is a portable seat or throne upon which Yahweh sits as he travels about with his people. The book of Numbers narrates how the Ark goes before the nation to disperse its enemies (Num 10:33–36). Failure to take the Ark into battle was failure to follow Yahweh and spelled certain defeat (Num 14:39–45). But to the Deuteronomist the Ark is nothing more than a box in which to carry the tablets of the Mosaic law (Deut 10:1–5). All of its significance as the portable throne of Yahweh is removed. Sacrifice in the Temple is likewise awarded a different significance.

Sacrifices are not for the deity himself. In Leviticus, again part of the Priestly traditions, the sacrifices are "the food of their God" (Lev 21:6, 8, 17). Not so in Deuteronomy. Afterall, the deity is in heaven, not in a house made with human hands. Rather, sacrifices offered in the chosen place are to be consumed by the ones who offer them. The sacrifices are to be shared with one's family, with the poor, and the Levite (Deut 12:12). In observing the festivals at the central place and offering the sacrifices pertaining thereto, worshippers were to remember that they were slaves in Egypt, oppressed and poor (Deut 16:12). With this reminder the Deuteronomist invokes a rationale that legitimizes the social significance of sacrifice, diminishing any other-worldly significance.

---

[18]See the especially clear summary of Josiah's reformation in light of Deuteronomy in E. W. Nicholson, *Deuteronomy and Tradition* (Oxford: Basil Blackwell, 1967) 1–17.

[19]See M. Weinfeld's "Introduction," in *Deuteronomy 1–11* (AB 5; New York: Doubleday, 1991) 1–84.

Perhaps nothing captures the desacralizing sentiment like the Deuteronomic provision for the nonsacrificial slaughter of animals. In recognizing that the distance to the cultic center might be too great to travel in order to slaughter animals for meat, the Deuteronomist allows that slaughter may be made in local settings (Deut 12:15, 20–22) and that the blood may be poured out like water instead of sprinkled upon the altar (Deut 12:16). By contrast, the Priestly view is that the shedding of the blood of domesticated animals is a sacred act (Lev 17:1–7). The priest is to sprinkle the animal's blood against the altar of the Lord. The provision that it should only be done at an appropriate shrine with a priestly official is to avoid the possibility of offering the animal to another deity (Lev 17:7). The Deuteronomist's revision simply removes any possible religious significance from the shedding of blood.

The dating of the legislation of Deuteronomy is crucial in determining the social text of the Deuteronomistic historian. Similarly, knowing something about the social text is crucial for dating the book itself. The circularity of the problem is clear in the two following examples and further contributes to the difficulties of knowing exactly how to understand the policies of centralization. For instance, scholars tend to date the origins of the Deuteronomic law code in the seventh century BCE.[20] Weinfeld dates the book to this time period because of form critical parallels between the book and the "Vassal Treaties of Esarhaddon," which are dated to around 672 BCE, early in the seventh century. These treaties were "oaths imposed by the retiring king on his vassals with respect to his successor."[21] If one can rely upon a seventh-century date for the Deuteronomic legislation, then indeed it might have been a model both for the reforms of Hezekiah (2 Kgs 18:1–8) as well as those of Josiah (2 Kgs 23:4–20). Their ideals of a pure cult devoted to Yahweh alone and exclusively represented by the royal cult in Jerusalem could then have derived from this legislation.

However, readers should note that all scholars do not agree with Weinfeld and the seventh-century dating of the centralization law. Some assert that the social text of the Josiah narrative in 2 Kings 23 could also suggest that the law of centralization itself is a later addition to the Deuteronomic law code, and thus was not itself a part of the original seventh-century legislation.[22] The account of Josiah's reforms in 2 Kings 23 seems to Clements, for instance, to be much more of a political legitimization to annex the former territories to the north, which had been held by the Assyrians, than an account of religious reform. Its primary emphasis is not so much the law book or the reforms as much as its antagonism toward Bethel, the rival cult to the north (2 Kgs 23:15–20). Further, the idea of making the Jerusalem cult exclusive was so radically new (in view of the practice of toleration of other Yahwistic shrines), it seems much more plausible to suppose that the policy derives from a time when the Temple was actually gone; thus, the time period would have to be after its destruction in 587 BCE, and during a time when there was a reason to restore the Temple. Only in the context of such diminished significance could a desacralizing theology (*name theology* diminished the sacrality of sacrifice and increased emphasis upon social well-being, etc.) flourish.[23]

---

[20]Thus, Weinfeld, *ibid.,* 17; Nicholson, *Deuteronomy and Tradition,* 38.

[21]*Ibid.,* 6.

[22]See the argument in R. E. Clements, "The Deuteronomic Law of Centralisation and the Catastrophe of 587 BCE," in *After the Exile* (eds., J. Barton and D. Reimer; Macon, GA: Mercer University Press, 1996) 5–25.

[23]*Ibid.,* 16–20.

The problem of dating the origins of centralization as the Deuteronomistic historian asserts it in 2 Kings 23 and throughout his history is singularly important. The consensus view, however, is still that the legitimization of centralization dates from an earlier period in the seventh century. However, such dating, as readers can see, has significant impact in one's understanding of the history of Israel's religion. Assuming a seventh-century date for the law of centralization, the Deuteronomistic historian, writing the first edition shortly after Josiah's reforms, is dealing with a completely different social text than the Chronicler. He is responding to the failure of the northern kingdom, its capture by Assyria, and then Assyria's eventual demise. What is more, he is profoundly influenced, very likely, by the thinking of the Deuteronomic theologians who understood the significance of the Temple in a way quite different from the Chronicler.

The Temple and the Eternal Hope of Restoration
Sirach 50:1–5; Tobit 14:4–5; Selections from the Dead Sea Scrolls

Learning Goals

- To understand that rereading of the Temple continues in "sacred" texts well beyond the canonical scope of the Bible.
- To understand the social text of the Dead Sea Scrolls.
- To understand that the Temple itself is a central image in late Jewish eschatological thought.

Guiding Study Exercises

1) How does Tobit's view of the Temple compare and contrast with that of Sirach?
2) Explain how the specific language of Tobit indicates that the Second Temple was not the restoration Temple.
3) Write a paragraph identifying the Dead Sea Scrolls.
4) Describe how the Essenes of Qumran reread the Temple traditions in order to legitimize their rejection of the literal Temple and priesthood of Jerusalem.

When readers reach the end of Ezra-Nehemiah not only do they wonder whether the people of Jerusalem will keep the law and prolong the forged unity between Levite and Zadokite, but also whether they will keep the Temple service properly, as well. Readers wonder whether the Second Temple, rebuilt under the leadership of Zerubbabel and the prophets Haggai and Zechariah (Ezra 1–6), truly reflects the glorious institution about which the Chronicler had spoken: David planned it, Solomon built it, and Moses legitimized it. Three final examples, drawn from Deuterocanonical and extra-biblical texts, provide some idea of how future generations of Hellenistic Jews answered these questions. These texts preserve both the hopes and the conflicts already encountered in the development of Israel's Temple story. Returning to a previously examined text, Sirach 50, the text mentioned in Chapter 2, readers see a portrait of the glory of the Aaronide/Zadokite priest Simon Onias walking through the courts of the Temple. A comparison of this passage with another third-century BCE text contributes to the understanding of the diversity of perspectives contrasting Ezra-Nehemiah's grand vision of restoration.

Sirach and Tobit

The concluding chapter of Sirach provides a glorious image of the Temple service that dates to around 185 BCE. This image attests to Sirach's belief that the Temple played a central role in the nation's relationship with God. Sirach includes his hymn of praise to Simon Onias II, along with the other heroes of Israel's story, because Simon was also involved in repairing the Temple. Readers cannot miss the fact that Simon's contribution to the Temple is one of the main reasons for Sirach's praise (See Sir 50:1–5).

The reference to repairs probably alludes to damages to the Temple done in the Syrian-Egyptian wars, between the Ptolemaic and the Seleucid dynasties over control of Palestine.[24] More important, in Sirach readers have a written document that gives some indication of the status of the Temple and Temple worship near the beginning of the second century BCE. Sirach expresses his exalted view of the Temple quite explicitly in his praise of Zerubbabel and Joshua the priest in Sir 49:11–12. He says of the Temple: "[T]hey built the house and raised a temple holy to the Lord, destined for everlasting glory." Note how Sirach believes that Zerubbabel's Temple (the **Second Temple** that stood during Sirach's time) is "destined for everlasting glory." Clearly, for Sirach the Second Temple is *the* restored Temple. According to Sirach, Simon had recently repaired this Temple and provided strong leadership for the glorious service of the Temple. Readers should also recall from the earlier treatment of Sirach (Chap. 2) the writer's favoritism toward the Aaronide/Zadokite control of the Temple, even to the extent that the high priest takes on the trappings of royalty (Sir 45:24–26). It may well be that Simon enjoyed such freedom both because of the initial favor bestowed upon the Jews by their Egyptian overlords, the Ptolemies, and because of Simon's willingness to embrace Hellenism. Simon, as other priests before him, very likely found it convenient to cooperate with Hellenistic culture, a calculated risk to maintain the freedom for Temple worship.

Not all Jews of this period, however, were as optimistic about the contemporary Temple as was Sirach. Some gave expression to the belief that a fuller restoration was yet to come, implicitly suggesting that even Sirach's Temple did not represent the fullness of the Temple's significance. Readers find this idea expressed in the Deuterocanonical book of Tobit. As a careful reading shows, the second-century author depicts his main character, a pious Jew named Tobit who lives in the eighth century BCE, as "predicting" the destruction of Jerusalem and the Temple in 587 BCE and the return back to Judah, which began ca. 539 BCE. However, the author, living roughly around the era of Sirach, did not believe that the homecoming and rebuilding of the city

---

[24]See J. H. Hayes and J. M. Miller, eds., *Israelite and Judaean History,* 570–580 for background.

and sanctuary had brought about *the* restoration. Rather, the author of Tobit insisted that the grand and glorious restoration about which the prophets had spoken was to find its fulfillment in a yet-to-be realized future—a future that included a glorified Jerusalem and Temple. The key language reads: "But God will again have mercy on them, and God will bring them back into the land of Israel; and they will rebuild the temple of God, but not like the first one until the period when the times of fulfillment shall come. After this they all will return from their exile and will rebuild Jerusalem in splendor; and in it the temple of God will be rebuilt, just as the prophets of Israel have said concerning it" (Tob 14:5).

Note how Tobit clearly looks forward to the end of Exile ("God will bring them back into the land of Israel") and the rebuilding of the Temple when the Jews return to their land ("and they will rebuild the Temple of God"). But Tobit is just as emphatic that the Temple rebuilt upon the return—the Temple rebuilt under the leadership of Zerubbabel, Joshua the High Priest, and the prophets Haggai and Zechariah—was *not* a Temple "like the first one," that is, the Temple Solomon built. Somehow, Tobit thought this rebuilt Temple to be less than what it should be. The Temple that was to be "like the first one" would not be built "until the period of the times of fulfillment shall come." Then, and only then, would the grand and glorious Temple—the one of which the prophets spoke and the one Sirach evidently equated with the Second Temple—be rebuilt. Tobit offers clear evidence that some Jews did not believe that the actual Temple that had been rebuilt in 515 BCE was the real Temple of the restoration. It simply did not live up to the expectations of those Jews looking forward to the restoration promised to God's people through prophets such as Second Isaiah, Haggai, and Zechariah. Thus it became necessary to reinterpret the present Temple. These Jews, while disappointed that the current Temple fell short of the grandeur they felt was promised by the prophets, did not abandon the hope that one day the restored and glorified Temple would exist. That hope achieved expression in the anticipation of a yet more glorious Temple.

The Witness of Qumran

At yet a later time period there is a new synthesis of these ideas of restoration, both of the Temple and of the rightful priestly leaders of that Temple. To appreciate this story readers must recall the previous examination of the story of the **Maccabees** in Chapter 5. The plot of the story turns on the conflict between Greek and Jewish cultures in the second century BCE. The government of Palestine was in the hands of Antiochus IV, the Seleucid ruler of Syria. It is evident that many of the priestly leaders in Judea sympathized with the Greek way of life—**Hellenism**—that was influencing the Mediterranean world at this time. Not only this, but Antiochus was willing to use his political power to install into the office of high priest men who were not only sympathetic to his cultural agenda, but who were also willing to offer him sufficient bribes. In the year 172 BCE, a certain Menelaus, who was perhaps *not a Zadokite*,[25] secured the office of high priest by bribing

---

[25] According to 2 Macc 3:4, Menelaus' ancestor, Simon, was from the tribe of Benjamin, though some ancient mss. have other tribal names here, many of which sound like they may have derived from the Hebrew *Bilgah*. Bilgah was one of the priestly families (1 Chron 24:14). Thus, Menelaus may have been a priest, but he was not of the line of Zadok. See J. A. Goldstein, *II Maccabees,* (AB 41A; Garden City: Doubleday, 1983) 183.

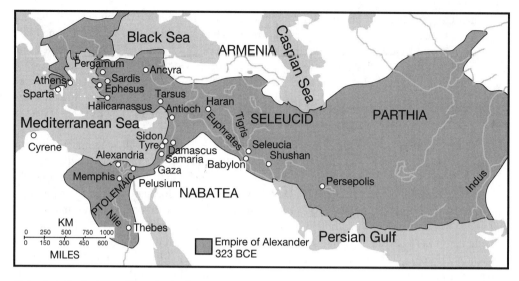

Alexander's Empire. When Alexander the Great conquered Persia in 333 BCE he asserted the superiority of Greek culture across its vast expanse. (From John Rogerson and Philip Davies, *The Old Testament World,* © 1989, p. 113. Reprinted by permission of Prentice Hall, Upper Saddle River, NJ)

Antiochus (2 Macc 4:23–25). If, indeed, Menelaus was not a Zadokite, his ascension marks the beginning of the end of the Zadokite monopoly on the office of high priest. Menelaus' rise to this position diminished the stature of this office in the eyes of many Jews.

Shortly after Menelaus' ascension, an extraordinary persecution of the Jews ensued as a result both of this cultural conflict and the political domination of Antiochus. In an attempt to Hellenize his domain fully, Antiochus issued decrees that prevented the Jews of Palestine from observing their religious customs, making such religious observances crimes punishable by death (1 Macc 1: 41–62). As a result, a family by the name of Hasmon (so named for their ancestor, Hasmoneus, according to the Jewish historian Josephus[26]), also nicknamed the "Maccabeans," sparked a revolt against this oppression (1 Macc 2:1–14). According to 1 Macc 2:1, the **Hasmoneans** were priests, but they were of the priestly line of Joarib (see 1 Chron 24:7). The priestly line of Joarib was also not of the line of Zadok (Neh 11:10–11).[27] The Hasmoneans, or Maccabeans, won not only the Jews' independence from Antiochus IV, but secured the high priesthood in Jerusalem as well, thereby pushing the Zadokites even farther from power. The Hasmoneans would rule the Jews until 63 BCE when Rome conquered Judea. Even after Rome conquered Judea, it allowed the Hasmonean family to maintain its hold on the high priestly

---

[26]*Jewish Antiquities,* 7.6.1. Josephus traces the genealogy of Mattathias of Modin, the grandson of Hasmoneus, a priest of the order of Joarib.

[27]Note how Neh 11:11–12 distinguishes the priestly families Jedaiah, the son of Joiarib (v. 10), and Seraiah, the son of Hilkiah (v. 12). If one compares Neh 11:11 with 1 Chron 6:1–15, one will see that Seraiah (v. 14) is of the line of Zadok (v. 8). The Joarib line was not of the Zadokite line.

office. Their hold on this office did not end until the rise of King Herod (37 BCE), who systematically executed the last remnants of this old family.[28]

When the Hasmoneans secured the office of the high priesthood in 153 BCE, the Zadokites lost all hope that they might regain control of this position. Though the Hasmoneans were not Zadokites, most Jews, grateful for the independence this family had given them, went along with the Hasmonean control of the high priestly office. But some Jews, particularly Zadokite priests, perceived the Hasmoneans as illegitimate, even evil usurpers.

It may well be that this struggle between these two priestly families, the Zadokites and the Hasmoneans, caused certain priests of the Jerusalemite priesthood to flee to the desert village of Qumran and there establish a community in which the highest ideals of the priesthood, at least as they understood things, could be realized. Ancient sources refer to a group know as the *Essenes,* the "purified ones," and many believe that these are the covenanters of Qumran. The term Essene may well describe them sociologically, while **ideologically** they reflect the perspectives of extremely conservative Zadokite priests. It is therefore not difficult to hypothesize the equation of Essenes with Zadokites,[29] and to suppose that the village of Qumran became home to this religious party of priests who fled from Jerusalem after the Hasmoneans seized control ca. 153 BCE. This settlement existed until around 68 CE.[30] It was this community that produced the writings now known as the **Dead Sea Scrolls**, a collection of biblical and **sectarian** writings that give expression to the life and faith of this desert-dwelling Jewish community. Space allows an examination of only a small selection of texts from Scrolls that suggest their anticipation of a new literal Temple.[31]

The conflict between the supposed Zadokite and Hasmonean priestly families explains much of what is found written in the literary texts of the Dead Sea Scrolls. The texts found in the caves near Qumran portray a community anticipating the coming of a priestly Messiah, whom this community ranked above the traditional Davidic Messiah.[32] Furthermore, the priestly members of the sect referred to themselves as "Sons of Zadok," thus claiming to be the legitimate heirs to the Jerusalemite priesthood (remember the Chronicler's story). The texts of the Dead Sea Scrolls also make numerous references to the impurity of both the priesthood and the sacrificial offerings of the Jerusalem Temple. Finally, these sectarians developed meaningful substitutes for animal sacrifices since they refused to offer sacrifice at the corrupt Temple of Jerusalem. Note the following excerpts from the sect's own literature:

> Its interpretation [Hab 2:5–6 is the biblical text being interpreted here] concerns the Wicked Priest, who is called by the name of loyalty at the start of his office. However, when

---

[28]The history of the Hasmonean dynasty and the rise of the Herodian family is fully explored in Chap. 9.

[29]F. M. Cross, "The Early History of the Apocalyptic Community at Qumran," in *Canaanite Myth and Hebrew Epic,* 326–346.

[30]See Hershal Shanks, *Understanding the Dead Sea Scrolls* (New York: Random House, 1992). See also, James C. VanderKam, *The Dead Sea Scrolls Today* (Grand Rapids, MI: Eerdmans, 1994).

[31]Y. Yadin, *The Temple Scroll: The Hidden Law of the Dead Sea Sect* (London: Weidenfeld and Nicolson, 1985) 235.

[32]Remember that Jesus ben Sirach extends to the Aaronide (Zadokite) priesthood a covenant that is itself like the covenant extended to David (Sir 45:24–25).

he ruled over Israel his heart became conceited, he deserted God and betrayed the laws for the sake of riches (1QpHab 8.8–11; Martínez).[33]

When these exist in Israel in accordance with these rules in order to establish the spirit of holiness in truth eternal, in order to atone for the fault of the transgression and for the guilt of sin and for approval for the earth, without the flesh of burnt offerings and without the fats of sacrifice—the offering of the lips in compliance with the decree will be like the pleasant aroma of justice and the correctness of behavior will be acceptable like a freewill offering—at this moment the men of the Community shall set themselves apart (like) a holy house of Aaron, in order to enter the holy of holies, and (like) a house of the Community for Israel, (for) those who walk in perfection (1QS 9.3–6; Martínez)[34]

Three observations are important from these brief excerpts. One, note how the first text (1QpHab) betrays an utter rejection of the established Hasmonean priesthood of Jerusalem. To refer to the officially ruling High Priest as "the Wicked Priest" needs no commentary to emphasize the hostility held by the sectarians of Qumran. The second text (1QS) is interesting for a number of reasons. Note how it insists that one obtains atonement not through literal sacrifices of "flesh" or "fat." What God accepts as atoning sacrifices are "the offering of the lips" (probably prayer) and "the correctness of behavior" (probably righteous living in obedience to God's law). The sectarians, who would not participate in the corrupt literal Temple of Jerusalem, substituted for literal sacrifices their own prayers and righteous living. These, they insist, "will be acceptable like a freewill offering" to God. The third important feature is found in the words "the men of the Community shall set themselves apart (like) a holy house of Aaron, in order to enter the holy of holies." Most interpreters of the Scrolls believe that, just as the community viewed its prayers and righteous living as the substitutes for the Temple sacrifices, it viewed itself, the community, as a substitute for the Temple building itself. And not only this, but the Qumran sectarians also viewed their community as the glorified Jerusalem described by Isaiah.[35] Recall the previous brief discussion of Deutero-Isaiah's description of the glorified Jerusalem in Chap. 5 (Isa 54:11–17). Observe carefully how the Qumran community reread this text about the glorified Jerusalem and applied it to themselves.

And your foundations are sapphires. [Its interpretation:] they will found the council of the Community, the priests and the peo[ple . . .] the assembly of their elect, like a sapphire

---

[33]This text is from a commentary on the book of Habbakuk found in the first of eleven caves that yielded texts that scholars refer to collectively as "the Dead Sea Scrolls." The technical way that scholars refer to this document is 1QpHab 8.8–11, an academic shorthand way of saying, "the commentary ["p" abbreviates the Hebrew word for "interpretation," *pesher*] on Habakkuk ["Hab"] found in cave one from Qumran ["1Q"], the eighth column, lines 8–11 ["8:8–11"].

[34]This text is known popularly as "The Rule of the Community." The "S" in the scholarly title stands for the Hebrew word "Sedeq" ("Rule").

[35]O. Betz, "Jesus and the Temple Scroll," argues that there was no uniform belief on this issue among the sectarians of Qumran. Some of the sectarians did anticipate the restoration of the literal Temple, while others maintained that the spiritualized Temple *permanently* replaced the literal Temple. See *Jesus and the Dead Sea Scrolls: The Controversy Resolved* (ed., J. Charlesworth; New York: Doubleday, 1992) 91–97.

stone in the midst of stones. [I will place] all your battlements [of rubies]. Its interpretation concerns the twelve [chiefs of the priests who] illuminate with the judgment of the Urim and the Thummim. . . . And a[ll your gates of glittering stones.] Its interpretation concerns the chiefs of the tribes of Israel in the las[t d]ays . . . (4QpIs^d; Martínez).[36]

Evidently, the interpreters at Qumran applied the text from Isaiah to themselves. The foundation of sapphires refers to the founding of "the council of the Community." The battlement of rubies refers to "the twelve [chiefs of the priests]," or the leadership of the Community. Once the Qumran covenanters became convinced that they were the true Temple with their deeds and prayers being the true sacrifices, they had no trouble going to the Jewish scriptures, finding texts about the Temple and Holy City, and applying these texts directly to themselves.

The previous readings on the Hasmoneans and the Zadokites following as they do the foregoing discussion of the Levites and Zadokites may leave the impression that the last word regarding the Temple was one of antagonism and hostile alienation. Readers should not minimize the fact that true voices of opposition to this symbol of power did exist. However, it is clear that these ideas that give expression to views born of antagonism simultaneously expressed a word of hope. Despite the fact that the Qumran community clearly maintained a negative attitude with regard to the Temple of the Hasmonean priesthood, they held forth the hope that in the age when God brought about the full restoration of Israel, he would also restore the Temple of Jerusalem.

One of the scrolls found in the Qumran library was the "Temple Scroll." This scroll is essentially a rewriting of much of the Jewish Torah, especially the book of Deuteronomy. In this rewriting, an ideal picture is painted of what life in God's holy city is supposed to be like. In the midst of this scroll, readers find clearly expressed the hope that sometime in the future God will rebuild the Temple:

I shall sanctify my Temple with my glory, for I shall make my glory reside over it until the day of creation, when I shall create my Temple, establishing it for myself for ever, in accordance with the covenant which I made with Jacob at Bethel (11QTemple 29.8–9; Martínez).

Even though the community at Qumran rejected the actual Temple of Jerusalem because they believed it to be in the wrong hands, they did not reject the principle of the Temple. Consequently, they believed that when the "day of creation" (recreation?) dawned, God would create his Temple anew.

At a different level, readers' ability to examine the conflict between Qumranic and Hasmonean priests provides a window on the much larger process by which the story of the Temple came to be. The ongoing reinterpretations of written texts and oral traditions considered in these pages bear witness to the reality that even the deepest and most cherished religious convictions are themselves inextricably bound to the changing tides of social, political, and historical circumstances. As readers proceed with the study of the New Testament, they will discover that rereadings of the significance of Jerusalem, the Temple, and the priesthood continued. The early

---

[36]The square brackets indicate places where scholars have had to reconstruct the text. These manuscripts are very old and it should not be surprising that we find lacunae in some places. Even with these emendations, the overall meaning of the text is clear enough.

followers of Jesus, like the covenanters of Qumran, would be required to reconcile their theological social texts with the many literary texts of the Jewish scriptures that held the Jerusalem Temple and its priesthood in high regard.

Conclusion

In this series of readings one of the central concerns of the post-Exilic religious and political debate becomes evident: What was the role of the Temple and who would preside over its service? It was these questions that prophets such as Haggai and Zechariah, Third Isaiah, and Malachi sought to answer. The Chronicler's vision of the Temple was one that had both priest and Levite working side by side. This, according to the Chronicler, stemmed both from the elaborate plans laid down by David as well as the Mosaic law, which David interpreted. The promise of Davidic rule on the throne in Jerusalem is significant for the Chronicler because this Davidic kingdom was to exist within the Temple. Ezra-Nehemiah gives expression to such a vision also, incorporating the importance of the Mosaic law in the governance of the post-Exilic Temple community. The Chronicler's grand vision further seeks to portray the Northern and Southern kingdoms as politically united, and to end centuries of hostilities between Levitical and Zadokite priests. Isolating these two families, with their accompanying traditions and literature, helps readers see that grand visions are often forged out of conflict.

The Chronicler's rereading of the Temple is no more radical, however, than that of the Deuteronomistic historian who organizes Israelite/Judean history around the establishment of the Temple as the exclusive place of worship to the exclusion of worship sites, and their priests, which had been valid for centuries. Under the influence of the Deuteronomic Code, the historian sought to assert a more rational and ethically central religion. The grand vision of the Temple, which was the culmination of these two great historians, continued to live on, especially after it was clear that the program of restoration of Ezra-Nehemiah did not live up to expectations. But it was only through yet more conflict and disagreement that new visions of the Temple would be produced and its place of importance would be pushed off further into some future time.

For Further Reading

David and the Temple: Ezra-Nehemiah and the Chronicler

Ackroyd, P. "Faith and its Reformulation in the Post-Exilic Period." *TD* 27 (1979) 323–346. (*Recommended for beginning students.*)

Wright, G. E. "Cult and History: A Study of a Current Problem in Old Testament Interpretation," *Int* 16 (1962) 3–20. (*Recommended for beginning students.*)

Wright, J. W. "The Founding Father: The Structure of the Chronicler's David Narrative." *JBL* 117 (1998) 45–59.

———. "The Legacy of David in Chronicles: The Narrative Function of 1 Chronicles 23–27." *JBL* 110 (1991) 229–242.

The Temple in the Deuteronomistic Historian's View

Cross, F. M. and Freedman, D. N. "Josiah's Revolt Against Assyria." *JNES* 12 (1953) 56–68.

Friedman, R. E. "From Egypt to Egypt; Dtr1 and Dtr2." In *Traditions in Transformation: Turning Points in Biblical Faith.* Edited by B. Halpern, J. D. Levinson. Winona Lake, IN: Eisenbrauns, 1981. Pp. 167–192.

Lohfink, N. "Deuteronomy." *IDBSup,* 229–232. (*Recommended for beginning students.*)

Weinfeld, M. "Cult Centralization in Israel in Light of New-Babylonian Analogy." *JNES* 23 (1964) 202–212.

The Temple and the Eternal Hope of Restoration

Golb, N. "Who Hid the Dead Sea Scrolls?" *BA* 48 (1985) 68–82. (*Recommended for beginning students.*)

Schiffman, L. "The Temple Scroll and the Systems of Jewish Law in the Second Temple Period." In *Temple Scroll Studies.* Edited by G. Brooke. Sheffield: JSOT Press, 1989. Pp. 239–255.

CHAPTER SEVEN

The Story of Kingship

Introduction

Review

The Temple occupies a central place in Israel's story. The Chronicler's story of the Temple remembers King David as having played a key role in the establishment of the Temple despite the Deuteronomistic History's recollection that Solomon, David's son, acted alone. The Chronicler's social text made it timely to bring together two divergent theologies, one Davidic, the other Mosaic, in order to reassert the importance of an all-Israel perspective in the Second Temple period. The social text of the Chronicler is implied by his rereading of the priestly officiants who served in the Temple. In his story, both Levite and Zadokite are legitimized as servants. The generations of interpreters following the Chronicler, such as those Jews under the political domination of Antiochus IV and those at Qumran, would continue to reread the Temple in ways that reflected their own unique social and political situations.

Preview

This chapter focuses closely upon the development of various ideas of kingship within the Hebrew Bible. The ancient Israelite understandings of kingship eventually became a rich theological and historical resource for post-Exilic and especially later Jewish messianic thought. Readers will examine texts that help them to see the socio-political, sacral-theological, and the eschatological significance of Israel's story of kingship. As before, Ezra-Nehemiah and the Chronicler are crucial beginning points in understanding the development of this line of thought.

"I Shall Build Him a House . . ."
The Davidic Promise
2 Samuel 7:4–17; 1 Chronicles 17:3–15

Learning Goals

- To understand reasons for the different portrayals of Zerubbabel in the post-Exilic texts.
- To understand the centrality of Nathan's promise of kingship to David in the Hebrew Bible's tradition of kingship.
- To recognize key language within the promise that indicates the transition from human king to divine king.

Guiding Study Exercises

1) Describe how Ezra's portrayal of Zerubbabel's significance compares and contrasts with that of Haggai and Zechariah. Explain how awareness of the social text of Ezra-Nehemiah can help one to understand the contrasts.
2) In a paragraph identify and explain the variations in wording between the Chronicler's version and the Deuteronomistic version of the Davidic promise.
3) List and explain three defining metaphors of the Davidic promise.

The Problem of Restoration

As has been evident in preceding chapters, the post-Exilic Jewish community faced a dilemma of redefinition. Under the political domination of Persian kings, there could be no independent state, and thus no Davidic monarch. And yet, as readers of Ezra-Nehemiah now know, the story of this post-Exilic community opens with the character of Zerubbabel, who causes readers to remember the question of kingship. These documents actually reflect a transitional understanding of the role of the king—or kingship—within the community. Recall, for instance, in Ezra 1:8 Sheshbazzar is called "prince of Judah." It is not necessary, of course, to interpret the term *prince* (translated from *nasi'*) as "king." It is a generic term and can mean leader or chief of leaders. In fact, in Ezra 5:14 readers see that Cyrus actually appoints Sheshbazzar as governor of Jerusalem.

Of more interest is the character Zerubbabel. Readers encounter him in Ezra 3:2 as one of a group that is beginning to rebuild the altar of God in Jerusalem. Reading through the narrative, one sees that, unlike the treatment of Sheshbazzar, the writer has included a genealogy for Zerubbabel (e.g., 3:8) that corresponds intertextually to the genealogy in the Chronicler's work (1 Chron 3:18–19). In Chronicles Zerubbabel is unambiguously a member of the Davidic royal lineage. Shealtiel, Zerubbabel's ancestor, was the son of a king, Jeconiah. This King Jeconiah,

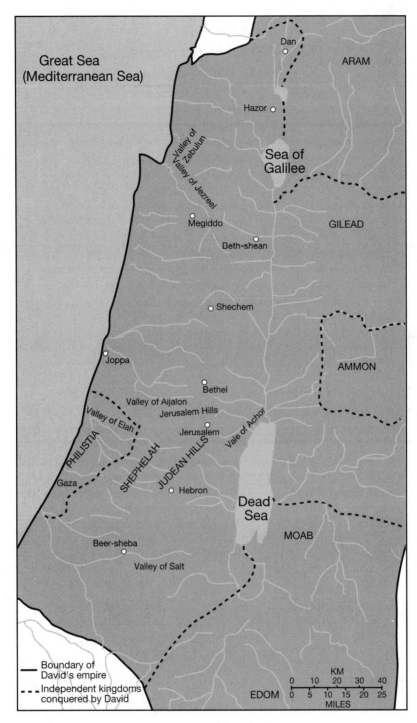

(From John Rogerson and Philip Davies, *The Old Testament World,* © 1989, p. 130. Reprinted by permission of Prentice Hall, Upper Saddle River, NJ)

whose genealogy traces back to David, was taken into captivity by Nebuchadnezzar, the Babylonian king. The story in Ezra-Nehemiah therefore opens hopefully with an authentic prince of Judah rebuilding the Temple. His absence as an important character in the latter part of the book of Ezra implies that the hoped-for kingship failed to materialize in the Second Temple period.

First, there seems to be a great deal of confusion in Ezra 1–6 about Sheshbazzar and Zerubbabel. Readers only get a summary of Sheshbazzar's actual work in the letter of Tattenai in Ezra 5:6–17. Remember that Tattenai, the governor of "Beyond the River," was questioning the work that Zerubbabel and his associates were doing on the Temple. In this letter to Darius, Tattenai reports that "Sheshbazzar came and laid the foundations of the house of God in Jerusalem" (v. 16). This would seem to contradict Ezra 3:2, which states that it was Zerubbabel who set out to build the altar of the Temple in the seventh month. Verse 8 continues that in the second year after their arrival Zerubbabel and his colleagues "make a beginning." Then v. 10 states, "When the builders laid the foundation of the temple of the Lord . . ." suggesting that, in fact, it was Zerubbabel who laid the foundation, not Sheshbazzar.

Scholars believe that the two characters' careers have very likely been telescoped into one. But, there is no reason to think that there was not a person named Sheshbazzar who led an initial group from Babylon back to Jerusalem and began to lay the foundation of the Temple. The telescoping may actually have its origins in the same motives that caused the writer to write Zerubbabel out of the story altogether after Ezra 1–6. The writer was concerned to downplay the involvement of Davidic characters in the restoration, especially in the rebuilding of the Temple. Scholars have long remarked that in Ezra 7 suddenly the main character is a Zadokite priest rather than a Davidic prince. As readers now know, for all of the importance attached to David and his throne in earlier history, the story of Ezra-Nehemiah concludes with a reestablishment of Mosaic law and priestly rule rather than with a literal Davidic monarchy.

Secondly, materials outside of Ezra-Nehemiah imply a genuine expectation of the restoration of a Davidic king in the Second Temple period. Recall how both Haggai and Zechariah, though concerned primarily with the Temple, both announce Zerubbabel's claim to the throne (see Chap. 5). Haggai acknowledges that Zerubbabel is the Persian governor (*pehah*), but then Haggai announces that the day is near when he would attain his status as the chosen of Yahweh. In Hag 2:20–23 the prophet envisions a day of cosmic upheaval and social reversals when Yahweh overthrows the political powers of the world. Then he says in verse 23, "On that day, says the Lord of hosts, I will take you, O Zerubbabel my servant, son of Shealtiel, says the Lord, and make you like a signet ring; for I have chosen you, says the Lord of hosts." Clearly, the language is veiled, but the allusions to the genealogical backgrounds ("son of Shealtiel"), the naming of Zerubbabel as the Lord's "servant," and the statement that he has been "chosen" suggest a heightened significance far beyond that of a mere Persian appointee. And yet in Ezra 1–6, there is simply no reference to the fact that this character Zerubbabel is to take his place as a real Davidic king.

What these texts indicate, in other words, is both an awareness of the importance of the tradition of Davidic kingship and the need to rectify that tradition with the post-Exilic socio-historical circumstances. Haggai and Zechariah refer to the restoration of the king, but in varying ways reread that position. Ezra knows of the Davidic lineage, but relegates the Davidic prince to the role of Temple establishment since the social reality behind the text made it impossible to have a Judean king. Perhaps one of the clearest expressions of the rereading of kingship, like the Temple, comes as the Chronicler rereads the Deuteronomistic historian.

The Chronicler's Interpretation of Nathan's Promise

It is not only in biblical books such as Ezra-Nehemiah and the minor prophets such as Haggai and Zechariah that the post-Exilic understanding of kingship changes. The treatments of kingship in the two major histories of the Bible, the Chronicler's History and the Deuteronomistic History, reveal a similar struggle. This struggle between literary text and social text is never clearer than in the episode of Nathan's promise to David that there would always be a Davidic heir on the throne in Jerusalem. There is a shift in the Chronicler's understanding of the king as an earthly, political ruler, to the king as a representative of Yahweh, who is himself the king. A simple way of conceptualizing this development is to set out the opposing political models of autocracy versus **theocracy**: a state ruled by an individual (human) versus a state ruled by God.[1] Students should take caution, however, as they reflect on categories that seem so mutually exclusive. It is quite likely that the human figure of the king was always considered a vice-regent of the deity, and thus imbued himself with divinity. Of course, the Deuteronomistic historian saw the king as one who, though the supreme ruler, nevertheless had to keep the law as any other human would (e.g., 2 Samuel 12). But long before the Deuteronomistic historian included Nathan's promise, the tradition of Davidic kingship had already undergone some important transformations. It seems the relationship between king and Temple provoked several rereadings throughout history.

David's Kingdom and the Temple. Reading these two versions of the promise of kingship intertextually immediately reveals great similarities, including the larger narrative context, the sequencing of events, and the various rationales for the deity's response to David (see Table 7.1).

Focusing on the version in the Deuteronomistic History first (2 Sam 7:1–17), the exact wording of the promise is of special interest. The promise is a kind of "Magna Charta" of kingship in the biblical tradition,[2] which later writers return to again and again, utilizing its very specific language quite intentionally. Notice that the chapter may be broken into two main parts: vv. 1–17 contain the dynastic promise, and vv. 18–29 contain the prayer of David. The present discussion is concerned with the first half of the chapter. One scholar has isolated three defining features of the promise characterized by vegetation imagery, sonship imagery, and images of perpetuity. Examine carefully vv. 11–14: First there is the assertion that the royal lineage comes from the "seed" of David, imagery associated with vegetation; second, there is a "father-son" relationship between the king and deity; and third, there will be an "eternal reign of the Davidic lineage on the throne in Israel," language guaranteeing the perpetuity of the promise.[3] Readers will see this kind of imagery recurring through later rereadings of the promise.

The promise to David through the prophet Nathan is quite complex, though, and full of its own internal contradictions. These internal contradictions require that readers consider its pre-Deuteronomistic History before making too much of it in its present form. Most immediately evident is that the rationale for Yahweh's rejection of David's building a Temple in vv. 5–7 seems to contradict the statement in v. 13a, where David's son is to build the Temple. Why, if the Lord

---

[1] We follow such treatments as Joachim Becker's for the sake of introducing mutually illuminating categories. *Messianic Expectation in the Old Testament* (Philadelphia: Fortress, 1980).

[2] Becker, *ibid.,* 25.

[3] See David Duling, "The Promises to David and Their Entrance into Christianity — Nailing Down a Likely Hypothesis," *NTS* 19 (1973–74) 56.

Table 7.1

The Promise to David

2 Samuel 7:8–13	1 Chronicles 17:7–14
8Now therefore thus you shall say to my servant David: Thus says the Lord of hosts: I took you from the pasture, from following the sheep to be prince over my people Israel;	7Now therefore thus you shall say to my servant David: Thus says the Lord of hosts: I took you from the pasture, from following the sheep, to be ruler over my people Israel;
9and I have been with you wherever you went, and have cut off all your enemies from before you; and I will make for you a great name, like the name of the great ones of the earth.	8and I have been with you wherever you went, and have cut off all your enemies before you; and I will make for you a name, like the name of the great ones of the earth.
10And I will appoint a place for my people Israel and will plant them, so that they may live in their own place, and be disturbed no more; and evildoers shall afflict them no more, as formerly,	9I will appoint a place for my people Israel, and will plant them so that they may live in their own place, and be disturbed no more; and evildoers shall wear them down no more, as they did formerly,
11from the time that I appointed judges over my people Israel; and I will give you rest from all your enemies. Moreover the Lord declares to you that the Lord will make you a house.	10from the time that I appointed judges over my people Israel; and I will subdue all your enemies. Moreover I declare to you that the Lord will build you a house.
12When your days are fulfilled and you lie down with your ancestors, I will raise up your offspring after you, who shall come forth from your body, and I will establish his kingdom.	11When your days are fulfilled to go to be with your ancestors, I will raise up your offspring after you, one of your own sons, and I will establish his kingdom.
13He shall build a house for my name, and I will establish the throne of his kingdom forever.	12He shall build a house for me, and I will establish his throne forever.
14I will be a father to him, and he shall be a son to me. When he commits iniquity, I will punish him with a rod such as mortals use, with blows inflicted by human beings.	13I will be a father to him, and he shall be a son to me.
15But I will not take my steadfast love from him, as I took it from Saul, whom I put away from before you.	I will not take my steadfast love from him, as I took it from him who was before you,
16Your house and your kingdom shall be made sure forever before me; your throne shall be established forever.	14but I will confirm him in my house and in my kingdom forever, and his throne shall be established forever.

moves exclusively about in the tent as his people move about, is he willing to grant the building of a Temple at all? Yet further complications arise in view of the language in v. 12. That language seems to imply a generic promise to *all* of David's offspring. The word translated "offspring" in v. 12 is "your seed" and frequently implies more than a single generation. However, in v. 13a there is the implication that only a single son is to build the Temple for Yahweh.

The explanation for these two contradictions is to be sought in the hypothesis of multiple stages of tradition long before either the Deuteronomistic historian or the Chronicler reinterpreted the Davidic promise for their own particular generations of readers. One scholar's reconstruction of the compositional history of this promise asserts three different stages with three separate social texts. The first stage is a simple prophetic oracle promising David a dynasty because of the king's intent to build Yahweh a Temple. This stage of composition would include verses 1a, 2–3, 11b-12, and 13b-15a. Isolating these verses from the rest leaves the reader with the impression that David's rationale for building a Temple was his awareness of the success that Yahweh had given him (vv. 1a and 2–3). David's dynasty then originates in Yahweh's response to David's act of piety and blessing (vv. 11b-12). Of special interest here is the promise of a father-son relationship and that David would retain divine favor unconditionally (vv. 13b-15a).[4] The image of sonship is significant since it implies that the king himself is divine. The association of kingship with divinity further implies a sympathetic understanding of the much larger ancient Near Eastern kingship **ideology**. That ideology understands kings to be sons of god, therefore giving them the prerogatives of gods. While this is an interesting belief, and Israel's view of kings comes very close to this at times (as indicated in Psalms 2 and 45), readers must be aware that the language of sonship is also used to denote a covenant relationship. Such sonship imagery may only be functioning to define the commitment of Yahweh to the king, his vassal.[5] The setting for this first and oldest stage of the kingship tradition would very likely be the reign of David himself. Its purpose would have been to legitimize the Davidic dynasty by linking that reign with David's pious initiative to offer to build a Temple.

The second stage of the composition is thought to be the addition of vv. 4–9a and 15b to the previous verses. These verses contain Yahweh's rationale for rejecting David's request—the deity moves around in a tent and does not live in houses (vv. 4–9a). There is also the reminder that Yahweh is one who has removed favored status from previous kings (v. 15b). The promise of a dynastic house is no longer an unconditional promise. The king like any other "mortal" must keep the law, and will bear punishment when he breaks the law (v. 14). These additional verses further indicate that the king's status only comes from Yahweh, David's pious initiative notwithstanding. The historical context is not clear for these additions, but the theory is that it is consistent with a prophetic view that was largely unsympathetic with kingship and suspicious of Temple religion (see Chap. 6). This prophetic stage of the composition would be attempting to say that David's success came entirely at the hands of Yahweh and that Yahweh does *not* actually need a Temple.[6]

[4]See the discussion of P. K. McCarter, *II Samuel* (AB 9; Garden City, NY: Doubleday, 1984) 223–231; also A. A. Anderson, *2 Samuel* (WBC 11; Waco, TX: Word Books, 1989) 116. See especially M. Fishbane's reconstruction of this material in *Biblical Interpretation in Ancient Israel* (Oxford: Basil Blackwell, 1985).

[5]Becker, *Messianic Expectation,* 27–29

[6]Anderson, *2 Samuel,* 122.

This model of the Temple offers a reliable reconstruction of what the Temple might have looked like in King Herod's day. (Chance and Horne)

A final stage of composition adds vv. 1b, 9b-11a, 13a, 16 and possibly some linking editorial language. These verses contain references to "rest from enemies," (v. 1b and 11a), the "greatness of David's name" (vv. 9b), Israel's history (v. 11a), and to "one son of David who would build the temple" (v. 13a). The references to "rest from enemies," the great name of the king, and the building of the Temple seem to fit in with the knowledge that Solomon, David's son, did in fact build it. Thus, this final stage of composition comes after Solomon and attempts to reiterate the importance of kingship by again tying it to the Temple.[7] In its final form there is a promise of an everlasting dynasty, the king as the son of Yahweh, and the centrality of the Davidic heir. The explanation of the contradiction in the rationale for Temple building is simply one of right timing. It was not the right time for David, but it was for his son Solomon.

The various stages of composition of this promise do not alter the fact that the promise was understood to legitimize a Davidic king on the throne forever. Nor does it alter the fact that as long as the king was obedient to Yahweh he would be on the throne. The various additions to the hypothetical core prophecy do not, in other words, reflect any abandonment of kingship altogether. The reinterpretation of the Chronicler, however, makes some drastic changes, due mainly

[7]*Ibid.,* 122.

to the social text in which he was reading this ancient promise. While the Chronicler's changes seem subtle at first, their significance clearly betrays a time period when there could be no king as Israel had known kingship.

Kingship of David in the Temple. Readers have already seen how the Chronicler used the tradition of Davidic kingship to legitimize the Temple. To do so the Chronicler had to modify the notion of kingship to be one of mainly building and maintaining the Temple. The modifications are even more evident when reading the two versions of 2 Sam 7:8–13 and 1 Chron 17:7–14 comparatively (see Table 7.1). Readers will observe in the Chronicler's version that the promise of Nathan to David is intact at every point. There is still the emphasis placed upon the Davidic lineage (v. 11); the Davidic promise is one that extends into perpetuity (vv. 11, 12 and 14); and the image of a father-son relationship is ever-present (v. 13). One could say that the Chronicler strongly reaffirms the centrality of the Davidic promise, even though the Chronicler is writing his history during the Persian period. However, a careful reading surfaces some variation in language that gives pause for reflection.

For example, the Chronicler appeals to an ideal of a united northern kingdom and southern kingdom in the claims of 1 Chron 17:13. Here we see the intertext with 2 Sam 7:14a *only*. The insistence of the father-son relationship defining Yahweh's relationship to his king is indeed prominent

---

A Closer Look: The "House of David." A recent archaeological discovery at Dan, a royal city of the northern kingdom from the days of Jeroboam I to the Assyrian destruction (922–732 BCE), has uncovered an inscription on a basalt stele that makes reference to the "house of David." The unprecedented discovery, though disputed, is written in Old Hebrew script, called "paleo-Hebrew," and very likely dates from sometime in the early to mid-ninth century BCE. The author of the inscription is no Israelite and very likely claims to have been victorious over the "king of Israel" (also mentioned in the inscription) and the "house of David." The archaeologists who made the discovery cautiously hypothesize a conflict with the Aramaean state to the north against whom the states of Judah and Israel, with their kings, were allied. If the interpretation is valid, the find would be one of the oldest, if not the oldest, physical attestation to the Davidic monarchy. Yet another interpreter, however, believes these conclusions are too hasty and rest upon only the "wishful thinking" of the interpreters. This scholar believes it is just as likely that the words "house of David" (*bytdwd*) could be a place name.

For further reading, H. Shanks, Ed. "'David' Found at Dan." *BAR* 20.2 (1994) 26–39; A. Lemaire. "'House of David' Restored." *BAR* 20.3 (1994) 30–7; P. R. Davies. "'House of David' Built on Sand." *BAR* 20.4 (1994) 54–5.

For more advanced study, A. Biran and J. Naveh. "An Aramaic Stele Fragment from Tel Dan." *IEJ* 43.2–3 (1993) 81–98; W. Dever. "Archaeology, Ideology, and the Quest for an 'Ancient' or 'Biblical Israel.'" *NEA* 61.1 (1998) 39–52.

in Chronicles, but the assertion that Yahweh will discipline the king is conspicuously absent. This exclusion is all the more remarkable in comparison with the view offered by the Deuteronomistic historian. There, David is portrayed as an adulterer who will preserve his public image at any cost (2 Samuel 11–12), and Solomon holds political expedience above the traditional religious commitments of Israel (1 Kings 1–8). Leaving out the reference to punishment is in keeping with the Chronicler's general tendencies to rehabilitate the reputations of both David and Solomon.[8] Remember, these two characters function in the Chronicler's History to legitimize the institution of the Temple. It may be of further relevance that the Chronicler, though rehabilitating the reputations of these two kings, knows that in his day there was no king. The Chronicler's History functions for his contemporary audience as a kind of ancient prophecy. His story envisions a day when punishing the human king would be irrelevant since it is actually Yahweh himself who is the king.

Perhaps the most striking difference between these two versions is in the comparison of 2 Sam 7:16 with 1 Chron 17:14. The passage in 2 Sam 7:16 reads "Your house and your kingdom shall be made sure forever before me; your throne shall be established forever." The passage in 1 Chron 17:14 reads, "but I will confirm him in my house and in my kingdom forever, and his throne shall be established forever." Notice that the two passages are similar in their conclusions of an eternal throne. They differ in that the older promise speaks of David's house and kingdom, whereas the more recent reading in Chronicles speaks of Yahweh's house and kingdom. The implication of this latter reading is that the historian, knowing that there can be no literal political kingdom, rereads Davidic kingship as something that only exists through the Temple. The human king, who is the Davidic heir, fulfills his royal function by leading the nation to worship the heavenly king, Yahweh.

The rereading in these verses stems from a remarkably different social text. In addition to the political reality that there could be no king due to Persian political domination, there is a strong shift from monarchical ideology to theocratic ideology. Yahweh alone is the heavenly king who rules over the nation. His servants are priests and their work in the Temple is central to Yahweh's rule. This idea of theocracy and not monarchy seems to fit more precisely with the Chronicler's **theology**. It explains the elevation of David and Solomon as Temple builders, Yahweh's refusal to punish them if they sin, and above all, his emphasis that the Davidic lineage could only live on within the effective function of the Temple. The Chronicler's theocratic tendencies seem even clearer when readers compare the intertextual relationships between the endings of the two histories. In 2 Kgs 25:27–30 the Deuteronomistic historian describes the release of the captive king Jehoiachin. In this way the historian signals both the endurance of the Davidic line (thus the fulfillment of Nathan's promise earlier in the history) and the hope that such a king might again reign in Jerusalem. The Chronicler has no such vision. The final word from the Chronicler on Israel's history is that a foreign king rather than a Davidic king releases Yahweh's people (2 Chron 36:22–23). It is Cyrus the Persian, acting as a mere representative of the heavenly king, Yahweh, who releases the people and builds the Temple in Jerusalem.[9]

---

[8]R. Braun, *1 Chronicles* (WBC 14; Waco, TX: Word Books, 1986) 199.

[9]See Becker, *Messianic Expectation,* 81.

"I Shall Be his Father, and He Shall Be my Son . . ."
The King as a Sacral Figure
1 Samuel 8:1–22; Psalms 2, 110, 45

Learning Goals

- To understand the concept of the divinity of the king in the Hebrew Bible.
- To understand how the king as a sacral figure relates to the broader ancient Near Eastern kingship ideology.
- To understand how this idea of the elevation of the king was given expression in the poetry of worship.
- To understand some of the socio-political realities in tenth- and ninth-century BCE Israel that called for the sacralization of kingship.

Guiding Study Exercises

1) Review the specific objections to kingship that Samuel lists (1 Sam 8:10–16). How, *specifically*, would life under a king contrast with the old tribal system?
2) List and explain specific examples from the Royal Psalms in the Bible where the king seems to be described as either divine himself or nearly so.
3) How does awareness of ancient Near Eastern kingship ideology help one to understand the elevation of the king in the Royal Psalms?
4) Explain how these Royal Psalms function to legitimate kingly rule.

By studying the Deuteronomist's and Chronicler's reformulation of the Davidic promise, readers have seen the most important boundaries within which ancient Israel came to define kingship. The promise not only implicitly makes a statement about the future, it also uses language that elevates the status of the king to that of divine sonship. Under the potential influence of the social text of ancient Near Eastern kingship ideology, the idea of a king who was only a mortal, as Deuteronomic theologians insisted, was rather radical. Thus, not only did ancient Israel struggle with the boundaries between a political ruler and a spiritual ruler (monarchy vs. theocracy), but it also struggled with the ideas of the divinity and mortality of the king. That struggle becomes clearer in view of some of the aspects behind the story that scholars believe called for such elevation to divine sonship in the first place.

The Social and Political Fallout of Kingship

It is difficult to understand the monarchy and the need to legitimize it in Israel apart from an appreciation for the nature of political organization *prior* to monarchy. There were concurrent

This anonymous medieval representation of David's coronation attests to the abiding influence of Davidic kingship in the Christian era. (Corbis-Betmann)

competing views of political organization, which were the basis for intense opposition to the idea of centralized authority. Readers encounter one of those competing viewpoints in a narrative concerning David's predecessor, Saul. In 1 Sam 8:1–22, Samuel the prophet opposes the appointment of Saul as king. Scholars believe that, even though the Deuteronomistic historian has edited this episode into his narrative, it actually reflects the voice of opposition to kingship during the earliest days of the monarchy.[10] The reasons for opposing kingship are couched in theological terms (rejection of Yahweh), to be sure. However, behind the theological arguments there exist serious sociological and economic realities that most likely provided the real basis of the opposition.

Rights of the King. The episode makes an implicit comparison between the rule of kings and that of judges (v. 1). The people request that Samuel give them a king. Samuel thinks this to be ultimately disastrous. He prays to Yahweh and is instructed to heed the people's voice. Samuel is not to interpret the request as a rejection of himself but as a rejection of the deity: "just as they have done to me, from the day I brought them up out of Egypt to this day . . ." (v. 8). Here there is unmistakably a theological argument taking shape. Establishing kingship is rejecting the idea of Yahweh's kingship; the people are willing to compromise the notion of theocracy in order to have a central political leader. Samuel is also to instruct the people in the ways of kings. There are not just theological questions at stake, but deeply embedded social and political questions as well.

The social text for this narrative is directly related to the social organization the people had under judges during the years around 1150–1000 BCE. Understanding this background helps readers appreciate the nature of the sacrifice people were making by having a king. The village was the most basic political and economic unity in the "segmented agrarian society."[11] It was independent. There were no economic or permanent political alliances. Leadership within the village was based upon the dominant economic unit of the village, the household. The household consisted of the extended family. This extended family, called "the house of the father," or *bet-'ab,* consisted of the head of the family and his wives, his sons and daughters and their spouses, his slaves, and foreigners. This basic family unit might then join together into a larger unit called a "clan," or *mispahah.* These consisted of several family units that were related, or which linked together into associations. An entire village might be simply several extended families living and working together.[12] Several of these clans might join together to form tribes. Tribes tended to be territorial.[13] That is, they laid claim to a certain part of the land for the sake of their own tribal members. Elders from the clans or villages provided the leadership on a local basis, while leaders for the entire tribe, perhaps in times of crisis, would emerge on an *ad hoc* basis. The Bible refers to such *ad hoc* leaders as judges.

The overall effect of such a socio-politico-economic arrangement was one of extraordinary independence and local ownership of land. There was no "national" economy; there was no centralized government; there was no standing army. The threats to one clan or tribe were not necessarily a threat to another. In fact, intertribal warfare was also common. So when the people ask Samuel to give them a king, Samuel responds by explaining that kingship will cost them much of the independence and freedom that stemmed from their tribal political organization.

Looking carefully at 1 Sam 8:10–18 readers see that Samuel offers his people a warning about the "ways" of the king. The word "ways" translates the Hebrew word *mispat,* which is used

---

[10]K. W. Whitelam, "Israelite Kingship. The Royal Ideology and its Opponents," *The World of Ancient Israel* (ed., R. E. Clements; Cambridge: Cambridge University Press, 1989) 126–127.

[11]J. Callaway, "Settlement and Judges," *Ancient Israel* (ed., H. Shanks; Englewood Cliffs, NJ: Prentice Hall, 1988) 79

[12]*Ibid.,* 79.

[13]*Ibid.,* 80.

elsewhere to mean "judgment" or "right." The text is not therefore merely reflecting upon general characteristics of kingship. Rather, it is reflecting upon the judgments or rights given to the king by virtue of his office. He has the right to people's children, their land, their servants, and their produce. All of these rights of the king reflect some feature of the segmented agrarian society over which he would exercise control. In order to satisfy the people's desire to have a king to "fight our battles" the king had to muster an army. Armies would be created from the people's children. To maintain the king's court he would collect provisions from the people's fields, which not only implied a right to taxation but the right to own the land as well. Clearly, the text asserts in unambiguous terms the fact that kingship brings major socio-economic changes.

Does the Gain Outweigh the Cost? Examining the text again, readers may also see that the narrative does include references to some real advantages in having a king. The narrative actually begins with the report that Samuel himself had grown old and there was some question among the people about his leadership. Readers may follow on their own his story in its fullness from the beginning of 1 Samuel. Samuel is called a judge (e.g., 7:15), although his duties resemble much more those of a prophet or a priest (7:5–6, 16–17). The people's judgment against Samuel's sons as his successors parallels a similar judgment against the sons of Samuel's predecessor, Eli (2 Sam 2:12–17). The story in its entirety asserts that the problem of a succession of honest judges and priests is difficult. The people want a leader who will "rule" them "like other nations." The word translated in the NRSV as "rule" is from the root *sapat,* which means in other contexts "to judge." Thus the people ask for a king to "judge" them; Samuel warns them of the "judgment," or *mispat,* of the king. The noun *mispat,* "judgment," is based upon the root *sapat,* "to judge." The two verses, 5 and 9, create an irony that casts a negative light over the narrative's attitude toward kingship. Still, Samuel's own sons were no better.

The conclusion of the episode portrays the people reiterating yet again their desire for a king (vv. 19–20). Here a new element appears in the rationale for their request. They want a king both to govern ("judge") them and to fight their battles. Readers who have followed the story from the beginning of the book of Samuel know that there was a constant threat from the **Philistines**. The Philistines were constantly raiding the Israelite tribes and even took as one of the spoils of war the very **Ark of the covenant** (1 Sam 4:10–22). Thus, the cry of the people to Samuel in 1 Samuel 8 reflects both a growing vacuum in leadership and an ever growing external threat posed by surrounding nations such as the Philistines. All of this is simply to say that the narrative depicts the people of Israel in dire circumstances, providing at least some legitimization for their request for a king.

The Elevation to Sonship

It is easy now to see some of the causes of the Deuteronomist's ambivalence toward kingship. As he composes his history, he knows how the story turns out in the sixth century BCE. From that perspective the gains of kingship did not outweigh its costs. The kings are partly to blame for leading Israel and Judah astray. For those who favored kingship it was necessary to legitimize it. The tradition of worship in ancient Israel, especially worship that was devoted to the celebration of kingship, illuminates the heights to which such legitimization of kingship could go. In the same way that the Chronicler connected the Temple with Davidic kingship in order to obtain legitimization, the king could be connected with Yahweh himself. The only way the gains of kingship could outweigh the costs is if Yahweh himself ordained the institution. A series of so-called Royal

Psalms within the book of Psalms reflect the basic assumptions of the importance of the king. Royal Psalms had the function of calling down blessings of Yahweh upon the king and his office, thus making clear the Lord's legitimization of the king's position. If Yahweh was behind kingship, so the argument goes, even though it results in radical redistribution of land, wealth, political organization, and economy, then the people could not so readily oppose it.

The Ancient Near Eastern Social Text. Readers cannot overlook that ancient Israel was a part of its larger Near Eastern context. Israel shared ideas about kingship with the nation-states that surrounded it. (Remember, 1 Sam 8:5 is conscious of the influence of "the nations.") It was common in that setting for peoples to conceive of the reign of the king as they did the reign of their deities. If gods were to reign with power and justice over the earth, so were kings. If gods were to reign eternally, ensuring the stability of the social order, then so were kings. It should come as no surprise that the same or nearly the same images of perpetuation and sonship that the Bible associates with Israel's Davidic kings are also found in the royal ideology of the larger ancient Near Eastern social text.

Most well known is the case of Egypt. The Pharaoh was called a god. He was celebrated as the son of Re. While he was alive he was the incarnation of the god Horus; upon death he was then incorporated into Osiris. The stele of Sehetep-ib-Re ascribes to king Ni-maat-Re these words:

Worship King Ni-maat-Re, living forever, within your bodies

And associate with his majesty in your hearts.

He is Perception which is in "(men's) hearts,"

And his eyes search out every body.

He is Re, by whose beams one sees,

He is one who illumines the Two Lands more than the sun disc.[14]

Clearly, in this poem the king is the god Re, and the people are to worship him as one who gives life and maintains life as the sun does.

The idea of the divine king was not so widely celebrated in **Mesopotamia**. There is clearly a distance between the earthly king and the heavenly deity. Readers will see below the language that associates the king with the deity nevertheless maintains the view that the king is *like* a deity in certain respects. In the following "Petition to a King," the language of sonship appears as the suppliant refers to the king as the "son of Anu," the chief god of the Sumerian **pantheon**, in his petition for justice.

To my king with varicolored eyes who wears a lapis lazuli beard, Speak;

To the golden statue fashioned on a good day,

The . . . raised in a pure sheepfold, called *to* the pure *womb* of Inanna,

The lord, hero of Inanna, say:

---

[14]*ANET,* 431

A Closer Look: The "Akitu" Festival in Babylon. Scholars' ability to piece together ancient state ceremonies also offers insight into the beliefs of ancient societies. The first day of the new year (the vernal equinox) was the day on which ancient Babylonians renewed the king's role in the cult. Through the ceremony of the Akitu festival the king was said to be "taking the hand of Bel-Marduk," the chief deity of the city of Babylon. During the ceremony the king knelt before the deity and confessed his innocence of any crime or abuse of office, thus declaring his fitness for the office. It was only through such annual renewal of king and cult, the effective reestablishment of the order of the world, that there could be assurance of a successful agricultural season. The significance of the yearly festival is attested in the Babylonian record, which speaks of how the last king of the Neo-Babylonian empire, Nabonidus (555–539 BCE), left the capital city, thus preventing the celebration from taking place. The antipathy this created between Nabonidus and the priesthood of Marduk, not to mention the citizens of the city, may explain why Cyrus' annals report the Babylonians to have welcomed him as conqueror into their city. He says he entered Babylon "as a friend."

For further reading, "Cyrus," *ANET,* 315–316; J. N. Postgate. "Royal Ideology and State Administration in Sumer and Akkad." *CANE* I, 395–411.

For more advanced study, D. Johnson. "The Wisdom of Festival Akitu: Babylonian New Year." *Parabola* 2.2 (1977) 20–23.

"Thou (*in*) thy judgment thou art the son of Anu,

Thy commands, like the word of a god, cannot be *turned back,*[15]

This is not the full text of the poem, but the excerpt suffices to illustrate again the idea of the close affinities between king and deity, even in ancient Mesopotamia. As the son of the deity, the king has the authority to make binding judgments. (See the Hammurabi stele on page 91).

Readers of the biblical materials must be cautiously aware that language asserting the role of the king as savior, as warrior, as judge, and as son of god is language that parallels imagery in other cultures contemporary with Israel. This does not mean that Israel adopted this imagery in whole, but it does require that readers keep in mind the broad macro-level intertextuality between Israel's notions of kingship and those of the larger ancient Near Eastern social text. Recall that the Davidic promise contains imagery of vegetation, perpetuity, as well as sonship. To these specific motifs readers must turn in their reading of the following psalms.

Psalm 2. This psalm is one of about ten or eleven such psalms that functioned to glorify the king.[16] Obviously, such psalms would have been composed for a time when there was a king, so

---

[15]*Ibid.,* 382.

[16]W. H. Holladay, *The Psalms Through Three Thousand Years* (Minneapolis, MN: Fortress, 1993) 38–39; compare K. Seybold, *Introducing the Psalms* (Edinburgh: T&T Clark, 1990) 115, who lists nos. 2, 18, 20, 21, 45, 72, 89, 101, 110, 132. Holladay adds no. 144.

scholars tend to date them to the pre-Exilic period. Psalm 2 is of particular interest because of the macro-level intertextuality on "sonship" it forms with the Davidic promise in 2 Sam 7:14. The psalm assumes Yahweh's reign in the heavens as king and extols the earthly king in language that would appear to raise him above the level of mere mortals.

The context in which such a psalm functioned was most certainly the Temple. It may well have been composed for the ceremony of the coronation of the Davidic king upon succession to the throne. If this is so, then the celebration of kingship through coronation had the task of legitimizing the act of declaring a king. It should be no surprise, given this possible setting, that the Royal Psalms also make clear the social responsibilities of the reigning king.

Notice, first of all, the voice of the narrator alternates both with the voice of the raging kings, who deride Yahweh (v. 3), and the voice of Yahweh (v. 6), who announces his confidence in his king. Then vv. 7–9 quote Yahweh's announcement to his earthly king. The language is of interest in that it suggests that the earthly king himself is speaking, thus causing readers to revise their assumption that the narrator of vv. 1–6 is someone other than the king. Verses 10–12 close the psalm with an admonition, presumably from the king himself, for all kings of the earth to serve Yahweh.

Notice especially v. 7, where the earthly king announces Yahweh's proclamation of sonship. Remember 2 Sam 7:14—"I will be a father to him, and he shall be a son to me"—where the Davidic promise asserts sonship and then expands on the idea by asserting that Yahweh will discipline the king as a father disciplines his son. Nothing like that appears in Psalm 2. In the psalm, Yahweh asserts the king's sonship and this status then becomes the basis for the earthly king's dominion over the nations. Most certainly this is poetic language and readers are cautioned about the extent to which literal claims can rest upon metaphoric language. But one cannot escape the metaphorical implication that sonship is a status that offers special privilege. In other words, if Yahweh would grant the king the inheritance of all nations, he would not hold back from him the ownership of all Israel.

Psalm 110. Yet another psalm that celebrates the reign of the king, and very likely functioned as a hymn for coronation day, is Psalm 110. The opening verse is significant for two reasons. The phrase "The Lord says to my lord" is characteristic prophetic messenger language (see Chap. 5). Therefore, readers could infer that this is an oracle that has come from Yahweh through his prophet. There is therefore macro-level intertextuality with 2 Sam 7:1–17, which also comes as a prophetic oracle to David. Further, v. 1 also quotes Yahweh as urging his king to sit at the Lord's right hand. The *right* hand is an image of strength and power as well as one of favor. But readers encounter the reverse of this imagery in v. 5 when the poet has Yahweh sitting at the right hand of the king. This shifts the relationship of the king to the deity as seen in v. 1, implying that the earthly king has assumed the position of deity.

The language of sonship is problematic in this psalm. It is possible to translate the **Masoretic text** of v. 3 as saying, "With you is princely dominion from the day of your birth in holy splendor; from the womb of the morning you have the dew of your sonship."[17] Addressed to the king, such language clearly assumes the king's elevation to divine status. But this is a disputed translation; NRSV translates v. 3 instead as, "Your people will offer themselves willingly on the

---

[17]Becker, *Messianic Expectation,* 43.

day you lead your forces on the holy mountains. From the womb of the morning like dew, your youth will come to you." The difference between the translations is significant. The first translation speaks of a "birth in holy splendor" and "sonship." The latter only uses nature very broadly ("the womb of the morning") as an image of blessing upon the king ("like dew").

The imagery of the perpetuation of the king's reign, so characteristic of the promise in 2 Sam 7:13, also takes a slightly different turn in Psalm 110. Verse 4 is another difficult passage. The Lord swears an oath that the king is of a priestly order. This kind of phrase certainly accomplishes the goal of elevating kingship by **sacralizing** the king's office. On the other hand, the passage is most enigmatic in that scholars do not understand exactly what the "order of Melchizedek" refers to. The most immediate intertext is with Gen 14:18 where Abraham encounters a king of Salem by this name. With this royal tradition standing behind the name, it might be that "the order of Melchizedek" is an order of priesthood that combines both kingship and priestly responsibilities. In the context of ancient Israel's families of priests, it would be an order that is neither Levitical nor Aaronic (see Chap. 6). However, the image is provocative enough that later poets and prophets reread this passage to give the figure of Melchizedek still fuller significance.

Psalm 45. Psalm 45 differs from the preceding psalms in the hypothesized occasion of its composition. Rather than the observance of the royal coronation, this psalm appears to be written for a royal wedding. The glory and strength of the king still take a central place in the poetry. However, the ultimate function is changed when the poet then admonishes the new queen to respond appropriately to her husband. Verses 10–11 make this clear: "Hear, O daughter, consider and incline your ear; forget your people and your father's house, and the king will desire your beauty. Since he is your lord, bow to him."

The specific language of the king's sonship is absent in this psalm. However, there is no lack of language that elevates the king nearly to the level of deity. Consider v. 6, which says: "Your throne, O God, endures forever and ever." Obviously, the idea of the perpetuation of this king's throne is unambiguous. The notion of an eternal reign also concludes the psalm. Verses 16–17 state that the king's sons will be "princes in all the earth." There is also the statement that Yahweh will cause the king's name to be celebrated "in all generations." Unlike the promise oracle in 2 Samuel, there is no condition of obedience to Yahweh attached to this claim of perpetual reign. What is perhaps most problematic to modern readers is the address of the king as "God." There are alternative translations of this Hebrew phrase. Another translation is "Your throne is a throne of God." In this latter case, the poet is not asserting the actual deity of the king. Nevertheless, readers encounter language that celebrates the sacrality of the king or of the king's office. Verse 7b seems to make a distinction between the king and God by speaking of the act of selection through "anointing." Verse 7b says, "Therefore God, your God, has anointed you with the oil of gladness beyond your companions." While the language of "anointing" is the same as that used of kings and priests, in this context such language may function as both a play on the tradition of anointing for public service as well as a reference to an "anointing" to the delights of being a husband.

"The Throne of His Kingdom Forever":
Between Now and Then
Isaiah 7:1–17; 9:1–7; 11:1–10; Selections from Daniel,
The Dead Sea Scrolls, and the Pseudepigrapha

Learning Goals

- To understand within the Hebrew Bible the widening gap between the historical present and the messianic future.
- To understand how the various messianic oracles of Isaiah shift from realistic, historical hope to utopian idealism.
- To understand that late Jewish messianism formed the basis for early Christian reinterpretations of the Messiah.

Guiding Study Exercises

1) Using the three Isaianic oracles studied in this unit as evidence, describe how expectations for an ideal king were increasingly pushed into a more remote future.
2) What is the meaning of the figure of the "son of man" in the vision of Daniel?
3) "Post-Exilic Judaism held to a common understanding of 'the coming Messiah.' " Respond to the adequacy of this statement in a paragraph.
4) Write a short answer explaining the function of a *Pesher.*
5) Write a paragraph summarizing the social text of the Psalms of Solomon.

One strategy in the post-Exilic period for reinterpreting kingship resembles what has already been encountered in reference to the Temple (see Chap. 6). That is, ancient theologians pushed the restoration of the Temple off into the future and associated it with a new age that was yet to come (recall Tob 14:5). The combination of a heightened significance of kingship in general, in the framework of social texts that did not allow historical political rulers, provided the background for similar ways of rereading the Davidic promise. In fact, readers may see this already at work in the oracles associated with Isaiah, and taking a yet more elaborate form in Daniel.

The Isaiah Trilogy and Daniel

This section begins by examining three different oracles within the book of Isaiah, as found in Isa 7:10–17, 9:2–7, and 11:1–10, all dating from successively later time periods. While it is not for certain when to date the latter two oracles, scholars are fairly certain, based upon the context, when to date the first. The latter two allow only the roughest estimation. Nevertheless, all three are linked intertextually by the royal language of sonship, and the latter two by the vegetation imagery alluding to the theme of the perpetuation of the Davidic line. Remember, sonship is one of the key features of the promise Yahweh makes to David. Of further significance, the figure about whom each oracle speaks—that messianic son—is gradually *dehistoricized*.[18] That is, he becomes less and less a figure of immediate historical reality and more and more an ideal figure projected into an indefinite future.[19] This trend toward dehistoricization is already beginning with the canonical biblical literature. The trend continues, as shall become evident, in Hellenistic and Qumranic Jewish literature. The literature that results forms a foundation for Christian messianism in the first century CE.

Isaiah 7:10–17. This is a passage of some import to the evangelist who wrote the New Testament book of Matthew. Recall from Chapter 5 that prophetic books, especially the book of Isaiah, are collections of prophetic oracles. These collections not only confront readers with the challenges of the prophet, but with the interpretations of the editors who did the collecting. While Matthew's gospel only cites one verse from the passage (v. 14), it is of more concern why he quotes it. It seems he is influenced by a tradition of rereading the ancient prophets. The author is concerned with tracing the lineage of Jesus the Christ (Matthew 1) through a royal descent that includes King David. His use of Isa 7:14 in Matt 1:23, then, confirms his understanding of this old oracle as announcing some future hope of a royal savior. But it is of special interest how the oracle functioned ostensibly in its own context late in the eighth century BCE. Knowing the oracle's original function underscores for readers the extent to which the first-century CE evangelist Matthew has reread the prophet.

Beginning with Isa 7:1, the larger context of the present focal passage, readers are able to piece together bits of the setting in which the prophet delivers the oracle. Ahaz is king (see appendix, Chap. 5) and Jerusalem is under attack from the king of Israel, called Pekah, and the king of Syria (Aram), called Rezin (v. 1). The aim of the attack on Jerusalem was to overthrow king Ahaz and replace him with another king, Tabeel (v. 6). One infers from other sources that their overall purpose was to put together an anti-Assyrian coalition to oppose the Assyrian king **Tiglath-Pileser** (2 Kgs 16:5–9). In order to withstand the attack on Jerusalem, one of the options before King Ahaz was to make a treaty with the Assyrians (which is what he eventually did, according to 2 Kings 16). The prophet Isaiah, however, admonishes the king to "stand firm in faith" (v. 9), thus doing nothing.

The oracle about the child named "Immanuel" comes from the prophet as a sign. The child named Immanuel, meaning "God is with us," will be born to a young woman to signify the defeat of the armies laying siege against Jerusalem. In addition to the unambiguous setting within the framework of the siege against Jerusalem during Ahaz's day, there are two further details that remind readers of the immediate historical implications of this oracle. First, there is nothing in the oracle that suggests that the woman is a virgin, as Matthew's gospel has it. The word translated in the NRSV as "young woman" in v. 14 is the Hebrew word *'alma*. While the word might well imply virginity, one would guess that if the prophet had intended for virginity to play a decisive

---

[18]This term is used by S. Talmon in his article, "The Concepts of *masiah* and Messianism in Early Judaism," *The Messiah* (ed., J. Charlesworth; Minneapolis, MN: Fortress, 1992) 95.

[19]On the further distinction between restorative and utopian messianism see L.H. Schiffman, "Messianic Figures and Ideas in the Qumran Scrolls," *The Messiah* (ed., J. Charlesworth) 116–129.

role in the meaning of the oracle, he would have used the more technical term for virgin, *betulah.* Second, there is nothing miraculous about the birth itself. In other words, the young woman is not "barren," nor does God's holy spirit come upon the young woman as in Matthew's gospel. Rather, the child is apparently born through the usual biological means. What is miraculous about this oracle is that Yahweh will deliver his city, Jerusalem, if king Ahaz will only trust in the Lord and not make an alliance with Assyria.

Whereas Christian readers familiar with Matthew immediately identify "Immanuel" with Jesus, scholars are not in agreement with regard to the identity of the child *in the originating context of the Isaianic oracle.* Some argue that there is good reason to read the child as the son of the prophet.[20] The larger context of the oracle portrays the prophet as conveying his messages through the symbolic naming of his other children as well. Two of the prophet's children are identified unambiguously in 7:3 and 8:1 as Shear-jashub and Maher-shalal-hash-baz. Notice that the first one's name means "a remnant shall remain" and thus could function as a symbolic word of salvation. The second one's name means "spoil speeds, prey hastens," and thus is a symbolic word of doom. The two names then parallel the tone of the prophet's oracles. The first is a call to trust in Yahweh; the second is the result of failing to trust in Yahweh.

On the other hand, the prophet could be talking about the son of the king, in which case Immanuel is the royal heir.[21] The difficulty here is that, as a sign, how could the prophet then have control over the naming of the child? Nevertheless, one of the earliest interpreters of this passage evidently thought that the Immanuel child was indeed a reference to a royal heir. Isaiah 8:8 is a concluding segment of a later oracle. Notice that it actually speaks of Immanuel. What is so distinctive in this later addition is that the oracle refers to the land as belonging to him. Ownership of the land could only be relevant if Immanuel were a king.

Regardless of *who* Immanuel was in the originating context of this oracle, it is clear that Isaiah envisions the "fulfillment" of his prophecy in the *immediate* and historical future. Read carefully v. 16: "For before the child knows how to refuse the evil and choose the good, the land before whose two kings you are in dread will be deserted." The meaning would have been clear to King Ahaz: Before this Immanuel child reaches the age of moral discernment (late childhood? early adolescence?) the nations of the two kings whom Ahaz so dreaded, Israel and Syria, "will be deserted." Presumably the prophet recognizes that the threatening nation of Assyria would very likely conquer these smaller kingdoms besieging Jerusalem. Readers who recall that Israel fell to Assyria in the year 722 BCE (see v. 17), and thus that Assyria was conquering nations at the time of the oracle, will understand that the immediate historical context vindicated the prophet's word, even though King Ahaz did not follow the prophet's advice.

Isaiah 9:2–7. These oracular verses display some striking macro-level intertexts with Isaiah 7, but unlike that former passage, it is lacking a narrative context (note there is no "story" surrounding the oracle as in Isaiah 7). Clearly the language of the oracle refers to the birth of a king and in v. 7 there is a strong connection with the throne of David. Notice especially in v. 6 the language of "sonship." The passage sounds more like the kind of elevated language in the Royal

---

[20]This is the approach of R. Clements, *Isaiah* (NCB; Grand Rapids, MI: Eerdmans, 1979) 87–88.

[21]Such is the approach of J. Hayes and S. Levine, *Isaiah* (Nashville, TN: Abingdon, 1987) 132. J. Blenkinsopp, *A History of Prophecy in Israel* (London: SPCK, 1984) 110, also acknowledges that this identity was an early interpretation.

Psalms (see Psalms 2, 110, and 45) and invites speculation as to the relationship between prophetic oracles and cultic language. It could well be coronation language for a son or grandson of Ahaz who was following his father on the throne. The phrase "a son has been given to us" both recalls the idea of God's adoption of his son at enthronement, as well as the Immanuel oracle in Isa 7:14. However, it is clearly a forward-looking oracle, capturing in a prophetic vision the hopes of what kingship would bring in the future.

The social text for this oracle is somewhat difficult to determine, however. Keeping in mind that later, post-Exilic, editors are responsible for the final form the whole book of Isaiah, it is possible that the oracle *could* have originated after the time of Isaiah of Jerusalem (similar to the oracles of Second and Third Isaiah). If, on the other hand, the oracle refers to Ahaz's son, then it is a rather immediate rereading of the Immanuel oracle. This would imply that the prophet is not attempting to envision anything beyond his immediate setting, that is, the rule of an ideal king. However, the poetic language is historically nonspecific, offering a much more general understanding of the historical circumstances. This could be any king in the Davidic line. Indeed scholars do not agree whether this oracle speaks of Ahaz's son, Hezekiah, or his grandson, Josiah, or some other general future messianic figure.[22] Whether or not the oracle itself dates to the time of Isaiah of Jerusalem or long after, or whether the oracle is intended to offer a portrayal of an ideal king yet to come in the indefinite future, is not clear. This ambiguity, drawn from the rather general nature of the oracle, may be an example of how prophetic oracles regarding the king could gradually expand the time between prophetic announcement and expected fulfillment.[23]

Isaiah 11:1–9. This oracle is still later since it assumes that the house of David is nothing more than a "stump." The oracle could, therefore, reasonably be dated to the period after the fall of Jerusalem and the virtual collapse of the Davidic dynasty in 587 BCE.[24] There are not any specific intertextual connections on the theme of "sonship" with either Isaiah 7 or 2 Samuel 7 as in the preceding two oracles. At a macro-level, however, the vegetation imagery of the "shoot" may well allude to similar imagery in Ps 132:17 ("There I will cause a horn to sprout up for David"). That notwithstanding, the oracle is unambiguously concerned with the Davidic king since there is a reference to David's father, Jesse (see 1 Sam 16:1–6), and it is very likely post-Exilic.

Notice that the oracle looks forward to a much more indefinite, nonhistorical future when it uses idealized language concerning the king. The prophet seems not to have any clear idea about *when* this coronation will take place. The oracle in vv. 1–5 precedes a vision of a utopian age when mortal enemies such as the wolf and the lamb, the calf and the lion, and the little child and the asp shall coexist in peace (Isa 11:6–9; cf. Isa 65:25). What is more, there are also the typical descriptions of the king's responsibilities toward righteous rule, but couched in highly poetic language. Verse 5 begins: "He shall strike the earth with the rod of his mouth, and with the breath of his lips he shall kill the wicked. Righteousness shall be the belt around his waist, and faithfulness the belt around his loins."

There is no possibility of understanding a social text for this oracle. Though it is clearly about David, there is no clue as to any historical event that informs the prophet's words. It is not

---

[22]Clements, *Isaiah,* 104

[23]S. Talmon, "The Concepts of *masiah,*" 98–101

[24]Some commentators take this to refer to the only remaining portion of Jerusalem and Judah after the Assyrian conquest of 722 BCE. See Hayes and Irvine, *Isaiah,* 211–212.

possible, as in Isa 9:2–7, even to suppose some historical figure such as Hezekiah or Josiah. This oracle reflects a total dehistoricization of the image of the royal figure.

Hence, within these three oracles in Isaiah that concern a "son" or a "king," readers can trace a movement from an expectation that is imminent in Isaiah 7 to an expectation that would find its fulfillment in a more ideal, utopian, and indeterminate future in Isaiah 11. The oracle of Isaiah 9 may stand somewhat between these two poles, depending upon how one dates the oracle and who one understands the ideal king portrayed in the oracle to be. But editorially, the seeds are being planted in the social text of the people for the view that the fulfillment of God's promise to David will come in the indefinite future (2 Sam 7:16).

Daniel. Readers might readily hypothesize at this point that Exilic and post-Exilic Jewish messianism defined itself only within the orbit of the promise of a *Davidic* king. The trajectory of thought growing from the promise given to David by Nathan the prophet certainly is an influential touchstone for many rereadings of kingship. But the notion of messianism that provided the background for first-century CE Christian evangelists was far more complex.

This section of the discussion concludes with a brief review of Daniel to illustrate how varied Jewish expectations regarding kingship in the future age of restoration could be. Readers will recall that in Dan 7:13–14 there is a figure referred to as the "son of man" (Chap. 5). Significantly, this figure is not traced to any royal lineage, even though the vision in Daniel 7 speaks of his "kingship." However, the angel's interpretation of the vision explains that this "son of man" is not really an individual at all. Rather, he represents the *community* of the "holy ones" (see Dan 7:18, 27), paralleling the earlier visions of the chapter where figures of beasts were used to represent worldly kingdoms opposed to God. This is significant, for this text allows readers to see that some Jews could speak of the coming restoration and of God's rule without appeal to any particular human ruler at all. Chapter 11 will subsequently show that both Jews and Christians eventually did come to identify this son of man figure with the Messiah. However, it must be acknowledged that the text of Daniel itself makes no such identification.

The Messianic Promise in the Dead Sea Scrolls and the Pseudepigrapha

The following discussion explores further how messianic expectation continued to be reread within Judaism during the second and first centuries BCE. Readers will see that the idea that this messianic leader might be a priestly figure came to expression among some Jewish communities. At the same time, many Jews continued to cling to the more traditional Davidic model.

The Messiah(s) of Qumran. The emphasis on a priestly leader is a special feature of the writings from the Qumran community (the **Dead Sea Scrolls**). Readers should recall, initially, Haggai and Zechariah. While these two prophets certainly placed high hopes and expectations in the Davidic descendant Zerubbabel, they also assumed that ruling alongside this Davidic heir was the priest Joshua (Hag 1:1; 2:2, 4; Zech 4:3–4, 12–14). In short, these two prophets, while giving prominence to the Davidic heir, offer a portrait of *dual* leadership, or what is called a *dyarchy.* The community of Qumran further developed this notion of dyarchy. Yet, unlike Haggai and Zechariah, this *priestly* community gave prominence to the priestly leader who was to come. Hence, while the royal, Davidic figure continues to play a role in the expectations of the Qumran community, the main messianic figure at Qumran is a Zadokite priest.

Readers already know from Chapter 6 some of the background of the Qumran community. The conflict between Zadokite priests and the Hasmonean priesthood may well have been the source of much of the Qumran community's writing. Among the Dead Sea Scrolls there are, broadly speaking, three types of texts. First, there are biblical texts. These have afforded scholars some insight into the status of transmission of biblical documents. Second, there are texts, such as "The Rule of the Community" (see Chap. 6), which laid out the rules and laws by which members of the community were to live their lives. Third, there were texts of biblical interpretation. These were texts that offered explicit interpretations, or rereadings, of biblical texts. These interpretive texts come in one of two forms: translations (**targums**) of biblical texts and contemporary interpretations (known as **pesherim**). The former interpret biblical texts by paraphrasing, and often greatly expanding, the biblical text. The latter tended to resemble the form of modern Bible commentaries where the biblical text would simply be quoted, to be followed by the text's interpretation or *pesher.*

In one of the texts, to which readers were introduced in Chapter 6 ("The Rule of the Community"), there are explicit references to the Qumran community's belief that there would actually be two messiahs: "They [members of the community] should not depart from any counsel of the law in order to walk in complete stubbornness of their heart, but instead shall be ruled by the first directives which the men of the Community began to be taught until the prophet comes, *and the Messiahs of Aaron and Israel*" (1QS 9.9–11; Martínez; emphasis added). The text actually shows that the Qumran community looked forward to the coming of *three* **eschatological** rulers, the prophet, the Messiah of Aaron, and the Messiah of Israel. While it would be interesting to pause and discuss this prophetic leader, space dictates that the focus of the discussion be on the two messianic figures.

That the Messiah of Aaron is a priestly figure is obvious given this messianic leader's explicit association with Aaron. But who was this "Messiah of Israel"? Other texts from among the community's Scrolls allow the conclusion that this messianic leader was thought to be a *Davidic* descendant. Two texts are revealing in this regard.

First, the text known as 4Q 161 (*Pesher Isaᵃ*) is an interpretation of Isaiah. One statement in 4Q 161 reveals the Qumran community's belief that they were living in "the last days." Fragments 5–6, for example, offer an interpretation of Isa 10:28–32. Verse 22 states: "[The interpretation of] the word concerns the final days, when the [king of the Kittim] comes. . . ." The biblical Isaiah passage itself speaks of the Assyrian army and its conquest of the lands near the sea. The pesher rereads this as having to do with the end of time and the armies of those who oppose and perhaps persecute the members of the Qumran community. In the same pesher, fragments 8–10 and beginning with line 11, readers encounter an interpretation of Isa 11:1–5, the passage considered above. While the biblical passage itself is left rather indefinite in its context, the Qumran rereading makes clear that this community read the text as referring to the coming in the last days of the Davidic messianic ruler.

> [Isa 11:1–5 A shoot will issue from the stu]mp of Jesse and [a bud] will sprout from its ro[ot.] Over him [will be placed] the spi[rit] 12of the Lord; a spirit of knowledge 13[and of respect for the lord, and his delight will be in respecting the] Lord. [He will not judge] by appearances 14[or give verdicts on hearsay alone;] he will judge [the poor with justice and decide] 15[with honesty for the humble of the earth. He will destroy the land with the rod of his mouth and with the breath of his lips] 16[he will execute the evil. Justice will be the belt of] his loins and lo[yalty the belt of his hips.] 17[. . .] *Blank* [. . .] 18[The interpretation of the word concerns the shoot] of David which will sprout [in final days, since] 19[. . .] (Martínez).

The micro-level intertextuality with the biblical Isaiah is striking. Note especially that lines 18–19 interpret the text of Isaiah to be speaking about "the shoot of David." Further, it is clear that this interpretation understands that the "shoot of David" will arise only in the "final days."

A second text offers the community's interpretation of the significant promise of 2 Samuel 7 to which this chapter has repeatedly referred.

> 10And [2 Sam 7:12–14] "YHWH de[clares] to you that he will build you a house. I will raise up your seed after you and establish the throne of his kingdom 11[for ev]er. I will be a father to him and he will be a son to me." This (refers to the) "branch of David," who will arise with the Interpreter of the Law who 12[will rise up] in Zi[on in] the last days, as it is written: [Amos 9:11] "I will raise up the hut of 13David which has fallen." This (refers to) "the hut of David which has fallen," who will arise to save Israel (4QFlorilegium 1.10–13; Martínez).

Again, the pesher reveals that the community reads its scriptures with the belief that the words of the ancient prophets were to be applied to the "last days" (see line 12). The Qumran covenanters apparently gave no credence to the fact that, in its original context, the descendant of David to whom Nathan was referring was Solomon. But, further, the text also makes clear that the community of Qumran did look forward to the time, in the last days, when the "hut of David"—the Davidic kingdom—would be reestablished. They *did* look forward to the coming of a Davidic messiah.

But this Davidic messiah would not be the prominent leader within the community of the restored Israel. The prominent role would be played by "the Messiah of Aaron." One particular text that allows this conclusion is entitled "The Rule of the Congregation" (1QSa). The text describes in some detail how the eschatological community is to assemble for its sacred meal.

Although space does not permit an extensive quote, it suffices to note that this text does not make explicit reference to the "Messiah of Aaron," but it does assume that at the gathering of the community in the last days there will be two leaders, the priest and the Messiah of Israel. Given 1QS 9.9–11, which does make explicit reference to "the Messiahs of Aaron and Israel," it is reasonable to conclude that the priestly leader at the eschatological banquet is the priestly Messiah. It is the priestly figure who has the prominent role. It is he and his entourage that enter the assembly first (lines 12–14a), then to be followed by the entrance of the Messiah of Israel (line 14b). After the priestly leader has blessed the bread and wine (lines 19–20a) the Messiah of Israel extends his hand out over the bread (lines 20b-21). The primary role that the priest plays in this significant gathering allows the conclusion that this messianic figure played the more important role in the leadership of the restored, eschatological Israel.

A Portrait of the Jewish Messiah from the Pseudepigrapha. To conclude the discussion, readers' attention is directed to an expression of messianism that scholars believe to have originated in Jerusalem sometime in the middle of the first century BCE. This comes within a collection of hymns called "The Psalms of Solomon." These psalms come from writings that scholars have come to call, primarily for convenience, the Pseudepigrapha. They are a somewhat miscellaneous collection of Jewish religious writings, dating roughly from the second century BCE to the first century CE. Scholars attempting to reconstruct the thought of Judaism during this period find the literature quite useful. The psalms are attributed to Solomon, even though there is unambiguous evidence within them of their first-century BCE setting. Readers should not think, however, that such an attribution makes an attempt to ascribe literal authorship to Israel's famous king, the son of David. Rather, such attributions simply reflect the ancient literary convention of **pseudonymous authorship**.

The psalms in general betray recent traumatic events within the life of the city of Jerusalem. They speak of invasion and occupation of the country by a foreign, gentile ruler. References to corrupt religious leaders become a basis for a yearning for the days when a righteous ruler would appear to stand and defeat all enemies. The scholarly consensus is that the calamities that the psalms assume grow from the invasion of the Roman leader Pompey, who in 63 BCE captured Jerusalem. Palestine at that time became a district of Roman political rule. The references to "sinners" very likely concern the Hasmoneans, Sadducees, and other aristocratic leaders who easily gave in to foreign practices. References to the righteous are not so easy to identify, however. Scholars thought at one time that these referred to the Pharisees in Jerusalem. But this is no longer widely held, and it must suffice simply to acknowledge that, as in the Hellenistic period generally, conflict between Jewish and non-Jewish culture seems to precipitate the writing of these psalms.

Out of the midst of this conflict the devout make the appeal to the coming of a righteous king. The portrait of the king in Psalms of Solomon 17 and 18 results from a rereading of various biblical texts about the Davidic kings and the promises made to David. While the extant texts are written only in Greek and Syriac, scholars believe that the original language was Hebrew. In the Greek text, the phrase used to describe this king, ***christos kurios,*** is translated as "Lord Messiah." Interestingly, this messianic title offers a striking micro-level intertext with Lk 2:11. The following excerpts from two of the psalms reveal the assumption of a *single* messiah of Davidic origins who fulfills the promise to David in 2 Sam 7:1–17 in some future event. The royal figure, furthermore, is no mere human. He is idealized in terms of his spiritual power, sinlessness, and holiness. Note, first, the opening of Pss Sol 17:1–4. It begins by referring to the relationship between God's kingdom and David's kingdom.

> 1Lord, you are our king forevermore, for in you, O God, does our soul take pride. 2How long is the time of a person's life on the earth? As is his time, so also is his hope in him. 3But we hope in God our savior, for the strength of our God is forever with mercy. And the kingdom of our God is forever over the nations in judgment. 4Lord, you chose David to be king over Israel, and swore to him about his descendants forever, that his kingdom should not fail before you.

Verse 4 clearly alludes to the promise that God made to David that his kingdom would endure forever (cf. 2 Sam 7:13, 16; Ps 132:11–12). It is a strong affirmation of God's kingship and David as his earthly representative. Note especially in verses 3–4 the connection between the eternity of God's kingdom and David's kingdom, a connection already encountered in the Chronicler's rereading of 2 Sam 7:1–17. This opening emphasis upon kings and kingship suggests a deliberate attempt to imitate the Royal Psalms of the Hebrew Bible.[25]

---

[25]See R. B. Wright, "Psalms of Solomon: A New Translation and Introduction," *The Old Testament Pseudepigrapha* (2 vols.; ed., J. H. Charlesworth; Garden City, NY: Doubleday, 1985) 2.639–734.

The psalm then proceeds to describe in vivid terms the suffering of the community of the righteous ones and Jerusalem generally. On that basis the psalmist then appeals to God with these words:

> [21]See, Lord, and raise up for them their king, the son of David, to rule over your servant Israel in the time known to you, O God. [22]Undergird him with the strength to destroy the unrighteous rulers, to purge Jerusalem from gentiles who trample her to destruction; [23]in wisdom and in righteousness to drive out the sinners from the inheritance; to smash the arrogance of sinners like a potter's jar (Pss Sol 17:21–23).

Again, notice the explicit reference to the Davidic lineage of this king. His task is to come as a warrior and destroy the "unrighteous rulers" and to "purge Jerusalem from gentiles." There is not, however, any language of sonship per se, which might indicate the view that this king is no ordinary human being. But this person is a holy king. The poet says, "And he will be a righteous king over them, taught by God. There will be no unrighteousness among them in his days, for all shall be holy, and their king shall be the Lord Messiah" (v. 32). Further, he shall not accomplish his reign in the usual ways: "(For) he will not rely on horse and rider and bow, nor will he collect gold and silver for war. Nor will he build up hope in a multitude for a day of war. The Lord himself is his king, the hope of the one who has a strong hope in God" (vv. 33–34).

Conclusion

Kingship, like the Temple, played a vital role in ancient Israel's self-understanding and theology. The strong association of David with the Temple likely originates as a means of legitimizing the existence of an institution that required persons to sacrifice their independence. Such elevation of the king performed the vital function of idealizing kingship and in particular reinforcing the king's authority to maintain justice and righteousness throughout society. In periods when there could no longer be a literal political king, kingship became a means of redirecting hopes from a dismal present to a future when Yahweh would reign on earth. Generation after generation found the promise to David in 2 Sam 7:1–17 open for reinterpretation, filling it fuller with possible implications. It will become evident that various Christian communities, like their Jewish ancestors just studied, would also utilize this promise in its attempt to understand Jesus of Nazareth.

For Further Reading

"I Shall Build Him a House": The Davidic Promise

Brueggemann, W. *David's Truth in Israel's Imagination and Memory.* Philadelphia: Fortress Press, 1985. (*Recommended for beginning students.*)

Tsevat, M. "The House of David in Nathan's Prophecy." *Bib* 36 (1965) 353–356. (*Recommended for beginning students.*)

Weinfeld, M. "Covenant, Davidic." *IDBSup,* 188–192. (*Recommended for beginning students.*)

"I Shall Be His Father , and He Shall Be My Son": The King as Sacral Figure

Cooke, G. "The Israelite King as Son of God." *ZAW* 73 (1961) 202–226.

Johnson, A. R. *Sacral Kingship in Ancient Israel.* 2nd ed. Cardiff: University of Wales Press, 1967.

Kapelrud, A. S. "Tradition and Worship: The Role of the Cult in Tradition Formation and Transmission." *Tradition and Theology in the Old Testament.* Edited by D. A. Knight. Philadelphia: Fortress, 1977. Pp. 101–124. (*Recommended for beginning students.*)

"The Throne of His Kingdom Forever": Between Now and Then

Charlesworth, J. H. "Pseudepigrapha, OT" *ABD* 5.537–40. (*Recommended for beginning students.*)

Collins, J. J. "A Pre-Christian 'Son of God' Among the Dead Sea Scrolls." *BibRev* 9.3 (June 1993) 34–39.

DeJonge, M. "Messiah." *ABD* 4.777–88.

Ellis. J. Y. "Messiah/Messianism" *MDB.* Pp. 571–572. (*Recommended for beginning students.*)

Wise, M. O. and Tabor, J. D. "The Messiah at Qumran." *BAR* 18.6 (1992) 60–63; 65. (*Recommended for beginning students.*)

CHAPTER EIGHT

The Story of the People of God

Introduction

Review

The story of the Hebrew Bible is a composite of many stories told from multiple points of view, shaped by everchanging social texts that create new and innovative interpretive texts. The tradition of Mosaic law as promoted by the prophets achieved a new prominence in the post-Exilic period. Likewise the traditions of king and Temple provide rich metaphors by which the post-Exilic community could claim a new identity. That identity sought to retain contact with the pre-Exilic Israel and its institutions, while accommodating a social reality in which there could be no king, no national independence, and the restrictive boundaries of political domination by the Persian empire. These accommodations revived and recharged the ideals that would become the seedbed of Christianity in the first century CE.

Preview

Kingship necessarily leads to a consideration of the theme of the people of God. Who belongs to the people of God becomes an acutely difficult question in the Second Temple period. It was a time when exiles not only returned to Jerusalem, but also continued to live in Babylon and in Egypt. The term *Diaspora* denotes the scattering of Jews around the world and is an apt descriptor for this time period. The present discussion will consider the world reflected by the books of Ezra-Nehemiah and how the criteria for belonging to the community of God were quite narrow. Not only did one need to be of proper ethnic origins, but great importance was attached to having passed through the Babylonian Exile. The notion of covenant comes to play a decisive role in the biblical understanding of the people of God. The closing two discussions trace the development of two different kinds of covenant: one in relationship to the patriarch Abraham, the other in relationship to the Mosaic law. In the former instance, Yahweh lays obligation upon himself in the form of promise. In the latter, Yahweh lays obligations upon his people.

Ezra-Nehemiah and the Exiles
Ezra 9; Jeremiah 31; Ezekiel 23; Isaiah 49:1–6

Learning Goals

- To understand that terms such as "Israel" have very different meanings within the biblical story, depending upon the social and political backgrounds.
- To understand that Post-Exilic Jews still perceived themselves as living in exile.
- To understand how the narrowness of Ezra-Nehemiah represents a departure from the idealistic visions of the late oracles of Jeremiah and Ezekiel.

Guiding Study Exercises

1) Write a 250-word essay in which you explain the meanings of the term *Israel* in Ezra-Nehemiah and the prophets.
2) Identify how the prophet Jeremiah (in chaps. 30–33) indicates his awareness of the political meanings of Jacob/Israel and Zion/Jerusalem while giving them a nonpolitical significance.
3) Examine the four servant songs of Deutero-Isaiah. List the evidence that the servant is both an individual and a group.
4) What does it imply that those living in Jerusalem still think of themselves as in exile?

The historical narrative of Ezra-Nehemiah opens with the announcement of the edict of Cyrus, the Persian king, that "the God of Heaven" was allowing any who were "of his people" to return to Jerusalem. In other words, those who claimed to be his people could leave Babylon. The plot of the story that follows takes many twists around the identity of those persons who returned. Scarcely two verses after reference to Cyrus' edict, readers learn that "the heads of the families of Judah and Benjamin," traditional names of ancient tribes that had populated the countryside surrounding Jerusalem, were stirred in spirit to return. The narrative clearly attempts to portray some connection with the older tribal lineages so common in narratives about pre-Exilic times. After the notification of the return in 2:1–2, the narrator begins to enumerate the "Israelite people" (2:2b). While there are not any lineages tracing back to the twelve tribes of Israel, the alert reader will remember that Israel was the name of the northern tribes that had been deported long before the tribes in the southern kingdom of Judah (2 Kgs 17:5–18). Obviously, the term *Israelite* can no longer have political significance in this time period. In the story of Ezra-Nehemiah its political significance has been exchanged for religious and ethnic significance.

The concern to describe these returnees as heirs of legitimate pre-Exilic families takes a more serious tone as the narration addresses the individuals who could not prove that they were descendants of some Israelite tribe (2:59). The concern is slightly more important in the case of the priests who had trouble proving that they came from priestly families (2:61–63). This meant that they could not serve until there was a priest who could consult the **Urim and Thummim** (2:63). Clearly, their status as priests consisted of more than mere religious affiliation. In the cases of those "people of the land" who requested to help build the Temple along with Zerubbabel (4:1–3), neither proper worship nor theological affinity could suffice to make them legitimate. These persons' ancestors had very likely lived in the cities of the northern kingdom after the deportation by Sargon II in 721 BCE, but, according to the story, they were not of the ethnic stock that had originally lived there. They had been settled there as colonists by the Assyrian kings Esarhaddon (681–669 BCE) and Ashurbanipal (668–627 BCE; named Osnappar in Ezra 4:10).[1] No reason is given for their exclusion by Zerubbabel and his men; however, the reader knows from recalling the edict of Cyrus that the identity of the true people of God is at stake.

Israel: A Remnant of Exiles; Ezra 9

In Ezra 9 readers encounter the first announcement of trouble for Ezra's leadership in the newly reconstituted community of Jerusalem. Ezra gets word that "The people of Israel, the priests, and the Levites have not separated themselves from the peoples of the lands," provoking the need for Ezra to address the question of intermarriage (see Chap. 4). What is so interesting here is the language used to identify these persons. The narrator, Ezra, relates that this announcement provoked acts of mourning. But notice in v. 4 his identification of the people in Jerusalem as "exiles." The NRSV translates the Hebrew word *hagolah* as "returned exiles," but in the Hebrew text there is no adjective that can be translated "returned." It is simply "the exiles," the implications of which will be addressed shortly. The choice of that word takes on an even more interesting dimension in view of the clarification already offered in Ezra 8:35, where the narrator uses the word "exile" (*bene' hagolah*) in parallel with "those who had come from captivity," (*habba'im mehassebi*). Here there is no question that the subject is the persons who have returned from Babylon. The Hebrew word for "captivity," *sebi,* makes this clear. In the case of Ezra 9:4 the term "returned" is added by the translator in order to clarify that these persons were not still in exile; they are actually in Jerusalem. But in making the clarification, the English translation smoothes over the rather abrupt description of the people—who are in Jerusalem—yet as exiles! This raises an intriguing question: why are the people considered exiles when they are no longer actually in exile?

Two possible explanations provide insight into the larger question regarding Israel's identity. First, the writer of Ezra is concerned to identify the true people of God as those who have come through the Babylonian Exile. Such an identification would both revitalize the links with the Judah and Jerusalem of the pre-Exilic period—since they were the ones exiled to Babylon—as well as localize the true Israel to the traditional geographical regions of Judah and Jerusalem in the author's day.[2] Recall from reading Ezra 1–6 the strong emphasis placed upon the tribes of

---

[1] See J. H. Hayes and J. M. Miller, *Israelite and Judean History* (London: SCM Press, 1977) 433–434.

[2] See H. G. M. Williamson, "The Concept of Israel in Transition," *The World of Ancient Israel* (Cambridge: Cambridge University Press, 1989), 141–161; see also R. J. Coggin, "The Origins of the Jewish Diaspora," *The World of Ancient Israel,* 163–187.

Judah and Benjamin (e.g., 1:5; 4:1), as well as the reference to David and the Jerusalemite royal lineage (3:10–11). Further recall the narrative's remembrance of the Temple that had stood in Jerusalem prior to the Exile (3:12). These allusions and references provide the reader with the indication that anyone not previously associated with this very specific community (such as those adversaries mentioned in 4:1–3) could not presently be so associated.

The historian emphasizes this connection to pre-Exilic Judah by referring to the group as an "escaped remnant." Three times within the body of Ezra's prayer (vv. 6–23) this happens (vv. 8; 13; and 15). In all three cases the idea that a people have lived through the event of the Exile, that is, have "escaped," is treated as an expression of Yahweh's mercy and grace. Actually, the idea of a remnant preserved through the Exile provides an important theological touchstone for Exilic and post-Exilic prophets' understanding of why the Exile happened to begin with. What is even more interesting is the relatively few persons who actually were exiled. Recall from Chap. 6 that, although the Babylonians did destroy Jerusalem and the Temple and deport the upper echelon of citizens, by no means was the land empty.[3] Many persons remained behind, escaping the Babylonian deportation.

As an example of some precedent for differentiating between those persons who were exiled and those who were not, readers should consider briefly a revealing passage in Jeremiah. The tradition remembers him as a prophet of the Exile, and thus whose words originated some 130 years prior to the ministry of Ezra.[4] Jeremiah 24:1–10 is a vision of two baskets of figs, one with "good figs" and the other with "bad figs." The vision is set in the interim between the first deportation of 597 BCE and the second, some ten years later (Jer 24:1, 8). The explanation of the vision given to the prophet is that the exiles taken from Judah to Babylon are the "good figs"; those who escaped the Exile are "bad figs." Notice the specific language: "exiles" (v. 5) is used in reference to the ones transported to Babylon, and the word "remnant" (v. 8) is used in reference to the ones who remained in Jerusalem, thereby avoiding the Exile. Very likely, this recollection reflects the prophetic response to the presumption and overconfidence of those who had not been taken in the first deportation of 597 BCE. Recall also the treatment of Ezekiel's prophecies as having a bearing upon post-Exilic restoration (Chap. 5). He, like Jeremiah, offers an oracle of denunciation to persons who had escaped the Exile and remained in the land of Judah. Unlike the oracle of Jeremiah, Ezekiel's oracle is dated to a period after the second deportation (Ezek 33:21). The prophet, one of Ezra's priestly predecessors, makes it clear that those who are left behind in this second deportation, and thus led to believe that *they* are the true children of Abraham, are sorely mistaken (Ezek 33:23–29). The land will be desolate and judgment will also come upon those who remain. Thus, even the earlier, exilic prophets would seem to reinforce the distinction between those who went into exile and those who remained behind. However, it will become clear below that neither Jeremiah nor Ezekiel conceived of the community of Israel as exclusively as the writer of Ezra-Nehemiah did. Nevertheless, the writer of Ezra-Nehemiah seems to have reread some idea from earlier prophets that persons who went through the deportation to Babylon represent the pure heirs of Israel.

---

[3]See also J. H. Hayes and J. M. Miller, 478–479.

[4]The passage in Jeremiah 24 is regarded as coming from later readers of the prophet Jeremiah, rather than from the prophet himself. See R. Clements, *Jeremiah* (IBC; Atlanta, GA: John Knox Press, 1988) 144–148.

A second reason to portray the inhabitants of Judah and Jerusalem as exiles has certainly to do with the historian's interest in implying that the Exile has not ended. Indeed, the glorious restoration has not yet occurred, a motif encountered in references to the Temple and which occurs again and again in later biblical literature. In Ezra 9 the priest's prayer portrays the people in slavery. Not only does he mention the shame of this slavery, but its immediacy. That is, the slavery has not ended just because the people are in Jerusalem. Twice in v. 7 the phrase "to this day" (*'ad hayyom hazzeh*) occurs (NRSV translates the very similar second phrase as "as is now the case" [*kehayyom hazzeh*]). The activity of the return and the repossession of "the holy place" are seen as a grant of mercy from God who wishes to "brighten our eyes and grant us a little sustenance in our slavery" (9:8). Greater emphasis is added by repeating the assertion that, even situated in Jerusalem, the returned exiles were in slavery (v. 8). Verse 9 opens by saying "we are slaves . . . ," though not forgotten by God. This language is very similar to that encountered in Nehemiah 9, where Ezra is again remembered as offering a prayer of confession. He says, "Here we are, slaves to this day—slaves in the land that you gave to our ancestors to enjoy its fruit and its good gifts" (v. 36).

Recall that Nehemiah 9 employed numerous times the Deuteronomistic pattern of apostasy, punishment, crying out for mercy, and deliverance (Chap. 2). The prayer concludes with the people in slavery, not with deliverance. In other words, by concluding the prayer—a prayer of confession and repentance—with an assertion of the people's slavery, the next step after repentance should be God's deliverance. The same kind of assumption may well be at work in Ezra 9. By portraying the present moment as one of slavery in a prayer of confession and repentance, the next step in the cycle should be God's deliverance. In Nehemiah 9 the people affirm an oath regarding the keeping of the law, intermarriage, Sabbath observance, and maintenance of the Temple. In Ezra 9 the people are ready to set their foreign wives aside.

This is further reinforced by the accompanying imagery of the Exodus that precedes the prayer in Ezra 9. One has but to remember that the narrative portrays Ezra as a kind of Moses figure. Like Moses in Exodus 32, Ezra leads people out of slavery and intercedes for them when they have committed sin. Now it is only appropriate for him to admonish the people about keeping the law as a necessary prerequisite for being free of the slavery in which they find themselves. Clearly, the post-Exilic historian is recapturing the old traditions of Moses to elevate the significance of the work of Ezra. But by drawing connections between the Exodus and Exile, he is making a claim about the identity of his Jerusalem community. For this historian, just as Israel of old came out of Egypt, the true Israel of Ezra's day came out of the Babylonian Exile. One cannot avoid the conclusion, therefore, that with the allusions to Moses and the Exodus, this historian's conception of the people of God is quite narrow.

Ezekiel 16 and 23, Jeremiah 31, and Deutero-Isaiah

Even though Ezekiel and Jeremiah differentiate between the exiles and those who remained in the land of Palestine, their conception of Israel in the restoration is not nearly as narrow as in Ezra-Nehemiah. Rather, as well as envisioning a restoration that includes both the northern and southern kingdoms (Israel and Judah), both prophets give emphasis to the common history for both.[5] In

---

[5]Williamson, "Concept of Israel," 141–143.

fact, in Ezekiel, the oracle avoids any specific reference to the political divisions that once existed between North and South, supplying unifying, familial language instead. North and South are simply two sisters who come from the same parentage. It is only in Deutero-Isaiah, the exilic prophet to the exiles in Babylon, that readers begin to see some narrowing of the meaning of Israel.

Ezekiel 23. Recall that Chapter 5 indicated Ezekiel's prophesying to have spanned a period before and after the deportations of 597 and 587 BCE. He was himself deported and lived among the exiles in Babylon. In addition to both oral and visionary oracles, the prophet makes use of other kinds of literary genres. The poems in chapters 16 and 23 are **allegories**. With this form of writing the prophet is able to draw an explicit parallel between the cities of Jerusalem and Samaria, as well as to develop the notion that their political treaties are tantamount to a prostitution of their distinctive identity. There is a strong similarity between the poem in chapter 16 and that in chapter 23. The later poem of chapter 23 was very likely built off Ezekiel 16. While both are allegories focusing upon the capital cities of the old Judean and Israelite nations, chapter 16 is concerned more with religious crimes, whereas chapter 23 is concerned with political crimes. Look more closely at Ezekiel 23.

The oracle in Ezekiel 23 consists of one section. The introductory statement, "The word of the Lord came to me," occurs only in v. 1 and the allegory holds the whole poem together through v. 49. This does not mean that the chapter is free of expansions and additions by later interpreters, however.[6] Verses 2–4 refer to the sisters' childhood in Egypt; vv. 5–10 narrate the story of the older sister, Oholah; vv. 11–21 narrate the story of the younger sister, Oholibah. The original judgment, vv. 22–27, is introduced as an oracle with the familiar prophetic phrase, "Thus says the Lord God" (v. 22). The two daughters, both of one mother, represent Samaria and Jerusalem (v. 4). The sexual prostitution of the daughters stands for the political relationships formed by each nation. Ezekiel, like other of his prophetic predecessors, favored a policy of political isolation.[7] Thus, the inevitable political treaties and alliances that were formed as the two kingdoms became more internationally viable formed the basis for their own demise. The political alliances robbed the two daughters of their virginity, as well as the purity and fidelity of their relationship with their husband, Yahweh. Their punishment, therefore, rightly comes at the hands of their lovers (vv. 22–27).

This oracle of judgment is remarkable, further, in that it makes no reference to Israel as the northern kingdom, nor Judah as the southern kingdom. Rather, the two daughters, although clearly signifying the North and the South, only represent the two capital cities. "Oholah is Samaria, and Oholibah is Jerusalem" (v. 4). Far more significant is that they are of the same family, "daughters of one mother" (v. 2). Both daughters also have a common beginning in Egypt (v. 2). It is from there that Yahweh takes them as his wives, even after their virginity is lost. But by avoiding reference to the two nations, the prophet's vision of one family provides a basis for a vision of the future restoration of both kingdoms as one. The possibilities for inclusiveness that this interpretation offers later interpreters are immense. The same allegory occurs in Ezekiel 16.

Jeremiah 30–31. These chapters are an important collection of oracles for a number of reasons. One of the most well known is their assertion of a "new covenant" that Yahweh would make

---

[6]J. W. Wevers, *Ezekiel* (NCB; Grand Rapids, MI: Eerdmans, 1969) 132, where Wevers lists at least three further additions in the form of judgment announcements: 28–30, 31–34, and 35.

[7]*Ibid.,* 133; recall Isaiah's advice to Ahaz, Isa. 7:8–14; see Chap. 6.

with his people (Jer 31:31–34; see below). The theme of a new covenant is revisited by first-century CE Jews, for instance, as they struggled to understand Jesus as their Messiah and thus the founder of this new covenant. Jeremiah 31 falls within a larger collection of salvation oracles concerned with the restoration (Jeremiah 30–33). The restoration they envision is no less than a full return to a national existence in the land Yahweh had given to his people, complete with a Davidic king (e.g., Jer 33:19–26). It is unlikely that these are the exact words of the prophet Jeremiah, however, given that so much of the material in Jeremiah came from the hands of later collectors and editors of that prophet's words (see previous comments in Chap. 5). These later collectors and editors give expression, in Jeremiah's name, to a remarkable restoration of all the families of Israel.

The language in Jer 31:1–6 contains striking imagery that both betrays the writer's knowledge of Israel as an ethnic entity as well as indicating his subtle awareness of her political history.[8] Verse 1 actually concludes an oracle that begins in 30:22. Note that both Jer 30:22 and 31:1 form a thematic framework on the theme of God's people. Within the framework is the assertion of Judah's punishment. The contrast between God's judgment in 30:22–31:1 and restoration in 31:2–6 sets in stark relief the power of the oracle of restoration and hope. Notice in v. 1 the deity's claim that "all families of Israel" shall be his people. As in Ezekiel there is familial imagery followed by reference to both the Exile and Israel.

Jeremiah 31:2 opens the second oracle extending through v. 6. Notice v. 2 refers to those who "survived the sword," a reference to the punishment and exile spoken of in 30:23–24. The next reference is to "Israel" who sought for rest. The use of *Israel* to refer to those who were exiled means that the term that once was used to refer to the northern political kingdom now refers both to the exiles as well as to all of the families that might be included in Israel. The language "virgin Israel" seems to reflect the prophetic appeal to an idealized day when the people of Israel were young and were Yahweh's bride. This imagery reminds readers of the language of yet an earlier prophet, Hosea. Hosea pictures Israel as Yahweh's bride whom he courted in the wilderness after liberating her from slavery in Egypt (Hosea 1–3).

Notice the mix of geographical locations in vv. 5–6. The oracle not only envisions days of agricultural bounty "on the mountains of Samaria," but a day when people of the northern kingdom shall say "let us go to Jerusalem," the capital of the southern kingdom. The language envisions a time when there was no political division between North and South. The subtle allusion is to an age when Jerusalem was the capital of both North and South, and also the center of Yahwistic worship. Against such a prophetic background, readers get a further idea of the narrowness of understanding of Ezra-Nehemiah. The visions of the exilic prophets such as Jeremiah and Ezekiel give the idea of a much broader definition. But readers may hypothesize that the social text of Ezra-Nehemiah, when there were actual returned exiles living in the mix of peoples that had populated Judah, called for dramatic redefinition of the prophetic vision.

Deutero-Isaiah. A later prophet living much closer to the time of the return to Jerusalem, Deutero-Isaiah (see Chap. 5), does begin to reveal some narrowing of possible meanings of the term *Israel*. Williamson's linguistic treatment of the question of the identity of Israel in

---

[8]Williamson, "Concept of Israel," 144, notes that, while Jeremiah also envisioned a unified Israel, he was far more aware of the political differences of North and South. This is expressed in Jeremiah 30–31 in the distinction between Ephraim/Israel and Zion/Judah parallels. The distinction is even more pronounced in the early oracles of Jeremiah 1–25.

Deutero-Isaiah is instructive here.[9] The prophet's oracles are contained in Isaiah 40–55, chapters 56–66 coming from the hand of a yet later post-Exilic prophet, who spoke in the Isaianic name. Deutero-Isaiah announced his visions of restoration toward the end of the Exile. This is especially evident in Isaiah 40–48, which unambiguously indicate the fall of Babylon (e.g., 46:1–2; 47:1). It was that prophet's visions of a glorious restoration, scholars believe, that played an important role in motivating certain groups of refugees to return to Jerusalem. The prophet's location in Babylon provides important insight therefore into his use of traditional language to address his people.

To summarize Williamson's study, of the total forty-two occurrences of the word *Israel* in Deutero-Isaiah, nineteen function to indicate Israel's relationship to the deity (as in the phrase "the Holy One of Israel") and are not of concern here. Seventeen of the remaining twenty-three are used in parallel with the name *Jacob,* the traditional ancestor of Israel (whose name was changed to Israel; Gen 32:22–32; 35:9–15). The remaining five occurrences do not have the parallel term Jacob in such immediate proximity and provoke questions as to the meaning of the term when used alone.[10] The use of both names, Israel and Jacob, in seventeen of the occurrences,

---

A Closer Look: Linguistic Analysis of the Bible. The appeal to the distinctive terms used in the Hebrew text not only reminds readers of the interpretive text of a translator, but of the task of linguistic analysis in biblical investigation. The meticulous counting of the occurrences of words, the definition of the subtle nuances that obtain in the coupling of terms with other words and modifiers, and the careful cataloging of contexts reveal the kinds of methods scholars use to systematize their interpretations of the Bible at the linguistic level. The most basic tool of such reading is a concordance. A concordance lists the occurrences of a term in various passages throughout the Bible. An exhaustive concordance lists all occurrences of all terms through the Bible. When readers learn the biblical languages, an exhaustive concordance in those languages both lists the words' meanings and then all of the occurrences through the Bible that define that meaning. Since the meanings of words are not inherent in the words themselves, but defined as much or more by context and conventional usage, a concordance allows readers to identify and explore the contexts in which words are used so as to define a word's meaning. This chapter's study of the word *Israel* will illustrate for students the linguistic analysis of the Bible.

For further study, G. B. Caird. *The Language and Imagery of the Bible.* London: Duckworth, 1981. Pp. 37–84; F. Danker. *Multipurpose Tools for Bible Study.* Minneapolis, MN: Fortress, 1993. Pp. 1–21; E. Würthwein. *The Text of the Old Testament: An Introduction to the Biblica Hebraica.* Grand Rapids, MI: Eerdmans, 1992.

For more advanced study, J. Barr. *The Semantics of Biblical Language.* Oxford: Oxford University Press, 1961. Pp.107–160; J. F. A. Sawyer. *Semantics in Biblical Research.* SBT 24; London: SCM Press, 1972.

---

[9]*Ibid.,* 141–161.
[10]*Ibid.,* 144–145.

would suggest that the prophet is, like his predecessors Jeremiah and Ezekiel, moving beyond the possible political significances of Israel to more religious significances. But on closer examination, it is even more certain that this prophet is speaking to exiles alone with such designations.

The context in which the dual terms occur make this clear. Examine Isa 40:27, for instance. This is an example of prophetic diatribe, where the prophet quotes the objections of his opponents. "Why do you say, O Jacob, and speak, O Israel, 'My way is hidden from the Lord, and my right is disregarded by my God'"? The people's question is an accusation and complaint that indicates the people are suffering, most likely from the loss of hope stemming from their circumstances in Babylon. This becomes a basis for the prophet to offer in response a message of hope, as in v. 28. Likewise, Isa 42:24 indicates the prophet's engagement in dialogue with his people, who apparently are accusing Yahweh of betraying them into the hands of their Babylonian tormentors. The prophet acknowledges Yahweh's involvement, but shifts the blame to the people. "Who gave up Jacob to the spoiler, and Israel to the robbers? Was it not the Lord, against whom we have sinned, in whose ways they would not walk, and whose law they would not obey?" As in Isa 40:27, the use of both *Jacob* and *Israel* refers to those persons in the Exile in Babylon.

Isaiah 49:1–6 is of special significance in that it seems to indicate some transition is underway in the understanding of the identity of Israel. The passage is known among scholars as one of the "Servant Songs" of Deutero-Isaiah, along with Isa 42:1–4, 50:4–9, and 52:13–53:12. The common feature in all these songs is reference to some unidentified "servant of Yahweh." Exactly who this servant is remains a mystery; sometimes the poems describe him as an individual, as though he were a king (Isa 42:1–4), and other times the servant seems to be a plurality. Within the larger context of Deutero-Isaiah's visions, the poems suggest at one point rather explicitly that the servant is the nation: "But you, Israel, my servant, Jacob, whom I have chosen, the offspring of Abraham, my friend; you whom I took from the ends of the earth, and called from its farthest corners, saying to you, 'you are my servant, I have chosen you and not cast you off'" (Isa 42:8–9).

In 49:1–6 there is an interesting development. In v. 3 the identity of the servant is Israel, as in 42:8–9. The name *Israel* stands alone here without the parallel term *Jacob,* as it occurs most frequently. In vv. 1–2 the purpose of the servant seems to be that of ministering to the nations: "O coastlands, pay attention, you peoples from far away!" But notice that in v. 5 the task of the servant also turns *toward* Jacob and Israel. Here there is a return to the double terminology for Israel to which readers grow familiar throughout Isaiah 40–48. But Israel as the servant of Yahweh, without the parallel term *Jacob,* is to minister to Jacob/Israel. Again, scholars do not know whether this servant denotes an individual or a group within the exiles. Still, readers can at least see that there seems to be a different understanding of Israel in this passage. And further, not only is this individual or group within and among the exiles to bring God's people back to him, this servant is also to bring the nations back to him. The passage closes with a most remarkable vision: "It is too light a thing that you should be my servant to raise up the tribes of Jacob and to restore the survivors of Israel; I will give you as a light to the nations, that my salvation may reach to the ends of the earth" (Isa 49:6).

God's People and the Covenant with Abraham
Ezra 9; Nehemiah 10; Genesis 15, 17, and 49

Learning Goals

• To understand covenant as a concept that defined the people of God.
• To understand that there are different, perhaps competing, ways of defining the idea of covenant within the biblical story.
• To understand the importance of the Abraham traditions in defining the people of God in pre- and post-Exilic social texts.
• To understand how circumcision became connected with the idea of Yahweh's covenant with his people.

Guiding Study Exercises

1) Write a short essay summarizing the different ways Ezra-Nehemiah understands the concept of covenant.
2) Summarize the key evidence that links the promise to Abraham (Genesis 15) with the Davidic promise (2 Sam 7:1–17) and the monarchy.
3) How might such a "divine grant" as the promise to Abraham function within the sociological framework of a community establishing a monarchy?
4) How does the sign of circumcision indicate the relative lateness of Genesis 17 as a rereading of Genesis 15?
5) Review Neh 9:7–8. Describe how this text combines *both* Genesis 15 and 17 in its rereading of those traditions.

Moving beyond the titles designating the people of God and their emerging significances, the next step is to consider the actual terms of being the people of God. One of the most central ideas of the entire biblical story is that of covenant. Tracing its history and development through the Bible provides another perspective on the varying understandings over time of what it meant to be the people of God. But unlike the themes of kingship, Temple, and the law, the various rereadings of the idea of covenant comprehend all of the others. As will be shown, both law and kingship, with the accompanying "promises" concerning Temple, are all components of the much larger notion of God's covenant with his people. The discussion begins with a brief definition and exposition of the broad boundaries of the term's application in the Bible.

The Meaning of Covenant in Ezra and Nehemiah

As in previous discussions, the post-Exilic book of Ezra-Nehemiah is a helpful beginning point because it refers to the act of "making a covenant." The handful of references in Ezra-Nehemiah, including Ezra 10:3, Neh 9:8, 38, and Neh 10:29, form the point of departure for the present discussion. Scholars generally define *covenant* as "an agreement enacted between two parties in which one or both make promises under oath to perform or refrain from certain actions stipulated in advance."[11] The special word *berit,* translated as "covenant," occurs in Ezra 10:3. After Ezra's prayer of repentance on behalf of his people, the people who heard the prayer were overcome with grief and said, "So now let us make a covenant with our God to send away all these wives and their children, according to the counsel of my lord and of those who tremble at the commandment of our God." It is not clear what exactly the term means in this context, though readers suspect that the people entered into some kind of firm resolve, or promise among themselves, to change their behavior. Notice in v. 5, however, that Ezra responds to the call for a covenant with God by making the people "swear." This would seem to illuminate the meaning of making a covenant in this passage. The people swear to abide by some kind of agreement.

Recall in Neh 9:38 a similar kind of event where the people make a "firm agreement in writing." The setting there is Jerusalem after Ezra's prayer (see Chaps. 2 and 3), and the people are signing a document formally committing themselves to keep the law. The formality of such a commitment seems clear, but it is not until Neh 10:29, when the people joined "with their kin, their nobles," and entered "into a curse and an oath to walk in God's law, which was given by Moses the servant of God," that readers realize this also to be a kind of solemn promise. The promise is initiated by the people and is solemnized by appeal to the deity to enforce it. But notice that the actual agreement in Nehemiah 9 and 10 is not an agreement *with* God. Rather, it is an agreement between people, and the deity only enters into the picture as one who witnesses the agreement to enforce it. What is more, the Hebrew word for "covenant," *berit,* does not occur in the passage in Neh 9:38 nor in 10:29.

With these two post-Exilic examples—one defining relationship between God and persons using the word *berit* ("covenant" or "promise"), another defining relationships between persons only, either with or without the term *berit,* there is a basis to inquire further into the function of the concept of covenant in the biblical story. Keeping in mind the broad definition set out above, "an agreement enacted between two parties . . . ," the passages clearly focus on one aspect of the definition. There are indeed promises that certain parties make to others, but little in the way of two-sided agreements.

But therein is one of the important components of understanding how covenant functions in the biblical story. To be sure, it functions as a determinative idea in defining the relationship between God and his people. But is covenant mainly about God's promises *to* people or is it about some kind of mutual agreement *between* God and his people? In the former case, the relationship seems somewhat one-sided. God makes a promise, the people benefit from it. In the latter case, however, people enter into an agreement with God where there are obligations that bind both parties. Actually, both understandings of covenant shape major portions of the biblical story.

Genesis 15 and Yahweh's Promise

The episode of covenant-making contained in Gen 15:1–21 occurs in a much larger literary context scholars refer to as the patriarchal narratives. In fact, Genesis 12–50 is devoted entirely to

---

[11]G. E. Mendenhall, G. A. Herion, "Covenant," *ABD* 1.1179–1202.

several episodes concerning four major patriarchs: Abraham, Isaac (one of his two sons), Jacob (one of Isaac's two sons), Joseph (one of Jacob's twelve sons), and their families. As in previous biblical narratives encountered (e.g., Nathan's promise to David, 2 Sam 7:1–17), readers see how very ancient stories have been reshaped to reflect the social, political, and theological circumstances of a much later time period. What were originally separate family traditions, stemming from different clans, have been woven together into a continuous narrative plausibly to support the political and theological aims of monarchy and its accompanying religio-political nationalism. Alternatively, if composed in the period of the Exile as other scholars believe (see Chap. 4), the narratives were written to function as a prologue to the Deuteronomistic History, and to transform that national story based upon ownership of a land into a story of a people and a promised land.[12]

The overall narrative in Genesis 12–50 gives evidence of a thoughtful process of editing. While the family motif pervades all of the narrative episodes, the interactions among the families and their neighboring nations reflect the governing theme of Yahweh's threefold promise of family, nationhood, and land. The opening narrative in Gen 12:1–3, for instance, relates the deity's promises to Abraham[13] of land and family. The narratives about Abraham (Genesis 12–26) are largely about how Yahweh will fulfill his promise of family. Sarah, Abraham's wife, cannot have children. But she does have a son when she is very old and this son, Isaac, carries the promise forward to the next generation.

Isaac has sons, Jacob and Esau, and the struggle then becomes one between brothers. The concern for building a family recedes into the background.[14] The narratives in Genesis 27–36 raise the question of how Yahweh's promise can possibly be fulfilled when brothers quarrel among themselves. Questions about legal rights among brothers, ownership of land, and justice pose a different kind of threat to Yahweh's promise as brothers live with brothers in the same land. None of these matters is of import in the episodes about Abraham; they only come to the forefront as the family grows.

The final part of Genesis (Genesis 37–50) incorporates yet another element. While the conflict among brothers, here the sons of Jacob (the ancestors of the twelve tribes), intensifies in these episodes, they all must reckon with kingship. It is in these narratives that the sons of Jacob first encounter the power of a king in the form of the Egyptian Pharaoh. One of the younger sons of Jacob, named Joseph, is quite precocious (Gen 37:1–4). His older brothers hate him and sell him as a slave to traders (Gen 37:26–28), who eventually take him to Egypt. There, Joseph prospers (Genesis 40–41) and becomes, unknown to his brothers (who tell their father that Joseph is dead), a key officer in the Egyptian government. Ironically, he rules over his brothers.

Covenant as Divine Promise in Genesis 15. A careful reading of Genesis 15 reveals complexities that suggest a composite nature not unlike that encountered in 2 Sam 7:1–17. Note that there is more than one promise in these verses. Verses 1–6 concern the promise of offspring,

---

[12]The discussion of Gen 15 and 17 relies upon the important and very different works of C. Westermann, *Genesis 12–36* (Minneapolis, MN: Augsburg, 1985) and J. Van Seters, *Prologue to History* (Louisville, KY: Westminster/John Knox, 1992).

[13]In the course of the narratives, Abram's and Sarai's names are changed to Abraham (Gen 17:5) and Sarah (Genesis 17:15). For convenience's sake, this discussion will use the name Abraham to refer to the character in episodes that precede the name change. Only in quotations from scripture will the differentiation be observed.

[14]Westermann, *Genesis 12–36,* 28–30, offers a helpful discussion of the composition of the patriarchal story.

while vv. 7–21 concern the promise of land. Both passages differ from the other in their description of how the deity communicates with Abraham. Note in 15:1–6 the use of the phrase "the word of the Lord came to Abram" (vv. 1 and 4). In vv. 7–21, however, Yahweh's speech to Abraham is introduced simply as, "Then he said to him," without any indirect reference to "the word of the Lord" (e.g., vv. 7, 9, 13). The use of the phrase "the word of the Lord" is usually associated with prophetic speech, implying the influence of a social text that was influenced by such speech, certainly much later than the patriarchal period itself. Readers do not encounter such references to "the word of the Lord" anywhere else in the Pentateuch.[15] Rather, the phrase occurs in narratives that originate much later in the period of the monarchy (e.g., 1 Sam 15:10; 1 Kgs 12:22; 16:1; 17:2, 8), most notably in 2 Sam 7:4, when Nathan receives the word from Yahweh. This intertext is yet another that implies the reworking of the Abraham narrative after the establishment of and perhaps in order to support the Davidic monarchy.

Verses 1–6 deal mainly with the question of offspring. Abraham receives the word of the Lord, which opens as an oracle of salvation. In v. 2 the patriarch rejects the oracle, questioning how he can prosper when he is childless. His counterproposal to the deity is that not his own flesh and blood, but someone from his house, perhaps a slave, would be the heir and carry on his name. Yahweh rejects this and assures Abraham that, indeed, he would have a son and that his offspring would be many. His descendants would be as numerous as the stars in the sky. Abraham's response is important, both in its expression of the patriarch's faith and in the absence of any kind of attending obligation that is laid upon the patriarch and his descendants. Later readers idealize Abraham's response in that here he simply trusts Yahweh's promise. Readers will see in Chapter 13, for instance, Paul's remarkable rereading of this promise to Abraham and its contingency upon Abraham's faith.

The second part of the passage turns to the theme of possession of land. Notice that the structure of the opening of this episode parallels that of vv. 1–6. Yahweh initiates the encounter by identifying himself and offering a word of salvation (compare vv. 7 and 1b). Abraham's response to Yahweh's initial assurance is one of uncertainty and doubt (compare vv. 8 and 2). The Lord then responds with another word of assurance (compare vv. 9 and 4). The only rhetorical feature that prevents the reader from considering these as two separate, though parallel, events is the use of the personal pronoun "he" in v. 7. The verse conveys the idea that the antecedent subject of the pronoun has already been introduced; the materials in vv. 7–21 are therefore just the continuation of the same story.

It is in this second episode that readers encounter the actual word "covenant" used in the context to describe what actually transpires between the Lord and Abraham (v. 18). When Yahweh responds to Abraham's question, he instructs him to prepare a sacrifice of animals, arranging them by cutting them in two (vv. 9–10) for the purpose of a ritual ceremony. The mysterious description of events requires some reflection upon other parts of scripture in order to understand the symbolic actions. The darkness is important since one cannot see God and live (Exod 33:20). Yet that it is terrifying suggests the presence of God. Also in other parts of scripture fire and smoke symbolize the presence of the deity (Exod 20:18). Thus, when the "smoking fire pot" and the "flaming torch" pass between the halves of the animals, the reader is to understand that

---

[15]Westermann, *ibid.,* 217–218.

Yahweh is passing in between them. In so doing he is making an oath or a promise to Abraham. Abraham's part in the agreement is simply to receive the gift of Yahweh.

The Social Text of the Covenant Promise. The affinities between the Abraham materials and 2 Sam 7:1–17 exist at several levels, both in form and content. **Form critical** analysis of the materials in Gen 15:1–21 and 2 Sam 7:1–17 show what scholars refer to as a "divine grant or charter."[16] The key feature is the deity's stark promise to his servant. Although the word *covenant* does not occur in 2 Samuel 7, the context makes unambiguous God's grant of grace, his provision of descendants, and his gift of land to both David and Abraham. Such parallelism suggests a social text of the Solomonic era, which reinterpreted the tradition of Nathan's promise in favor of the pro-Temple Solomonic court.[17] The idea of using the Abraham materials is to seek legitimization for monarchy in the ancient promises made to the patriarchal fathers.

Yet other intertexts strengthen the hypothesis of a Solomonic social text for Genesis 15. Notice that Gen 15:18 refers specifically to the boundaries of the land that Abraham's progeny will possess: "To your descendants I give this land, from the river of Egypt to the great river, the river Euphrates." The parallel between that statement and the boundaries given by the history of the Solomonic era in 1 Kgs 4:21 are striking. There it states, "Solomon was sovereign over all the kingdoms from the Euphrates to the land of the Philistines even to the border of Egypt." The common features in the two are the boundaries of the Euphrates river in Mesopotamia and the border of Egypt.[18] In this geographical detail, the Abraham narrative seems to presuppose the boundaries of the Solomonic era, or at least those mentioned in the court history.

More recent interpreters regard the Abraham materials not to have entered into the sacred story until the Exilic period (see Chap. 4). This view begins with the observation that there is no reference to Abraham in any pre-Exilic material. Even the prophets make no reference to Abraham until Deutero-Isaiah. The implication is that the Abrahamic traditions could not have been used by historians in the Solomonic period in order to legitimize monarchy by appeal to any patriarchal promise.[19] Yet another macro-level intertext between Genesis 15 and a late eighth-century prophet reinforces the hypothesis of a much later date for the social text of the Abraham passage. That comes in what is one of the most important verses in the entire passage, v. 6. Recall that in v. 6 the narrative affirms that Abraham believed Yahweh and the Lord "reckoned it to him as righteousness." First, that the narrator takes note of Abraham's trust—"And he believed the Lord"— is distinctive and reflects the religion of a time when such behavior would have itself been noteworthy. For example, to return to the passage considered in Chapter 6, the prophet Isaiah forewarns King Ahaz that "If you do not stand firm in faith, you shall not stand at all" (Isa 7:9). The word for "stand firm in faith" here is the same root as in Gen 15:6, the causative stem of the word *'aman,* meaning "to confirm," or "support" (often denoting faith). The Isaiah narrative depicts a king who has no faith; he refuses to believe Yahweh. The occurrence of the word in such

---

[16]Mendenhall and Herion, "Covenant," 1189–1190.

[17]See F. M. Cross, for instance, "The Ideologies of Kingship in the Era of the Empire: Conditional Covenant and Eternal Decree," *Canaanite Myth and Hebrew Epic* (Cambridge, MA: Harvard University Press, 1973) 262.

[18]*Ibid.,* 262.

[19]As in Chap. 4, see J. Van Seters, "Tradition and Social Change," *PRS* 7 (1980), 96–113; see also J. Blenkinsopp's summary, *The Pentateuch* (New York: Doubleday, 1992) 111–116.

a context suggests to scholars that the attribution to Abraham reflects the understanding of faith in the time of Isaiah (eighth century BCE), clearly later rather than in the Solomonic period.[20]

A second theological reflection of the narrator also seems to form an intertext with a later social text than that of the Solomonic period. That the deity declares such an attitude in some sense "correct"—"and the Lord reckoned it to him as righteousness"—is also from a much later period. The word "righteousness" in the sense of some morally correct behavior before Yahweh does not occur in literature before the Deuteronomist (e.g., Deut 24:13). In other words, this statement about the character Abraham reflects the religious assumptions of the prophets and the Deuteronomist who did not write before the eighth century BCE.[21] If these materials were written in the Exilic period, well after the Deuteronomistic History, then the notion of covenant as obligation is being radically revised in these narratives (see below).

The point here is that the narrative about Abraham, even though it concerns a very ancient character who no doubt lived and received a promise of a child from his deity, was not *written* until a time in Israel's existence when it was immediately relevant. The intertexts with the narratives about the Davidic monarchy, including the parallels in the form of the promise, suggest that the story was used in some sense to provide religious legitimization of a nationalistic movement, perhaps the monarchy itself. The intertexts with much later religious features leave open the possibility that the Abrahamic materials were not written until the Exilic period. But what is so important for the immediate purpose is that the notion of covenant is clearly defined in this passage as Yahweh's promise of blessing to the heirs of Abraham. In receiving that promise of land they became God's people.

Genesis 17 Rereads Genesis 15

This discussion of covenant as promise concludes with a brief consideration of Genesis 17 as a rereading of Genesis 15. Readers who press forward through the biblical narrative come to Genesis 17 and wonder why there is yet another episode on covenant-making. The similarities, and thus the redundancy created, between chapters 17 and 15 are unmistakable: There is the recurrence of "covenant"; there is the appearance of the deity to Abraham; there again is the promise of offspring (vv. 4–5); there is also the promise of land (v. 8). The episode follows the Hagar story, where Sarah's maid, Hagar, runs away due to the mistreatment she receives from Sarah because of jealousy. Perhaps narratively a reprise is called for since the promise has not yet been fulfilled through Sarah. From a narrative point of view, repetition reinforces the reader's suspense about Yahweh's fulfillment of his promise. Still, there is the theological question of whether God has to repeat his promises. Readers should therefore also keep in mind that for later readers (subsequent to the tradition of Genesis 15) there may well have been the need for clarification of what such promises might mean in social texts that differed from the earlier ones.

The differences between the two episodes of Genesis 15 and 17 are even more striking. Notice that in Genesis 17 there are references to Abraham's age (vv. 1, 17). The character of Abraham is different, too. He does not speak back to God. Rather, God merely makes an announcement. Notice, further, that the name for the deity is "God," only once being called Yahweh (v. 1). This

---

[20]Westermann, *Genesis 12–36*, 222–223.

[21]*Ibid.*, 223. See Westermann's fuller discussion and bibliography on this point.

episode, though making the same promises as in Genesis chapter 15, repeats the word "covenant" several times. A quick count reveals at least thirteen occurrences. In this narrative the deity's promise is now called an "everlasting covenant" (e.g., 15:8; 17:7). The episode also rereads the patriarch's name. After the covenant-making, Abram becomes Abraham, "ancestor of a multitude of nations." There is also a very explicit treatment of the mother of all nations, Sarah. Whereas Genesis 15 simply made the promise that a child would come from Abraham's loins, the promise of Genesis 17 emphasizes that Abraham's wife, Sarah, would conceive and bear a child. In effect, she too is a bearer of Yahweh's promise.

Taking both the similarities and the variations between Genesis 15 and 17 together, one easily suspects a different version of the same story. (Note the nature of covenant, the name change, and the genealogical and itinerary information.)[22] The nature of covenant is of special interest in the consideration of the possibility of a still later rereading of Genesis 15. Notice that not only does the word covenant recur more frequently, but also that the structure of the story reinforces the emphasis on defining covenant as Yahweh's promise. There is an introduction in vv. 1–3 followed by the divine speech itself in vv. 4–21. The speech also may be subdivided. Verses 3b–8 emphasize God's promise; vv. 9–14 emphasize Abraham's obligation; vv. 15–21 emphasize the promise, only this time through Sarah, Abraham's wife. With this structural arrangement the strong emphasis is still on God's promise. In fact, the promise aspect of covenant provides a framework for the material on Abraham's obligation. So even though there is an obligation laid upon the patriarch, that response is still contextualized by Yahweh's own obligation to Abraham and Sarah.

It is revealing to look more closely at Abraham's obligation to the deity. Here readers get the most definitive insight into the social text behind this passage. In verses 9–14 God lays down for Abraham his part of the covenant. Abraham must circumcise himself and all of the male members of his family. Further, this ritual must be performed on all future males born into the family on the eighth day after they have been born. The cutting away of the foreskin of the penis is to be a sign of God's promise of both offspring and land to Abraham and all of his descendants. In other words, in this narrative the act of circumcision takes on some very important religious significance. But its very inclusion here in reference to a text on God's covenant indicates how the understanding of God's promises were changing at the time this version of the story was written.

Circumcision was widely practiced in ancient Israel, as in other cultures around Israel. However, there was no *religious* significance attached to the operation until the Exilic or post-Exilic periods. The most telling evidence within the Bible for this is the absence of its provision in any of the old law codes. (Recall the relative dating of the origins of these codes in Chapter 4: the **Covenant Code**, the oldest, precedes the eighth-century BCE **Deuteronomic Code**; the **Holiness Code** may also be as early as the eighth century.) Reference to circumcision occurs in passing in Lev 12:3 in relationship to the birth of a male child. Admittedly, arguments from silence are weak. However, given the importance of this particular sign in the narrative in Genesis 17—given to Abraham, no less—one should expect the law codes to make more of it than they do. But they do not. That suggests that the narrative in Genesis 17 is actually later than most of the materials in the codes and the act of circumcision is incorporated into the narrative text as a means of

---

[22]*Ibid.*, 256–271; also N. Sarna, *Genesis* (Philadelphia and New York: The Jewish Publication Society, 1989) 123.

signifying this idea of God's promise to his people. In the Exilic and post-Exilic period, when maintaining identity as the people of God was made even more difficult, circumcision became an important identifying mark among the male population.[23] Reading the significance of circumci sion back into the story of Abraham, and the covenant Yahweh made with him, served to give legitimacy to this ritual of identification.

God's People, Covenant, and the Obligations of the Mosaic Law Deuteronomy 1–11; 26:16–34:12

Learning Goals

- To understand that the Hebrew Bible also knows of covenant in terms of mutually binding obligations between two parties.
- To understand the complexity of the book of Deuteronomy as the result of a process of several stages of rereading by historians influenced by Deuteronomic theology.
- To understand the possible influence Assyrian treaty forms might have had on the idea of covenant in Deuteronomy.

Guiding Study Exercises

1) Outline the broad structure of the book of Deuteronomy. Delineate between the original framework and additions by later historians.
2) What are the chief differences between the original framework to Deuteronomy and later Deuteronomistic additions?
3) Describe the key features in Deuteronomy that give evidence of being influenced by Assyrian treaty forms.
4) How does the later stage of the framework to Deuteronomy address its social text?

It is appropriate that the concluding discussion returns to the Deuteronomistic History and its introductory book Deuteronomy. Readers recall how Ezra's prayer in Neh 9:6–37 is so profoundly influenced by Deuteronomic theology. It should come as no surprise that this great Deuteronomistic historical corpus is regarded by some as the central panel of the biblical story. Not only does it reread the old Covenant Code of Exod 21:1–23:33 and preserve the traditions of Moses, but it asserts one of the most influential theological statements in the biblical story. That statement affirms that the extraordinary relationship between Yahweh and his people rests

---

[23]See a fuller discussion in R. DeVaux, *Ancient Israel* (London: Darton, Longman and Todd, 1961) 46–48.

upon mutual love as expressed in moral obligation. Those who would be the people of God must enter into a covenant of obligation with the deity, who has chosen them to keep his religious and social laws.

The theological significance of the Deuteronomic conception of covenant is only surpassed by the complexity of the book of Deuteronomy itself. At the heart of its complexity is its origins, behind which is reflected many years of development and multiple layers of tradition. In this closing section, the brief summary of the complex structure of Deuteronomy functions to illustrate how, in relationship to law, covenant takes on a meaning quite different from its application to the patriarchal stories. That different meaning would be all the more rich if a definite social text could be established. Unfortunately, this is as inconclusive as any in biblical studies. However, scholars continue to promote two or three different social texts that provide the background for the origins of covenant as obligation.

The Framework of the Deuteronomic Code

Attention must be directed to the so-called framework of the Deuteronomic Code since readers encounter here the language of covenant. Readers will recall from Chapter 4 that the code itself consists roughly of Deuteronomy 12–26. Within these chapters are laws similar to those in Exod 21:1–23:33, the Covenant Code. Quickly scanning the boundaries of the Deuteronomic Code, notice that the code begins and ends with related themes of worship. Deut 12:5 follows an admonition to destroy the local foreign cultic places and asserts worship at the one place where Yahweh causes his name to dwell. Similarly, Deut 26:1–15 is a concluding act of worship, again emphasizing the one place where Yahweh has chosen his name to dwell (Deut 26:2). This theme therefore functions as an apparent literary boundary delimiting the legal material within it and thereby clearly separating the code from the framing material.

The varying materials surrounding the law code contribute to this chapter's study of covenant since they provide the clearest indication of a process of rereading the significance of law. Perhaps the point of departure for the discussion grows from the observation that covenant terminology occurs in the framework surrounding the law-code but not in the law-code itself. The word for "covenant," *berit,* only occurs one time in the law code (17:2), while it occurs over twenty times in the framework.[24] In other words, while the law code proper is originally framed by a concern for worshipping Yahweh in the appropriate place, the larger framework imposes the concept of covenant.

Reading through the book of Deuteronomy, there is a complex series of introductions, sermons, conclusions, and farewells. While chapters 1–11 seem to stand on their own as introductory material, there are at least two introductions: 1:1–4:43 and 4:44–11:32. Further, while there is a clear break between the materials in Deuteronomy 26 and those that conclude the book (chaps. 27–34), they are quite diverse. Blessings and curses follow the law code in 27:1–28:68, with a ceremony of covenant-making in 29:1–30:20, a song of Moses in 32:1–43, a blessing by Moses in 33:1–29, and a further appendix on Moses' death in 34:1–12.[25]

---

[24]See, for example, 4:13 , 23, 31; 5:2, 3; 7:2, 9, 12; 8:18; 9:9, 11, 15; 10:8; 29:1, 9, 12, 14, 21, 25; 31:9, 16, 20, 25.

[25]Helpful introductions into this material are in M. Weinfeld, *Deuteronomy 1–11* (AB 5; Garden City, NY: Doubleday, 1991) 9–14; B. Childs, *Introduction to the Old Testament as Scripture* (Philadelphia: Fortress, 1979) 204–207.

Generally, scholars believe that the original book consisted of 4:44–28:68. In this case, surrounding the law code is a series of introductory admonitions to keep the law and a series of blessings and curses serving as threats if people did not keep the law. To this original book of law was later added further framing material, not so much to introduce the law book as much as to connect it to the larger work of history (the Deuteronomistic History) it was to introduce. Thus, Deuteronomy 1–3 was a later addition, as was Deut 31:1–8. Readers will notice that both of these are concerned about inheritance of the promised land. A comparative reading with Joshua 1 reveals similarities in language that suggest their larger purpose in the historical narrative that follows the book of Deuteronomy. Likewise, Deut 4:1–40 corresponds to Deut 30:1–10 in their apparent concern for the people's repentance and return from Exile. That they seem to presuppose the Exile gives scholars some indication about the date at which they were added. They bear a great affinity with Solomon's prayer in 1 Kgs 8:44–53. While there is not space to explore all of these connections and their supposed social texts, readers will observe a roughly symmetrical structure between law code and the various frameworks of the book (see Table 8.1).

Covenant in the Introduction to the Law: Deuteronomy 6:20–25; Deuteronomy 5:1–4

The writer of the original introduction to the law code seems to know of the Lord's promise to Abraham, Isaac, and Jacob. But he incorporates a different understanding of what accompanies this idea of covenant. For unlike the promises to the patriarchs, covenant takes on special obligations that must be observed in order for Yahweh's promise to be fulfilled.

Deuteronomy 6:20–25. In the broader context of this first instruction on the first commandment (6:1–25), the writer knows of Yahweh's promise to the patriarchal fathers. Verse 10 makes this clear: "When the Lord your God has brought you into the land that he swore to your ancestors, to Abraham, to Isaac, and to Jacob, to give you. . . ." Obviously, there is not the accompanying language of covenant here, which was evident in Genesis 15 and 17. Nevertheless, the language indicates that Yahweh "swore" this to the ancestral fathers. This is furthermore not the only occurrence in the older framework of a reference to Yahweh's promise to those ancestors. In Deut 7:12–13 there is another reference, this one making more explicit the contingent nature of the Lord's covenant. In Deut 8:18 there is yet another reference to the covenant Yahweh swore to

Table 8.1

The Structure of Deuteronomy

A. 1:1–3:29: Introduction to the Deuteronomistic History
  B. 4:1–11:32: Introduction and admonitions to keep the law
    C. 12:1–28:68: The laws with attending blessings and curses
  B'. 29:1–30:20: Covenant-making ceremony (presupposes the Exile)
  A'. 31:1–34:12: Transition of power from Moses to Joshua

the ancestors. Apart from the larger context, this one seems more in keeping with the earlier reading of covenant as promise. However, the larger context in which these instructions occur, while acknowledging that Yahweh made a covenant with the patriarchs, nevertheless makes it impossible to understand that covenant as merely a one-sided promise.

The conclusion to this first instruction, 6:20–25, could not make clearer the accompanying obligations. The setting is itself instructional: "When your children ask you in time to come, 'What is the meaning of the decrees and the statutes and the ordinances that the Lord our God has commanded you?'" This balances the admonition earlier in the instruction to recite Moses' words to one's children (v. 7). Verses 21–23 narrate very briefly the story of deliverance from Egypt. Notice how v. 23 provides the interpretation that the deliverance from Egypt was both so Yahweh could give his people the land and so he could thereby keep the promise he swore to the ancestors. But the final verse makes clear that Yahweh also commanded his people to observe his commandments, which, one reads later, are contained in the laws that follow.

Deuteronomy 5:1–4. The idealism of this writer is even more evident in the introductory words to the Decalogue (vv. 6–21). Within these verses readers see clearly that the covenant of obligation is made at Horeb, the Deuteronomist's name for Sinai. These statutes and ordinances are presented as being given to the people at that place and time. Verse 1 concludes with the directive to "learn them and observe them diligently." Notice that the concluding verse in the chapter (v. 33) says virtually the same thing, clearly indicating that living long in the land depends upon careful commitment to the commandments.

What is of special interest, however, are vv. 2–3: "The Lord our God made a covenant with us at Horeb. Not with our ancestors did the Lord make his covenant, but with us, who are all of us here alive today." Now this is a remarkable statement indeed, since, as readers have already read, the people standing on the east side of Jordan is a new generation of people (see Deut 2:14–16). In an intriguing way the writer of this older framework to the law code sees the people who were getting ready to claim the land of Canaan as the ones with whom Yahweh made his covenant of law at Horeb/Sinai. Reasoning historically, readers know that these persons could *not* have even been born or were at least very young at the time. But, readers may be missing the original writer's point if they tarry too long over this discrepancy. The writer is rather concerned about how this covenant at Horeb is binding upon people of successive generations. In other words, it is his way of both acknowledging (tacitly) that something new is being introduced into the traditional understanding of relationship to Yahweh. Hearers and readers alike should not appeal to older understandings of covenants with ancestors, or to the failures of previous generations. Each successive generation, rather, must see itself as standing on the east side of Jordan ready to cross into the promised land and as remembering that the covenant at Horeb is also binding upon them.

Only in this way do these ordinary people become the people of God. In 7:6 it says, "For you are a people holy to the Lord your God; the Lord your God has chosen you out of all the people on earth to be his people, his treasured possession." The word "holy" is an important word in the Hebrew Bible. It means "set apart" or, in reference to the deity, "other." Thus, God's people are to be different from the peoples of the other nations. The verse reiterates the idea by stating that Yahweh has "chosen" the people from among all other peoples. Israel is to be a "treasured possession." This idea recurs throughout both the law-code and at the conclusion in a covenant formulation (e.g., 14:2; 26:18). These ideas of holiness, "chosenness," and even the very possession of Yahweh all combine to create the important theological idea of election. Yahweh chose

Israel to be a special people, and their unique identity as his chosen people derives from their observance of his "statutes and ordinances."

The Social Text of the Covenant of Obligation

The social text behind the idea that Yahweh enters into a covenant of mutual obligations with his people raises a series of complex questions. To summarize the nature of the problem, there is an apparent opposition between the meaning of the word *covenant* in the Abraham narratives and the meaning of that word in the book of Deuteronomy and in the Deuteronomistic History about Israel, God's people. Providing a social text for either requires both offering a date for their origins as well as a social context. The hope for this discussion would be to suggest which tradition is rereading the other. However, no such suggestion is possible here. Nevertheless, it is clear that within the corpus of the book of Deuteronomy there are multiple layers of rereading. It is clear that the framework to the collection of laws imposes the notion of covenant obligation, *berit,* upon a document that originally was not so conceived. Are the writers of Deuteronomy rereading an old covenant tradition that stood behind the Abraham-David tradition, or is the sequence just the reverse? Are the writers of the Abraham tradition actually doing their work quite late and thus rereading the notion of covenant obligation as it is connected to land for a still later setting?[26] Only aspects of the ongoing scholarly debate can be included in what follows.

Covenant as an Ancient Idea. To a certain extent the question turns on scholars' ability to date the origins of the idea of covenant itself. One of the most influential arguments to support the antiquity of covenant in Israel comes from those who have argued for intertextuality between the biblical traditions and various ancient Near Eastern treaty forms. As the thesis was argued by G. E. Mendenhall, for example, ancient, second-millennium Hittite treaties between kings and their vassals formed the bases for Israelite theologians' reflections upon the relationship between Yahweh and his people.[27] Through what was fundamentally a form-critical argument, Mendenhall sought to show a macro-level intertextual relationship between the treaty pattern and the Decalogue in Exod 10:1–17. The pattern itself consists of six elements, as follow: (1) a preamble where the sovereign initiating the treaty gives his name; (2) a historical prologue leading up to the making of the treaty; (3) the actual stipulations or obligations laid upon the **vassal**; (4) a deposit of the treaty in the sanctuary for regular reading; (5) an appeal to deities to enforce the treaty; and (6) various cursing and blessing formulas.[28] Mendenhall admitted that though all of the elements were not present in the Decalogue itself, they nevertheless were evident in the fuller episode of covenant at Sinai (Exodus 19–24). He believed that there were parallels with the biblical phrase "I am the Lord your God" (Exod 20:2), forming the identification formula; the historical

---

[26]See. R. Davidson, "Covenant Ideology in Ancient Israel," *The World of Ancient Israel,* 323–348, for a broad summary of the contrasting views and the evidence they are based upon; two very helpful overviews of the history of the scholarly debate are, R. A. Oden, Jr. "The Place of Covenant in the Religion of Israel," *Studies in Israelite Religion* (eds., P. D. Miller, Jr., P. D. Hanson, S. D. McBride; Philadelphia: Fortress, 1987) 429–447; W. Zimmerli, "The History of Israelite Religion," *Tradition and Interpretation* (ed., G. W. Anderson; Oxford: Oxford University Press, 1979) 351–383.

[27]The classic formulation is in G. E. Mendenhall, "Covenant Forms in Israelite Tradition," *BA* 17 (1954) 50–76.

[28]Zimmerli, "History of Israelite Religion," 374.

The black obelisk of Assyrian King Shalmanesar III (859–824 BCE) depicts Jehu (842–816 BCE; 2 Kgs 9:1–10:31) offering tribute to the Assyrian King. Such tribute would be offered by all the king's vassals with whom the king had made a treaty. (Basalt bas-relief. British Museum, London, Great Britain)

preamble was in the phrase, "who brought you out of the land of Egypt, out of the house of slavery" (Exod 20:2); the stipulations consisted of the laws that followed the Decalogue.

While there is no space to expatiate Mendenhall's work, nor to elaborate the extensive study it provoked, it is important for the present discussion that readers realize his hypothesis has made plausible the claim for the antiquity of the covenant obligation idea based upon these treaty forms. Dating the Hittite treaties to the mid-to-late second millennium BCE corresponded well with other claims regarding the origins of ancient Israel in the land of Canaan.

Covenant As a More Recent Idea. On the other hand, the antiquity of the idea of covenant as mutual obligation has not been persuasive to all. Criticism of Mendenhall's ideas have therefore led the way to reappraisals of the evidence of antiquity and assertions of hypotheses that, in fact, the covenant idea was really quite late in Israel's existence rather than ancient. Not the least of the objections was the observation that neither the Decalogue nor the larger legal section (Exodus 19–24) contained all of the elements of a vassal treaty, and that the apparent resemblances could be explained in other ways. Furthermore, the appeal to ancient Near Eastern vassal treaties dating from the middle of the second millennium BCE was not necessarily a clear indication of antiquity. Such treaty forms continued to be used well into the first millennium BCE, allowing the possibility of a much later influence, if there was any at all.

A further criticism paralleled the argument in reference to the Abraham tradition. In much the same way as prophetic reticence on the Abraham tradition led to the supposition of that tradition's lateness, so it was argued that similar prophetic silence regarding covenant and law indicated the same thing. It was not until the eighth century BCE that prophets began to speak of the notion of covenant relationship to the deity. Then it was only in northern kingdom prophets such as Hosea and the later seventh-century Jeremiah. The implication, whatever the origins of the term *covenant,* was that the idea of covenant relationship with Yahweh entered through late prophetic preaching. That Deuteronomy itself was dated to the seventh century BCE was further reinforcement of the argument that the covenant concept was late. Recall from Chapter 6 the discussion that the discovery of the law in the Temple was thought by many scholars to have some degree of factuality to it and to have been the discovery of the lost Deuteronomic Code. That discovery brought the law code with its early framework into public and official view. It became a manifesto for reform in Jerusalem and Judah and especially for the reclamation of land that had been lost to Assyria in the late eighth and seventh centuries BCE.

Treaty, Cultic Instruction, Wisdom

It is not only the relative date of the concept of covenant that is problematic. Identification of the social milieu out of which it might have come also poses challenges to readers and scholars alike. Some scholars acknowledge the late origins of the book, and thus of the notion of covenant obligations, but persist in their insistence upon the treaty form as having influenced Deuteronomy's composition. Others, by contrast, suggest that the exhortatory forms imply a cultic setting, indicating that the origins of the covenant idea should be located there. Likewise, other scholars recognize an implicit didacticism in Deuteronomy's exhortation and promote the wisdom movement as a background.

The Rhetoric of Treaty. That the treaty form continued to be in use through the first millennium BCE allows the supposition that the writers of Deuteronomy might still have been influenced by such a form in their understanding of covenant. Even those who criticized Mendenhall's thesis affirmed the possible influence of the treaty form upon Deuteronomy.[29] For instance, M. Weinfeld has argued that the book reflects the pledges of loyalty within the vassal treaties of Esarhaddon, a late Assyrian king (681–669 BCE). Such treaties were attempts by retiring Assyrian kings to secure loyalty from their vassals for their successors. Weinfeld observes that the literary structure of Deuteronomy reflects the form of the treaty: historical prologue (Deuteronomy 1–11); stipulations (Deuteronomy 12–16:15); mutual obligations (Deut 26:16–19); and blessings and curses (Deuteronomy 27–28).[30]

[29]D. J. McCarthy, *Treaty and Covenant* (AnBib 21A; Rome: Pontificio Istituto Biblico, 1978) for instance; also see M. Weinfeld's recent application in *Deuteronomy* 1–11, 8–11.
[30]*Ibid.,* 6–9.

These claims, while provocative, do not go without criticism.[31] Not the least of these is the unlikelihood that, in the supposed context that is ascribed for the production of the original book of Deuteronomy, an Assyrian treaty form might have been a helpful way of conveying the people's relationship to Yahweh. Weinfeld still places this transformative time period around the reforms of king Josiah (at the end of seventh century BCE). The reforms take place as Judah seeks to break away from 150 years of Assyrian domination in Israel and Judah. Readers have to wonder whether an Assyrian treaty would have been well received by people who were struggling to overthrow such influence, especially those who were trying to rid themselves of Assyrian religious domination.

Oration and Cult. Alternatively, the laws within the book of Deuteronomy are presented as a final address or admonition of Moses. Their presentation pictures a people gathered together, who respond by entering into a covenant sealed by a sacred ceremony before Yahweh (Deuteronomy 29–30). In fact, many scholars continue to treat materials within the framework as sermonic material.[32] The idea is that the materials in the framework originally stem from the exhortations of levitical priests charged with the responsibility of cultic instruction of those who came to worship. The exhortations found in Deuteronomy preserved those old sermons, based upon the Decalogue and the law code generally, in a new form that attributes them to Moses.

The notion of covenant, then, is not a political idea at all. Rather, it stems from the context of worship. Without denying the existence and even the influence of the treaty pattern, Von Rad, for instance, admitted the free use of such patterns within the context of the exhortations and homilies that served cultic festivals. In particular, he believed that the form of Deuteronomy reflected a supposed covenant renewal celebration that took place during the feast of Succoth in the autumn of the year.[33] The weakness of the view stems largely from the failure to find evidence for the existence of such a covenant renewal festival.

The Rhetoric of Wisdom. Readers have encountered Israel's wisdom tradition only once before in this text. That was in reference to the affinities between wisdom instructions and **apodictic** law (see Chap. 4). The exhortative and sermonic rhetoric of the book of Deuteronomy invite reconsidering wisdom circles as a possible social text. Recall that the framework passages concerning covenant (above) place the admonitions about covenant in the context of concern for the education of children. Deut 6:7 reads, "Recite them to your children and talk about them when you are at home and when you are away, when you lie down and when you rise." Likewise, Deut 6:20 says, "When your children ask you in time to come, 'What is the meaning of the decrees and the statutes and the ordinances that the LORD our God has commanded you?'" Such concern for education invites comparison with similar rhetorical situations in Proverbs 1–9, where readers encounter parents teaching the ways of wisdom to their children. In fact, in Deut 4:6 the laws are identified with wisdom.

While the idea of covenant is not found in wisdom literature at all, its approach being more humanistic and noncultic, the wisdom setting might have provided a catalytic context, making a

---

[31]The most thorough recent criticism is that of E. W. Nicholson, *God and His People* (Oxford: Clarendon Press, 1986) 56–82.

[32]P. Miller, *Deuteronomy* (IBC; Louisville, KY: John Knox, 1991) 1–17; G. Von Rad held this view quite strongly in *Deuteronomy* (OTL; London: SCM Press, 1966) 28–30.

[33]*Ibid.*, 28–30; see also E. W. Nicholson, *Deuteronomy and Tradition* (Oxford: Basil Blackwell, 1967) 42–45.

A Closer Look: Israel's Wisdom Tradition. When scholars speak of a wisdom tradition they are referring to the deposit of literary, historical, and sociological artifacts both within and without the biblical story, that define the phenomenon known as *wisdom.* Unfortunately, little is said about the topic in this text (and many texts) since one of the defining features of the wisdom tradition is its reticence on the biblical story. Rather, in the Bible, wisdom is characterized by the literary works of Proverbs, Job, some Psalms, Jesus ben Sirach, and the Wisdom of Solomon. Historically those works of literature are thought to derive from the post-Exilic period, but reflect a long history of development (see Prov 25:1 for references to Hezekiah's men). Sociologically, wisdom's precise origins are not clear. There is evidence that the family and clan stand behind a concern to inculcate values. Likewise, court and school, as they might have maintained a symbiosis, could have broadened and developed the concern for educational and political efficacy. Even the cult, dominated by court and its international concerns, could have engaged in the promotion of a worldview (based upon creation, for instance) that maintained order and emphasized the social status quo. It was, after all, the educated scribes and priests who sought to write Israel's traditions and teach them to succeeding generations.

For further reading, J. Crenshaw. *Old Testament Wisdom.* Atlanta, GA: John Knox Press, 1983. Pp. 11–25; 42–65; ———. "The Concept of God in Old Testament Wisdom." *In Search of Wisdom.* Edited by L. G. Perdue, et. al. Louisville, KY: Westminster/John Knox Press, 1993. Pp. 1–18; R. N. Whybray. "The Sage in the Israelite Royal Court." *The Sage in Israel and the Ancient Near East.* Edited by J. G. Gammie and L. G. Perdue. Winona Lake, IL: Eisenbrauns, 1990. Pp. 133–339.

For more advanced study, R. E. Murphy. "Wisdom and Creation." *JBL* 104.1 (1985) 3–11; R. B. Y. Scott. "Solomon and the Beginnings of Wisdom in Israel." *VT*Sup 3 (1955) 262–279.

transition from covenant as a quaint, localized cultic idea to a broader theological notion that had more universal and transcendent appeal.

Conclusion

The idea of the people of God develops in relationship to the everchanging social and historical contexts surrounding it. In the post-Exilic period the notion of Israel had become very narrow in the story-world of Ezra-Nehemiah. This is quite a contrast from the prophetic view of those who spoke on Yahweh's behalf just a century and a half prior to this. But time and circumstances change everything. The notion of covenant, so determinative in the story of the Hebrew Bible, is itself fraught with multiple meanings, applications, and complexities. Is it late? Is it early? Is it Abrahamic? Davidic? Mosaic? Deuteronomic? There are no clear answers, only hypotheses and the provocative groundwork for more research.

Such complexity and diversity calls all the more for readers to grasp the process of reread-ing that gives such complexity to the scriptures. It was indeed the task of each generation to grap-ple with the meaning of their identity as God's people, God's nation, holding God's future. The biblical story attests great disagreements (e.g., Levites vs. Aaronides). But the Bible comes into being as these disagreements assume the forms of reinterpretation that span generations. Not only, then, do later generations of Yahweh's people inherit a complex story, handed on by genera-tions who affirmed faith in Yahweh, but they also inherit an understanding that they too must reread the story that defines who they are and then pass on that new understanding to the next generation. It is not only how God's people came to be, it is how the Hebrew Bible came to be.

For Further Reading

Ezra-Nehemiah and the Exiles

Ackroyd, P. R. "The Jewish Community in Palestine in the Persian Period." *CHJ* I, 130–361. (*Recom-mended for beginning students.*)

Herion, G. A. "The Impact of Modern and Social Science Assumptions on the Reconstruction of Israelite History." *JSOT* 34 (1986) 3–33.

Kearney, M. "Borders and Boundaries of State and Self at the End of Empire." *Journal of Historical Sociol-ogy* 4 (1991) 52–74.

Williamson, H. G. M. "The Concept of Israel in Transition." *The World of Ancient Israel.* Edited by R. E. Clements. Cambridge: Cambridge University Press, 1989. Pp. 141–162.

God's People and the Covenant with Abraham

Childs, B. S. "The Etiological Tale Re-examined." *VT* 24 (1974) 387–397.

Dever, W. G. "The Contribution of Archaeology to the Study of Canaanite and Early Israelite Religion." *An-cient Israelite Religion.* Edited by P. D. Miller, Jr., P. D. Hanson, S. D. McBride. Philadelphia: Fortress, 1987. Pp. 209–248. (*Recommended for beginning students.*)

Mendenhall, G. E. "The Nature and Purpose of the Abraham Narratives." *Ancient Israelite Religion.* Edited by P. D. Miller, Jr., P. D. Hanson, S. D. McBride. Philadelphia: Fortress, 1987. Pp. 337–356. (*Recom-mended for beginning students.*)

Van Seters, J. "Confessional Reformulation in the Exilic Period." *VT* 22 (1972) 448–459.

God's People, Covenant, and the Obligation of the Mosaic Law

Clements, R. E. *Deuteronomy.* OTG; Sheffield: JSOT Press, 1989. (*Recommended for beginning students.*)

Gerstenberger, E. "Covenant and Commandment." *JBL* 84.1(1965) 38–51.

Miller, P. *Deuteronomy.* IBC. Louisville, KY: John Knox Press, 1990. Pp. 1–17. (*Recommended for begin-ning students.*)

PART THREE

The Story
of
Jesus
and
His
Earliest Followers

CHAPTER NINE

The World of Jesus and His Followers

Introduction

Review

One might summarize the story of Israel as found in the scriptures of Israel as follows: God had called a people, Israel, to be *his* people. He led these descendants of the patriarchs out of Egypt, through the wilderness, and into the land flowing with milk and honey. He made a covenant to bless and protect Israel, so long as Israel was loyal to him, obeying his commandments and worshipping him in a fitting manner. But Israel rebelled against God. Thus, God punished them, sending them far away into the Exile. But there was a grand "homecoming"—a return from the Exile. Certainly, while different readings, or understandings, of this story existed among the Jewish people, many Jewish people believed the story to be unfinished. For example, Ezra-Nehemiah understands that, despite the rebuilding of the Temple and the city wall, the Jewish people still live in slavery (Ezra 9:9). To some extent, they are still "exiles." In light of this, N. T. Wright's assessment of Judaism in the Greco-Roman era is on target:

> Most Jews of this period, it seems, would have answered the question "where are we?" in language which, reduced to its simplest form, meant: we are still in exile. They believed that, in all the senses which mattered, Israel's exile was still in progress.[1]

This "big story" as found *in* the Bible constitutes a macro-level social text for those who embraced as their own the story of Israel. Parts Three and Four of this text will focus attention on how followers of Jesus intersected their understanding of Jesus with the larger story and smaller stories that they inherited from their scriptures.

Preview

Previous chapters have emphasized that one's understanding the literary text of the Bible is greatly enhanced by one's understanding of the social text out of which and in the context of

---

[1]N. T. Wright, *The New Testament and the People of God* (Minneapolis, MN: Fortress, 1992) 268–269.

which the scriptures were written. Given that the NT was composed over a more compressed period of time than the Hebrew Bible (with most NT documents composed in the second half of the first century CE), a very focused investigation of the social text of the first century CE is in order. Chapter 2 surveyed the historical social text of Israel's story up to the beginning of the Roman period. Subsequent chapters of Parts One and Two offered more detailed historical investigation of the various phases of Israelite, Judean, and **post-Exilic** Jewish history up through and including the Maccabean Revolt (167 BCE). The following historical survey will begin with the end of this revolt. First, the chapter surveys the world of **Palestine** in Jesus' time, including significant features of Jewish history up to the time of Jesus' birth. Second, the chapter examines Palestine after Jesus. Third, the chapter explores the world of Jesus' followers beyond the land of Palestine—the larger world of the Roman Empire. Readings from the Gospel of Luke and the Acts of the Apostles will provide points of departure for the study of the world of Jesus and his followers. With foundational knowledge of the social text of Jesus and his earliest followers in place, subsequent chapters will survey the story of Jesus and his followers and offer a more detailed study of the ways that early **Christians** reread the traditions that they inherited from Israel's stories and scriptures.

Palestine in Jesus' Time
Luke 1–4

Learning Goals

- To learn the basic history of the Jews of Judea from the end of the Maccabean revolt to the birth of Jesus of Nazareth.
- To learn the essentials of the complex political structures that influenced Palestine in Jesus' day.

Guiding Study Exercises

1) Write a summary of Jewish history from the rise of Simon Hasmon up to the rise of Herod the Great. Include the names of key rulers, events, and their dates.
2) Explain how Herod came to power and how his family continued to wield political influence even after his death.
3) Describe how the following institutions of power related to one another in Judea during the period of Jesus' ministry: the Emperor, the Sanhedrin, the house of Herod, and the Roman governors.

Jewish History before the Ministry of Jesus

Luke 1–4 presents a number of historical notices in the opening chapters of the narrative (see esp. Lk 1:5; 2:1; 3:1–2). Luke 1:5 offers an almost casual reference to King Herod, as though the reader would know exactly who he was. By means of such notices, Luke places the Jesus story squarely into the world of the larger history of **Judea** and the Roman Empire.

In the year 142 BCE, under the leadership of Simon Hasmon, "the yoke of the Gentiles was removed from Israel" (1 Macc 13:41 [see Chap. 2]). This independence gave rise to the **Hasmonean** Dynasty, which continued to exert influence over Judea even after the establishment of Roman rule in 63 BCE. When Simon died in 134 BCE, his son, John Hyrcanus I, assumed the rule of the Jews, holding both the offices of high priest and the political throne (see Figure 9.1). Employing mercenaries, he extended the boundaries of Judea into both the regions of **Samaria** to the north and Idumea to the south. Ironically, even though the Maccabean revolt began as a defense of traditional Jewish piety, Hyrcanus was not perceived as being very religious by the more pious people under his rule. There were severe tensions, therefore, between Hyrcanus, the descendent of the Maccabean leadership, and many of the pious people who had formed the Maccabean army in the previous generation.

After Hyrcanus died (134 BCE), one of his sons, Aristobulus I, seized control, though he died after a brief reign (104–103 BCE). Intrigue was now part of the court of Hasmon, for Aristobulus threw his mother and his brothers in prison and assassinated another brother in order to secure his position. After Aristobulus died, his widow, Salome Alexandra, released his brothers from prison, married the eldest of these (Alexander Jannaeus), and placed him on the throne. Jannaeus continued to expand Judea's territory, making his kingdom about the same size as that of Solomon's centuries before. The gap between pious Jews and the Hasmoneans grew wider during his reign. It was not uncommon for Jannaeus to employ both terror and torture to enforce his policies on his increasingly disillusioned subjects.

Upon Jannaeus' death, his wife, Salome, took over the reigns of secular power. She could not serve as high priest, since she was a woman, so she placed her son Hyrcanus II in this office. Wisely, Salome sought reconciliation with the pious Jews of her country. She made steps in this direction by placing **Pharisees**, scrupulously pious layperons who had most vehemently opposed Jannaeus, on the ruling council, known as the **Sanhedrin**. When she died (67 BCE), her son, the high priest Hyrcanus II, assumed her place on the secular throne. However, his brother, Aristobulus II, engaged him in war and succeeded in overthrowing Hyrcanus II. At this stage in the story a certain Antipater, from the region of Idumea, came to the aid of Hyrcanus II. Antipater persuaded nearby rulers to support Hyrcanus II and, as a result, helped him to resecure his position as both high priest and ruler. It was also at this time that the Roman general Pompey entered Judea with his Roman forces (63 BCE). Henceforth, the Romans would be establishing policy in Judea and the surrounding regions of Palestine.

Pompey sided with Hyrcanus II and Antipater. However, he restored Hyrcanus II only to the office of high priest and greatly reduced the boundaries of the territory over which Hyrcanus II had control. Roman politics continued to influence Judea and Palestine. Pompey and forces loyal to him grew alarmed at the expanding power of Julius **Caesar**, the leading general in the west and formerly Pompey's ally. Civil war erupted between the armies of the two generals (49–45 BCE), with Caesar emerging as the victor. In return for the support that Hyrcanus II and Antipater offered Caesar, he granted Antipater the office of governor of Judea. The Antipatrid

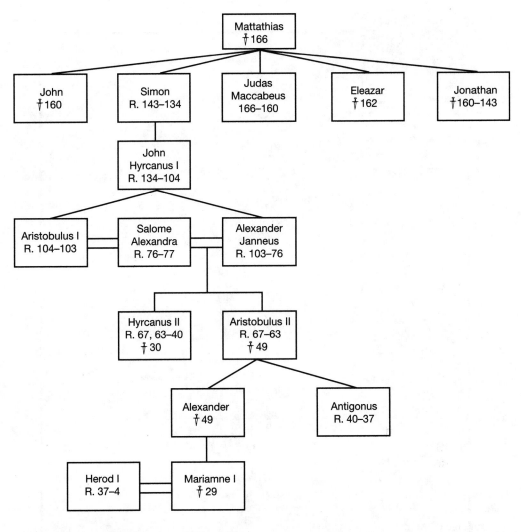

Figure 9.1

The Hasmonean Dynasty

family now had a secure foothold of power in the region. It was from this family that the King Herod of Lk 1:5 emerged.

Herod was one of the sons of Antipater. After Antipater suffered a violent death, Antigonus, the son of Aristobulus II, Hyrcanus II's old rival, succeeded in wresting control of the high priesthood from Hyrcanus II. As a consequence, Antigonus ruled Judea from 40–37 BCE, and Herod

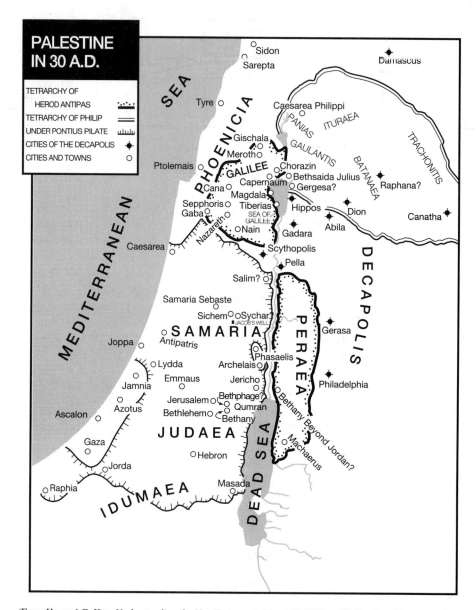

(From Howard C. Kee, *Understanding the New Testament*, 4th ed. © 1983, p. 83. Reprinted by permission of Prentice Hall. Adapted from *The Westminster Historical Atlas to the Bible* (rev. ed.), George Ernest Wright and Floyd Vivian Filson, eds. Copyright 1956, by W. L. Jenkins. Adapted and used by permission of The Westminster Press, Philadelphia, PA)

was forced to flee to Rome. In 40 BCE, Herod persuaded the Roman senate to make him king of the Jews. Backed by Rome, Herod returned to Palestine and succeeded in overthrowing the forces of Antigonus in 37 BCE. He ruled until 4 BCE over a large territory, extending from Caesarea Philippi in the north to the region of Idumea in the south (see Map of Palestine in 30 CE). According to both Luke (Lk 1:5) and Matthew (Matt 2:1), Jesus of Nazareth was born in the final years of Herod's reign.

Herod employed any means necessary to maintain his secure hold on his power. For example, in an effort to appease the supporters of the old royal Hasmonean family, he married the granddaughter of Aristobulus II, Mariamne, who became only one of Herod's several wives. He even appointed her brother, Aristobulus III, to the high priesthood. Yet Herod, ever fearful that even those closest to him would attempt to overthrow him, concluded that the inclusion of the Hasmonean family into his household was not enough to secure his position. He had Aristobulus III murdered and, eventually, ordered the assassinations of Mariamne and their two sons. Herod did, however, spare his young grandchildren and decades after King Herod's death one of these grandsons, Herod Agrippa, would rule the former territory of Herod the Great.

Palestine in Jesus' Day

Luke 2:1 makes reference to Caesar Augustus, again almost in passing, as though Luke assumed that readers knew of whom he spoke. Caesar's defeat of Pompey and his allies resulted in Caesar's quick ascension to dictatorial power. Yet former supporters of Pompey, whom Caesar had pardoned, still feared his power and conspired successfully to assassinate Caesar within the senate chambers in Rome in 44 BCE. Supporters of the senate coup aligned themselves against the forces of Antony and Caesar Octavian, the latter being Julius Caesar's adopted son and legal heir. Antony and Octavian defeated the senatorial forces (42 BCE), but then turned on each other. Octavian defeated the combined forces of Antony and Cleopatra, the last queen of Egypt, in 31 BCE. In 27 BCE, the Roman senate bestowed on Octavian the title of "the August One," or Augustus. Henceforth, the vast territory under the dominance of Rome would be the Roman Empire, ruled by the Emperor. Upon the death of Augustus, Tiberius, mentioned in Lk 3:1, became the Emperor of Rome.

Luke 3:1–2 refers to several other political and religious rulers who affected the religio-political world of Jesus. Behind this passing reference to these rulers lies a complex network of power relationships. The following discussion outlines the most significant matters for introductory readers. Luke 3:1 refers to Emperor Tiberius (see Table 9.1), the governor Pontius Pilate, Herod (the ruler of Galilee), and Herod's brother Philip (the ruler of two smaller regions). Luke 3:2 refers to "the high priesthood and Annas and Caiaphas." The text also mentions Lysanias (3:1), though he plays no significant role in Luke's story of Jesus or his followers.

Herod and Philip. Following the death of King Herod in 4 BCE, Emperor Augustus honored the legal will of Herod, who had divided his kingdom between three of his sons: Archelaus, Herod Antipas, and Philip. Archelaus was given the regions of Samaria and Judea. However, Rome was not pleased with his rule and he was deposed and exiled in 6 CE. Since Archelaus had been out of power for almost a quarter century by the time Jesus began his public ministry, Luke has no need to mention him in Lk 3:1. Herod Antipas, whom Luke simply refers to as Herod in Lk 3:1, inherited the rule of the regions of Galilee and Perea. According to the **Synoptic Gospels**, Jesus focused his ministry on the region of Galilee. Hence, Jesus would have spent most of his time under Herod's jurisdiction. Not surprisingly, stories about Herod recur frequently in Luke's

Table 9.1

The Roman Emperors of the NT Era

Date	Emperor	Connection with NT
27 BCE–14 CE	Augustus	Mentioned in Lk 2:1. According to Luke, Augustus' worldwide tax registration required Jesus' parents to journey to Bethlehem. This specific registration cannot be confirmed from extra-biblical sources.
14–37 CE	Tiberius	Mentioned in Lk 3:1. He was Emperor during the ministry of Jesus and the early years of the Jesus movement following Jesus' death.
37–41 CE	Caligula	Not mentioned in the NT. It was he who made Herod the Great's grandson, Agrippa I, king of the Palestinian territory.
41–54 CE	Claudius	Mentioned in Acts 11:28 in connection with a prophecy of a worldwide famine. Extra-biblical sources speak of a Judean famine in the year 46 CE (Josephus, *Antiquities*, 20.51–53). Claudius is also mentioned in Acts 18:2, which says that Claudius ordered the Jews to leave Rome. Extra-biblical sources speak of Claudius expelling a significant number of Jews from Rome in 49 CE (Suetonius, *Life of Claudius*, 25).
54–68 CE	Nero	Not mentioned in the NT. According to church tradition, both Peter and Paul, influential leaders of the early church, were executed during his reign. Ironically, this is the emperor to whom Paul appealed his legal case (Acts 25:11).
68–69 CE	Galba; Otho; Vitellius	None is mentioned in the NT. That there were three emperors within one year shows that this brief period was tumultuous.
69–79 CE	Vespasian	Not mentioned in the NT. However, the NT alludes several times to the destruction of Jerusalem and the Temple (see, e.g., Luke 21). This occurred in 70 CE, while Vespasian was emperor.
79–81 CE	Titus	Emperor Titus is not mentioned in the NT. Titus was the general who led the Roman forces that destroyed Jerusalem in 70 CE.
81–96 CE	Domitian	Not mentioned in the NT. The intense persecution of Christians under his reign provided the social text for the Apocalypse, the final book of the NT.

narrative (see 3:19–20; 9:7–9 [cf. Mk 6:17–29]; 13:31–32; 23:6–12). Herod Antipas was deposed in 39 CE. The regions granted to Philip lay in the northeastern extremities of King Herod's domain. According to the Synoptic Gospels, Jesus ventured on occasion into his territory (Matt 16:13–23; Mk 8:27–30 [Caesarea Philippi was under Philip's rule]; Lk 9:10; 10:13 [Bethsaida was also under Philip's administration]). Philip died in 34 CE. Students should study carefully the Map of Palestine in 30 CE to acquaint themselves with the regions of these rulers.

Pontius Pilate. After Archelaus was deposed in 6 CE, Rome thought it best to place his territory under direct Roman administration. Hence, there followed the appointment of a series of governors to rule over Samaria and Judea. Pontius Pilate was the fifth of these governors, ruling the regions from 26–36 CE. During this period of direct Roman administration, tensions often ran high between the Judean populace and the Roman prefect. There was even a short-lived rebellion instigated by some Jewish radicals in the year 6 CE (Acts 5:37 makes reference to this revolt). Tensions remained high under Pilate. His practice was to respond to Jewish unrest, or even hints of unrest, quickly and ruthlessly (see, e.g., Lk 13:1, which speaks of Pilate's slaughter of some Galileans, whom he apparently believed were up to subversive behavior). The fact that he ultimately chose to deal with Jesus by ordering his crucifixion is consistent with his pattern of rule. He was relieved of his post in 36 CE, in large measure because of his ruthlessness.

Annas and Caiaphas. Luke notes that Jesus' ministry began "during the high priesthood of Annas and Caiaphas" (3:1). This might imply that Luke saw these two as sharing some type of joint priestly rule. That would be misleading. During the period of Jesus, Caiaphas was actually the ruling priest, having held this position from 18 to 36 CE. Annas had held the office of high priest from 6 to 15 CE. Annas, however, continued to wield great influence. John 18:13 notes that Caiaphas was his son-in-law and, according to extra-biblical sources, five of Annas' sons also held the office (Josephus, *Antiquities,* 20.198). More important than naming these office holders is understanding the important role of the high priest.

During the period of Roman administration, the high priest was appointed by representatives of the Roman government. The high priest served as the leader of the Jerusalem ruling council, or Sanhedrin, the Jewish governing body of Judea. This council consisted of seventy-one members, made up of leading priests, elders (lay aristocratic leaders), and **scribes** (legal experts; cf. Mk 15:1). Recall that Salome Alexandra appointed Pharisees to the version of the ruling council as it had existed in her day. According to the NT, Pharisees continued to be represented on the council during the Roman period (cf. Acts 5:34; Jn 11:47). If so, the Pharisees likely would be included within the group designated above as "the scribes." In addition to overseeing the Temple and settling disputes in matters regarding Jewish law, it was also the responsibility of this council to assist the Roman administration in the maintenance of public order. This duty likely explains why the Sanhedrin brought Jesus to the attention of Pontius Pilate (Lk 23:1–5).

Hence, behind Luke's reference to the numerous leading authorities in Lk 3:1–2 lies a complex governing system. As part of the Roman Empire, Palestine would ultimately be under the rule of the Emperor Tiberius. Some regions in which Jesus worked were governed locally by the sons of King Herod (Herod and Philip). The heartland of Palestine was under direct Roman administration (Pontius Pilate). And since Jesus was Jewish he would also have fallen under the jurisdiction of the Jerusalem Sanhedrin, working in conjunction with the Roman administration, most especially after Jesus made his appearance in Jerusalem toward the end of his life.

The World of Jesus' Followers:
Palestine after Jesus
Acts 12; 21; 23–26

Learning Goals

- To learn about the continuing influence of the House of Herod in Palestine.
- To learn about the causes and results of the Jewish revolt against Rome.

Guiding Study Exercises

1) Offer a description of how the House of Herod continued to exert influence in Palestine in the generation after Jesus. Cite specific names and events.
2) Describe the primary causes of the revolt against Rome and offer a basic outline of the course of that revolt.

Under the orders of Pontius Pilate, Jesus was executed ca. 30 CE. His followers, however, believed that Jesus' death was not the end of his story, for they believed that God had raised Jesus from the dead. The NT narrative that tells the story of Jesus' followers is the Acts of Apostles. Like the gospels, Acts makes many references to the socio-political world of its story, references that provide readers with a point of departure to understand better the larger social text of the early Christianity.

The House of Herod

Acts 12:1–5 and 18–23 relate two short accounts involving a King Herod. One unfamiliar with the history of Palestine might assume this Herod to be identical with Herod Antipas, whom Luke also refers to simply as "Herod." Actually, the King Herod of Acts 12 is a different person. This Herod, more commonly referred to as Agrippa I, was the grandson of Herod the Great. Agrippa's grandmother was Mariamne, the Hasmonean whom Herod had married and then later murdered. Agrippa was friends with Caligula, who became the Roman emperor in 37 CE. Caligula quickly appointed Agrippa I ruler of Philip's (d. 34 CE) territory, which had been under direct Roman administration since Philip's death. Agrippa I was also granted the region of Abilene, located to the north of Philip's former territory. When Herod Antipas was deposed in 39 CE, Agrippa was given the regions that he had ruled, Galilee and Perea. Agrippa's fortunes were not yet complete, for two years later (in 41 CE), he became the ruler of Samaria, Judea, and Idumea as well, territories that had been under direct Roman administration through governors such as Pontius Pilate since 6 CE. More important, Agrippa was granted the title of "king" (see Acts 12:1, which refers to him as King Herod).

Agrippa I was generally accepted by the Jewish leadership, for, first, he was a descendant, through his grandmother Mariamne, of the old Hasmonean line. Second, Agrippa was outwardly an observant Jew, at least when in Jerusalem. Perhaps it was his desire to show his loyalty to Judaism that led him to execute James, one of the original followers of Jesus (Acts 12:1–5). The narrator of Acts, of course, shows no sympathy for Agrippa and reports that, while in Caesarea, he willingly accepted divine accolades (12:22), an act of impiety that led immediately to his death (44 CE).

Agrippa I's son, Agrippa II, was too young to assume leadership when his father died. Hence, his father's territory was again placed under direct Roman administration. Later, however, in 53 CE, Agrippa II was given a portion of his father's territory, the regions that had once been ruled by Philip, located to the northeast of Galilee. He was also given supervision of the Temple, including the power to appoint the high priest. One finds numerous references to Agrippa II (referred to simply as Agrippa) in Acts 25–26, events that can reliably be dated to the late 50s CE. Acts 25:13 and 23 allude to a titillating bit of ancient gossip, with the passing reference to Bernice. She was Agrippa II's sister and the widow of Agrippa II's uncle. Rumor had it that she and Agrippa were involved in an incestuous relationship (Josephus, *Antiquities,* 20.145–46). She was married, though only briefly in the early 60s, to King Polemon of Cilicia, perhaps to deflect rumors about her incestuous affair. Sometime in the early 70s, Bernice became the mistress of Titus, the Roman general who had just recently sacked Jerusalem (70 CE). The affair continued until Titus became the Emperor (79–81 CE). Apparently, Titus ended the affair for political expediency. Ever-loyal to the Roman Empire, it fell to Agrippa II to try to play the role of mediator and dissuade Jewish rebels from revolting against Rome. In this role he failed, for the Jews revolted against Rome in 66 CE, details of which will be presented later. Agrippa II died sometime in the 90s (scholars are not sure of the exact date). With his death, both the Hasmonean and Herodian houses pass from the stage of history.

The Successors of Pilate

As one reads Acts 25–26, one finds not only numerous references to Agrippa, but also many references to (Porcius) Festus. Introduced in Acts 24:27, Festus is described as the successor of Felix. Who were Felix and Festus?

After Herod the Great's son Archelaus was deposed by the Romans in 6 CE, his territory came under direct Roman administration. It was in this capacity that Pontius Pilate governed from 26–36 CE. After Pilate was removed from office, he was succeeded by numerous other governors who ruled over the heartland of Palestine (Samaria and Judea). Except for the brief period when Agrippa I was given rule of these regions (41–44 CE), a Roman appointed governor ruled over the Jews who lived in this territory. Felix and Festus are two of these governors, the only ones mentioned in Acts.

Serving as the governor of Judea and the surrounding regions was not a pleasant task. The Jewish historian Josephus reports that the countryside was regularly being disturbed by Jewish insurrectionists who wanted to throw off the power of Rome. The NT shows little direct interest in the larger political disturbances taking place in Palestine in the decades of the 40s, 50s, and 60s. As noted above, only Felix and Festus are mentioned in the NT, and this only because these two governors played a role in Paul's legal trials. Yet, when one understands something of the political

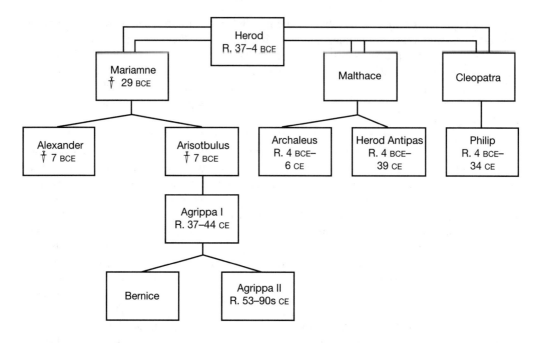

KEY: This chart is quite abbreviated. For example, Herod actually had 10 wives. Parallel lines denote marriage. Vertical and diagonal lines denote lines of descent.

✝ = year of death. R. denotes period of rule

Figure 9.2
The House of Herod

unrest in the area, one can immediately understand why these governors would become involved in a dispute over a man whom history remembers primarily as a preacher of the message about Jesus of Nazareth.

Felix, who governed from 52–60, had a number of encounters with Jewish revolutionaries. Felix, himself a former slave, was not an able administrator. Even the Roman historian Tacitus characterized him as "practicing every kind of cruelty and lust; he exercised royal power with the instincts of a slave" (*Histories,* 5.9). During his administration, a Jewish terrorist group, known as the **Sicarii,** specializing in political assassination, was especially active. Felix even secretly conspired with these enemies of the Roman Empire to assassinate the high priest Jonathan, with whom Felix was having serious political disagreements (Josephus, *Antiquities,* 20.173–78). It was also during his administration that a major disturbance erupted under the leadership of an Egyptian, the Jewish followers of whom gathered near Jerusalem to witness the miraculous liberation of the city (Josephus, *Antiquities,* 20.169–72). While the Egyptian escaped, Felix killed 400 of his followers. Later, when a disturbance arose in the Temple precincts involving Paul (Acts 21:27–36), Paul was actually mistaken for this fugitive Egyptian (v. 38). Even if that case of mistaken identity was quickly dispelled, one can understand why Felix, anxious to put to an end any hints of unrest, would want to look into Paul's case. He therefore had Paul imprisoned. Acts 24:26 indicates that Felix was hoping that Paul would offer him a bribe in order to secure his release from prison. This is not out of character for Felix.

Little is known of Felix's successor, Festus (60–62 CE), allowing readers to conclude that the region experienced relative calm during his administration. Such calm, however, would come to an end with successive administrations. Most important for understanding Palestinian history during this period is the administration of Gessius Florus (64–66 CE). According to Josephus, Florus deliberately provoked the Jews to hostilities, in hopes of diverting the attention of his superiors away from his own failings and toward the troublesome populace. He openly laughed at the Jews when they petitioned him with various grievances. He intentionally failed to quell tensions between Jews and Greeks in the city of Caesarea in the year 66 CE. When Florus stole some funds from the Jerusalem Temple treasury, claiming that the Emperor wanted the funds, some Jews mockingly took to begging through the streets for the "impoverished" governor. Florus responded with a bloody massacre in Jerusalem, not even sparing women or infants (Josephus, *War,* 2.280–308). It was now only a matter of time before the region would explode in all-out war against the Roman Empire.

The Jewish Revolt

The clearest NT references to this revolt are found in prophetic utterances of Jesus (see Matthew 24; Mark 13; Luke 21). The fact that each of these gospels alludes to this event testifies to its importance. The tone of the gospels' references to the revolt indicates that Jewish followers of Jesus were not sympathetic to the rebels' methods. In fact, many Christian Jews migrated to Pella, located on the east side of the Jordan, to escape involvement in the revolt.

Initially, the rebellious factions of the Jews were led by disgruntled aristocrats, among whom was the Jewish historian Josephus. Aristocratic leaders who were opposed to the revolt, assisted by Agrippa II, attempted at the beginning of the insurrection (early in the summer of 66 CE) to come to a negotiated settlement of the uprising. Negotiations failed, and by the end of the summer of 66, Jerusalem and much of the larger countryside were in the rebels' hands. At this time, there arose within the rebel movement a radical wing of insurrectionists, known as **Zealots**. Led by John of Gishala, this *nonaristocratic* rebellious force was driven by a religiously charged **ideology** that tolerated no compromise with the hated Romans. Unfortunately for the rebels' cause, such a zealous ideology could tolerate little compromise even with different factions of rebels. Internal disputes among rebel leaders were common.

When Emperor Nero fully realized the extent and seriousness of the revolt, he placed Vespasian, who would one day himself become the Emperor, in command of the campaign to put down the revolt. Vespasian, together with his son Titus, who would also one day be Emperor, gathered together three legions of troops, forming an army of 18,000 men. In the spring of 67, Vespasian began in earnest his campaign to recapture Palestine. Galilee, which was under the military command of Josephus, was the first to fall. Josephus was forced to surrender, whereupon he prudently switched loyalties. Many Galilean rebels, now led by John of Gishala, fled to Jerusalem where John and his forces quickly took control of the city. Internal divisions and infighting among the rebels hampered the success of the revolt. John, for example, found that he had

The Arch of Titus, located in Rome, commemorates his destruction of Jerusalem in 70 CE. (Courtesy of Larry McKinney)

to share control of Jerusalem with the leader of a rival rebel faction, Simon bar ("son of") Giora. Such in-fighting, combined with the sheer might of Roman power, inevitably doomed the revolt.

When Vespasian became the Emperor in 69 CE, he handed the Palestinian campaign over to Titus. Titus began the siege of Jerusalem in the spring of 70 and by early autumn of that year, Jerusalem and the Temple were destroyed. The surviving rebels fled to the fortress of Masada, originally constructed by Herod the Great. Masada eventually fell (73 CE), and the revolt was over. Jerusalem was renamed *Aelia Capitolina,* and Jews were forbidden entry into the city. The Torah, together with the Temple, had formed the basis of Jewish life in the post-Exilic period, but the Temple was now gone. Fading away as well was the priesthood, the core of Jewish leadership during the whole post-Exilic period, for it had lost its base of power. A new group of leaders would now emerge, the **Rabbis**, under whose leadership Judaism would continue as a faith focused exclusively on obedience to the law.

The World Beyond Palestine
Acts 17–19

Learning Goals

- To learn the general characteristics of popular religions in the Greco-Roman world.
- To acquire essential acquaintance with philosophical schools that influenced the Greco-Roman world.
- To acquire a basic understanding of Diaspora Judaism and the relationship between Jews of the Diaspora and the larger culture.

Guiding Study Exercises

1) Discuss the impact that the idea of *Fate* had on many people of the Hellenistic world.
2) Building on your response to the previous exercise, describe some of the significant ways that popular Greco-Roman religion and Greek philosophy tried to address the issue of Fate.
3) Read 2 Macc 6:12–7:42 and 4 Maccabees 1. Describe how 4 Maccabees attempts to justify Jewish piety through the use of philosophical concepts. As specifically as possible, relate the content of 4 Maccabees 1 to ideas of Greek philosophy you learned about in this chapter.

The followers of Jesus did not remain confined to the regions of Palestine. The message of the early Christians quickly spread throughout the Roman Empire. In the assigned texts from Acts for this unit, Acts 17–19, readers encounter a number of stories that illustrate the complex religious and philosophical world of early Christianity.

Religion in the Hellenistic World

In the book of Acts, one encounters numerous references and allusions to popular religious ideas and personalities. For example, Acts 14:8–18 tells a story where the populace of Lystra hail Paul and his companion, Barnabas, as manifestations of the Greek gods Hermes and Zeus. Reference is made to "the priest of Zeus" and a temple dedicated to Zeus in that city. Acts 17:23 refers to various objects of worship, earlier identified by the narrator as idols (v. 16), that Paul found in Athens. Later in Acts 19:11–16, readers encounter just one of several examples of a story involving unclean spirits. Just a few lines later, reference is made to people who practice magic (v. 19). In the same chapter, one finds numerous references to the god Artemis, the patroness deity of the city of Ephesus. The world beyond Palestine into which early Christians went to spread the message about Jesus was a very religious world. While beginning students cannot be expected to become experts on the great varieties of popular religious expression that influenced the Greco-Roman world of first-century Christianity, basic familiarity with the general features of the religious social text of popular, traditional religion can enrich one's understanding of the NT itself.

The Nonexclusive Character of Greco-Roman Religion. Student readers influenced by even a passing familiarity with the major Western religious traditions of Judaism, Christianity, and Islam would tend to think of religions as being exclusive, meaning that the god of one's particular tradition is the only true god. Popular religious belief of the Hellenistic world tended not to be exclusive. One could quite legitimately show homage at the same time to different deities and even deities of varied traditions. For example, showing appropriate devotion to the Greek goddess Aphrodite would not preclude one from also giving devotion to the Egyptian goddess Isis. Jews and Christians, who insisted on strict loyalty to only one god, would not have been the norm.

Blending the Identities of Various Deities. The nonexclusive character of Greco-Roman religious thought led commonly to the practice of equating different deities. Many are familiar, for example, with the fact that gods of the Roman pantheon were identified with comparable Greek gods (e.g., Jupiter was identified with Zeus). Isis, noted above, was regularly identified with the Greek goddesses Demeter and Aphrodite.

Concern for the Power and Influence of Deities. The great empires that dominated during the Hellenistic age, those of Alexander and his successors and subsequently the Roman Empire, made one's world a bigger place. Local cities and regions, formerly the center of one's world, were now displaced and subjugated to a massive empire. Consequently, the individual, cut loose from local bonds, emerged as a more important entity. This led to an increased concern for the power and influence of the various deities: What difference could the deities make in one's *individual* life? Such interest in the power and influence of deities actually led to the deification of "power" itself. Such powers as Peace (Pax) or Victory (Victoria) became personified deities. Luck, Chance, or Fate, came to be viewed as the deity (*Tyche*) that most influenced one's life.

Demons. Belief in demons was widespread and quite intellectually acceptable (the great philosophers Socrates and Plato both accepted the idea of demons). Demons were thought of as spiritual beings that, though supernatural, ranked lower than the gods. They were thought of as being everywhere, affecting individuals' lives, for better or worse. It is not coincidental that Jewish belief in the activities of both good and bad intermediary divine beings increased during the Hellenistic age. Angels, while not absent in pre-Exilic biblical literature, become quite prevalent in post-Exilic and especially Hellenistic Jewish texts, most especially apocalyptic texts. Though there were evil, or fallen, angels who were allied with evil spirits (commonly called demons), angels were generally viewed as godly.[2] As belief in demons progressed, demonic beings increasingly came to be associated exclusively with what harmfully affected human beings. Demons came to be thought of as spiritual forces that could actually take possession of individual humans and do them great harm. The many stories in the NT of Jesus and his followers casting out demons, shows how this popular belief of the Hellenistic world influenced Jewish and Christian views of reality.

Fate. There emerged in the Hellenistic world a strong belief in Fate. The essential idea was that one's own destiny was beyond one's control. This belief is related to the rise in the influence of massive structures of political power (such as the Roman Empire), which seemed to diminish the control that one had over her or his own life. Fate came to be viewed as an increasingly influential god. While the pervasive belief in Fate might lead to a rather despondent view of life, fatalism actually brought comfort to many people of the Hellenistic age. If one were simply to resign oneself to the fact that one's destiny was beyond one's control, one could actually find peace of mind. "Since he does not long for things beyond his reach, he bears what is decreed for him with self-discipline and, renouncing both pleasures and penalties, becomes a good soldier of Fate" (Vettius Valens, 5.9.2).[3]

Astrology and Oracles. While fatalism might have been the pervasive belief, that did not deter many people from trying to learn as much as they could about their destinies, in order that they might at least know what to expect. Astrology and oracles helped people to learn something of their destinies. Astrology finds its most influential roots in Babylonian astral religion, which included the idea that the heavenly bodies surrounding the earth were gods. In the Hellenistic age, these gods increasingly came to be viewed as deities who controlled one's destiny. By learning how "to read the stars" and to chart one's horoscope, one could gain some insight into one's destiny and perhaps (as logically inconsistent as it might seem) avoid total disaster. For example, if one's horoscope for a given day appeared foreboding, one might avoid beginning a long journey on that day.

Oracles were another way that people would try to learn something of their destinies. One could visit a shrine, the most famous of which during the Hellenistic age being the shrine of Apollo, located at Delphi, to consult the prophetess on practical matters, such as marriage, business, or travel. While one might not be able to control Fate, consulting the stars or heeding the oracles might at least offer one guidance as to the best course of action, thereby, at least, not "tempting Fate."

Magic. Belief in the power of supernatural forces that controlled humans' lives gave rise to attempts to control these very powers. Magic was a means of such control. Given the widespread belief in fatalism, magic was often viewed pejoratively: It was not right for one to try to control the powers that were supposed to control the individual. Still, belief in magic existed throughout the Greco-Roman world. The magician was viewed as one who, because of special knowledge, could actually make the supernatural powers work for one's own benefit. Knowledge of the proper incantations or formulas could induce the spiritual powers to bring one healing, power, and even love, and also to do harm to one's enemies.

---

[2]D. S. Russell, *Divine Disclosure: An Introduction to Jewish Apocalyptic* (Minneapolis, MN: Fortress, 1992) 50–51.

[3]Quoted from E. Ferguson, *Backgrounds of Early Christianity* (2nd ed.; Grand Rapids, MI: Eerdmans, 1993) 226.

Mystery Religions. Even as magic was practiced by many in an effort to liberate themselves from Fate, there arose during the Greco-Roman period religious communities that also promised liberation from the deterministic powers. These religious communities were almost like secret societies, guarding closely the content and meaning of their beliefs and rituals. Many ancient gods from various ancient civilizations took on new roles and functions with the advent of these mystery religions. The Egyptian deities Isis, Osiris, and Sarapis; the Phoenician deities of Astarte and Adonis; and the Persian deity Mithras, for example, were all transformed due to the influence of mystery religions. The **cult** of Isis was the most pervasive non-Greek or Roman deity to influence popular religion. She was transformed from a national deity to a cosmopolitan deity, supreme over all the forces that might direct one's life. She speaks of herself as follows in a vision to one of her initiates, Lucius, the protagonist in an ancient religious novel devoted to the cult of Isis:

> I am she that is the natural mother of all things, mistress and governess of all the elements, the initial progeny of worlds, chief of the powers divine, queen of all that are in hell, the principal of them that dwell in heaven, manifested alone and under one form of all the gods and goddesses.[4]

Initiation into one of the many mystery religions offered the initiate personal fellowship and communion with the deity. Such fellowship gave the initiate a divine ally and benefactor. And this alliance offered "the appropriation of power and the securing of the protection of higher authorities in the adversities of life and for the passage of the soul into a better world after death. . . ."[5] This can again be illustrated by the words of Isis to her follower Lucius:

> Behold, I am come to take pity of thy fortune and tribulation; behold I am present to favour and aid thee; leave off thy weeping and lamentation, put away all thy sorrow, for behold the healthful day which is ordained by my providence. . . . Thou shalt live blessed in this world. . . . And if I perceive that thou art obedient to my commandment and addict to my religion, meriting by thy constant chastity my divine grace, know thou that I alone may prolong thy days above the time that the fates have appointed and ordained.[6]

Civic-mindedness. The belief in the power of the gods and various other supernatural powers to control life had implications not only for individuals, but for the larger social order as well. The same powers that controlled an individual's destiny also controlled the destiny of a city or even a whole empire. Showing proper homage to the gods could affect positively the welfare of the larger community. Social disaster was regularly viewed as divine chastisement for not giving the gods their due. Hence, religious groups such as Christianity or Judaism, which were often perceived by the larger populace as not showing appropriate reverence to the gods, were regularly viewed as socially dangerous and subversive.

---

[4]Apuleius, *Metamorphoses,* Book 11. (Translated by W. Adlington; revised by S. Gaselee, Loeb Classical Library; Cambridge, MA: Harvard University Press, 1915).

[5]H. Koester, *Introduction to the New Testament.* Volume 1: *History, Culture, and Religion in the Hellenistic Age* (Philadelphia: Fortress, 1982) 203.

[6]*Metamorphoses,* Book 11.

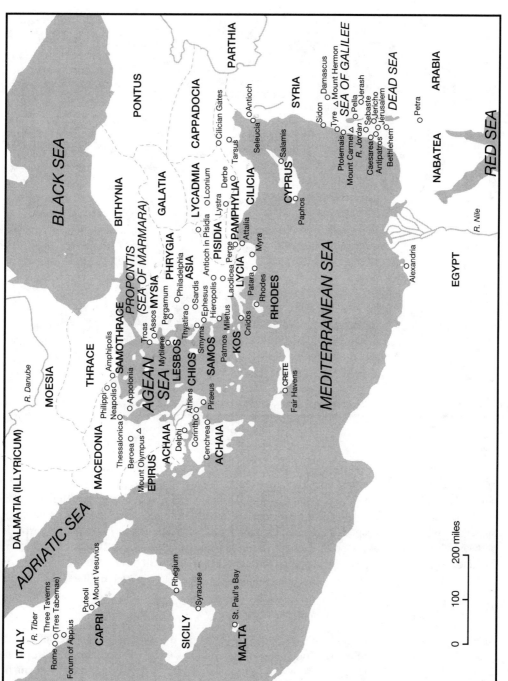

Map of the Roman World of the First Century. (From the frontispiece of the book *Fishers of Men*, photographs by Gordon N. Converse, text by Robert J. Bull and B. Cobbey Crisler, © 1980. Reprinted by permission of Prentice Hall, Upper Saddle River, NJ)

Many of the Greco-Roman gods were personifications of abstract powers such as Peace or Fate. The stone carving above, located in Ephesus, depicts the god Nike, or Victory. (Courtesy of Larry McKinney)

The above overview of the general characteristics of popular religion in the Greco-Roman period reveals a common theme: People believed that they inhabited a world that was controlled by powers beyond the human sphere. Coping in such a world was the goal of popular religious sentiments. For many, one was to accept the "Fate" dictated by the gods. Such coping might come through resignation to accept one's destiny. Or one might seek to learn one's Fate through astrology or the oracles and then take appropriate steps that might at least help one avoid total disaster. Others dared to attempt to control the divine powers through magic, while still others sought a personal, divine ally by seeking communion with a deity through initiation into a mystery religion.

Philosophy in the Hellenistic World

Acts 17:16–34 tells a story of Paul's encounter with two of the more influential philosophical schools within the Roman Empire, Epicureanism and Stoicism (v. 18). Paul even quotes from one Greek philosopher, Aratus, in v. 28b; words that have a distinctly religious focus.[7] Hellenistic

---

[7]Acts 17:28 does not identify the source of the quote. But it is from the opening lines of Aratus' *Phaenomena*. The quotation in v. 28a is generally credited to Epimenides.

A Closer Look: The Greek Novel and Popular Religion. Novels, in modern as well as ancient settings, can offer insight into widely held cultural assumptions and beliefs. A particular Greek novel, authored under the pen name of Xenophon (the actual name of the author is unknown) and entitled *An Ephesian Tale,* offers an entertaining look at how people of the Greco-Roman world viewed the pervasive influence of the gods. The plot centers around the trials and adventures of a young couple of Ephesus, Habrocomes and Anthia, whom the god Eros compels to fall madly in love during the religious festival honoring Artemis. The parents, concerned for the welfare of their love-sick children, seek an oracle from Apollo and, based on that oracle, decide that the children should marry and be sent on a voyage. Their ship is attacked by pirates and the couple is separated. The story then follows the adventures of the separated lovers as they attempt to reunite. In the course of their travels Habrocomes, on one occasion, escapes execution by praying to the Egyptian god of the sun, Helios. Anthia also regularly prays to Isis for deliverance and receives a divine oracle promising her ultimate reunion with Habrocomes. Upon their happy reunion in the city of Rhodes, they offer prayers of thanksgiving to the goddess Isis. And upon their return to their home of Ephesus, they pay homage to Artemis as well. The story aptly illustrates the popular belief in the power of the gods to shape human destiny, the belief in oracles, and the nonexclusive character of popular religion (the characters pray and give homage to many gods). The tone of the novel reveals as well the widespread sentiment of the Greco-Roman world that individuals live in a big and even hostile world, for the separated lovers often find themselves in situations over which they have little control (imprisonment, torture, and forced servitude). Despite their strivings to be reunited, in the end what brings them together is a series of "coincidences," which, the narrator makes clear, is all under the watchful control of the gods.

For further study, A readable translation of *An Ephesian Tale* and other Greek novels is found in B. P. Reardon, Ed. *Collected Ancient Greek Novels.* Berkeley: University of California Press, 1989; ———. *The Form of Greek Romance.* Princeton, NJ: Princeton University Press, 1991; Thomas Hägg. *The Novel in Antiquity.* Berkeley: University of California Press, 1983.

philosophy had a strong religious orientation as it attempted to offer people a holistic view of the world, including how one was to understand the relationship between (the) god(s) and human beings. Philosophy, like religion, attempted to help people live in a world generally perceived as controlled by supernatural powers. Philosophy was also quite concerned with ethics, tending to emphasize as virtues the attainment of the goals of self-sufficiency, freedom, and individual happiness. Of course, to attain these goals, one must understand the nature of reality, leading back again to fundamentally religious questions.

The Roots of Philosophy. Socrates (fifth century BCE) is regularly credited as standing at the headwaters of the various philosophical streams that made their way through the Hellenistic world. Central to Socrates' concerns were individual conscience and personal religion. While loyal to the larger community (or city-state), Socrates would not surrender individual conscience to the community. Consequently, when faced with charges of disloyalty to Athens, he freely accepted the sentence of death by poisoning, showing simultaneously his loyalty both to the city—refusing to participate in the plot of his followers to help him escape—and to his principles of freedom and self-determination.

The most influential student of Socrates was Plato (429–342 BCE), who founded his philosophical school, the Academy, in 387 BCE. Plato's philosophical system focused on the world of "forms" or "ideas." By "ideas" Socrates did not mean those thoughts that exist in human minds, which is what the word has come to mean. For Plato, ideas were objective realities and truths that existed *independently* of the human mind or of material reality, although, through reflection and contemplation, the human mind could grasp these realities. For example, the "idea" of justice existed independently of human conceptualization of any form of justice. The existence of justice in this material world was but an imperfect shadow or replica of the pure form of justice.

Plato's ethical theory began with his contemplation on the nature of the soul. The soul for Plato belonged to the sphere of the immaterial and spiritual, whereas the body belonged to the sphere of the material and physical. Just as the perfect forms or ideas existed independently of material reality, the soul existed independently of the body, both *before* and *after* it inhabited a body. Indeed, because the soul belongs to the realm of the immaterial, the soul enables the human being to understand the immaterial world of ideas. Through soulful contemplation, one comes to know what is virtuous: wisdom, courage, and self-control.

Aristotle (384–322 BCE), Plato's pupil, established his own school, known as the Peripatetics, in 334 BCE. Aristotle did not totally reject Plato's notion of forms, but he did reject the premise that forms could exist independently of their material manifestations. The material cannot exist without the immaterial form, to be sure; but, equally important, the immaterial form cannot exist without the material. Consequently, Aristotle believed that understanding the form began not with contemplation on the immaterial world of forms, but by actual observation of material reality. In short, the quest for truth begins by studying that which is physically observable.

Aristotle emphasized moral virtue in his discussion of ethics. At the core of his ethical theory was the idea that moral action consists of freely choosing actions that avoid extremes. For an action to be moral, it must be free or voluntary, not compulsory. For an action to be moral it must be a chosen action, with such choice being the product of reflection and deliberation. For an action to be moral, it must avoid the extremes, which Aristotle labeled "excess" or "deficiency." Courage, for example, is a moral virtue, if done freely and deliberately, for it avoids the extremes of both foolhardiness or cowardice.

While many philosophical schools emerged during the late classical and subsequent Hellenistic period, it is fortuitous for the purposes of studying early Christianity, that Acts mentions Stoics and Epicureans. Acquaintance with these two philosophical schools will allow student readers a flavor of the different ways that philosophy helped persons of the Empire to develop a holistic sense of life and develop a rationale for ethical behavior.

Stoicism. This school was established by Zeno (335–263 BCE). Zeno was influenced by Diogenes of Sinope, the founder of another philosophical school, the Cynics. The Cynics radically emphasized individual freedom by displaying utter disdain for social convention and custom. Use of abusive language, the intentional maintenance of an unkempt appearance, begging, and even public acts of defecation, masturbation, and sex were some of the ways that Cynics celebrated their freedom. Zeno and his followers dissociated themselves from these more abrasive features of Cynicism. Yet they did maintain Cynicism's emphasis on certain aspects of individual freedom, while, at the same time, affirming the legitimacy of the larger social order.

Stoics taught that the divine reality, which had many names, such as Reason (Logos), Spirit, or Providence, permeated all of material reality. One can clearly see in this idea a rejection of Plato's radical dichotomy between material and immaterial reality. The Stoics' **pantheism** led logically to the conclusion that all things are interconnected by a higher intelligence that providentially guides all things to an intended goal. Because Stoics believed that the Logos permeated all things, including all other human beings, respect for other people was a hallmark of their ethical ideal. Their strict view of Providence led to the belief that ethical behavior found its roots in living life in harmony with the Logos that guided all of life, including one's own. One's social or economic station, which belonged the "external circumstances" of one's life, were of no intrinsic significance. What was important was to understand that one's external circumstances were in accordance with the providential Logos. Given this, Stoics taught that one should not exert energy trying to change these circumstances. They were beyond one's control anyway. What one could

---

A Closer Look: Stoicism in the First Century CE. The pervasive influence of Stoic philosophy during the birth of the Christian era is evidenced by the fact that leading Stoic teachers came from a wide spectrum of society. One prominent Stoic was Seneca (1–65 CE), a Roman aristocrat whose brother was the governor of Achaea (see Acts 18:12). Seneca was the teacher of Emperor Nero, illustrating that this philosophy was welcomed in the royal court, even if not followed consistently. Another influential Stoic was Epictetus (55–135 CE), who came from the other end of the spectrum, being both a former slave and physically handicapped, conditions that the ancient world did not tend to view with sympathy. Below is a sampling of Epictetus' teachings:

- "There are things which are within our power, and there are things which are beyond our power. Within our power are opinion, aim, desire, aversion, and in one word, whatever affairs are our own. Beyond our power are body, property, reputation, office, and in one word, what are not properly our own affairs."
- "Men are disturbed not by things, but by the views which they take of things."
- "Remember that you are an actor in a drama of such sort the author chooses. . . . If it be his pleasure that you should enact a poor man, see that you act it well; or a cripple, or a ruler, or a private citizen. For this is your business—to act well the given part; but to choose it belongs to another." These quotes are from Epictetus' *Enchiridion*. Quoted from E. Ferguson. *Backgrounds of Early Christianity.* 2nd Ed. Grand Rapids, MI: Eerdmans, 1993, p. 345, following the translation of T. W. Higgonson and A. Salomon. Macmillan: New York, 1955.

control and, hence, what one should focus on was the way one responded to these circumstances. Apathy regarding one's external conditions was the highest virtue.

Epicureanism. Epicurus (341–270 BCE) and his followers lived an austere lifestyle in seclusion from the world. Epicurus' philosophy emphasized personal fulfillment by seeking the pleasures of the mind and body and the fellowship of friends.

Epicurus offered a materialistic philosophy of life. The universe, which was eternal—hence there was no "creation"—was made up of small building blocks called atoms. These atoms, which were eternally existent solids that had shape, size, weight, and motion, came together to form objects. While particular objects may cease to exist, such as one's body, or even one's soul (Epicurus denied that the soul was immortal), the atoms themselves continued to exist. Epicurus' materialism was also evident in his belief that one comes to understand reality through observation, perception, and individual experience. His way to knowledge was quite different from Plato's path of detached contemplation on the immaterial world of ideas.

It was Epicurus' view of the gods that was most controversial. He maintained that the gods too were made up of atoms, though of a more refined sort. But, more important, he believed that the gods were not concerned with human beings or with matters of this world. This is quite distinct from Stoicism, for if the gods have no interest in human welfare, it is meaningless to speak of Providence. Still, one was to give proper reverence to the gods, not to earn their favor, but because, as gods, they deserved basic respect.

Epicurus' view of the gods shaped his ethical theory. The Epicureans disagreed with the Stoics, who argued that the divine permeated and guided all reality, thereby legitimizing one's lot in life or the social order in which one lived. Hence, for the Epicureans, the highest good was not to accept what Providence had given one, but to seek personal pleasure. While they did not mean by this mindless hedonism, Epicureans did advocate that one should seek the physical pleasure of satisfying hunger with good food and enjoying the pleasures that came from rest and good health. Yet pleasure of the soul and mind was the highest sort. Such pleasure comes not from seeking wealth, power, community influence, or even family. To seek pleasure in such things led inevitably to frustration and disappointment, for in seeking pleasure in these things one is dependent on the actions of others. Rather, one should seek peace of mind. This came, first and foremost, by ridding oneself of the superstitious notion that one should revere the gods in hopes of getting their attention, earning their favor, or spending eternity with them. Realization that the gods did not care was actually liberating. Where one found ultimate peace and contentment was in the rich fellowship of friendship.

These two philosophies, Stoicism and Epicureanism, show two very different ways that people sought to cope in a world where life seemed to be moved by forces bigger than the individual. The idea of Fate could make people feel rather small and helpless in a big world, tossed about by the seeming whims of the gods. Stoicism offered solace by teaching that what happened to one was, indeed, beyond one's control. But one could rest assured that a benevolent Providence moved things along. Epicureanism offered solace with a radically different message. It boldly challenged the common assumption of popular religion, saying that one's life is *not* dictated by either divine whim or concern; the gods simply do not care. Hence, one should view oneself as a totally free being who should find meaningful ways to enjoy one's life.

Judaism of the Diaspora

Acts 17–19 speaks of Paul's encounters with Jewish people in the **synagogues** of various cities located throughout the Empire: Thessalonica (17:1), Beroea (17:10), Athens (17:17), Corinth (18:1–4), and Ephesus (19:1, 8). Students would benefit from locating these cities on the "Map of the Roman World of the First Century" (p. 231). Clearly the narrative of Acts assumes that Jews do not live only in Judea. Jews who lived outside the land are referred to as Jews of the **Diaspora**. The fact is, only some ten to fifteen percent of the total Jewish population of about five million people, actually lived in Palestine.

There were many reasons why the majority of Jews found themselves living in the Diaspora. Chief among these was the Babylonian Exile. Many Jews chose to remain in Babylon even after the Persians granted them permission to return to Judea. Babylon actually became an important center of Jewish learning, with some of the most influential Jewish teachers of the Hellenistic age either coming from Babylon or studying under the tutelage of Babylonian Jews. In addition, the Babylonian conquest of Judah and Jerusalem led to many other Jews fleeing to Egypt, where, again, most of their descendants remained. By the first century CE, a thriving Jewish community existed in Alexandria. The Jewish people endured a series of dominant political masters: Persians, Greeks (Alexander the Great), Alexander's successors (the Ptolemaic and Seleucid empires), and the Romans. With each succeeding political shift, Jews would regularly find themselves having to migrate, for various reasons, to locales throughout the larger world. Sometimes the transfer of power would lead to forced migration, as victorious powers would regularly round up some slaves from conquered populations to ship back home to do the menial work. Other Jews would have relocated to different cities throughout the Mediterranean world for the same reasons that people relocate today: economic opportunity.

As Jews settled into cities throughout the world, they invariably came into contact with non-Jewish people. Because Judaism was an ancient religion, Jews were generally free to practice their faith, for Rome's policy was to respect the individual customs of ancient and established religions. Judaism's status as an established religion, recognized for its high moral standards and monotheism, led many non-Jewish people to find something attractive about this tradition. Despite the continued popularity of traditional Greco-Roman religions, with their many gods, monotheism was increasingly attractive to growing numbers throughout the Empire. Acts 17:1–5, for example, refers to "devout Greeks" being present at the Jewish synagogue where Paul preached. Apparently such "devout Greeks," whom the author of Acts refers to as "God-fearers" in other places in his narrative (e.g., Acts 13:16, 26), were not actual converts to Judaism, or **proselytes**, but gentiles sympathetic to Jewish religious beliefs. As one can easily surmise, such "God-fearers" would logically have been seen as good prospects for the early Christian missionaries, for these people already had an essential understanding of Judaism upon which the preachers of Jesus could build their Christian proclamations.

Yet Jews and their religion were not universally respected and this led regularly to anti-Semitic attitudes and even persecution. Many non-Jews might view the Jews' strict monotheism, which denied the reality of the other gods of the Greco-Roman world, as actually impious, or even a form of atheism. And while Jewish ethical standards were quite noble, they practiced what many gentiles considered to be strange and even barbaric customs. Jews did not work on the **sabbath**; they refused to eat certain kinds of food; they practiced the rite of **circumcision**, which many gentiles considered to be nothing more than mutilation. Ancient sources speak of a number of instances when the Jewish community of a particular city would suffer anti-Semitic persecutions. For example, the influential Jewish philosopher **Philo** of Alexandria once had to lead a delegation of Jews to Rome to appeal to Emperor Caligula to put an end to Jewish persecution in Egypt (ca. 40 CE).

Living within the larger social text of the Greco-Roman world would also have an impact on the Jews. It was not uncommon for Diaspora Jews to interpret, or reread, their traditions in the context of Greek philosophy, attempting to show that the essential features of Jewish religious belief were actually harmonious with the best of that philosophical tradition. Philo of Alexandria, noted above, dedicated his intellectual life to such pursuits. For example, through **allegorical** interpretation of the scriptures, he argued for the similarities between Jewish faith and the Platonic concept of forms or ideas, asserting that God created the prototypes, or forms, of all the things that one encounters in this material world. In 4 Maccabees, which likely dates to the first century CE and which was composed by an anonymous Diaspora Jew, there is another illustration. The basis for 4 Maccabees is the story of the torture and martyrdom of Eleazar, the seven brothers, and their mother (4 Macc 1:8). Their heroic faithfulness to the Jewish law was almost legendary in Judaism (see 2 Macc 6:12–7:42). The writer of 4 Maccabees argues that such devotion, even to

A Closer Look: The Jewish Synagogue. One finds no references to the synagogue in either the Hebrew Bible nor the Apocrypha. Yet, one finds literally scores of references to this institution in the NT, and the literature contemporary with the NT. The origins of this institution are shrouded in mystery, though scholars generally agree that the synagogue emerged in the context of Diaspora Judaism.

The term *synagogue* comes from a Greek word meaning "to gather together." Hence, it denoted the gathering place of the Jewish community. If one were to limit one's study of the synagogue's function to the NT, one would conclude that it was primarily a place for religious gatherings. Indeed, the synagogue did play an important role in the religious life of Jews, being the place where they would gather for prayer (in Egypt the synagogue was commonly called "the place of prayer") and the study of scripture. Such study would consist of scriptural readings and sermonic exposition.

The synagogue also played an important role in other aspects of Jewish life. It served as the "house of interpretation," where one was formally educated in the scriptures and traditions of Judaism, and the "house of meeting," where Jews could gather for social occasions and to discuss matters of interest to the Jewish community. In this context, the synagogue could provide a place where traveling Jews could find lodging. Further, the synagogue served as the "house of judgment," where the leaders of the Jewish community could settle legal disputes that arose within the Jewish community.

For further study, E. Ferguson. *Backgrounds of Early Christianity.* 2nd Ed. Grand Rapids, MI: Eerdmans, 1993. Pp. 539–546; L. I. Levine. "The Nature and Origin of the Palestinian Synagogue Reconsidered." *JBL* 115.3 (1996) 425–448. E. M. Meyers and R. Hachlili. "Synagogue." *ABD* 6.251–263.

The ruins of the synagogue of Gamala, located a few miles east of the northern edge of the Sea of Galilee, date from about 40 BCE and represent the oldest surviving ruins of a synagogue. (Chance and Horne)

the death, was actually evidence of the martyr's choosing to follow reason rather than emotion, in accordance with the highest standards of rational judgment taught by philosophy.

Conclusion

The larger social text of Jesus and his followers was quite rich. This historical social text of the Hasmonean dynasty and its eventual demise under Rome and Herod reveals that the quest to secure and maintain power was at that time, even as it is today, what drove politics. The political world of Jesus was a complex network of institutions of power: the rule of the Herodian house, the administration of a succession of Roman governors, and the Jewish ruling council of the Sanhedrin, headed up by the high priest. As the followers of Jesus moved out into the Hellenistic world beyond the borders of Palestine, they encountered a variety of religious and philosophical traditions. Within most of these traditions ran a common theme: Individuals have little control over much of their lives. Finding ways to make sense of a life that seemed so much out of one's control drove many of these religious and philosophical traditions. Jews were not unaffected by this larger world; they lived in that world, influencing and being influenced by it. Having come to a basic understanding of this larger social text, Chapter 10 will explore two significant literary texts that tell the story of Jesus and his followers: Luke and Acts.

For Further Reading

Given the common subject matter of historical and social backgrounds of the three subsections of this chapter, the following reading list will not offer a separate bibliography for each subsection. Readers may easily find the appropriate sections to supplement their understanding of relevant topics within the tables of contents of the following reading list.

Cumont, F. *Oriental Religions in Roman Paganism.* New York: Dover, 1956.

Ferguson, E. *Backgrounds of Early Christianity.* 2nd Ed. Grand Rapids, MI: Eerdmans, 1993. (*Recommended for beginning students.*)

Koester, H. *Introduction to the New Testament.* Volume 1: *History, Culture, and Religion of the Hellenistic Age.* Philadelphia: Fortress, 1982. (*Recommended for beginning students.*)

Lohse, E. *The New Testament Environment.* Nashville, TN: Abingdon, 1976. (*Recommended for beginning students.*)

Nock, A. D. *Conversion: The Old and the New in Religion from Alexander the Great to Augustine of Hippo.* London: Oxford University Press, 1933.

Safrai, S. and Stern, M., Eds. *The Jewish People in the First Century.* 2 Volumes. Philadelphia: Fortress, 1974.

Schürer, E. *The History of the Jewish People in the Age of Jesus Christ (175 BC–AD 135).* Revised and Edited by G. Vermes and F. Millar. 3 Volumes. Edinburgh: T&T Clark, 1973–1987.

CHAPTER TEN

The Story of Jesus and His Followers

Introduction

Review and Preview

Chapter 9 explored selections from the Gospel of Luke and the Acts of the Apostles, noting the narratives' references to political leaders and groups, as well as religious and philosophical traditions and schools. These texts revealed something of the complex social text out of which early Christianity and its literary texts emerged. This chapter will narrow the scope of investigation. Having learned something of the broader historical and social text of Jesus and early Christianity, attention will now focus specifically on the story of Jesus and his earliest followers. The NT itself provides two narratives, penned by the same author, that tell the story of both Jesus and his followers, Luke-Acts. While separated in the final form of the NT by the Gospel of John, scholars believe these two narratives to have originally been a single narrative, composed in two volumes (cf. Acts 1:1–2). This chapter will offer only a preliminary survey and overview of Jesus' and the early **Christians'** story, saving more focused investigation for subsequent chapters.

Chapter 10 is divided into three sections, plus an Excursus. The first section introduces Luke–Acts, giving special attention to the value of this narrative as a historical source about Jesus and his followers. The second section presents an overview of the Gospel of Luke, with the third section providing a similar overview of the Acts of the Apostles. The Excursus returns to the issue of the employment of NT narratives for the reconstruction of the historical social text that lies behind the literary text, presenting a case study to illustrate how tedious such historical reconstruction can be. It concludes with a summary table that outlines the chronology of Jesus' life and the early **church**.

Introducing Luke-Acts

Learning Goals

- To learn about the literary relationships that exist among the gospels and how scholars explain these relationships.
- To understand why scholars believe that the NT narratives must be used cautiously when attempting to reconstruct the historical social text of Jesus and his followers.
- To learn introductory information regarding the authorship and date of Luke-Acts.

Guiding Study Exercises

1) Explain why scholars believe there exists a direct literary relationship between the Synoptic Gospels.
2) Summarize the two hypotheses that attempt to resolve "the Synoptic problem."
3) State and succinctly summarize three things you learned in the section that might help you to understand why historians must be cautious when using the NT narratives to reconstruct history.
4) Read Lk 16:18, Matt 5:32, 19:9, Mk 10:11–12, and 1 Cor 7:1–10. Also read Deut 24:1–4. How would you employ the Criteria of Authenticity to argue either for or against the authenticity of this saying attributed to Jesus?
5) Read the "We Passages." Do you think that these provide evidence that Luke-Acts was written by an eyewitness? By Luke?

The fact that the NT begins with narratives makes it comparable to the beginning of the Hebrew Bible. The initial books of the Hebrew Bible, the Torah (Genesis through Deuteronomy) and the Former Prophets (Joshua through Kings), offer an extended *narrative* of the story of ancient Israel. Yet, while both the Hebrew Bible and NT begin with narratives, they are very different kinds of narratives. The Torah, in its *present* form, represents a single narrative, from the creation of the world to the encampment of Israel on the eastern side of Jordan River, preparing to enter the land that God had promised to Israel's ancestors. The Former Prophets continue the narrative, telling the story of Israel from its settlement of the land to the fall of Judah and the deportation of its leading citizens to Babylon in the sixth century BCE (review Chap. 2).

The four gospels and Acts do *not* present a continuous narrative. Rather, the gospels offer four individual narratives about Jesus, telling of his life and ministry, with each culminating in the story of his death and resurrection. Each gospel was composed with the intention of being read on its own. Of these four gospels, only Luke is connected with a subsequent narrative, the Book of Acts, which tells the story of Jesus' earliest followers. What is more, while the narratives that initiate the Hebrew Bible cover centuries of time, the initial narratives of the NT speak of events that are confined to the first few decades of the first century CE.

> ***A Closer Look: What Is Gospel?*** The term *gospel* is an old English translation of the
> Greek word *euangelion,* meaning literally "good news." The Latin equivalent of the
> term was *evangelium*. The Romans regularly used *evangelium* to denote the "good
> news" of the accomplishments of the Roman emperors, such as the bringing of peace
> and stability—salvation even—to the Roman Empire. When the early Christians em-
> ployed the term *euangelion* to summarize their message of the "good news" of the sal-
> vation that God offered in Jesus Christ, one suspects that the Christians were aware
> that they were presenting Jesus in a competing role with the emperor. It is *Jesus,* not
> the emperor, about whom one should proclaim the "good news."
>
> Originally, therefore, the term *gospel* did not refer to any specific literary texts about
> Jesus, such as the four gospels, or the Gospel of Luke. Rather, early Christians used
> the word *gospel* to refer to the *message* about Jesus: the "good news" that God has
> offered salvation through him. However, by the middle of the second century, Justin
> Martyr (*1 Apology* 66.3) used the term *gospel* to denote the *books* about Jesus' life.
>
> ***For further study,*** H. Koester. *Ancient Christian Gospels: Their History and Devel-
> opment.* Philadelphia: Trinity Press, 1990.

The Sources behind the New Testament Narratives

There exist many micro- and macro-level intertexts among the gospels. Table 10.1 shows the
abundance of micro-level intertexts in the **pericope** popularly called "The Cleansing of the Temple." Micro-level intertexts have been noted by the italicized words and phrases.

One immediately notices that there exist many more micro-level intertexts between
Matthew, Mark, and Luke than between John and the other three gospels. The high degree of intertextuality that one finds between the first three gospels, as illustrated in Table 10.1, may be
found throughout these narratives. Consider the following:

- Matthew, Mark, and Luke have eighty-six pericopes in common with one another. On the
  other hand, John shares only a small number of pericopes with the other gospels. Further,
  when John does share a pericope, one finds low micro-level intertextual correlation, similar to what is seen in Table 10.1.[1]

- Matthew and Luke share an additional fifty pericopes with one another that are not found
  in Mark's gospel, rendering a total of 136 pericopes that Matthew and Luke share with
  one another.

- The first three gospels share a common outline of Jesus' ministry: (1) the birth of Jesus
  (Matthew and Luke only); (2) the ministry of John the Baptist, Jesus' baptism and
  temptation; (3) Jesus' ministry around Galilee; (4) Jesus' journey to Jerusalem; (5) Jesus'

---

[1]Statistics on the Synoptic Gospels may be found in J. B. Tyson, *The New Testament and Early Christianity* (New
York: Macmillan, 1984) 151. R. B. Brown lists only six pericopes that the Gospel of John shares with the Synoptic
Gospels. *The Gospel according to John (I–XII)* (AB 29; Garden City, NY: Doubleday, 1966) xliv.

Table 10.1

The Cleansing of the Temple

Matthew 21:12–13	Mark 11:15–17	Luke 19:45–46	John 2:14–17
12 *Then* Jesus *entered the temple and drove out* all *who were selling* and *buying in the temple, and he overturned the tables of the money changers and the seats of those who sold doves.*	15 *Then* they came to Jerusalem. And *he entered the temple and began to drive out those who were selling* and those who were *buying in the temple, and he overturned the tables of the money changers and the seats of those who sold doves.*	45 *Then* *he entered the temple and began to drive out those who were selling things there;*	14 In *the temple* he found people *selling* cattle, sheep, and *doves,* and the *money changers* seated at their *tables.*
(overturned the tables— see above)	(overturned the tables— see above)		15 Making a whip of cords, he drove all of them out of the temple, both the sheep and the cattle. He also poured out the coins of the money changers and *overturned* their *tables.*
	16 and he would not allow anyone to carry anything through the temple.		
13 *He said* to them, *"It is written, 'My house shall be called a house of prayer';* *but you* are *making it a den of robbers."*	17 *He* was teaching and *saying,* *"Is it* not *written, 'My house shall be called a house of prayer* for all the nations'? *But you have made it a den of robbers."*	46 and *he said,* *"It is written, 'My house shall be a house of prayer';* *but you have made it a den of robbers."*	16 *He* told those who were selling the doves, "Take these things out of here! Stop making my Father's *house* a marketplace!" 17 His disciples remembered that it was written, "Zeal for your house will consume me."

ministry in Jerusalem; (6) Jesus' **passion**; (7) Jesus' resurrection. While John shows very general agreement with items 2, 5, 6, and 7, he is quite different from the other gospels with regard to items 3 and 4. Whereas Matthew, Mark, and Luke divide Jesus' ministry rather neatly between Galilee and Jerusalem, with Jesus making one trip to Jerusalem toward the end of his life, John's gospel portrays Jesus in Jerusalem quite frequently before he makes his last, fateful trip (see Jn 2:12–22; 7:14–8:59; 10:22–39).

The Sources of the Gospels. Because of the similarity in form and content between the first three gospels, scholars call these the **Synoptic Gospels.** *Synoptic* comes from the Greek words "with" (*syn*) and "eye" (*optic* [cf. "optical"]). The three are similar enough that one can, at least in a sense, read them "with one eye." And, because of these similarities, most scholars conclude that some type of direct literary relationship exists between the Synoptic Gospels. But how does one explain this literary relationship? Scholars refer to this question as "the Synoptic problem."

Critical scholars have offered many hypotheses to address the Synoptic problem. Most scholars today explain the literary relationship with one of two hypotheses. The **Two-Gospel Hypothesis** is maintained by a minority of scholars. It states that Matthew composed his gospel first. Luke used this gospel, thereby accounting for the abundance of material that Matthew and Luke have in common with one another (136 pericopes). Later, Mark used *both* Matthew and Luke, condensing the two longer gospels and, because of such editing, left out much that he found in his two sources (the fifty pericopes that are in Matthew and Luke, but not in Mark).

The **Two-Source Hypothesis** is the majority view. It argues that Mark wrote his gospel first. Matthew and Luke then each used Mark *independently* of one another. This accounts for the eighty-six pericopes found in all three gospels. In order to explain the fifty pericopes that are found in Matthew *and* Luke, but are absent from Mark, this hypothesis proposes that Matthew and Luke each made independent use of a common source. For the sake of convenience, scholars call this now lost source "**Q**," derived from the German word for source, *Quelle.*

The question of sources that possibly lie behind John's gospel will be explored more thoroughly in Chapter 15. For now, it is sufficient to understand that whatever literary sources might lie behind the Fourth Gospel, most scholars believe this narrative to be literarily independent of the Synoptic Gospels.

The Sources of Acts. Most critical interpreters do believe some sources lie behind the Acts of the Apostles.[2] Some scholars have tried to identify within the narrative itself such sources, arguing that key urban centers of early Christianity, such as Jerusalem and Antioch, had records or sources that the author of Acts could have used. Others also believe that the writer of Acts used some sort of itinerary that tracked the journeys of Paul from city to city. Finally, several sections of Acts employ a first person plural narrator (see, e.g., Acts 16:10–17.) These so-called We Passages[3] may indicate places where the author himself was present, or they may indicate a source used by the author, but compiled by an eyewitness other than the author. Despite the belief that sources do lie behind Acts, attempts by source critics to identify and specify such sources have failed to reach a consensus among scholars.

[2]D. A. Koch, "Source Criticism (NT)," *ABD* 6.170.
[3]The other We Passages are found in Acts 20:5–15; 21:1–18; 27:1–28:16.

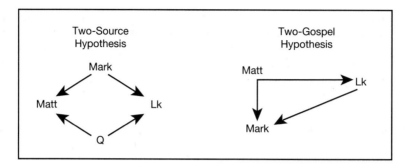

Figure 10.1
Gospel Source Hypotheses

The New Testament Narratives as Sources for
the History of Jesus and the Early Church

Parts One and Two of this text have regularly argued that there is no simple identification between the literary text and the historical social text. One cannot simply paraphrase the story in the literary text and assume that she or he is offering a record of what happened. This lesson applies to the NT narratives as well.

The Genre of the Gospels and Acts. Chapter 1 introduced the gospels in a very general way to readers, suggesting that one who reads the gospels might associate them most readily with the literary **genre** of biography. Chapter 1 also suggested that one would likely associate the Acts of the Apostles with the genre of historical narrative. While there is not universal agreement on the question of the genre of these narratives, many scholars who have compared the gospels with ancient biographies, or "Lives," as they tended to be called, have noted enough similarities to conclude that "the gospels are biographies, albeit ancient ones."[4] Similarly, scholars have made good arguments that the Acts of the Apostles is very much like the historical narratives of the period.

Association of the gospels and Acts with biographical and historical works of the day provides informed readers, ancient and modern, with a word of caution, especially as they attempt to address the question of the value of these narratives as sources for the history of Jesus and his followers. Ancient biographers and historians did not play by the rules of strict accuracy that most people expect of historians and biographers today. Lucian, a most prolific writer of the second century CE, wrote a scathing attack on the carelessness of historians of his time (*How to Write History*). The Greek historian Xenophon (fifth to fourth centuries BCE) composed a biography of Cyrus, the same Cyrus who allowed the Jews to return from Babylon. It is noteworthy that ancient readers of Xenophon's *Cyropaedia*, as much as they appreciated its teachings, recognized that it played fast and loose with the facts. Cicero, the Roman orator of the second century BCE, stated that "the great Cyrus was portrayed by Xenophon not in accord with historical truth, but as a model of just government" (*Letters to Quintus,* 1.1.23). Diogenes Laertius, the biographer of the great philosophers of the Greek tradition, claimed that Plato described the *Cyropaedia* as

---

[4]C. H. Talbert, *What Is a Gospel? The Genre of the Canonical Gospels* (Philadelphia: Fortress, 1977) 135.

"fiction" (*Plato,* 3.34). The fact that the ancients themselves recognized that the biographers and historians of antiquity were not always careful and accurate should encourage students to read the gospels cautiously and critically as historical reports.

The Gospels and the History of Jesus. Chapter 5, "The Story of the Prophets," spoke of how one finds a number of voices in the prophetic books, corresponding to the development of the material. That chapter focused attention on two voices: that of the prophet himself, who spoke his message to his actual listeners, and that of the final editor of the prophetic book, who was responsible for arranging the traditions he received into the present literary text.

One can understand the composition of the gospels in a similar manner. The gospels present not only the voice of Jesus, but the voice of the evangelist who is, finally, responsible for the literary text in which the words of Jesus are embedded. Table 10.1 reveals that the words Jesus spoke during the "Cleansing of the Temple" do not come to readers directly, but through the literary compositions of the gospel writers. Note that none of them quotes Jesus in exactly the same way. Further, John places the entire scene of the Cleansing at the beginning of Jesus' ministry, while the Synoptics place it at the end of his ministry. Interpreting the gospel narratives requires that one ask what each evangelist may have been wanting to communicate about Jesus by offering the narrative portrait as he did. Reading the gospels with sensitivity to the author's possible intentions in arranging the material as he did is referred to as **redaction criticism**.

Within the prophetic materials, one finds not only the words of the prophet (literarily arranged by the final editor), one also finds words *attributed to the prophet,* either implicitly or explicitly; words that actually represent subsequent interpretations (rereadings) of the prophet's message by later followers of that prophet.[5] Second and Third Isaiah, for example, present oracles that date to the Exilic and early post-Exilic periods, respectively, long after the death of Isaiah of Jerusalem. Their inclusion in the literary text of Isaiah *implies* that Isaiah spoke these words, even though close and critical readers know that Isaiah of Jerusalem did not do so. The question is whether one finds a similar phenomenon in the gospels. Are there words attributed to Jesus in the literary texts of the gospels that, from a strictly historical point of view, he did not actually say? Are many words attributed to Jesus actually rereadings of the *meaning* of his ministry and message?

When one wades into the terrain of attempting to reconstruct what Jesus actually did and did not say, one is immediately confronted with a host of questions. For example, should one looking for what Jesus actually said explore only the biblical materials or take into account extra-biblical sources as well? When one brings into consideration both the biblical and extra-biblical materials, one discovers that the Christians of antiquity attributed a plethora of sayings to Jesus.[6] Should one consider *any* saying attributed to Jesus in *any* ancient writing to be authentic? If not, by what criteria does one separate the authentic from the inauthentic sayings? Should one assume a saying to be inauthentic unless one can demonstrate its likely authenticity; or should one assume it to be authentic, requiring that its inauthenticity be demonstrated?

---

[5]See Chap. 5, pp. 106–107.

[6]J. D. Crossan has compiled an anthology of the known sayings attributed to Jesus in antiquity from both biblical and extra-biblical sources. *Sayings Parallels: A Workbook for the Jesus Tradition* (Philadelphia: Fortress, 1986).

Candidly, it is impossible to offer any simple answer to this host of questions that could do justice to the wide range of conclusions reached by NT scholars. However, student readers can at least be introduced to some of the different perspectives of NT scholarship. Some NT scholars believe that one finds in the literary texts of the gospels a large amount of subsequent rereading and interpretation of Jesus' words; that is, *most* of the words attributed to Jesus in the gospels were not actually spoken by him. In recent years, the work of the Jesus Seminar probably best represents this school of thought. This group of scholars gathers regularly to study the many sayings attributed to Jesus in both the **canonical** and extra-canonical materials, trying to reach some consensus on what Jesus actually said. Generally, they have concluded that the vast majority of sayings attributed to Jesus in both the canonical and extra-canonical sources were not actually said by him. Within the extra-canonical materials, only a paltry handful of sayings are authentic. In the biblical gospels, the record is a bit better, with a little less than about 20 percent of the sayings attributed to Jesus considered to be authentic.[7]

Within academic circles, responses to the work of the Jesus Seminar have not been universally positive. Some critics regularly call into question the criteria that many scholars employ to extract the authentic sayings of Jesus from the sea of sayings attributed to him (see the box "A Closer Look: Finding the Real Words of Jesus"). For example, why should one privilege the authenticity of sayings attributed to Jesus that are *dissimilar* to Jewish beliefs or subsequent Christian beliefs? Scholars who differ with the Jesus Seminar do not believe that it is necessary to approach the canonical gospels with the degree of skepticism that these researchers employ.[8] As for the extra-biblical materials, interpreters who are more inclined to accept the veracity of the biblical gospels will argue that the extra-biblical material, both Christian and non-Christian, cannot displace or be given historical priority over the canonical gospels. Noncanonical gospels, some argue, are either so obviously legendary or spurious that no one can expect to find reliable historical information within them. Further, some argue that noncanonical gospels are later and, in many instances, actually dependent upon the canonical gospels. Hence, they are of no real historical value for reconstructing a historical portrait of Jesus.[9]

The Acts of the Apostles and the History of Jesus' Followers. Debate also ensues regarding the historical value of the Acts of the Apostles. One school of thought argues that Acts, while written in the form of a historical narrative, is not very good history, for the author was more concerned to promote a **theological** message than to convey historical information. The monumental commentary by E. Haenchen represents this perspective.[10] Recently, Richard Pervo has taken this

---

[7]R. E. Brown, *An Introduction to the New Testament* (New York: Doubleday, 1997) 819–823 offers an overview of the work of the seminar.

[8]Students may find a very accessible dialogue between two scholars, one representing the Jesus Seminar (R. J. Miller) and one critic of the Seminar (B. Witherington, III) in "Battling Over the Jesus Seminar," *BibRev* 13/2 (April 1997) 18–26.

[9]E.g., E. M. Yamauchi, "Jesus Outside the New Testament: What Is the Evidence?" *Jesus Under Fire: Modern Scholarship Reinvents the Historical Jesus* (ed., M. J. Wilkins and J. P. Moreland; Grand Rapids, MI: Zondervan, 1995) 207–229. See also, H. C. Kee, *Jesus in History: An Approach to the Study of the Gospels* (2nd ed.; New York: Harcourt Brace Jovanovich, 1977), especially chaps. 2 and 8.

[10]E. Haenchen, *The Acts of the Apostles: A Commentary* (Philadelphia: Westminster, 1971).

A Closer Look: Finding the Real Words of Jesus. Scholars who argue that one must demonstrate the authenticity of sayings attributed to Jesus in the ancient sources have developed criteria for isolating the real words of Jesus. First, students must understand what scholars mean by "the real words of Jesus." Generally, they do not mean verbatim quotes, what, technically, scholars call the *ipsissima verba,* or "authentic words" of Jesus. Most interpreters concede that the closest scholars can come to "the real words of Jesus" are close paraphrases of what he said, what they call the *ipsissima vox,* or "authentic voice" of Jesus.

By what criteria do scholars isolate the *ipsissima vox* of Jesus?

• The Criterion of Dissimilarity. This states that one can assume the authenticity of sayings that are dissimilar to traditional Jewish ideas or ideas that would have held currency in the early church. The idea is that it is reasonable to conclude that sayings attributed to Jesus that are *distinctive* in their content can be considered authentic. For example, sayings that claim the presence of God's reign due to Jesus' work (e.g., Lk 11:20) are so distinctive, given his social text, that such sayings are likely authentic.

• The Criterion of Coherence. This states that sayings attributed to Jesus that cohere and are consistent with sayings established as authentic by the criterion of dissimilarity may be considered authentic. For example, if one concludes that Jesus claimed the presence of God's kingdom, then Jesus' claim that he saw Satan fall like lightening (Lk 10:18) might also be considered authentic, since the idea of the fall of Satan *coheres* with the idea that God's reign has come.

• The Criterion of Multiple Attestation. A saying attributed to Jesus in different sources or within different types of material may be considered authentic. For example, multiple sources offer versions of the parable of the mustard seed: Mark (Mk 4:30–32), Q (Lk 13:18–19; Matt 13:31–32), and the extra-canonical Gospel of Thomas (Th 20:1–4). Therefore, this parable could likely be deemed authentic.

• The Criterion of Language and Environment. Obviously, sayings attributed to Jesus that show signs of having originated in a non-Palestinian environment or after Jesus was executed cannot be considered authentic. For example, one might conclude that Jesus' specific instructions on how to remove someone from the church (Matt 18:15–17) could not have been spoken by Jesus since the church did not come into existence until *after* Jesus.

For further study, A more complete discussion of the criteria of authenticity may be found in D. Dulling and N. Perrin. *The New Testament: Proclamation and Perenesis, Myth and History,* 3rd Ed. Fort Worth, TX: Harcourt Brace College, 1994. Pp. 520–523. For the Jesus Seminar's thorough discussion of the criteria that it employed to locate the authentic words of Jesus, criteria that are more complex than the summary above, see *The Five Gospels: The Search for the Authentic Words of Jesus.* Edited by R. W. Funk, R. W. Hoover, and the Jesus Seminar. New York: Macmillan, 1993. Pp. 1–38. For a critique of these criteria and the Jesus Seminar's employment of them, see D. L. Bock, "The Words of Jesus in the Gospels: Live, Jive, or Memorex?" *Jesus Under Fire: Modern Scholarship Reinvents the Historical Jesus.* Edited by M. J. Wilkins and J. P. Moreland. Grand Rapids, MI: Zondervan, 1995. Pp. 73–99.

approach one step further and argued that one should not read Acts as a historical narrative at all. He argues that Acts is an edifying and entertaining historical novel; that is, Acts is an intentional piece of fictional narrative only minimally based on history.[11] Scholars such as Gerd Lüdemann essentially agree with Haenchen's view that the final narrative of Acts is the literary construction of the author and cannot be relied upon in and of itself for historically valuable information. However, Lüdemann believes that behind the narrative are valuable historical *traditions* that the author has employed in the construction of his narrative. With careful and critical reading one can extract from the narrative of Acts valuable pieces of historical information.[12] Finally, one may find critical scholars, such as Martin Hengel,[13] who argue that Luke's overall historical narrative—not just the traditions that lie behind it—offers a historically reliable portrait of the early church. To be sure, such scholars do not read Acts naively or uncritically. They do not, for example, try to argue that Acts is an absolutely accurate and reliable narrative. Still, this approach insists, Acts measures up rather well to other histories of its time and should be taken seriously as a good source of historical information.

The case study presented in the Excursus within this chapter will illustrate one specific historical problem that one encounters in Luke's narrative. When the chapter is complete, students will at least have a better understanding why critical scholars can disagree so thoroughly on the issue of the historical reliability of NT narratives.

The Authorship and Date of Luke-Acts

The title, "The Gospel of Luke," clearly implies that the author of this gospel was a person named Luke. This has been the consistent view of church tradition for centuries. The narrative itself identifies no author. The consensus view of both tradition and critical scholarship is that the author of the gospel is identical with the author of the book of Acts. The book of Acts may offer clues as to the identity of the author. A number of sections within Acts are written from a first person perspective. Scholars refer to these as the "We Passages" (see "A Closer Look: The 'We Passages' of Acts"). If one assumes that the We Passages indicate a true eyewitness to Paul's travels, one can conclude that the author was at least an occasional companion of Paul's. Several letters bearing Paul's name mention persons who traveled with Paul or assisted him in his work (see, e.g., Rom 16:21–24; 1 Cor 1:1; 2 Cor 1:1; 16:19–20; Eph 6:21–22; Phil 1:1; Col 1:1; 4:7–16; etc.). There is a passing reference to a certain Luke in Col 4:14 and Philem 24, allowing the conclusion that a man named Luke was, indeed, an occasional companion of Paul. But can one be sure that this companion named Luke wrote the gospel and Acts? Though the tradition has been around since the second century, many critical scholars prefer to hold judgment, saying that there is simply not enough evidence to conclude that the writer of Luke-Acts was, in fact, Luke, the companion of Paul. But scholars regularly refer to the author as Luke for the sake of convenience.

---

[11]R. Pervo, *Profit with Delight: The Literary Genre of the Acts of the Apostles* (Philadelphia: Fortress, 1987).

[12]G. Lüdemann, *Early Christianity according the Traditions in Acts: A Commentary* (Minneapolis, MN: Fortress, 1989).

[13]M. Hengel, *Acts and the History of Earliest Christianity* (Philadelphia: Fortress, 1979).

A Closer Look: The "We Passages" of Acts. One finds within Acts a number of passages written in the first person plural, the so-called We Passages (see Acts 16:10–17; 20:5–15; 21:1–18; 27:1–28:16). It would appear that the most obvious way to read these passages is to conclude that the author of Luke-Acts was actually present and an eyewitness to the events narrated in the first person, whether that author is identified with Luke or not. Many scholars do read these passages this way (e.g., B. Witherington III [see bibliography below]). However, this is not the only way that scholars understand these passages. S. E. Porter surveys various ways interpreters have understood the We Passages: (1) Some argue that the We Passages serve as a literary device to give the narrative a feel of historical veracity or literary vividness (e.g., Haenchen); (2) Others contend that first person narration was a stock literary convention employed by ancient authors to narrate sea voyages (Robbins); (3) Finally some, including Porter, argue that the author employed a source penned by an eyewitness, though the author of this source was not the author of Luke-Acts.

For further study, B. Witherington III. *The Acts of the Apostles: A Socio-Rhetorical Commentary.* Grand Rapids, MI: Eerdmans, 1998. Pp. 480–486; S. E. Porter. "The 'We' Passages." *The Book of Acts in Its First Century Setting.* Edited by B. W. Winter. 6 Volumes. Grand Rapids, MI: Eerdmans, 1993–97. Vol 2:545–574. Porter surveys the various approaches to the We Passages. E. Haenchen. *The Acts of the Apostles: A Commentary.* Philadelphia: Westminster, 1971. See comments on relevant passages; V. Robbins. "By Land and By Sea: The We-Passages and Ancient Sea Voyages." *Perspectives on Luke-Acts.* Edited by C. H. Talbert. Danville, VA: Association of Baptist Professors of Religion, 1978. Pp. 215–242.

When and where did Luke write Luke-Acts? The response here is very much thoughtful conjecture, as anything else. Luke seems to know about the fall of Jerusalem in 70 CE, given that his descriptions in Luke 21 of the event are far more detailed than in the parallel version of this material in Mark 13, Luke's likely source. If this is sound logic, he must have written after 70 CE. Historians of early Christianity believe that Paul's letters were in circulation as a collection by around 100 CE. The author of Luke-Acts shows no awareness of such a collection, which is quite strange given the attention he gives to Paul. That might imply that Luke wrote Luke-Acts *before* the collection and distribution of Paul's letters; hence, before 100 CE. These kinds of inferences lead most scholars to date Luke-Acts to the last third of the first century CE. As to the place of composition, guesses have included Antioch, Rome, or other urban centers of Christianity.

Luke's Story of Jesus:
The Gospel of Luke

Learning Goals

- To understand that Luke constructs his narrative to portray Jesus as the fulfillment of Israel's scriptures and hopes of liberation and restoration.
- To learn that Luke emphasized God's concern to offer liberating salvation to both Israel and the gentiles.
- To understand Luke's employment of the theme of the division of Israel.

Guiding Study Exercises

1) Write two or three paragraphs that describe how Luke, *throughout his gospel,* portrays Jesus as the fulfillment of Jewish scripture and hopes of liberation.
2) Describe how Lk 4:16–30 introduces the theme of God's concern for non-Jews. List and briefly summarize three other texts from the gospel that keep this theme before readers.
3) Simeon prophesies "the falling and rising of many in Israel" (Lk 2:34). How does Luke's narrative portray the fulfillment of this prophecy?
4) Review the resurrection narrative of Luke 24. Write a short essay analyzing how this chapter pulls together important themes found throughout Luke.

The following overview of Luke's gospel will divide the gospel into seven sections: (1) the births of Jesus and John, (2) the ministry of John and the baptism and temptation of Jesus, (3) the Galilean ministry of Jesus, (4) Jesus' journey to Jerusalem, (5) Jesus' ministry at the Temple, (6) Jesus' passion, and (7) Jesus' resurrection.

The Births of Jesus and John (Luke 1–2)

After a formal prologue that resembles the formal prologues of other ancient biographical and historical narratives (1:1–4), Luke tells the story of the priest Zechariah's vision in the Temple of Jerusalem (1:5–23). The Temple setting is important, for it informs readers that the story that ensues is a thoroughly Jewish story. The angel Gabriel tells the pious and elder priest that he and his formerly barren wife, Elizabeth, will have a son. This son's mission is clearly defined as one who is "to make ready a people prepared for the Lord" (1:17).

The scene shifts to Nazareth where the young virgin Mary also receives a heavenly visitation (1:26–38). She is informed that "the Holy Spirit will come upon" her (1:35) and that she will bear a son, Jesus, who "will reign over the house of Jacob forever" (1:33). This son who will be king is also said to be a descendant of David and the son of God (1:33–34), implying that Jesus is the one who will fulfill the promise that God made to David centuries before: that one of his descendants, who would also be a son of God, would rule David's kingdom forever (see 2 Sam 7:12–16). This notice further informs the reader that the story of Jesus is closely connected with the story of Israel: this Jesus who is coming is to be Israel's king.

Following this heavenly vision, Mary visits her kinswoman, Elizabeth (1:39–45), and while there offers a hymn of praise to God, the Magnificat (1:46–55). The content of the hymn reinforces the message that Jesus is to be one who fulfills the promises that God made to the ancestors (see especially vv. 54–55).

Luke 1:57–80 narrates the story of John's birth and **circumcision** ceremony. In this context, the priest Zechariah also offers a hymn of praise (vv. 68–79), the Benedictus. This hymn also emphasizes that the actions God is taking will bring to fulfillment the promises of liberation that God made to the Jews' ancestors (vv. 72–73). Jewish hopes for the end of the Exile and the coming of the grand restoration clearly seem to be in view here. With the arrival of John and Jesus, Jewish hopes for liberation can find realization.

Luke 2 narrates the story of Jesus' birth and the events immediately thereafter. The journey of Mary and Joseph to Bethlehem (2:1–7) reminds readers that Jesus is "descended from the house and family of David" (v. 4; cf. 1:32). The angelic visitation to the shepherds (vv. 8–14) further reinforces that this Jesus will be a deliverer, the Savior and **Messiah** (v. 11). The fact that lowly shepherds are privileged to receive this angelic announcement reminds readers that God has a favored place for the lowly of the world, a theme that was first voiced explicitly in Mary's Magnificat (1:50–53). Jesus is circumcised (v. 21), indicating that he is born into a pious Jewish family. The Jewish piety of Jesus' family is further reflected in the fact that the parents journey to the Temple of Jerusalem to dedicate Jesus to the Lord (vv. 22–24). There they meet a devout Jewish elder named Simeon who offers an inspired utterance, the Nunc Dimittis (vv. 29–32). The words of Simeon provide yet another word of assurance that Jesus has come for the benefit of Israel (v. 32b). But he adds an important feature: Jesus has also come as "a light for revelation to the **Gentiles**" (v. 32a). Yet Simeon offers a further and ominous word: this Jesus "is destined for the falling and rising of many in Israel, and to be a sign that will be opposed" (v. 34). This foreshadows that not all in Israel will accept this one in whom their hopes of salvation are finding realization.

The Ministry of John, Jesus' Baptism and Temptation (Luke 3:1–4:13)

The story of John's birth told of his mission to prepare Israel for the coming of the Lord. In Lk 3:1–20 John fulfills his mission. He preaches of the coming salvation *and* judgment of God (vv. 16–17). What one receives from God hinges on whether one repents (vv. 7–8). With John's mission of preparing the people complete, he exits the stage, being thrown in prison for his moral condemnation of Herod Antipas (vv. 19–20). Jesus now makes his appearance, being baptized. During this event, God personally affirms Jesus as his son, in the form an intertextual echo of Ps 2:7, a Royal Psalm. The echo of a Royal Psalm provides a subtle, but real, reminder that Jesus is God's anointed one, Israel's king. Following Jesus' baptism, Luke presents a genealogy of Jesus (3:23–38), reaffirming the Davidic (v. 31) and Jewish (v. 34 refers to Abraham, Isaac, and Jacob) lineage of Jesus. In tracing Jesus all the way back to Adam (v. 38), the ancestor of all human

Madonna and Child with the Infant Saint John (1510–1512), by Giuliano Bugiardini (1475–1554). It is not uncommon for portraits of John and Jesus as children to portray them as precocious and even acting out in their infancy their missions as adults. In this painting by Bugiardini note that John is depicted anachronistically as wearing the camel hair clothing that he would wear as an adult (cf. Mk 1:6). As the viewer looks at John's staff, it appears to be a cross, for which the child Jesus reaches with one hand while offering the traditional priestly blessing—the uplifted fingers—with his other hand. The artist appears to be saying that even as a child Jesus knew his destiny was to die a sacrificial death. The story of Jesus at the Temple, portraying the youth Jesus as something of a prodigy in matters of Jewish law (Lk 2:41–51), may represent that same kind of anachronistic tendency that would become most prevalent in extra-canonical narratives about Jesus and later art. (Oil with traces of tempera, transferred to Masonite 491/2″ diameter (125.7 cm). Nelson-Atkins Museum of Art, Kansas City, Missouri [Purchase: Nelson Trust])

The excavated ruins of a house in Capernaum that dates back to the first century CE. Tradition maintains that Peter's house originally sat on this site. Today a modern church is situated above these ruins. (Courtesy of Larry McKinney)

beings, Luke offers readers another reminder that Jesus has come to offer salvation not only to Israel, but to the gentiles as well.

The scene now shifts to the desert where Jesus is tempted by the devil (4:1–13). This is an important scene, for it reveals that Jesus' messianic work of liberating Israel has far-reaching implications. Jesus' work to offer liberation for Israel and the gentiles will require that Jesus confront the one who, in Jewish thought of the first century CE, was the ultimate oppressor, God's nemesis and adversary, the Satan. Foreshadowed here are the many conflicts that Jesus will have with the allies of Satan: sin, sickness, and demonic possession. Foreshadowed as well is Jesus' eventual victory over the Satanic powers of oppression, for Jesus comes forth from this confrontation unscathed.

Jesus' Galilean Ministry (Luke 4:14–9:50)

In this section, several of the themes that the narrative has introduced to this point begin to find fuller elaboration.

Jesus Fulfills the Jewish Scriptures and Hopes of Liberation. Luke begins the Galilean section with Jesus returning to his hometown of Nazareth and preaching in the **synagogue** (4:14–30). Jesus' first public act is to read from the prophet Isaiah (vv. 18–19; Isa 61:1–2; 58:6) and to claim boldly that "today this scripture has been fulfilled in your hearing" (v. 21). With this declaration, Luke's Jesus affirms that in him the scriptures find their fulfillment. The text from Isaiah emphasizes the liberating aspects of Jesus' work, with its declaration that Jesus is to "proclaim release to the captives . . . to let the oppressed go free" (v. 18). Just what kind of "release" or liberation that Jesus offers becomes clear as the narrative progresses.

Upon leaving his hometown, Jesus immediately casts a demon out of a possessed man (4:31–37) and heals the mother-in-law of Simon, who will soon become one of Jesus' followers (4:38–39). The reader begins to suspect that such exorcisms and healings demonstrate the liberative power of Jesus. The following summary of 4:40–41 reiterates the exorcising and healing power of Jesus, with v. 41 explicitly associating this work with Jesus being the Messiah. Finally, in v. 42, Jesus employs the phrase "the kingdom of God." The manifestation of the ruling power of God was to bring for Israel the liberation and restoration for which it had been longing. By the time readers come to the end of Luke 4, they should recognize that this liberating power is manifesting itself in Jesus' mighty deeds. Luke keeps such deeds before his readers in this Galilean section. Notices and stories of other exorcisms are found in 6:18, 8:2, 26–39, and 9:37–43. Jesus also regularly heals people throughout this section (5:12–16; 6:6–11; 7:1–10; 8:42b–48).

Jesus' liberating work also offers "release from" or "forgiveness of" sin. The story of the healing of the paralytic makes this clear (5:17–26). As the story begins, readers suspect yet another healing story. While Jesus does heal in this story, the narrative indicates that Jesus' liberative work includes release from sin, for Jesus declares to the paralytic in 5:20 that his sins are forgiven. Significantly, the word denoting "forgiveness" (*apheōntai*) shares the same root as the word Jesus read from Isaiah in 4:18 (*aphesis*), translated in the NRSV as "release" and "go free." This pericope allows readers to see that the same authority that allows Jesus to liberate people from sickness also allows him to liberate them from sin. Luke keeps before readers Jesus' concern to offer forgiveness to sinners (5:27–32; 7:36–50).

The liberation that Jesus brings in his preaching the reign of God includes release from the ultimate oppressor of human beings, death. Twice in the Galilean section Jesus raises people from the dead (7:11–17 and 8:40–42a, 49–56). The first story of resuscitation (7:11–17) concludes with an affirming word from those who witnessed Jesus' mighty deed: "A great prophet has risen among us! God has looked favorably on his people" (v. 16). The latter phrase echoes Zechariah's Benedictus, where the father of John declared that God "has *looked favorably* on his people and redeemed them" (1:68).

At the end of Luke 4, Jesus summarized his liberating work of healing and exorcism by saying that his purpose was to "proclaim the good news of the kingdom of God" (4:43). This "good news" included Jesus' invitation to receive the blessings of God's forgiveness of, or "release from," sin. Yet, Luke makes clear that receipt of the blessings of forgiveness is linked to repentance (see 3:3, 8; 5:32). That is, God's offer of forgiveness can only be received by people who recognize their need of his liberating power and who are willing to turn back to him and direct their lives in accordance with God's will. This is the context in which one can understand Jesus' so-called Sermon on the Plain (6:17–49). These words of Jesus offer specific guidance for those who respond affirmatively to the liberating power of God's reign (note the opening words of this address in 6:20). In Jesus, the reign of God promises to liberate people who experience oppression (vv. 20–23) and to turn the tables on the oppressors (vv. 24–26; cf. Mary's Magnificat, 1:50–53). Yet those who experience the power of God's redemptive mercy must themselves display mercy to others. They are to love their enemies (vv. 27–36), not pass disparaging judgment on others (vv. 37–43), live lives that demonstrate their transformation (vv. 43–45), and follow Jesus' way in obedience (vv. 46–47). It is only people such as these who can survive the judgment that is coming (vv. 48–49; cf. 3:7–8).

Jesus performs his work of liberation as "the Messiah," the descendant of David and son of God (cf. Lk 1:32–33). Fittingly, before the Galilean section concludes, Jesus' followers come to recognize that he is the Messiah (9:18–20). With this recognition by his followers, Jesus twice informs his followers, and the readers, that central to the messianic work is his mission to suffer, be **crucified**, and resurrected (9:21–22, 44–45). Also fitting is the scene in the last chapter of the Galilean section where Jesus is gloriously transfigured before three of this **disciples** (9:28–36). Appearing with him are Moses and Elijah, likely representing the law and the prophets. In the presence of Jesus' followers and the apparitions of those who represent the scriptural heritage of Israel, the voice of God affirms once again that Jesus is his son (cf. 3:22), whose words his followers are to heed (v. 35). When the story concludes, "Jesus was found alone" (v. 36), as though with his appearance and God's affirming word of him, Moses and Elijah can now fade from the stage; the scriptures that they symbolize are now finding fulfillment.

Jesus Works for the Liberation of Gentiles, as well as Jews. There is a clear emphasis in the Galilean section on Jesus' ministry to offer liberation to Israel. Yet, the word of Simeon in 2:32a that Jesus would be "a light for revelation to the Gentiles" is not forgotten. The pericope describing Jesus' visit to his hometown synagogue (4:16–30) expresses the theme of gentile inclusion in the blessings of God. Though the people at the synagogue initially respond favorably to Jesus' declaration that the scripture of Isaiah is fulfilled before them (4:21–22), by the end of the story they turn on Jesus (v. 29–30). Between the crowd's initial acceptance of Jesus and their rejection of him, Jesus makes clear that the blessings of God are not limited only to Israel. He tells of how two prophets of the scriptures, Elijah and Elisha, offered miraculous assistance to non-Israelites, even though many people of Israel were also in need of God's help (vv. 25–27). The implication is not that God abandoned Israel to help non-Israelites, but that God is equally concerned for the welfare of non-Jews. The people of the synagogue respond to such a suggestion in rage (v. 28).

In the Galilean section Jesus offers to a gentile the same liberation of healing that he offered to the Jews. Luke 7:1–10 tells the story of a Roman centurion who wanted Jesus to heal his slave. Jesus commends the centurion's faith in Jesus' healing power, saying that he had not witnessed such faith even among his own people (vv. 8–9). The story of the exorcism of the Gerasene demoniac (8:26–39) may also point to Jesus' offering liberation to gentiles from demonic possession. Luke does not explicitly say that the demoniac was a gentile, but the presence of a swineherd in the immediate vicinity of the demoniac likely implies that the story is taking place in "gentile country," since it strains credulity to suppose that one would have a large herd of pigs in Jewish territory. Thus, just as Jesus offers liberating healing and exorcism to the people of Israel, he offers the same to gentiles.

"The Falling and Rising of Many in Israel." Simeon spoke these words in 2:34a, adding that Jesus was "to be a sign that will be opposed" (v. 34b). Simeon's ominous word portends the fact that not all in Israel will accept Jesus' liberating word and mission. In some measure, such rejection of God's messenger is consistent with Israel's pattern of behavior. Ezra's confessional

prayer of Nehemiah 9 made note of Israel's tendency to reject God's prophets (Neh 9:26, 30). And while the Lukan Jesus is ultimately the Messiah and son of God, he is also prophet who, like his prophetic ancestors, is not accepted among his own (4:24). Jesus' rejection by the people of his hometown of Nazareth seems to foreshadow ominously the fact that many within Israel will reject his message.

Throughout the Galilean section, Israel divides into two camps: those who accept Jesus (those who "rise" within Israel) and those who reject him (those who "fall"). Luke 7:29–30 offers a clear statement that summarizes the division that marks Israel. The ordinary people seem open to Jesus; the leadership essentially rejects him, for the former "acknowledge the justice of God," whereas the leaders "rejected God's purposes for themselves." The Jewish leadership regularly opposes Jesus (5:17–32; 6:1–11; 7:30; 9:22). They question Jesus' authority to forgive sins (5:21), his association with sinners (5:30; 7:39), and his seeming violation of **sabbath** laws (6:2, 7). As Luke narrates the story, the one who comes to offer Israel its liberation ironically meets most of his resistance from those who are supposed to lead Israel. On the other hand, the larger populace appears more open to Jesus. They are amazed by his works of power (4:36; 5:26; 7:16). They press in to hear his preaching and witness his work (5:2; 6:17; 7:1, 11; 8:4, 40; 9:11). Yet, the fact that the people of Jesus' hometown rejected Jesus leaves the reader with the sense that even the larger populace of Israel might, in the end, also reject Jesus. In Lk 7:31, Jesus appears to condemn the whole of what he calls "this generation," comparing them to children who condemn both John and Jesus (vv. 32–34). Still, up to this stage of the story, the people as a whole are open to Jesus, not yet fully appropriating the attitude of "this generation."

Among those who clearly accept and follow Jesus are the twelve apostles (6:13), a special group whom Jesus sets aside to assist him in his work. This group shares most explicitly in Jesus' work of preaching, healing, and exorcising (9:1–2). It is also this group that explicitly recognizes Jesus as the Messiah (9:20). But even they have much to learn, for as the Galilean section draws to a close, these disciples do not understand what Jesus is talking about as he speaks of his mission of death and resurrection (9:45). They, quite unlike their master, quibble over greatness (9:46–48), and they seem to insist that only *they* be privileged to share Jesus' power to liberate people from demons (9:49–50).

The Journey to Jerusalem (Luke 9:51–19:44)

This section is regularly punctuated with reminders that Jesus and his followers are making their way toward Jerusalem (9:51, 53; 13:22, 33; 17:11; 19:28, 41). During the course of Jesus' gradual and deliberate journey, Luke's Jesus engages in teaching and actions that further reinforce the subthemes of the preceding Galilean section: Jesus is the fulfillment of Jewish hopes of liberation, Jesus offers God's liberating reign to non-Jews as well as Jews, and Jesus' mission of liberation divides Israel into two camps, those who accept and those who reject the liberating work of God in Jesus.

Jesus Fulfills Jewish Hopes of Liberation. On the course of his journey to Jerusalem, Jesus continues to liberate people from the power of sickness (e.g., 13:10–17; 14:1–6; 17:11–19; 18:35–43) and demonic possession (e.g., 11:14–23). Even the exorcising work of Jesus' followers serves to break the power of Satan. When some of Jesus' followers return to him, speaking of their power to cast out demons, Jesus reports a visionary experience in which he saw Satan fall like lightening from heaven (10:17–19). The enemy of God's people, from whom Zechariah had prophesied God's people would be liberated (1:71), is loosing his grip on this age. Liberation from the power of sin is also prevalent in this section. Jesus calls on his listeners to repent (13:1–9), offers parables that emphasize God's willingness to forgive those who repent (15:1–32), and openly receives and shares fellowship with sinners who do repent (19:1–10).

The somewhat enigmatic saying of Lk 16:16 also echoes the theme that Jesus fulfills the hopes of the scriptures: "The law and the prophets were in effect until John came; since then the good news of the kingdom of God is proclaimed, and everyone tries to enter it by force." Scholars have wrestled with the precise meaning of this saying, but one thing appears clear. With the coming of John and Jesus' proclamation of God's liberating reign, a significant shift has taken place: The law and the prophets have moved from center stage, to be replaced by the message of God's liberating reign. Luke 10:23–24 says much the same thing, for here Jesus explicitly tells his followers that that which is taking place before them is what the prophets and kings of old had longed to witness, but were not privileged to behold.

As Jesus' journey to Jerusalem draws to a close, he approaches the city riding on a colt, an apparent macro-level intertext with Zech 9:9: "Rejoice greatly, O daughter Zion! Shout aloud, O daughter Jerusalem! Lo, your king comes to you; triumphant and victorious is he, humble and riding on a donkey, on a colt, the foal of a donkey." The Lukan characters appear to recognize the scriptural allusion of Jesus' action, for "the whole multitude of the disciples began to praise God joyfully with a loud voice for all the deeds of power that they had seen, saying, 'Blessed is the king who comes in the name of the Lord! Peace in heaven, and glory in the highest heaven!' " (19:37–38).

Jesus Offers God's Liberating Reign to Jews and non-Jews. This theme is rather subtly presented in this section, but it is present. Three pericopes, for example, speak of the **Samaritans**, a group despised by the Jews of Jesus' time. The journey section begins with Jesus attempting to pass through Samaria, but he is rebuffed by the Samaritans (9:51–56). Jesus' followers want to call down divine punishment on the Samaritans, but Jesus "rebuked" their vengeful plan. This short story offers a clear indication that Jesus does not reject the Samaritans, as most Jews did. In the famous parable of the Good Samaritan (10:25–37), Jesus portrays a Samaritan as the hero of the story, when he fulfills the divine commandment of loving one's neighbor. Finally, Luke tells a story where Jesus healed ten lepers, only one of whom, a Samaritan, returned to thank him and offer praise to God (17:11–19). Cumulatively, these stories indicate that even a group despised by Jews can receive and respond positively to the liberating blessings of God.

Luke 13:22–29 also affirms that the blessings of God's liberating power are to reach beyond the boundaries of Israel. In response to a question of whether only a few people will be saved, Jesus exhorts his listeners to "strive to enter through the narrow door; for many, I tell you, will try to enter and will not be able" (v. 24). Merely having had some fellowship with Jesus or hearing his teachings is no guarantee that one will be able "to enter" the kingdom (vv. 26–27). In fact, Jesus warns his listeners that they will be thrown out of the kingdom of God (v. 28), while people "from east and west, from north and south, . . . will eat in the kingdom of God" (v. 29). There is debate among interpreters regarding the precise identity of those from the four corners of the earth. Does the phrase denote Jews of the **Diaspora** or *all people,* Jews and gentiles, who live scattered throughout the world? If the latter, readers find in this saying of Jesus a clear affirmation that people from all over the earth can be welcomed to the great victory banquet of God's kingdom.

The Division of Israel. During Jesus' journey to Jerusalem, the division of Israel continues. Jesus' call to repentance (13:1–9), his exhortations to weigh seriously the costs that accompany following him (14:25–35), his calls to diligent and faithful service (12:35–48), and his warnings of the great judgment that is coming (12:49–59; 17:20–37) cumulatively function to demand that those who hear his word make a decision. Jesus is God's son, anointed one, and prophet, and his word must be heeded (cf. 9:35). Failure to do so results in judgment.

The loyalty that Jesus demands in heeding his word and following him is absolute. Such loyalty is to take precedence over one's concern for financial security (12:13–21; 16:19–31; 18:18–30) and even familial obligations (9:59–62; 14:26). This kind of loyalty will bring division: "Do you think that I have come to bring peace to the earth? No, I tell you, but rather division! From now on five in one household will be divided, three against two and two against three; they will be divided: father against son and son against father, mother against daughter and daughter against mother, mother-in-law against her daughter-in-law and daughter-in-law against mother-in-law" (12:51–53).

As in the Galilean section, Jesus condemns "this generation" (11:29–32). In this pericope, this generation is described as evil (v. 29). Jesus compares this generation to the evil ancient city of Nineveh to whom God sent the prophet Jonah, demanding repentance (v. 30). Those knowledgeable of the biblical story know that this city did repent and experienced the forgiveness of God (Jonah 3:1–10). Will this generation follow the example of Nineveh or will it be condemned "at the judgment" (v. 32)?

As in the Galilean section, it is primarily the Jewish leadership that embodies most the characteristics of "this evil generation," while the ordinary people continue to be most open to Jesus' work of liberation (13:10–17, especially v. 17). Jesus' strong condemnation of the "scribes and Pharisees" (11:37–12:3) clearly places this group in the camp of those who are "falling" in Israel, for they are opposed to Jesus (cf. 2:34). The implication is that one must separate oneself from the official religious leadership of the Jews and be a loyal follower of Jesus if one is to be among those who are "rising" in Israel.

The polemic of Jesus against the institutions and symbols of Jewish leadership carries over into sayings that bode ill for Jerusalem, a major institutional symbol of Jewish leadership in Jesus' world. In Lk 13:31–35, Jesus speaks again of his prophetic identity, declaring that as a prophet it is necessary that he die in Jerusalem (v. 33). He summarizes the character of the city as one which "kills the prophets and stones those sent to it" (v. 34). Clearly, Jesus' hope is that he can gather Jerusalem under his protective wing, presumably so that it could share in the blessings of God's coming reign. But that is not to happen, at least in the foreseeable future, for Jerusalem is not willing (vv. 34–35). Just after Jesus receives the accolades of his followers as he descends from the Mount of Olives (19:36–38), he receives a predictable rebuke from the Pharisees (v. 39). Then Jesus launches into another tearful lament over the city that is doomed to destruction (vv. 41–44), for it failed to recognize "the time of [its] visitation from God" (v. 44). Tragically, it is on this note that Jesus' journey to Jerusalem reaches its end. Much of Israel, most especially that represented by the persons and institutions of leadership, is not accepting the liberation that God is offering. Readers of Jesus' many warnings, found throughout the journey section, know that judgment is the destiny of those within Israel who reject God's prophet, Messiah, and son.

Jesus' Ministry at the Temple (Luke 19:45–21:37)

Jesus' first act once he enters Jerusalem is to take possession of the Temple (19:45–46). Luke then states that "every day [Jesus] was teaching in the temple" (v. 47a). The division between the Jewish leadership and the people is reiterated, as Luke explicitly states the leadership sought to kill Jesus while the people "were spellbound by what they heard" (v. 47b). Verse 47 is carefully balanced in the Lukan narrative by the concluding verses of this section. In 21:37–38, Luke closes this section of the gospel by stating that Jesus taught daily in the Temple and that his teaching attracted "all the people." Hence, this introduction (19:47) and conclusion (21:37–38) frame the narrative of Jesus' Jerusalem ministry, guiding the reader to understand this whole section as Jesus' last attempt, as God's prophet and Messiah, to offer Israel at its Temple God's saving word.

Much of Jesus' teaching reveals intense conflict with the Jewish leadership. In 20:1–8, "the chief priests and the scribes" question the legitimacy of Jesus' authority. Jesus roundly condemns this group with his parable of the wicked tenants (20:9–19). This parable portrays the leaders as those to whom God had entrusted the care of his vineyard, Israel—a trust that they had violated by abusing the various servants that the owner of the vineyard (God) had sent to the tenants. The parable climaxes with Jesus speaking of how the tenants even abused the son of the vineyard owner, going so far as to kill him (v. 15). Verse 16 promises that, as a result, the vineyard's owner "will come and destroy those tenants and give the vineyard to others." This parable clearly functions in Luke's narrative as an **allegory** about God, Israel, the Jewish leadership, and the leadership's treatment of God's servants and son, Jesus. Significantly, this parable does *not* say that God destroys the vineyard of Israel, but that he will destroy the tenants (leaders) and give the vineyard over to others, presumably another group of leaders. Israel will continue, but only under new leadership. Readers are not yet told who this new leadership will be. The balance of Luke 20 offers further stories of conflict between Jesus and the leadership (vv. 20–44), concluding with a severe indictment of the leadership's pomposity and even heartlessness (vv. 45–47).

Luke 21:5–36 devotes close attention to the impending destruction of Jerusalem. If Luke was composed after the destruction of Jerusalem in 70 CE, Luke's readers would view the bulk of Luke 21 as fulfilled prophecy. Jerusalem had suffered destruction for its rejection of Jesus, just as the Messiah had predicted.

Jesus' Passion (Luke 22–23)

Readers know that the Jewish leadership wants to kill Jesus, an ominous theme reiterated in Lk 22:2. It is perhaps ironic that all of this plotting to kill the Messiah is said to be taking place during the festival of **Passover** (22:1). The Passover should remind readers of God's act of liberating Israel when he led his people out of Egypt. Now that God is trying to offer Israel its ultimate liberation, its leadership is trying to destroy the one who brings that liberation.

The liberating theme of Passover continues as Jesus and his disciples gather together to celebrate the feast (vv. 7–23). Verse 16, where Jesus says that he himself will not actually participate in this meal "until it is fulfilled in the kingdom of God," allows readers to see the explicit connection between God's past act of liberation at the **Exodus** and his ultimate act of liberation through the coming of God's reign. Tragically, Jesus announces that there will be betrayal (vv. 21–23) and denial (vv. 31–35), even among the ranks of his followers. Though Peter will deny Jesus, Jesus promises that he will be restored after he has repented ("turned back," v. 32), and that he will actually be a source of strength for the rest of Jesus' followers.

In vv. 28–30 Jesus promises his followers that they, like Jesus, will be given a kingdom. In the context of their participation in Jesus' kingdom, they are told that they "will sit on thrones judging [or "ruling"] the twelve tribes of Israel" (v. 30). This likely connects back with 20:16, where Jesus prophesied in the parable of the Wicked Tenants that God would destroy the tenants (the traditional Jewish leadership) and give the vineyard to others. The "others" appear to be the twelve apostles who, despite their own weaknesses and imperfections, have prevailed with Jesus through his trials.

The betrayal of Jesus by Judas brings the leadership of the Temple out to arrest Jesus (22:47–53). Jesus' word to his captors explicitly aligns them with the cosmic power of demonic darkness that Jesus has been battling against during the whole of the gospel narrative (v. 53). These representatives of the power of darkness take Jesus away and the following morning they take him to Pilate. Though Pontius Pilate finds Jesus guilty of no crime, he succumbs to the pressure of the Jewish leadership and condemns him to death.

Though Luke emphasizes the guilt of the Jewish leaders for Jesus' execution, the people, who had to this point kept their distance from their leaders, fail to stand with Jesus during his moment of trial. Luke 23:18 appears to say that the people join their leaders in calling out for Jesus' execution. It is clear that many among the people regret what is happening to Jesus, for some women mourn for him as he goes to the cross (23:27). And while the Jewish leaders mock Jesus as he hangs from the cross, the people do not join in the verbal abuse (23:35). In fact, when Jesus dies, the people leave the scene, beating their breasts in sorrow and, perhaps, even repentance (23: 48). Still, Jerusalem and its children will suffer for what its leadership has done (vv. 28–31).

The Resurrection (Luke 24)

The story of Jesus ends in triumph with the narration of his resurrection from the dead. In the context of these resurrection narratives, characters within the story and readers in front of the story are reassured that what happened to Jesus was in fulfillment of the scriptures (vv. 26–27, 44–46). Jesus is reunited with "the eleven," Judas, Jesus' betrayer, presumably being the one who is absent (v. 33). Most important is Jesus' final command to his followers. Their forthcoming mission is to preach "forgiveness of sins . . . in [Jesus'] name to all nations, beginning from Jerusalem" (v. 47). Jesus' work of offering liberation from sin is to continue, though now it will continue through his followers. What is more, this liberating message is to be offered to all nations, continuing the theme that was first voiced by Simeon that Jesus would be a light of revelation to the gentiles (2:32). That the apostles are instructed to begin their mission of preaching from Jerusalem also implies that the people of Jerusalem will also be offered, despite Jesus' execution, another opportunity to repent and receive the liberating power of God's forgiveness.

Luke's Story of the Early Church: The Acts of the Apostles

Learning Goals

- To recognize that the Acts of the Apostles continues to develop the themes introduced in the gospel.
- To understand with greater depth why critical scholars must use caution when employing NT narratives to reconstruct history.

Guiding Study Exercises

1) Select three passages from Acts and analyze how they develop the theme that Jesus fulfills Jewish scriptures and hopes of liberation.
2) Discuss how the literary structure of Acts *and* the mission work of Paul illustrate Luke's concern to demonstrate that God's salvation is for all people, Jews and gentiles.
3) Describe how the two major Jerusalem sections of Acts (1–7 and 21–23) portray the "division of Israel."
4) Discuss how the whole of this chapter, including the case study of the Excursus, has or has not influenced your own self-text regarding the question of the historical reliability of the NT narratives.

Acts 1:8 offers a general outline of the book of Acts, as the resurrected Jesus informs his followers that they will be his "witnesses in Jerusalem, in all Judea and Samaria, and to the ends of the earth." The summary below will follow that outline.

The Witness to Jerusalem (Acts 1:1–8:1a)

The opening verses of Acts 1 offer in more detail the story of Jesus' ascension to heaven to assume his position on the messianic throne (1:1–11). The apostles then return to Jerusalem where their first order of business is to replace the vacancy left by Judas who, subsequent to his betrayal of Jesus, committed suicide (1:12–26). On the day of the festival of **Pentecost**, Jesus' promise that his followers would receive power from the Holy Spirit (Lk 24:49; Acts 1:8) is fulfilled (2:1–4). Following this empowerment, Peter offers the first public preaching of the gospel message to Jews from all over the world, who had gathered in Jerusalem for the Pentecost festival (2:5–47).

This opening sermon accomplishes two important things. First, it quotes frequently from the scriptures in an effort to show that the death and resurrection of Jesus was, indeed, the fulfillment of these scriptures. Second, Peter calls upon his audience to repent for the execution of Jesus, with the promise that if they do repent, they too will receive the Holy Spirit (v. 38). Significantly, Peter explicitly exhorts his hearers to "save [themselves] from this corrupt generation" (v. 40). The Gospel of Luke had identified "this generation" primarily with the Jewish leadership, which rejected Jesus. Hence, one finds in this exhortation an implied call to the people to separate themselves from their official leadership and to follow their new leader, Jesus the Messiah and his witnesses, the apostles. Significantly, the text reports that 3,000 persons accepted Peter's challenge (v. 41).

Acts 3 offers yet another sermon by Peter, wherein he again calls his audience to repent for having killed the Author of life (vv. 15, 19). Verses 19–21 make explicit that such repentance will result in receiving God's liberation from sin and the eventual return of the Messiah, who will bring to completion the work of restoration that he began during his ministry on earth. Verses 22–26 explicitly identify Jesus with the prophet like Moses, who, Moses had prophesied, God would one day "raise up." Peter asserts that only those of Israel who listen to this new prophet, Jesus, can experience the restorative work of God; for those who do not listen to him "will be utterly rooted out of the people" (v. 23). Verse 25 reiterates the theme of the gospel, that God's liberating salvation was for *all* people. Here Peter quotes from the scriptures the promise God made to Abraham that through his descendants "all the families of the earth shall be blessed." Hence, the first three chapters clearly offer the people of Jerusalem a second opportunity to receive the blessings of God's liberating salvation.

At this point, the Jewish leadership enters the stage and continues its task of opposing the message of the gospel. Acts 4–5 devotes much of its attention to the conflict between the apostles, the new leaders of Israel, and the official Jewish leadership. Significantly, despite the power of the Jewish leadership to arrest and even imprison the apostles, it cannot stop the apostles from preaching the gospel; a proclamation that continues to meet with great success among the larger Jewish populace (4:4; 5:14–16).

Acts 6–7 concludes the witness to Jerusalem on a tragic note, for it reports the arrest and execution of Stephen, one of Jesus' followers. Stephen's accusers charge him with speaking "blasphemous words against Moses and God" (6:11), claiming that he spoke against the law and the Temple (6:13). As though history repeated itself, many of the people turn against Stephen (6:12), much like many of the people of Jerusalem turned against Jesus in the gospel narrative. Stephen addresses the charges against him by offering a summary of Israel's story (Acts 7). This summary tells of an Israel that has consistently been disobedient toward God, rejecting the leaders—especially Moses— whom God had sent to Israel to rescue and liberate them (7:25, 27, 35). The implied comparison with Jesus is obvious: just as Israel rejected their liberator Moses, they have rejected Jesus. Stephen is careful in his summary of Israel's story to note that Aaron, the ancestor of the Aaronic priesthood, led the ancient Israelites into idolatrous worship (7:39–43). Likely, this reminder of Aaron's actions that led to idolatry serves implicitly to condemn the priesthood of Stephen's day. These descendants of Aaron also have led the people in false worship in the Jerusalem Temple, over which they have had responsibility. As a result of Stephen's powerful invective, he is killed.

Hence, the Jerusalem witness offers to the people of the city the opportunity to receive the liberating salvation of God, manifested primarily through their receipt of the Holy Spirit and the forgiveness of sins. While the story ends on a tragic note, with the leadership and many of the people coming together to kill Stephen, Acts 1–7 makes clear that literally thousands of Jerusalem's inhabitants (2:41; 4:4; 5:14; 6:7) heeded the message of repentance and chose to follow Jesus, the prophet like Moses whom God had sent as their ultimate liberator. Much of Israel is, indeed, experiencing the salvation and redemption that God had promised their ancestors. Regrettably, many are refusing the salvation that God offers. Simeon's prophecy of the division of Israel (Lk 2:34) continues to find fulfillment.

The Witness to Judea and Samaria (Acts 8:1b–11:18)

The death of Stephen sparked "a severe persecution . . . against the church in Jerusalem" (8:1), requiring that all the followers of Jesus, except the apostles, flee the city. It seems curious that the apostles would not need to flee the city, but this only reinforces Luke's idea that they are the *true* leaders of God's restored people. As Luke narrates the story, the flight of the followers from Jerusalem serves the larger purpose of advancing the message of the gospel, for those who fled "went from place to place, proclaiming the word" (8:4).

Acts 8 narrates the exploits of Philip, one of the associates of Stephen (cf. 6:5). Philip goes to the region of Samaria and proclaims the message of God's salvation, offering not only the message of liberation, but also releasing people from demonic possession and sickness (8:4–13). When word of Philip's success reaches the apostles as Jerusalem, Peter and John go to Samaria where they lay hands on the Samaritans (vv. 14–25), whereupon they too receive the Holy Spirit (v. 17). "An angel of the Lord" (v. 26) directs Philip to head south, toward Gaza, where he leads an Ethiopian eunuch to be baptized and receive God's salvation (vv. 27–40). This offers further testimony that God's salvation for all people, prophesied in the scriptures, is achieving realization. Isaiah 56:3–5 looked forward to the day when foreigners and eunuchs would be welcomed among God's people. With the salvation of this eunuch from a foreign land, this scripture finds its fulfillment.

Acts 9:1–30 narrates in some detail how Saul, first introduced at Stephen's execution (8:1a), persecutes the church. Not surprisingly, he operates as an agent of the **Sanhedrin**, the "official" ruling body of the Jews bent on putting an end to the mission of Jesus' followers. On his way to Damascus to round up some disciples of Jesus and bring them back to Jerusalem, Saul has an encounter with the resurrected Jesus, who calls Saul to a new mission. Rather than oppose Jesus and his church, Saul is to be "an instrument . . . to bring [Jesus'] name before Gentiles and kings and before the people of Israel" (v. 15). Saul immediately becomes a loyal follower of Jesus, preaching the gospel in Damascus, from which he eventually flees, for now *he* is persecuted. Saul returns to Jerusalem where the church eventually accepts him as a true follower.

Luke offers a brief transitional statement, noting that the church was experiencing success throughout the regions of Judea, Galilee, and Samaria (9:31). He then redirects attention to Peter (9:32–11:18). First, he describes briefly the travels of Peter to Lydda and Joppa, where Peter manifests the liberating power of God through a miracle of healing and even a resuscitation (9:32–43). Then, Luke offers a detailed description of Peter's conversion of the gentile Cornelius and his household (10:1–48). This event is most significant, for with this conversion of a gentile by Peter, the leader of the apostles, the stage is now set for the next phase of the church's mission to the ends of the earth. Readers see how God directs the action, providing visionary experiences to both Cornelius and Peter (vv. 3, 9–16). As Peter is preaching the gospel to Cornelius and his household, the Holy Spirit comes upon them, just as the Spirit came upon the initial followers of Jesus in Acts 2 (vv. 44–47). Peter can only conclude that God has, indeed, offered the gentiles the same liberating salvation that he has offered the Jews.

When Peter returns to Jerusalem, he initially encounters opposition from the church there for having associated with gentiles (11:1–18). But when Peter shares his experience, and most especially when he reports that God gave to the gentiles the Holy Spirit, resistance crumbles: "When they heard this they were silenced. And they praised God saying, 'Then God has given even to the Gentiles the repentance that leads to life'" (v. 18). With this affirmation, the witness to the ends of the earth can begin in earnest.

The Witness to the Ends of the Earth (Acts 11:19–28:31)

The sheer size of this section indicates the importance of this part of the story. The offering of God's salvation to Jews of the Diaspora and the gentiles who inhabit the larger world can now bring to realization the initial prophecy of Simeon that Jesus brings God's salvation both to Israel and the gentiles (Lk 2:32). While Peter does not exit the stage entirely, Luke focuses attention primarily on Saul, also known as Paul, as the main character who serves as Jesus' instrument to preach the gospel both to Israel and the gentiles, all in fulfillment of the mission Jesus assigned to Saul/Paul in Acts 9:15.

Christianity Spreads to Antioch of Syria (Acts 11:19–12:25). With Peter and the Jerusalem church now having affirmed the mission to the gentiles, Luke can report the success of the gospel in the city of Antioch in **Syria**, a major urban center of that region (11:19–25). Yet, Luke does not want readers to conclude that Christianity leaves Jerusalem behind. Hence, he narrates how the church at Antioch sent famine relief to the Jerusalem church through Saul and another disciple, Barnabas (11:27–29). In this larger context, Luke reminds readers that opposition to Jesus' followers in Jerusalem is still a matter of concern, as he describes how Herod Agrippa executed James, one of the apostles, and imprisoned Peter (12:1–23). Yet the message of the gospel cannot be thwarted, for "the word of God continued to advance and gain adherents" (v. 25).

Paul's First Missionary Journey (Acts 13–14). The church of Antioch, under the explicit direction of the Holy Spirit, commissions Saul and Barnabas to preach the gospel throughout the region of Asia Minor. Saul visits the synagogues, preaching both to the Jews and the gentile "God-fearers." Luke gives focused attention to Paul's sermon preached at Antioch of Pisidia (13:13–52). Similar to Peter's first sermon in Acts 2, Paul outlines how Jesus fulfills the hopes of the Jewish scriptures. Response to Paul's sermon reveals how the division of Israel continues, for while "many Jews and devout converts to Judaism followed Paul" (v. 43), many Jews on the following week opposed Paul (vv. 44–45). Luke specifically states that "as many [gentiles] as had been destined for eternal life became believers" (v. 48). The incident at Antioch of Pisidia sets a pattern for the Lukan narrative, as 14:1–2 makes clear: "The same thing occurred in Iconium, where Paul and Barnabas went into the Jewish synagogue and spoke in such a way that a great number of both Jews and Gentiles became believers. But the unbelieving Jews stirred up the Gentiles and poisoned their minds against the brothers." The first journey concludes with Paul and Barnabas returning to Antioch of Syria where they "related all that God had done with them, and how he had opened a door of faith for the Gentiles" (14:27).

The Council of Jerusalem (Acts 15:1–35). The success of Paul among the gentiles had raised the question of whether gentiles had to become circumcised and keep the law of Moses— that is, become **proselytes**—in order to truly become followers of Jesus and, hence, be saved (vv. 1–5). The meeting in Jerusalem settled the issue with James, the brother of Jesus (though Luke never so explicitly identifies him as such), who had assumed leadership of the Jerusalem church,

According to Acts 18:12–17, Paul was brought before Gallio, the proconsul of Achaia. Shown in the foreground are the ruins of the seat of judgment of ancient Corinth. (Courtesy of Larry McKinney)

declaring that gentiles did not have to be circumcised, though they were to obey the most minimal features of the Jewish law (vv. 19–21).

Paul's Second Missionary Journey (Acts 15:36–18:22). Paul decides to revisit the churches established during the first journey (15:36). Yet Paul not only visits churches in Asia Minor. Obedient to a visionary experience, he presses on across the Aegean Sea into Macedonia, signaling the entry of the gospel into Europe (16:9–10). Typically, Paul preaches to both Jews and gentiles in fulfillment of his mission (cf. 9:15). The pattern of the division of Israel continues, in that some Jews accept the gospel (e.g., 17:4, 11–12), while others oppose Paul (e.g., 17:5, 13). This mission takes Paul to some major urban centers such as Philippi (16:11–40), Thessalonica (17:1–10), Athens (17:16–34), and Corinth (18:1–17). At the conclusion of the journey, Paul makes a brief stop in Jerusalem, then returns to Antioch of Syria (18:22).

Paul's Third Missionary Journey (Acts 18:23–21:16). Paul begins this journey with an extended stay in Ephesus, again preaching in the synagogue (19:1–41). Paul then moved on to Macedonia and Greece. Meeting strong resistance from the Jews in Greece (20:1–3), Paul, wanting to return to Jerusalem, heads east. After a brief stay in Troas of Asia Minor (20:5–16), Paul gathers the church leaders of Ephesus in Miletus and there offers something of a farewell address (20:17–35), passing the mantle of leadership on to the elders and overseers (vv. 17, 28) of the church, exhorting them to be on guard against wolves who, in the future, would attempt to distort the truth of the gospel (vv. 29–30). His farewell to the church complete, Paul then sets sail for Jerusalem, making a brief layover in Caesarea (20:36–21:16).

Paul's Trials in Jerusalem and Caesarea (Acts 21:17–26:32). Paul's return to Jerusalem is fraught with conflict. Just as Jesus and the apostles encountered resistance from the Jewish leadership and some of the people in Jerusalem, so too would Paul. The trouble begins when certain Jews from Asia, who happened to be in Jerusalem, accused Paul of bringing gentiles into the Temple (21:27–28). The charge is false, but it contributes to a pattern that the careful reader can discern in Acts.

Throughout the Acts narrative, opposition to Paul is instigated by Jews who oppose the gentiles' acceptance of God's liberating salvation (see 13:45; 17:5, 12–13). Here again, in Acts 21, it is the thought that non-Jews might have entered the sacred precincts of the Jewish Temple that sparks an outbreak of violence. Careful readers might recall Lk 4:16–30, where Jesus is at first warmly received by the synagogue audience in Nazareth *until he speaks of God's concern for non-Jewish people.* The reader may suspect that herein lies a crucial issue for Luke. Luke has pressed the argument that God offers his salvation both to Jews and gentiles. He has made equally clear that too often Jewish characters in his narrative are resistant to this divine agenda. The people's reaction to Paul's speech in defense of his position seems to confirm this (22:1–21). Paul affirms his loyalty to his Jewish heritage, but explains that he was changed after he had his encounter with the resurrected Jesus. The people of Jerusalem seem to listen attentively to Paul until he tells of a vision that he had on one occasion in the Temple, in the context of which Jesus said to Paul, "Go, for I will send you far away to the Gentiles" (v. 21). Luke states, "Up to this point they listened to Paul, but then they shouted, 'Away with such a fellow from the earth! For he should not be allowed to live'" (v. 22). Though Luke reminds readers that there are thousands and thousands of Jews living in Jerusalem who are faithful followers of Jesus (21:20), the bulk of the population has chosen not to separate itself from "this generation" and to follow Jesus as their Messiah.

From this point on, Paul meets with continued threats against his life as the Jews of Jerusalem and their official leadership try to kill him (23:12–15; 25:3). Paul, in the protective custody of the Roman forces, goes through a number of legal hearings before the Jewish Sanhedrin (23:1–10), the Roman appointed governors, and even Agrippa II (24:1–26:32). Throughout all of Paul's defense speeches before the people, the Jewish leadership, and the Roman governors and Agrippa II, he denies that he is disloyal to his own Jewish heritage (e.g., 22:3; 23:6; 24:12, 16–17; 25:8). His only crime is that he believes that in Jesus God's promises as revealed in the scriptures are finding their fulfillment (24:14–15, 21). Believing that he cannot get a fair hearing in the region, Paul appeals his case to the Roman emperor (25:11–12).

Paul Journeys to Rome (Acts 27–28). Luke-Acts ends as Paul takes the gospel to the center of the Roman Empire. Symbolically at least, the gospel has now reached the ends of the earth. After arriving in Rome, Paul has the opportunity to preach the liberating message of God's reign, arguing that in Jesus one finds the fulfillment of the hopes of the Jewish scriptures (28:23, 31). With his proclamation, the division of Israel continues, for "some were convinced by what he said, while others refused to believe" (28:24). Luke ends his narrative on an ominous note regarding Israel, as he depicts Paul quoting from Isaiah to the effect that much of Israel is still burdened by hardness of heart and spiritual blindness (28:26–27, quoting Isa 6:9–10). In the future, the focus of the gospel's proclamation will be the gentiles (28:28).

Excursus
Reading the New Testament Narratives
for Historical Information
A Case Study: The Birth of Jesus

Throughout Luke-Acts, the narrator offers an abundance of historical clues that should provide scholars with helpful information to reconstruct the historical social text behind the narrative. He reports that John was conceived in the days of Herod (Lk 1:5), and that Jesus was conceived just six months later (1:26). He further specifies that Jesus was born in the days when Emperor Augustus decreed "that all the world should be registered. This was the first registration and was taken while Quirinius was governor of Syria" (Lk 2:1–2). Luke states that Jesus began his public ministry "in the fifteenth year of the reign of Emperor Tiberius" (Lk 3:1), when "Jesus was about thirty years old" (Lk 3:23).

The Acts of the Apostles also offers numerous historical clues. Paul and Barnabas journey to Jerusalem to deliver relief in response to a worldwide famine (11:27–30). Acts implies that this famine relief journey to Jerusalem occurred around the time of the death of Herod Agrippa I, since Luke speaks of that death in the context of his narration of the journey that Paul and Barnabas made to Jerusalem (Acts 12:20–23). Acts 18 refers to two specific historical events that should help scholars date the time of Paul's stay in Corinth. Acts 18:1–2 indicates that Paul arrived in Corinth around the same time that Emperor "Claudius had ordered all Jews to leave Rome." Acts 18 also states that while Paul was in Corinth, "Gallio was the proconsul of Achaia" (v.12). Finally, Acts mentions two specific governors of Judea, before whom Paul had legal hearings: Felix (Acts 23:24 and other texts) and Festus (Acts 24:27 and other texts). Student readers may wonder, then, why, with so many clues, NT historians cannot with more confidence offer a solid reconstruction of early Christian history and chronology.

The following case study will guide students through some of the intricacies involved in attempting to reconstruct a chronology of NT events. The following study does not attempt to resolve the historical dilemmas. It will attempt to lead students to see why reconstructing the history and chronology of Jesus and his followers is more complex than merely reading the literary text and taking what it says at face value.

As noted above, Luke offers two important historical clues for dating Jesus' birth. First, he indicates that the conception of John occurred during the days of King Herod (Lk 1:5). He then reports that Mary conceived six months later (1:26). This allows the conclusion that Jesus would have been born either during Herod's reign or, at most, shortly after his death. Ancient sources allow historians confidently to date the year of Herod's death to 4 BCE. It should be noted that Matthew's gospel is quite explicit that Jesus was born while Herod was still alive (Matt 2:1), placing Jesus' birth in 4 BCE, at the latest. Further, Matthew implies that Herod did not die until at least a couple of years after Jesus' birth (Matt 2:16, 19), pushing the date of Jesus' birth back to ca. 6 or 7 BCE.

Second, Luke reports that Jesus was born during the worldwide registration ordered by Augustus "while Quirinius was the governor of Syria" (2:1–2). The term Luke employs that the NRSV translates as "registration" denotes a registration for the purpose of paying taxes. The records of ancient historians, such as the Jewish historian **Josephus** and the Roman historian

Tacitus, allow for a rather thorough accounting of Quirinius' career as well as a good reckoning of those who governed Syria in the closing year's of Herod's reign. The governor of Syria from 10/9 BCE until 7/6 BCE was Sentrus Saturninus. He was succeeded by Quinctilius Varus, who governed from 7/6 BCE until 4 BCE, serving a few months beyond Herod's death. Quirinius did not become the governor of Syria until 6 CE. One can immediately see the problem. Not only was Quirinius not the governor of Syria in the final days of Herod, he did not even assume this office until ten years after Herod's death. Clearly, Jesus could not have been born in or before 4 BCE (the last years of Herod) *and* also during the governorship of Quirinius, which did not begin until at least ten years later.

There are other problems. Luke states that Jesus' family had to journey to Bethlehem, the ancestral home of Joseph, to participate in the worldwide tax registration that Augustus had ordered. Ancient annals offer no indication that Augustus ordered a *worldwide* registration. To be sure, the Roman government regularly oversaw regional or provincial registrations in order to secure population and property records for taxation. But there is simply no evidence, aside from Luke's passing comment, that a worldwide registration was conducted. Furthermore, it was Roman practice to require people to register for taxes where they actually lived, worked, and held property, not to return to their ancestral home for such a registration. Such a massive relocation of the population, requiring all the people of a region or province—not to mention the whole Empire!—to return to their ancestral home, would have created social and economic chaos. Jesus' parents were from Nazareth (Lk 1:26; 2:4, 39, 51); hence, it was in Nazareth that they would have registered for taxes, not in Bethlehem.

Finally, Quirinius did oversee a tax registration while he was the Syrian governor. When Herod's son Archaleus was deposed in 6 CE (see Chap. 9), his territory came under direct Roman administration. It was in this context that Quirinius conducted the tax registration. However, this registration involved only the territory that had formerly been ruled by Archaleus. The hometown of Jesus' family was Nazareth, which was situated in the region of Galilee. Galilee was still under the rule of another of Herod's sons, Herod Antipas. Jesus' parents and other residents of Galilee would not, therefore, have been affected by Quirinius' registration.

So, when was Jesus born? Many scholars believe that notices in both Matthew and Luke that date the birth of Jesus toward the end of Herod's reign are more reliable than locating Jesus' birth at the time of Quirinius' governorship. Assuming the Two-Source Hypothesis, Matthew and Luke are independent of one another and since these independent witnesses both date Jesus' birth toward the end of Herod's reign, that data should be taken seriously. But this requires that one acknowledge that Luke is mistaken to associate the birth of Jesus with the tax registration under Quirinius. Some have attempted to argue that Quirinius held the office toward the end of Herod's life and then held the office again ten years later, after Archaleus was deposed. Such arguments are based on inscriptional evidence that alludes to Quirinius. But even if one could establish this (and most historians are not persuaded by these arguments), one is still left with the other problems noted, namely, the worldwide census and the requirement that Joseph return to Bethlehem. Further, this attempted solution only raises another problem, for it proposes that Quirinius, during his supposed first tenure as governor, oversaw a tax registration within the boundaries of Herod's kingdom. While Herod answered ultimately to Rome, it would have been inconsistent with Roman policy to have had the governor of one province (Syria) oversee the tax registration within the territory of Herod's kingdom.

Once one acknowledges Luke's historical confusion, believing that Herod was King of Judea and Quirinius was governor of Syria at the same time, one must regard Lukan historical notifications with caution. One cannot simply read his narrative at face value, assuming that all chronological and historical notices are accurate. Consequently, reconstructing a chronology of Jesus' life and a basic outline of the history of earliest Christianity must be tentative. Students should note, as they study the table below, that dating events of the early church actually revolves around dating key events in Paul's life, about whom scholars have considerable information. With such cautionary statements in mind, the following table offers an approximate chronology of Jesus' life and the history of his followers.

Conclusion

While Luke offers a number of historical markers, his primary purpose is not to provide a thorough chronology or history of either Jesus or his followers. Thus, one must employ Luke, as well as other gospel narratives, with critical caution when reconstructing history. Even if one interprets the We Passages to indicate that Luke was an occasional companion of Paul and eyewitness to some events, he was present only for a very limited number of these events. He relied on other sources for his narrative, sources that he employed to construct a narrative portrait of the significance of Jesus and the movement he began.

Luke's narrative portrait takes readers from the births of Jesus and John to the proclamation of the gospel message in Rome itself. Luke has tried to show through his narrative that Jesus is the fulfillment of Jewish hopes of liberation and salvation. Such liberation comes primarily in the release that God offers from sickness, Satan, and sin. Many within Israel accept the liberating reign of God that has come in Jesus. They have received forgiveness and the Holy Spirit, the latter being the sure sign that they are part of God's restored people. Yet many within Israel do not accept God's liberating reign. These Jews, Luke appears to believe, have been rooted out of the people of God for they have followed the way of "this generation" in rejecting God's offer of salvation, even as did many of their ancestors who rejected Moses and the other prophets whom God sent to them. But Luke is equally clear that this liberating salvation of God is for all people, gentiles as well as Jews. While the gospel narrative offered clear hints and foreshadowings of this universal feature of God's salvation, the narrative of Acts brings to realization the offering of salvation to non-Jewish people. God has brought to fulfillment the words spoken by Simeon as he first laid eyes on Jesus: "My eyes have seen your salvation, which you have prepared in the presence of all peoples, a light for revelation to the Gentiles and for glory to your people Israel" (Lk 2:30–32).

The narrative of Luke-Acts often touches bases with the "smaller stories" that Part Two analyzed (the law, the prophets, the Temple and priesthood, kingship, and the people). Luke insists that Jesus is the fulfillment of "the law and the prophets." Further, he portrays Jesus as a prophet, more specifically, the prophet like Moses, whom Moses prophesied God would raise up. The opening of the gospel at the Temple, important prophetic announcements regarding Jesus when his parents took him to the Temple, Jesus' final teaching of Israel at the Temple, and the conflict between Jesus and his followers and the official Jewish leadership, including the Sanhedrin and priesthood, all serve to connect the story of Jesus and his followers with the story of the Temple. Jesus' identity as the Messiah, who fulfills the promises God made to David, as well as Jesus'

Table 10.2

A Chronology of Jesus and the Early Church (Paul)

Date Ranges	Event	Explanation
7–4 BCE	Birth of Jesus of Nazareth	Both Matthew and Luke, independently of one another, date Jesus' birth toward the end of the reign of Herod the Great. Matthew implies that Jesus was actually born a couple of years before Herod died.
28/29 CE	Jesus' public ministry begins	Luke 3:1 states that Jesus began his ministry in the fifteenth year of the reign of Emperor Tiberius (14–37 CE).
30 CE	Death of Jesus	The Synoptic Gospels offer no specific indication of the length of Jesus' ministry. John's gospel indicates a ministry of two, possibly three, years, if one can accept as historically reliable this gospel's record of Jesus' frequent trips to Jerusalem during various Jewish festivals.
30–33 CE	Early period of the Jerusalem church	Assuming the accuracy of Acts 1–8, these events must occur prior to the time of Paul's call.
33 CE	Call of Paul	Dating Paul's call requires that one work backwards from dates that one can ascertain with more assurance, such as Paul's work in Corinth (see below).
36 CE	Paul visits Jerusalem	Acts 9:23–26 is very imprecise regarding the time-span between Paul's call and his first trip to Jerusalem. Yet Paul says in Gal 2:18 that he did not visit Jerusalem until three years after his call, a trip to Arabia, and his return to Damascus. (Acts makes no mention of these last two events.)
33–47/50 CE	Expansion of Christianity into Judea, northern Syria, and Asia Minor	Events of Acts 10–14 would be placed between the call of Paul (33 CE) and Paul's second trip to Jerusalem.
47 or 50 CE	Paul visits Jerusalem a second time. The council meeting of Acts 15	Paul says in Gal 2:1 that he returned to Jerusalem "after fourteen years." But does he mean fourteen years after the first visit (36 CE) or after his call experience (33 CE)? Scholars are not sure. Most scholars equate this second visit with the meeting described in Acts 15. That creates a problem, however, for Luke reports that Paul visited Jerusalem a second time sometime around the death of Herod Agrippa I (44 CE; Acts 11:27–12:23). But it is very difficult to have Paul visiting Jerusalem ca. 44 CE, even fourteen years after his call, unless one pushes the date of Paul's call back to 30 CE. Many historians believe that Luke is confused in his report that Paul visited Jerusalem around the time of Herod Agrippa's death.

Date Ranges	Event	Explanation
47/50 to 58 CE	Paul's missionary travels	The travels of Paul narrated in Acts 16–20 would fall into this period, after the council meeting of Acts 15 and before Paul's final trip to Jerusalem.
51 CE	Paul in Corinth	Acts 18:12 indicates that Paul was in Corinth when Gallio was proconsul. Roman records allow historians to date the likely tenure of Gallio from the spring of 51 to the autumn of 52 CE. This provides a touchstone date around which to date other events.
58 CE	Paul returns to Jerusalem, where he is arrested and imprisoned	Assuming the reliability of the reports in Acts regarding Paul's imprisonment under Felix (52–60 CE) and Festus (60–62 CE), Paul arrived in Jerusalem ca. 58 CE, given that Acts 24:27 implies that Paul was imprisoned in Caesarea during the last two years of Felix's reign. Paul's letters confirm that he was planning a trip to Jerusalem (e.g., Rom 15:25).
Fall 60 CE	Paul leaves for Rome	Acts 26 implies that it was not long after Festus assumed leadership that Paul left for Rome. Acts 27:9, with the reference to the Fast (the Day of Atonement), indicates that the voyage began in the autumn.
Early 61 CE	Paul arrives in Rome	Acts 27:1–28:14 states that the voyage to Rome took place over the winter season. The voyage was interrupted by a shipwreck that required the crew and prisoners to holdover on Malta for the winter.
61–63	Paul's stay in Rome	Acts ends with reference to Paul's preaching in Rome for two years, offering no word on the outcome of Paul's trial. Later church traditions asserted that Paul was released and continued his missionary work. He was then martyred during Emperor Nero's persecution of Christians.

announcement of the "good news" of God's kingdom, provides a connection with the story of kingship. And finally, Luke's story of the division of the people of Israel and the incorporation of the gentiles into the circle of God's blessings have direct connections with the biblical story of the people. Luke's narrative shows that the NT assumes, builds on, and rereads the significant stories of the Jewish scriptures. Part Four will now explore how the NT continued the work of rereading the sacred traditions of Israel and its scriptures.

For Further Reading

Introducing Luke-Acts (All immediately below are recommended for beginning students.)

Brown, R. E. *An Introduction to the New Testament.* New York: Doubleday, 1997. Chapters 9–10. (Includes thorough bibliography.)

Marshall, I. H. *Luke: Historian and Theologian.* Grand Rapids, MI: Zondervan, 1971.

Powell, M. A. *What Are They Saying about Acts?* New York: Paulist, 1991.

———. *What Are They Saying about Luke?* New York: Paulist, 1989.

"The Sources behind the New Testament Narratives"

Bellinzoni, A. J. *The Two-Source Hypothesis: A Critical Appraisal.* Macon, GA: Mercer University Press, 1985.

Dupont, J. *The Sources of Acts: The Present Position.* New York: Herder and Herder, 1964.

Farmer, W. R. *The Synoptic Problem.* 2nd Ed. Dillsboro, NC: Western North Carolina, 1976. (Advances Two-Gospel Hypothesis.)

Stein, R. *The Synoptic Problem.* Grand Rapids, MI: Baker, 1987. Advances Two-Source Hypothesis. (*Recommended for beginning students.*)

"The New Testament Narratives as Sources for the History of Jesus and the Early Church"

Aune, D. E. *The New Testament in Its Literary Environment.* Philadelphia: Westminster, 1987. Chapters 1–4. (*Recommended for beginning students.*)

Burridge, R. A. *What Are the Gospels? A Comparison with Graeco-Roman Biography.* SNTSMS, 70. Cambridge: Cambridge University Press, 1992.

Johnson, L. T. *The Real Jesus: The Misguided Quest for the Historical Jesus and the Truth of the Traditional Gospels.* San Francisco: HarperCollins, 1995.

Winter, B. A., et. al., Eds. *The Book of Acts in Its First Century Setting.* 6 Volumes. Grand Rapids, MI: Eerdmans, 1993–1997. (Especially Vol. 1.)

Luke's Story of Jesus: The Gospel of Luke (Commentaries)

Fitzmyer, J. A. *Luke.* AB 28/28A. Garden City, NY: Doubleday, 1981, 1985.

Johnson, L. T. *The Gospel of Luke.* SacPag 3. Collegeville, MN: Glazier/Liturgical Press, 1991.

Stein, R. H. *Luke.* NAC 24. Nashville, TN: Broadman, 1992. (*Recommended for beginning students.*)

Tannehill, R. C. *The Narrative Unity of Luke-Acts.* 2 Volumes. Volume 1: *The Gospel according to Luke.* Minneapolis, MN: Fortress, 1986.

The Acts of the Apostles (Commentaries)

Conzelmann, H. *Acts of the Apostles.* Hermeneia. Philadelphia: Fortress, 1987.

Johnson, L. T. *Acts of the Apostles.* SacPag 5. Collegeville, MN: Glazier/Liturgical Press, 1992.

Polhill, J. B. *Acts.* NAC 26. Nashville, TN: Broadman, 1992. (*Recommended for beginning students.*)

Tannehill, R. C. *The Narrative Unity of Luke-Acts.* 2 Volumes. Volume 2: *The Acts of the Apostles.* Minneapolis, MN: Fortress, 1990.

"Excursus: The Birth of Jesus"

Brown, R. E. *The Birth of the Messiah: A Commentary on the Infancy Narratives of Matthew and Luke.* Garden City, NY: Doubleday, 1979. Pp. 547–556. (*Recommended for beginning students.*)

Schürer, E. *The History of the Jewish People in the Age of Jesus Christ (175 BC–AD135).* Revised and Edited by G. Vermes and F. Millar. 3 Volumes. Edinburgh: T & T Clark, 1973–1987. Volume 1: 399–427.

Special Studies in Luke-Acts

Below are special studies of issues and themes that have influenced the reading of the Lukan narrative presented in this chapter.

Chance, J. B. *Jerusalem, the Temple, and the New Age in Luke-Acts.* Macon, GA: Mercer University Press, 1988.

Garrett, S. *The Demise of the Devil: Magic and the Demonic in Luke's Writings.* Minneapolis, MN: Fortress, 1989.

Jervell, J. *Luke and the People of God: A New Look at Luke-Acts.* Minneapolis, MN: Augsburg, 1972.

Juel, D. *Luke-Acts: The Promise of History.* Atlanta, GA: John Knox, 1983. (*Recommended for beginning students.*)

Tiede, D. L. *Prophecy and History in Luke-Acts.* Philadelphia: Fortress, 1980.

Tyson, J. D. and Parsons, M., editors. *Luke-Acts and the Jewish People: Eight Critical Perspectives.* Minneapolis, MN: Augsburg, 1988.

Tyson, J. D. *Images of Judaism in Luke-Acts.* Columbia, SC: University of South Carolina Press, 1992.

PART FOUR

The
Revisitation
of
Israel's Traditions
in the
New Testament

CHAPTER ELEVEN

Rereading the Story of Kingship

Introduction

Review

Chapter 10 introduced readers to two features of the story of kingship. Central to Jesus' message and ministry was the kingdom of God. First, the reign of God brought the longed-for liberation both to Jews and gentiles. Central to this liberation was forgiveness of sins. Second, Chapter 10 introduced Jesus as the Messiah who fulfills the promises made to King David that one of his descendants would rule forever over Israel.

Preview

This chapter will examine in more detail how selected NT texts reread the story of kingship. First, Matthew 13 is viewed with an eye to how Jesus used the parable to talk about the liberating kingship of God. Second, Mark's passion narrative is explored to illustrate how one Christian reread the story of kingship in light of Jesus the Messiah's execution. Finally, a close reading of 1 Corinthians 15 will show how Paul spoke of the coming reign of God and the role that Jesus played in God's triumphant and liberating reign.

"The Kingdom of God is Like . . ."
Speaking in Parables
Matthew 13; Compare Mark 4

Learning Goals

- To understand the meaning and use of the parable in the teachings of Jesus.
- To learn essential knowledge about the extra-canonical literary text, the Gospel of Thomas.
- To understand how Jesus could reread his own scriptural traditions in order to talk about the kingdom of God.
- To understand how followers of Jesus could reread inherited traditions of Jesus' parables in order to apply Jesus' message to their own social texts.

Guiding Study Exercises

1) Offer a concise definition of *parable,* showing awareness of the Greek word from which it comes.
2) Summarize how Matthew has reread Mark 4 and identify the key issues that such a rereading of Mark allows Jesus' parables to address.
3) Identify the Gospel of Thomas.
4) Write two paragraphs describing how Jesus reread various scriptural portrayals of kingdoms in order to present his distinctive portrayal of "the kingdom of God."
5) Focusing on the parable of The Mustard Seed, describe how subsequent interpreters of Jesus' parable reread this parable and offer suggestions as to how one might explain these rereadings.

"Hear then the Parable . . ."

So Jesus says to his **disciples** in Matt 13:18 as he begins to interpret for them the meaning of the **parable** of the sower (Matt 13:3–8). The reader encounters seven parables of Jesus in this chapter: The Sower (13:3–8), The Weeds (13:24–29), The Mustard Seed (13:31–32), The Yeast (13:33), The Hidden Treasure (13:44), The Pearl (13:45–46), and The Net (13:47–50). There are also some interludes where Jesus talks to his disciples about parables. In one instance he explains why he uses parables (13:10–17). In two instances he explicitly interprets the parables (13:18–23, 36–43). There is a brief interlude in 13:34–35 as Matthew pauses to tell the reader that Jesus' use of parables fulfills scripture. Finally, there is a concluding comment where Jesus asks for assurance that his followers (including the readers) will understand the parables (13:51–53). The concluding comment is particularly important for it invites the disciples and readers to seek out the meaning of the parables.

Clearly, parables invite interpretation; it is part of the very **genre**. The Greek word *parabole* literally means "to lay alongside." The parables presented in Matthew 13 illustrate this simple definition: Jesus takes the phrase "the kingdom of heaven"[1] and in a literary sense "lays it alongside" a story about a sower, or a field of wheat and weeds, or a mustard seed, or finding a hidden treasure. As stories of comparison, parables then function as extended metaphors or similes. The kingdom of God is not literally a mustard seed planted in a field; it is *like* a mustard seed planted in a field.

Parables as metaphors and similes invite interpretation. Consequently, Matthew did not merely regurgitate the parables of Jesus. He *interpreted* them. For example, most scholars believe that Matthew inherited the basic structure of Matthew 13 from Mark 4.[2] Table 11.1 shows the

---

A Closer Look: Parables. Parables are not unique to the NT. Aristotle spoke of parables as realistic fictional stories that made comparisons. The Hebrew Bible also refers to parables (*masal*), but the term is used to denote not only short narratives but also proverbs and allegories. The comparative nature of parables invites their hearers/readers to explore multiple levels of meaning. There is the literal surface-level meaning, such as stories about fishers catching fish or a lucky man finding a treasure (see Matthew 13 for examples). Beneath this surface-level meaning is a more complex meaning, which requires interpretation on the part of the hearer/reader. For example, it is regularly left to the reader of the gospels to interpret how the short story of a man finding a treasure is like the kingdom of God. Jewish teachers employed parables, regularly attaching explicit interpretations to their stories. In this regard, Jesus tends to be different than Jewish teachers, for the gospels rarely depict Jesus as explicitly interpreting his own parables. Because the gospels regularly portray Jesus as *not* interpreting his parables, many scholars believe that such explicit interpretations actually represent rereadings of Jesus' parables by his followers—rereadings subsequently attributed to Jesus himself.

For further study, J. D. Crossan. "Parables." *ABD* 5.146–152; P. R. Jones, "Parables," *MDB*, 643–645; R. H. Stein. *An Introduction to the Parables of Jesus.* Philadelphia: Westminster, 1981; P. Perkins. *Hearing the Parables of Jesus.* New York: Paulist, 1981; J. Jeremias. *Rediscovering the Parables.* New York: Scribner's, 1966.

For more advanced study, B. Young. *Jesus and His Jewish Parables: Rediscovering the Roots of Jesus' Teaching.* New York: Paulist 1989; C. W. Hedrick. *Parables as Poetic Fictions: The Creative Voice of Jesus.* Peabody, MA: Hendrickson, 1994.

---

[1]Matthew tends to use the phrase "kingdom of heaven," whereas Mark and Luke use the phrase "kingdom of God." There is no difference in meaning. See J. D. Kingsbury, *The Parables of Jesus in Matthew 13: A Study in Redaction Criticism* (Richmond, VA: John Knox, 1969) 17.

[2]Recall that most scholars believe that the Two-Source Hypothesis best explains the literary relationship between the Synoptic Gospels (Chap. 10).

common overall structure of the two chapters. Matthew, however, has not merely copied Mark. He has *added* parables to the Markan chapter (see rows 6, 10–14) and he has *deleted* some of the material he acquired from Mark (see rows 4–5).

Matthew's Rereading of Mark. While Matthew's structure is similar to Mark's, Matthew rereads the Markan source. By adding certain parables to Mark, Matthew gives a distinctive interpretation to the Markan parables. For example, the parables of The Weeds and The Net, which are added to Mark (see rows 6, 10, and 13), show that Matthew gives attention to the *final judgment* that the kingdom would bring.[3] By adding the parables of The Hidden Treasure and The Pearl (rows 11 and 12), Matthew adds to Mark an emphasis on *seeking* the kingdom and being willing to sacrifice anything necessary to acquire it.

Matthew has not only adapted the overall *structure* of Mark, he has actually altered the sayings of Jesus in order to allow Jesus to say more clearly what Matthew wishes to emphasize. Matthew emphasizes how important it is that Jesus' followers "understand" his parables. Matthew 13:13 incorporates Mark's lone reference to "understanding" from Mk 4:12. However, Matthew then *adds* the word four additional times (see vv. 14, 19, 23, and 51).[4] Hence, Matthew

Table 11.1

Matthew 13 and Mark 4

Matthew 13	Mark 4
1 The Sower (vv. 1–9)	**1** The Sower (vv. 1–9)
2 The Reason for Parables (vv. 10–17)	**2** The Reason for Parables (vv. 10–12)
3 Interpretation of Sower (vv. 18–23)	**3** Interpretation of Sower (vv. 13–20)
4 *Not in Matthew 13*	**4** Hiding the Light (vv. 21–25)
5 *Not in Matthew*	**5** The Secret Growing Seed (vv. 26–29)
6 The Weeds (vv. 24–30)	**6** *Not in Mark*
7 The Mustard Seed (vv. 31–32)	**7** The Mustard Seed (vv. 30–32)
8 The Yeast (v. 33)	**8** *Not in Mark*
9 Jesus' Use of Parables (vv. 34–35)	**9** Jesus' Use of Parables (v. 33–34)
10 Interpretation of The Weeds (vv. 36–43)	**10** *Not in Mark*
11 The Hidden Treasure (v. 44)	**11** *Not in Mark*
12 The Pearl (vv. 45–46)	**12** *Not in Mark*
13 The Net (vv. 47–50)	**13** *Not in Mark*
14 Exhortation to Seek Treasure (vv. 51–52)	**14** *Not in Mark*

[3]"Still, the chief tendency in chapter 13 is to cast Jesus Son of Man into the future role of Judge. In this capacity Jesus will visibly come again in great power at the End of the Age . . . to separate the righteous from the wicked . . ." (Kingsbury, *Parables of Jesus in Matthew 13,* 133).

[4]The Greek word is *suniemi.* Some English translations may not reflect that the same Greek word is used. Both the RSV and NRSV do, however.

has not just heard the parables from Mark. He has heard them with care and critical appropria-tion, adapting the structure and content of his source to allow the words of Jesus to speak as Matthew would think appropriate.

Realization that Matthew viewed the parables of Jesus as sayings to be adopted and adapted allows one to ask how much freedom followers of Jesus employed in preserving and transmitting the sayings of Jesus. Is Jesus' message of the kingdom as it is now presented in the *finished* gospels identical with or even consistent with what Jesus himself may have been trying to convey as he told his parables? The following study of one parable in its differing versions will illustrate how the parables of Jesus underwent transformation in their transmission.

Reading Jesus Rereading the Tradition: The Mustard Seed

Among the ancient sources, both biblical and extra-biblical, there exist four distinct versions of the parable of The Mustard Seed. Study Table 11.2 carefully.

Two introductory matters require explanation. First, it is likely that both Mark *and* **Q** (Luke) contained a version of this parable.[5] Observe that Luke's version of the parable has nu-merous features that are different from Mark's. Luke's version states that the mustard seed be-comes a tree, not a shrub (row 3). Also, Mark speaks of the birds making nests in the *shade* of the shrub, while Luke speaks of birds nesting in the *branches* (row 4). There are enough differences in detail to suggest that Luke had an alternate version of the parable. A comparison with Matthew allows the conclusion that Q provided this alternate version, for both Matthew and Luke refer to the seed becoming a "tree" (row 3) and birds making nests in its "branches" (row 4).

Second, most student readers will not be familiar with the Gospel of Thomas. This gospel, which consists almost entirely of sayings attributed to Jesus, was discovered in 1945, along with a number of other Christian and non-Christian religious texts near an Egyptian town called Nag Hammadi. The document itself dates from middle of the fourth century CE. The document is not the original Gospel of Thomas, but a later copy of a document that was written as early as the first century. Even if one dates its time of composition later, many scholars argue that the Gospel of Thomas represents an *independent* line of tradition of the sayings of Jesus. That is, the author of Thomas[6] did not rely on any of the **canonical** gospels, meaning that Thomas would represent a separate version of the parable.[7] NT scholars, trying to reconstruct what Jesus actually said, in-clude the Gospel of Thomas within their data base. This makes sense, given that scholars want to take into consideration all relevant data.

There are enough differences among the versions to justify asking, "What did Jesus actually say?" What did he intend to convey? Was the seed sown in a garden (Q), a field (Matthew), the ground (Mark), or tilled soil (Thomas)? Did Jesus offer an explicit contrast between the smallness of the mustard seed and the greatness of the shrub or plant (Matthew, Mark, Thomas)? Or did he not mention anything at all about the size of the seed or resulting plant (Q)? Did Jesus speak of the

---

[5]A. D. Jacobson, *The First Gospel: An Introduction to Q* (Sonoma, CA: Polebridge, 1992) 203–205.

[6]Scholars do not believe that Thomas, one of Jesus' disciples, actually wrote this gospel. "Pseudonymous author-ship," where one would write in the name of another, was widely practiced in antiquity.

[7]See C. W. Hedrick, "Thomas, Gospel of," *MDB* 913–914. There is disagreement, however, among NT scholars re-garding Thomas' independence of the Synoptic Gospels. See Chap. 10, n. 9.

Table 11.2

The Mustard Seed (4 Versions)

	Matthew	Mark	Q (Luke)	Thomas
1	The kingdom of heaven is like a grain of mustard seed which a man took and sowed in his field;	The kingdom of God . . . it is like a grain of mustard seed, which when sown upon the ground,	The kingdom of God . . . it is like a grain of mustard seed which a man took and sowed in his garden	The kingdom of heaven . . . it is like a mustard seed, the smallest of all seeds. But when it falls on tilled soil
2	it is the smallest of all seeds,	is the smallest of all the seeds on earth;		[the smallest of all seeds (*see above*)]
3	but when it has grown is the greatest of shrubs and becomes a tree,	yet when it is sown it grows up and becomes the greatest of all shrubs,	and it grew and became a tree,	it produces a great plant
4	 so that the birds of the air come and make nests in its branches.	and puts forth large branches, so that the birds of the air can make nests in its shade.	and the birds of the air made nests in its branches.	and becomes a shelter for birds of the sky

mustard seed becoming a plant or shrub (Mark and Thomas); a tree (Q); or both (Matthew)? Most important, do these variations make any difference with regard to the meaning of the parable?

Scholars who note the variations and are interested in what Jesus of Nazareth was trying to communicate through his telling of parables, believe that it is necessary to reconstruct as closely as possible what he actually said—the ***ipsissima vox*** of Jesus.[8] The balance of this discussion will rely on a reconstruction of the parable of The Mustard Seed offered by Bernard Brandon Scott.[9] He reconstructs the "originating structure" (as he calls it) of the parable as follows:

---

[8]Review Chap. 10, "A Closer Look: Finding the Real Words of Jesus."

[9]B. B. Scott, *Hear Then the Parable: A Commentary on the Parables of Jesus* (Minneapolis, MN: Fortress, 1989).

The grand cedar of Lebanon commonly symbolized stately kingdoms (e.g., Ezek 17:23; 31:3). Jesus' comparison of the kingdom of God with a mustard weed rather than the grand cedar would have created quite a startling image for his original hearers. (Courtesy of Larry McKinney)

[The kingdom of God is] like a grain of mustard seed which a man took and sowed in his garden and it grew and became a great shrub and puts forth large branches so that the birds of heaven make nests in its shade/shelter.[10]

Jesus is up to something by telling a story about a man who plants a mustard seed in a garden. His hearers would immediately have sensed that "there is something wrong with this [word] picture," for this phrase actually offers a macro-level intertext to Jewish law. The Jewish Torah explicitly forbade mixing different kinds of seed in the same field.[11] Based on these scriptural injunctions, the **Rabbis** ruled *quite specifically* that mustard seed was not to be planted in a garden: "Not every kind of seed may be sown in a garden-bed, but any kind of vegetable may be sown

---

[10]*Ibid.,* 373.

[11]Lev 19:19 says, "You shall not sow your field with two kinds of seed." Deut 22:9 offers a similar rule: "You shall not sow your vineyard with a second kind of seed, or the whole yield will have to be forfeited, both the crop that you have sown and the yield of the vineyard itself."

therein. Mustard and small beans are deemed a kind of seed and larger beans a kind of vegetable."[12] Why would Jesus compare the kingdom of God to a man intentionally planting a mustard seed where it did not belong?

Second, the mustard plant grew rampantly. One ancient student of nature commented as follows:

> It grows entirely wild, though it is improved by being transplanted: but . . . when it has once been sown it is scarcely possible to get the place free of it, as the seed when it falls germinates at once.[13]

Adding this information to the fact that Jewish law forbade planting mustard seed in a garden makes the parable more intriguing. Jesus is actually comparing the kingdom of God to a man who intentionally plants in a garden a wild plant—something akin to a weed. The picture is clear: this mustard seed, planted where it should not be in the first place, has the capacity to take over the garden. One interpreter of Jesus' parables, Stephen Patterson, interprets well the implications of Jesus' comparison of the kingdom of God to a mustard seed planted in a garden.

> One should call this the Parable of the Mustard *Weed,* rather than the Mustard Seed. And yet that is what the kingdom is like: it grows from the smallest of seeds to become the most loathsome of weeds. . . . A small thing can be a very large nuisance. Such is the kingdom. . . . It is small, yet insidious, and impossible to control once it has been implanted. It stands to take over, to invade, to change the way things are. . . . This is a subversive kingdom.[14]

Jesus could not help but to provoke some contrasting images in the minds of his original hearers. Who would dare to compare something as grand and glorious as God's kingdom to a weed *illegally* planted in a garden where it would immediately take root and take over? Jesus would seem to be implying, particularly in the larger context of his ministry, that this seed had already been sown. The weed was already beginning to spread, taking over the vegetable patch of people's neatly ordered lives. The invasion of God's reign into the world, while apparently innocuous—after all, what harm can a seed do?—is all-consuming. And the consumption has already begun.

But Jesus is not done teasing his listeners. He speaks of this large, weedy shrub as sprouting large branches in which the birds of the air can make nests and find shelter. The image of a larger shrub would not shock Jesus' hearers, for mustard plants grew to be rather large; some reports say as much as six to eight feet high.[15] What perhaps would have caught the attention of Jesus' hearers is the picture of birds making nests or finding shelter in its shade, for as Table 11.3

---

[12]This statement is found in a portion of the Mishnah, a collection of rabbinic legal interpretations. See Herbert Danby, *The Mishnah* (Oxford: Clarendon Press, 1933) 31.

[13]Pliny, *Natural History,* 29.54.170. Quoted from Scott, *Hear Then the Parable,* 380.

[14]S. J. Patterson, *The Gospel of Thomas and Jesus* (Sonoma, CA: Polebridge Press, 1993) 240.

[15]I. Jacob and W. Jacob, "Flora," *ABD* 2.812.

Table 11.3

Biblical Traditions for The Mustard Seed Parable

Jesus' Parable	Ezekiel 17:23	Ezekiel 31:3, 6	Daniel 4:12
[The kingdom of God is] like a grain of mustard seed which a man took and sowed in his garden and	On the mountain height of Israel I will plant it, in order that it may produce boughs and bear fruit,	Consider Assyria,	
it grew and became a great shrub and puts forth large branches	and become a noble cedar. (see reference below to branches)	a cedar of Lebanon, with fair branches and forest shade, and of great height, its top among the clouds.	The tree grew and became strong, its top reached to heaven, and it was visible to the ends of the whole earth.
so that the birds of heaven make nests in its shade/shelter.	Under it every kind of bird will live; in the shade of its branches will nest winged creatures of every kind.	All the birds of the air made their nests in its boughs; under its branches all the animals of the field gave birth to their young; and in its shade all great nations lived.	Its foliage was beautiful, its fruit abundant, and it provided food for all. The animals of the field found shade under it, the birds of the air nested in its branches, and from it all living beings were fed.

shows, Jesus' reference to "birds" and "making nests" in "branches" offers yet another macro-level intertext with images from the Jewish scriptures.

Jesus' hearers who were familiar with their scriptural traditions could have noted the intertexts between Jesus' parable and the scriptures, all of which use the image of birds taking refuge in branches and/or shade. In the scriptures, however, these branches are said to be in *trees.* Furthermore, these trees represented *kingdoms,* much in the same way that the mustard shrub of Jesus' parable represented a kingdom, the kingdom of God. In the example from Ezekiel 17, the "noble cedar" is an image for the mighty and restored kingdom of Israel. In the second example from Ezekiel, the great cedar denotes the kingdom of Assyria. In the example from Daniel, the great tree represents Babylon, more specifically the king of Babylon himself, Nebuchadnezzar. Jesus' hearers were quite accustomed to hearing about grand kingdoms, represented by stately trees, in which nations and people, represented by birds and other animals, could find shelter. Jesus also claims that the kingdom of God will be a place where nations and people, represented by birds, can find shelter. But Jesus' vision of God's kingdom does not match up with popular images provided from his Jewish heritage.

For Jesus, the reign of God manifests itself in his proclamation of the "good news" (Lk 4:43) and his offering release from disease, demons, and even sin (Chap. 10). It is a mighty kingdom, binding as it does even the power of Satan (Lk 11:17–23). But this kingdom defies expectations. As this kingdom is planted in the garden and spreads like the obnoxious mustard weed, it provides shelter for "the poor, the crippled, the blind, and the lame" (Lk 14:21). Yet, the mighty kingdoms opposed to Israel, Rome in Jesus' day, do not fall with the dawning of God's kingdom. All evil is not vanquished. The truth is, only those who "have the eyes to see" or "ears to hear" can discern the presence of the kind of kingdom Jesus portrays. There is something different about the kingdom that Jesus proclaims and brings. It is the kingdom for which his Jewish contemporaries were looking; hence it is appropriate for Jesus to use images from the scriptures to describe this kingdom of God: a place where birds of the air make nests and find shelter in the shade. Yet there was something very *different* about this kingdom—different from what his listeners were expecting. Thus, Jesus must employ shockingly new images; not a great tree set high on a hill, but a mustard bush—a weed!—planted, quite illegally, in the midst of a garden. Hence, one who wants to receive the liberation that this kingdom offers must be prepared to accept new definitions of kingship and messiahship.

Rereading Jesus. Parables invite interpretation. Jesus' followers interpreted this parable. One can see this by comparing the four different versions that are now extant (Table 11.2). *Just as Jesus reread Jewish tradition to talk about his understanding of the kingdom, his followers reread him as they attempted to make sense of his words for their contemporaries.* For example, Q apparently read the line about the "birds making nests in the shade" as an intertextual echo of the great tree images from the Jewish scriptures. Q then changed the "shrub" of Jesus' parable *back to a tree*! Did the compilers of Q not get the "punch line" of the parable, failing to recognize that Jesus was quite intentionally comparing the kingdom of God to a weedy bush, rather than a stately tree? And why did Matthew change the "garden," which was likely in his Q source, to "field"? Could it be because he was aware of the Jewish laws forbidding the planting of mustard seed in gardens, and those laws permitting the planting of mustard seeds in larger fields?[16] Was Matthew offended at what he read in Q, which suggested that the kingdom of God is like a mustard seed planted *illegally* in a garden plot? Obviously, one cannot know for sure what the motives were for these changes and alterations—these redactions—of the tradition. But **redaction criticism** notes the editorial changes and then, at least, attempts to uncover possible motives for such emendations. Clearly, even if one cannot fully understand these redactional motives, one can see how the Bible itself offers evidence that the early Christians did not merely memorize the traditions they received. They reread these traditions. Jesus reread the biblical traditions about grand

---

[16]This was allowed, since in a larger field the mustard could be kept separate from the other crops. Hence, the law of "not mixing" was not violated. See Scott, *Hear then the Parable,* 383.

cedars representing kingdoms and transformed them into an image of a mustard shrub representing God's kingdom. Q reread Jesus, changing the shrub back into a tree. Matthew reread Q, changing the garden to a field. And each time a reader interprets today, another rereading takes place.

"Are You the Messiah?"
The Markan Passion Narrative
Mark 14–15

Learning Goals

- To understand the problems scholars have in identifying the date of Jesus' crucifixion.
- To understand how Mark has reread scriptural traditions about the Davidic king in light of the fact of Jesus' execution.
- To understand how Mark and non-Christian interpreters of scriptural traditions came to identify the Messiah, the son of man, and the son of God.
- To understand how Mark reread the connections between the king and the Temple that are found in the scriptures.

Guiding Study Exercises

1) Explain why one cannot simply paraphrase the canonical gospels' portrayals of Jesus' crucifixion in order to determine the date of Jesus' execution.

2) How does Jesus' statement that he gives his life "as a ransom for many" serve to reread scriptural traditions about the liberating role of the king?

3) Trace how the author of 2 Esdras has reread Daniel 7 so as to collapse into one figure the Messiah, the son of man, and the son of God. Reflect on how the rereading of 2 Esdras compares with that of Mark.

4) Identify and offer a brief interpretation of key texts in Mark's gospel that serve to redefine the relationship between the king and the Jerusalem Temple.

The Text behind the Text of Mark's Passion Narrative

"Passion" derives from the late Latin word *passion,* meaning "to suffer." Hence, the passion narratives tell the story of Jesus' suffering as he was arrested, tried, and executed. Mark's account of Jesus' passion is found in chapters 14–15 of his gospel.

Authorship, Date, and Sources. Tradition, going back to the early second century CE, ascribes the second gospel to Mark, a companion of Peter (1 Pet 5:13).[17] The gospel itself is anonymous and, thus, many scholars are content to leave the question of authorship unsettled. One must infer a likely date for the text based on **internal evidence**. Frequently, scholars note that Mark 13 gives extensive attention to the issue of the destruction of Jerusalem and the Temple by the Romans (13:1–2, 4, 14) and the bloody Jewish revolt that precipitated the Temple's destruction (vv. 7–8, 17–20).[18] This allows the inference that at the time Mark wrote, the destruction of Jerusalem and the Temple was a significant issue. Hence, most date Mark's composition to around 70 CE, the year the Romans burned the Temple and sacked Jerusalem.

Regarding possible sources employed by Mark, scholars ask whether the evangelist composed his passion narrative on the basis of discrete traditions or made use of a *narrative* that someone composed prior to the composition of the gospel. Many scholars believe that Mark did have access to a narrative that he redacted (reread) to suit his own **theological** ends. However, despite broad agreement on this conclusion, scholars cannot agree as to the precise content of this pre-Markan narrative.[19]

The Date of Jesus' Execution. Exploring the issue of the date of Jesus' execution illustrates again what was regularly noted in the study of the Hebrew Bible: the story *in* the literary text regularly does not match up with the historical social text that stands behind the narrative. "What happened" historically is often different from "what happens" in the narrative world of the literary text.

There is agreement among the canonical gospels that Jesus was **crucified** on Friday, the day of *preparation* for the Jewish **Sabbath** (Matt 27:62; Mk 15:42; Lk 23:54; Jn 19:31). But on what *date* was Jesus executed? Mark's narrative and those of Matthew and Luke, which follow Mark, offer a clear answer to this question. Mark 14:12–16 explicitly states that Jesus commanded his disciples to make preparations for the celebration of the Jewish **Passover** feast. Verse 12 even provides a specific chronological reference, stating that it was the day "when the Passover lamb is sacrificed." The date on which the lamb was sacrificed was, by the reckoning of the Jewish calendar, 14 Nisan. In the days of Jesus, the priests sacrificed the Passover lambs at the Temple after the sun began to set, which Jewish legal authorities interpreted to mean after noon, when the sun had reached its highest orb. Thus, on the afternoon of 14 Nisan, Jesus' disciples began preparations for the Passover.

Mark continues his narrative, reporting that when evening came, Jesus gathered with his disciples to eat the Passover meal (14:17–25, note especially v. 14). Since the Jewish calendar begins a new date at sunset, not midnight, it is now 15 Nisan. After the meal, Jesus goes with his

---

[17]The church historian, Eusebius, records a statement from a second-century bishop named Papias that credits Mark, whom he calls "Peter's interpreter," with the second gospel (*Ecclesiastical History,* 3.39.15–16). See R. E. Brown, *An Introduction to the New Testament* (New York: Doubleday, 1997) 158–161.

[18]Chap. 9 offered the historical background to this significant event. Chap. 12 will explore the implications of the Temple's destruction in more detail.

[19]See R. E. Brown, *The Death of the Messiah: From Gethsemene to the Grave,* (2 vols.; New York: Doubleday, 1994) 1.53–57.

A Closer Look: The Last Supper as a Passover Meal. If one follows the Synoptic Gospels and interprets the Last Supper as a Passover meal, one can see how Jesus rereads the significance of this meal. There were four stages to the meal, which was presided over by the head of the family (the *paterfamilias*) or, in the case of Jesus and his followers, the head of the community of disciples. The preliminary course consisted of a blessing, the serving of the first cup of wine, and the eating of herbs and fruit purée. This was followed by the Passover liturgy. Here the *paterfamilias* told the Passover story, in the context of which the *paterfamilias* interpreted the symbolic significance of the elements of the meal. Participants then sang the first part of the Passover hymn, the *hallel* (Ps 113 [or 113–114; this is debated]), and concluded with the second cup of wine. The main meal began with a grace, followed by the distribution and eating of the feast, and concluded with a final grace over the third cup of wine. The ceremony concluded with the singing of the second part of the *'hallel* (Ps 114–118 [or 115–118]) and a final cup of wine.

In the Synoptic portrayal of the Last Supper (Mk 14:22–26; cf. Matt 26:26–30 and Lk 15–20; see also 1 Cor 11:23–26), one finds a greatly abbreviated recounting of the Passover meal, as the writers focus in on the main meal and, most especially, Jesus' rereadings of the significance of the feast as he offers the grace at the beginning and the conclusion of the meal. In the context of the initial grace, Jesus reinterpreted the meaning of the unleavened bread and, as he offered the grace over the third cup of wine, he further reread the significance of the cup. In both instances, he redirected attention to himself and his impending death. Given the whole purpose of the Passover meal—remembering God's liberation of Israel from the bondage of Egypt—Jesus' explicit rereading of the bread and wine with reference to himself served to portray him as the one through whom God's final liberating salvation was to come.

For further study, A very thorough treatment of the Last Supper as a Passover meal may be found in J. Jeremias, *The Eucharistic Words of Jesus.* Philadelphia: Fortress, 1966. Especially pp. 84–88, 218–237.

disciples to the Mount of Olives (14:26), situated just to the east of Jerusalem. There, a delegation from the Jewish authorities arrests Jesus (14:46), and takes him before the high priest, chief priests, elders, and scribes—the **Sanhedrin** (14:53)—who interrogate Jesus (14:60–61) and find him guilty of blasphemy (14:63–64). The following morning (it is still 15 Nisan), the Jewish authorities take Jesus to Pontius Pilate (15:1–2), the Roman governor who eventually sentences Jesus to death (15:15). On that same day, Jesus is executed (15:25, 34–37) and buried (15:42–46).

While there are broad agreements between Mark and John regarding the basic order of events, there is disagreement regarding the *date* of Jesus' execution. First, though John speaks of a last meal, this narrative says nothing to indicate that the meal was a Passover feast. In fact, Jn 13:1 explicitly says that the setting of this meal was *before the festival of Passover,* clearly indicating that this last meal was *not* a Passover meal. Second, according to Jn 18:28, the Jewish leadership refused to enter Pilate's headquarters "so as to avoid ritual defilement and to be able to eat the Passover." This indicates that the Jewish leadership, in contrast to Jesus as presented in Mark, had *not yet* eaten the Passover meal. Third, Jn 19:14 explicitly states that the day on which Jesus was tried before Pilate "was the day of *Preparation for the Passover.*" These three notices from John lead to the conclusion that John's gospel portrays the date of Jesus' arrest, trial, and execution as the day of Preparation for the Passover, or 14 Nisan.

The literary texts of Mark and John present two different portraits of the *date* of Jesus' Passion. Mark dates these events to 15 Nisan; John to 14 Nisan. The narratives agree on main points: Jesus died on the order of the Roman government at the urging of the Jewish leadership around the Passover season. Yet these inconsistencies in the literary texts of Jesus' Passion allow student readers to see that reconstructing the historical social text requires more than merely paraphrasing the literary texts.

There exist many solutions to the discrepancies between Mark and John.[20] Some scholars have argued that different Jewish groups of Jesus' time did not agree on the calendar and, therefore, they celebrated Passover on different days. According to this solution, Jesus and his disciples followed one calendar while the Jewish leadership, following a different calendar, celebrated Passover on a different day. The evidence for this solution, however, is meager, leading most scholars to conclude that theories of different calendars do not offer a satisfactory solution. Other scholars, probably the majority, simply acknowledge that there is confusion in these early Christians' literary texts and that either Mark or John (or both!) are simply confused regarding the actual date of Jesus' execution. As to which gospel, if either, is "right"—this is an ongoing debate in scholarly circles.[21] *The main issues for introductory readers to understand are (a) that the literary text simply does not match up with the historical social text and (b) what the evidence is for this conclusion.*

The Literary Text of Mark's Passion Narrative: The Death of the King

The following discussion will compare various and relevant intertexts relating to kingship, some of which were explored in Part Two of this text. This intertextual reading will allow readers to see how Mark has "reread the story of kingship" as it applied to Jesus, whom he believed to be the Messiah.

Jesus: the Crucified Messiah. It would have been difficult for early Christians to ignore the seemingly embarrassing fact that the one whom they claimed was the Messiah had died the shameful death of crucifixion.[22] Mark's passion narrative offers a glimpse at how one early Christian dealt with this potential embarrassment.

---

[20]See Brown, *Death of the Messiah,* 2.1350–73 for a thorough survey of the problems of dating Jesus' execution and various attempts to solve the riddle of the discrepancies between Mark and John.

[21]Brown, *ibid.,* 2:1356–61 surveys the various strengths and weaknesses of following either Mark's or John's chronology. He concludes that probably the majority of scholars believe John's dating of the crucifixion to be more probable than Mark's.

[22]Not all early Christians so clearly emphasized the death of Jesus. Below, this chapter discusses how the Corinthians seemed to downplay the significance of Jesus' death. Some non-canonical Christian texts even go so far as to deny that Jesus actually died on the cross. See E. Pagels, *The Gnostic Gospels* (New York: Random House, 1979) 70–101.

As Mark tells the story of Jesus' Passion, he emphasizes the idea that Jesus is crucified *because he is the Messiah* and that *through his death, Jesus carries out his messianic mission of liberation.* As Mark tells the story, the high priest asks Jesus: "Are you the Messiah, the Son of the Blessed One?" (Mk 14:61). Jesus responds, "I am; and 'you will see the Son of Man seated at the right hand of Power,' and 'coming with clouds of heaven'" (14:62). Note that according to Mk 14:63–64, Jesus' admission that he is the Messiah is what convicts him before the Jewish authorities.

As Mark proceeds with his narrative, he keeps before the reader the theme of Jesus' kingship. Pilate's initial question to Jesus is "Are you the King of the Jews?" (15:2). As Jesus' trial proceeds, Pilate refers to him twice as "King of the Jews," asking the crowd, gathered together and incited by the Sanhedrin, what they want done with Jesus (15:9, 12). The response is "crucify him" (15:13, 14). The soldiers mock Jesus as "the King of the Jews" (15:16–20) and the official charge against Jesus for which he is crucified is that he is "the King of the Jews" (15:26). Finally, Mark records that the crowd mocks Jesus as "the Messiah, the King of Israel" (15:32). Clearly, as Mark tells the story, Jesus is interrogated, tried, condemned, and executed as "the King of the Jews."

One who has read the whole of the Markan narrative is not surprised that Jesus fulfills his role as the messianic king through suffering, death, and, ultimately, resurrection. Mark has prepared the reader for the passion narrative. As Mark tells his story, Jesus' followers first recognize him as the Messiah in 8:29: "[Jesus] asked them [the disciples], 'But who do you say that I am?' Peter answered him, 'You are the Messiah.'" Immediately after this confession of faith, Mark records the following. "Then he [Jesus] began to teach them that the Son of Man must undergo great suffering, and be rejected by the elders, the chief priests, and the scribes, and be killed, and after three days rise again" (8:31). Note how Mark's Jesus comments on what his messianic role will be: as the son of man he will experience death and resurrection. On two other occasions, Mark's Jesus again defines precisely his role as the son of man in terms of suffering, death, and resurrection (9:31; 10:33–34).

As to *why* Jesus has to die, Mark offers a clue in 10:45: "The Son of Man came not to be served, but to serve, *and to give his life as a ransom for many.*" Chapter 10 spoke of the liberating work of Jesus, manifested in ministry of healing and exorcism that set people free from the corrupting powers of God's nemesis, Satan. It is telling to note that the word translated as "ransom" (*lutron*) in Mk 10:45 derives ultimately from the Greek word *luō,* meaning "to loose." One can immediately see the connotations of liberation in this word. To be sure, *lutron* speaks of a more specific kind of "loosing," one that implies that some kind of price be paid (hence, the use of the English word "ransom"). From Mark's perspective, the death of Jesus is the price to be paid for this "loosing," or setting people free. The liberating work of the kingdom of God, initially manifested in the healings and exorcisms of Jesus, reaches its climax in the death of Jesus. Hence, for Mark the Passion of Jesus is not a fluke, but *the* means by which Jesus acts out his kingly mission of liberation.

The idea that the king served as an instrument of liberation, deliverance, or salvation of the people of God is a familiar one in the Hebrew Bible. One of the early stories of Saul's anointing as king speaks clearly of his liberating work: "You shall anoint him to be ruler over my people Israel. He shall save my people from the hand of the Philistines" (1 Sam 9:16b). The Royal Psalms speak of this work of liberation through the deliverance of God's people from their enemies (Ps

This model of ancient Jerusalem shows Herod's palace in the middle foreground. The Roman governors, such as Pontius Pilate, lived here when visiting Jerusalem. This palace, located on the western edge of ancient Jerusalem, would have been where Jesus of Nazareth was tried and sentenced to be crucified. (Courtesy of Larry McKinney)

2:8–9; 45:5; 110:1–3). The king also plays a liberating role as he gives "deliverance to the needy" (Ps 72:4, 12) and the poor (Ps 72:12), saves the lives of the needy (Ps 72:13), and "from oppression and violence . . . redeems their life" (Ps 72:14).

Christian rereadings of the story of kingship can be understood as the result of numerous intertextual connections. The historical social text of Jesus' execution under the Roman charge that he was "King of the Jews" clearly influenced the earliest Christians whose literary texts now constitute the NT. The literary texts of the Christians' Jewish heritage, texts that portrayed the king as an instrument of God's liberation, also played a role in shaping the portrait of Jesus as an instrument of liberation. The two come together in Mark: through his death as King of the Jews, Jesus performs God's work of setting God's people free.

Messiah, Son of God, and Son of Man. Note again the high priest's question to Jesus and Jesus' response. "Again the high priest asked him, 'Are you the Messiah, the Son of the Blessed One?' Jesus said, 'I am; and "you will see the Son of Man seated at the right and of Power," and "coming with the clouds of heaven"'" (Mk 14:61b-62). Coming together, therefore, are three titles, all of which serve in some way to identify Jesus: Messiah, son of the Blessed One (God), and son of man. How can one explain this collapsing of three titles into a single figure, Jesus? This short text offers an intriguing intertext with the Jewish scriptures.

One can see in Table 11.4 how the Markan text collapses together two texts from separate portions of the scriptures, a Royal Psalm, that in its original context was in reference to the Davidic king, and a vision from the apocalyptic visionary text of Daniel. Jesus' opening remark, "you will see the Son of Man," forms a micro-level intertext with the phrase from Daniel "I saw one like a son of man." The statement that this son of man would be "seated at the right hand of the Power" is an intertext with the line from the Royal Psalm, "sit at my right hand." Finally, Jesus' speaking of this son of man as "coming with the clouds of heaven" provides an intertext with the last line quoted from Daniel. Using these micro-level intertexts, Mark's Jesus has combined biblical images of the son of man (Daniel) and the Davidic king (Psalm 110) into one another, and applied both to himself, the son of the Blessed One (God). Such a weaving of texts, which in the Jewish scriptures appear to refer to two *different* persons, the Davidic king and the son of man, gives expression to the theological social text of early Christian thought that, in fact, the Davidic king and the son of man are one and the same person. Was this kind of rereading a peculiarly Christian reading? Or did other Jewish interpreters reread the Bible similarly?

Recall from Chapters 5 and 7 that Daniel 7 presents a vision of four beasts that represent successive worldly kingdoms (Dan 7:1–8). The fourth beast, representing the Seleucid kingdom of Antiochus IV, is of special interest to Daniel, for this kingdom persecutes God's people (7:23–25). Daniel also conveys a vision of "one like a son of man" (7:13). The vision *does* interpret this son of man as a *royal* figure: "To him was given dominion and glory and kingship" (7:14a). However, in Daniel, this son of man is *not* said to be the Messiah, but rather stands as a figure of *God's people* (see 7:18, 27). Thus, in the originating context of Daniel 7, the "son of man" is, indeed, a royal figure representing God's people whose kingdom supersedes that of the monstrous beasts; but this son of man is *not* the Messiah, nor is he said to be a son of God.

Table 11.4

Messiah, son of God, and son of Man

Mark 14:65	Intertexts from the Jewish Scriptures
Jesus said, "I am [the Messiah, the son of the Blessed One]; and 'you will *see the Son of Man seated at the right hand of the Power'*	The Lord says to my lord, *"Sit at my right hand until I make your enemies your footstool"* (Ps 110:1)
and *'coming with the clouds of heaven.'"*	As I watched in the night visions, I *saw one like a son of man coming with the clouds of heaven* (Dan 7:13)

This vision from Daniel, however, provided a rich text for subsequent rereadings within Judaism. The **Apocryphal** book of 2 Esdras dates to the late first century CE, after Mark composed his gospel. Thus, one cannot argue that Mark knew this literary text and, therefore, used it as a source. However, 2 Esdras offers a window into how at least one Jewish writer roughly contemporary with Mark reread the vision of Daniel 7.[23]

2 Esdras 11:1–12:3a narrates Ezra's (the supposed author of the text) detailed vision of an eagle that eventually "gained control of the whole earth, and with much oppression dominated its inhabitants" (11:32). As the vision continues, Ezra sees a lion who confronts the eagle and eventually destroys it (11:36–12:3a). Typical of the apocalyptic genre, the vision is interpreted for Ezra (and the reader). 2 Esdras 12:11–12 *explicitly* informs the reader that Ezra's vision of the eagle was a re-presentation of Daniel's vision of the fourth beast in Daniel 7; hence, there is no doubt as to what scriptural text 2 Esdras is rereading. The interpretation of the vision explains that the eagle represents a terrifying kingdom (12:13), undoubtedly Rome, given the social text out of which 2 Esdras emerges. More important, 12:31–32 explicitly interprets the conquering lion as "the Messiah." Hence, in 2 Esdras the Messiah conquers the beast of Daniel 7. This is a significant rereading of Daniel for, recall, Daniel itself does *not* identify the conqueror of the beast with the Messiah.

Then, 2 Esdras 13 continues with yet another vision about a "man" who "flew with the clouds of heaven" (v. 3), a clear intertext with Dan 7:13. This man does battle with and eventually destroys the peoples of the earth who oppose him (vv. 5–11). Though not actually called "the son of man," it is clear that the text about the son of man from Daniel inspires the picture of the figure of 2 Esdras 13:3. When Ezra receives the interpretation of the vision from God himself, God refers to this "man" explicitly as "my Son" (13:32; cf. v. 37). There is *no* reason to suppose that "the man" of 2 Esdras 13 is a different figure from the lion/Messiah of 2 Esdras 12. The "man" who flies on the clouds of heaven, a clear allusion to the son of man of Daniel 7, and the Messiah are the same figure. Further, God refers to this messianic man as his son.

This allows one to see that while the figure of the son of man in Daniel was not, in Daniel itself, interpreted to be the Messiah or the/a son of God, later Jewish rereadings could offer such an interpretation. Clearly the figure of Daniel 7 has the trappings of royalty (Dan 7:14), allowing one to understand how later readers of Daniel could associate this figure with a king. One can also understand how Jewish rereadings would not associate this royal figure with just any king, but with a specific king: the ideal Davidic king—the Messiah—who was yet to come in order to deliver God's people from their oppressors. Finally, the scriptures themselves offered ample testimony that the Davidic king shared a filial relationship to God, being described in many texts as God's son (see 2 Sam 7:11–14; Ps 2:6–7; 89:20, 26–27). Subsequent Jewish rereadings of texts such as 2 Sam 7:11–14 continued to note the filial relationship between David's heir and God. Frequently, this Davidic heir was identified with a messianic deliverer.[24]

[23]Chap. 12 will say more about this Jewish text. Other Jewish texts that speak of the son of man include 1 Enoch and 2 Baruch.

[24]D. Duling, "The Promises to David and their Entrance in Christianity—Nailing Down a Likely Hypothesis," NTS 20 (1973) 55–77.

A Closer Look: Did Jesus Explicitly Refer to Himself as the Son of Man? In the Gospel of Mark, sayings attributed to Jesus employ the term *son of man* in three ways: (1) the son of man on earth (Mk 2:1–12, 23–28); (2) the suffering, death, and resurrection of the son of man (Mk 8:31; 9:9–12, 31; 10:33–34, 45); (3) the glorious return of the son of man in the future (Mk 8:38; 13:26–27; 14:62). Jesus consistently employs the term in the third person, as though speaking about someone else, though the Markan context makes clear that Jesus is referring to himself. The last two categories of sayings, addressing the death and resurrection of Jesus and his triumphal return as the vindicated eschatological judge, strike some interpreters as so explicitly Christian that they fail the authenticity test of the Criterion of Dissimilarity (see Chap. 10, "A Closer Look: Finding the Real Words of Jesus"). One might object, noting that, with rare exceptions (Acts 7:56; Rev 1:13; 14:14), one finds the phrase "son of man" in the NT only on the lips of Jesus, implying that the term *son of man* was *not* a favorite term by which the early followers of Jesus referred to him. Additionally, the phrase son of man is found in various streams of the gospel tradition (Q, material peculiar to Matthew, material peculiar to Luke, and John), allowing one to conclude that the term satisfies the Criterion of Multiple Attestation. It is safe to conclude that there is no scholarly consensus on the question raised in the title of this box. Students should note that even if one concludes that Jesus employed the phrase "son of man," that does not automatically allow the inference that any particular "son of man" saying in the gospel tradition is authentic.

For further study, G. W. E. Nickelsburg. "Son of Man." *ABD* 6.137–150; B. Witherington III, *The Christology of Jesus.* Minneapolis, MN: Fortress, 1990. Especially pp. 233–262.

For more advanced study, D. R. A. Hare. *The Son of Man Tradition.* Minneapolis, MN: Fortress, 1990; N. Perrin, *A Modern Pilgrimage in New Testament Christology.* Philadelphia: Fortress, 1974.

Thus, one can see that both Mark and 2 Esdras could reread the scriptures so as to collapse the Messiah, the son of man, and the son of God into one figure. The macro-level intertextuality between these two texts, one Christian and one non-Christian, allows the conclusion that identifying the Messiah with the son of man and God's son was not a distinctively Christian idea. The distinctive Christian contribution to the equation was to identify this figure with Jesus and to identify this Messiah's primary work of liberation with his crucifixion.

The King and the Temple. Recall from Chapters 6 and 7 that in many of the literary texts of the scriptures, there was a close association between the king and the Temple. The Chronicler emphasized King David's involvement in the preparation of the building of the Temple and the organization of the priesthood. One could summarize a major theme of Chapter 6 with the statement: "kings build temples." The Chronicler also proposed that it was through the Temple and priesthood that the legacy of David lived on (Chap. 7).

The biblical story of the relationship between the king and the Temple provides an intertextual background for Mark's story of Jesus' last week in Jerusalem. Mark 11:15–19 portrays Jesus' opening act in Jerusalem as shutting down the Temple because it did not serve as a place of prayer for all the nations (v. 17a, a micro-level intertext with Isa 56:7). Mark has "sandwiched" Jesus' shutting down the Temple between a story about Jesus' cursing a fruitless fig tree (vv. 12–14, 20–24). This leads interpreters to conclude that Mark wishes to portray the Temple as a fruitless institution that Jesus *judges*.[25] This reading is confirmed by Jesus' explicit prediction in Mark 13 that the Jerusalem Temple will be destroyed (13:1–2).

The conflict between the Messiah and the Temple is also a central feature of Jesus' interrogation before the Sanhedrin. Mark records that "false witnesses" claimed that Jesus said he would destroy the Temple made with *hands,* and in three days build another, one *not* made with hands (14:57; cf. 15:29). On the *literal* level the charge made against Jesus is "false," for Mark nowhere records that Jesus *literally* said such a thing. On a deeper, more ironic level, however, the charge is "true," for Jesus has judged the Temple (11:15–17) and claimed that it would be destroyed (13:1–2).[26] The cryptic reference to "in three days" is assuredly an allusion to Jesus' resurrection. With this resurrection, the text implies, Jesus will build a new, spiritual, Temple; one *not* made with hands. According to Mark, at the time Jesus dies, "the curtain of the temple was torn in two, from top to bottom" (15:38). The torn curtain is likely an image of the Temple's eventual destruction.[27]

Mark is offering some provocative rereadings of Jewish texts that describe the relationship between the king (the Messiah) and the Temple. Whereas "kings build temples" in the Hebrew Bible, Mark's Jesus is the king who destroys the literal Temple made with hands and replaces it with another one, not made with hands.

Conclusion. The Jewish scriptures speak of the liberating work of the Davidic king. For Mark, Jesus is this Davidic king. But Jesus' crucifixion requires that Mark make sense of the fact that this king suffered and died. Thus, he has reread the scriptures to say that Jesus fulfills his kingly mission of liberation primarily through his death as a "ransom for many." Yet Jesus is not only the Messiah; he is also the son of man and the son of God. Finally, Mark rereads the traditional connection between the king and the Temple, virtually turning this connection upside down. As Messiah, Jesus does not affirm or restore the literal Temple of Jerusalem. He judges it, implying that he will replace it with a spiritual Temple.

---

[25]W. R. Telford, *The Barren Temple and the Withered Tree. A Redaction-Critical Analysis of the Cursing of the Fig-Tree Pericope in Mark's Gospel and its Relation to the Cleansing of the Temple Tradition* (Sheffield: JSOT, 1980); J. J. Kilgallen, *A Brief Commentary on the Gospel of Mark* (New York: Paulist, 1989) 210–216.

[26]Following D. Juel's interpretation, which he offers in *An Introduction to New Testament Literature* (Nashville, TN: Abingdon, 1978) 145–151. Juel's fuller treatment of this enigmatic charge is found in his work, *Messiah and Temple: The Trial of Jesus in the Gospel of Mark* (SBLDS 30; Missoula, MT: Scholars Press, 1977) 143–157.

[27]Brown, *Death of the Messiah,* 2.1099–1102.

All Things under His Feet
Defeating the Enemies of God
1 Corinthians 1–4, 15

Learning Goals

- To learn basic information regarding Paul's letters.
- To understand how Paul's interaction with the social texts of his readers shaped the literary texts he produced.
- To learn about Paul's understanding of how Jesus, and especially of how Jesus' death and resurrection, ushers in the kingdom of God.
- To understand how Paul has reread certain scriptural texts in light of specific theological social texts affirming Jesus as the messianic king and the new Adam.

Guiding Study Exercises

1) Be able to list the seven indisputably Pauline letters and to know the decade in which they were composed.

2) What did the Corinthian Christians think about the issue of the resurrection of the dead, and how did their beliefs on this issue shape how Paul constructs his discussion of the topic in 1 Corinthians 15?

3) How does Paul understand "the enemies of God," and how has his understanding of this group shaped the way he interprets the meaning of Jesus' death and resurrection, and the parousia?

4) Explain the logic behind Paul's collapsing together of the literary texts of Psalm 8 and Psalm 110.

Paul and His Letters

Chapter 10 introduced Paul as an important figure, for he was very influential in carrying the gospel beyond Palestine to Jews of the Diaspora and gentiles. When speaking of his mission in the context of his own writings, Paul focused special attention on the call God gave him to preach to gentiles (Gal 1:13–17). After Paul established a **church**, an effective way for him to maintain contact with this church was through his letters. When Paul would write a letter, it was because some specific issue or set of issues had come to his attention that he believed demanded a response from him. His letters reflect his thoughtful and theological responses to real situations facing churches for which he felt responsibility and accountability.

Several letters that he wrote to churches have survived and are now found in the NT. In all, thirteen letters in the NT bear this **apostle's** name. Most critical scholars do not believe that Paul actually wrote all thirteen letters. These scholars believe that *followers* of Paul wrote some of these letters several years after Paul died in an attempt to reread and apply Paul's message to changing occasions and circumstances (social texts) in the church. Subsequent chapters will examine some of these "disputed" letters.

The Text behind the Text of 1 Corinthians (1 Corinthians 1–4)

Paul composed this letter around the year 56 or 57 CE. Careful reading of the text reveals that Paul's relationship with the Corinthian congregation was complex and stormy. Paul, as the founder of this congregation, believed he was obliged to offer guidance to his spiritual children

---

A Closer Look: The Letters of Paul. The table below summarizes critical scholarly consensus regarding the authentic and disputed letters of Paul. The dates after each letter represent approximate dates of composition, following R. E. Brown, *An Introduction to the New Testament* (New York: Doubleday, 1997). When two dates appear in the second and third columns, the first date represents the approximate date of composition if the letter is authentic, whereas the second date represents the approximate date offered by scholars who believe the letter to be post-Pauline.

Authenticity Accepted by Vast Majority of Scholars	Authenticity Disputed by Majority of Scholars	Authenticity Disputed by Vast Majority of Scholars
1 Thessalonians (50/51)	2 Thessalonians (51/52 or late first century)*	1 Timothy (65 or late first century)
Galatians (54/55)	Colossians (61–63 or 80s)**	2 Timothy (65 or late first century)
Philemon (55)	Ephesians (60s or 90s)***	Titus (65 or late first century)
Philippians (56)		
1 Corinthians (56/57)		
2 Corinthians (57)		
Romans (57/58)		
	*Brown estimates that 50% of critical scholars dispute authenticity (*Introduction,* 591).	Scholars refer to these collectively as the "Pastoral Epistles."
	**Brown estimates that 60% of critical scholars dispute authenticity (*Introduction,* 600).	Brown estimates that 80–90% of critical scholars dispute the authenticity of the Pastorals (*Introduction,* 639, 654, 673)
	***Brown estimates that 80% of critical scholars dispute authenticity (*Introduction,* 621).	

(1 Cor 4:14–21, especially v. 15). Paul vehemently disagreed with the Corinthians over a number of important issues.

Division. The text of 1 Cor 1:10–13 makes clear that the church was divided. This division explains many of the other problems that this church encountered: lawsuits (6:1–11), debates about eating meat offered to idols (8:1–13), about proper worship practices (Chap. 11), and about spiritual gifts (Chaps. 12, 14). Paul believed that such divisions violated the fact that all the believers had been baptized into the one Christ (1: 13).

Maturity and Ethics. Division within the church led Paul to conclude that the individual members were quite immature, or babies in Christ, as he called them (3:1–4). The lack of ethical behavior was further evidence that this congregation was not mature. The fact that Paul had to tell the Corinthians explicitly that it was not acceptable for a man to have a sexual relationship with his stepmother (5:1–13), or for the Corinthians to have sex with prostitutes (6:12–20), evidenced their need of his guidance.

The Corinthians' Self-Perceptions. While Paul views the Corinthians as very immature and unspiritual in their orientation to the Christian life, they had quite the opposite view of themselves. In words dripping with sarcasm, Paul scolds the Corinthians for their spiritual presumptuousness: "Already you have all you want! Already you have become rich! Quite apart from us you have become kings! Indeed, I wish that you had become kings, so that we might be kings with you!" (4:8). According to Paul, the Corinthians perceive themselves as "wise," "strong," and persons of "honor" (4:10). Already they presume to share in the royal honor of the exalted Christ.

Perhaps it is Paul's desire to calm the Corinthians' spiritual enthusiasm that prompts him to emphasize in the early chapters of the letter the crucifixion of Jesus (1:18–2:5). The presumptuous Corinthians, who were too quick to focus on the images of Christ's glory as well as their own, needed to be reminded that death must precede resurrection, both for Jesus and for them. From Paul's point of view, the Corinthians are nowhere near attaining their presumed status as royal practitioners of powerful honor and wisdom, for they are still, metaphorically speaking, on the milk bottle (3:2).[28]

The Resurrection and the Kingdom of God (1 Corinthians 15)

Paul saved his discussion of resurrection until last, highlighting the importance of this issue for the apostle.[29] He begins by summarizing the central feature of the Christian message: Jesus' death and resurrection (15:3–11). There is no evidence that the Corinthians did not affirm this essential confession and attempt to claim that Jesus was really dead. Strangely, while affirming the essential Christian confession of Jesus' death and resurrection (emphasizing the resurrection!), what they seemed to deny was the *future resurrection of believers.* At least, this is the way that some scholars interpret what Paul says in 1 Cor 15:12–19.[30]

What lies behind the Corinthian denial of the resurrection of the dead? This denial may very well link up with the Corinthians' understanding of spiritual reality. *Already,* they say, we

---

[28]Chap. 14 will say more about the Corinthians' and Paul's disagreements regarding spirituality.

[29]"The heart of our 'first' letter to Corinth lies here—perhaps because [Paul's] readers required 14 chapters of preparation." R. A. Harrisville, *I Corinthians* (Minneapolis, MN: Augsburg, 1987) 248.

[30]E.g., C. H. Talbert, *Reading Corinthians* (New York: Crossroads, 1987) 96–99.

A Closer Look: "Afterlife" in the Hellenistic World. A small minority of ancients disputed the idea of an afterlife (e.g., the Epicureans [Chap. 9]). But most ancients believed in some fashion that one's soul, once separated from the body, continued to exist. In early thought, the souls of the dead gathered beneath the earth in a special place, called by various names: *hades* (Greek), *sheol* (Hebrew), or *inferi* (Latin). There was no distinction, based on whether one lived a good or bad life, among the souls of the dead. Later thought differentiated between the fate of the souls of good or bad people (cf. Lk 16:19–31), with the souls of the good continuing in the celestial regions (compare the popular idea of "going to heaven") and the souls of the bad remaining in the underworld.

While there was not uniformity, generally Jews and Christians were distinct from the larger Hellenistic population in that many affirmed the idea of resurrection. Those who believed in resurrection asserted that the soul did not remain separate from the body, but the body also shared in the blessings or punishments of afterlife. One can find in some Jewish texts belief in the older idea that there was no differentiation among souls after death (e.g., Sir 14:16–19). Other texts do not speak of resurrection, but of the rewards offered to the immortal souls of the righteous (4 Macc 13:16–17; 15:3; 16:25; 17:12). Other Jewish texts affirm the resurrection of the body (Dan 12:1–3; 2 Maccabees 7). The debate that Paul has with the Corinthians shows lack of uniform belief even among Christians regarding the nature of the afterlife.

For further study, E. Ferguson. *Backgrounds of Early Christianity.* 2nd Ed. Grand Rapids, MI: Eerdmans, 1993. Pp. 228–234, 519–521; G. W. E. Nickelsburg. "Resurrection: Early Judaism and Christianity." *ABD* 5.684–91.

For more advanced study, J. Bremmer. *The Early Greek Concept of the Soul.* Princeton, NJ: Princeton University Press, 1983. Pp. 70–124; G. W. E. Nickelsburg. *Resurrection, Immortality and Eternal Life.* Cambridge, MA: Harvard University Press, 1972.

have become rich! *Already* we are kings! *Already* we are wise! *Already* we are powerful! The Corinthians evidently believed that already they had attained a glorified status in the present. Yet for Paul, believers truly come to possess royal power and glory only at the *future* resurrection of the dead. For him, the present was a time of sharing in the *sufferings* of Christ. His own words, drawn from another of his letters, say it best: "If [we are] children [of God], then [we are] heirs, heirs of God and joint heirs with Christ—if, in fact, we suffer with him so that we also may be gloried with him. I consider that the sufferings of the present time are not worth comparing with the glory about to be revealed to us" (Rom 8:17–18).

Paul wanted to emphasize that while Christ has been raised, his followers have *not yet* attained this glory. Believers are still living in an age very much influenced by "the enemies of God," which God has not yet subdued, with the main enemy being death. Paul's description of the future subjugation of God's enemies by Jesus the Messiah offers insight into how Paul has reread the Jewish story of kingship.

Identifying the Enemies of God. Jewish stories of kingship regularly speak of the king as conquering God's enemies. Royal Psalms clearly express this triumphal theme: "The LORD is at your right hand, he will shatter kings on the day of his wrath" (Ps 110:5; cf. Ps 2:8–9). Later Jewish tradition picked up on such images of conquering and used them to describe the work of the end-time anointed one of God: "Raise up unto them their king . . . that he may purge Jerusalem from the nations that trample (her) down to destruction" (Psalms of Solomon 17:23–25).

Paul shares with his Jewish ancestors and contemporaries the hope that God's anointed king will conquer the enemies of God (1 Cor 15:24–26). But Paul likely understands God's enemies to be spiritual forces opposed to God. As Jerome Neyrey states: Paul's "cosmos is crowded with . . . personified malevolent figures" who wage war against God and his creatures.[31] Paul had different names for these spiritual forces: Death (1 Cor 15:26; Rom 5:14, 17); Sin (Rom 5:21; 6:12; 7:11–23); Satan (Rom 16:20; 1 Cor 5:5; 2 Cor 2:11); Rule (1 Cor 15:24; Rom 8:38); Rulers (1 Cor 2:6, 8); Authority (1 Cor 15:24; Rom 13:1); Power (1 Cor 15:24; Rom 8:38).[32]

Jesus: God's Anointed Agent. Recall that the Synoptic Gospels describe Jesus' battling the forces of evil through his works of healing, exorcism, and the forgiveness of sin. The battle culminates in Jesus' crucifixion. Colossians testifies to Paul's, or a follower's, belief that Jesus' historical messianic work contributed to the conquering of God's enemies. Colossians does not speak, however, of miracles of healing and exorcism. For Colossians, the crucifixion of Jesus was *the* primary event that inaugurated and ensured the eventual defeat of evil: "He disarmed the rulers and authorities and made a public example of them, triumphing over them in it [the cross]" (Col 2:15). The death of Jesus inaugurated God's victory over God's enemies, the oppressive forces of evil and especially Sin. "Since all have sinned," Paul writes in his letter to the Romans, "and fall short of the glory of God; they are now justified by his grace as a gift, through the redemption that is in Christ Jesus, whom God put forward as a sacrifice of atonement by his blood" (Rom 3:23–25a). From Paul's perspective, the messianic warrior manifests his power initially through his death.

Yet Paul believed that the *final* victory of Christ lay in the future. The present is a time of ongoing struggle against the cosmic forces that oppose God. This struggle will not be over for Jesus the Messiah or his people until Jesus destroys Death, "the last enemy" (1 Cor 15:26). And this has not yet happened. This awaits the triumphant coming of Christ at the end of history, at which time "those who belong to Christ" will be resurrected from the dead (1 Cor 15:23). The Corinthians who believe that *already* they are powerful, wise, and rule as kings are naively premature in their optimism. Christ must win the final battle—defeat the enemy of Death—before the soldiers of Christ can talk of sharing in the rule of the king.

In 1 Cor 15:20–28 Paul shows that he believed this future victory to be assured. The ultimate victory of God is achieved with the conquering of Death, the primary enemy of God. Such conquering has already begun, for Christ has already been resurrected, the "first fruits" of those who will share in God's victory over death (v. 23a). Sometime in the near future the **parousia** would occur.[33] *Parousia* is often translated as "coming" in English Bibles, and it refers to what

---

[31]J. Neyrey, *Paul, In Other Words: A Cultural Reading of His Letters* (Louisville, KY: Westminster/John Knox, 1990) 162–63.

[32]*Ibid.,* 162.

[33]It appears that Paul believed "the end" to be near. Note Paul's explicit words from an earlier section of 1 Corinthians: "The appointed time has grown short" (7:29b); "the present form of this world is passing away" (v. 31b).

many modern people call "the second coming." The word was regularly used to denote the arrival of a royal figure. It makes sense, therefore, that the followers of Jesus adopted the term to denote the arrival of their messianic king at the end of history. Coinciding with the parousia was the resurrection of "those who belong to Christ" (v. 23). "Then comes the end," Paul says in v. 24, "when he hands over the kingdom to God the Father, after he has destroyed every ruler and every authority and power." Paul goes on to say that Christ "must reign until he has put all his enemies under his feet. The last enemy to be destroyed is death" (vv. 25–26). Most likely, the destruction of Death would coincide with the resurrection "of those who belong to Christ" (v. 23b) at the parousia. From this, it follows that Paul understood the present time—the time between Jesus' resurrection and parousia—as the reign of Christ.[34] With the resurrection of believers, the reign of Christ comes to an end, for "when all things are subjected to him [Jesus], then the Son himself will also be subjected to the one [God] who put all things in subjection under him, so that God may be all in all" (v. 28). Paul associates this era when God is "all in all" with the transformation of creation itself. In 1 Cor 15:22–28, this is implied, when Paul talks of the destruction of all the powers opposed to God.

For Paul the reign of Christ, culminating in his defeat of the cosmic enemies of God, including Death, would eventuate in the transformation of the created order (Rom 8:20–21). Other NT writers share a similar theological social text, speaking of "the new heaven and the new earth" (2 Pet 3:11–13; Rev 21:1). With this total transformation of creation, God's reign, God's being "all in all," would be realized. Christ's work as the kingly Messiah would be accomplished.

Rereading the Scriptures. In 1 Cor 15:25 and 27 Paul offers micro-level intertextual echoes of two passages from the Psalms. Verse 25 echoes Ps 110:1, while v. 27 echoes Ps 8:6 (see Table 11.7). Paul is not precisely quoting the Psalms, but interpreting and paraphrasing them. For example, he interprets the phrase from Ps 110:1, "sit at my right hand," as "he must reign." Further, he has altered "your footstool" to "under his feet." The phrase, "under his feet" clearly comes from Ps 8:6. Thus, it appears that Paul has actually merged the two Psalms, allowing the language of Ps 8:6 to shape his paraphrase of Ps 110:1.

Psalm 110 is obviously a Royal Psalm; that is, it is about God's chosen king. Given that Christians believed Jesus to be God's anointed king, they were drawn to this psalm to give expression to their faith in Jesus as the Messiah. The opening line affirmed for them the royal dignity of Jesus who ruled from God's right hand, his enemies serving as a stool for his feet.[35]

But why does Paul bring in Psalm 8? Is it a Royal Psalm? While it does use the language of royalty, it is *not* a Royal Psalm. It is a psalm of praise about humanity and its relationship to God and the rest of creation. The language of Psalm 8 is quite reminiscent of the Genesis story of God's creation of human beings, as Table 11.8 shows.

These two macro-level intertexts employ similar traditions regarding humanity, with each affirming the special status of human beings. Genesis speaks of God creating humans in God's

---

[34]Not all scholars interpret these verses in this manner. Some see the time of subjugating the powers as not taking place until *after* the parousia, at which time Paul envisioned the establishment of an earthly kingdom. For a close examination of the various interpretations see L. J. Kreitzer, *Jesus and God in Paul's Eschatology* (JSNTSup 19; Sheffield: JSOT Press, 1987) 131–154.

[35]D. M. Hay, *Glory at the Right Hand: Psalm 110 in Early Christianity* (Nashville, TN: Abingdon, 1972) offers a thorough study of the use of this psalm by early Christians.

Table 11.7

Echoes of Scripture in 1 Corinthians 15: 25, 27

1 Corinthians	Psalms 110 and 8
25For he must reign until he has put all his enemies under his feet.	110:2 The Lord said to my lord, "Sit at my right hand until I make your enemies your footstool." (Ps 109:1 in LXX).
27For God has put all things [in subjection]* under his feet.	8:6You have set him over the works of your hands; you have put all things under his feet.
*"in subjection" added to NRSV for clarity, it is not in the Greek New Testament text.	

Table 11.8

**Genesis 1 and Psalm 8: A Comparison
(Based on LXX)**

Genesis 1:26	Psalm 8:5–8
26And God said, Let us make man according to our image and likeness,

and let them have dominion over the fish of the sea, and over the flying creatures of heaven, and over the cattle and all the earth, and over all that creep on the earth. | 5You have made him [human kind] a little less than angels, you have crowned him with glory and honor; 6you have set him over the works of your hands: you have put all things under his feet: 7sheep and all oxen, indeed, even the cattle of the field; 8the birds of the sky, and fish of the sea, the things which pass through the paths of the sea. |

image. The psalm speaks of God creating humans just lower than the angelic beings and crowning these humans with honor and glory. Both traditions affirm that humankind has dominion over the earth since God has set humans over the other creatures. It is in this context that the psalmist speaks of how God has "put all things under his feet."[36] It is clear that the psalmist is not thinking about the Messiah or any future king. Rather, he is reflecting on the place of human kind—"man"—in the scheme of things. So how did Paul come to associate this text with Jesus, *the Messiah,* and merge it with Psalm 110, which clearly is a Royal Psalm?

Christ: The New Adam and the New Humanity. In 1 Cor 15:21 words are spoken about how death has come "through a man"; in the same verse Paul says that "also through a man has come the resurrection out of the dead." He clarifies what two men he is talking about in v. 22: "for as all die in Adam, so all will be made alive in Christ." In 15:45–49 Paul again compares Adam and Jesus, portraying them as two particular human beings who serve as progenitors of the whole human race. In Adam is found the old humanity, those "of the dust," while in Christ there exists a new humanity, "those of heaven" (v. 48). For Paul, the story of Adam served as a **typological** macro-level intertext to help him interpret the significance of the story of Jesus. Paul believed Jesus to be the head of a new humanity, even as the character from the scriptures, Adam, was the head of the old humanity, a race dominated by sin and guilt and, therefore, destined for Death, God's ultimate enemy. Paul's belief that Jesus, the messianic king, was a "second Adam" (cf. v. 45) could prompt intriguing new readings of his scriptures. Psalm 8 offers a good example.

Psalm 8 was originally about Man to whom God gave dominion over all things. Any reader, such as Paul, who read Psalm 8 as being about Man would easily connect the text with the Genesis story and the creation of Man—or "Adam,"[37] as later readers of the story came to call him. Adam is the one created a bit lower than the angels and crowned with glory and honor. Adam is the one under whose feet God has placed all things. It is easy to imagine how Paul might reread this text, *once he affirms that Jesus the Messiah is the "second Adam."* Paul could apply *typologically* to the "second Adam" this psalm that originally referred to the "first Adam." Hence, in its fullest sense, the psalm gives testimony to Christ as the one whom God has crowned with glory and honor. Christ is the one whom God has set over all the works of God's hands (the Creation). Christ is the one under whose feet God has set all things. While the psalm, in its original reference to humankind, understood "all things" to mean the other creatures (fish, birds, cattle, etc.), Paul understands the term "all things" far more absolutely as referring to "every ruler and every authority and power" and, ultimately, even Death (1 Cor 15:24, 26). Paul can make this association because he has blended Ps 8:6, which speaks of "all things" being "under his feet," with Ps 110:1, which speaks of God making the king's "enemies his footstool." By merging the two psalms, "all things" (from Psalm 8) blends with "enemies" (Psalm 110), allowing Paul to identify "all things" with the cosmic spiritual forces opposed to God.

Conclusion. The preceding discussion has been complex, but if readers will study Figure 11.1 and work through the intertextual connections of Psalm 8, Psalm 110, the story of Adam, and 1 Corinthians 15, the results are rewarding. Paul has blended a Royal Psalm (Psalm 110) with

---

[36]Contemporary English does not prefer the generic use of the masculine pronoun. However, a literal translation is necessary in order to see how Paul is reading the text. Paul did not have a Greek text or speak a Greek language that was "gender neutral"; it would be a gross anachronism to expect that he would. If one's goal is to understand *Paul,* one must bear with his masculinized text for this portion of the discussion.

[37]In Hebrew *'adam* meant "human being." As folk retold the Genesis story, they came to understand *'adam,* "human being," as "Adam," the proper name of the first human.

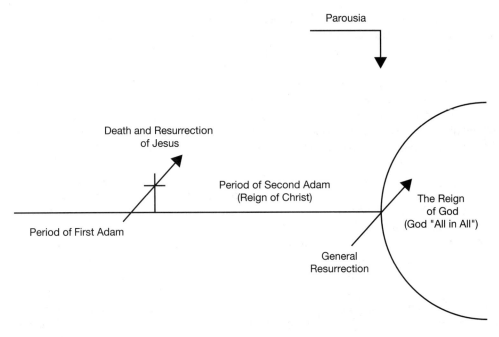

Figure 11.1
Paul's View of History

a psalm about humankind (Man/Adam in Psalm 8), reading both as ultimately referring to Christ, who is *both* the anointed king of God and the last Adam. When the last Adam, the messianic king, has conquered all things, he will then give them to God, submit himself to God and God will be "all in all" (1 Cor 15:28). God will make right once again the world that God created. *This* is the final chapter in the "story of kingship" as reread by the followers of Jesus.

Conclusion

"When your days are fulfilled and you lie down with your ancestors, I will raise up your offspring after you, who shall come forth from your body, and I will establish his kingdom" (2 Sam 7:12). As Chapter 7 showed, this is one of the more important literary texts from the early chapters of the social text of the story of kingship. Making sense of how God would remain true to this promise through Israel's and Judah's tumultuous history required ongoing rereading.

For Jesus, talk of kingship focused on the kingship of *God*—or **theocracy**. While Jesus was not the first to speak of God's reign, he had distinctive things to say about this kingdom. God was the king and he was demonstrating his reigning power even in the midst of Roman oppression, for through Jesus, God was taking on the ultimate sources of human oppression: disease, demons, and sin. While this kingdom was very real, it was not exactly what people expected. Like a seemingly innocuous mustard seed that finds its way into a garden, it germinates, sprouts, grows, and eventually takes over, offering shelter for birds of the sky. This curious image of the kingdom displaces the grand images of the mighty cedar of Lebanon in the OT tradition.

Mark continued to reread of the story of kingship, addressing specifically the fact of Jesus' execution. Through his death as a "ransom," Jesus carries out the work of the Davidic king who was to deliver God's people.

The resurrection of Jesus heightened his followers' perceptions of the centrally significant role that Jesus himself was to play in this kingdom. The present reality of God's reign, which manifested itself in the conquering of disease, demons, and sin was not forgotten. Yet the exaltation of Jesus to the messianic throne gave added importance to the role that *Jesus* was playing now and in the future as the anointed king of God. Even now he reigns, Paul affirmed, continuing to subjugate the enemies of God, the evil forces of spiritual darkness. The ultimate enemy that this king and progenitor of a new race is to conquer is Death and its pervasive influence of corruption and decay. This he will do finally at the parousia when those who belong to him will be raised and creation itself will be set free from its own bondage. Then too another promise made to David will find its ultimate realization: "I will give you rest from all your enemies" (2 Sam 7:11b).

For Further Reading

"The Kingdom of God is Like . . ."

Footnotes and the "Closer Look" box on parables offer basic bibliography on the parables. The following bibliography focuses on the kingdom of God. Immediately below are representative scholars who interpret Jesus' message of the kingdom from within an explicit Jewish eschatological and apocalyptic context.

Allison, D. C., Jr. *The End of the Ages Has Come: An Early Interpretation of the Passion and Resurrection of Jesus.* Philadelphia: Fortress, 1985.

Sanders, E. P. *The Historical Figure of Jesus.* London: Penguin, 1993. (*Recommended for beginning students.*)

———. *Jesus and Judaism.* Philadelphia: Fortress, 1985.

Wright, N. T. *Jesus and the Victory of God.* Minneapolis, MN: Fortress, 1996.

———. *Who Was Jesus?* Grand Rapids, MI: Eerdmans, 1993. (*Recommended for beginning students.*)

Some scholars argue that while Jesus used the phrase "kingdom of God," he did not intend to be understood from within an eschatological or apocalyptic context. Rather, the reign of God was a noneschatological symbol that Jesus employed to confront his hearers with the present reality of God. The following are representatives of this school of thought.

Borg, M. *Jesus, A New Vision: Spirit, Culture, and the Life of Discipleship.* San Francisco: HarperSanFrancisco, 1987.

———. *Meeting Jesus Again for the First Time: The Historical Jesus and the Heart of Contemporary Faith.* San Francisco: HarperSanFrancisco, 1994. (*Recommended for beginning students.*)

Crossan, J. D. *Jesus: A Revolutionary Biography.* San Francisco: HarperSan Francisco, 1994. (*Recommended for beginning students.*)

———. *The Historical Jesus: The Life of a Mediterranean Jewish Peasant.* San Francisco: HarperSanFrancisco, 1991.

Perrin, N. *Jesus and the Language of the Kingdom: Symbol and Metaphor in New Testament Interpretation.* Philadelphia: Fortress, 1976.

The Markan Passion Narrative

Kelber, W., Ed. *The Passion in Mark.* Philadelphia: Fortress, 1976.

Senior, D. *The Passion of Jesus in the Gospel of Mark.* Wilmington, DE: Michael Glazier, 1984. (*Recommended for beginning students.*)

Commentaries on Mark

Collins, A. J. *The Beginning of the Gospel: Probings of Mark in Context.* Minneapolis, MN: Fortress, 1992. (*Recommended for beginning students.*)

Taylor, V. *The Gospel according to Mark.* London: Macmillan, 1953.

All Things under His Feet

Beker, J. C. *Paul the Apostle: The Triumph of God in Life and Thought.* Philadelphia: Fortress, 1980.

———. *The Triumph of God: The Essence of Paul's Thought.* Minneapolis, MN: Fortress, 1990. (*Recommended for beginning students.*)

Dunn, J. D. G. *The Theology of Paul the Apostle.* Grand Rapids, MI: Eerdmans, 1998. Especially pp. 167–315.

Ridderbos, H. *Paul: An Outline of His Theology.* Grand Rapids, MI: Eerdmans, 1975. Especially pp. 44–90, 487–562.

Commentaries

Barrett, C. K. *The First Epistle to the Corinthians.* HNTC. New York: Harper & Row, 1968. (*Recommended for beginning students.*)

Conzelmann, H. *1 Corinthians.* Hermeneia. Philadelphia: Fortress, 1975.

Witherington, B. *Conflict and Community in Corinth: A Socio-Rhetorical Commentary on 1 & 2 Corinthians.* Grand Rapids, MI: Eerdmans, 1995

CHAPTER TWELVE

Rereading the Story of the Temple

Introduction

Review

Solomon's Temple, built in the tenth century BCE, was a significant feature of religious and political life in Judah. Religiously, it was the place God had chosen for his name to dwell (1 Kgs 8:29). Politically, it undergirded the legitimacy of Jerusalem as the capital of the Davidic house. Destroyed by Nebuchadnezzar in 587 BCE, the rebuilding of the Temple after the Exile served as a sign that the larger restoration envisioned by many of the prophets was underway. Yet many Jews believed that the **Second Temple** was a far cry from the glorious visions of the prophets. A number of Jewish interpreters concluded that the Second Temple was not *the* Temple of the time of restoration—the Temple of the time of restoration was yet to come (see Tob 14:5).

Chapters 10 and 11 showed that the story of the Temple was an integral part of the telling of the Jesus story. Luke begins his narrative of Jesus' life in the Temple and portrays Jesus as teaching the people of Israel on the Temple grounds during the last week of his life. The Temple also played a role in the passion narrative of Mark, which portrays Jesus as cursing the Temple, predicting its destruction and replacement by another Temple "not made with hands."

The Story Continues

When Herod came to power (37 BCE), the Jewish people did not widely accept him as a legitimate king (Chap. 9). In order to enhance his legitimacy, he refurbished the Second Temple, making it into a grand architectural structure encompassing roughly 25 percent of the area of city of Jerusalem![1] There is some evidence that this refurbishing was an attempt by Herod to portray

---

[1] See N. T. Wright, *The New Testament and the People of God* (Minneapolis, MN: Fortress, 1992) 225–226.

himself as a kind of Solomonic figure. Few Jews fell for his scheme, but it shows that Herod knew that the Temple continued to be central to Jewish understandings of God's presence with his people.

After Herod died (4 BCE), work on the Temple continued, finally being finished ca. 66 CE. Tensions between Jews of Judea and the Roman government, however, continued to mount, culminating in the outbreak of an all-out revolt in 66 CE (Chap. 9). Many Jews saw this revolt as the battle to usher in the longed-for time of restoration. Significantly, Jewish revolutionaries seized control of the Temple and the priesthood in an act reminiscent of the Maccabean revolt 200 years earlier. These actions by the rebels reveal that they too understood their legitimacy to be connected with control of the Temple.[2] But the Romans, under the leadership of Titus, put down the revolt and destroyed Jerusalem and the Temple. For Jews, it was as if they were experiencing the agony of 587 BCE all over again.

Preview

The actions of both Herod and the Jewish revolutionaries show that the story of the Temple formed a significant theological social text for the Jews. The Christians' claims about Jesus carried with them implied claims about the Temple, for Jewish hopes of restoration were closely tied to the Temple (Chap. 6). Hence, Christian claims about Jesus formed yet another theological social text that Jesus' followers would have to integrate with the story of the Temple. Again, rereading the Bible becomes necessary.

This chapter will look at the Christian rereading of the Temple story. First, to be examined is Luke's interpretation of the significance of the destruction of the Second Temple, comparing and contrasting Luke's interpretation with that of a contemporary Jewish text, 4 Ezra. Second, a study of the epistle to the Ephesians will explore how the author of this document reread both Jewish traditions of the new Temple and the earlier letters of Paul. Third, the book of Hebrews' rereading of the story of the priesthood and the sacrificial system will be presented. Finally, a study of the vision of the New Jerusalem offered in Revelation 21–22 will illustrate how this text reread and rewrote scriptural and Jewish traditions regarding the restored Temple and city.

---

[2]See J. B. Chance, *Jerusalem, the Temple, and the New Age in Luke-Acts* (Macon, GA: Mercer University Press, 1988) 17–18.

Not One Stone on Another:
Two Responses to the Destruction of
Jerusalem and the Temple

Learning Goals

- To understand different theological (Jewish and Christian) explanations for the destruction of Jerusalem and the Temple.
- To learn basic information about 4 Ezra.

Guiding Study Exercises

1) Write a paragraph summarizing the key introductory issues of 4 Ezra, including its date, genre, and theological perspective.

2) In what ways do Luke and 4 Ezra agree in their explanations regarding the destruction of Jerusalem and the Temple? In what ways do they disagree?

3) Compare and contrast the expectations in Luke and 4 Ezra regarding the ultimate future of Jerusalem and the Temple.

4) Explain how one's knowledge of the respective theological social texts that inform these two writers can help one to understand what these texts say about the destruction and restoration of Jerusalem and the Temple.

The Response of 4 Ezra (4 Ezra 3; 9:26–10:59; 13:1–58)

In the previous chapter, readers were exposed to the book identified in the Apocrypha as 2 Esdras. The text has a complex history of composition, with scholars agreeing that it was composed in stages. Chapters 3–14 represent the earliest stage, being composed by a *non-Christian* Jew toward the end of the first century CE.[3] Scholars who wish to refer only to 2 Esdras 3–14 will regularly speak of 4 Ezra. Even a quick reading of the opening verses of 4 Ezra 3 will convince most readers that at one time these verses introduced the book. 4 Ezra represents, like Daniel, an example of the apocalyptic **genre** of literature. The text was actually written ca. 100 CE, though it presents itself as being composed by Ezra in "the thirtieth year after the destruction of the city" by Babylon, which would be 557 BCE (see 4 Ezra 3:1).[4]

---

[3] 2 Esdras 1–2 and 15 are later Christian expansions. Scholars refer to these chapters as 5 Ezra and 6 Ezra, respectively.

[4] The supposed date of composition (557 BCE) creates immediate problems, for Ezra, who arrived in Jerusalem decades *after* the Exile ended, would not even have been born yet. Such glaring historical problems should remind readers that the real authors of these documents were hardly trying to write "real history."

The historical social text that the real author wishes to address, therefore, is the destruction of Jerusalem by the Romans in 70 CE. Since the author addressed the issue of the destruction of the *Second* Temple by composing a document that supposedly was about the destruction of the *First* (Solomonic) Temple, it is clear that the author saw a connection between the two tragic events of Jewish history.

The Cause of the Destruction of Jerusalem and the Temple. In 4 Ezra 3, reminiscent of Nehemiah 9, the narrator, Ezra, offers a prayer to God. This prayer shows the clear influence of the **Deuteronomic perspective**. Just as the first Temple was destroyed because of disobedience to God's law, so the Second Temple was destroyed. The prayer of 4 Ezra 3 states that God had called Israel as his special people, promising Abraham "that you [God] would never forsake his descendants" (v. 15). But Israel sinned, for "you did not take away their evil heart from them, so that your law might produce fruit in them" (v. 20). Thus, "you handed over your city to your enemies" (v. 27).

Ezra wrestles with some tough theological problems, such as why God would use an enemy who is far more sinful than Israel to punish Israel (vv. 28–36). Furthermore, Ezra is quite pessimistic about the possibility that any nation or people is able to keep the law, for all of human history is marked by total rebellion and disobedience (3:5–27). Ezra is convinced that humanity, beginning with Adam, is "burdened with an evil heart," a "permanent disease," and "evil root" (3:21–22). He concludes that "you may indeed find individuals who have kept your commandments, but nations you will not find" (3:36). These are severe theological problems, for the whole Deuteronomic perspective rested on the assumption that God gave the law for Israel to obey and that, indeed, it was not difficult to obey (see Deut 30:11–14). If, in reality, no nation can obey this law, curse is inevitable. Despite these harsh theological questions, the author of 4 Ezra can only make sense of the destruction of Jerusalem from within the Deuteronomic perspective: Israel's enemies destroyed Jerusalem because of the Jews' disobedience.

The Future of Jerusalem and the Temple. While Ezra has a pessimistic view of the ability of persons to obey the law, he does not conclude that God has abandoned Jerusalem or the Temple. In 4 Ezra 9:43–10:4, a vision is presented concerning Zion's, or Jerusalem's, future. Ezra has a vision of a woman mourning the loss of her son (9:43–10:4). Ezra, who is grieving for the loss of Zion, breaks off the woman's cries and, with some impatience, reminds the woman that there are more important things to mourn about, namely, the loss of Jerusalem (10:5–24). He tells her to "acknowledge the decree of God to be just" (10:16) with regard to the fate of her son. Ezra then sees the woman transformed into a vision of a great city (10:25–27).

The angel, introduced earlier as Uriel (4:1), now comes to interpret the vision for Ezra (10:29–59). The angel tells Ezra that the woman of his vision is Zion (10:44); her son represents the period of Jerusalem's habitation (10:47), and the death of her son, Jerusalem's destruction (10:48). But the story does not end there. The woman's transformation into a city represents "the city of the Most High [that] was to be revealed" (10:54).

A brief glance at 4 Ezra 13 completes the story. Here the reader sees a vision of a certain "man from the sea," interpreted as a messianic figure (13:25–26; cf. also 12:31–32).[5] Note how he is said to stand atop Mount Zion/Jerusalem (13:35). "And Zion shall come and be made mani-

---

[5]Review the discussion in Chap. 11 regarding the identity of this savior figure with the Messiah, the son of God, and the son of man.

fest to all people, prepared and built, as you saw the mountain carved out without hands" (13:36). Then 4 Ezra 13:6 says that this man from the sea carved out this mountain that represents Zion. When all the visions are put together, one sees that Ezra hoped for a restored Zion, which a messianic figure, the "man from the sea," would build ("carve out"). He will not only restore the city, but there he will judge the nations (13:37–38) and gather together the people of God (13:39–50). What is more, 4 Ezra leaves the reader with the impression that the glorious restoration of Zion is near. For "the age has lost its youth, and the times begin to grow old" (14:10).

Though 4 Ezra finds the Deuteronomic perspective troublesome, given the text's conclusion that "whole nations" cannot keep God's law (3:36), he still clings to the basic idea that God has punished Israel for its disobedience. In a very real sense, Israel still lives in Exile, just as it was forced into Exile after the destruction of the Solomonic Temple. But just as the Deuteronomic theological social text affirmed that God would eventually restore Israel and its holy city and its Temple, 4 Ezra hopes for the ultimate restoration of Jerusalem and the Temple. Further, the Messiah would play a key role in this restoration. With some rereading, the author of 4 Ezra has retained and reapplied to his new social text this Deuteronomic tradition.

The Response of the Gospel of Luke (Luke 19:41–44; 21:5–36)

Readers need no extensive introduction to the Gospel of Luke (review chap. 9). Suffice it to say that most interpreters believe Luke wrote Luke-Acts not too many years after the destruction of the Second Temple in 70 CE.

The Cause of the Destruction of Jerusalem and the Temple. Luke 19:41–44 offers one of the clearest explanations in the NT regarding the cause of Jerusalem's destruction: "because you [Jerusalem] did not recognize the time of your visitation from God" (19:44). Luke believes that this divine visitation has come in the person of Jesus Christ. For example, in Lk 7:16, after Jesus had raised a young man from the dead, the people declared, "A great prophet has risen among us" and "God has 'looked favorably on' (Greek = 'visited') his people." In this pericope, God manifests his visitation in the work of Jesus. Jesus' statement in Lk 19:44 that Jerusalem's destruction is due to the failure of Israel to recognize the arrival of God's visitation is tantamount to saying that Israel had failed to recognize that Jesus was the agent of God's visitation. It was for this reason that the Romans destroyed Jerusalem, according to the Lukan gospel.

Luke, like 4 Ezra, sees the destruction of Jerusalem as divine punishment. But it is not failure to obey the law that leads to the city's destruction but failure to recognize God's visitation in Jesus. Rejection of Jesus, not disobedience of the **Torah**, is what concerns God.

Luke 21:5–36 also speaks of the destruction of Jerusalem and the Temple. Verses 5–6 clearly predict the Second Temple's destruction. Other predictions are offered as well when the people ask Jesus "Teacher, when will this be?" (v. 7). Jesus speaks of the rise of false messiahs, wars, insurrections, international struggles, famines, and other disasters (vv. 9–11). Luke's readers could find allusions here to the struggles that faced those in Judea (cf. v. 21) during the time of the revolt against Rome. Jesus also predicts persecution for his followers (vv. 12–19). The book of Acts narrates the fulfillment of these predictions of persecution. Then Jesus specifically addresses the destruction of Jerusalem (vv. 20–24). He describes the punishment of Jerusalem and its inhabitants in harsh terms, speaking of Jerusalem's "desolation" (v. 20), the "days of vengeance," "great distress," and "wrath against this people" (vv. 22–23). The people will be

"Not one stone will be left upon another" (Lk 21:6). One can see in Jerusalem to this day stones from the Roman destruction of the Herodian Temple. (Chance and Horne)

"taken away as captives among all nations," calling to mind, once again, impressions of the Exile. Finally, "Jerusalem will be trampled on by the Gentiles, until the times of the Gentiles are fulfilled" (v. 24).

The Future of Jerusalem and the Temple. Whereas much attention was paid in 4 Ezra to Zion's restoration, Luke, like other Christians, says nothing explicit about such a restoration. Luke agrees with 4 Ezra that Jerusalem was destroyed as divine judgment. Yet, the text disagrees with 4 Ezra over the cause of Jerusalem's judgment, and its ultimate restoration. Some interpreters see a hint of Jerusalem's restoration in the phrase "until the times of the Gentiles are fulfilled" (v. 24b). The "until" might imply that Jerusalem's trampling will one day end and that Jerusalem will once again be free.[6] But one must concede that this is a very subtle hint of restoration.

After the announcement of Jerusalem's destruction, attention shifts to the triumphant coming of the son of man (vv. 25–27), whom Luke identifies with Jesus. With Jesus' **parousia** comes the redemption of Jesus' listeners (v. 28). These listeners certainly include the Jewish multitudes who have gathered at the Temple to hear Jesus speak (see 21:37–38). Hence, hope is held forth for the redemption of Jews who hear Jesus' words and, presumably, eventually come to recognize him as the Christ, the agent of God's visitation (cf. 19:41–44). But aside from the hint of v. 24b,

[6]One of the authors of this text has argued this way. See Chance, *Jerusalem, the Temple, and the New Age,* 127–138. Personally speaking, I am not so confident any more, only proving that scholars are quite prone to change their minds about things.

the text gives no attention to the restoration of Jerusalem per se. And the text is silent regarding the restoration of the Temple. The Second Temple, it appears, was the *last* Temple.

There is one important similarity between Luke and 4 Ezra. 4 Ezra leaves the impression that the time of Jerusalem's restoration is near. Luke also leaves the impression that the time for the coming of the son of man and the redemption of those who follow Jesus is near. Notice that immediately after Jesus speaks of the destruction of Jerusalem, he speaks of cosmic signs that will precede the parousia of the son of man (v. 25). From the perspective of Luke's readers, the destruction of Jerusalem is an accomplished fact. Therefore, all that remains for the parousia are the cosmic signs. Verse 28 tells readers to know their "redemption is drawing near" when "these things begin to take place." Verse 31 says much the same thing. Readers of Luke's gospel have seen most the things of chapter 21 occur. Like readers of 4 Ezra, Luke's original readers probably felt that *their* redemption was drawing near.

But unlike the **implied readers** of 4 Ezra, who are Jewish, Christians did not look beyond the destruction of the Second Temple to the glorious restoration of a new *literal* Temple or city. The return of Jesus the Messiah as the son of man was the object of their hope. For the Jewish readers of 4 Ezra, the messianic "man from the sea" was not an insignificant figure. But part of his significance was rooted in his intention to rebuild Zion and there judge the nations and bless God's people. For Luke's readers, Jesus, not the Temple or city he builds, is central. Jesus *alone* has taken center stage.

What about the Temple and city? What of all the grand prophecies of restoration offered by the Jewish scriptures? Are these merely left unfulfilled? If Christians wished their claims to be taken seriously that, in Jesus, God had visited and redeemed his people, they could not avoid what the Jewish scriptures said about the glorious restoration of the Temple and Jerusalem. Christians did not avoid these expectations, but they did reread them.

A Holy Temple in the Lord:
Ephesians 2

Learning Goals

- To learn how Ephesians reread traditional Jewish expectations regarding the Temple in light of a Christian theological social text.
- To understand how the changing social text of Ephesians accounts for this text's rereading of the earlier letters of Paul.

Guiding Study Exercises

1) Describe how the writer of Ephesians has reread traditional Jewish expectations so as to affirm the fulfillment of these hopes, while, at the same time, *not* expecting the rebuilding of a *literal* Temple.
2) What is distinctive about the historical social text of the author of Ephesians that accounts for his rereading of Paul and his embracing of "realized eschatology"?

Rereading the Expectations of a New Temple

Going back at least as far as the time of Third Isaiah, some Jews hoped for a time when gentiles and Jews would experience the salvation of God at the restored Temple of Jerusalem (Isa. 56:6–7). A review of texts such as Tob 14:5–7 shows that this belief continued to form an extremely influential theological social text for many Jews of the Second Temple period.

The author of Ephesians believed that the new age of salvation had dawned. He speaks of God's "plan for the fullness of time, to gather up all things in him [Christ], things in heaven and things on earth" (Eph 1:10). He talks of how this plan, "the mystery of his will" (1:9), has been "made known to us," the church (1:9). What is more, this "plan of the mystery hidden for ages in God" (3:9) is now, "through the church," being "made known to the rulers and authorities in the heavenly places" (3:10). The church plays a very important role in the revealing of this cosmic plan of God. Additionally, God has resurrected Christ and he now sits at the right hand of God in the heavenly places (1:20), "far above all rule and authority and power and dominion . . ." (1:21). God "has put all things under his feet and has made him head over all things for the church, which is his body, the fullness of him who fills all in all" (1:22–23). *Already* Christ rules over all things, God having put all things "under his feet." Jesus, the cosmic king, *now* rules from the heavenly places.

The body of Christ, the church, shares in this cosmic victory of Christ. Note that it was *for the church* that God has put all things under Christ (1:22). And just as Christ already reigns over all things from the heavenly places, his people *already* "have been saved" (2:5, 8) and *already* God "has raised us up with [Christ] and seated us with him in the heavenly places in Christ Jesus" (2:6). The age of salvation is here and even now the church, God's people, share in its blessings and God's "glorious inheritance" (1:18) and "immeasurable greatness" (1:19). The belief that God's salvation is present informs readers' understandings of what Ephesians says about the Temple.

The writer focuses on the Temple motif in 2:19–22. Statements made to the gentile readers (cf. 2:11–12) address them as "citizens with the saints" and "members of the household of God" (2:19), built on the apostolic foundation, with Christ himself as the corner or keystone (2:21). In Christ "the whole structure is joined together and grows into a holy Temple in the Lord" (2:21), constituting a "dwelling place for God" (2:22). The building imagery employed by Ephesians to talk about God's people is obvious: household, cornerstone, structure, God's dwelling place, Temple.

God has joined together gentile believers with Jewish believers to form "one new humanity in the place of the two" (2:15). In contemporary terminology, Christians are a people who transcend former racial and ethnic identities. Before the gentiles were joined in Christ to form a new humanity, they were aliens in regard to Israel, strangers to the **covenant**, and a people far away from God and without hope (2:12–13). Now, however, these gentiles are brought near to God and "are no longer strangers and aliens," but "citizens with the saints" (2:19).

It is significant that the text describes the gathering place of this new humanity consisting of Jew and gentile as "a holy Temple in the Lord" (2:21). Ephesians rereads an important scriptural expectation regarding the salvation of both Jews and gentiles in God's Temple. Ephesians understands the Temple where Jews and gentiles find salvation not as a specific building located in a specific city, but as the fellowship of God's people, the church.

The self-portrait of the Christian community as the Temple provides a macro-level intertext with the community of Jews who lived at **Qumran,** who also viewed themselves as a Temple (recall

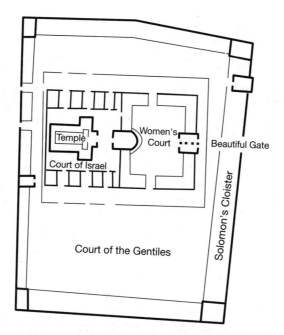

Temple

Women's Court

Beautiful Gate

Court of Israel

Solomon's Cloister

Court of the Gentiles

This diagram of the Temple area in Jesus' time shows that the gentiles were restricted in their access to the Jewish Temple (note the "Court of the Gentiles" outside the main Temple area). Ephesians envisions Jews and gentiles *together* constituting the "new Temple" of the church (Eph 2:17–22). (Adapted from Robert A. Spivey and D. Moody Smith, *Anatomy of the New Testament: A Guide to Its Structure and Meaning,* 5th ed, © 1995, p. 152. Used by permission of Prentice Hall, Upper Saddle River, NJ)

Chap. 6). However, they saw themselves as an *interim* Temple to function only until God built a literal new Temple in the future to replace the corrupt Second Temple (Chap. 6). Ephesians does not view the church as merely an interim Temple awaiting some future golden age of salvation. According to Ephesians, the time of salvation and Christ's cosmic rule are now here. The time of the church's sharing of this cosmic triumph is also now here. And with this coming of God's age of salvation comes his new Temple, where Jew and gentile find salvation in Christ: the church.

Rereading Paul

The author of Ephesians is not only rereading Jewish tradition as he speaks of the church as God's new Temple for the age of salvation, he is also rereading Paul. Just as the Chronicler could reread an earlier source, such as the Deuteronomistic History, so in the NT the author of one text could reread earlier texts. Most scholars believe that the author of Ephesians is rereading earlier texts written by Paul.[7]

---

[7]R. E. Brown, *An Introduction to the New Testament* (New York: Doubleday, 1997) 621, states that 80% of critical scholars conclude that Ephesians is pseudonymous. See pp. 627–30 for a fuller discussion.

To be sure, the letter to the Ephesians claims to be written by Paul (see 1:1). Consequently, many beginning critical readers may feel uncomfortable questioning the stated authorship of this biblical document. However, **pseudepigrapha** were quite common in antiquity, as previous study of Daniel (Chap. 5), Tobit (Chap. 6), and 4 Ezra (just above) demonstrates. Christians, like Jews, could practice **pseudonymous authorship**, writing documents under the pen name of a worthy figure of either the recent or distant past in order both to honor the one in whose name the text was written and to enhance the authority of the pseudonymous text.

Most scholars believe for the following reasons that Ephesians was written by a follower of Paul. First, the letter exhibits differences in style, language, and even content and perspective when compared with the core of the indisputably authentic letters of Paul. Second, Paul wrote letters to address *specific* occasions and situations, as the study of 1 Corinthians in the previous chapter indicates. Ephesians, however, is a thoughtful and provocative presentation of some of the great themes of Paul's other letters. Yet, unlike the indisputably authentic letters, it does not address a *specific* occasion. If Paul did write Ephesians, one must conclude that he thought it would be valuable to compose, in a more formal style than his earlier letters, a kind of general summary of some of the great theological themes of his earlier letters. This scenario is not impossible, but it does not impress most critical readers as probable or as being the most reasonable conclusion to be drawn based on the evidence. Finally, "Ephesians" is actually something of a misnomer, for the earliest and best manuscripts of this letter do not have the words "in Ephesus" in the superscription of 1:1. That is, this letter originally circulated to no specific church at all, but was originally a general encyclical letter. That is quite out of character for Paul.[8]

Most believe, therefore, that the real author is an interpreter who rereads Paul. Scholars agree that the author of Ephesians quotes from every other letter attributed to Paul in the NT (excluding the Pastorals), and most especially from Colossians. This author had access to Paul's letters and attempted to present a distillation of Paul's theology *for his own time.* The author is not bound by the original meaning of what Paul wrote in his letters a generation earlier. Rather, he lifts from Paul's letters important themes and reinterprets them for and applies them to the generation of Christians who lived a couple of decades after Paul died.[9] In short, the historical social text that informs the author of Ephesians is to be found in the generation following Paul.

An Example of Rereading. A study of some intertexts between Ephesians and Paul's indisputably authentic letters (see Table 12.1) can illustrate how Ephesians is rereading Paul (italics added for emphasis).

In row 1, Ephesians speaks of the victory of Christ as *complete* and *accomplished* for the sake of the church: "he *has put* all things under his feet and *has made* him the head over all things for the church." *Already* God has subjected all things to Christ. This offers an interesting comparison and contrast with the intertext from 1 Corinthians. The Corinthian text leaves the impression

---

[8]M. Barth, *Ephesians 1–3* (AB 34; Garden City, NY: Doubleday, 1974) 36–50, offers a thorough defense of traditional Pauline authorship.

[9]Scholars generally date Ephesians broadly to the last third of the first century (C. L. Mitton, *Ephesians* [Grand Rapids, MI: Eerdmans, 1973] 24–25, with most dating it toward the end of this period (R. E. Brown, *Introduction,* 621).

Table 12.1

Ephesians and the Authentic Letters of Paul: A Comparison

Ephesians	Other Pauline letters
1. God put this power to work in Christ when he raised him from the dead and seated him at his right hand in the heavenly places, far above all rule and authority and power and dominion, and above every name that is named, not only in this age but also in the age to come. *And he has put all things under his feet and has made him the head over all things for the church* (1:20–22).	*For he must reign until he has put all his enemies under his feet. The last enemy to be destroyed is death. For "God has put all things in subjection under his feet."* But when it says, "All things are put in subjection," it is plain that this does not include the one who put all things in subjection under him. When all things are subjected to him, then the Son himself will also be subjected to the one who put all things in subjection under him, so that God may be all in all (1 Cor 15:25–28).
2. But God, who is rich in mercy, out of the great love with which he loved us even when we were dead through our trespasses, *made us alive together with Christ—by grace you have been saved—and raised us up with him and seated us with him in the heavenly places in Christ Jesus,* so that in the ages to come he might show the immeasurable riches of his grace in kindness toward us in Christ Jesus. For *by grace you have been saved* through faith, and this is not your own doing; it is the gift of God (2:4–8).	Much more surely then, now that we have been justified by his blood, *will we be saved* through him from the wrath of God. For if while we were enemies, we were reconciled to God through the death of his Son, much more surely, having been reconciled, *will we be saved* by his life (Rom 5:9–10). For if we have been united with him in a death like his, *we will certainly be united with him in a resurrection like his* (Rom 6:5).

that Christ has *not yet* subjected all things to himself. Such subjugation will not occur until Christ's parousia, when he conquers Death, the last enemy, through the resurrection. What 1 Corinthians is *anticipating,* Ephesians views as already *realized.*

Row 2 of Ephesians states that Christians *"have been* saved" and have *already* been "raised up" with Jesus to sit with him in the heavenly places. Romans 5 speaks of the *future* of the believers' salvation ("we *will* be saved"). Similarly, Paul speaks in Romans 6 of the *future* of the believers' resurrection and subsequent union with Christ. Again, what are *future* expectations in Paul have become *realized* for the author of Ephesians.

Scholars use the phrase **realized eschatology** to denote the idea that eschatological hopes and expectations generally associated with the *future* are actually *realized* in the present. That is precisely what one finds in Ephesians. What are future expectations in the indisputably authentic letters, such as Jesus' subjection of all things and the believers' salvation and resurrection, are, in Ephesians already realized and effective. What has changed to lead the author of Ephesians to reread Paul?

The Need for Rereading. The historical Paul believed the parousia to be near (Chap. 11). However, Ephesians does not speak of the imminent parousia.[10] The implication of the tone of Ephesians is that the church is settling in for the long haul of history, preparing itself for "the ages to come" (Eph 2:7). In short, Ephesians shows evidence of a change in the church's theological social text, from one that affirmed an imminent parousia to one that viewed the parousia as more remote. Consequently, the *church,* joined in union with Christ as a wife to a husband (Eph 5:31), is what is important to the author.[11] As the focus shifted from the imminent parousia to the long haul of history, Christians needed to make relevant the early Christian hope for Jesus' parousia and the believers' sharing in his cosmic triumph through their own resurrection. By affirming that God and Christ have *already* won the cosmic victory over evil, Ephesians instills within persons who had lost a sense of future imminence a sense of present confidence and assurance. Christians could be assured that *already* they have been saved and *already* they have been raised up with Christ and seated with him. Thus, when the readers hear the author's closing exhortation to "put on the whole armor of God, so that you may be able to stand against the wiles of the devil" (Eph 6:11), they can follow such counsel, confident that God has already won the cosmic victory. It is much easier to go into battle if one knows that the enemy has already been so badly battered that one's own victory is assured.

In short, a new historical social text, a text concerned not with preparing the church for the imminent return of Christ but for its mission in the world for the ages to come, requires a rereading of Paul. The author of Ephesians has taken Paul's message, tied as it was to his own historical social texts, and reshaped it into a message for the church that transcends any particular time and any particular historical situation. Ephesians' "aim is to present the *abiding* truths of the Christian gospel as they are to be found in Paul's letters."[12] (Re)readers of the Bible have been doing this ever sense.

---

[10]Mitton, *Ephesians,* 28.

[11]See J. C. Beker, *Heirs of Paul: Paul's Legacy in the New Testament and in the Church Today* (Minneapolis, MN: Fortress, 1991) 70.

[12]Mitton, *Ephesians,* 29 (emphasis added).

"You Are a Priest Forever"
The New Priesthood and New Covenant
Hebrews 1; 7:1–28; 8:1–10:18

Learning Goals

- To learn about the social text that informs the author and audience of Hebrews.
- To understand how the author of Hebrews reread the scriptures to portray Jesus as a superior priest in an attempt to address the social text of his audience.
- To understand how Hebrews' employment of the scriptural idea of "the new covenant" compares to other Jewish rereadings of the idea.

Guiding Study Exercises

1) Summarize the social text of the audience of Hebrews as explained by this textbook.
2) Explain how the author of Hebrews has reread the biblical traditions about Melchizedek in order to argue for the superiority of the priesthood of Christ.
3) How does Hebrews interpret the idea of a heavenly temple in order to try to convince his readers that Christ's priesthood is superior to the levitical priesthood?
4) Compare Hebrews use of the "new covenant" idea with what one finds in the scrolls of Qumran. How do they compare and contrast? How do you account for these similarities and differences? (Review Chaps. 6 and 7 if you need to recall more specific information about this Qumranic group.)

The Text behind the Text of Hebrews (Hebrews 1)

The author of Hebrews quickly makes clear his eschatological and christological perspective: "in these last days [God] has spoken to us by a Son" (Heb 1:2). Note the two key ideas that shape the author's theological social text as he talks of how God communicates with his people: he and his readers are living in "the last days" and God's son is the one through whom God now speaks. The author's christological perspective clearly guides his reading of the Jewish scriptures. Verses 5–13 reveal the author's assumption that these texts from the scriptures either address Jesus (as, e.g., in v. 5a, quoting Ps 2:7) or speak about him (as, e.g., in v. 5b, quoting 2 Sam 7:14).

Scholars do not know who the author of Hebrews was. Church tradition has said it was Paul, but the letter is anonymous and there is no concrete evidence that Paul wrote this letter. Hence, the following discussion will refer to the author simply as "the author" or as "Hebrews."

Careful and nuanced reading allows some conclusions regarding the audience of the letter. First, it is quite apparent that the implied readers of the text are Christians (v. 2). Second, the saturation of the letter with motifs from and quotations of the scriptures points to an audience for whom the story and scriptures of Judaism were meaningful. Third, the heroes of Hebrews 11, whom the author calls "ancestors," are the heroes of the Jewish scriptures. The author obviously assumes that his readers would view these persons as authoritative models. Fourth, the text sternly warns its audience against "falling away" (6:6) and "spurning the Son of God" (10:29). Both warnings imply that the author views his audience as standing on the edge of a dangerous precipice, as though they may take a step that will lead to their own destruction. Finally, the text insists that Christ represents a whole new priesthood (cf. 4:14–5:10), offers a perfect sacrifice that mediates a new covenant (9:11–15), and effects a permanent forgiveness (10:12–18). This points to an audience living in the symbolic world of the covenant and the sacrificial means of atonement found in the scriptures.

Cumulatively, these features allow some description of the social text of this letter. The letter appears to address a Christian audience very much at home in Jewish tradition and scripture but, in some way, in danger of "falling away" or "spurning the Son of God." Scholars regularly suggest, therefore, that the audience consists of Christian Jews who are having second thoughts about leaving behind their non-Christian Jewish community of faith.[13] While most critical readers appear to embrace such a relatively general portrait of the audience, others, such as Barnabas Lindars, are more explicit. He suggests that the addressees are concerned that the death of Jesus, which they understand as a sacrifice for sin, is *not* effective in dealing with sins committed *since* they became Christians and were baptized. Lindars argues that these Christian Jews were beginning to believe that they needed to look to the Jewish sacrificial services of the Temple of Jerusalem to deal with sins committed *since* baptism. Thus, they wished to maintain very close ties with the Jewish community on whose behalf the Jerusalem Temple services offered atonement. Obviously, Lindars assumes the letter was written before 70 CE while the Temple still stood.[14]

The New Priesthood (Hebrews 7:1–28)

Some Jewish texts composed prior to Hebrews conceived of the Messiah in priestly categories (e.g., the Dead Sea Scrolls [Chap. 7]). Investigation of the motif of a new priesthood actually begins with a glance at Psalm 110, which the author used to conclude the opening string of scriptural quotations in Hebrews 1. Early Christians frequently quoted this particular Royal Psalm, particularly the first verse: "The LORD said to my lord, 'Sit at my right hand until I make your enemies your footstool.' "[15] Of course, they reread it in light of their conviction that Christ was the "lord" whom the "LORD" God placed at his right hand. This captured well the early Christian conviction that even now Jesus reigned as Messiah "in the heavenly places" (cf. Eph 1:20). The

---

[13]See R. M. Wilson, *Hebrews* (Grand Rapids, MI: Eerdmans, 1987) 10–11.

[14]B. Lindars, *The Theology of the Letter to the Hebrews* (New Testament Theology; Cambridge: Cambridge University Press, 1991) especially 4–15. There is debate among critical scholars whether Hebrews was written before or after the destruction of the Second Temple. Brown, *Introduction,* 696–97, notes that scholars are equally divided regarding this issue.

[15]See, e.g., Matt 22:44; Mk 12:36; 14:62; Lk 20:42–43; Acts 2:34–35. Chap. 11 examined Mark's and Paul's use of the psalm in Mk 14:62 and 1 Cor 15:25, respectively.

Christ on the Cross (ca. 1655), by Philippe de Champaigne (1590–1650). This portrait of Jesus' crucifixion interprets the death of Jesus in a manner similar to that of the author of Hebrews. Jesus is portrayed as a priest, offering a priestly blessing—note the uplifted fingers of Jesus' right hand—even as he dies. (Oil on canvas; 35½″ × 22″ (90.3 × 56.0 cm). Nelson-Atkins Museum of Art, Kansas City, Missouri [Purchase: Nelson Trust])

A Closer Look: Baptism in the Early Church. The Greek word *baptizō* literally means "to dip." The rite of baptism was widespread in the ancient world, commonly understood as a ritual associated with purity. Baptism could be practiced either as a rite of initiation into a community or to offer ongoing purification to persons. Some mystery religions (Chap. 9) practiced the rite, as did the Jews of Qumran. John was known for calling Jews to be baptized as a sign of repentance to prepare for the coming eschatological judgment of God (cf. Lk 3:7–17). Scholarly consensus argues that baptism was practiced by the earliest Christians as a rite of initiation (Acts certainly assumes this to be the case [cf. Acts 2:38–41; 8:12, 35–39, etc.]), perhaps as a direct outgrowth of John's practice, which included baptizing Jesus (Mk 1:9). In Rom 6:1–14, Paul interprets baptism as a participation in the death and resurrection of Jesus, which he applies to the moral behavior of Christians: they have died to sin and are to walk in a newness of life. In 1 Peter there is a similar understanding of the rite, if one assumes, as many scholars do, that much of the letter is a reflection on an early Christian baptismal liturgy. In 1 Peter the stress is on rebirth with the resulting transformation of life (1:3, 23) that is to issue in a life of holiness and obedience (1:11–17, 22; 2:1–10). Receiving the Holy Spirit was also associated with baptism (Acts 1:5; 11:16), with the Spirit serving as the initiated Christian's guarantee of ultimate salvation at the close of the age (2 Cor 5:5).

For further study, L. Hartman. "Baptism." *ABD* 1.583–94; G. R. Beasley-Murray. "Baptism." *MDB* 85–86.

For more advanced study, G. R. Beasley-Murray. *Baptism in the New Testament.* London: Macmillan, 1963; O. Cullmann. *Baptism in the New Testament.* Philadelphia: Westminster, 1978; R. C. Tannehill. *Dying and Rising with Christ: A Study in Pauline Theology.* Berlin: Töpelmann, 1967.

second half of the verse acknowledged the important fact that the battle was not yet won and that God and Christ had not yet subjected all the enemies of God—that awaited future fulfillment.[16]

The author of Hebrews also was drawn to this passage. He went beyond his Christian contemporaries, employing not only v. 1 of the psalm, but v. 4 as well. "The LORD has sworn and will not change his mind, 'You are a priest forever according to the order of Melchizedek'" (Ps 110:4). In its original historical context of pre-Exilic Judah, when the family of David sat on the throne, the psalm affirmed the close relationship that existed between the king and the Temple cult. Christian readers, however, applied to Jesus these texts referring to the King and the priesthood of Melchizedek. The author of Hebrews, moved by his concern to convince his readers that they need not return to the sacrificial cult of Judaism, sees in this psalm the basis for arguing for the existence of a whole new priestly order that actually supersedes the **levitical** priesthood of the Jewish scriptures.[17] If he can convince his readers that Jesus belongs to a priestly order that

---

[16]This idea that the final victory of Christ awaits *future* fulfillment is, of course, different from what Ephesians says. Significantly, Ephesians does *not* quote or paraphrase Ps 110:1b.

[17]Readers should recall the issue of the relationship between the levitical and Aaronide priests (Chap. 6). Hebrews appears to collapse the two. Note Heb 7:11, where Hebrews speaks of "the levitical priesthood" as being of "the order of Aaron."

supersedes that of Judaism, he can make great headway in undercutting their rationale to return to the Temple cult of Judaism.

The author knows his scriptures well enough to be familiar with a very short story about Melchizedek found in Gen 14:18–20 (see Table 12.2). Rows 1–3 of the Genesis column quote the text from Gen 14:18–20. Rows 1–3 of the Hebrews column shows how the author of Hebrews has paraphrased and quoted from the passage. Row 4 reveals how Hebrews interprets the meaning of the name and office of Melchizedek. The first half of the priest's name comes from the Hebrew word for "king" (*melek*), while the second half comes from the Hebrew word for "righteousness" (*sedeq*); hence, the translation "king of righteousness." Hebrews takes *Salem* to be the equivalent of *shalom* ("peace") and translates it, accordingly, as "king of peace." Hebrews clearly is associating Melchizedek with Christ, whom he views as both "the king of righteousness" and "king of peace."

Hebrews also observes that Abraham tithed to Melchizedek (rows 6–8) and draws significant conclusions from this fact. First, a priest who did not belong to the descendants of Abraham or Levi collected tithes from Abraham. This establishes that there exists a priestly order apart from the levitical order. Second, row 7 affirms the superiority of Melchizedek over Abraham by

---

A Closer Look: Melchizedek in Jewish Tradition. Melchizedek sparked numerous interpretations among various Jewish writers. One of the Dead Sea Scrolls portrays Melchizedek as an eschatological figure who brings salvation and liberation to God's people and the final judgment to God's opponents (11QMelchizedek). Some scholars argue that 11QMelchizedek assumes the identification of Melchizedek with the archangel Michael, whom Daniel portrays as the protector and deliverer of God's people (Dan 10:21; 12:1). R. H. Pfeiffer proposed the provocative, though not widely held thesis that Psalm 110 originated during the late Maccabean period. The portrayal of Melchizedek as priest, king, and warrior served to legitimate Simon's status as the first ruler of the Hasmonean dynasty.

Both the Jewish philosopher Philo and the Jewish historian Josephus interpreted Melchizedek's name as did Hebrews: the king of righteousness (Philo, *Allegorical Interpretation* III.79–82 and *On Mating with Preliminary Studies,* 99; Josephus, *Antiquities* 1.180). Like Hebrews, Philo also finds symbolic significance in the tithe that Abraham offered to Melchizedek. Philo interprets the symbolic significance of the bread and wine Melchizedek offered to Abraham. While there was no common way to interpret the significance of Melchizedek, this curious figure did inspire various rereadings.

For further study, M. C. Astrour. "Melchizedek (Person)." *ABD* 4.684–86; G. J. Brooke. "Melchizedek (11QMelch)." *ABD* 4.687–88; R. H. Pfeiffer. *Introduction to the Old Testament.* Rev. Ed. New York: Harper, 1948.

For more advanced study, F. L. Horton. *The Melchizedek Tradition: A Critical Examination of the Sources to the Fifth Century A.D.* SNTSMS 30. Cambridge: Cambridge University Press, 1976; J. A. Fitzmyer. "Further Light on Melchizedek from Qumran Cave 11." *JBL* 86 (1967) 25–41; M. de Jonge and A. S. van der Woude. "11QMelchizedek and the New Testament." *NTS* 12 (1966) 301–326.

Table 12.2

The Melchizedek Story

Genesis 14:18–20	Hebrews 7:1–10
1. And King Melchizedek of Salem brought out bread and wine; he was priest of God Most High.	This "King Melchizedek of Salem, priest of the Most High God, met Abraham as he was returning from defeating the kings
2. He blessed him and said, "Blessed be Abram by God Most High, maker of heaven and earth;	and blessed him";
3. and blessed be God Most High, who has delivered your enemies into your hand!" And Abram gave him one tenth of everything.	and to him Abraham apportioned one-tenth of everything.
4. King Melchizedek of Salem	His name, in the first place, means king of righteousness; next he is also king of Salem, that is, king of peace.
5. (Cf. Ps 110:4 for allusion to "high priest forever.")	Without father, without mother, without genealogy, having neither beginning of days nor end of life, but resembling the Son of God, he remains a priest forever.
6. And Abram gave him one tenth of everything.	See how great he is! Even Abraham the patriarch gave him a tenth of the spoils. And those descendants of Levi who receive the priestly office have a commandment in the law to collect tithes from the people, that is, from their kindred, though these also are descended from Abraham. But this man, who does not belong to their ancestry, collected tithes from Abraham
7. He blessed him and said, "Blessed be Abram by God Most High,	and blessed him who had received the promises. It is beyond dispute that the inferior is blessed by the superior.
8. And Abram gave him one tenth of everything.	In the one case, tithes are received by those who are mortal; in the other, by one of whom it is testified that he lives. One might even say that Levi himself, who receives tithes, paid tithes through Abraham, for he was still in the loins of his ancestor when Melchizedek met him.

observing that Melchizedek blessed Abraham: "It is beyond dispute that the inferior is blessed by the superior" (row 7). Third, the existence of a priestly order other than that of the levitical order *and* the superiority of the specific priest Melchizedek over Abraham, the ancestor of the levitical priests, allows Hebrews to imply that Levi is inferior to the priest Melchizedek, "for he [Levi] was still in the loins of his ancestor [Abraham] when Melchizedek met him" (row 8). This sets the stage for Hebrews' argument that the priesthood of Jesus, which is of the order of Melchizedek and not that of Levi, is superior to that of Levi.

Christ represents not only a superior priesthood, he performs his priestly service in a superior sanctuary. Hebrews believes that the earthly sanctuary of the levitical priestly service is but "a sketch and shadow of the heavenly one; for Moses, when he was about to erect the tent, was warned, 'See that you make everything according to the pattern that was shown you on the mountain'" (Heb 8:5, quoting Exod 25:40). Many Jewish interpreters believed that the pattern God showed Moses, on the basis of which the Israelites constructed their earthly Temple, existed in heaven. This "heavenly" Temple or sanctuary was the object of much speculation by Jews in the time around which Hebrews was written,[18] speculation that the author of Hebrews uses to his advantage. Most important, since this heavenly sanctuary was located in heaven and was not an earthly creation, it was superior. Hebrews claims that the superior priest, Jesus, offered the sacrifice not in the earthly sanctuary, but the heavenly sanctuary itself: "For Christ did not enter a sanctuary made by human hands, a mere copy of the true one, but he entered into heaven itself, now to appear in the presence of God on our behalf" (Heb 9:24). Hebrews, unlike Ephesians, speaks not so much of a *new* Temple, but of a *heavenly* Temple, which has always existed and of which the earthly sanctuary of Jerusalem was but an imperfect copy. Jesus is the perfect sacrifice offered by Jesus himself, the perfect priest, in the perfect heavenly sanctuary. Given this, the readers of Hebrews no longer have need of a cultic system that was only a sketch and shadow of the perfect sacrifice.

Many texts intersect in Hebrews. The author's own Christian self-text has intersected with a particular historical social text (that of his readers, who are considering returning to their former Jewish practices) and the literary text of the scriptures. The author's desire to persuade his readers that there exists a priesthood other than and superior to the levitical priesthood leads him to read the scriptures the way he does. This rereading allows him to conclude that the priesthood of Jesus offers much more than the levitical priesthood could offer. In a word, what the priesthood of Jesus offers is perfection: "Now if the perfection had been attainable through the levitical priesthood— for the people received the law under this priesthood—what further need would there have been to speak of another priest arising according to the order of Melchizedek, rather than one according to the order of Aaron?" (Heb 7:11). Clearly, Hebrews believes that the old order could not provide such perfection (7:19; 9:9; 10:1), whereas the new priesthood of Christ can (6:1; 10:14; 12:23).

Hebrews does not understand "perfection" to denote moral perfectionism, as in Western ethical thought. Lindars is helpful in his suggestion that perfection denotes "the completion of God's plan of salvation."[19] At the heart of this plan of salvation is the access of God's people to

---

[18]Jewish texts that speak of a heavenly counterpart to the Temple or sanctuary found on earth include Wis 9:8 and, in the Pseudepigrapha, 1 Enoch 14:10–20, Testament of Levi 3:2–4, and 2 Baruch 4:5. The Jewish philosopher Philo also spoke at length about this heavenly sanctuary. See, e.g., *Life of Moses* ll.74–75.

[19]Lindars, *Hebrews,* 44. See his larger discussion, 42–58.

the presence of God himself: "and since we have a great priest over the house of God, let us approach with a true heart full of assurance of faith, with our hearts sprinkled clean from an evil conscience and our bodies washed with pure water" (10:22–23). The sacrifice of the high priest Jesus, who "offered for all time a single sacrifice for sins, . . . for by a single offering he has perfected for all time those who are sanctified" (10:12, 14), *does* provide God's people with access to the deity. On the other hand, "since the law was only a shadow of the good things to come . . . it can never, by the same sacrifices that are continually offered year after year, make perfect those who approach" (10:1). Simply put, the law, which authorizes the levitical priesthood and the Temple worship, does not provide the means of direct access to God's presence that is provided by the new high priest, Jesus, who offers a better sacrifice. "For it is impossible for the blood of bulls and goats to take away sins" (10:4). But Jesus, the new high priest, "entered once for all into the Holy Place, not with the blood of goats and calves, but with his own blood, thus obtaining eternal redemption" (9:12). Christ, for Hebrews, is both the priest and the sacrifice whose work purifies "our conscience from dead works to worship the living God" (9:14). This worship of the living God results from the people's direct access to God, who had said in the scriptures "I will remember their sins and their lawless deeds no more" (10:17, quoting and expanding upon Jer 31:31b).

The New Covenant (Hebrews 8:1–10:18)

The "new covenant" finds its earliest biblical expression in Jer 31:31–34, a text quoted in full in Heb 8:8–12. Though the idea of new covenant was not foreign to other early Christian writers,[20] none of these other texts actually quotes or makes *specific* allusion to the text from Jeremiah.[21] Nor did Jeremiah's passage receive much thought or treatment from Jewish thinkers who were contemporaries of the early Christians.[22] Probably the Jews who most highlighted the idea of new covenant were the priests at Qumran. Yet, they did "not think of the new covenant as abrogating the Sinai covenant but as carrying it forward for a more faithful observance of it according to the precepts of [their leader] the Teacher of Righteousness."[23] The author of Hebrews offers a more radical interpretation: "In speaking of a 'new covenant,' he has made the first one obsolete. And what is obsolete and growing old will soon disappear" (8:13).

It is not likely that Jer 31:31–34, understood in its original context, intended to prophesy the *displacement* of the Sinai covenant. The author of this text looked forward to a time when God would inscribe on human hearts his law, resulting in human beings truly knowing God and living as God's people ought to live.[24] However, the author of Hebrews rereads Jeremiah from the context of his own self-text, which is his belief that Jesus offers the fulfillment of God's plan of salvation, *and* from the context of trying to persuade Christian Jews that "the Jesus story" offers them all for which they could hope: perfection and direct access to God.

Consequently, Hebrews offers a radical interpretation of the new covenant idea. The new covenant initiated by Jesus' sacrifice displaces both the old covenant and the sacrificial system

---

[20]See, e.g., Matt 26:28–29; Mk 14:24–25; Lk 19:20; Rom 9:4; 11:26–27; 1 Cor 11:25; 2 Cor 3:6, 14; Gal 3:15, 17; 4:21–31. Chap. 13, "Rereading the Story of the Law," will further explore the idea of the new covenant.

[21]See S. Lehne, *The New Covenant in Hebrews* (JSNTSup 44; Sheffield: JSOT, 1990) 63–91.

[22]*Ibid.,* 35–61.

[23]Lindars, *Hebrews,* 83.

[24]Lehne, *New Covenant,* 32–34.

that accompanied it. Hebrews 9:1–10 speaks of the first covenant and the "regulations for worship" (9:1) that supported it. Verses 11–14 describe Christ's dual role as both priest and offering, whose work "purif[ies] our conscience from dead works to worship the living God" (9:14). Hebrews links this work of Christ explicitly with talk of a new covenant: "For this reason he is the mediator of a new covenant, so that those who are called may receive the promised eternal inheritance, because a death has occurred that redeems them from the transgressions under the first covenant" (9:15).

Hebrews' argument is quite compelling. By saturating the text with numerous micro- and macro-level intertexts from the scriptures, the author shows the affinity that the new covenant has with the old. This new covenant is not new in the sense that it is something totally without preparation or foundation. The old covenant itself laid the foundation for the new one by speaking specifically of the establishment of a new covenant. Yet the covenant is new in that it displaces the old cultic system and the covenant that undergirded it. The reader who accepts the author's argument could leave behind the old Jewish cultic system, still resting assured that the scriptures of Judaism looked forward to this new covenant. This, the author hopes, will dissuade his readers from feeling the need to return to their former Jewish practices and modes of worship; after all, "what is obsolete and growing old will soon disappear" (8:13b).

A Bride Adorned for Her Husband:
The New Jerusalem of Revelation 21–22

Learning Goals

- To learn basic introductory information regarding Revelation.
- To understand what Revelation believes the New Jerusalem to be.
- To understand how Revelation has reread several texts from the scriptures and other Jewish writings to offer a word picture of the New Jerusalem.

Guiding Study Exercises

1) Write a paragraph summarizing the essential introductory information about Revelation.

2) Exactly *what* does the author of Revelation understand the New Jerusalem to be? How has the Seer reread scriptural and other texts to offer his understanding of the New Jerusalem?

3) Study carefully the various tables that lay out the micro- and macro-level intertextual connections between Revelation and the scriptures and other Jewish texts. Select what you consider to be the three most significant rereadings of the images offered by the Seer. Explain why you think the texts you chose are "significant."

4) Reflecting on the whole of this chapter, what have you learned about the way that early Christians "reread the Bible"? In what way, if any, has your study of the way early Christians reread the Bible reshaped your own self-text as a reader of the Bible?

Introduction

The first section of this chapter explored how 4 Ezra looked forward to the restoration of the destroyed city of Jerusalem. Tobit also looked forward to a Jerusalem that would be built in splendor, resulting in a great pilgrimage of the nations to the restored city (Tob 14:5 [Chap. 6]). The hope of a new Jerusalem was firmly embedded in the eschatological social and literary texts of Judaism. Early Christians, of course, believed that the time of restoration had begun, though they said little, if anything, regarding a *literal* restoration of the city of Jerusalem. Rather, early Christians spoke of the church as the new Temple (Ephesians), and of heaven as the seat of the true sanctuary where Christ offers himself as the perfect sacrifice (Hebrews). This study of Christian rereadings of the story of the Temple will conclude with a brief analysis of the portrait of the New Jerusalem offered by the author of Revelation.

The Text behind the Text of Revelation. The Apocalypse, or Revelation, belongs to the genre of apocalyptic literature studied in Chapter 5. Revelation presents visions interpreted by an angelic being and intends to encourage God's people who are undergoing persecution to remain faithful. "They have conquered him [Satan] by the blood of the Lamb and by the word of their testimony, for they did not cling to life even in the face of death" (12:11). "Let anyone who has an ear listen: If you are to take captive, into captivity you go; if you kill with the sword, with the sword you must be killed. Here is a call for the endurance and faith of the saints" (13:9–10). Popular readings of Revelation emphasize the predictive elements of the book, intersecting the literary text of Revelation with the *contemporary* social text, while ignoring the originating social text of the book. Mainstream biblical scholars, on the other hand, focus on the originating social text of the book and ask how its originating author and audience might have understood these visions. In this context, the book is not so much a foretaste of tomorrow's headlines, as it is a call for faithful endurance based on the assurance that the final victory will belong to God and his Christ. "The kingdom of the world has become the kingdom of our Lord and his Messiah, and he will reign forever and ever" (11:15b). It is, in short, a story, mediated through the popular ancient genre of apocalypse, about the end of the world and the final victory of God over evil and corruption.

Most scholars date the writing of the book to the end of the first century, when the Christians were being persecuted by Emperor Domitian.[25] The author, moved by a powerful visionary experience, was compelled to share his experience with his readers through this popular literary medium. He himself was living in exile on the island of Patmos, apparently because of his Christian testimony (1:9). Following his experience, and in obedience to the command of the vision itself, he composed this book so that the reader could, at least vicariously, experience what the Seer had: a vision of the final triumph of God and Christ. The Seer identifies himself simply as "John" (1:1, 4, 9). This makes Revelation different than other examples of the genre, for the author feels no need to write in the name of an ancient worthy. One reason that this early Christian could write in his own name was because the early Christians believed that the spirit of prophecy, which included visions (see Acts 2:17), was active in God's new people.[26] Church tradition has identified

---

[25]Brown, *Introduction,* 802–804.

[26]Chap. 14 will explore early Christian prophecy in more detail.

The harbor of the isle of Patmos where John received his vision that prompted the writing of Revelation. Perhaps the fact that John experienced persecution on this island surrounded by water helped to inspire him to picture the new heaven and new earth as having no sea (Rev 21:1). (Courtesy of Larry McKinney)

this John with the son of Zebedee, one of Jesus' original followers. Readers should understand, however, that nowhere does the author claim to be the son of Zebedee.[27]

The Image of the Bride. John introduces Revelation 21 with a vision of "the holy city, the new Jerusalem, coming down out of heaven from God, prepared as a bride adorned for her husband" (21:2). Later, John again refers to the city as "the bride, the wife of the Lamb" (21:9). Earlier in the book, a "hallelujah chorus" rejoices over "the marriage of the Lamb" and "his bride [who] has made herself ready" (19:6–7). A few lines later, the text describes this bride as clothed "with fine linen, bright and pure," with this "fine linen [being] the righteous deeds of the saints" (19:8). The symbolic and metaphorical character is apparent: a bride, clothed in the righteous deeds, is preparing to marry the Lamb! This metaphorical language makes sense once readers realize that the Lamb is a symbol of Christ and the bride of the Lamb a symbol of the church, the people of God. The church, made up of those who live righteously, is preparing for her union with Christ.

The depiction of the people of God as a bride is found in other biblical texts. Ephesians 5:25–33 employs the image of a husband and wife to speak of Christ and the church. In the

---

[27]Some scholars defend the tradition that John, son of Zebedee, wrote this book. D. Guthrie, *New Testament Introduction* (Downers Grove, IL: Inter-Varsity Press, 1976) 934–949 offers a thorough discussion of the authorship of Revelation.

Jewish scriptures, the prophet Hosea compared the relationship between God and his people to that of a husband and wife (Hos 2:16–20). Another prophet, Second Isaiah, uses the image of the wife to denote the city of Jerusalem, which God temporarily abandoned because of her sin (Isa 54:4–8). It appears that the author of Revelation has pulled together a number of these images from both Christian and pre-Christian tradition to form a picture of the Church as "the bride, the wife of the Lamb . . . the holy city Jerusalem coming down out of heaven from God" (21:9–10).

For John, therefore, the New Jerusalem is very much a hope and expectation, even as it was for the author of 4 Ezra. But the Seer does not look forward to the coming of a *literal* city, but of "a bride adorned for her husband" (Rev 21:2). This New Jerusalem is the church, the people of God.[28] The portrait of the New Jerusalem that John paints offers a magnificent metaphor for the church. Yet, as new as this idea is, John's portrait is rich in micro-level and macro-level intertextual allusions drawn from Jewish tradition.

Rereading Jewish Textual Traditions

The Seer of Revelation has drawn from a wealth of imagery to paint his portrait of the bride of the Lamb, the New Jerusalem. The following analysis will make apparent how the author has employed intertexts from the Jewish scriptures to weave his tapestry of the New Jerusalem as the church of God and the bride of Christ. Readers will benefit from a careful, comparative reading of the following intertexts.

Table 12.3 shows that both Revelation and Ezekiel speak of twelve gates associated with the names of the twelve tribes of Israel. Both present the picture of three gates on each side of the city. Ezekiel even offers the names of each tribe. Revelation is different in one significant detail. It speaks of the city wall having twelve foundations on which are found the names of the twelve apostles. This detail can have no parallel in Ezekiel, for the notion of "twelve apostles" is a thoroughly Christian concept unavailable to Ezekiel. The Seer's idea of the apostles as the foundation of the Christian community of faith forms a macro-level intertext with Eph 2:20. Ephesians describes the household of the church as "built upon the foundation of the apostles and prophets, with Christ Jesus himself as the cornerstone." The Seer of Revelation has intersected one social text coming from Christian tradition (the apostolic foundation of the church) with images from the literary text of the scriptures (Ezekiel) to paint his metaphorical portrait of the walled city, the church of the Lamb. The New Jerusalem, the bride of the Lamb, is the glorious Jerusalem of Ezekiel's vision. Yet it is more than a city, it is a people.

The texts of Table 12.4 describe the new Jerusalem as constructed of rare jewels and metals. The precise details do not always match in the intertextual comparisons. Revelation names a separate precious stone for each of the foundation stones, while Isaiah speaks only of sapphires. Revelation identifies the gates as consisting of pearls, while Isaiah speaks of jewels in general, and Tobit speaks of sapphires and emeralds. Revelation says not only that the streets are paved with pure gold (row 2, [Tobit envisions rubies and stones of Ophir, with the towers and battlements being made of gold]), but that the whole city is built of pure gold (row 1). The depiction of the city as pure gold forms a macro-level intertext with the description of the Solomonic Temple in 1 Kings 6 (row 2), which states that Solomon overlaid the inner sanctuary and "the whole

---

[28]R. W. Wall, *Revelation* (Peabody, MA: Hendrickson, 1991) 243–245.

Table 12.3

The Wall of the New Jerusalem

Revelation	Jewish Scriptures
It has a great, high wall with twelve gates, and at the gates twelve angels, and on the gates are inscribed the names of the twelve tribes of the Israelites; on the east three gates, on the north three gates, on the south three gates, and on the west three gates. And the wall of the city has twelve foundations, and on them are the twelve names of the twelve apostles of the Lamb (Rev 21:12–14).	These shall be the exits of the city: On the north side, which is to be four thousand five hundred cubits by measure, three gates, the gate of Reuben, the gate of Judah, and the gate of Levi, the gates of the city being named after the tribes of Israel. On the east side, which is to be four thousand five hundred cubits, three gates, the gate of Joseph, the gate of Benjamin, and the gate of Dan. On the south side, which is to be four thousand five hundred cubits by measure, three gates, the gate of Simeon, the gate of Issachar, and the gate of Zebulun. On the west side, which is to be four thousand five hundred cubits, three gates, the gate of Gad, the gate of Asher, and the gate of Naphtali (Ezek 48:30–34).

house" with gold. Such intertextuality invites readers to compare the New Jerusalem with the Solomonic Temple and to recognize the New Jerusalem, the people of God and the bride of the Lamb, to be the place of God's presence.

The tapestry woven in Table 12.5 offers a picture of the New Jerusalem drawn primarily from intertexts with Isaiah 60, though one can also see traces of other portions of Isaiah. Row 1 finds no counterpart in Isaiah, for the idea that God himself *and the Lamb* (Christ) would form the Temple of the New Jerusalem is distinctively Christian. This might appear initially to contrast with Rev 3:12, which states that the victorious saint will be made "a pillar in the Temple of my God." One who reads with wooden literalism may object that a person cannot be a pillar in a Temple in a place where there is no Temple. Actually, the two images fit together quite nicely, so long as one recognizes the highly symbolic and metaphorical character of Revelation. With God and Christ as the Temple, the image of saints serving as pillars in that Temple portrays these folk as living in *union* with God in Christ. They are part of the very Temple that is God and Christ.

Other features of the portrait show clear affinities with portraits of the New Jerusalem drawn from Isaiah. Both Revelation and Isaiah say that there is no sun, for the deity serves as the

Table 12.4

The Splendor of the City

Revelation	Jewish Texts
1. The wall is built of jasper, while the city is pure gold, clear as glass. The foundations of the wall of the city are adorned with every jewel; the first was jasper, the second sapphire, the third agate, the fourth emerald, the fifth onyx, the sixth carnelian, the seventh chrysolite, the eighth beryl, the ninth topaz, the tenth chrysoprase, the eleventh jacinth, the twelfth amethyst. And the twelve gates are twelve pearls, each of the gates is a single pearl,	O afflicted one, storm-tossed, and not comforted, I am about to set your stones in antimony, and lay your foundations with sapphires. I will make your pinnacles of rubies, your gates of jewels, and all your wall of precious stones (Isa 54:11–12). The gates of Jerusalem will be built with sapphire and emerald, and all your walls with precious stones (Tob 13:16b)
2. and the street of the city is pure gold, transparent as glass (21:18–21).	[H]e overlaid it [the inner sanctuary] with pure gold. He also overlaid the altar with cedar. Solomon overlaid the inside of the house with pure gold, then he drew chains of gold across, in front of the inner sanctuary, and overlaid it with gold. Next he overlaid the whole house with gold, in order that the whole house might be perfect; even the whole altar that belonged to the inner sanctuary he overlaid with gold (1 Kgs 6:20b-22). The towers of Jerusalem will be built with gold, and their battlements with pure gold. The streets of Jerusalem will be paved with ruby and stones of Ophir (Tob 13:16c).

light of the city. Of course, in Revelation, both the Lamb *and* God serve to light the city. This feature is not found in Isaiah (unless John understood the phrase "the LORD will be your everlasting light" to be a reference to the *Lord* Jesus). Row 3 of both columns speaks of nations and kings making pilgrimage to the new city. Isaiah makes mention of the "wealth" being brought to the glorious city (see rows 3 and 5). Revelation speaks of the people bringing "glory" to the city. The polemical attitude that John displays toward riches may explain why he is reticent to speak of

Table 12.5

The Character of the City

Revelation	Jewish Scriptures
1. I saw no Temple in the city, for its Temple is the Lord God the Almighty and the Lamb (21:22).	
2. And the city has no need of sun or moon to shine on it, for the glory of God is its light, and its lamp is the Lamb (21:23).	The sun shall no longer be your light by day, nor for brightness shall the moon give light to you by night; but the LORD will be your everlasting light, and your God will be your glory (Isa 60:19).
3. The nations will walk by its light, and the kings of the earth will bring their glory into it (21:24).	³Nations shall come to your light, and kings to the brightness of your dawn. ⁵Then you shall see and be radiant; your heart shall thrill and rejoice, because the abundance of the sea shall be brought to you, the wealth of the nations shall come to you (Isa 60:3, 5).
4. Its gates will never be shut by day— and there will be no night there (21:25).	Your gates shall always be open; day and night they shall not be shut, . . . (Isa 60:11a)
5. People will bring into it the glory and the honor of the nations (21:26).	. . . so that nations shall bring you their wealth, with their kings led in procession (Isa 60:11b).
6. But nothing unclean will enter it, nor anyone who practices abomination or falsehood, but only those who are written in the Lamb's book of life (21:27).	A highway shall be there, and it shall be called the Holy Way; the unclean shall not travel on it, but it shall be for God's people; no traveler, not even fools, shall go astray (Isa 35:8). Awake, awake, put on your strength, O Zion! Put on your beautiful garments, O Jerusalem, the holy city; for the uncircumcised and the unclean shall enter you no more (Isa 52:1).
7. He will wipe away every tear from their eyes. Death will be no more; mourning and crying and pain will be no more, for the first things have passed away (21:4).	I will rejoice in Jerusalem, and delight in my people; no more shall the sound of weeping be heard in it, or the cry of distress. No more shall there be in it an infant that lives but a few days, or an old person who does not live out a lifetime for one who dies at a hundred years will be considered a youth, and one who falls short of hundred will be considered accursed (Isa 65:19–20).

people bringing wealth to the New Jerusalem. After all, riches and wealth were characteristic of the city of Babylon, the antithesis of God's pure and holy city (Rev 18:3, 15, 17, 19). In row 3 Revelation lacks another feature from Isaiah. Isaiah says that "the abundance of the sea shall be brought to you." Such a statement would be thoroughly inappropriate in Revelation, for in the "new heaven and new earth," of which the New Jerusalem is a part, "the sea was no more" (Rev 21:1). Some interpreters understand the sea as a symbol of evil, or, at least the chaos that inflicts the creation with turmoil. Significantly, the monstrous beast that opposes God's people is said to rise up out of the sea (Rev 13:1). This, perhaps, explains the absence of the sea from John's vision of the new creation. Regardless of one's precise understanding of the meaning of the sea, one can see how John's conviction that the new creation would be free of evil and chaos has led him to reread Isaiah and strike the prophet's reference to the sea.[29]

Row 4 also shows clear intertextual connections between Revelation and Isaiah. Both texts say that the gates of the city remain open. The image of an open gate depicts the peace and security that come to God's people who live in the new creation. But note a difference: Isaiah says that the gates will be open day *and night*. In Revelation, there is no night; hence, John simply says that the "gates will never be shut *by day*."

Row 6 shows that in both pictures of the New Jerusalem, God's pure and clean people will dwell in the city. One can observe here further rereadings of Isaiah by the Seer. For example, Revelation says that to enter the New Jerusalem, one's name must be written in the Lamb's book of life; that is, one must be a faithful follower of Jesus. Obviously, Isaiah cannot speak of "the Lamb's book of life," for this is a specifically Christian phrase. Isaiah, however, does say that uncircumcised people will not enter the city, which is his way of saying that the city is a place of refuge for God's people. However, Revelation makes no mention of circumcision. John understands that one becomes a part of God's new people by virtue of her or his faithfulness to Christ, not on the basis of circumcision.[30] Thus he strikes this Isaianic detail from his rereading.

Finally, Row 7 speaks of the new Jerusalem as a place of joy, with both Revelation and Isaiah saying that crying/weeping will be no more. Yet, there is a distinctive difference between the intertexts. Revelation says in absolute terms that "death will be no more." The theological social text affirming that God would resurrect his people to eternal life (Chap. 11; cf. Rev 20:4–6) informs the author of Revelation. This particular idea is not part of the theological beliefs of Third Isaiah, thus, he cannot speak of "eternal life." Yet Isaiah does speak of *long* life: no longer will babies die in infancy or righteous people before 100 years of age. The author of Revelation rereads this text about *long* life in the light of his Christian social text of resurrection to speak more absolutely of the end of Death.

The literary and social texts of the Seer's religious tradition and heritage very much influence his vision of the New Jerusalem. It would appear that whatever the Seer "saw" in his revelatory experience, he also had in mind, as he wrote his visions, the texts and traditions of visionaries and prophets who had preceded him. Out of the dynamic combination of his personal experience, which would have shaped his self-text, and his familiarity with earlier traditions and texts that constituted his social text, he wove a whole tapestry, to portray for his contemporary and future readers a picture of the New Jerusalem. It is a very Christian portrait, requiring exten-

---

[29]C. B. Caird, *A Commentary on the Revelation of St. John the Divine* (HNTC; New York: Harper & Row, 1966) 262.

[30]Chap. 13, "Rereading the Story of the Law," will discuss the issue of circumcision in more detail.

sive rereading of his traditions. Most evident in John's rereadings are his inclusion of the Lamb (Christ), where earlier biblical traditions spoke only of God, and his equating of the New Jerusalem with the bride of this Lamb, that is, God's people, the church. Put bluntly, John did not envision God's people as *walking* the golden streets, but as *being* the golden streets. In fulfillment of the hopes and expectations of the scriptures, there would be a New Jerusalem—a glorious new city in which God would dwell. However, the city is now a people. From the Seer's Christian perspective, it is a people, not a literal city, in whom God would find his ultimate dwelling place.

Conclusion

In rereading the story of the Temple, early Christian texts interacted with many antecedent Jewish texts, both literary and social. The authors of these Christian literary texts reread these earlier expectations in the context of the key Christian theological social text, which stated that the age of restoration had dawned in Jesus Christ. With the reinterpretation of these expectations, the Christian authors did not look to the literal city of Jerusalem as the place where God would reside in the age of restoration. This city and its Temple, destroyed in 70 CE, were "history," as one might say today. Certainly the author of Luke-Acts felt that way. To the author of Ephesians, the future belonged to a new Temple, the church. The church lives in the context of a new covenant that Christ established when he, as the new high priest, offered himself as the perfect sacrifice in the perfect heavenly sanctuary (Hebrews). And when the restoration comes in all of its fullness with the appearance of the new heavens and new earth, God's people, the church, will be the New Jerusalem where God will dwell (Revelation).

For Further Reading

Not One Stone on Another: Luke and 4 Ezra

Giblin, C. H. *The Destruction of Jerusalem according to Luke's Gospel.* AnBib 107. Rome: Biblical Institute Press, 1985.

Mattill, A. J. *Luke and the Last Things.* Dillsboro, NC: Western North Carolina, 1979.

Stone, M. E. "Esdras, Second Book of." *ABD* 2.611–614. (*Recommended for beginning students.*)

———. "Reactions to Destructions of the Second Temple: Theology, Perception, and Conversion [4 Ezra]." *JSJ* 12 (1982) 195–204.

A Holy Temple in the Lord: Ephesians

Lincoln, A. T. and Wedderburn, A. J. M. *The Theology of the Later Pauline Letters.* New Testament Theology. Cambridge: Cambridge University Press, 1993. Pp. 75–166. (*Recommended for beginning students.*)

Perkins, P. *Ephesians.* ANTC. Nashville, TN: Abingdon, 1997. (*Recommended for beginning students.*)

You Are a Priest Forever: Hebrews

Cody, A. *Heavenly Sanctuary and Liturgy in the Epistle to the Hebrews.* St. Meinrad, IN: Grail, 1960.

Käsemann, E. *The Wandering People of God.* Minneapolis, MN: Augsburg, 1984.

MacRae, G. W. "Heavenly Temple and Eschatology in the Letter to the Hebrews." *Poetics and Faith: Essays Offered to Amos Niven Wilder.* Edited by W. A. Beardslee. *SBLSS* 12 (1978) 179–199.

A Bride Adorned for Her Husband: Revelation

Bauckham, R. *The Theology of the Book of Revelation.* New Testament Theology. Cambridge: Cambridge University Press, 1993. Especially pp. 126–43. (*Recommended for beginning students.*)

Court, J. M. *Myth and History in the Book of Revelation.* Atlanta, GA: John Knox, 1979.

Freyne, S. "Reading Hebrews and Revelation Intertextually." *Intertextuality in Biblical Writings: Essays in Honor of Bas van Iersel.* Edited by S. Draisma. Kampen: Uitgeversmaatschappij J. J. Kok, 1989. Pp. 83–94.

Michaels, J. R. *Interpreting the Book of Revelation.* Guides to New Testament Exegesis. Grand Rapids, MI: Baker, 1992. (*Recommended for beginning students.*)

CHAPTER THIRTEEN

Rereading the Story of the Law

Introduction

Review

In its present form, the story of the law in the Hebrew Bible reads as a set of commandments offered by God to the people of Israel through his servant Moses. It was during and after the Exile that the Torah came to take on its present form and authority, providing for the Jews a sense of common identity, and explaining to them *why* they had suffered as a people: they had disobeyed God (the Deuteronomic perspective).

Preview

Within early Christianity, the followers of Jesus made sense of the law in relation to Jesus, and vice-versa. Believing Jesus to be the realization of Jewish hopes as contained in scripture required that his followers take account of the law and their relationship to it. Being Jewish, Jesus would have had to address the subject of the law in order to enter into public conversation and to espouse his message of God's kingdom. His followers would also have had to address the issue of the law.

This chapter will offer two studies to examine the rereading of the story of the law by early Christians and, at least indirectly, by Jesus himself. First, portions of Paul's letter to the Galatians will be examined. Central to this letter's theme is the question: "Do gentiles who follow Jesus have to observe the Jewish law?" Second, attention will be given to the Sermon on the Mount, found in Matthew's gospel and presented as Jesus' definitive statement on the law of God.

"The Law Was Our Disciplinarian"
Paul and the Galatians
Galatians 1:1–5:12

Learning Goals

- To understand the social text of conflict that lay behind Paul's letter to the Galatians.
- To understand how people with different theological social texts could read the literary text of the scriptures differently.
- To understand the essentials of Paul's argument regarding the law and the law's application to those who believed in the gospel.

Guiding Study Exercises

1) What did the people whom Paul opposed want the gentile believers to do?
2) What most distinguished the theological social texts of Paul and his opponents?
3) How might Paul's opponents have justified their insistence on circumcision from the scriptures? What does their way of reading the scriptures have to do with their theological social texts?
4) How does Paul's theological social text, which he summarizes as "the gospel," drive his rereading of the story of the law? Address such issues as the following: (a) Why, according to Paul, did God give the law? (b) What was the law's function? (c) For how long was this law to remain in force?
5) Is Paul's interpretation of the Abraham story "typology" or "allegory"? Explain your answer, making clear that you understand what typology and allegory are and how they are similar to and different from each other.

The Text behind the Text of Galatians

Scholars debate the date of this letter. Some interpreters argue that Galatians is Paul's earliest surviving letter, dating to around the late 40s CE. Other scholars note that Paul refers to his recipients as "Galatians" (3:1) and argue that Paul is sending the letter to the descendants of Celtic immigrants who settled in the north-central region of Asia Minor—a region Paul did not visit until later in his missionary career. That would tend to date the letter later, perhaps closer to the mid-50s. This textbook will follow the majority of NT historians and suggest a date for the letter around the mid-50s.[1]

---

[1]See "A Closer Look: The Letters of Paul" in Chap. 11 for a summary of the dates of Paul's letters.

Paul's Message to the Galatians. One can only infer from hints found in Paul's surviving letters what the **apostle** preached to his Galatian listeners when he established their churches. Central to Paul's message was the "good news," or gospel, that, through the death and resurrection of Jesus, God had offered salvation and liberation to people from the dark cosmic and spiritual forces that enslave humanity, chief among them Sin and Death (Chap. 11). Paul believed that God was offering this liberation both to Jews and gentiles *on the same terms*: faith, or belief, in the God who had acted through the death and resurrection of Jesus. Paul had received a call from God to preach this message of salvation to gentiles (1:15–16). They too could find salvation and liberation by believing in the story, the gospel, of what God had accomplished in Jesus. Paul did *not* require these gentiles to become Jewish converts, or **proselytes**, to receive **circumcision**, or to practice other "works of the law" (Gal 3:2, 5), such as dietary regulations and sabbath observance.

The "Other" Gospel. As scholars attempt to reconstruct the historical social text of Paul's letters, they must make inferences from the hints and clues that survive in what Paul says in these letters. Galatians 1:6–9 indicates that someone had introduced the Galatians to "another gospel." Whatever this other gospel proclaimed, it apparently included the idea that the gentile Christians must adopt the practice of circumcision (5:2–4) and observe special days (4:10). These facts, combined with Paul's consistent polemics against "works of the law" (i.e., distinctively Jewish practices), led scholars to conclude that the preachers of this "other gospel" were Christian Jews. Like Paul, these Jews believed Jesus to be the **Messiah**. Yet unlike Paul, they continued to believe that being circumcised and living by the law were necessary if gentiles wanted to be included among God's people.

The Jewish preachers' argument must have been compelling since the Galatians were apparently willing to consider seriously undergoing circumcision. Perhaps the Christian Jews based their arguments on the Jewish scriptures themselves, particularly Genesis 17. This literary text outlines some important features that might have persuaded gentiles to be circumcised:

1. God establishes his covenant with Abraham and his descendants (v. 7).
2. Abraham and his descendants are to keep the covenant with God through circumcision (v. 10), which is quite explicitly said to be a literal, physical circumcision of the flesh (v. 11).
3. The covenant of circumcision is everlasting—there are no hints that this requirement of God to Abraham and his descendants would ever be set aside or abrogated (vv. 12, 13b).
4. Any male who "is not circumcised in the flesh of his foreskin shall be cut off from [God's] people; he has broken [God's] covenant" (v. 14).[2]

The implications of the Genesis 17 story are clear: if one wishes to be one of the "covenant people of God," one is to be a descendant of Abraham, and the descendants of Abraham are to be circumcised. Paul is emphatically opposed to this line of argument, but the clarity of the Abraham story means that Paul must propose a strong counterargument if he wants to persuade his readers not to be circumcised.

---

[2]E. P. Sanders offers a readable reconstruction of the situation that faced Paul in Galatia and the kinds of arguments that the preachers of "the other gospel" might have used (*Paul* [Oxford: Oxford University Press, 1991] 54–55).

Other Attacks on Paul and Paul's Self-Defense. The preachers of the "other gospel" attempted in other ways to persuade the Galatians to move away from Paul's version of the gospel. They minimized the legitimacy of Paul's authority as an apostle, claiming that he was only a sub-apostle, who derived his authority from the true apostles, like James (Jesus' brother), Peter, and John. Paul bristles at these claims, arguing that his authority is based on revelation from God and **Christ**, not other human beings (1:1, 11–12, 15–16). Paul points out that he defended the gentiles, challenging Peter and the other Christian Jews at Antioch, who segregated themselves from eating with gentile Christians by giving in to people from James (2:11–14). Perhaps the Christian Jews of Antioch segregated themselves from the gentile Christians because gentiles did not serve food that would be considered *kosher,* that is, acceptable to eat according to the Jewish laws of purity. Technically, these Christian Jews would have been breaking the law by eating with these gentiles.

Yet it is precisely Paul's point that a new day has dawned for God's people. People are "justified" by believing in Christ, "not by doing works of the law" (2:16). For, after all, "if justification comes through the law, then Christ died for no purpose" (2:21). Paul was convinced, based on his own *experience* of revelation, that what God had accomplished in Christ restored humanity's relationship with God. The restoration God had accomplished in Christ, Paul summed up in the word "gospel." This gospel provided for Paul *the* social text by which he reinterpreted and reread the Jewish social text of the law.

The law, whatever its purpose, was not to restore the fellowship between God and humanity. Christ and his death accomplished that. Thus, from Paul's perspective, to accept circumcision, to subscribe to dietary restrictions, or to practice other "works of the law," effectively nullifies the grace of God (2:21a). Thus, Paul is uncompromising in his words to the Galatians: "If you let yourselves be circumcised, Christ will be of no benefit to you. . . . You who want to be justified by law have cut yourselves off from Christ" (5:2, 4). Yet the Jewish scripture itself seems so clearly to say that those who *refuse* circumcision are to be "cut off" from the people of God (Gen 17:14). So which is it? And if people are not to follow works of the law, "why then the law?" (Gal 3:19). Some close rereading is in order to make sense of the purpose of the law in the light of the gospel.

"The Promises Were Made to Abraham"

Paul's strategy to undercut the arguments of those insisting on circumcision is not to address the circumcision issue directly but to speak more broadly of the law and its role. If Paul can show that the law itself no longer imposes its authority on the Galatians, then the issue of circumcision becomes moot. In Galatians 3, Paul attempts this line of argument.

The Appeal to Experience (3:1–5). Paul first appeals to the Galatians' own experiences, to their self-texts, and asks, rhetorically, whether their current participation in the Holy Spirit came from their hearing in faith or their doing works of the law (see esp. vv. 2, 5). Why then, Paul asks simply, are they considering turning back (v. 3)? Having reminded the Galatians that nothing in their own experience affirms works of the law, Paul now moves to offer his own rereading of the Abraham story.

The Promise to Abraham (3:6–18). The first section of Paul's argument is found in 3:6–9. Paul presents two micro-level intertexts to the Jewish scriptures. Verse 6 quotes Gen 15:6 while

A Closer Look: Justification. The Greek word translated as "justification" or "righteousness" and its verbal equivalent ("to justify" or "to make righteous") are related to the legal world of antiquity. To be declared justified in court is to be found to be in the right, or to be vindicated. Within a Jewish context, the term was also related to the idea of covenant and eschatological hope. In the end, Jews believed, the ultimate judge (God) would hold court—the final judgment. Those found *justified* in God's court would share in the deliverance, blessings, and salvation that God had promised to his covenant people. In short, to be justified is to be found to be a part of God's covenant people who participate in God's liberating reign.

A close reading of Gal 3:24–26 shows how Paul can use "be justified" to denote being one of God's people. Study the following parallelism:

A. Therefore the law was our disciplinarian until Christ came,

    B. so that we might be *justified by faith.*

A′. But now that faith has come, we are no longer subject to a disciplinarian,

    B′. for in Christ Jesus you are all *children of God through faith.*

In comparing lines B and B′, one can see that being "justified by faith" stands parallel with being "children of God through faith." To be justified means to be found within God's people: the family of God (and a descendant of Abraham). This is precisely the point Paul wants to make to the Galatians. They are not justified, found to be part of God's people—or descendants of Abraham—by virtue of accepting the marks of Judaism or "doing the works of the law" (Gal 2:16). They are justified, found to be a part of this people, by virtue of faith.

For further study, R. B. Hays. "Justification." *ABD* 3.1129–33; N. T. Wright. *What Saint Paul Really Said: Was Paul of Tarsus the Real Founder of Christianity?* Grand Rapids, MI: Eerdmans, 1997.

For more advanced study, K. Stendahl. *Paul among Jews and Gentiles.* Philadelphia: Fortress, 1976; J. A. Ziesler. *The Meaning of Righteousness in Paul: A Linguistic and Theological Enquiry.* Cambridge: Cambridge University Press, 1972.

verse 9 combines Gen 12:3 and 18:18. Verse 8 makes the point that *from the beginning,* when God first called Abraham, God envisioned the blessing of the gentiles. Furthermore, what made Abraham right before God was his faith. From this Paul concludes "those who have faith are blessed with the faithful Abraham" (v. 9, author trans.). The people of faith, and not those who do the works of the law, such as circumcision, are Abraham's descendants.

In verses 10–14, Paul moves to drive a wedge between the law and faith, presenting them as two mutually exclusive options. The Galatians must follow the way of law or the way of faith. Verses 11–12 present two key micro-level intertexts. "Now it is evident that no one is justified before God by the law; for 'the one who is righteous [justified] will live by faith'" (quoting Hab 2:4b). This is significant, for here Paul uses scripture itself to say that those who are right with God *live by faith.* On the other hand, scripture itself goes on to say, "the one who does these things will live by them [these things]" (v. 12). Here Paul is quoting Lev 18:5. The context of Lev 18:5 makes clear that "these things" refer to "ordinances" and "judgments," that is, commandments of the law. Scripture itself sets up the contrast that Paul needs: those who live by faith are said to be righteous (or "justified"); those who live by works of the law are not said by scripture to be righteous, but only to be living in accordance with the law's requirements.

Galatians 3:10 quotes Deuteronomy, saying "cursed is everyone who does not observe and obey all the things written in the book of the law" (Deut 27:26; 28:58). In Deuteronomy, Moses threatened a curse to *encourage* the people of Israel to follow the law. Yet Paul threatens a curse to *discourage* the doing of the law, and to encourage his readers to seek a better option. Christ provides this option for the Galatians, for he "redeemed us from the curse of the law by becoming a curse for us" (3:13b). In "becoming a curse" Christ paved the way for the gentiles to receive the blessing God had promised when he called Abraham: "the promise of the Spirit through faith" (3:14). By regularly associating the word "curse" with the law (vv. 10, 13) and words like "righteousness" (v. 11), "blessing," and "promise" (v. 14) with faith, Paul is setting up a clear contrast for the Galatians. Essentially, they have two options: follow the way of law and cursing or follow the way of faith and blessing.

Verses 15–18 elaborate on the promise God made to Abraham. Paul wants to make clear that the law does not compromise the promise and its fulfillment. God made a promise to Abraham and to his offspring. The law, which was given to Israel through Moses 430 years later, "does not annul a covenant previously ratified by God, so as to nullify the promise" (v. 17). The promise made to Abraham and his offspring remains intact and valid. In exploiting the singular "offspring" and identifying this offspring not with Abraham's physical descendants, the Jews, but with one person, Christ, Paul is again attacking the premise of his opponents.[3] The promise to Abraham (the blessing of the Spirit for the gentiles) finds its realization not in those who are circumcised, but in Christ alone. If one wishes to be a part of the promise, one must find a way to be associated with Christ.

"Why then the Law?" (3:19–29). This question initiates the last section of Paul's rereading of the story of God's promises to Abraham. The argument is complex and interpreters are not united regarding its interpretation. But two points are clear. First, Paul consistently presses the *temporary* character of the law (vv. 19, 23, 24). Could the Galatians come to any conclusion but that the law played a role only *until* the coming of Christ? Second, the law played the role of "disciplinarian" (vv. 24, 25). The word translated as "disciplinarian" is the Greek word *paidagōgos,* a term used to denote a person, often a slave, whose job it was to give guidance to younger children. Paul is asserting that the law played an important role in guiding humanity, to keep it in line, so to speak, until it came of age. Humanity "came of age" with the arrival of Christ and the way of faith that he brought. "But now that faith has come, we are no longer subject to a disciplinarian" (v. 25).[4]

---

[3]Paul's identification of the "seed" with Jesus the Messiah is not just a *tour de force,* but may show that he assumes a Jewish tradition that connected "the seed" of Genesis 17 with the Messiah. "Paul truly believed, as did various other early Jews, that the messianic king would be a true, indeed the truest, descendant of Abraham, the one who would establish or at least renew the everlasting covenant." B. Witherington III, *Paul's Narrative Thought World: The Tapestry of Tragedy and Triumph* (Louisville, KY: Westminster/John Knox, 1994) 47. His chapter on Paul's reading of the Abraham story (Chap. 4) is a clear and quite readable discussion.

[4]D. L. Lull, "The Law Was Our Pedagogue: A Study in Galatians 3:19–25," *JBL* 105/3 (1986) 481–498.

Paul returns to this theme of minor and adult children in 4:1–7. Here the apostle speaks of minors who, though they may be heirs to the estate, have no real rights so long as they are minors. Rather, "they remain under guardians and trustees" in a state similar to children under the watchful eye of a "disciplinarian." Humanity was like this. But with the coming of Christ, those who have been "under the law" have been redeemed, or set free (4:5), and are now children with full rights of inheritance. Prior to the coming of Christ, "we were imprisoned and guarded under the law" (3:23). Now people have the opportunity to be full heirs. But how?

One's connection with Christ makes one an heir. Paul uses a number of expressions to denote this connection with Christ: "in Christ" (3:26), "baptized into Christ" (3:27a), and being "clothed with Christ" (3:27b). By virtue of being "in Christ you are all children of God through faith" (3:26). This status as God's child is independent of one's status as a Jew or gentile, one's social status as slave or free, or even one's sexual status (3:28). Verse 29 presents Paul's bold conclusion: "If you belong to Christ [*the* offspring of Abraham in whom the promise finds realization], then you are Abraham's offspring, heirs according to the promise." Paul's rereading of the scriptures argues that being a descendant of Abraham comes solely through one's attachment to Christ and not by virtue of adopting the Jewish legal custom of circumcision. Attachment to Christ comes through *faith,* through trusting in the gospel message that tells what God has accomplished through Christ.

By setting up two mutually exclusive options for the Galatians, either faith that attaches one to Christ or works of the law that have nothing to do with associating one with Christ, Paul attempts to undercut the very foundation of his opponents' line of argument. One could paraphrase Paul's argument as follows: Even if the Jewish scriptures say that one must be circumcised to be a descendant of Abraham and a recipient of the blessings of a covenantal relationship with God, one must understand how and to whom the law applies. The law, with its demands of circumcision, is actually unrelated to the promise of the blessing of the Holy Spirit to be given to you gentiles. For those who lived before this time of fulfillment, the law was necessary. It served an important role as a disciplinarian. But now is the time of fulfillment. We have come of age and are ready to become heirs of the promise. This, however, comes only through faith, through believing in what Christ has done on our behalf. Through this faith you gentiles are joined to Christ, *the* offspring of Abraham, and by virtue of this spiritual union, *and only by virtue of this union,* you have also become children of Abraham and of God.

Paul argues that if the Galatians choose circumcision they will be rejecting the God-given means to righteousness and blessing. Christ will be of no benefit to them (5:2). To follow the way of the law will only enslave the Galatians again to those dark cosmic forces from which Christ had liberated them (see 4:8–9). To follow the way of circumcision will remove the Galatians from the protective enclave offered by Christ (they will cut themselves off from Christ [5:4a]) and expose them once again to the dangers of living in a world still dominated by evil (they will have fallen away from grace [5:4b]).

An Allegory Based on Sarah and Hagar (4:21–5:1)

Paul offers in these verses an **allegory** (see 4:24) based on the story of Hagar and Sarah. The stories of these women, both of whom bore children to Abraham, can be found in Genesis 16 and

A Closer Look: What Is Allegory? Allegorical interpretation was a type of intertextual reading widely practiced in Paul's day. It attempted to reinterpret literary texts in a highly *symbolic* manner in order to apply these texts directly to the situation or social text of the interpreter. According to Robert Grant, one ancient interpreter defined allegory as "saying one thing and signifying something other than what is said" (Grant and Tracy, 19). This quest for "something other than what is said" often led to a lack of concern for the historical character of the interpreted narrative. The allegorical interpreter looked primarily, perhaps exclusively, for the hidden, *symbolic* meaning of the literary text.

To be compared with allegory is another method of biblical interpretation that came to be called typology (see Chap. 1). This type of interpretation seeks to find "correspondence between people and events of the past and of the present or future." It "does not ignore the historical meaning of a text, but begins with the historical meaning" (Dockery, 33). Like allegory, typology is a kind of intertextual reading that attempts to apply what is found in a literary text directly to the reader's context, or social text. Unlike allegory, it takes more seriously the historical character of the interpreted text. Both, however, represent intertextual rereadings, attempting to intersect what is found in literary texts with the reader's own social text.

For further study, J. E. Alsup. "Typology." *ABD* 6.682–85; D. S. Dockery, *Biblical Interpretation Then and Now: Contemporary Hermeneutics in the Light of the Early Church.* Grand Rapids, MI: Baker, 1992; R. M. Grant with D. Tracy. *A Short History of the Interpretation of the Bible.* 2nd Ed. Philadelphia: Fortress, 1984.

For more advanced study, L. Goppelt. *Typos: The Typological Interpretation of the Old Testament in the New.* Grand Rapids, MI: Eerdmans, 1982.

21. Readers of this text who are unfamiliar with the story would do well to read these narratives from Genesis before proceeding.

Paul's Rereading of the Story of Sarah and Hagar.[5] Paul has already associated the law with such words as "imprisoned" (3:22, 23), "guarded" (3:23), and "disciplinarian" (3:24–25)— words that communicate putting restrictions on people. On the other hand, the gospel and faith are liberating, bringing humanity into a full familial relationship with God as his children (3:26, 29; 4:5–7). This framework of thought, which *contrasts* the covenants of law and promise, allows Paul to discern a meaning that the Sarah and Hagar narratives, read only literally, could not bear.

While Paul is assuming the historical character of the narrative, he is *not* reading the story literally. Paul is well aware that Sarah and Hagar are not literally "two covenants" (4:24). Further, one cannot construe the Genesis story to mean that the *literal* descendants of Hagar and her son

[5]Witherington, *Paul's Narrative World,* Chap. 4, has guided this discussion.

Ishmael are the Jews who observe the Mosaic law. *Literally,* the Jews are the descendants of Sarah and her son Isaac. Paul knows this, but he wants to reflect on what the two women represent or symbolize. He posits that each represents one of the two covenants about which he has been speaking: the Mosaic covenant of law (represented by Hagar, a slave woman) and the Abrahamic covenant of promise (represented by Sarah, a free woman).

Paul associates the slave Hagar with Mt. Sinai and the covenant of law given through Moses. As such, she corresponds with the literal Jerusalem, the place of Judaism that follows the Mosaic law. Since Paul has already associated life under the Mosaic covenant of law with slavery and imprisonment, Hagar the slave serves for him as an apt representation of this covenant. Her son is a literal descendant of Abraham, just as Jews who do not follow Christ are literally descendants of Abraham. But these Jews, Paul believes, live in slavery, not because they are literally descendants of the slave son Ishmael (they are not), but because the legal covenant that Hagar represents enslaves them.

Sarah, the free woman, also bears a son. This son "was born through the promise" (4:23). By reminding his readers of the promise, Paul connects the birth of Sarah's son, Isaac, with the original covenant of promise God made with Abraham—the promise that found its fulfillment in Christ (3:16–17, 27–29). She corresponds, Paul says, to the heavenly Jerusalem, the place of God's free children. "She is our mother," Paul says in verse 26. All who participate in the covenant of promise are her descendants. Again, Paul is not being literal. The Galatian gentiles are not *literally* the descendants of Sarah. Sarah is the mother of the people of faith because she represents the covenant of promise. And *anyone* can be an heir of this promise, Paul believed, in and through Christ and the response of faith (3:29; 4:7, 28).

Concluding Application. Readers familiar with the Sarah and Hagar stories know that Sarah drove "out the slave and her child" (4:30, quoting Gen 21:10). Perhaps Paul is encouraging the Galatians literally to drive out those insisting on circumcision, or slavery. Even if Paul is not advocating such literal expulsion, he is quite emphatically calling upon the Galatians to "stand firm . . . and not submit again to the yoke of slavery" (5:2). They are to reject circumcision. It belongs to a covenant that has outlived its usefulness. This is surely a most radical rereading of the story of the Jewish law. Was it a reading shared by all the followers of Jesus? The very presence of the Christian Jews whom Paul was opposing in this letter is proof that not all shared Paul's interpretation. Can we find any voices in the rest of the NT affirming the ongoing authority and validity of the law?

Fulfilling the Law and the Prophets:
Matthew and the Sermon on the Mount
Matthew 5–7

Learning Goals

- To learn about the social text that stood behind the literary text of Matthew's gospel.
- To reflect critically on how different social texts can lead to different rereadings of significant theological texts.
- To learn different approaches scholars have taken to interpret the Sermon on the Mount.
- To interpret some key texts within the Sermon on the Mount.

Guiding Study Exercises

1) Summarize the historical social text Matthew is addressing. In the context of this social text, why does Matthew give so much attention to the group he identifies as "the scribes and Pharisees"?

2) How might the different social texts of Matthew and Paul explain their different approaches to the law?

3) List and define the approaches to the Sermon on the Mount discussed by Joachim Jeremias (including his own view). Which one seems most reasonable to you and why?

4) Describe ways that one can understand the phrase "righteousness that exceeds that of the scribes and Pharisees."

5) Describe how the idea of the "new covenant" helps one to understand the Antitheses.

6) Reflect on your own "self-text" in light of the discussions of this chapter. Are you inclined to agree more with Paul, or Matthew, or both on the issue of the law? Explain your answer.

The Text behind the Text of the Sermon on the Mount

The "Scribes and Pharisees" and the Destruction of Jerusalem. Matthew's gospel devotes attention to a group that he designates the "**scribes** and **Pharisees**," a phrase unique to Matthew.[6] By referring to the "scribes and Pharisees" as though they represented a single group, Matthew offers a clue concerning a key social text standing behind the writing of his gospel.

---

[6]Matthew employs the phrase "scribes and Pharisees" or "the scribes and Pharisees" eight times. While Luke (5 times) and Mark (3 times) may talk about both scribes and Pharisees in the same verse, they do not make use of this distinctive phrase. Both Luke and Mark leave the distinct impression that the scribes and the Pharisee are two closely related, yet still distinct groups of the Jewish leadership.

The Pharisees were a pious lay movement that likely originated during the period of the Maccabean revolt. At the heart of their piety was the law and its rigorous application to the particulars of daily life. Since the law of Moses did not directly address every conceivable situation, the Pharisees were open to expansive rereadings of the written law so that this literary text could remain relevant in everchanging social texts. The scribes were the recognized scholars of the law. It is reasonable that Pharisees would turn to these persons for guidance in the interpretation and application of the law. While some scribes would have associated themselves with the priestly class, many aligned themselves with the lay Pharisaic movement (see Mk 2:16 and Lk 5:30).

Jacob Neusner argues that an even more solid alliance formed between the scribes and Pharisees following the destruction of Jerusalem.[7] Given that the Pharisees had developed an understanding of piety centering on the Torah rather than on the Temple, it is understandable that many Jews would look to them to offer guidance regarding the Jewish faith after the Temple was destroyed. Scribal interest in the study of the Torah, combined with the diminishing power of the priesthood that accompanied the loss of the Temple, contributed to the solidification of this alliance between scribes and Pharisees, resulting in their becoming the core of the new leadership of Judaism. By the end of the second century BCE, rabbinic Judaism was beginning to emerge as *the* normative expression of Jewish religion. The **Rabbi**, the recognized authoritative teacher of Jewish religion to this day, is a religious descendant of the scribes and Pharisees who began to consolidate Judaism after the fall of Jerusalem. Matthew's portrayal of the scribes and Pharisees as *one* group may indicate that he recognized these emerging leaders to be those whom he had to address and engage in debate if his readers were to take him seriously.

Matthew's Community and Post-70 CE Judaism. Matthew sees himself as a participant in the debates that occurred *within* Judaism after 70 CE. While modern readers may read Matthew as a *Christian* text that talks *about* Judaism from an outsider's perspective, Matthew saw himself as an insider who, when he talked "about" Judaism, was talking about his own faith and heritage.

> The Matthean group is a fragile minority still thinking of themselves as Jews and still identified with the Jewish community by others. . . . Matthew's Jewish community of believers-in-Jesus had been engaged in a lengthy conflict with Jewish authorities and had recently withdrawn from or been expelled from the Jewish assembly. . . . Matthew still hoped that he would prevail and make his program normative for the whole Jewish community.[8]

The theological social text through which Matthew interpreted events of his time was Jewish. As such, he was engaged in the debate of the significant issues facing Jews of his time, chief among which was the role and meaning of the law.

For Matthew, *the law is important.* He offers no statements, as does Paul in Galatians, that it was a temporary covenant sandwiched between the covenant promised to Abraham and its fulfillment offered in Christ. The law is something God's people are to understand and obey, *especially* now that the Messiah has come. But for Matthew, one looks to this Messiah, not the scribes and Pharisees, to discern the proper understanding of God's law. These scribes and Pharisees may have the right idea, namely, that one is to do what the law says. But they themselves are not to be

---

[7]J. Neusner, "The Formation of Rabbinic Judaism: Yavneh from A.D. 70–100," *ANRW* ll.19.2., 22.

[8]A. Saldarini, *Matthew's Christian-Jewish Community* (Chicago: University of Chicago Press, 1994) 1–2.

followed, for they do not interpret or apply the law properly (see Matt 23:2–3).[9] The evangelist even disparages the title "rabbi," a term beginning to become associated with the master teachers of the law. Through Jesus, Matthew exhorts his readers not to look to anyone as "rabbi" or "teacher," for the evangelist's community has but one teacher, Jesus the Messiah (see Matt 23:8, 10).

Though Matthew struggled to convince *Jews* that the proper course for Judaism to take was that offered by Jesus the Messiah, history would determine his to be a loosing cause. The vast majority of Jews followed the way of the scribes and Pharisees. But recognition of this debate offers a lens through which to read the Sermon on the Mount. Andrew Overman is helpful in saying that "Matthew 5–7 amounts to something like a constitution for the community, which instructs and guides the members."[10] A significant part of this "constitution" was the Torah. One could not know how to live properly in the community of faith if one did not understand and follow the law as properly interpreted. Matthew's Jesus offers this interpretation in the Sermon on the Mount.

Table 13.1

An Outline of the Sermon on the Mount[11]

Introduction: Blessing as the Basis of Jesus' Interpretation of the Law (5:3–16)
  1) The Beatitudes (5:3–12)
  2) Being Salt and Light (5:13–16)
Central Section: Jesus the Messiah's Interpretation of the Law (5:17–7:12)
  1) Fulfilling the Law and Prophets (5:17–20)
  2) Antitheses (5:21–48)
  3) Piety (6:1–18)
  4) Other Significant Issues (6:19–7:11)
  5) The Law and Prophets (Reprise) (7:12)
Conclusion: Doing What God Requires ("Dualing" Pictures) (7:13–27)
  1) The Picture of Two Ways (7:13–14)
  2) The Picture of Two Kinds of Fruit (7:15–20)
  3) The Picture of Two Kinds of Folk (7:21–23)
  4) The Picture of Two Kinds of Houses (7:24–27)

---

[9]See the article by M. A. Powell, " 'Do and Keep What Moses Says' (Matthew 23:2–7)" *JBL* 114/3 (1995) 419–435.

[10]*Matthew's Gospel and Formative Judaism* (Minneapolis, MN: Fortress, 1990) 95.

[11]The basic outline offered by G. Stanton (*A Gospel for a New People: Studies in Matthew* [Louisville, KY: Westminster/John Knox, 1993] 297–298) served as this text's beginning point. D. A. Carson's discussion (*The Sermon on the Mount: An Evangelical Exposition of Matthew 5–7* [Grand Rapids, MI: Baker, 1978] 115–136) of the dual structure of the last section guided this text's structuring of the conclusion, though many other readers have noted the dual structure here.

A view of the Sea of Galilee from the traditional location of the Sermon on the Mount. (Courtesy of Larry McKinney)

The Gospel as the Framework for Interpreting the Sermon

Meaningful interpretation takes place within a larger framework, (con)text, or story. Throughout history, interpreters have wrestled to locate the most appropriate context for making sense of the Sermon on the Mount. Warren S. Kissinger, for example, has devoted a book length investigation to the history of the interpretation of the sermon. Each of the thirty-four chapters is devoted to *at least* one approach to reading the sermon.[12] Joachim Jeremias, in his own helpful study of the sermon, offers four essential approaches that will offer students a sufficient survey of the various frameworks for interpretation.[13]

Jeremias called the first approach "the perfectionist conception." The sermon outlines the absolute demand of God in the form of law. It stands in conformity with the Jewish scriptures and their own demands for absolute obedience. One result of this approach is that nothing has really changed: the sermon is primarily another interpretation of the law, offering nothing new. Consequently, the sermon has nothing to do with the gospel. He labeled a second framework the "preparation-for-the-gospel approach." The rigorous demands of the sermon, when laid before the hearer, drive one to realize that she or he cannot keep God's radical commandments, thereby driving one to the gospel of grace. This approach is often popular among Protestants influenced by the thought of Martin Luther. The implication of this approach is that the sermon, while cer-

[12]*The Sermon on the Mount: A History of Interpretation and Bibliography* (Metuchen, NJ: Scarecrow Press, 1975).
[13]*The Sermon on the Mount* (Philadelphia: Fortress, 1963).

tainly rhetorically powerful, is actually irrelevant, for it is not intended to be followed but avoided by substituting the gospel of grace for the demand of law. A third framework is called the "interim ethic approach." Jesus (and Matthew) believed the world was ending soon and the radical demands of the sermon served as a *short term* ethic for the immediate crisis just before the final salvation comes. An implication of this approach is that the sermon has literally outlived its relevance since it was based on a false assumption, namely, that the world was soon coming to an end. It is not an ethic for Jesus' followers for the long haul of history.

The fourth approach, which Jeremias adopts, approaches the sermon as early *Christian* teaching (or **didache**). Such teaching explicates what God expects of those who say "yes" to the gospel of the reign of God. This has a number of implications for interpretation. First, the sermon assumes the reality and authority of the gospel message. As such, the sermon's intended audience is people who have already said "yes" to Jesus, the gospel, and the kingdom. Second, one is not to contrast the demands of the sermon with the gospel (as with both the "perfectionist" or "preparation-for-the-gospel" approaches), but to hear the sermon's demands *in the context of the gospel*. Third, the sermon offers ongoing guidance to the community of Jesus' followers. It is not just a short-term radical ethic for the last generation before the end of the world.

Blessing as the Basis of Jesus' Interpretation of the Law (5:3–16)

The beatitudes, which pronounce God's blessing, precede any statement of God's demand. These beatitudes are quite consistent in their form: "Blessed are . . . because." "*Blessed are* the poor in spirit, *because* the kingdom of heaven is theirs" (author's trans.). These are not conditional sentences: "If you are poor in spirit, then the kingdom of heaven is yours." Nor are they commands: "Be poor in spirit, that the kingdom of heaven might be yours." They are not explicit calls to action, but explicit pronouncements of what *is*: "Blessed *are*" certain people, not because of what they have done, but because of what God is doing and will do. Indeed, the very word "blessed" can be translated as "happy," rendering the idea, "the happiness which is the result of God-given salvation."[14] It is, after all, God who offers his kingdom (5:3, 10) and the rewards of his kingdom (5:12). It is God who offers comfort (5:4), inheritance (5:5), filling (5:6), mercy (5:7), a vision of himself (5:8), and adoption as children (5:9). God's people are not blessed *because* they are pure in heart, merciful, and peacemakers. Such people are blessed because God has chosen to offer them the reward and goodness of his reign. To be sure, the beatitudes express *implied* conditions and imperatives. If *God's* future belongs to the meek, merciful, and peacemakers, strong incentive is offered *to be* meek, merciful, and a maker of peace. Still, one is to understand the strong moral imperatives the beatitudes imply as grounded in what God has done and will do.

Verses 13–16 make clear that the sermon speaks to those who *are* the salt of the earth (v. 13) and the city on the hill (vv. 14–16). These words, then, are addressed to those who *are* followers of Jesus. They are addressed to those who have said "yes" to the proclamation of God's dawning reign. But with such *being* comes responsible *doing*. Salt must retain its flavor. The shining light or city must act in a manner that brings glory to God. Though the law of Jesus the Messiah is for those who have embraced the gospel, it is still law. It is demand. The law of Jesus the Messiah illustrates how his followers are to live.

---

[14]Stanton, *Gospel for a New People*, 298.

Conclusion: Doing What God Requires ("Dualing" Pictures) (7:13–27)

The introduction of the sermon consists primarily of the pronouncements of God's blessings and focuses on the "blessed ones'" participation in God's future offerings of inheritance, filling, mercy, and the like. The conclusion of the sermon also points readers to God's future. However, the future includes God's judgment. Matthew offers four word pictures to conclude the sermon. Each presents a duality, two contrasting pictures juxtaposing images of judgment or reward. Matthew makes clear that such judgment or reward rests on how one responds to the teachings of Jesus.

The Picture of Two Ways (7:13–14). The road leading to life and reward is narrow and hard. Conversely, the way to destruction is wide and easy. The word picture clearly implies that the positive response to Jesus is for those willing to take the road less traveled—and that, by definition, will be few. One can take little comfort that one's way of understanding God's will conforms to the understanding of the majority. Given Matthew's immediate context, this picture offers a warning: Though the majority of Jews of Matthew's time were following "the way" of the scribes and Pharisees, this is the wide path leading to destruction. The way that leads to life is the harder way of understanding God's will as Jesus the Messiah presents it.

The Picture of Two Kinds of Fruit (7:15–20). The **parable** of the fruit, which speaks of good fruit coming from good trees and bad fruit coming from bad, is almost self-explanatory. Clearly, the fruit serves in the context of Matthew's gospel as an image for one's deeds (see Matt 3:8, 10b). It is by one's fruits, or deeds, that others can recognize whether one is good or bad. There is also an interest here in recognizing false prophets. This appears to be an allusion to persons *within* the Christian community, indicating evidence of persons—would-be leaders, perhaps—who do not follow the ways of God as Jesus the Messiah presents them. Clearly, the picture of two kinds of fruit serves as a call to live consistently with the demands of God.

The Picture of Two Kinds of People (7:21–23). This picture is closely related to the immediately preceding one. The "bad people" exist *within* the Christian community, for they are described as referring to Jesus as "Lord, Lord." The picture painted indicates that claiming Jesus as Lord requires *doing* the will of God. Certainly, there is nothing wrong per se with what these identified as "evil doers" do: prophesying, casting out demons, and doing mighty works. Yet one looks in vain in the sermon for any hints that *these* kinds of activities stand at the center of *doing* the will of God. It is *avoidance* of the doing of God's will as interpreted by Jesus in the central section of the sermon that marks one as an evildoer, not casting out demons and other similar activities.

The Picture of Two Kinds of Houses (7:24–27). The houses serve as metaphors for one's life and the storm as a metaphor for God's judgment. Thus, the sermon ends with an unmistakable allusion to the eschatological judgment of God, the event referred to in the preceding picture as "that day." Those who build their lives by doing what Jesus teaches, build their lives on the solid foundation that can withstand the onslaught of God's final judgment. Those who fail to heed the word of Jesus will not survive. One can scarcely imagine a more powerful picture with which to conclude the sermon if Matthew wanted his readers to take seriously the understanding of God's law as offered by Jesus the Messiah. The central section of the sermon presents Jesus' interpretation of this law.

Fulfilling the Law and the Prophets (5:17–20)

These four verses probably offer some of the most difficult texts to interpret in all of the NT. The NT regularly denotes the whole of the Jewish scriptures by referring to the "law and the prophets" or a similar phrase.[15] While Matthew can share in this way of referring to the whole of the scriptures, he also recognized the law as something existing in its own right to give specific and concrete expression to the will and commandments of God (Matt 5.18, 12.5, 23.23). This is the primary meaning of the law in Matt 5:17–20, which refers specifically to "the law," "commandments," and "righteousness." Matthew understands Jesus as the one who fulfills the law in the sense of fulfilling God's commandments. "The *telos* [goal] which the Torah anticipated, namely, the Messiah, has come and revealed the law's definitive meaning."[16]

   How Does Jesus Fulfill the Law (5:17)? How does Jesus "fulfill" the law? In what sense, precisely, does he reveal the law's definitive meaning? Does the whole of Jesus' life and ministry, including his death and resurrection, offer a new kind of righteousness (see 5:20) that satisfies the demands of the law, thereby fulfilling the law's role and function in the sense of bringing it to completion?

   This interpretation, effectively, would lead to the conclusion that Jesus fulfills the law by bringing about its end; a view similar to that offered by Paul in his letter to the Galatians.[17] Such an interpretation, attractive as it might be to contemporary readers influenced by the thought of Paul, does not fit well into the larger context of Matthew's gospel and especially the more immediate context of the Sermon on the Mount. Matthew is too concerned with matters of the Torah to have embraced the idea that "now that Christ has come we are no longer subject to the Torah" (cf. Gal 3:23–25). Certainly, Matthew is in agreement with Paul that *Jesus,* and not the Torah itself, is now on center-stage. But as Jesus occupies center-stage, he devotes much speech and action to the subject of the Torah.

   In Matthew, Jesus fulfills the law not to displace it, but to give it proper understanding. This happens not only in his teachings, such as in the Sermon on the Mount and in other discourses that Jesus offers on the law (such as Matthew 15 and 23), but in his actions, such as those involving healing on the sabbath (Matt 12:1–14). Most important, he offers this proper understanding so that his followers might *do* this law, as made clear by the emphatic utterance of Jesus near the conclusion of the sermon: "Everyone then who hears these words of mine and *acts on them* will be like a wise man who built his house on the rock" (Matt 7:24).

   The Enduring Validity of the Law (5:18). Jesus begins Matt 5:18 with solemn declaration, "Amen [truly], I say to you." The very formula speaks to the solemnity and seriousness of the matter under discussion.[18] It is probably not coincidental that Jesus first employs this formula in Matthew's gospel to address the issue of the Torah (Matt 5:18). According to Matthew's Jesus, the Torah endures "till heaven and earth pass away"; it is not a temporary covenant, as Paul argued in Galatians.

   One might argue that "until all things take place" (found at the end of v. 18) is a reference to the completion of Jesus' ministry, culminating in his death and resurrection. The idea would be

---

[15]See, e.g., Matt 5:17; 7:12; 11:13; 22:40; Lk 16:16; 24:44; Jn 1:45; Acts 13:15; 24:14; 28:23; Rom 3:21.

[16]W. D. Davies and D. C. Allison Jr., *A Critical and Exegetical Commentary on the Gospel according to Saint Matthew* (3 vols., ICC; Edinburgh: T & T Clark, 1988/1991/1998) 1.486.

[17]U. Luz, *Matthew 1–7: A Commentary* (Minneapolis, MN: Augsburg/Fortress, 1989) 260–265.

[18]The expression "Amen [or "amen, amen," typical of John's gospel], I say to you . . ." is found in sixty-six verses in the gospels. It was a typical expression employed by Jesus to indicate that he believed his words conveyed authoritative teaching.

that with the completion of Jesus' ministry, this "heaven and earth" are, in a very real sense, "passing away." This way of reading allows one to harmonize Matthew and Paul, for Paul says in one of his letters that "the present form of this world *is* passing away" (1 Cor 7:31b). In another letter he says that for those who are in Christ, "everything old *has passed* away; see, everything *has become* new!" (2 Cor 5:17). Yet Matthew uses the phrase "until all things take place" elsewhere in his gospel. "Truly I tell you, this generation will not pass away *until all these things have taken place*" (Matt 24:34).[19] The context of Matthew 24 is Jesus' discourse on his **parousia** at the *end* of the age. From Matthew's perspective, the phrase "until all things take place" was a way of talking about the end of this age. It is clear, therefore, that Jesus is affirming that the law endures only "until [this] heaven and earth pass away" and "all things take place." That is, Jesus does not affirm that the law is eternal. Still, it is valid for the world in which Matthew and his readers find themselves, for all things have *not yet* taken place.

"The Least of These Commandments" (5:19). The phrase "the least of these commandments" places this text squarely in the middle of *Jewish* debates about the Torah. Later Rabbis (and presumably their religious ancestors whom Matthew referred to as the "scribes and Pharisees") actually discussed "light" (meaning least) and "heavy" commandments. For example, the Rabbis said that the commandment to honor one's parents (Deut 5:16) was a "heavy commandment." The commandment regarding whether one could eat a bird "sitting on her fledglings or on the eggs" (Deut 22:6–7), was a "light commandment." While Jewish legal scholars debated "light" and "heavy" commandments, they did *not* offer such distinctions to justify avoiding the lighter ones while heeding only the heavier ones. The leading Rabbi of the late second century CE, Judah the Prince, is credited with a statement that the scribes and Pharisees of Matthew's day likely would have affirmed: "Be heedful in a light precept as in a grave one."[20] This teaching is consistent with 5:19 where Jesus explicitly says that one is to teach and do the "least of the commandments." Failure to do so, according to 5:19, does not result in expulsion from the kingdom of heaven but produces a lesser role or reward (Matt 5:12; 10:41–42; 20:23).

Righteousness Exceeding the Scribes and Pharisees (5:20). Knowledge of the larger historical social text of Matthew's gospel helps to make sense of the literary text of Matt 5:20. The scribes and Pharisees, as representative of the emerging leadership of post-70 CE Jewish religion, offered the Jewish community one way to understand and apply the Torah. Through Jesus, Matthew is saying that this way is unacceptable. To follow the way of the scribes and Pharisees, as opposed to the way, teaching, and example of Jesus, is to exclude oneself from the kingdom of heaven. Matthew clearly is offering a serious warning to the readers of his day as he insists that the way of Jesus the Messiah is the way that God's historic people, the Jews, need to follow.

But what *exactly* did Matthew mean by "exceeding the righteousness of the scribes and Pharisees?" Again, one might offer a Paulinized reading here. By righteousness, Paul meant to be vindicated before God, with such vindication being attained only on the basis of faith in Jesus and the gospel, having nothing to do with observance of the Jewish law. Read this way, Jesus in Matthew would be saying something like, "Unless you have a righteousness different from that of

[19]The NRSV translations of the phrase in question in Matt 5:18 and 24:34 are not identical. However, the Greek text is, except that 24:34 reads "these things," rather than simply "things."

[20]See D. J. Harrington, *The Gospel of Matthew* (Collegeville, MN: Liturgical Press, 1991) 81.

the scribes and Pharisees, a righteousness based on faith in God and unrelated to doing works of law, you will not be saved."

Once again this way of reading does not make the best sense of the text, given its *Matthean* context. The subject matter under discussion is the Torah, which is to endure until the end of the age, and commandments, even the least of which God's people are to observe. What is more, immediately following Matt 5:20 are the so-called **Antitheses**, all of which have to do with Jesus' comment on specific texts from the Mosaic Torah. However one understands "righteousness," it must be connected with what Jesus is talking about in the larger literary context. Jesus is talking about the Torah and commandments, and the *doing* of these. " 'Righteousness' is therefore Christian character and conduct in accordance with the demands of Jesus—right intention, right word, right deed. Hence, 'righteousness' does not refer, even implicitly, to God's gift. The Pauline . . . connotation is absent."[21]

The righteousness that exceeds that of the scribes and Pharisees has both a quantitative and qualitative element to it.[22] Quantitatively, Jesus calls on his followers to do *more* than the scribes and Pharisees. At the same time, he expects a kind of righteousness that is qualitatively different, permeating the very core and being of the **disciple**. He expects those who practice the "excessive righteousness" to be meek (5:5), pure in heart (5:8), and even perfect (5:48). This kind of righteousness involves "purity of motive, rather than mere outward observance."[23] To allude to one of the word pictures that Jesus employs to conclude the sermon, Jesus demands that his followers be the kind of wholly good trees (*qualitatively* exceeding the scribes and Pharisees) that produce an abundance of good fruits (*quantitatively* exceeding these same Jewish leaders). It is to those who hunger and thirst for this kind of righteousness that the kingdom of heaven belongs (5:6).

A brief quotation by Anthony Saldarini sums up well the discussion of 5:17–20. "The law is not to be changed but 'fulfilled' in two ways: in Jesus' life, which corresponds to God's promises in the Bible, and in Jesus' teachings, which lay bare the true meaning and requirements of the law. . . . Matthew means for his group to obey fully the demands of the law as they are understood through Jesus' teaching."[24]

The Law and the Prophets (Reprise) (7:12)

The central section of the sermon concludes with the so-called Golden Rule: "In everything do to others as you would have them do to you; for this is the law and the prophets." Here one finds yet another reference to "the law and the prophets." Jesus is not unique in the ancient annals in attempting to summarize the essence of the divine demand as expressed in scripture. An often-told story involves the Jewish legal scholar Hillel, who lived during the late first century BCE. The story tells of a gentile who challenged Hillel to summarize the law while the gentile stood on one foot. In reply, Hillel is reported to have said: "What is hateful to you, do not do to your neighbor: that is the whole of the Torah, while the rest is commentary thereon; go and learn it."[25] Even Paul

[21]Davies and Allison, *Matthew,* 1.499.

[22]Luz, *Matthew,* 270–271.

[23]Stanton, *Gospel for a New People,* 303.

[24]*Matthew's Christian-Jewish Community,* 161.

[25]*Babylonian Talmud, Sabbat,* 31a. The saying may be found in any number of secondary sources; quoted here from Davies and Allison, *Matthew,* 1.687.

offered his own summary of the essence of the Torah's teaching: "For the whole law is summed up in a single commandment, 'You shall love your neighbor as yourself' " (Gal 5:14).

The Principle of Love. Though located outside the context of the Sermon on the Mount, Matthew offers another summary of the essence of "the law and the prophets" (see Table 13.2).

Matthew's rereading of his Markan source reveals Matthew's concerns. Mark has Jesus say "there is no other commandment greater than these" (12:31b). Yet Matthew specifically links the discussion about the love of God and neighbor with "the law and the prophets" (22:40). This phrase, framing as it does the central section of the Sermon on the Mount, is important to Matthew. Further, it is significant that he uses the phrase when summarizing the essence of "the greatest commandment." Matthew's rereading of Mark allows the conclusion that what Matthew *implies* in 7:12 (that love is the essence of "the law and the prophets"), he makes explicit in chapter 22. Love of God and love of neighbor summarize the content of the law and the prophets. Herein lies the key to attaining the righteousness that exceeds the scribes and Pharisees. It is through the application

Table 13.2

"The Greatest Commandment"

Matthew 22:34–40	Mark 12:28–31
34When the Pharisees heard that he had silenced the Sadducees, they gathered together,	28One of the scribes came near and heard them disputing with one another, and seeing that he answered them well,
35and one of them, a lawyer, asked him a question to test him.	he asked him,
36"Teacher, which commandment in the law is the greatest?"	"Which commandment is the first of all?"
37He said to him, " 'You shall love the Lord your God with all your heart, and with all your soul, and with all your mind.'	29Jesus answered, "The first is, 'Hear, O Israel: the Lord our God, the Lord is one; 30you shall love the Lord your God with all your heart, and with all your soul, and with all your mind, and with all your strength.'
38This is the greatest and first commandment.	
39And a second is like it: 'You shall love your neighbor as yourself.'	31The second is this, 'You shall love your neighbor as yourself.'
40On these two commandments hang all the law and the prophets."	There is no other commandment greater than these."

of the principle of love of God and neighbor, as taught and exemplified by Jesus, that Matthew's community can come to a right understanding and application of the law of God.

How does the principle of love, functioning as a summary of "the law and the prophets," apply itself to specific issues of the Torah? The story found in Matt 12:9–14, describing Jesus' healing on the sabbath, illustrates how the principle of love summarizes the law and the prophets.[26] From the perspective of the Jewish leaders in the story, who represent for Matthew the real Jewish leaders of his own time, Jesus stands in violation of the sabbath commandment: "Remember the sabbath day, and keep it holy" (Exod 20:8). The Torah itself goes on to define such holiness as refraining from labor (Exod 20:9). The (implicit, to be sure) application of the criterion of love, combined with specific issues of legal conversation, guides Jesus as he engages in debate with the Jewish leaders over what the appropriate *legal* action is on the sabbath day. First, Jesus asks the question, "Suppose one of you has only one sheep and it falls into a pit on the sabbath; will you not lay hold of it and lift it out?" (Matt 12:11). There is no specific commandment in the Torah permitting such activity (see Deut 22:4, for the closest related text), hence, there was considerable debate among the Jews whether one could rescue an animal on the sabbath. *Some* Jews did argue that one could do so, and Matthew clearly assumes this position here.[27] Next in Jesus' argument is the implicit application of the love principle: "How much more valuable is a human being than a sheep" (12:12a). Here, Jesus is arguing from the lesser (the value of an animal) to the greater (the value of a human being), a common mode of scribal argument in Judaism during the first century CE. Guiding the use of logical argument is the principle of love for the human being. Finally Jesus concludes, "So it is *lawful* to do good on the sabbath" (12:12b). The conclusion is important. Jesus does not say anything like, "Given the principle of love, one need not be concerned with the specifics of what the law requires." Rather, through logical argument employing the principle of love, Jesus comes to conclude what is *lawful* to do on the sabbath. The love principle does not allow for nullification of the law, but offers concrete guidance in concluding what the *lawful* action is.

The Love of God and Neighbor and the Central Section of the Sermon. The principle of love, implicit in the Golden Rule and made explicit in Matt 22:34–40, also offers a perspective through which to understand the central section of the Sermon on the Mount. One can see this in the so-called Antitheses (5:21–48). The term *antitheses* is based on the consistent form of this series of sayings: "You have heard that it was said . . . but I say to you." One cannot ignore, however, that each of the sayings derives from the Torah and Jesus has explicitly said that he has come to *fulfill* and not to abolish the Torah. Matthew 5:17–20 must control one's reading of the Antitheses, understanding them not as antithetical to the Torah, but the fulfillment of it.

The Antitheses offer specific legal declarations and commentary related to the "greatest commandment" of loving one's neighbor. The last of the Antitheses (5:43–48) has *explicitly* to do with the love of one's enemies. This Antithesis requires that one "exceed" in righteousness (5:20) by loving not only one's neighbor, but one's enemy. The other Antitheses, while not addressing

---

[26]See Saldarini, *Matthew's Christian-Jewish Community,* 126–134 for a discussion of Matthew's treatment of sabbath laws.

[27]There was not agreement among Jewish interpreters of Jesus' day whether it was legal to pull an animal from a pit on the sabbath. The Qumran Jews state in one of their legal texts that it was not.

"love" explicitly, also offer specific commentary on how to apply the legal demands of God when taking into consideration the principle of loving the neighbor. The requirements that one not be angry but, rather, seek reconciliation (5:21–26), not look at a woman lustfully (5:27–30), not divorce his wife (5:31–32), practice consistent honesty (5:33–37), and not engage in retaliatory action (5:38–42) all offer specific commentary and application to commandments from the Torah that demonstrate the "excessive righteousness" and love of one's neighbor.

Matthew 6 concerns itself primarily with proper piety, dealing with such issues as almsgiving, prayer, and fasting (6:1–18). The first verse serves as a fitting introduction to all the topics: "Beware of practicing your piety before others in order to be seen by them; for then you have no reward from your Father in heaven." Piety is to offer genuine expression of devotion to God. The pictures of pious behavior offered by Jesus, void of public recognition or fanfare, provide illustration of "purity of heart" (5:8) and "excessive righteousness" (5:20). They also offer illustration of the kind of love of God "the greatest commandment" describes. Piety that is wholly directed toward God manifests loving God with one's heart, soul, and mind (Matt 22:37). Similarly, the complete dependence on God's merciful care and lack of concern about personal wealth (6:19–34) also reflect the radical love toward God called for in Matt 22:37.

The righteousness exceeding that of the scribes and Pharisees, therefore, is not to be made up as one goes along, with one *subjectively* deciding what the right thing to do is in this or that situation. For Matthew, such righteousness is rooted in his assumption, which he shares with fellow Jews of his time, that the doing of righteousness begins with the doing of the Torah. As one hungers for this higher righteousness, Jesus the Messiah offers guidance by way of specific word (e.g., the Antitheses), example (e.g., healing on the sabbath), and principles that summarize the essence of "the law and the prophets" (e.g., the Golden Rule and "the greatest commandment"). In following his word and deed, one can find the narrow way that leads to life. So Matthew hoped to persuade his reading audience.

The New Covenant and the Law (Matt 1:1–17; 26:26–29)

The Sermon on the Mount presents ethical demands that seem to require something of an inner transformation of the disciple. The Beatitudes, for example, call "blessed" those who possess a certain type of inner-character such as "poverty of spirit" (5:3), "meekness" (5:5), "mercy" (5:7), and "purity of heart" (5:8). It is often recognized that the so-called Antitheses go to the core of a person's being. It is not sufficient that one not murder, but one must not be "angry" toward or contemptuous of other people (5:21–22). One cannot think of himself as righteous simply because he has never committed adultery; one must not even lust in the heart (5:27–30). One is not righteous simply because she "tells the truth" when she has sworn to do so; true righteousness resides in persons of such integrity that they always speak the truth (5:33–37). Further, true righteousness is so motivated by love that one even loves and prays for one's enemies (5:43–48). In the conclusion of the Sermon on the Mount, Jesus uses the image of "good trees" to describe those who are truly righteous: "good fruit" symbolizes the good works that flow from the inner being and character of the good person (7:15–20). True righteousness stems from persons who have been transformed from within.

Are there any macro-level literary or social texts from Matthew's Jewish heritage from which he could have drawn to emphasize such an inner transformation? Matthew believed that the Jesus who came to fulfill the law also came to bring a "new covenant."[28] This is seen most explicitly in Matthew's narrative of the last meal Jesus shared with the disciples. In the context of this meal, Jesus speaks of the cup, which represents his "blood of the covenant, which is poured out for many for the forgiveness of sins" (Matt 26:28).

It is true that this text makes no explicit reference to a "new covenant."[29] Yet the setting of the story allows the inference that Matthew sees the death of Jesus as inaugurating a new covenant for his followers. This last meal, as Matthew presents it, was a **Passover** feast (Matt 26:17–19), celebrating God's liberation of the Jews from Egypt.[30] In Matthew's telling of the story, Jesus offers a rereading of this Passover celebration, as he takes the elements from the Passover meal and reinterprets them in light of his upcoming death. In so doing, Jesus is saying that through his death, people will now be offered liberation or release, manifested primarily through the forgiveness of sins.[31]

Matthew's Jewish tradition looked forward to God's establishing a new covenant with his people. The clearest expression of this hope is found in Jer 31:31–34, which readers should review carefully. Jeremiah's talk of a new covenant is explicitly connected and contrasted with the **Exodus** event (Jer 31:32). The new covenant as Jeremiah spoke of it also concerned forgiveness, and prophesied that God would no longer remember his people's sin (Jer 31:34). This is similar to Matthew's story of the meal Jesus is having with his disciples: the Passover setting itself relates the meal to the Exodus event and Jesus speaks explicitly of forgiveness of sin. Jeremiah also says that with this new covenant God would put the "law within them" and "write it on their hearts" (31:33), with the result that God's people "shall all know me" (31:34). This sounds very much like something of the inner transformation that Matthew's Sermon on the Mount assumes.

Another prophetic voice spoke of the transformation of the heart following the Exile. The prophet Ezekiel saw that a "new heart" would provide the ultimate solution to the problem of Israel's pattern of disobedience toward Yahweh. "Cast away from you all the transgressions that you have committed against me, and get yourselves a new heart and a new spirit! Why will you die, O house of Israel?" (18:31). God will give his people this new heart, a soft heart of flesh to replace a hard heart of stone, when he restores them after the Exile: "A new heart I will give you, and a new spirit I will put within you; and I will remove from your body the heart of stone and give you a heart of flesh" (36:26).

Matthew believed that the time for the restoration of Israel had come. The Exile was finally coming to an end. This is made clear in the way he begins his gospel. In presenting the genealogy of Jesus (Matt 1:1–17), the evangelist divides the genealogy into three sections (v. 17). Using this genealogical division, the evangelist divides the history of God's people into three periods: the period of the patriarchs (from Abraham to David), the period of the monarchy (from David to the deportation to Babylon [the Exile]), and the period of Exile (from the deportation to the coming of the Messiah). This is important, for it communicates that Matthew believed that the period of

---

[28]Recall the discussion of the new covenant in Hebrews (Chap. 12).

[29]Some ancient copies of Matthew's gospel insert the word "new" before covenant in v. 28. Most scholars believe this not to have been in Matthew's original gospel. The insertion reveals that later copiers of Matthew (re)read the text to say that Jesus established a new covenant through his death.

[30]Review Chap. 11 on the topic of Jesus' last meal as a Passover feast.

[31]See D. C. Allison, *The New Moses: A Matthean Typology* (Minneapolis, MN: Fortress, 1993) 256–261.

Israel's history immediately preceding the coming of the Messiah was the period of Exile. However, with the coming of the Messiah, Israel has entered into a new period of history: the time of the Messiah *and the end of the Exile.* With the coming of the time of restoration and the end of Israel's Exile there would also come the time when God would give his people a new covenant and write his law on their transformed hearts.

Matthew is in conversation with this macro-level social text from his Jewish heritage. With the coming of the Messiah, the time has come for the end of the Exile. And with the end of the Exile comes the new covenant and new heart that the prophets had foreseen. The excessive righteousness the followers of Jesus are to observe, therefore, is grounded in a transformation of the hearts of his disciples. With this transformation comes the kind of people who have purity of heart and who, to use Matthew's own metaphor, are the kind of good trees who bear the good fruit of a righteousness that exceeds that of the scribes and Pharisees.

Conclusion

The NT presents two different ways of rereading the law. For Paul, the law was a temporary covenant designed to be followed only until the fulfillment of the covenant of promise made to Abraham and his offspring (Christ). For Matthew, the law endures and is to be obeyed until "everything is accomplished," by which he meant the parousia of Christ. These contrasting ways of rereading are rooted in the different social texts confronting Paul and Matthew. Paul was addressing a gentile audience whom certain Christian Jews were attempting to persuade to become Jews, or at least to adopt minimal Jewish practices. Paul could not accept this premise, for this would have implied that nothing had really changed with the coming of Christ. Gentiles had always had the option of becoming Jews and if this were still required, it would mean that Christ died for no reason (Gal 2:21). This is a conclusion Paul cannot accept.

Matthew, on the other hand, was addressing a Jewish audience. What is more, the social text confronting him was one in which he was in active debate with the emerging leadership of Judaism following the destruction of Jerusalem in 70 CE. Central to Jewish identity, including Matthew's own identity, was that God gave the Torah to be obeyed. The issue, then, is not whether one is to obey the law, but *how* one is to obey the law. And to whom is one to look to know how to interpret and apply the law? Most Jews were looking to the emerging leadership of the scribes and Pharisees. Matthew encourages his readers to look to the Messiah, not as one who has come to "abolish the law and the prophets, but to fulfill them" (Matt 5:17). Thus two different NT authors offered two different rereadings because each practiced his own reading of the Jewish scriptures in the context of two differing social texts.

For Further Reading

The Law Was Our Disciplinarian: Galatians

Dunn, J. D. G. *The Theology of Paul the Apostle.* Grand Rapids, MI: Eerdmans, 1998. Pp. 128–161 and 334–389.

Murphy-O'Connor, J. *Paul: A Critical Life.* Oxford: Clarendon, 1996. Pp. 185–210. (*Recommended for beginning students.*)

Sanders, E. P. *Paul, the Law, and the Jewish People.* Philadelphia: Fortress, 1983.

Thielman, F. "Law." *Dictionary of Paul and His Letters.* Edited by G. F. Hawthorne and R. P. Martin. Downers Grove, IL: InterVarsity Press, 1993. (*Recommended for beginning students.*)

Ziesler, J. A. *Pauline Christianity.* Rev. Ed. New York: Oxford University Press, 1990. (*Recommended for beginning students.*)

Fulfilling the Law and the Prophets: Matthew

Carter, W. *What Are They Saying about Matthew's Sermon on the Mount?* New York: Paulist, 1994. (*Recommended for beginning students.*)

———. *Matthew: Storyteller, Interpreter, Evangelist.* Peabody, MA: Hendrickson, 1996. Pp. 77–102. (*Recommended for beginning students.*)

Davies, W. D. *The Setting of the Sermon on the Mount.* Cambridge: Cambridge University Press, 1964.

Deutsch, C. M. *Lady Wisdom, Jesus, and the Sages: Metaphor and Social Context in Mathew's Gospel.* Valley Forge, PA: Trinity Press, 1996.

Lambrecht, J. *The Sermon on the Mount: Proclamation and Exhortation.* Good News Studies 14. Wilmington, DL: Michael Glazier, 1985. (*Recommended for beginning students.*)

Strecker, G. *The Sermon on the Mount: An Exegetical Commentary.* Nashville, TN: Abingdon, 1988.

CHAPTER FOURTEEN

Rereading the Story of Prophecy and the Prophets

Introduction

Review

The prophets emerged in ancient Israel as a group who proclaimed the word of God independently of specific references to the Torah. Later, they were reread to be concerned with calling Israel back to obedience to God's Torah. Still later, they came to be understood as offering predictions of the end-time. By the time of Jesus, the eschatological reading of the prophets was normative for many Jews. Central to such eschatological reading were the prophets' predictions of Israel's future glorious restoration. Clearly, the early Christians also read the prophets in an eschatological manner. The study of Luke-Acts (Chap. 10) showed how the early Christians read the prophets with the conviction that the last days had dawned because of the life, death, and resurrection of Jesus.

Preview

This chapter will explore further Christian rereadings and interpretations of the prophets and the whole phenomenon of prophecy by focusing on three sets of texts. First, the study of Matthew's gospel will continue, giving attention to the first two chapters of the gospel. Second, readers will explore the idea of prophecy in early Christianity by examining 1 Corinthians 11–14. Third, the Pastoral Epistles will be examined to see what they contribute to understanding prophecy and prophets in early Christianity.

"This Happened to Fulfill What Was Spoken by the Prophets": Matthew's Rereading of the Prophets
Matthew 1–2

Learning Goals

- To understand how Matthew reread Isaiah in order to show Jesus to be the fulfillment of Jewish scriptures.
- To understand that early Christians employed more than one method of (re)reading scriptures, and to learn the essentials of these methods.
- To understand how Matthew employed the idea of "the prophet like Moses" to present Jesus to his readers.

Guiding Study Exercises

1) Offer your own paraphrase of what Isaiah's words *as recorded in Isa 7:14* would have meant to King Ahaz, and what those same words, *as recorded in Matthew's gospel,* would have meant to Matthew's readers. Reflect on what one might mean by this phrase: context influences one's interpretive text of a literary text.

2) Make a list of ways in which *charismatic exegesis* and *midrash* are similar to one another *and* ways in which they are distinctive from one another. How does understanding Matthew's social text help one to understand why he was more sympathetic with midrash than charismatic exegesis?

3) In light of your response to the previous question, reflect on this question: How might understanding your own social text help you to better understand why you read the Bible the way you do, whatever that particular way might be?

4) List some ways that Matthew shaped his narrative of Jesus' birth to show that Moses was a "type" of Jesus. Recalling what you know about Matthew's historical social text, why might Matthew have thought that a typological comparison of Moses and Jesus would have been useful in persuading his readers to become disciples of Jesus?

Readers have already had some exposure to material from Matthew 1–2 (review Chaps. 1 and 13). This section will show that Matthew not only read the prophets through the lens of the Jesus story, but that he also understood and retold the Jesus story in light of his understanding of the prophets and other Jewish scriptures. In other words, the social text of the Jesus story and the literary text of the Jewish scriptures created intertexts out of which emerged a distinctive interpretive text.

"Look, the Virgin Shall Conceive."

Matthew 1:23 offers the first of five fulfillment texts presented in chapters 1 and 2 of his gospel.[1] Throughout the balance of his gospel, Matthew offers nine additional fulfillment quotations.[2] The idea of Jesus "fulfilling" the scriptures or the prophets is clearly important to the first evangelist.

The Identity of Jesus. In Matt 1:1–17, Matthew has presented the genealogy of Jesus in order to show that Jesus is "the son of David, the son of Abraham" (1:1). By tracing Jesus' lineage through the royal line of David, beginning with reference to Solomon in v. 6b and culminating with "Joseph the husband of Mary" in v. 16, Matthew portrays Jesus as the legitimate heir to the messianic throne. It initially strikes one as curious that Matthew points out that three sets of fourteen generations make up the genealogy of Jesus (v. 17). This is a contrived number, for Matthew must omit names from the known descendants of David in order to arrive at the number of fourteen generations from David to the deportation.[3] Matthew is more interested in the *meaning* conveyed by the pattern of three sets of fourteen generations than the accuracy of Jesus' lineage. Apparently, Matthew wished to convey by the artificially constructed genealogical pattern his conviction that Jesus' coming into the world was according to a divinely ordered plan.

Though Matthew can present the human genealogy of Jesus, he also believes that Jesus was miraculously conceived. For Matthew there is no contradiction. Because Joseph, who was of the royal line of David, took Mary as his wife and named Jesus in accordance with the divine command, he is the *legal* father of Jesus—Jesus is legally descended from the line of David. Because Jesus is miraculously conceived through the power of the Holy Spirit (1:18, 20), Jesus is also the son of God. Jesus is both the son of David, the heir to the throne, and the son of God, the one through whom God is present to save his people from their sins (1:21, 23).

The Use of Isaiah 7:14. (NOTE: Readers should reread Isa 7:10–17 *and* review the treatment of Isaiah 7 in Chapter 7 to reacquaint themselves with this oracle *in its originating context* before proceeding with the following study of Matthew's rereading of Isaiah.) Read in the context of Matthew's narrative, the statement from Isaiah appears straightforward: The Lord, through the prophet, predicted the virginal conception of Jesus. Yet, when readers observe the originating context of Isaiah, the oracle about Immanuel is addressed to King Ahaz, offering him a sign that within the *immediate* future the kings of Syria and Israel, his nation's enemies, will fall.

Nothing in the text of Isaiah itself implies that the conception of this child would be miraculous (note that the Hebrew text says that a "young woman" will conceive). It is true that the translators of the **Septuagint** chose to use the Greek word *parthenos* to translate the Hebrew word for "young woman" (*'alma*). The more appropriate Greek word to translate *'alma* would have been *neanis,* though in one other instance the Septuagintal translators used *parthenos* to translate *'alma* (see Gen 24:43). The word *parthenos* generally does mean "virgin." However, even the use of "virgin" in the LXX need not imply that the Septuagintal translators were intend-

---

[1]The others are 2:5b–6, 15b, 17–18, and 23b.

[2]See Matt 3:3; 4:14–16; 8:17; 12:17–21; 13:14–15, 35; 21:4–5; 26:56; 27:9–10.

[3]Note that Matt 1:8 says that Jehoshaphat, Joram, Uzziah, then Jotham belonged to Jesus' genealogy. 1 Chronicles 3:10–12 presents this portion of the royal genealogy as Jehoshaphat, Joram, Ahaziah, Joash, Amaziah, Azariah (= Uzziah), then Jotham. Matthew has left out three names (Ahaziah, Joash, and Amaziah), a necessary move to allow the number of generations to equal fourteen. There exists no genealogical list with which to compare the names in the last set of fourteen generations, so one cannot know if Matthew deliberately altered the number of generations here.

A Closer Look: The Virgin Birth. The miraculous conception of Jesus is popularly known as "the virgin birth." The term *virgin birth* actually has a more technical meaning than that intended by many who employ the term. The virgin birth refers not only to belief in the miraculous conception of Jesus, but also to his miraculous birth. According to Catholic tradition, Mary remained a virgin, having never had sexual relations with Joseph. Traditional Protestantism affirms the miraculous conception of Jesus, but neither the miraculous birth nor the perpetual virginity of Mary.

One of the earliest narrative expressions of Jesus' miraculous *birth* is found in the extra-biblical gospel, *The Proto-Evangelium of James,* 19.2–3:

> And he [Joseph] went to the place of the cave, and behold, a dark [bright] cloud overshadowed the cave. The midwife said: "My soul is magnified to-day, for my eyes have seen wonderful things; for salvation is born in Israel." And immediately the cloud disappeared from the cave, and a great light appeared, so that our eyes could not bear it. A short time afterwards that light withdrew until the child appeared, and it went and took the breast of its mother Mary. . . . And the midwife . . . said to her [sister]: "Salome, Salome, I have a new sight to tell you; a virgin has brought forth, a thing which her nature does not allow." And Salome said: "As the Lord my God lives, unless I put (forward) my finger and test her condition, I will not believe that a virgin has brought forth." (Quoted from R. Cameron, Ed. *The Other Gospels: Non-Canonical Gospel Texts.* Philadelphia: Westminster, 1982. P. 118).

For further study, P. D. Simmons. "Virgin Birth." *MDB* 948–949.

For more advanced study, R. E. Brown. "Virginal Conception." *The Birth of the Messiah: A Commentary on the Infancy Narratives in Matthew and Luke.* Garden City, NY: Doubleday, 1979. Pp. 517–533.

ing to convey a miraculous conception. One can easily understand the LXX to be saying that a maiden who is *now* a virgin (at the time Isaiah uttered the words) would, in the near future, conceive and bear a son.

If one grants the Matthean social text, however, one can easily understand his way of reading Isa 7:14. He may have observed that the sign offered by Isaiah was offered not simply to Ahaz, but to the whole "house of David" (see 7:13), thereby allowing Matthew to find significance for this text beyond the generation of Ahaz. That could have led him to understand the text as a *messianic* text. And if it is a messianic text, Matthew would see it as being about Jesus, the one whom he believed to be the Messiah. Additionally, the oracle as a whole concerns God's word of assurance and salvation to both the house of David and God's people of Judah. Matthew understood Jesus to be God's instrument of salvation, as made clear by his explanation of Jesus' name in Matt 1:21 ("he will save his people from their sins"). Some scholars have argued that Matthew read Isa 7:14 in the even larger context of Isa 6:1–9:7, a passage culminating in the oracle of the birth of the ideal king to come.[4]

---

[4]C. H. Dodd, *According to the Scriptures* (rev. ed.; Philadelphia: Fortress, 1971) argues that Christian interpreters of the scriptures regularly took into account the larger literary context of the biblical passages they applied to Jesus.

For a child has been born for us, a son given to us; authority rests upon his shoulders; and he is named Wonderful Counselor, Mighty God, Everlasting Father, Prince of Peace. His authority shall grow continually, and there shall be endless peace for the throne of David and his kingdom. He will establish and uphold it with justice and with righteousness from this time onward and forevermore. The zeal of the LORD of hosts will do this (Isa 9:6–7).

If Matthew read this larger literary text of Isaiah 7–9 **intertextually** with his own theological social text, which affirmed that Jesus was the ideal messianic king, one can understand why he would have interpreted all these references to the royal child as applying to Jesus. The reference to the virgin may also have drawn Matthew to this text. His awareness of the tradition of the miraculous conception of Jesus made this literary text from Isa 7:14 very inviting. Thus, it was not the historical social text of the ancient prophet, but Matthew's own that informed his reading of Isaiah.

Matthew's Way of Interpreting the Scriptures

Charismatic Exegesis. David Aune has employed the phrase "charismatic **exegesis**" to denote the early Christian practice of biblical interpretation. This way of reading the scriptures was based on two presuppositions:

(1) The sacred text contains hidden or symbolic meanings which can only be revealed by an interpreter gifted with divine insight, and (2) The true meaning of the text concerns eschatological prophecies which the interpreter believes are being fulfilled in his own day.[5]

Clearly, the sectarians at **Qumran** practiced this approach to biblical interpretation, as the following excerpt from the commentary on the prophetic book of Habakkuk, found among the **Dead Sea Scrolls**, shows:

And God told Habakkuk to write down the things which will come to pass in the last generation, but the consummation of time He made not known to him. And as for that which He said, *That he may read it easily that reads it* [Hab 2:2], the explanation of this concerns the Teacher of Righteousness to whom God made known all the Mysteries of the words of His servants the prophets (1QpHab 7:1–5).[6]

This text assumes both the mysterious character of the scriptures, which need special illumination, and the "end-time" character of this prophetic text.

There is evidence that early Christians also practiced charismatic exegesis. Luke 24:45 records that the resurrected Jesus "opened their minds to understand the scriptures." In 2 Cor 3:12–18 Paul stated that a veil lay over the minds of non-Christian Jews, preventing them from understanding the reading of their scriptures. This veil, Paul asserted, is lifted only when one turns to the Lord. Special insight is needed for the veil to be lifted, and this insight comes from the illumination offered by turning to Christ, the resurrected Lord who bestows the Spirit upon believers. Though Paul offers no systematic treatise on his philosophy of scriptural interpretation,

[5]D. E. Aune, *Prophecy in Early Christianity and the Ancient Mediterranean World* (Grand Rapids, MI: Eerdmans, 1983) 339.

[6]Quoted from Aune, *ibid.,* 341.

he did believe that persons of faith had the Spirit of God (1 Cor 2:10), by which they could discern the once-hidden mysteries of God "now disclosed" and "through the prophets . . . being made known" (Rom 16:25–26). Scriptural interpretation was very much a *spiritual* exercise.

Did Matthew employ charismatic exegesis? Matthew believed that the scriptures were primarily about the coming of Jesus, the Messiah. The coming of the Messiah was eschatological by definition. Thus, Matthew does satisfy the *second* presupposition of charismatic exegesis: "The true meaning of the text concerns eschatological prophecies which the interpreter believes are being fulfilled in his own day."[7] But does Matthew satisfy the first presupposition, the idea that "the sacred text contains hidden or symbolic meanings which can only be revealed by an interpreter *gifted with divine insight*"?[8]

Matthew does believe in the reality of direct divine revelation, as is evidenced by the abundance of dreams and visions through which God speaks in the first two chapters of his narrative. Matthew also affirms that the Spirit can give speech to God's people as they face situations of trial (10:20). Finally, Matthew believed that God himself spoke directly through the scriptures (see, e.g., 1:22; 22:43). *But, significantly, he makes no explicit claim that divine insight is what leads one to the proper interpretation of scripture.* As in Lk 24:45, Matthew believes that the key to understanding scripture is Jesus. But, unlike Luke, Matthew does not state that the *resurrected* Jesus offers the insight into understanding the scriptures properly. Rather, it is the *historical* Jesus who offers guidance to the community of faith. Through his teachings as found in the great discourses of the gospel, such as the Sermon on the Mount, Jesus offers the proper interpretation of the Jewish scriptures. The historical Jesus, who argued with **scribes** and **Pharisees** and taught the masses, is the teacher and the instructor of the **disciples** (Matt 23:8, 10). The distinction is subtle, but it is important. While Matthew clearly believed the *teachings* of Jesus to be key to understanding properly the meaning of scripture, he does not appeal to any type of special spiritual or divine illumination given to the interpreter, as Paul and Luke did. Scriptural interpretation appears to be more a matter of careful study, guided by the teachings of the Rabbi Jesus, than a product of inner illumination.

Midrash and Matthew's Reading of the Scriptures. **Midrash** designates a manner of reading Jewish texts employed by many Jews of Matthew's time. It comes from the Hebrew word *darash,* meaning "to search out," "seek," or "investigate."[9] It denotes, therefore, a type of interpretation. Midrashic interpretation was quite free in its application. In employing midrash, interpreters were most concerned to offer readings of scripture that provided for a meaningful and *contemporary* application of the text. In other words, midrashic interpretation intentionally intersected the literary text of the Jewish scriptures with the social text of the interpreter.[10]

The scribes and Pharisees, who formed the core leadership group of Judaism after 70 CE (Chap. 13), practiced midrashic interpretation. These interpreters, while quite concerned to offer an interpretation of scripture that spoke to the contemporary context, did not follow either of the presuppositions of charismatic exegesis. They did not believe that special divine illumination was

---

[7]*Ibid.,* 339.

[8]*Ibid.* (Emphasis added).

[9]T. C. Smith, "Rabbinic Literature," *MDB,* 733.

[10]Midrashic interpretation can be contrasted to a way of reading, also practiced within ancient Judaism, called *peshat. Peshat* focused attention on the plain, literal sense of the text. While Jewish interpreters were aware that a text had a plain and literal sense, they were most interested in its *contemporary* application and meaning (its midrashic meaning).

necessary to understand the Bible, nor did they assume that the "end-time" was the only frame-work in which to interpret the Bible.[11] Matthew therefore stands in partial disagreement with these other Jewish interpreters of his time in that he believes that one is to interpret scripture in an *eschatological* context. However, he appears to stand in agreement with midrashic interpretation in that he does not make claims to special divine insight as he offers the contemporary interpreta-tion of the text. Just as the scribes and Pharisees (and the **Rabbis** who were emerging from this group) looked to the authoritative teachers within their communities to provide guidance for the meaning of scripture, Matthew looked to Jesus the Messiah as the authoritative teacher to give guidance for scriptural interpretation.

The historical social text of Matthew helps one to understand why the evangelist would show some affinities with scribal/rabbinic approaches to scripture. Matthew was vying to have a voice in the reconstruction of post-70 CE Judaism (Chap. 13). He was, in part, attempting to per-suade Jews that the authoritative interpreter of the law was Jesus the Messiah, not the scribes and Pharisees or Rabbis. Matthew, that is, was attempting to appeal to readers who were inclined to understand Judaism according to the traditions and ideas of the scribes, Pharisees, and Rabbis.

It is perhaps significant that many within the scribal/Pharisaic/rabbinic circles of Judaism were rather skeptical of charismatic claims of insight offered directly by the Spirit. One reason that they might have been skeptical of such charismatic claims was their belief that *they* were the legitimate interpreters of God's Torah, a role once filled by the prophets of earlier biblical days. But the Rabbis asserted that those days, the days of prophetic inspiration by the Spirit, were over. The Rabbis, guided by tradition and careful reading of the written text, were now responsible for interpreting God's law for the people.[12] Clearly, it would undermine their legitimacy as the sole interpreters of the Torah if they were to grant legitimacy to the claims of inspired interpretation being made by competing Jewish groups, such as the Christians. If Matthew was attempting to appeal to Jewish readers who were generally sympathetic with the scribal/Pharisaic/rabbinic ap-proach to scripture, complete with their skepticism of inspired interpretation, he would not have helped his own cause to claim that access to special inspiration justified his reading of the scrip-tures. Persons skeptical of such ways of reading would have been even less inclined to hear Matthew's appeal were he to have made such claims.

Jesus: The Prophet like Moses

A figure, described as "the prophet like Moses," is first encountered in Deut 18:15, 18–19:[13]

> 15The LORD your God will raise up for you a prophet like me from among your own peo-ple; you shall heed such a prophet. . . . 18I will raise up for them a prophet like you from among their own people; I will put my words in the mouth of the prophet, who shall speak to them everything that I command. 19Anyone who does not heed the words that the prophet shall speak in my name, I myself will hold accountable. . . . [Also relevant is a con-cluding statement found in Deuteronomy]: Never since has there arisen a prophet in Israel like Moses, whom the LORD knew face to face (Deut 34:10).

[11]Aune, *Prophecy,* 340.

[12]*Ibid.,* 103–106.

[13]The following introductory discussion relies on the work of Aune, *ibid.,* 124–135.

Hopes for an Eschatological Prophet. Long before the lifetime of Jesus, some Jews interpreted this prediction of a prophet like Moses eschatologically. Within some circles, Elijah was believed to be this "prophet like Moses." The idea that Elijah would return before "the day of the Lord" to prepare the people for the Lord's coming finds expression in later portions of the Jewish scriptures.

> Lo, I will send you the prophet Elijah before the great and terrible day of the LORD comes. He will turn the hearts of parents to their children and the hearts of children to their parents, so that I will not come and strike the land with a curse (Mal 4:5–6).

A review of Sir 48:10–11 offers additional testimony that some Jews anticipated the eschatological return of Elijah. The historical narrative of the Maccabean conflict with the Seleucid dynasty makes two references to a prophet who is to come (1 Macc 4:46; 14:41). These brief texts do not provide many details regarding this prophet to come, but it is likely that this prophet has some connection with the eschatological prophet spoken of in Malachi and Deuteronomy. The sectarians of Qumran also spoke of the prophet who is to come to give clear explication of the law. One Qumranic text (the so-called Messianic Anthology), cites Deut 18:18–19 within a collection of other texts that the sectarians read as "messianic." Some early Christian circles associated John the Baptist with the eschatological Elijah (Matt 17:11–13; Lk 1:15–17), though other Christian texts challenged such an identification (Jn 1:19–21).

While hopes regarding the coming of an eschatological prophet were not monolithic, there was a widely held belief, grounded in such scriptural texts as Deut 18:18–19 and Mal 4:5–6, that a prophet would come "in the last days." Some followers of Jesus made use of such expectations to speak of Jesus. In two sayings of Jesus, he explicitly associates himself with the prophets (Mk 6:4 [‖ Matt 13:57 ‖ Lk 4:24]; Lk 13:31–33). There is evidence that people of Jesus' time perceived him as a prophet (Mk 6:14–15; 8:28; Lk 7:16; Jn 6:14). In some instances, the prophetic work of Jesus is more like that of Elijah than Moses. For example, the story of his raising the widow's son in Lk 7:11–17 offers a macro-level intertext with the story of Elijah, who also raised a widow's son from the dead (1 Kgs 17:8–24). In other instances, such as Acts 3:22–23, the NT associates Jesus with the *Mosaic* eschatological prophet.

Part Four of this book has shown that the conviction that Jesus fulfilled the hopes and expectations of Jewish scriptures influenced the way his followers read these scriptures. However, association of Jesus with specific Jewish hopes also influenced the way his followers told the Jesus story. In other words, just as the social text of the Jesus story shaped the way Jesus' followers reread the Jewish scriptures, Christian rereadings of the Jewish scriptures shaped the way the Christians told the story of Jesus. Influences moved in two directions. How, specifically, did the conviction that Jesus was the eschatological prophet like Moses shape the way that Matthew told the story of Jesus' birth?[14]

Matthew's Birth Narrative: Mosaic Characteristics of Jesus and Intertexts from Jewish Scripture. At least four features of Matthew's story about Jesus' birth show relevant micro- or macro-level intertexts with scriptural statements regarding the birth of Moses. First, Matthew records the story of King Herod's attempt to slaughter the male children of Bethlehem. Exodus 1:15–22, which introduces the story of Moses' birth, records the orders of the Pharaoh of Egypt to

---

[14]The following discussion is based on W. D. Davies and D. C. Allison, Jr., *Matthew* (3 vols., ICC; Edinburgh: T & T Clark, 1988, 1991, 1998) 1.190–196.

kill the male children of Israel. Second, Jesus escapes death because he and his family fled their homeland and went to Egypt. As a child, Moses escapes death because his mother places him in a basket and places it in the Nile River of Egypt (Exod 2:1–10). Later in life, Moses again escapes death by fleeing from his homeland of Egypt (Exod 2:15). Third, after the death of Herod, Joseph was commanded to return to his homeland, being told that "the ones who are seeking the life of the child have died" (Matt 2:20, author's trans.). After the death of Pharaoh, Moses receives a divine command to return to his homeland with the words "for all the ones who are seeking the life of you have died" (Exod 4:19, author's trans. of LXX). One can hear a clear micro-level intertextual echo between Matt 2:20 and Exod 4:19. Fourth, according to Matthew, Joseph returned to his homeland with his wife and son (2:21). According to the Jewish scriptures, Moses took his wife and sons and returned to his homeland (Exod 4:20).

Matthew's Birth Narrative: Mosaic Characteristics of Jesus and Intertexts from Jewish Legends. Matthew's infancy narrative also reveals intertexts with texts about Moses found in non-scriptural legends and stories about the ancient leader. First, **Josephus** relates that Moses' father, Amram, was fearful upon finding out about his wife's pregnancy. God, however, appeared to him in a dream and counseled him not to despair (*Antiquities,* 2.210–216). Matthew records that Joseph was distraught, having found out about Mary's pregnancy, only to be put at ease through an angelic appearance in a dream. Second, a **pseudepigraphical** text attributed to **Philo** (*Biblical Antiquities,* 9.10), tells of a revelatory dream of Moses' sister, Miriam, that God would save his people through her brother. Josephus tells of a dream vision Moses' father had that conveyed the same message (*Antiquities,* 2.216). Matthew tells of Joseph's dream that Jesus would save God's people from their sins (Matt 1:21). Third, Jewish tradition expanded the story of Pharaoh's motives for wanting to kill the male children of Israel: he had heard of the birth of Israel's future liberator (Josephus, *Antiquities,* 2.205–209). Herod wanted to kill Jesus because he heard that Jesus was to be "king of the Jews" (Matt 2:2–3). Fourth, Pharaoh learns of the birth of the future liberator of Israel from the sacred scribes (Josephus, *Antiquities,* 2.205, 234). According to Matthew, Herod learns the details of Jesus' birth from chief priests and scribes (Matt 2:4–6).

The Significance of the Intertextual Parallels. Each of these intertexts between the Gospel of Matthew and the Jewish stories about Moses are found *only* in Matthew's birth narrative. That is, Luke's birth narrative does not contain these specific intertexts. It would appear highly probable that either Matthew, or a traditional source he was employing, wanted to tell the story of Jesus to make explicit the micro- and macro-level intertextual connections between Jesus and Moses. By showing how characteristics and events of Moses' life prefigured characteristics and events of Jesus' life, Matthew, apparently, understood Moses to be a "type" for Jesus. By painting a literary portrait of Jesus' birth as he did, Matthew leads readers to see such macro-level intertextual and typological connections. Readers would now carry with them through the rest of their reading of Matthew the awareness that Jesus is to be compared with Moses. Thus, when Jesus associates himself with the prophets (Matt 13:37), or when characters in the story associate Jesus with the prophets (14:5; 16:14; 21:11), readers can understand Jesus to be not only *a* prophet, but *the* prophet like Moses.

Yet Jesus supersedes Moses. In the transfiguration story of Matt 17:1–8, the two characters of old with whom Jesus appears are Moses and Elijah, both figures who were associated with the eschatological prophet. By the time this story ends, Moses and Elijah have disappeared and "no one except Jesus himself alone" remained (17:8). The hopes associated with these eschatological figures find their fulfillment in the Jesus story. The hopes associated with Elijah found their fulfillment in John the Baptist, as Matthew makes patently clear in the verses immediately following the transfiguration story (17:9–13). Hopes circulating about Moses find their realization in Jesus, who shows many affinities with the figure who was Israel's first prophetic redeemer. But the identification of Jesus with the Mosaic prophet is not the primary feature of Matthew's understanding of Jesus. Certainly, Jesus as the Messiah and son of God are far more important to the evangelist. Still, followers of Jesus understood him to be the realization and fulfillment of *all* Jewish eschatological hopes, including those of the eschatological prophet. It is fitting, therefore, that Matthew, in portraying Jesus as the Messiah and son of God, also offers a portrait of Jesus that portrays him as the eschatological Mosaic prophet.

Prophecy among the Early Christians
1 Corinthians 11–14; Selections from
the Pastoral Epistles

Learning Goals

- To learn about early Christians' differing understandings of prophecy and other "gifts of the Spirit."
- To learn that women's active roles within the early church created tension between two ideals: equality and harmony/order.
- To learn how selected NT texts employed the Jewish scriptures to silence women in the early church.
- To learn that the gift of prophecy lost its influence with the institutionalization of the church, and to understand why this happened.

Guiding Study Exercises

1) What would you identify as the fundamental disagreements that existed between Paul and the Corinthians regarding the issue of "gifts of the Spirit"?

2) What criterion did Paul employ to assess the value of a spiritual gift? What criterion did the Corinthians employ, insofar as we can discern from Paul's letters?

3) Given what Paul says in 1 Corinthians, was the apostle opposed to women or supportive of harmonious relationships within the church? What about the author of the Pastorals? Was he opposed to women or supportive of harmony/order?

4) Paraphrase how Paul and the author of the Pastorals employed the Genesis story to define women's roles in the life of the church. Respond to their use of Genesis in the context of your own self-text.

5) What evidence do the Pastorals provide that prophecy and the Spirit had ceased to be influential sources of authoritative teaching? Why do you think this happened?

6) As you think about your own self-text, do you tend to promote equality for all, at the expense of harmony and/or order, or do you promote harmony and/or order at the expense of equality for all? Give some examples and a rationale.

Introduction

Prophecy was a live and viable phenomenon in early Christianity. First, the early Christians assumed the dynamic presence of the Spirit in their midst (e.g., Acts 1:8; 2:4; 1 Thess 1:5–6; 1 Cor 12:7–11). Second, some NT texts associate this Spirit with prophetic activity (Acts 2:17; 19:6; 1 Thess 5:19–22). Third, the NT contains nineteen references to persons within the early Christian movement designated as prophets.[15]

Was the presence of prophets and of prophetic activity a distinctive feature of early Christianity? The consensus among biblical scholars is that Judaism believed prophecy had ceased in Israel with the last of the OT prophets (Haggai, Zechariah, and Malachi). If one wanted to hear the voice of a prophet, one was to turn to the words of the prophets recorded in the Jewish scriptures. This, at least, was the view of the Rabbis. As noted above in the previous discussion of Matthew, scribal circles viewed skeptically claims to prophetic inspiration made by persons in their own time; prophets belonged to Israel's *past*. Given that the Rabbis eventually became the dominant voice within Judaism and, thereby, produced much of the surviving literature, many scholars have taken the rabbinic view regarding prophecy to be the norm.

Some interpreters, such as David Aune, have challenged the scholarly consensus that most Jews no longer considered prophecy a viable phenomenon.[16] Certainly, there were Jews who lived on the "margins" of Jewish society, such as the sectarians of Qumran, who believed the prophetic Spirit to be active in their midst. But after an exhaustive survey of the data, even Aune must concede that the "evidence for prophetic activity in the popular religion of . . . early Judaism [is] paltry."[17] It is important to point out, however, that many Jews, including the Rabbis, *did* believe that with the coming the eschatological restoration, the spirit of prophecy would return. Because the early Christians believed that this time of restoration had dawned with the coming of Jesus, they believed that the "spirit of prophecy" had returned (Acts 2:17–21).

Prophecy in Corinth (1 Corinthians 11–14)

Chapter 11 introduced some of the conflicts Paul had with the Corinthian Christians. The Corinthians were a sorely divided community. Additionally, they had a very enthusiastic spirituality, wherein they emphasized the *present* reality of their glorious life in Christ, even to the extent of denying the need for their own future resurrection from the dead. The Corinthians' belief that they shared in the *present* reality of the eschatological life would provide a ready social text within which they would understand the early Christian emphasis on the presence of the Spirit. Through this Spirit, Christians could receive divine revelations, visions, and other experiences of divine possession. Yet, just as Paul believed that he needed to redirect the thinking of the Corinthians regarding their understanding of the resurrection of the dead, he also needed to redirect their thinking with regard to their understanding of the power of the Spirit and its relationship to prophecy and other manifestations of divine illumination and inspiration. Differences over the

---

[15]Aune, *Prophecy*, 195.

[16]*Ibid.*, 103–152.

[17]*Ibid.*, 189. A recent discussion confirming the scholarly consensus that "Jews in the Second Temple period ceased to believe in the continued existence of prophecy" may be found in B. D. Sommer, "Did Prophecy Cease? Evaluating a Reevaluation," *JBL* 115/1 (1996) 31–47.

Some of the ruins of ancient Corinth may be seen in the foreground. Careful reading of Paul's letters to the church located in this city reveals many insights regarding real life in the first-century church. (Courtesy of Larry McKinney)

understanding of the Spirit and the Spirit's manifestations in human beings also contributed to the divisions that were part of Corinthian religious life.

Paul's Picture of Prophecy. The tone and content of 1 Corinthians 11–14 reveal that Paul is engaged in a debate with his readers. Through careful reading of Paul's input into the debate, a picture emerges regarding how he believed prophecy *should* operate in the Corinthian congregation.[18] First, Paul understands prophecy in the context of a diversity of spiritual gifts that God offered to the church: "Now there are varieties of gifts, but the same Spirit" (12:4). In v. 10 Paul lists prophecy as one among several examples of such gifts, all of which "are activated by one and the same Spirit" (12:11). Second, the Spirit provides the gift of prophecy, like all spiritual gifts, "for the common good" (v. 7). These two observations provide the foundation for what Paul will say regarding spiritual gifts in 1 Corinthians 11–14.

Paul wished to accomplish simultaneously two things that stood in tension with one another. On the one hand, he wants to offer a clear *distinction* between various types of gifts. The list of gifts offered in 12:8–11 and Paul's careful differentiation of prophecy and tongues in chapter 14 point in this direction. On the other hand, Paul wants to point the attention of the readers to

[18]See J. J. Kilgallen, *First Corinthians: An Introduction and Study Guide* (New York: Paulist, 1987).

the *unifying* function of these distinct gifts. The body metaphor that Paul offers in 12:12–26 comes into play here. The body consists of many distinct members (12:14), yet the totality of the various members forms one body (12:20). Hence, while Paul wants in principle to affirm the *intrinsic* worth of the many and varied gifts, the contribution of each gift to the common good of the church determines the *functional* value of these gifts.

This allows Paul to offer a critique of the actual value of various spiritual gifts. Paul does precisely this in 12:27–31. Paul's use of "first," "second," "third," and "then" shows that he is prioritizing the value of the gifts God offers to the church. The exhortation of 12:31 to "strive for the *greater* gifts" betrays Paul's assumption that some gifts are more valuable than others. For Paul, what determines the value of a gift is the degree to which a gift serves the common good (12:7).

This criterion of the common good complements Paul's discourse on love in 1 Corinthians 13. Verses 1–3 indicate that spiritual gifts practiced apart from love are worth nothing. Verse 8, which speaks of how prophecies, tongues, and knowledge will eventually end, reinforces Paul's point that spiritual gifts, including prophecy, are of less-than-ultimate value. Paul is not offering naive platitudes. He is quite serious that the lifestyle demanded by love is the prerequisite to the true viability of any spiritual gift. Traits described in vv. 4–7, among which are not being arrogant, rude, or insistent on having one's own way, characterize this lifestyle of love. Such characteristics are quite consistent with Paul's insistence that the Corinthians are to employ spiritual gifts for the common good (12:7).

Having provided a criterion for the evaluation of the usefulness of spiritual gifts, Paul proceeds in chapter 14 to offer a discussion of two gifts in particular, prophecy and tongues.[19] Paul understands tongues to denote a kind of ecstatic speech. First, he describes tongues as speaking not "to other people, but to God" and "speaking mysteries in the Spirit" that "nobody understands" (14:2). Verse 9 clearly says that tongues offer "speech that is not intelligible"; it is "speaking into the air." In v. 14 Paul says that "if I pray in a tongue, my spirit prays but my mind is unproductive." Such talk, implying that the mind is not involved in tongue speech, implies a kind of ecstatic speech as though the person is under some type of divine possession. Finally, Paul says that if a non-believer were to attend a church gathering and "the whole church comes together and all speak in tongues, . . . will [non-believers] not say that you are out of your mind?" (v. 23). This also implies a kind of talking that persons would not perceive as normal language.

Paul readily acknowledges that such ecstatic experiences can be beneficial to the one having the experience: "Those who speak in a tongue build up themselves" (v. 4). The problem, from Paul's point of view, is that other persons are not "built up." Those observing the other person speaking in tongues gain no spiritual enrichment from the experience of the other person. Since the degree to which a spiritual gift serves the common good determines the gift's value, Paul does not value tongues as much as prophecy: "Strive for the spiritual gifts, and especially that you may prophesy" (14:1).

Paul values prophecy for a number of reasons. First, people prophesy in ordinary, intelligible speech. Whereas, the one who speaks in tongues addresses God and not other people (v. 2), the one who prophesies "speak[s] to other people" (v. 3). Paul contrasts "tongues," which the

---

[19]K. Quest, *Reading the Corinthian Correspondence: An Introduction* (New York: Paulist, 1994) 84–86 offers a very readable overview of Paul's discussion of tongues and prophecy.

spirit generates, with praying, singing, and praising "with the mind" (14:14–19). Given that Paul is contrasting tongues and prophecy throughout the chapter, one can only conclude that he thinks that the *mind* generates prophecy. This implies that he does not see prophecy as an ecstatic experience of divine possession. Second, because one prophesies in ordinary speech prophecy can serve the common good more readily: "Those who prophesy speak to other people for their upbuilding and encouragement and consolation" (v. 3). Thus, Paul can say, "in church I would rather speak five words with my mind, in order to instruct others, than ten thousand words in a tongue" (v. 19). Third, Paul values prophecy more highly because it can have a more positive impact on nonbelievers who visit a church gathering. Whereas nonbelievers would think the congregation mad if all spoke in tongues, the opposite is true if all prophesy: "But if all prophesy, an unbeliever or an outsider who enters is reproved by all and called to account by all. After the secrets of the unbeliever's heart are disclosed, that person will bow down before God and worship him, declaring, 'God is really among you' " (vv. 24–25).

Paul's conviction that spiritual gifts, including prophecy, are to serve the community leads him to conclude his discussion of gifts with some practical guidance for the utilization of gifts in communal worship (vv. 26–33a). Paul states explicitly in v. 26 that, when employing any spiritual gift, one must take into account the criterion of service to the whole church. The congregation is also to practice *orderly* worship. "Let two or three speak in tongues or let two or three prophesy," Paul instructs in vv. 27–31. Additionally, since community edification is the goal of spiritual gifts, Paul counsels those having the tongues experience to keep it private if there is no one to interpret for the larger community (vv. 27–28). Even those who prophesy are to subject their prophecies to the evaluation of others (v. 28). The larger community of faith was to test the validity of a claim to prophetic insight. The community is to provide for the person claiming a revelation the opportunity to speak, and, thus, the one who may currently be speaking is to yield. The fact that Paul speaks of revelation in v. 30 and then immediately returns to the subject of prophecy in v. 31, implies that he understands prophetic speech to be a channel of divine revelation.[20] Paul appears to have a very practical view of inspired prophecy, given his explicit declaration that "the spirits of the prophets are subject to the prophets" (v. 32). He seems to mean here that the prophet is never so divinely possessed that he (or she? [to be discussed below]) cannot prophesy in an orderly manner. After all, Paul concludes, "God is not a God of disorder but of peace" (v. 33).

In summation, Paul understands the Spirit of God to be active in the life of the Christian community. Among the many manifestations of the presence of God's Spirit is the phenomenon of prophecy, which Paul understands as sober, human speech. Though prophecy employs ordinary language, Paul believed it served as a channel of divine revelation offering edification to the *whole* Christian community. Prophecy for Paul was not something belonging only to the past. Through his Spirit, God spoke through prophets in the present time.

The Corinthian View of Prophecy and Spiritual Gifts.[21] Paul's concern to differentiate the various spiritual gifts implies that the Corinthians did not distinguish all that much between the

[20]Cf. also 14:26. There Paul says "each one has a hymn, a lesson, a revelation, a tongue, or an interpretation." Note he does not list "prophecy." It is possible that he views in this context "revelation" and "prophetic speech" as synonymous or, at least, that he believes prophetic speech to include, if not always equate with, the offering of divine revelation.

[21]The following discussion does not pretend to offer a summary of the whole of A. Wire's *The Corinthian Women Prophets* (Minneapolis, MN: Fortress, 1990). Still her work offers one example of how a careful reading of Paul's letter can offer helpful insight into the perspectives of those whom Paul was addressing.

various manifestations of the Spirit. For them, any activity offering a spiritual manifestation was considered valid. For them, ecstatic tongues and prophetic revelation may have been virtually one and the same. Given that within some religious movements of Greco-Roman culture "there was an increasing tendency to equate states of ecstatic frenzy with divine inspiration,"[22] it is understandable that certain Corinthian believers would interpret manifestations of the Spirit in a similar vein. The ecstatic experience itself (tongues) is the avenue to divine inspiration (prophecy). Finally, Paul's insistence that spiritual gifts are to function for the common good and not for the edification of the individual implies that the Corinthians placed supreme value on the *personal* experience provided by the ecstasy of tongues/prophecy.

1 Corinthians 13:4 may indicate that Paul attributed such focus on the *personal* experience to self-centered envy, boasting, or arrogance. Likely the Corinthians did not view their understanding of the personal benefits of spiritual experiences in that manner. Such experiences, manifesting themselves in speaking, praying, singing praises, and offering blessings *to God* (14:2, 14–16), are not, after all, *self*-centered acts in and of themselves. The Corinthians may have believed that the direct experience of the spiritual presence of God and the resurrected Christ in the life of each *individual* believer was the proper focus and goal of Christian worship. For Paul, the fact that there were divisions among the Corinthians (1 Cor 1:10), which manifested themselves in jealousy and quarreling (3:3) and even lawsuits (6:1–8), offered partial justification for his critique of the Corinthians' understanding of manifestations of God's Spirit. Apparently, he believed that if the Corinthians came to understand that the Spirit functioned primarily for the good of the community, they too would direct their own energies to the community's welfare, thereby bringing an end to the divisions existing in the Corinthian church.

Special Concern about Women Prophets.[23] In two places, Paul focuses attention on women prophets (11:2–16; 14:33b-40). The first passage, wherein Paul insists that women pray or prophesy with heads covered, is challenging to modern readers. While it is clear that Paul wants the women to wear a covering when prophesying, his rationale requires some explanation. Precisely how, as Paul claims, does the lack of a cover on a woman's head disgrace her head (the man)? And why were the women praying and prophesying with their heads uncovered in the first place? Were they trying to make a statement and, if so, what?

It is likely that the women prophets' failure to wear a cover was an intentional act through which they were attempting to make a point. A. Wire argues that the women prophets took with all seriousness the Christian claims that in Christ persons are new creations. She argues that Gal 3:28, which says, in part, that "there is no longer male and female," comes from an early Christian baptismal formula that offered intertextual echoes and, hence, a rereading of Genesis. According to Genesis, God created humanity in his image, male *and* female he created them (Gen 1:27). The new creation in Christ has eradicated such a distinction, for in Christ all are one: there is *no* male or female. By not wearing the traditional women's attire of a head covering, the women were giving expression to their status as new creatures, where there is no distinction between male and female.

Paul opposes such lack of distinction. Paul appeals to the creation story of Genesis itself to argue that there is a hierarchy in creation: Christ is the head of man, man is the head of woman,

---

[22]Aune, *Prophecy,* 47.

[23]Wire, *Corinthian Women,* offers thoughtful and provocative insight on this issue.

and God is the head of Christ (11:3). 1 Corinthians 11:7 offers a macro-level intertextual allusion to and rereading of Gen 1:27. Genesis speaks of "man" being created in the image of God. It is clear from the whole verse that Genesis means "human being." But Paul takes it to mean "male." The *male* "is the image and reflection of God" (v. 7). Since the man is to reflect the glory of God, he is to pray with his (physical) head *uncovered* so as not to "cover over" the glory of God that his head reflects. Woman, however, "is the reflection of man" (v. 7). Paul does not derive this directly from the Genesis story, but infers it from his belief that "the man is the (metaphorical) head of the woman" (v. 3). Consequently, if she prays or prophesies with her (physical) head uncovered, she will be reflecting the glory of *her* (metaphorical) head, which is man, thereby distracting the proper glory that is due God. Since it is the proper duty of the male to reflect the glory of God, un-veiled prophesying by a woman has the capacity to shame, or disgrace, the man since such activity directs the honor toward *him* and away from God. What could be more disgraceful to a man than for his own wife, or any woman for that matter, to do anything that would direct honor away from God and toward the man?

1 Corinthians 11 appears to grant women the "authority" to prophesy, since the veil they are to wear serves as their authority to engage in this practice. "For this reason a woman ought to have an *authority* on her head, because of the angels" (1 Cor 11:10).[24] Theoretically, Paul ac-knowledges, women prophets, properly attired, are *authorized* to pray and prophesy. Yet Paul may not actually be granting the women license to practice such authorized activity. Several times earlier in 1 Corinthians Paul has spoken of "authority," only to assert that the proper thing to do is *not* exercise one's authority to do something. " 'All things are lawful (Greek = "autho-rized") for me', but not all things are beneficial. 'All things are lawful ("authorized") for me', but I will not be dominated by anything" (1 Cor 6:12; cf. 10:23). "But take care that this liberty (Greek = "authority") of yours does not somehow become a stumbling block to the weak" (1 Cor 8:9). Paul speaks of his own "authority" to do certain things, which he waives for the larger pur-pose of serving the good of the gospel. "Do we not have the right (Greek = "authority") to our food and drink? Do we not have the right ("authority") to be accompanied by a believing wife, as do the other apostles and the brothers of the Lord and Cephas?" (1 Cor 9:4–5). "Nevertheless, we have not made use of this right ("authority"), but we endure anything rather than put an obstacle in the way of the gospel of Christ" (1 Cor 9:12b). Given Paul's tendency in 1 Corinthians to insist that one's authorization to do something does not mean that one *should* do something, he may be implying in 1 Corinthians 11 that the women not exercise their authority to prophesy.

Paul's direct command to women in 14:33b-36 to "be silent in the churches" makes explicit his implicit appeal of 1 Corinthians 11. He declares that women "are not permitted to speak, but should be subordinate as the law also says" (a macro-level intertext with Gen 3:16d). Verse 36 ap-pears almost as an insulting affront to the Corinthian women: "Do they think that the word of God originated with them or that they are the only ones it has reached?" This appears a direct and al-most sarcastic attack on their claims to prophetic experience. Paul does not deny their technical authorization to prophesy. But it is an authority that they should relinquish, being totally submis-sive and silent in the church. In v. 37 he insists "anyone who claims to be a prophet [including the women] . . . must acknowledge that what I am writing to you is the command of God."

---

[24]NRSV reads "For this reason a woman ought to have *a symbol of* authority on her head, because of the angels." Yet the words "a symbol of" do not appear in the Greek text.

Paul paints the women prophets into a corner. Paraphrased, he appears to offer this argument: "If you are truly prophets you will recognize my authority and do what I say. You will not practice the gift of prophecy, even if you are authorized to do so. If you do not recognize that I speak the commandment of God, then we do not recognize you to be the prophets you claim to be. If you women are truly prophets, you will not prophesy!"

Why does Paul, who fights so zealously in his letter to the Galatians (Chap. 13) for the equality of Jew and gentile in Christ, struggle to keep the women silent? Apparently, Paul and the Corinthians operated within the context of conflicting ideological/theological social texts. For the Corinthians, the spiritual enrichment of the *individual* was of prime importance. Add to this that the Corinthian women prophets enthusiastically embraced the theological social text that affirmed the equality of men and women. Paul, on the other hand, was informed by a social text that affirmed the supreme value of the *community*. What brought conflict and dissension to the community violated his central principle that spiritual gifts operate for the common good. Paul be-

---

A Closer Look: Other Readings of Paul's Words to the Women Prophets. This textbook's interpretation of Paul's exhortations to the women prophets represents only one way to read these texts. Many scholars conclude that Paul is not only recognizing the authority of women to prophesy in 1 Corinthians 11, but is actually quite open to their practicing this gift, so long as they wear the veil to authorize their prophetic behavior. But if Paul is actually open to women practicing the gift of prophetic speech, how does one reconcile the explicit command to silence in 1 Cor 14:33b-36?

Generally, two solutions are offered. (1) Paul did not actually write the verses in question in 1 Corinthians 14. The verses do seem rather abrupt (the NRSV places them in parentheses, as though they are intrusive). Furthermore, in a very few manuscripts of 1 Corinthians, one finds vv. 33b–36 at the very *end* of the chapter. The intrusiveness and dislocation of these verses combine to lead some to conclude that the verses were added by a later copyist of 1 Corinthians who did not share Paul's openness to women prophets. In the parlance of this text, the later copyist "reread" (and rewrote) Paul's text in an effort to silence women. (2) Other scholars reject the first solution but offer a reading of 14:33b–36 that still allows the women to prophesy. These interpreters argue that what Paul is actually forbidding in vv. 33b–36 is not prophesying (note that these verses do *not* explicitly forbid prophesying), but disruptive "chattering" or more profane talking. A variation of this reading argues that Paul is forbidding the women only from questioning or "weighing" (cf. 14:29b) the prophecies of other male prophets or even of their own husbands who were prophets. This solution "in no way negates a woman's right to pray or prophesy in church but only restricts her from judging prophecy by men or speaking in some manner so as to lord it over either her husband or men in general" (Witherington, 176).

For further study, E. S. Fiorenza. *In Memory of Her: A Feminist Theological Reconstruction of Christian Origins.* New York: Crossroads, 1987. Pp. 226–236; B. Witherington III. *Women and the Genesis of Christianity.* Edited by A. Witherington. Cambridge: Cambridge University Press, 1990. Pp. 172–178.

lieved that the Corinthians, especially the women, needed to reevaluate their understanding of spiritual gifts. Their focus should be the good of the whole *community,* not *personal* spiritual enrichment. Paul had concluded that the divisions and quarreling within the church stemmed from the Corinthians' failure to devote sufficient focus to the welfare of the larger community. Redirecting their focus required that Paul convince the Corinthians to end behavior that was more concerned with the self than the church. Paul believed that it was *self*-promoting for women prophets to engage in behavior designed to communicate their equal status in the new creation.

This creates a perpetual dilemma. It is true that when any group that has traditionally been subordinate begins to believe and *act* like it is equal to the traditionally superior group, it will engage in assertive behavior. To those who had considered themselves superior, such behavior might appear "pushy," "uppity," or "self-promoting." It is valid for one to ask whether Paul's insistence that women begin to engage in behavior demonstrating their less-than-equal status is also not self-promoting and *to the advantage of the men.* It is easy for those in power to encourage those historically or currently out of power to practice self-sacrifice. Perhaps without even being aware of it, those in power who issue calls for those who are out of power to be sacrificial and to not insist on their own rights are really calling for the maintenance of the status quo. If those out of power adopt a way of life that never "insists on its own way" (cf. 13:4), they will forever remain "on the bottom." Ironically, a community in Christ where there are those "on top" and those "on the bottom" hardly reflects the ideal of Gal 3:28 where "all are one in Christ."

Paul was not simply seizing the opportunity to repress some women who were finally recognizing their equal role in God's new creation. However, in his own well-intentioned zeal to end the quarreling and divisions, he lay the blame on those whom he believed were partially responsible for stirring up the trouble: women who were breaking social convention and custom by daring to behave as though they really were members of a new creation where there is no longer male or female (cf. Gal 3:28). Paul, apparently, was far more influenced by a social text promoting the harmonious welfare of the community than a social text affirming that, in Christ, there was no male or female.

Silencing the Prophets: The Pastoral Epistles (1 Timothy 2:8–15; Titus 1:5–9)

Neither traditional nor institutional structures are totally comfortable when confronted with the voice of a prophet who claims the authority of divine inspiration. Prophetic voices regularly challenge given traditions and institutions. Consequently, social structures undergirded by tradition, custom, and institutions are often quick to silence the prophets. Even early Christianity provides evidence of this.

Most scholars believe someone who considered himself a follower and interpreter of Paul's thought wrote the Pastoral Epistles decades after Paul's death.[25] Strictly speaking, therefore, the letters are fictitious missives. Paul did not actually write the letters and Timothy and Titus were not the actual recipients. Yet one is to read the letters as though Paul actually wrote them to Timothy and Titus, just as one would read 4 Ezra *as though* Ezra wrote it. The use of fictional genres may appear strange to modern readers, but the practice has been encountered before.[26] Biblical

[25]See Chap. 11, "A Closer Look: The Letters of Paul."

writers were quite capable of employing differing literary devices, including the "fictional letter," which was a popular genre of literature in antiquity.[27]

One can see evidence in the Pastorals of an emerging *institutional* church led by bishops, elders, and deacons. Within this emerging institutional context one can see evidenced a concern to maintain control. Bishops and elders played extremely important roles in the churches addressed by the Pastorals, as a close reading of Titus 1:5–9 shows.

Titus reveals a number of insights into the church of late first or early second century. First, there was a fluid relationship between elders and bishops. "Paul" commands that *elders* be appointed in every town, whereupon he then begins to outline elders' qualifications. Immediately, the discussion regarding qualifications shifts to a discussion of *bishops,* with no indication that the writer is talking about some other group. Second, there is a concern for order and control. Elders are to serve as leaders who can oversee the functions of the churches everywhere. The elder/bishop is to "have a firm grasp of the word that is trustworthy in accordance with the teaching, so that he may be able both to preach with sound doctrine and to refute those who contradict it" (v. 9). This line is particularly telling. The text assumes a rather firm idea of what true Christian teaching is. It employs summary terms like "the word," "sound doctrine," and "the teaching," as though ancient readers would know how to define these words. Significantly, one of the responsibilities of the elder/bishop is to ensure that people do not stray from this "sound doctrine." The elders and bishops must be prepared to "refute those who contradict it."

Other texts within the Pastorals also show evidence of concern for order and control:

Excerpt One: Timothy, guard what has been entrusted to you. Avoid the profane chatter and contradictions of what is falsely called knowledge; by professing it some have missed the mark as regards the faith. Grace be with you (1 Tim 6:20–21).

Excerpt Two: Hold to the standard of sound teaching that you have heard from me, in the faith and love that are in Christ Jesus. Guard the good treasure entrusted to you, with the help of the Holy Spirit living in us (2 Tim 1:13–14).

Excerpt Three: You then, my child, be strong in the grace that is in Christ Jesus; and what you have heard from me through many witnesses entrust to faithful people who will be able to teach others as well (2 Tim 2:1–2).

Excerpt Four: But avoid stupid controversies, genealogies, dissensions, and quarrels about the law, for they are unprofitable and worthless. After a first and second admonition, have nothing more to do with anyone who causes divisions, since you know that such a person is perverted and sinful, being self-condemned (Titus 3:9–11).

The first two excerpts (1 Tim 6:20–21; 2 Tim 1:13–14) frequently exhort "Timothy," the fictitious recipient of the letter who serves as a model church leader, to "guard what has been entrusted to you"; "avoid profane chatter and contradictions of what is falsely called knowledge" (a

[26]See the discussions of Daniel (Chap. 5) and of Ephesians and 4 Ezra (Chap. 12).

[27]See W. G. Doty, *Letters in Primitive Christianity* (Philadelphia: Fortress, 1973) 6–7. He lists the fictitious letter, which he calls the "non-real letter," as one of several subgenres of letters commonly employed in antiquity.

likely reference to alternative interpretations of the Christian teachings); "hold to the standard of sound teaching"; and "guard the good treasure entrusted to you, with the help of the Holy Spirit." The emphasis on maintaining control and order by maintaining a fixed standard of teaching is obvious.

The phrase "with the help of the Holy Spirit" is quite interesting. This is one of only four references to the Spirit in the Pastorals (see also 1 Tim 4:1 and Titus 3:5, 6), a relatively sparse number, especially when one considers that 1 Corinthians alone has twenty-six references. Yet the scarcity of references is not all that is significant; important also is the description of the Spirit's function. In 1 Corinthians, Paul asserted that *all* Christians have the Spirit and "to each is given a manifestation of the Spirit for the common good" (1 Cor 12:7). Though Paul insisted on order in Corinthian worship, one cannot read 1 Corinthians 14 and be left with any other impression but that the Spirit was active in a very dynamic and even spontaneous fashion in the Corinthian church. However, in 2 Tim 2:14 the Spirit functions primarily to assist Timothy, the model bishop, to *guard* traditional teaching. There is no hint that the author of the Pastorals looks to the Spirit to offer new insights or revelation. In fact, the injunction to Timothy, in the first excerpt, to avoid what is falsely called knowledge implies a total skepticism of ideas that do not conform to the standard. One suspects that if anyone offered a revelation with which the elder/bishop disagreed, such a person would be dismissed. This is confirmed by the fourth excerpt (Titus 3:9–11). The author of these words has little patience for dissension of any sort. It would appear that the church membership is to conform to the teaching of the elder/bishop.

The third excerpt (2 Tim 2:1–2) is also informative. "Paul" is portrayed as the apostle who passes on to Timothy sound Christian doctrine. Note 2 Tim 1:13: "Hold to the standard of sound teaching that you have heard from me, in the faith and love that are in Christ Jesus." But what is Timothy to do with this "sound teaching" other than "guard" it and "hold to" it? According to 2 Tim 2:1–2 he is to pass it on—"entrust [it] to faithful people who will be able to teach others as well." Evidenced here is an early expressions of what became a fixture of second-century Christian institutionalization: the idea that the true apostolic teaching is handed on in an organized succession, in this case from Paul to Timothy to faithful people to others. Such an organized succession of apostolic teaching, which the church eventually came to call **apostolic succession**, was a primary way to *legitimize* what was taught in the churches by the elders and bishops. The "sound teaching" they were to learn and maintain (Titus 1:5–9) was understood as finding its roots in the teachings of the first-generation Christian apostles, such as Paul.

In a context where people perceive true teaching as handed down from the apostles to succeeding generations through recognized and authorized bishops and elders, there is not going to be much use for prophetic voices that claim immediate divine authority and inspiration. If the one claiming divine inspiration offers a revelation that conforms to traditional teaching, he is only being redundant and he is certainly not going to "rock the boat." This kind of revelation is harmless and actually serves to reinforce and legitimate the traditional teaching (cf. 2 Tim 1:14). If one claiming divine inspiration offers a supposed revelation "contrary to the sound teaching that conforms to the glorious gospel of the blessed God, which he entrusted to me [Paul]" (1 Tim 1:10–11), then one can be assured that such a person is a divisive trouble maker who is "perverted and sinful, being self-condemned" (Titus 3:11).

The stance of the Pastoral Epistles with regard to women in the church also evidences this concern for control. In the Pastorals, the seeds of the repression of women's voices planted by Paul himself in 1 Corinthians come to full bloom, as 1 Tim 2:8–15 aptly illustrates.

> *A Closer Look: From Charisma to Institution.* New religious movements regularly
> spring forth as sectarian movements from more established religions. The emergence
> of Christianity from Judaism illustrates this phenomenon. New religious movements
> are often "charismatic," meaning that the leader(s) of such nascent movements do not
> so much have any officially sanctioned authority but are perceived by their followers
> as somehow specially "gifted" (the Greek word *charisma* means "gift"), enabling them
> to offer revolutionary interpretations, or rereadings, of the more established religious
> traditions. Jesus and his earliest followers illustrate this feature of "charisma." Yet
> movements cannot long survive as purely "charismatic" movements. In time, these
> new movements themselves establish solid traditions and teachings that are to be
> handed down to the next generation of followers. When this happens, the once-sectar-
> ian movements themselves begin to become institutionalized. With institutionalization,
> leadership is increasingly viewed not as a charismatic gift directly bestowed by the
> deity (or the Spirit). Rather, leadership comes to be associated with an "office," or a
> formally sanctioned position that one holds. The idea of "charisma" may be main-
> tained, but the "gift" of leadership now comes from the institution.
>
> The Pastoral Epistles show evidence of emerging institutionalization within early
> Christianity. Rather than finding frequent references to the Spirit, one finds numerous
> exhortations to guard and pass on the received teachings and traditions of Christian-
> ity. 1 Timothy 3:1–7 lays out the specific qualifications that one must fulfill in order to
> hold "to the office of bishop" (v. 1). 1 Timothy 4:14 states, "Do not neglect the gift
> (*charismatos*) that is in you, which was given to you through prophecy with the laying
> on of hands by the council of elders." Here, the language of "charisma" and even
> "prophecy" is retained, but such charisma is given to Timothy, the model bishop, when
> the established leadership of the church (the elders) sanctions him through the laying
> on of hands.
>
> *For further study,* H. Fallding. *The Sociology of Religion: An Explanation of the
> Unity and Diversity in Religion.* Toronto: McGraw-Hill Ryerson, 1974. Pp. 153–166;
> C. Osiek. *What Are They Saying about the Social Setting of the New Testament?* Rev.
> Ed. New York: Paulist, 1992. Pp. 75–80; M. Weber. "Charisma: Its Revolutionary Char-
> acter and Its Transformation." *Sociology and Religion: A Book of Readings.* Edited by
> N. Birnbaum and G. Lenzer. Englewood Cliffs, NJ: Prentice-Hall, 1969. Pp. 184–196.
>
> *For more advanced study,* B. Holmberg. *Paul and Power: The Structure of Authority
> in the Primitive Church as Reflected in the Pauline Epistles.* Philadelphia: Fortress,
> 1980; M. Weber. *The Sociology of Religion.* Boston: Beacon Press, 1963. Pp. 46–94.

The author of the Pastorals is a rereader of Paul, employing macro-level intertextual allusions to 1 Corinthians and extending and applying them to silence women's voices once and for
all. Whereas men pray, women dress and adorn themselves so as not to draw any attention to
themselves. They are background fixtures in the house of God. In order to clarify the text's meaning, the Pastorals reread the command of 1 Cor 14:33b-36 for women to be silent. Women are not
only to be silent, but the text grounds such silence in the larger principle that women are to have

no authority over men. As Paul in 1 Corinthians 11 reread the Genesis story to establish that "man was the head of woman," the author of the Pastorals further rereads the story. The Pastorals note not only that God created Adam first, thereby making him the gender of authority, but also add that Eve was deceived first, making the female gender responsible for the fallen mess of creation. (Paul blamed Adam and each individual's own sinful behavior for the Fall [see Rom 5:12–14].) Finally, the author of the Pastorals alludes intertextually to Gen 3:16a ("I will greatly increase your pangs in childbearing; in pain you shall bring forth children") to conclude that women "will be saved through childbearing, provided they continue in faith and love and holiness, with modesty" (1 Tim 2:15). The woman's role is precisely defined. With no authority, no voice, and, effectively, no presence, she can attain salvation by maintaining faith and holiness and by bearing men's children.

Christianity began as a movement on the margins of the established social orders of both the Jewish and Greco-Roman cultures. In such a context, there existed in principle an openness to eradicate the differences that distinguished and classified human beings into superiors and subordinates: "Your sons and your daughters shall prophesy, and your young men shall see visions, and your old men dream dreams. Even upon my slaves, both men and women, in those days, I will pour out my Spirit; and they shall prophesy" (Acts 2:17). So, according to Luke, began the first Christian sermon ever preached. God shows no partiality, for all are one in Christ. Institutionalization is a sociological necessity for any movement to survive. But it brings with it inevitably the impulse for self-preservation, which is slow to accept new ideas and slow to share power equally with all persons within its boundaries. In such a context, it was quite difficult for Christianity to hold to the ideals of its first public sermon; ideals later summarized in early baptismal formulas and echoed by Paul in his more sublime moments: "There is no longer Jew and Greek, there is no longer slave and free, there is no longer male and female; for all of you are one in Christ Jesus" (Gal 3:28).

The NT offers some texts that appear liberating and egalitarian with regard to women. Peter's sermon, for example, quite explicitly speaks of both men and women prophesying. The NT also presents texts, such as 1 Corinthians and the Pastorals, that advocate the silencing of women. Readers today confront competing voices in the NT, even as the earliest Christians confronted competing voices in *their* scriptures. Those who wished to argue for the separation of Jews and gentiles had ample scriptural ammunition to offer (e.g., Neh 13:1–3). Those who advocated the inclusion of the gentiles also could appeal to scriptural tradition (e.g., Isa 56:3–8). Something other than "the Bible says so" moves readers in one direction or another. That "something else" is made up of the varied ideological social texts that inform, though they do not *determine,* the self-texts of every interpreter of the literary text of the Bible. The NT offers texts to support either the silencing or the promotion of women's prophetic voices. Finding a verse or two to support one's position proves little. The verses to which one is drawn, those promoting equality in the context of the gospel or those privileging one group over another in the name of that same gospel, speak volumes about the fundamental ideological and ethical social texts that guide the interpreter.

Conclusion

Prophecy was alive and well in earliest Christianity. Christians believed not only that the prophetic scriptures were finding their realization in the person of Jesus and the history of his followers, but also that prophetic inspiration itself was a viable phenomenon. According to some, such as Paul and the author of Luke-Acts, such inspiration allowed the followers of Jesus to interpret the Jewish scriptures with the insight necessary to understand them properly. This is not to say that every early Christian always warmly welcomed such prophetic activity. Paul appears skeptical of women prophets in Corinth. A later follower of Paul continues along this track. The Pastorals not only forbid women absolutely from any meaningful role in the life of the community, but view prophecy and the Spirit primarily as the means to legitimate traditional structures and ideas.

This is not unlike what one sees in the Hebrew Bible. The Spirit of prophecy was a source of direct revelation of the word of Yahweh, independent of the law. Yet after the law became normative, prophets were reread to point the people back to this law and to legitimate this law. Similarly, once a Christian tradition emerged that the bishop was to guard, the Spirit became primarily an instrument to preserve this tradition. Once the prophetic voice becomes primarily a voice to confirm tradition, it looses its vital force as an agent for change, for its voice looses both its fresh perspective and its boldness to challenge accepted patterns of thought. The controlling of the prophetic voice begun in Paul and the virtual silencing of that voice found in the Pastorals continued on into the second century. David Aune summarizes well the Christian prophets' ultimate fate:

> Prophets and their revelations played an integral role within early Christianity until the beginning of the second century A.D. Thereafter, the inevitable forces of institutionalization banished prophets from their roles as leaders and marginalized the revelatory significance of their proclamations.[28]

For Further Reading

This Happened to Fulfill What Was Written: Matthew

Review also the "Further Reading" on Matthew suggested at the end of Chapter 13.

Allison, D. C. *The New Moses: A Matthean Typology.* Minneapolis, MN: Fortress, 1993.

Brown, R. E. *The Birth of the Messiah: A Commentary on the Infancy Narratives in Matthew and Luke.* Garden City, NY: Doubleday, 1979.

Gundry, R. H. *The Use of the Old Testament in St. Matthew's Gospel with Special Reference to the Messianic Hope.* NovTSup 18. Leiden: E. J. Brill, 1967.

Stendahl, K. *The School of St. Matthew and Its Use of the Old Testament.* Philadelphia: Fortress, 1968.

Prophecy among the Early Christians: 1 Corinthians and the Pastorals

Review also the "Further Reading" on 1 Corinthians suggested at the end of Chapter 11.

Köstenberger, A. J., et al. *Women in the Church: A Fresh Analysis of 1 Timothy 2:9–15.* Grand Rapids, MI: Baker, 1995. (*Offers a sympathetic reading of women's subordination.*)

Toriessen, K. J. *When Women Were Prophets: Women's Leadership in the Early Church and the Scandal of Their Subordination in the Rise of Christianity.* San Francisco: HarperSanFrancisco, 1995.

[28]Aune, *Prophecy,* 189.

Verner, D. C. *The Household of God: The Social World of the Pastoral Epistles.* SBLDS 71. Chico, CA: Scholars Press, 1983.

Commentaries

Bassler, J. M. *1 Timothy 2 Timothy Titus.* ANTC. Nashville, TN: Abingdon, 1996. *Assumes pseudonymous authorship. (Recommended for beginning students.)*

Lea, T. D. *1, 2 Timothy Titus.* NAC 34. Nashville, TN: Broadman, 1992. *Assumes Pauline authorship. (Recommended for beginning students.)*

CHAPTER FIFTEEN

Rereading the Story of the People

Introduction

Review

The god of Abraham and the other patriarchs entered into a covenant with the people of Israel, whom God called to obey his law. Too often Israel did not follow God's law, however, and this resulted in punishment, especially the Exile. Though many Jews still considered themselves living in Exile,[1] they were confident that restoration to their home would come one day.

Luke-Acts offers a portrayal of Jesus as the one who came to initiate the universal restoration (Acts 3:21) to benefit both Israel and the nations (Lk 2:30–32). God's people would be inclusive of both groups, though inclusion in God's people involved acknowledging that Jesus was God's "anointed one" (Acts 2:38). Paul's letter to the Galatians also addressed "the story of the people" (Chap. 13). Gentiles, through their attachment to Christ, Paul argued, became descendants of Abraham and heirs of the promises God made to Abraham. Hence, gentiles and Jews can be part of God's people.

Preview

This chapter will focus attention on how selected NT texts reread the story of the people called Israel. The gentiles, through Christ, can now be included in the people of God. Yet the vast majority of Jews did not embrace the central Christian theological social text that Jesus was the anointed one through whom their god would bring about "the universal restoration that God announced long ago through his holy prophets" (Acts 3:21). Does the Jewish rejection of the gospel lead to the conclusion that God has rejected his people Israel? How two NT texts answer this question will be the focus of this chapter's study. First, a study of Romans 9–11 will show how Paul retold the story of Israel to explain historic Israel's refusal to recognize Jesus to be the Messiah. Second, a study of John 14–17, Jesus' farewell discourse, will explore how John's gospel addressed the issue of the Jews who had not recognized Jesus to be the Messiah. The concluding observations of the chapter will argue that these representative NT texts did not reread the story of the people of Israel in the same way.

---

[1]N. T. Wright. *The New Testament and the People of God* (Minneapolis, MN: Fortress, 1992) 268–272, 299–301.

"Has God Rejected His People?"
God's Salvation for Jews and Gentiles
Romans 15:7–13; 9:1–11:36

Learning Goals

- To learn about the situation Paul was addressing in this letter.
- To understand the essential gist of Paul's argument in Romans 9–11 regarding the current disobedience and eventual restoration of Israel.
- To understand how Romans 9–11 addressed the particular situation of the Roman church.
- To learn how Paul reread the Deuteronomistic pattern.

Guiding Study Exercises

1) What specific situation did this textbook argue Paul was attempting to address in this letter?
2) How does Paul employ stories and themes from the scriptures to explain Israel's current disobedience? Include, but do not confine yourself to, Paul's rereading of the Deuteronomistic pattern.
3) Based on your reading of Rom 9:30–10:21, what constitutes Israel's current disobedience?
4) What does Paul believe the ultimate destiny of Israel to be? How does he employ the Deuteronomistic pattern to express his view of Israel's destiny?
5) How does the argument of Romans 9–11 address the situation of the Roman church as you described that situation in question no. 1?

The Text behind Paul's Letter to the Romans

Most scholars believe that Paul wrote this letter around the years 57 or 58 CE[2] from the city of Corinth. Romans is different from the rest of Paul's indisputably authentic letters to churches in that Paul had never personally visited the Roman church (Rom 1:13). Now, he finally plans to visit Rome and then move on to Spain to continue his missionary work. But Paul first intends to go to Jerusalem to present to the church a financial gift that he has collected from various gentile churches (Rom 15:23–26). Paul's stated desire "to be sent on by you [the Roman Christians]"

---

[2]Review "A Closer Look: The Letters of Paul" (Chap. 11).

(15:24) to Spain may imply that he was hoping to secure support, spiritual as well as financial, from the Roman Christians.

But why would Paul write such a long letter to a church he did not establish? Paul's hope for future support may offer one motive. "Paul thought it necessary to elaborate his understanding of the gospel at length before he made his specific requests to the Roman Christians, on the assumption that they needed to give him the support he sought."[3] This might partly explain Paul's motives for writing this letter. Yet it was Paul's practice to apply his understanding of the gospel to *specific* situations confronting a particular community. The long list of greetings in chapter 16 implies that Paul knew many people.[4] With so many personal acquaintances, it is probable that Paul would have known about particular issues and problems facing the Roman Christians.

Paul seems especially concerned about divisions within the Roman congregation. Romans 14:1–15:6 speaks of conflicts between two groups whom Paul identifies as "the weak" and "the strong." Paul describes "the weak" as those who are scrupulous about dietary regulations and the observance of special days (Rom 14:1–6). Conversely, "the strong" appear to be those who believe they can eat anything and "judge all days to be alike." While certainty is not possible, many scholars conclude that those whom Paul describes as "weak" are Christian Jews who continue to observe certain Jewish practices. Following this reading, "the strong" likely denotes gentile Christians for whom these Jewish practices have no significance.[5] In short, the Roman church may very well have been experiencing ethnic divisions, with Christian Jews wishing to continue to practice their Jewish customs and gentile Christians making light of such customs.

In Rom 15:7–13, the apostle presents a collage of biblical texts that address directly the ethnic divisions within the Roman church. Employing scriptural allusions and quotations, Paul affirms that Christ has come to offer benefits to *both* Jews and gentiles. "Christ," Paul insists, "has become a servant of the circumcised . . . in order that he might confirm the promises given to the patriarchs" (v. 8). Yet the benefits of God's mercy also affect the gentiles: "Rejoice, O Gentiles, with his people" (v. 10). "In him the Gentiles shall hope" (v. 12). God has accepted both Jews and gentiles; Jewish and gentile believers, consequently, should accept each other.

Paul wants to lead his readers to understand that Christ welcomes both Jews and gentiles so that both groups together may worship God. But what about those Jewish people who did not rec-

---

[3]J. D. G. Dunn, "The Formal and Theological Coherence of Romans," *The Romans Debate* (ed., K. Donfried; rev. ed.; Peabody, MA: Hendrickson, 1991) 246.

[4]Given that Paul had not visited Rome, it seems strange that he would know so many people. This has led some scholars to argue that what we now call "Romans 16" was originally a brief letter of recommendation on behalf of Phoebe (see Rom 16:1–2) sent to the church at Ephesus. Paul spent many years in Ephesus, and it is not surprising that he would know so many people. The hypothesis goes on to say that, somehow, this short letter was later appended to the Roman letter. Among the many ancient copies of this letter that we possess, we do have some that do not contain Rom 16:1–24, providing some evidence for this hypothesis. It is equally likely, other scholars argue, that Paul knew many of the folk in Romans by reputation and that he was simply sending his greetings. See J. Gamble, Jr., *The Textual History of the Letter to the Romans: A Study in Textual and Literary Criticism* (Grand Rapids, MI: Eerdmans, 1977).

[5]See, e.g., C. E. B. Cranfield, *Romans: A Shorter Commentary* (Grand Rapids, MI: Eerdmans, 1985) 335–338, whose interpretation is representative of how many NT scholars identify the weak and the strong. Mark Nanos offers the strongest challenge to this consensus, arguing that "the weak" are non-Christian Jews and "the strong" are Christians, be they Jews or gentiles. *The Mystery of Romans: The Jewish Context of Paul's Letter* (Minneapolis, MN: Fortress, 1996) 85–165.

ognize Jesus to be God's Messiah? Numerous comments Paul makes in Romans 9–11 imply that some of the gentile Christians were claiming that God had rejected his historic people and replaced them with the gentiles. Is this true? "Has God rejected his people?" (Rom 11:1). Paul addressed this question in Romans 9–11.

Approaching Romans 9–11

Given that these chapters have created some of the most difficult reading for interpreters of the NT, a few preliminary remarks are in order.

- The disposition with which one reads these chapters will shape one's interpretive text. One who understands the god of the Bible to be inclusive, desiring to offer a salvation that is broad, even cosmic, in its reach, will read the text one way. Others who believe God to be concerned primarily with the salvation of a few individual souls will read it another. The following discussion will take seriously Paul's inclusive message (cf. Rom 8:21; 1 Cor 15:28; Col 1:19–20).
- C. E. B. Cranfield is quite right when he says, "We shall misunderstand these chapters, if we fail to recognize that their key-word is 'mercy.' "[6] God's mercy, made manifest in God's desire to save, drives these chapters.
- Paul is not presenting an abstract argument, but composes Romans 9–11 in order to address one of his larger concerns in the missive. Romans 9–11 assists Paul's appeal to both Jewish and gentile Christians to recognize the legitimacy of each other.

Reading Romans 9–11

The Call of God (9:1–13). Paul's comments on Israel are driven by personal anguish (9:1–3) and theological perplexity (vv. 4–5). How can the very people to whom the promises of salvation belong now stand outside the circle wherein the promises are finding realization? As perplexing as the problem may be, Paul does not conclude that "the word of God had failed" (v. 6a). Paul argues that there is distinction between being "out of Israel" due to one's physical descent and being a part of Israel, understood as God's people (vv. 6b–7). Paul states that physical descent from Abraham alone does not make one a part of God's people. The Jewish scriptures indicate that God has called people from *among* the physical descendants of Abraham: Isaac, not Ishmael, and Jacob, not Esau (vv. 7b-12). It is these who are called, the "children of promise," who are "the children of God" (vv. 8–9). Paul does not apply the argument to his current situation, but he is laying the foundation for the idea that not every Jew, not every physical descendant of Abraham, is a true child of Abraham, that is, a child of the promise and of God.

The Motive for Election: The Mercy of God (9:14–29). God's call is not based on an arbitrary whim. What moves God to call a people are his mercy and a desire to demonstrate his saving power. Verses 14–18 allude intertextually to the story of the Exodus, the event of liberation from slavery in Egypt and from the oppression of bondage to Pharaoh, who had stubbornly refused to release the people of Israel. God used the belligerence of Pharaoh to demonstrate that God can show his mercy and saving power so that his "name may be proclaimed in all the earth" (v. 17),

---

[6]Cranfield, *Romans,* 215.

even in the face of human hardheartedness. God can use human rebellion to advance his work of salvation.

Paul specifically applies this principle to his current time. God presently can make use of rebellious people, such as non-believing Jews, to accomplish his purposes of salvation (vv. 19–24). Because of his patience, God is enduring "vessels of wrath fit for destruction (v. 22) . . . in order to make known the riches of his glory for the vessels of mercy" (v. 23). Such vessels of mercy are those whom God has called, *both Jews and gentiles* (v. 24). Paul does not explain his logic. But apparently he believed that God was employing the non-believing Jews ("vessels of wrath," v. 22) to extend salvation to the gentiles as well as Jews (v. 24). He employs Jewish scripture to declare that gentiles, those who were once not God's people, are now called by God to be his people (vv. 25–26, employing Hos 1:10; 2:23). In applying the discussion to the Jews, Paul makes use of a tapestry woven from Isa 10:22, 28:22, and 1:9 to state that God has called out of Israel a remnant to be saved (v. 27). Without such a remnant, Israel's long-term future would have fared no better than Sodom and Gomorrah, the ancient wicked cities that God totally destroyed (v. 29; cf. Gen 19:24–25). This theme of the remnant will be important in the development of Paul's argument.

Righteousness and Law/Jews and Gentiles (9:30–10:4). History stands at a curious moment. Gentiles, who historically had not concerned themselves with the pursuit of righteousness, or being included within the covenant people of God, were now attaining this righteousness.[7] Ironically, Israel, which had historically sought to fulfill the law of righteousness, has failed to attain to this law. Verse 32 offers an answer to this curious state of affairs. The Jews failed to attain to this law of righteousness because they did not pursue it "out of faith, but as out of law" (literal trans.). From the beginning of Romans, Paul has argued that *faith* is the means of obtaining salvation for *both* Jews and gentiles (cf. Rom 1:16–17). The Jews pursued the "law of righteousness," unaware that the goal they wished to attain was available through faith *for everyone.* Paul's Jewish kinsfolk believed that righteousness was "out of works" (9:32). That is, they believed that inclusion within the people of God hinged on being Jewish and doing the necessary "works" to maintain Jewish distinctiveness. Thus when Christ came manifesting "the righteousness of God through faith in Jesus Christ for *all who believe*" (3:22), the Jews stumbled over this Christ, who brought this salvation to *all.*

Paul emphasizes the zeal the Jews have for God (10:2). But he insists it is an unenlightened and ignorant zeal (10:2b, 3a). Jews are ignorant concerning "the righteousness of God" (10:3a). As Paul tried to argue in the first four chapters of Romans, God demonstrates his saving righteousness by offering salvation to *all* who have faith, both the Jew and the Greek (Rom 1:16–17; 3:21–31; 4:9–12). Being the *god of all* (Rom 3:29–31), God offers his righteousness, his saving power, to *all.* Not knowing this, the Jews sought to establish a righteousness with God that was exclusively *their own* (10:3b). Consequently, they failed to submit to God's righteousness, his universal offer of salvation to all people (10:3b). Salvation for both Jew and Greek is the goal toward which the history of the law and the prophets had been moving. The coming of Christ makes the goal of righteousness "for everyone who has faith" (10:4) a reality. Lloyd Gaston sums

---

[7]When applied to human beings, Paul employs the term "righteous" and its cognates to denote those who stand vindicated before God's eschatological seat of judgment, resulting in being included in God's covenantal people. See "A Closer Look: Justification" (Chap. 13).

up well the point of this section of Paul's argument: "Israel was faithful to Torah as it relates to Israel, but with respect to the goal of the Torah as it relates to Gentiles, they stumbled and were not faithful. . . . The righteousness of God for Gentiles, which is the goal of the Torah, has now been manifested, and it is the failure of Israel to acknowledge this, which is what Paul holds against them."[8]

A Closer Look: The Righteousness of God. Chapter 13 spoke of righteousness and/or justification as it pertained to people (see "A Closer Look: Justification"). Paul also speaks regularly of "righteousness" in relation to God, employing the phrase "the righteousness of God" (Rom 1:17; 3:21; 10:3; 2 Cor 5:21). Paul's understanding of the righteousness of God was rooted in the Hebraic notion of righteousness, which understood righteousness as a relational and legal concept. To be righteous was to satisfy one's obligations. "[T]he righteousness of God . . . denotes God's fulfillment of the obligations he took upon himself in creating humankind and particularly in the calling of Abraham and the choosing of Israel to be his people" (Dunn, 342). Similarly, "'the rightousness of God' . . . denote[s] the faithfulness of God, who graciously maintains his covenant" (Kümmel, 196).

One of God's primary "obligations" is to save and deliver his people. Accordingly, one can find texts that reveal the close relationship between the salvation God offers and the righteousness that belongs to God:

> He [God] put on *righteousness* like a breastplate; and a helmut of *salvation* on his head (Isa 59:17a).

> If I stumble, the mercies of God shall be my eternal *salvation*. If I stagger because of the sin of the flesh, my justification shall be by the *righteousness of God* which endures forever. . . . Through *his righteousness* he *will cleanse me* of all the uncleanness of man and of the sins of the children of men (1QS 11:12, 14b–15 [Dead Sea Scrolls]).

> For I am not ashamed of the gospel; it is the *power of God for salvation* to everyone who has faith, to the Jew first and also to the Greek. For in it *the righteousness of God is revealed* through faith for faith; as it is written, "The one who is righteous will live by faith (Rom 1:16–17).

For further study, J. D. G. Dunn. *The Theology of Paul the Apostle.* Grand Rapids, MI: Eerdmans, 1998. Pp. 340–346; W. G. Kümmel. *The Theology of the New Testament According to Its Major Witnesses.* Nashville, TN: Abingdon, 1973. Pp. 193–203; N. T. Wright. *What St. Paul Really Said: Was Paul of Tarsus the Real Founder of Christianity?* Grand Rapids, MI: Eerdmans, 1997. Pp. 104–111.

For more advanced study, E. Käsemann. "'The Righteousness of God' in Paul." *New Testament Questions of Today.* Philadelphia: Fortress, 1969. Pp. 168–182; H. Ridderbos. *Paul: An Outline of his Theology.* Grand Rapids, MI: Eerdmans, 1975. Pp. 159–181.

---

[8]L. Gaston, "Israel's Misstep in the Eyes of Paul," *Romans Debate,* 316.

Summary of Paul's Argument to this Point. So far, Paul has focused his attention on his *Jewish* readers. He has reminded them that being a child of God is not a matter of physical descent, but a matter of God's electing promise and mercy. Paul goes on to argue that while most Jews are currently rejecting the gospel, God is using their rebellion, even as he once used the rebellion of Pharaoh against God, to further his salvational purposes: he is making out of the gentiles a people and calling out from Israel a remnant. Finally, he argues that the reason gentiles are attaining the righteousness of God is because they understand that God's salvation is available "out of faith." Faith in God is a possibility for all people; it does not depend on being Jewish. Most Jews, Paul believes, understand righteousness to be connected with being Jewish—one of the people of historic Israel and a descendant of Abraham. Being unaware that God's righteousness is demonstrated through offering salvation to *all* people, most Jews tripped over the Messiah, whom God put forward as the goal of his saving work.

The Word is Near, Preached, and Heard (10:5–21). In Rom 10:5–13, Paul employs scriptural allusion (Lev 18:5 and Deut 30:12–13) to continue to contrast the two ways of understanding righteousness. Verse 5 affirms that scripture itself writes about "the righteousness that is out of law" (literal trans.). Scripture says that this kind of righteousness focuses on *doing* things required by the law: "the person who *does* these things will live by these things." Persons who perceive that their inclusion within God's people is grounded in being Jewish and keeping the law that God gave to the Jews—"doing works of the law"—will live their lives focusing on the fulfillment of distinctively Jewish practices. But the scriptures implicitly *also* speak of "the righteousness out of faith" (10:6). Employing Deut 30:12–13, Paul makes clear that this righteousness is found in Christ, who has descended to earth to accomplish his God-assigned work and has been raised from the dead. One is to respond to what Christ has done by confessing and believing the word about Christ (the gospel) that is preached (vv. 8–10). Verses 9–12 reiterate the persistent theme of Romans, namely that this "way of faith" is universal and inclusive. "*Every one* who *believes* (= "has faith") in him will not be put to shame" (v. 10 [employing Isa 28:16]). Verse 12 says that there is no distinction between Jew and Greek and that the one true god is Lord of both. Verse 13 rounds out the argument with a quotation from Joel 3:5: "*Every one* who calls upon the name of the Lord will be saved." The way of faith is the way for *all* human beings to receive God's forgiveness and salvation and find themselves included within the covenant people of God.

Verses 14–21 offer a Pauline reflection on the fate of the word that he and others have preached. People cannot call upon God unless they hear the message (v. 14–15). But messengers who proclaim this good news have been sent (v. 15b), even though many have not believed their message (v. 16). In vv. 18–21, Paul reiterates that the message has gone forth (v. 18) and that Israel did not understand (v. 19a), being "disobedient and contrary" (v. 21). Many gentiles have found God, however, though they did not seek him (v. 20). Employing Moses, Paul says that Israel will respond with jealousy or zeal toward this gentile people (v. 19b, an intertext with Deut 32:21), a theme to which he will return in the next chapter.

The Elect Remnant and the Hardened Blind of Israel (11:1–10). This section elaborates on two themes already introduced, that of the remnant (9:27–29) and hardhearted rebellion (9:17–21). Paul emphatically asserts that the current rejection of the gospel by most Jews does not mean that God has rejected his people (11:1a). The remnant theme helps Paul to make his case. Paul and the many other Jewish people who embrace the gospel are Jews, physical descendants of Abraham. These who believe the gospel form "a remnant, chosen by grace" (v. 5). Paul compares his time to the time of Elijah when most of Israel was living disobediently before God

(vv. 2–4, an intertext with 1 Kgs 19:10, 18). Because God at that time preserved a remnant, Israel survived. Paul and the millions of Jews now living throughout the Roman empire were proof of Israel's survival. The remnant is God's way of *preserving* his people.

Paul concedes that the majority of Jews are blind to the reality of Christ (vv. 7–10). Paul's previous discussion allows readers to infer what exactly the Jews do not see: God's *universal* offering of salvation, forgiveness, and inclusion within his people, all by means of faith. Paul attributes this current blindness to the work and providence of God. But God's having mercy on some and hardening the hearts of others (9:18) is not arbitrary or capricious, as Paul will argue in the following verses. In short, history unfolds according to God's intention to *save*; history is the history of God's saving work, or **salvation history.**

Jews and Gentiles: Instruments of God's Inclusive Work of Salvation (11:11–24). The gentiles owe their salvation to the Jews. Perhaps that is something of an overstatement for, of course, ultimately, gentiles and Jews both owe their salvation to God. But Paul believes that God is using the Jews, both those who believe and those who do not believe, for the purpose of saving the gentiles. God is also using the gentiles for the eventual salvation of nonbelieving Israel. Both Jews and gentiles are instruments of God for his inclusive work of salvation.

Nonbelieving Jews and gentiles. First, gentiles owe their salvation to the Jews who have *rejected* the gospel. Verse 11 is emphatic: "through their [the Jews'] trespass salvation has come to the Gentiles." Paul equates the Jews' trespass with riches for the world and their failure with riches for the gentiles (11:12).

Believing Jews and gentiles. Second, gentiles are saved by virtue of being attached to historic Israel, "the holy root" of v. 16. Gentiles are now connected with the historic promises that God made to *Israel* long ago. "Remember," Paul says to his gentile readers (v. 13a), "it is not you that support the root, but the root that supports you" (v. 18). These gentiles should in no way believe that they have replaced the Jews as the people of God. God's people, whether they be Jew or gentile, are the people of faith. Jewish "branches" who have been broken off the tree, have been separated "because of their unbelief" (v. 20). Gentiles are attached to the root and will remain attached to the root only by virtue of their faith (v. 20). Significantly, this faith associates the gentiles with a historic people called Israel; gentiles' faith does *not* give birth to a whole new people who have replaced historic Israel.

Most scholars conclude that the "root" of v. 16 symbolizes the patriarchs.[9] The image makes clear that the gentiles' association with the people of God is based upon their attachment to the root of historic Israel's ancestors: "it is not you that support the root, but the root that supports you" (v. 18). Gentiles, Paul insists, have been grafted on to the olive tree that represents God's people. And only by virtue of their attachment to the olive tree can the gentiles hope "to share the richness" of the people of God (v. 17). This should silence any arrogant gentile claims that their newly acquired inclusion into the people of God spells the end of God's special relationship with his historic people, Israel.

Believing Jews and nonbelieving Jews. Believing Jews play a role in the eventual salvation of nonbelieving Jews. "If the dough offered as first fruits is holy, so is the whole lump; and if the root is holy, so are the branches" (v. 16). Many understand the "whole lump" to symbolize the

---

[9]See, e.g., J. A. Fitzmyer, *Romans* (AB 33; New York: Doubleday, 1993) 614; R. A. Harrisville, *Romans* (Minneapolis, MN: Augsburg, 1980) 177–178; Cranfield, *Romans,* 277.

whole of Israel, the "branches" to symbolize the people of faith, Jewish or gentile,[10] and the "dough" to symbolize the believing Jewish remnant.[11] If the "whole lump" denotes the *whole* of the Jewish people, Paul is claiming that the remnant (the "dough") sanctifies the whole of Israel (the "whole lump").

The remnant is God's means of preserving his people (9:27–29; 11:1–6). The remnant of believing Jews does not represent all of the Jews who will find salvation. The remnant is but the "first fruits" (v. 16), clearly implying that many more of God's historic people will experience salvation. The remnant of believing Jews is God's means of preserving his historic people for ultimate restoration. Paul makes several comments indicating that he understands the unbelief of the majority of Jews to be a temporary thing and that their restoration would eventually occur. He speaks of the Jews' "full inclusion" (v. 12b), their "acceptance" (v. 15b), and their being "grafted back into their own olive tree" (v. 24b). Paul envisions the eventual restoration of the whole of Israel. The current remnant stands as testimony that God's historic people will *not* experience the fate of Sodom and Gomorrah (9:29), being removed from the face of the earth.

Believing gentiles and nonbelieving Jews. Paul offers statements to indicate that the gentiles also play a role in the eventual restoration of Israel. "Inasmuch then as I am an apostle to the Gentiles, I magnify my ministry in order to make my fellow Jews jealous (cf. Rom 10:19), and thus save some of them" (vv. 13b–14). Paul believed that his mission to the gentiles would play a role in the eventual restoration of the Jews by "making them jealous." Paul apparently believed that when Jews began to see the gentiles receive God's blessings that they would become "jealous" and also want to share in the these same blessings.

Nonbelieving Jews play a role in the salvation of gentiles. Believing Jews play a role in the salvation of nonbelieving Jews and gentiles. Believing gentiles play a role in the salvation of nonbelieving Jews. Whether people are obedient or disobedient to the gospel, nothing will thwart God's intention to keep his promises to Israel and to bring this people to restoration and salvation.

The Restoration of Israel (11:25–36). Paul addresses the comments of this last section to gentile readers. He implies that the gentiles seriously misunderstand the meaning of the hardening of part of Israel (v. 25). The gentiles fail to see that "a hardening has come upon part of Israel, until the full number of the Gentiles come in, and so all Israel will be saved" (vv. 25b–26a). The present time of Paul's work is the time God has offered for gentiles to learn the way of faith. Nonbelieving Israel plays a role in this advancement of faith in ways that Paul has already described in the previous section. But Israel's final role is not merely to spur the advancement of faith among the gentiles. This hardening has come on part of Israel only *until* the full number of gentiles has been attained, that is, until the period of the gentile mission draws to a close. At the conclusion of this period, "all Israel will be saved." Scholars debate just what Paul means by "all Israel." Does he mean every single Jew who happens to be alive when the full number of gentiles come in? Does he mean Israel as whole? What about Jews who have lived before the conclusion of the gentile period? By what means are the Jews saved?

Regrettably, Paul does not answer these questions with the precision one might like. But some tentative responses are possible. It is unlikely that Paul envisions the coming of every single

---

[10]Cranfield, *ibid.,* 277; Harrisville, *ibid.,* 177–178; B. Byrne, *Romans* (Collegeville, MN: Liturgical Press, 1996) 339–340.

[11]Fitzmyer, *Romans* 614; Harrisville, *ibid.,* 177–178; Cranfield, *ibid.,* 277.

Jew to a righteousness of faith, just as it is unlikely that Paul expected every single gentile to come to faithful relationship with God. At the same time, Paul likely did not mean "all Israel" to denote only a small number of Jewish people who, after "the full number of Gentiles come in," would come to a relationship of faith. Ben Witherington charts a middle course, arguing that the Jewish scriptures use the term "all Israel" to mean "not absolutely all, but the corporate whole with some exceptions who are in the minority."[12]

The salvation of all Israel will involve their continuing *not* to persist in unbelief, as Paul asserted earlier, saying that those Jews who did not persist in unbelief "will be grafted in [to the olive tree], for God has the power to graft them in again" (v. 23). Scholars debate precisely what Paul means by not "persisting in unbelief." But Paul is clear that "all Israel," the "natural branches," will come to hold the kind of faith necessary, whatever that faith may be, to "be grafted back into their own olive tree" (v. 24). God has made promises to Israel's ancestors (v. 28) and God's call cannot be retracted (v. 29). The hardness of Pharaoh did not thwart God's intention to save Israel centuries before, and the hardness of part of Israel will not thwart God's same intentions in Paul's own day.

Verses 30–32 offer a good conclusion to Paul's argument. Jews and gentiles alike have lived in disobedience to God. Equally, Jews and gentiles also experience the mercy of God. Paul ultimately attributes all that is happening with regard to the Jews and the gentiles to "the depth of the riches and wisdom and knowledge of God" (v. 33a), for whom, through whom, and to whom are all things (v. 36).

Summary: Paul's Argument to the Roman Christians. It is now time to connect the foregoing discussion with Paul's more specific concern to encourage Roman believers, both Jews and gentiles, to "welcome one another . . . as Christ has welcomed you" (15:7). Paul's emphasis on the mercy of God should lead both groups to realize their mutual dependence upon God, and discourage either group from viewing itself as superior to the other. His argument that gentiles are dependent on both believing and nonbelieving Jews for their being grafted onto the root of God's people, together with Paul's reminder to these gentiles that God will restore Israel, should silence any misconceptions the gentiles had that God had replaced his historic people, Israel, with the gentile Christians. To the Jews, Paul encourages their acceptance of the gentiles by insisting that through their inclusion into God's people, nonbelieving Israel would experience "jealousy" and thus be moved to embrace the way of faith. The current inclusion of the gentiles into God's people serves as part of God's larger plan to save all Israel. Failure to embrace the gentiles whom God has accepted and is even using to save Israel can certainly not be in the best interest of believing Jews, who are concerned, even as Paul was, for the welfare of nonbelieving Jews.

Rereading the Deuteronomistic Pattern

Paul has done much rereading of the Jewish scriptures in Romans 9–11. The three chapters are saturated with texts from the Jewish Bible. But Paul has not only reread particular literary texts, he has also reread a larger social text, the **Deuteronomistic pattern**. Deuteronomic theology offered a pattern by which Israel could make sense of its experiences. It affirmed that (1) *God had called Israel to be his people*; and that (2) Israel was *to respond to this call through obedience* to

---

[12]*Paul's Narrative Thought World; The Tapestry of Tragedy and Triumph* (Louisville, KY: Westminster/John Knox, 1994) 70.

God's Torah. It further affirmed, however, that (3) *Israel rebelled against this Torah and rejected the prophets* whom God sent to warn her, and therefore, that (4) *God* removed Israel from the land and *sent Israel to live in Exile* until it should (5) *repent,* at which time (6) *God would restore the people.*[13] Paul employed the Deuteronomistic pattern to make sense of the story of Israel and particularly its refusal to recognize Jesus as Israel's hoped-for Messiah.

Israel as God's People. Paul affirms *God's call of Israel to be his people.* First, he says of Israel that "to them belong the adoption, the glory, the covenants, the giving of the law, the worship, and the promises; to them belong the patriarchs, and from them, according to the flesh, comes the Messiah, who is over all" (9:4–5). It is clear that Paul acknowledges the special role of Israel in the plan of God. Second, just after Paul has declared that "all Israel will be saved" (11:26a), he justifies his statement with the simple observation that "the gifts and the calling of God are irrevocable" (11:29). God has *called* Israel and that has serious implications for Paul. Third, Paul begins his discussion of Romans 11 with the question, "Has God rejected his people?" (11:1). The question only makes sense if one understands "people" to denote the historic, ethnic Israel.

Israel's Rebellion. Though Israel was to *respond with obedience* to God's call, *it rebelled against God and rejected the prophets and messengers sent to it to turn it back to God* (see items 2, 3, and 4 of the Deuteronomistic pattern, above). Paul explicitly states, in reference to Israel, that "they have now been disobedient" (11:31). In 9:29 Paul quotes Isaiah to compare Israel to Sodom and Gomorrah, the ancient cities of rebellion (9:29). Again quoting Isaiah, Paul announces that Israel is "a disobedient and contrary people" (10:21). In chapter 11, when Paul compares himself to the remnant of ancient Israelites who did not serve Baal, he is implicitly comparing the majority of present-day Israel who are rejecting the gospel with the ancient Israelites who worshiped Baal and "killed [God's] prophets" (11:3). Israel, Paul believes, is following the Deuteronomistic pattern of rejecting God's ways and his messengers.

The Punishment of Israel. Due to its persistent rebellion, God has required Israel to live in Exile. Paul never uses the word "Exile," but it is clear that he views Israel as *currently* living under the wrath and judgment of God. Paul quotes the words of Moses found in Deut 32:21 (10:19), applying them to the unbelieving Israel of the apostle's own day: "I will make you jealous of those who are not a nation." The Deuteronomic text Paul quotes is referring to the Exile, into which God sent Israel because of its rebellion. Several passages from Romans 11 make clear that Israel stands under the judgment of God: they now live with their backs forever bent (v. 10); they have now stumbled (v. 12a); they are defeated (v. 12b); and they are rejected (v. 15a). The whole **parable** of the olive tree (vv. 17–24) portrays the majority of Israel as being broken off, separated from the tree that symbolizes God's people. The image of separation from the tree is quite similar to the idea of being exiled and separated from the land. In the parable of the olive tree, Paul also speaks of how God "did not spare the natural branches" and notes God's "severity toward those [Jews] who have fallen" (v. 21–22). Finally, Paul even speaks of how Israelites currently "are enemies of God" (v. 28). Paul may not use the word *exile,* but the Exile denoted the experience of God's judgment, and Paul certainly believed that Israel was currently living under the judgment of God.

Repentance and Restoration. Israel's repentance would lead to its eschatological restoration. Paul believed that the members of Israel who had been cut off from the tree of the people

---

[13]This summary of the Deuteronomistic perspective and Paul's rereading of it in Romans essentially follows, with some modifications, the helpful discussion of J. M. Scott, "Paul's Use of Deuteronomic Tradition," *JBL* 112.4 (1993) 645–665.

would be grafted back into it "if they do not persist in unbelief" (11:23). Paul does not dwell on this issue or even use the word *repentance* in Romans 9–11. Yet he affirms that Israel will be restored if it begins to believe (have faith) in God as the god who accepts *all* people on the basis of faith. Paul appears quite confident that Israel will come to this faith and then experience the blessings of the restoration: "Have they stumbled so as to fall? By no means!" (11:11). "How

Paul used the image of olive tree to represent the people of God in Romans 11. The dense foliage, created by the many branches of the olive tree, allowed Paul to employ the image of branches being removed and added to the thick trunk. (Chance and Horne)

much more will their full inclusion mean?" (11:12). "God has the power to graft them in again" (11:23). "All Israel will be saved" (11:26).

Paul employs many micro-level intertexts as he rereads the story of Israel in Romans 9–11. These chapters also employ macro-level intertextuality as Paul rereads the Deuteronomistic pattern to help him interpret Israel's rejection of the gospel. Paul embraces the pattern that teaches that rebellion leads to judgment, which leads to repentance and restoration. In the context of this way of thinking, Paul interprets the present situation of Israel's rejection of the gospel as disobedient rebellion against God. But Paul is confident that God cannot break his promises to or rescind his call of Israel; thus, he looks forward to Israel's eventual repentance and restoration.

"That They May Be One":
The People in the Gospel of John
John 14–17

Learning Goals

- To learn the basic issues of introduction pertaining to the Gospel of John.
- To understand how the genre of Jesus' farewell discourse informs one's reading the text.
- To understand how the gospel rereads specific scriptural images of Israel to portray Jesus and his followers as displacing "the Jews" as the true Israel.
- To understand John's dualistic employment of the idea of "the world" to explain the antagonism between the Johannine Christians and the synagogue.

Guiding Study Exercises

1) Briefly describe the textbook's conclusions regarding each of the following introductory issues:
   a) the authorship of the gospel.
   b) the relationship between the Johannine community and the synagogue.
   c) the sources employed by the author of the gospel.
2) Identify the genre of Jesus' farewell discourse and explain how one's knowledge of this genre can inform a critical reading of the text.
3) Describe how John reread the image of the vine (John 15), so as to portray Jesus and his followers, rather than "the Jews," as the true Israel.
4) How does your understanding of the relationship between the Johannine community and the synagogue help you to make sense of John's portrayal of the Jews as "the world"?
5) Whose rereading of the story of the people do you find most persuasive, Paul's or John's? If you wish, you may answer "neither" and explain why. Or you may challenge the premise of the question and argue that Paul and John do *not* present two different rereadings at all.

The Text behind the Fourth Gospel

The Authorship, Date, and Setting of the Gospel. Since the end of the second century, Christian tradition has identified the author of the fourth gospel with John, son of Zebedee.[14] This tradition is based on a statement found in Jn 21:24–25 that states that "the disciple whom Jesus loved" (21:20) was the one who "has written these things." Nowhere does the gospel identify this so-called **Beloved Disciple**. Many infer that this Beloved Disciple must have been among the inner circle of Jesus' disciples. According to the **Synoptic Gospels**, Jesus' inner circle consisted of Peter, James, and John, leading some to surmise that the Beloved Disciple must come from this group. He cannot be Peter, since Peter appears in several scenes with the Beloved Disciple (e.g., 20:2). James has not been a regular candidate, since Christian tradition reported that he was killed early in the history of Christianity (Acts 12:2), too early to have written this gospel. This leaves John. For most modern scholars, the threads tying the inferences together are too thin to allow for a confident conclusion. Thus, most are hesitant to make any firm claims regarding the identity of the gospel writer. The ensuing discussion will use the traditional name of John, but primarily as a matter of convenience.

The questions of date and setting are related. Many believe that the social text of John is very similar to that of Matthew. Matthew wrote in the early decades after of the fall of Jerusalem, in a context of strained relations between his community and the **synagogue** (Chap. 13). The Gospel of John also reflects a context of conflict with the synagogue. However, the conflict appears to be even more harsh than that experienced by Matthew's community. A peculiar word, *aposynagōgos,* appears in John's gospel. It is generally translated as "being put out of the synagogue" (9:22; 12:42; 16:2). In Jn 16:2, Jesus predicts of his followers: "They will put you out of the synagogues."[15] The following line is even more ominous: "Indeed, an hour is coming when those who kill you will think that by doing so they are offering worship to God" (16:2). Assuming the fourth evangelist composed words that would speak to the issues facing his contemporary readers, Jn 16:2 may offer evidence of a very hostile relationship between the Johannine Christian Jews and the non-Christian Jews of the larger Jewish community. Even if the tension had not reached a point where people were literally put to death, the tone of the rhetoric indicates intense hostility.

The gospel provides further evidence of a hostile relationship between the Johannine community and the synagogue. First, a complex story in John 9 about Jesus healing a blind man concludes with Jesus severely condemning the Jewish leadership as both blind and guilty (9:39–41). Second, the term "the Jews" is used derisively to denote those who are opposed to Jesus (see 9:18; 10:31; 18:12, 36, 38; 19:12). Texts such as 8:42–44 even quote Jesus to say that the Jews' father is the devil, not God! This should impress readers as quite striking, especially given what

---

[14]See J. Kysar, "John, Gospel of," *ABD* 3.912. This is an excellent article on matters of introduction.

[15]Some scholars, following the work of J. L. Martyn in his book *History and Theology in the Fourth Gospel* (rev. ed.; Nashville, TN: Abingdon, 1968/1979), have argued that this expulsion from the synagogue was a formal "excommunication" enacted by the Jewish leadership to deal with Christian Jews. Others are more inclined to see the action as less formal, but still very real and theatening to the Johannine Christians. Hence, not all features of Martyn's thesis are fully embraced, but many Johannine scholars still recognize the overall validity of his reconstruction: Johannine Christians were being removed from their synagogue communities and this was creating hostile conflict between the two groups. See J. Kysar, "John, Gospel of," *ABD* 3.918.

Paul argued in his letter to the Romans. These and other similar texts lead Robert Kysar to conclude: "Such a stance in relationship toward Judaism is made understandable if the Johannine community stood in opposition to the synagogue from which it had been expelled."[16]

From the early days of Christian tradition, interpreters have believed that the gospel was written toward the end of the first century CE (ca. 90). Modern scholars tend to agree. The intensity of the hostile relationship between the Johannine community and the synagogue appears to fit better with the period after the destruction of Jerusalem (70 CE) than with the period before.

The Nature of the Conflict between the Johannine Christians and the Synagogue. In Matthew the conflict centered around the proper understanding of the law. Matthew urged his readers to understand that they were to look to Jesus, the new Moses and master teacher, and not to the scribes and Pharisees, for the proper understanding of the law (Chap. 13). The conflict in John's gospel revolves around the issue of Jesus himself. The gospel makes many bold claims about Jesus and his relationship to God. These claims, which speak of Jesus' oneness with God (see 10:30, "The Father and I are one"), would have sounded blasphemous to the non-Christian Jews of John's time. The gospel even records a unique story about how the Jews attempted to kill Jesus because he made himself equal with God (5:18). The rift between followers of Jesus and the other Jews is much deeper than in Matthew, for the issue is not "How does one understand the law?" but "Who is Jesus?" and "What is his relationship to God?"

The Sources of the Gospel. Some scholars have attempted to identify and reconstruct the possible sources that now lie embedded in the finished product of the gospel. Such source critics have noted that John refers to the miracles of Jesus as "signs,"[17] a curious phenomenon, given that the Synoptic Gospels refer to Jesus' miracles as "signs" only in a pejorative manner.[18] John's portrayal of miracles as signs intended to inspire faith in Jesus has led some scholars to argue that a source of miracle stories, or a "Signs Source," lies behind the fourth gospel. Interpreters have also recognized that Jesus speaks differently in John than in the Synoptics. Virtually gone are the pithy proverbs and provocative parables. The subject matter of Jesus' speech is also different. Rather than talking about the kingdom of God, as he does in the Synoptics, the Johannine Jesus talks about *himself* and his role as the revealer of God. The so-called *I am* sayings represent well this different style and focus of Jesus' discourse in the fourth gospel. Most notable are such sayings as "I am the bread of life" (Jn 6:35, 48, 51); "I am the light" (8:12; 9:5); "I am the good shepherd" (10:11, 14); "I am the resurrection and the life" (11:25).[19] This way of speaking is peculiar to the fourth gospel. The fact that Jesus speaks differently in John has led some scholars to conclude that John made use of a "Discourse Source."

There is consensus among critical scholars that John, being independent of the Synoptic Gospels, likely employed some unique sources. Yet most scholars have concluded that John's sources cannot be isolated and reconstructed with confidence.

[16]See Kysar, *ibid.*

[17]See, e.g., Jn 2:11, 23; 4:54; 6:2, 14, 26; 7:31; 12:37; 20:30.

[18]See, e.g., Matt 12:38–39; 16:1–4; 24:24; Mk 8:11–12; Lk 23:8.

[19]Other good examples are "I am the gate" (10:7, 9); "I am God's Son" (10:36); "I am the way, the truth, and the life" (14:6); "I am the true vine" (15:1, 5).

The Farewell Discourse of Jesus and the People of God

The farewell discourse of Jesus (John 14–17) provides a useful avenue to study the fourth evangelist's idea of the people of God. In broaching this subject three features require examination: (1) the **genre** of the discourse, (2) Jesus as the exclusive means to the Father, and (3) the relationship between God's people and "the world."

The Genre of the Farewell Discourse. This discourse offers an example of the so-called testamentary genre of ancient Jewish and Christian literature. Typical of the genre was the offering of a speech by a renown character of the past. This character is facing death and offers in this dramatic setting a farewell testament to his followers, children, or some such group. Through the farewell **testament**, the hero not only speaks of this death and its meaning but offers counsel to those he is leaving behind and to successive generations of followers. Peter Ellis states that "the discourse in Jn 13–17 fits this literary form perfectly. . . . The discourse . . . deals with the immediate and distant future–the approaching death of Jesus and the life of the Church up to and beyond the time of the evangelist."[20]

John 14–17 portrays Jesus as speaking to his followers who are with him during their last meal together. In reality, according to the conventions of the genre, the real audience of the speech is the reader of the gospel. Again, Peter Ellis summarizes clearly the implications of recognizing the genre of Jesus' discourse: "The words are addressed to the apostles, but in the ecclesiological context of the whole discourse and in John's mind and intention, the discourse is meant as Jesus' testament given from heaven and intended for Christians of all times."[21] The genre invites the reader to listen to the words of the Johannine Jesus to hear what the evangelist wanted to say to his readers toward the end of the first century. In so doing, readers can learn much about "the people of God" in the fourth gospel.

Jesus: The Way to the Father. In this discourse John says to his followers, "I am the way, the truth, and the life. No one comes to the Father, except through me" (14:6). The idea that Jesus is the way to God is not new to NT thought (see, e.g., Acts 3:23). But the Gospel of John adds a depth to this claim only implied in the other NT texts. Jesus is the way to God because he shares an absolutely unique relationship with God–one of absolute unity. "The Father and I are one" (10:30). Immediately after Jesus says that he is the way to God, he can immediately say, "If you know me, you will know my Father" (14:7). A couple of verses later he says, "Whoever has seen me has seen the Father" (14:9). The evangelist believes that Jesus is the way to God, for he is God in the flesh. "The Word [identified as God in Jn 1:1] became flesh and dwelt among us" (1:14). "No one has ever seen God. It is God the only Son, who is close to the Father's heart, who has made him known" (1:18). This view of Jesus, which emphasized his divine character, likely contributed to the intense conflict between the Johannine Christians and the larger Jewish community.

Jesus had become so absolutely central in the Johannine tradition that the gospel portrays him as personally *replacing* the significant institutions of Judaism. His first miracle, where he changed water into wine, is rich with symbolism communicating this idea (2:1–12). The story refers to the large jars that held the water used "for the Jewish rites of purification" (2:6). Jesus

---

[20]P. F. Ellis, *The Genius of John: A Composition-Critical Commentary on the Fourth Gospel* (Collegeville, MN: Liturgical Press, 1984) 210.

[21]*Ibid.,* 216.

replaces this water used for this Jewish ritual with wine, with the wine perhaps symbolizing the age of salvation and restoration.

> The time is surely coming, says the LORD, when the one who plows shall overtake the one who reaps, and the treader of grapes the one who sows the seed; the mountains shall drip sweet wine, and all the hills shall flow with it. I will restore the fortunes of my people Israel, and they shall rebuild the ruined cities and inhabit them; they shall plant vineyards and drink their wine, and they shall make gardens and eat their fruit (Amos 9:13–14).

The miracle at Cana portrays Jesus as replacing the water of the old Jewish rite of purification with an abundance of new wine, signifying that the eschatological age of salvation had dawned. "[T]he episode emphasizes the replacement of Jewish institutions by a new economy of salvation."[22]

The fourth evangelist places the story of Jesus cleansing the Temple (2:13–22) immediately after the Cana narrative. After Jesus had cleansed the Temple he made the bold declaration, "Destroy this temple and in three days I will raise it up" (2:19). The narrator goes on to explain that Jesus "was speaking of the temple of his body" (2:21). Jesus *himself* is the temple that replaces the sacred Jewish institution. The Synoptics place the Temple episode at the *end* of Jesus' ministry. But the Gospel of John places it in the earliest phases of Jesus' ministry to emphasize that *from the beginning* Jesus came to *replace* in his own person—his own body—the revered and holy institutions belonging to Judaism.

In his final discourse Jesus employs the image of the vine to describe himself (Jn 15:1–8). His words indicate that it is *exclusively* through union with Jesus that one lives in union with God. Attachment to Christ is essential to being one of the people of God: "Whoever does not abide in me is thrown away like a branch and withers; such branches are gathered, thrown into the fire, and burned." The image of judgment is clear. Further, bearing much fruit and being a **disciple** of Jesus glorifies the Father (v. 8). The clear implication is that one cannot glorify God without being a disciple of Jesus. The glorification of God and union with Jesus go hand-in-hand. Finally, Jesus explicitly declares that he is the *true* vine (v. 1). The picture of Jesus as the vine conjures up images of the "new wine" that symbolize the new age of restoration. The image of the true vine portrays Jesus as the one in whom Israel finds its eschatological restoration. The significance of the vine imagery is heightened when one notes the macro-level intertexts with the Jewish traditions of the vine as an image for *Israel.*

Israel as God's vine. Psalm 80:8–19, which students should read, illustrates the biblical use of vine imagery to denote Israel. Employing the image of the vine to symbolize Israel, the Psalmist tells the story of Israel from the now-familiar Deuteronomistic pattern. Verses 9–11 tell of God's rescue of Israel from Egypt, the Exodus. These initial lines go on to speak of God's blessing Israel, as its "branches" spread over the entire land, denoting the geographical expansion of the nation in the days of Israel's glory. Verses 12–16 speak of the current hardship that the vine is now enduring as its fruit is plucked and the vine itself is cut down and burned with fire. A reader familiar with the Deuteronomistic pattern would know that the reason for such hardship must be the rebellion of Israel, "the vine." Verses 17–19 offer a familiar word from Deuteronomic theology, the theme of restoration. God will be with the king (the one at his right hand),

---

[22]*Ibid.,* 44.

and the nation will turn back to God. The final words (v. 19) speak of Israel's restoration and salvation.

Another set of texts comes from Isaiah 5:1 7 and 27:2 6, both of which students should read carefully. Again, the vine/vineyard image refers to Israel. Israel was to bear fruit (5:4), interpreted as justice and righteousness (5:7). Yet the vines bear only wild grapes (5:2, 4), thorns, and briers (27:4). Consistent with the Deuteronomistic pattern, there will be judgment. God will break down the protective wall and the vineyard will be trampled down, overrun with thorns (5:5–6), and burned up (27:4). Isaiah 27 adds the regular note of ultimate restoration, stating that eventually Israel will bear fruit that will fill the whole earth (v. 6). Again, Israel is the vine that is to bear good fruit, but it does not.[23]

Jesus as the true vine. Within this macro-level intertextual framework, Jesus' claim that he is the *true* vine and that his followers are the branches who bear fruit for God subverts the picture of historic, ethnic Israel as the vine of God. Claiming to be the true vine, the Johannine Jesus claims to represent in his person the mission and destiny of Israel. Jesus not only replaces Jewish rituals and institutions (John 2), he replaces Israel itself. Whereas the Israel of old was marked by consistent disobedience and rebellion, Jesus as the true vine lives in perfect harmony with God's will: "But I do as the Father has commanded me" (14:31a). "I have kept my Father's commandments and abide in his love" (15:10b). "I glorified you on earth by finishing the work that you gave me to do" (17:4). The gospel offers other texts that communicate the same idea: Jesus follows the Father in the kind of obedience Israel was to offer (4:34; 5:19, 30; 6:38).

Since Jesus is the true vine, it follows that Jesus' disciples, through their attachment to Jesus, are the true Israelites. Further, as true Israelites the disciples would be expected to live obedient lives before God, bearing fruit fitting of the vineyard of Israel. Appropriately, Jesus emphasizes to his disciples the theme of bearing fruit (Jn 15:4–5). The Jewish scriptures regard *Israel* as the vine that was expected to bear fruit (Isa 5:2, 4; 27:6). According to the Johannine Jesus, only the disciples who abide in Jesus can bear the fruit that brings glory to the Father (15:8).

Such fruit comes from keeping the commandments of Jesus. It is through obedience to the commandments of Jesus that one shows his or her love for Jesus. "If you love me, you will keep my commandments" (14:15). "They who have my commandments and keep them are those who love me; and those who love me will be loved by my Father, and I will love them and reveal myself to them" (14:21). "Those who love me will keep my word, and my Father will love them, and we will come to them and make our home with them" (14:23). "If you keep my commandments, you will abide in my love, just as I have kept my Father's commandments and abide in his love" (15:10). This last statement shows that through obedience to Jesus' commandments one continues to abide in the love of Jesus and God. Conversely, "Whoever does not love me does not keep my words; and the word that you hear is not mine, but is from the Father who sent me" (14:24). In the farewell discourse and other Johannine texts, the commandment one is to keep is that of love for one another. "I give you a new commandment, that you love one another. Just as I have loved you, you also should love one another" (13:34). A bit later the gospel states, "This is my commandment, that you love one another as I have loved you" (15:12; see also 15:13–17).

A special feature regarding this commandment of love needs comment. "In Johannine theology, it is not so much love for all as for the covenanted brethren, who have been born from on

---

[23]Other texts that employ vine imagery for Israel include Jer 12:10; Ezek 15:1–6; 17:5–10.

high through the death of Jesus and through having been 'begotten of water and Spirit' (3:5)."[24] The tense and even hostile relationship with the synagogue appears to have created something of a fortress mentality within the Johannine community. This mentality gave rise to an understanding of the love commandment that focused the attention of the commandment on *fellow believers.* The Gospel of John offers no equivalent to what one finds on the lips of the Synoptic Jesus: "Love your enemies" (cf. Matt 5:44; Lk 6:27, 35). John believes the relationship between the follower of Jesus and "the world" to be one of antagonism. "If you belonged to the world, the world would love you as its own. Because you do not belong to the world, but I have chosen you out of the world —therefore the world hates you" (15:19). With regard to members of the community, love is to be total. With regard to "the world," the relationship is antagonistic.

   The Followers of Jesus and the "World." The fourth gospel uses the word "world" ambivalently. On the one hand, the world is the object of the Father's love. "For God so loved the world that he gave his only Son, so that everyone who believes in him may not perish but may have eternal life" (3:16). "Indeed, God did not send the Son into the world to condemn the world, but in order that the world might be saved through him." Jesus came into the world to be its light (8:12; 9:5; 12:46), take away its sin (1:29), offer it salvation (4:42; 12:47), give it life (6:33), and to testify to the truth before it (18:37). On the other hand, the gospel insists that "the world" rejects what Jesus has to offer. "The true light, which enlightens everyone, was coming into the world. He was in the world, and the world came into being through him; *yet the world did not know him*" (1:9–10).

   The world's rejection of Jesus is a dominant theme of the gospel. Though Jesus is the light of the world, "people loved darkness rather than light because their deeds were evil" (3:19). Thus, Jesus "came into this world for judgment" (9:39) so that those who recognize that they live in darkness can come to the light, while those who live in darkness but deceive themselves by thinking that they live in light will remain in their darkness. Further, Jesus judges and conquers the world by driving out the ruler of the world (12:31; 16:33). In brief, the world does not know God (17:25) or Jesus, whom God sent (1:10). Given the stark contrast between light (Jesus) and darkness (the world), the relationship between the two is thoroughly antagonistic. The world hates the Son (7:7) and actually rejoices that he will die (16:20).

   The world also directs its antagonism toward Jesus' followers. Neither Jesus nor his followers find their origins in the world. "They do not belong to the world, just as I do not belong to the world" (17:16), Jesus says. Thus, the world responds with hatred toward Jesus' followers, just as it responded to Jesus. "If you belonged to the world, the world would love you as its own. Because you do not belong to the world, but I have chosen you out of the world—therefore the world hates you" (15:19; cf. 17:14). The Gospel of John speaks through the voice of Jesus to the readers to remind them that they are separate from the world—a world that hates them, Jesus, and God. "If the world hates you, be aware that it hated me before it hated you" (15:18). "Whoever hates me hates my Father also" (15:24).

   The gospel portrays the disciples as pitted against the world. Scholars refer to this kind of intense antagonism as **dualism**. A dualistic perspective claims that two groups or powers exist in thoroughgoing opposition to one another: light vs. darkness; love vs. hate; good vs. evil; God vs. Satan; the disciples vs. the world. What is most important about Johannine dualism, especially as

---

[24]Ellis, *Genius of John,* 219.

it relates to "the story of the people," is that *John portrays "the Jews" as representing and embodying "the world."*

John 15:24–16:4 illustrates this quite clearly. This passage speaks of the Jews, as the reference to *"their* law" (15:25) affirms. When John wants to identify "the world" with a specific group, he directs the attention of the reader toward the Jews. The Jews are those who kill Jesus' followers and think that they are serving God (16:2b). As "the world," the Jews become in John's gospel the object of a number of damning charges. Most especially, they know neither Jesus nor the Father (1:10; 17:25), and they hate Jesus and God (15:18, 23). Since they neither know nor love the Father, it follows that God cannot truly be their god. John 8:42–47 asserts this most emphatically. This text asserts that God is not the father of the Jews, the devil is. The text declares

---

A Closer Look: Dualism in John and the Dead Sea Scrolls. The dualistic perspective that one finds in John is similar to the dualism of the Qumran community.

> [God] has created man to govern the world, and has appointed for him two spirits in which to walk until the time of His visitation; the spirits of truth and injustice. Those born of truth spring from a fountain of light, but those born of injustice spring from a source of darkness. All the children of righteousness are ruled by the Prince of Light and walk in the ways of light, but all the children of injustice are ruled by the Angel of Darkness and walk in the ways of darkness. . . . The nature of all the children of men is ruled by these (two spirits), and during their life all the hosts of men have portion of their divisions and walk in (both) their ways. . . . For God has established the spirits in equal measure until the final age, and has set everlasting hatred between their divisions. Truth abhors the works of injustice, and injustice hates all the ways of truth. And their struggle is fierce in all their arguments for they do not walk together (Excerpts from 1 QS 3:13–4:26; Vermes).

Such a dualistic perspective was not uncommon in sectarian groups, particularly those that viewed themselves as persecuted by the larger society or religious community. In this respect, the Qumran and Johannine communities shared a similar social text, contributing to their both holding to a dualistic perspective.

For further study, R. Kysar. *John: The Maverick Gospel.* Atlanta, GA: John Knox, 1976. Pp. 47–64; D. S. Russell. *Divine Disclosure: An Introduction to Jewish Apocalyptic.* Minneapolis, MN: Fortress, 1992. Pp. 104–115.

For more advanced study, J. H. Charlesworth. "A Critical Comparison of the Dualism in 1QS 3:13–4:26 and the 'Dualism' Contained in the Gospel of John." *John and the Dead Sea Scrolls.* Edited by J. H. Charlesworth. New York: Crossroad, 1990. Pp. 76–106; J. J. Collins. *Apocalypticism in the Dead Sea Scrolls.* London: Routledge, 1997. Pp. 30–51; M. Hengel. *Judaism and Hellenism: Studies in their Encounter in Palestine in the Early Hellenistic Period.* 2 volumes. Philadelphia: Fortress, 1974. 1. 218–224.

that the Jews pattern their way of living after that of the devil–the way of murder and deceit. The text charges that the Jews are not from God.

Some radical rereading of the story of the people has taken place within the Johannine orbit of Christianity. God's people are those who belong to Christ. That is a consistent message in the NT. But John has blended with this message the perspective of a radical dualism that manifests itself in a stringent "us vs. them" mentality. Much of this dualistic perspective is rooted in the concrete historical social text wherein the tensions between the followers of Jesus and the synagogue reached a fever pitch. In this context, loyalty to Christ is made the "acid test" of being one of God's people. And if one is not loyal to Christ, she or he must live on the dark side of the dualistic universe. That includes the Jews who are not followers of Jesus. Gone, it appears, is the consistent theme of the Deuteronomistic pattern that affirmed the last word in God's relationship with Israel to be restoration. The author of the fourth gospel might affirm that the last word with regard to Israel is restoration, but he would maintain with equal vigor that "the Jews" no longer have anything to do with "Israel." They are of "the world."

Conclusion:
"Disinheriting the Jews?"
John 8:31–49

The title of Jeffrey S. Siker's provocative book provides the title for these concluding comments.[25] Using the figure of Abraham, Siker traces the development of the idea of the people of God through the first 100 years of Christian history (roughly 50–150 CE).

Paul argues in Galatians that gentiles can be descendants of Abraham by virtue of their faith. Such inclusion of the gentiles does not *exclude* the Jews from such status, though Paul argues in Galatians 4 that Jews who do not live in faith live in a state of slavery to the law. In Romans, Paul distinguishes between being a physical descendant of Abraham and being a *child* of Abraham (Rom 9:6–7). To be a child of Abraham is to be more than a physical descendant; it is to be a child of "promise," which translates into being a person of faith (Rom 4:9–12). Paul recognizes that most Jews of his time do not live in such faith. But, he insists, the unbelieving Jews have *not* stumbled so as to fall (11:11). The current hardening that has come on "part of Israel" (11:25) is only temporary, serving God's purposes of offering gentiles the opportunity to attain to righteousness, which is to be included in the ranks of God's people. In the end, "all Israel will be saved" (11:26), for "they are beloved for the sake of their ancestors" (11:28) and "the gifts and the calling of God are irrevocable" (11:29).

Within 100 years, things had changed. Justin, a second century *gentile* Christian writer, used the Abraham story not as a means to *include* both Jew and gentile, but as means to *exclude* the Jews from the people of God. He rereads the Abraham story as being exclusively a story about the ancestor *of the gentile Christians and them alone.* As Jeffrey Siker states:

[F]rom Justin's perspective it is doubtful that the Jews were ever really the intended heirs of God's promises to Abraham. Christians become the true descendants, Christians the bless-

[25]*Disinheriting the Jews: Abraham in Early Christian Controversy* (Philadelphia: Westminster/John Knox, 1991).

John employed the image of the grape vine to denote Jesus as the true embodiment of Israel in John 15. The abundant fruit of the vine, pictured in the vinegrower's hand, served as an image of the fruitful life that one attached to Jesus was to live (Jn 15:2, 5). (Courtesy of Larry McKinney)

ing to the nations, and Christians the rightful heirs to the land. By redefining and redirecting the promises in this way, Justin seeks to preclude the Jews from making any legitimate appeal to the Abrahamic heritage. . . . The Jews stand completely dispossessed. They are stripped of their lineage from Abraham, which the Christians now justly claim. The Jews are like a sterile wasteland. They are no longer a light to the Gentiles; rather, the Gentiles now bear the torch and are a light to obstinate Jews. . . . Justin has no doubt that the Jews have no legitimate heritage from Abraham, nor can they lay claim to any of God's promises to Abraham.[26]

[26]*Ibid.*, 170–171, 178.

Texts such as Jn 8:31–59 place the Gospel of John closer to the position of Justin than that of Paul. The Jews claim to be "descendants" (literally "seed") of Abraham (v. 33). John concedes that the Jews are physical descendants of Abraham (v. 38), but this does not mean that they are *children* of Abraham (v. 39). Paul makes a similar distinction (Rom 9:6–7), *but Paul does not draw the same conclusion as John.*

John declares that the Jews have neither God nor Abraham as their father, but the devil himself (v. 44). This goes far beyond what Paul says. John does not say that the Jews *become* children of Satan because they reject Jesus; he asserts that they reject Jesus because they *are* children of the devil. "Why do you not understand what I say? It is because you *cannot* accept my word. You are from *your father the devil,* and you choose to do your father's desires. . . . If I tell the truth, why do you not believe me? Whoever is from God hears the words of God. The reason you do not hear them is that *you are not from God"* (8:43–44, 46b–47).

Read honestly, John's gospel does not say what Paul says. Paul does not dismiss the Jews. His whole argument of Romans 9–11 is intended to *prevent* his gentile readers from dismissing the Jewish people. To be sure, Paul acknowledges that most Jews are not believing the gospel. But Paul attributes such nonbelief to the mysterious workings of God to provide the gentiles an opportunity to be saved. Because of their unbelief, individual Jews have been cut off the tree of Israel. But Paul is quite confident that they will be grafted back (Rom 11:17–24). The promises God made to the ancestors of Paul's fellow Jews are irrevocable (11:28–29). For the fourth gospel, however, the Jews have no real promises rooted in the ancestors. Abraham is a physical ancestor only; the Jews are not really his children. Since their father is the devil, the ruler of this world (12:31; 14:30; 16:11), they *cannot* accept Jesus' word (8:43–44). John represents movement along a trajectory of early Christian thought that culminates in Christian interpreters like Justin: God is for us, the gentile Christians, and not for others—especially not the Jews. It bears asking whether the early Christians merely replaced one form of exclusivism (the Jews are in, others are out) with another (Christians are in, others [especially Jews] are out).

Paul reread the story of the people of God. As he rereads this story, he does so to include the gentiles and not to exclude the Jews. Paul cannot deny the current reality of the majority of Jews' unbelief. But this is not the final word for Paul. Consistent with his religious ancestors, he embraces the Deuteronomistic pattern where the last word is always restoration. John, probably because he and his community are caught up in a bitter struggle with the synagogue, has employed the Jesus tradition to reread the Jews *out of* the story of God's people. For modern readers who, for whatever reason, embrace a vision of the gospel that excludes the Jews, John's story of the people will be appealing. God has found a new people. A new exclusive group has replaced the old. For readers who embrace the vision of 2 and 3 Isaiah and of the earliest followers of Jesus— a vision of inclusion of Jew and gentile—Paul offers an alternative voice. His is a voice worthy of thoughtful attention.

For Further Reading

"Has God Rejected his People?" Romans

Barth, M. *The People of God.* JSNTSSup 5. Sheffield: JSOT, 1983.

Beker, J. C. *Paul the Apostle: The Triumph of God in Life and Thought.* Philadelphia: Fortress, 1980. Pp. 328–347.

Donaldson, T. L. *Paul and the Gentiles: Remapping the Apostle's Convictional World.* Minneapolis, MN: Fortress, 1997. Pp. 215–248.

Dunn, J. D. G. *The Theology of Paul the Apostle.* Grand Rapids, MI: Eerdmans. Pp. 499–532.

Witherington, B. *Paul's Narrative Thought World: The Tapestry of Tragedy and Triumph.* Louisville, KY: Westminster/John Knox, 1994. Pp. 57–72. (*Recommended for beginning students.*)

Commentaries

For commentaries on Romans, consult the footnotes of this chapter.

"That They May Be One": The Gospel of John

Brown, R. E. *The Community of the Beloved Disciple: The Life, Loves, and Hates of an Individual Church in New Testament Times.* New York: Paulist, 1979. (*Recommended for beginning students.*)

Fortna, R. T. *The Fourth Gospel and its Predecessor.* Philadelphia: Fortress, 1988. (*Source analysis of the gospel.*)

Käsemann, E. *The Testament of Jesus according to John 17.* Philadelphia: Fortress, 1968.

Kreitzer, L. *The Gospel according to John.* Regent's Study Guides 1. Oxford: Regent's Park College, 1990. (*Recommended for beginning students.*)

Commentaries

Brown, R. E. *The Gospel according to John.* AB 29/29A. Garden City, NY: Doubleday, 1966/1970.

Talbert, C. *Reading John: A Literary and Theological Commentary on the Fourth Gospel and the Johannine Epistles.* New York: Crossroad, 1992. (*Recommended for beginning students.*)

Epilogue:
The Rereading Continues

For those students who have now come to this point in the book through the discussions in each preceding chapter, there is one final text to offer in retrospect. It reads: "He [God] will teach him [Jesus] the Book, the Wisdom, the Torah, the Gospel, to be a messenger to the Children of Israel."[1] At first glance readers might suspect that the passage is yet another portion of the NT, some passage affirming the mission and ministry of Jesus Christ to the Jewish people of his day. But that is not the case. This passage comes from the Quran, the sacred scriptures of Islam. The text does indeed affirm the ministry of Jesus as a prophet, but the larger context of the passage makes clear that Jesus is not the final revelation, Muhammed is.

This macro-level intertext with the Bible, alluding to both Testaments, is a provocative reminder that the process of rereading the Jewish and Christian sacred scriptures continued beyond the canonization of both the Hebrew Bible and the NT. It even reached beyond the communities of the Jewish and Christian faiths. The Arabian followers of the seventh-century prophet Muhammed were taught the stories of Abraham, Ishmael, Jacob, Moses, Mary, and Jesus. These characters were a part of their received traditions. However, Muhammed made it clear that the final revelation rests in the Quran, where one reads, "The Christians say, 'The Messiah is the Son of God.' . . . God assail them! How they are perverted! . . . They were commanded to serve but One God; There is no God but He" (9:30–31).[2] Muhammed believed that the Christian view of the trinity—God in three distinct persons, Father, Son and Holy Spirit—had perverted the original monotheistic confession of faith. It was Muhammed's mission to reform it.

Several questions arise from this simple demonstration that allow readers now to reflect upon at least what one can observe about the origins, definition, and meaning of the Bible. For the process of reading and rereading has to do with the origins, definition, and, ultimately, the meaning of the Bible's story. The same kinds of processes are involved in the origins of the Quran and most likely other sacred books as well.

Origins of the Bible. The Bible comes into existence through a process of interpretation and reinterpretation. The idea of rereading attempts to capture this so that whatever other dimensions

---

[1]The Quran 3:48–49. Quoted in John L. Esposito, *Islam: The Straight Path* (Oxford: New York: Oxford University Press, 1991) 20.

[2]*Ibid.,* 20.

there may be to biblical origins (and to some of us readers, there are others), it is at least a collection of ancient literature written by persons giving expression to new experiences of their faith as they were in conversation with more ancient expressions of that faith. What readers are able now to observe is a very human process of reading and interpretation. Persons transmitted the biblical traditions, wrote them down, transcribed them, edited them, collected them, combined them, and passed them on to the next generation.

Some readers will ask whether this diminishes the significance of the idea of inspiration. Inspiration may still be a part of one's understanding of origins. But one must keep in mind two things. First, inspiration—and this can admittedly mean many things—is not something one can observe in the same way one has observed various kinds of intertextuality and rereading. Rather, inspiration is something readers bring to the text—the self-text—based upon the many social texts that influence them. Second, it may be necessary to redefine what is meant by inspiration in view of the intertextual nature of the biblical text. At the very least, notions of inspiration must include some rather frank admissions about the various literary conventions that grew from the ancient social texts that produced the scriptures. Perhaps it would be better to think of inspired persons rather than inspired texts. It was inspiration that caused people to give expression to their faith in the literary forms available to them in their days. Nevertheless, it is important to recognize how a careful reading of the Bible requires that one rethink (reread!) one's own understanding of biblical origins. How the Bible came to be shapes what readers understand the Bible to be.

Definition/Identity. Thinking about biblical origins provides some insight on what the Bible is. Of course it is a collection of teachings, hymns, prayers, stories, genealogies, apocalypses, laws, and so on. Since its origins are within the framework of human existence and experience, whatever else it is (and, again, it is much more to many people), it is at least such a collection of ancient literary genres. It is very difficult to think of the Bible as only one thing, or as a unity for that matter. Its multiplicity, complexity, and enormity are overwhelming. In order to read it one must know it in its parts. Each individual story and episode—each text—has a story of its own origins and purpose standing behind it, which is nearly lost to memory and virtually impossible to reconstruct. Each law has a connection, either real or symbolic, with ancient Israelite society or literature.

The fact that these ancient documents were passed on generation after generation attests to the reality of the power of interpretation. The communities that reread their sacred traditions did so because it gave expression to something they experienced as real and authoritative. This phenomenon allows the inference that many who have read the Bible have thought that there was more to it than just ancient literature. Many Christian communities have thought that these ancient texts spoke to them. One stark example comes from the instructions of a twentieth-century Christian pastor, Deitrich Bonhoeffer. In his instructions to young seminarians he urges them to pray the psalms, and in doing so they will find that the psalms themselves instruct the community to "pray as a fellowship."[3] He sees Psalm 5 as a good example, but when we look at the psalm itself, nothing in it says "pray as a fellowship." That is because Bonhoeffer is drawing this meaning from the "parallelism" of the poetic lines of the poem: "that remarkable repetition of the same sense in different words in the second line of the verse." From this he concludes there are always

[3]Dietrich Bonhoeffer, *Life Together* (New York: Harper & Row, 1954) 49.

"two voices," and thus, a fellowship within the psalm.[4] Clearly, the psalm does not say this, but Bonhoeffer brings to the text a way of reading that allows him to draw this meaning from it. In the remarkable social text behind Bonhoeffer's interpretation of Psalm 5—that of a community of seminarians illegally training to minister in Nazi Germany—Bonhoeffer found a way to hear some new meaning in the text.

Meaning. Taking seriously the origins and nature of the Bible that can be inferred from its own intertextuality and the process of rereading that produced such intertextuality, it is no longer appropriate to speak of meaning in the sense that many people do. For one thing, the text really has no meaning apart from those who are reading and rereading it. One implication is that reading the Bible is not merely a process of "mining it" for its nuggets of gold. There are no tools to ensure that one will get to the "mother lode." That is because meaning is created as readers find intersections between the story in the Bible and their own stories. Does that mean that the Bible is really completely contingent? Is there no bedrock, no absolute foundation from which readers have a beginning and ending point? If there is any such bedrock or beginning point, it is not within the text itself. Again, it is within the readers themselves.

But not readers as individuals so much as readers within communities. This is important, because through relationships communities are charged with a kind of spiritual vitality. This vitality forms a commonness of purpose and intent and makes such actions as reading and interpreting no mere "willy-nilly" activity. Rather, that common purpose and vital spirit provides the boundaries of meaning that may be derived from a text. In the case of the Jewish or Christian communities, it is the experience of the living God, as it has been transmitted through the community of faith, that assists the process of reading and interpretation. The creative vitality of the community as it practices love for each other and for those outside the community guides the interpretation of the sacred texts. Meaning, therefore, is an interrelational activity.

If determining the meaning of the biblical text is an interrelational activity, then it is also an ongoing activity—one that can never cease. As relationships and circumstances change, so do meanings, as illustrated by the following modern expression of this phenomenon. Christianity and its Bible played a great role in allowing the institution of slavery to exist for a long time. Even the NT did not come right out and oppose it. One has but to read what Paul says in his letter to Philemon regarding his slave, Onesimus: "Treat him not as a slave any more, but something much better than a slave, a dear brother." But Paul did not speak out against the institution of slavery, and this became a basis for the suffering of many African Americans in the early days of the United States. Needless to say, all know that slavery is wrong today, regardless of the shortfall of the Bible in this respect. It is not the clear and unambiguous teachings of the Bible that allow modern people to know that slavery is wrong, but the larger culture, or social text, of the real communities in which people live. Clearly, modern Christians, who are shaped as much by the social texts of their worlds as by the words of their sacred text, have reread the Bible and given it a new meaning. The process of rereading goes on.

[4]*Ibid.,* 49.

Glossary

Aaronic/Aaronide priests/priesthood Designates a family of priests who traced their lineage to Moses' brother Aaron. The Zadokites traced their lineage to Aaron. While they generally trace their lineage back to the patriarch Levi, the family of Aaron is singled out for special service according to Numbers 17.

AD see CE.

Allegory/allegorical A method of interpretation wherein specific items in a text are interpreted in a thoroughly symbolic manner with little regard for the literal or historical meaning. Compare TYPOLOGY.

Anachronism/anachronistically A chronological misplacement. Frequently this occurs as a writer attributes characteristics of a certain time period to an event or character from a different time period.

Antitheses Refers to Matt 5:21–48, where Jesus compares/contrasts his own teaching with that of the Torah.

Apocalyptic/apocalypticism/apocalypse These words are all related to the Greek word for "revelation," *apocalypsis,* the title of the last book of the Christian Bible.
"Apocalyptic" is an adjective used to describe ways of thought that look forward to a cataclysmic end of the world and the coming of new and better creation.
"Apocalypticism" is a noun denoting a social movement or perspective characterized by an apocalyptic worldview.
"Apocalypse" is generally used to denote a genre of literature that offers a narrative or story that "reveals" to the reader the mysteries of history and of the cosmos.
See ESCHATOLOGY, GENRE.

Apocrypha See DEUTEROCANONICALS.

Apodictic Describes a certain form of "law" that is more instruction than actual law. Its rhetorical features include direct address (using the second grammatical person), negative formulation ("you shall not"), and an appeal to deity for legitimation.

414

Apostasy Abandonment of or defection from previous commitments of faith.

Apostle Literally, "one sent out." Christians used the word to denote persons who had received a direct commissioning from the resurrected Jesus to proclaim the gospel.

Apostolic succession An idea that emerged in the early church tradition, asserting that church leaders were the authoritative heirs of the Apostles and, as such, were to guard the true Christian teaching.

Aramaic A semitic language closely related to Hebrew that, in its earliest forms, was in the Assyrian court and later became the official language of the Persian court. In the post-Exilic period it became the common language of Palestine. Parts of Ezra and Daniel are written in Aramaic.

Ark of the covenant A box that was built to contain the laws that Moses received atop Mt. Sinai. As a central religious artifact it functioned as a portable shrine.

Artifact/artifactual Refers to some piece of material. Archaeologists use the term to designate items found in the process of excavation. As a basis of evidence, "artifactual" evidence is that which is material evidence as opposed to literary evidence.

Assyria/Assyrian A significant Mesopotamian empire from ca. 1900–612 BCE. This empire conquered the northern kingdom of Israel in 721 BCE and made Judah a vassal state.

Babylonia/Babylon This ancient empire went through three major phases. The Old and Middle Babylonian periods extend roughly through the first millennium BCE. The biblical story is most concerned with the Late Babylonian empire, which reached its zenith of power in sixth century BCE. Babylon was the capital city of this empire. See EXILE.

BC see BCE.

BCE Denotes "Before the Common Era" and represents a way of dating that is not specifically Christian. Dates followed by BCE represent the same time as dates followed by BC (meaning "Before Christ").

Beloved Disciple Refers to the character in the Gospel of John who is simply identified as "the disciple whom Jesus loved." Tradition identifies this character with John, the son of Zebedee.

Benjamin One of the patriarchal ancestors and sons of Jacob/Israel, after whom one of the twelve tribes of Israel is named.

Caesar Aristocratic Roman family that ruled Rome beginning with Julius Caesar (d. 44 BCE) and ending with Nero (d. 64 CE).

Canon/canonical From the Greek word used to denote a carpenter's rule, the term came to be used metaphorically to denote a "norm" or "standard." To describe the Bible as "canonical" is to affirm that the Bible provides the standard or norm for the religious community that reads it.

Casuistic Designates a kind of law that has its setting in actual "cases" of dispute or arbitration. It is characterized by a double structure: one, a conditional clause, called a *protasis,* which defines the parameters of a case ("if two men struggle . . ."); two, a result clause, called an *apodosis,* which indicates the legal response.

CE Denotes "Common Era" and represents a way of dating that is not specifically Christian. Dates followed by CE represent the same time as dates preceded by AD (meaning *Anno Domini,* translated as "the year of our Lord").

Christ (or **christos**) See MESSIAH.

Christian(s) From the Greek, *christianos.* The term denotes one who is a follower of Jesus, believing him to be the Christ. The term appears only rarely in the New Testament (Acts 11:26, 26:28; 1 Pet 4:16). Can be used as an adjective to attribute to a noun ideas or characteristics commonly held among Christians, such as "Christian teaching."

Chronicler A shorthand term to refer to those who wrote the history contained in 1 and 2 Chronicles.

Church Translates the Greek word *ekklesia,* literally meaning "the called out assembly." Early Christians used the term to denote their local congregations as well the worldwide body of Christians.

Circumcision/circumcise Removal of the foreskin from the penis. In the Bible, circumcision represented a covenant between God and the people of Israel. (See Genesis 17.)

Covenant Designates a binding agreement between two parties. As it occurs in the Bible, it may refer both to a divine grant or charter or to a bilateral agreement with obligations binding both parties. As a bilateral agreement, it is central to the Deuteronomist's understanding of the nation's relationship to God.

Covenant Code One of the most ancient law codes in the Bible. It comprises Exod 21:1–23:33.

Crucifixion/crucify An ancient form of execution by asphyxiation whereby the victim was suspended from a wooden pole that sometimes included a cross bar.

Cult/cultic Refers to the officially sanctioned practice of worship.

Davidic house Is a term denoting the dynastic succession that reigned in Jerusalem until the first Babylonian siege in 597 BCE. In later periods the Davidic dynasty was thought to be the lineage through which the Messiah would trace his origins.

Dead Sea Scrolls Discovered in 1946 in caves around Qumran, these scrolls date from the second century BCE to the first century CE. They consist of the most ancient copies of the Hebrew Bible discovered to date as well as many additional documents that served to offer religious guidance to the Jewish sectarians who produced these scrolls. See SECT.

Decalogue Or "Ten Commandments." This term designates the short lists of general, categorical instructions. They do not specify how they will be enforced or what penalties are to accompany them. There are several Decalogues within the Hebrew Bible: Exod 20:1–17; Exod 34:11–26; Deut 5:6–21.

Desacralize/desacralization The removal of religious sanctification from activities or ideas that had once been so endowed in view of alternative and often nonsacred (secular, or profane) explanations for the same activities or ideas.

Deuterocanonicals Books in the Roman Catholic and Orthodox versions of the Christian Old Testament for which there are no corresponding books in the Hebrew Bible. Protestant Bibles may contain these Deuterocanonical books, though they are placed in a separate section belonging to neither the Old or New Testaments and labeled "Apocrypha," meaning "hidden" or "secret."

Deuteronomic Code Consisting of Deuteronomy 12–26, much of it assumes and rereads the Covenant Code.

Deuteronomistic pattern The pattern, found frequently in the literary texts of the Deuteronomist, that interprets the history of Israel as a cycle of the rebellion of the nation against Yahweh, repentance toward Yahweh, and restoration of the people by Yahweh.

Deuteronomic theology/perspective Describes the eighth-century BCE school of legal specialists whose theology was tied closely to Moses, emphasizing covenant law, and very likely also tied closely to prophets such as Hosea and later Jeremiah.

Deuteronomist/Deuteronomistic As both noun and adjective the term refers to persons who hold to Deuteronomic Theology, but who are more recent than the eighth century BCE. In most contexts the terms refer to the great history in the Bible, begun in the late sixth century BCE and completed during the fifth century BCE, by persons espousing this theology. See DEUTERONOMISTIC HISTORY.

Deuteronomistic History A narrative covering the history of Israel from the conquest of Canaan until the fall of Judah. It consists of the books of Joshua, Judges, Samuel, and Kings.

Diaspora Technical term to denote Jews who are "dispersed" throughout the world, not living in "the land."

Diatribe Designates the rhetorical relationship between a prophet and an opposing audience. Frequently the prophet's own words give the reader clear indication of what the audience's point of view is.

Didache From the Greek word for "teaching," New Testament scholars regularly use the term to denote specifically early Christian teaching—or doctrine—as it came later to be called.

Disciple In the New Testament the word is used most often to denote a follower of Jesus. More broadly, it can denote any devoted follower or student of some noteworthy teacher or figure.

Double tradition Similar narrative episodes presented by two different sources.

Dualism A word used by scholars of religion describing a worldview that understands the cosmos as involved in a struggle between two spiritual forces, those of good and evil.

Eschatology/eschatological Derived from the Greek words for "last" and "talk" or "word," the term denotes that which has to do with "last things." When used in relation to the Bible, it generally refers to something that is conceived of as new, displacing the present order of things. The biblical idea of the "kingdom of God" is an eschatological concept. See also APOCALYPTIC.

Essenes A first-century BCE group of sectarian Jews thought to have sought sanctuary in the village of Qumran from the persecutions of, what they felt to be, the corrupt religious leaders in Jerusalem.

Exegesis From the combination of two Greek words, rendering "to lead out of," it is a term used to denote strategies for interpreting the Bible—"to lead out of" the text its meaning.

Exile The period in Israel's history (587–539 BCE) when, after the fall of Jerusalem to Nebuchadnezzar of Babylon, the Jews of Jerusalem and Judea were away from their homeland, held captive by foreign rulers.

Exodus Is a Greek term referring to the dramatic escape of Hebrew slaves from Egypt under the leadership of Moses in the thirteenth century BCE.

Form criticism A method of reading that biblical scholars use that seeks to understand the origins of a literary passage in a preceding oral stage of tradition. The tacit assumption is that well-defined patterns of speech derive from historically accessible social contexts.

Genre Coming ultimately from the Greek word for "kind," the term denotes the "kind" of literature a work in question represents. Works belonging to the same genre are characterized by a particular rhetorical style, vocabulary, content, and function. Knowing the genre of a text gives readers a clue as to how to read and make sense of a text.

Gentiles The term denotes any persons in the Bible who are not Jewish. It is particularly used in the New Testament, translating the Greek word *ethne,* which literally means "nations."

Gospel The word is derived from an old English word, meaning "good news." It serves to translate the Greek word *euangelion,* which literally means "good news." Early Christians used this word to summarize their message: the "good news" that through the death and resurrection of Jesus, God was offering salvation to all people. The word eventually came to denote the narratives that told the story of Jesus' life, death, and resurrection: the Gospels of Matthew, Mark, Luke, and John.

Gymnasium Designates the Greek educational center, both for intellectual as well as physical education. The term *gymnos,* from which the term stems, means "naked" in Greek, and refers to the fact that all of the physical education activities were performed in the nude.

Hasmoneans More popularly referred to as "the Maccabees," this was the family that led the successful revolt against Syria in the second century BCE. Following the revolt, persons from this family ruled the Jews in Judea, holding both the high priesthood and political throne.

Hebrew Bible The Jewish scriptures, consisting of three parts: the Torah (Law), the Nebi'im (Prophets), and the Kethubim (Writings). They were composed over a long period of time throughout the first millennium BCE. These documents form the foundation of the Christian Old Testament. See DEUTEROCANONICALS.

Hellenistic/Hellenism Adjective/noun that from the fourth century BCE through the early Christian period denoted the pervasive influence of Greek culture. May be used more narrowly to denote the historical period from the fourth century BCE until the emergence of the Roman domination in the mid-first century BCE.

Historical recitals Brief summaries of the history of Israel and Judah. They usually occur in the contexts of prayers (e.g., Neh 9:6–38), speeches (e.g., 1 Sam 12:6–12) and cultic liturgies (Psalms 105 and 106). The narrative context in which they occur shapes their function and reason for being incorporated. They give modern readers some idea of the development of Israel's story.

Holiness Refers to the state of being holy. *Holy* literally means "separate" and leads to the idea of otherness. One way of practicing separateness was through moral purity.

Holiness Code Another ancient code of law now embedded within the book of Leviticus (see Leviticus 17–26).

Holy war A specific kind of warfare in which Israel engaged against its enemies, whereby all living things were to be slaughtered as an act of total devotion. It is rooted in the belief that such warfare was the will of God and served to accomplish his purposes (see Joshua 8).

Ideology/ideological A systematic set of ideas, be they political, economic, religious, or the like, that provides for an individual or a group an overall schema for understanding and interpreting events and experiences.

Implied reader A term from literary criticism denoting the reader that a given text implies, regardless of who the "real reader" might be. For example, the "implied reader" of a high school textbook is a high school student, even though anyone might actually read the textbook.

Institution An established, socially legitimate pattern of behavior or series of public or private relationships and priorities by which a community defines its central values and beliefs.

Internal evidence In biblical studies, the term is used to denote information derived from within a document that provides information about the document's social text. For example, an allusion to a historical event within a document allows one to conclude that the document was composed after the event.

Interpretive Text The interpretation that emerges as a reader intersects various types of texts.

Intertext "An intertext is a text found in another text (or echoing in another echo chamber). It may be transposed, absorbed, even reversed or transumed." (Danna Nolan Fewell, *Reading Between Texts* , 1992: 23.)

Intertextual/Intertextuality/Intertextually In this text, an approach to reading that explores the *inter*connecting relationships between various *texts* and the meaning that emerges from between these various texts.

Ipsissima verba/vox Technical term to denote "the authentic words" of Jesus and "the authentic voice" of Jesus, respectively. The latter is what most scholars believe is accessible to modern investigators.

Israel The Bible employs the term primarily in three, often overlapping, ways. First, to denote the descendants of Jacob, whose sons were the progenitors of the twelve tribes of Israel. Second, to denote the "people of God." Third, to denote the political nation that existed from 922–722 BCE.

Josephus A prolific first-century CE Jew whose histories of Judaism, entitled *Antiquities* and *War,* offer valuable information regarding Judaism of the Hellenistic period and the first century CE.

Josiah A king of Judah who reigned from 640 BCE to 609 BCE. He is most remembered for the wide-ranging cultic reforms that confined officially recognized worship of Yahweh to Jerusalem.

Judah One of the patriarchal ancestors after whom one of the twelve tribes of Israel is named. In Genesis 49 readers find this tribe to be one of the most important. Also denotes the geographical region in southern Palestine populated by this tribe and the nation that was ruled by the Davidic House.

Judea An Aramaic variation of the word Judah, Judea became the common term in the Hellenistic and Roman periods to denote the territory surrounding Jerusalem that was roughly the geographical equivalent of Judah.

Judges Designates an office in the loose tribal affiliation that settled in Palestine prior to kingship. Judges were *ad hoc* leaders chosen for their charismatic abilities.

Kerygma From the Greek work for "proclamation," the term was taken over by early Christians as a short-hand way of referring to the message "proclaimed" by the early Christians: the salvation offered through the death and resurrection of Jesus. See GOSPEL.

Levites/Levitical Members of the clergy in ancient Israel who descended from Jacob's son Levi. In some texts are considered rival families for control of the Temple service.

Literary Text The most common understanding of "text"; a text in its written form.

Liturgy/liturgical From a Greek word that means "public service," as in the service of a priest. The word came to designate the service of public worship within the Christian community. Used in this book generally to designate either worship or the set structures of public worship.

LXX See SEPTUAGINT.

Maccabees/Maccabean See HASMONEANS.

Macro-level intertextuality/intertext When one text compares broadly to the themes or ideas another text, be it a literary text or social text, yet with a low degree of verbal correspondence. See MICRO-LEVEL INTERTEXTUALITY.

Masoretes Identifies the generations of scribes whose work transmitting one form of the consonantal text of the Hebrew Bible is known only to us through the massive set of interpretive instructions which accompany that text. "Masorete" derives from the name of those instructions, "Masorah." See MASORETIC TEXT.

Masoretic text Denotes the particular version of the text that the Masoretes produced.

Mesopotamia Means "between rivers" and refers to that region of land to the east of Palestine between the Tigres and Euphrates rivers, corresponding to modern day Iraq. Three great cultures came from this region over the millennia: Sumeria, Babylon, and Assyria.

Messenger formula Refers to a typical phrase that introduces speech that is represented as coming from Yahweh. Most characteristic is "thus says Yahweh"; or the concluding phrase, "a saying of Yahweh."

Messiah This represents the English equivalent of the Hebrew word *masiah,* meaning "anointed one." The Greek word *christos* represented the Greek translation of "anointed one." *Christos* is transliterated into English simply as "Christ."

Micro-level intertextuality/intertext A close intersection between two texts, accompanied by a high degree of verbal correspondence, such as when one text quotes from or offers a near quotation of another text. See MACRO-LEVEL INTERTEXTUALITY.

Midrash From the Hebrew word meaning "to search out," it denotes a method of Jewish scriptural interpretation that was primarily concerned with the contemporary meaning and application of a scriptural text.

Minor prophets The designation reflects the length of the prophetic book, not the relative significance of the message or contribution. The "Twelve" minor prophets are grouped together at the very least because the collection fits on a single scroll.

Mishnah A collection of the teachings of the Rabbis gathered into written form toward the end of the second century CE.

New Testament The collective term used to denote the twenty-seven documents that make up the second half of the Christian Bible. The documents were written by followers of Jesus between ca. 50 and 150 CE.

Old Testament The collective term used to denote the documents that make up the first half of the Christian Bible. The documents of the Hebrew Bible provide its foundation.

Oracles against the Nations A distinct prophetic genre whereby prophets denounced political entities that were perceived as a threat to Israel or Judah.

Palestine A term used by Greeks and the Roman government (*Palaestina*) to denote the traditional homeland of the Jews.

Pantheism From the Greek words "all" (*pan*) and "god" (*theos*), it denotes the belief that god or the gods permeate all things.

Pantheon Designates all of the deities that function within the religious system of any polytheistic worldview.

Parable Most commonly, it denotes a simple story that compares one thing to another. Jesus employed this genre of story, often using it to compare the kingdom of God to the subject matter of the story he was telling.

Paraclete From the Greek term often translated as "counselor" or "advocate," it is the term used to denote the Holy Spirit in the Gospel of John. In some sense the Paraclete functions in John's gospel to represent Jesus after his departure from earth.

Parousia It is literally the Greek word for "presence." Early followers of Jesus used the term to denote the expectation of experiencing again in the future the full "presence" of Jesus, when he came at the designated time to manifest his cosmic lordship. Many people today refer to this idea by using the phrase "the second coming of Jesus."

Passion narrative(s) Early Christian narrative(s) about Jesus' arrest, trial, and execution.

Passover An Israelite festival that eventually came to celebrate God's deliverance of Israel from the bondage of Egypt (the Exodus).

Patriarchs The forefathers of the Israelites, usually restricted to Abraham, Isaac and Jacob.

Pentateuch Is a Greek term meaning "five" (*penta*) "scrolls" (*teuchos*). In scholarly parlance it refers to the first five books of the Hebrew and Christian Bibles (or the Torah).

Pentecost Originally an agricultural festival that took place fifty ("Pentecost" derives from the Greek word for fifty) days after Passover (Lev 23:15–22). In Acts it denotes the day when God gave the Holy Spirit to Jesus' disciples (Acts 2:1–13).

Pericope A term used by biblical scholars to denote a small, self-contained unit of biblical material. It is especially used to denote the individual stories about and the sayings of Jesus in the gospels.

Persian period Designates the period of ancient history when the Persian empire dominated the world. Their political influence extended from 539 to 333 BCE, when Alexander the Great conquered them.

Pesherim The singular form of which is *Pesher,* the word *Pesherim* comes from a Hebrew root that means "interpretation." Thus, a Pesher was an interpretation and was produced in the form of commentaries upon older biblical texts.

Pharisees Meaning "separated ones," the term denotes a pious lay movement of Judaism emerging most likely during the second century BCE. They focused their attention on the application of biblical law to all aspects of life. They often held opinions that contrasted with those of the Sadducees.

Philistines Refers to a people who lived along the cities of the southern coastal plain of Palestine. They were non-semitic, having migrated from the Aegean area in the twelfth century BCE.

Philo A Jewish philosopher who lived in Alexandria, Egypt, during the first century CE. His writings, which attempt to combine Jewish law and tradition with Greek philosophy, offer an example of how some Jews sought to relate their religion to the larger culture.

Polemic/Polemical Denotes conflict and struggle. Theological positions are often held in opposition to other conflicting points of view. Therefore those views are called polemical points of view.

Post-Exilic Designates that period of time in the history of Judah after the Babylonian captivity.

Pre-Exilic Designates that period of time in the history of Israel and Judah prior to the Babylonian captivity.

Priestly A term scholars use to describe certain characteristics of a particular theological or ideological point of view as expressed in a passage of scripture. The usage of the term in this way derives from the hypothesis that the Pentateuch reflects several different theological perspectives, one of which derives from priestly schools of thought.

Priestly Code This term can refer in some instances to the more expansive materials throughout the Pentateuch that come from the hands of priestly editors. In other contexts it may refer to the Holiness Code (Leviticus 17–26) itself.

Primary text A text that is the object of investigation. In this textbook, the primary text is the Bible. By contrast, this textbook is a secondary text, since it aims to help one study the primary text.

Proselyte A gentile who converts to Judaism.

Pseudepigrapha Generally, this term denotes writings attributed to an author who is different from the real author. More specifically, scholars can use the term to denote a somewhat miscellaneous collection of Jewish religious texts dating roughly from second century BCE to the first century CE. See PSEUDONYMOUS AUTHORSHIP.

Pseudonymous authorship A term to denote "falsely named" authorship of a text. For example, most critical scholars believe that certain letters (e.g., 1 Timothy) attributed to Paul in the New Testament were not actually written by him; thus, they are "pseudonymous."

Purity Designates the state of being clean, or holy (see HOLINESS). The Jewish religion was a purity system, that is, an institution for defining the boundaries of cleanliness and uncleanliness.

Q From the German word for source (*Quelle*), *Q* designates a source some believe Matthew and Luke used in the composition of their gospels. See TWO-SOURCE HYPOTHESIS.

Qumran A wadi (or dry river bed) near the northwest corner of the Dead Sea, which served as the communal headquarters of a Jewish apocalyptic sect from the mid-second century BCE to the mid-first century CE. The Dead Sea Scrolls were produced here.

Rabbi A term originally denoting respect, often used by pupils as a way of referring to their teacher. As Judaism evolved, Rabbis emerged as the leadership of the Jewish community of faith.

Realized eschatology Term used by scholars to denote an early Christian belief that "end time" (eschatological) hopes were currently being "made real" (realized) in the ministry, death, and resurrection of Jesus.

Redaction criticism A method of reading used by biblical scholars that seeks the origins of literary passages in a preceding process of editing and interpretive arrangement of tradition. The tacit assumption is that preexisting oral and written stages of a tradition were joined together subsequently by editors who shaped these traditions into their final forms.

Sabbath Denotes the seventh day of the week, the day of rest. The word *sabbath* is related to the Hebrew verb "to rest."

Sacralize To attribute religious meaning to activities, ideas, persons, or social institutions, usually as a means of elevating authority.

Sadducees The aristocratic element of Jewish society, closely aligned with the ruling priesthood. This group made up the majority "party" of the Sanhedrin from the second century BCE to first century CE.

Salvation history A view of history that guides the biblical story, according to some contemporary biblical interpreters. In this view, history moves according to providential care for the ultimate purposes of achieving God's goal of saving his people.

Samaria The capital city of the northern kingdom of Israel. It was destroyed by the Assyrians in 721 BCE. In the New Testament the term denotes the geographical region located between Judea and Galilee.

Samaritans Inhabitants of the region of Samaria, they were the descendants of the kingdom of Israel who had intermarried with their Assyrian conquerers. Relations between the Samaritans and descendants of Judah were hostile.

Sanhedrin The Jewish governing council made up of elders and officials within the Jewish community. See SADDUCEES.

Scribes Originally denoting those who worked with texts, the scribes emerged in Jewish life as the persons responsible for the preserving, transmitting, and copying the Torah. Some were aligned with the Sadducees while others were aligned with the Pharisees.

Second Temple The term given to denote the Temple rebuilt by the Jews after the Exile. It was completed ca. 515 BCE. Herod the Great thoroughly refurbished it. It was destroyed by the Romans in 70 CE.

Sect/sectarian Denotes a smaller, at times self-isolating, group within a larger religious tradition. The smaller group, the sect tends to see itself as the true expression of the larger tradition, thereby viewing suspiciously the more "mainstream" expressions of the religious tradition. Some would call the early Christians a sect of first-century Judaism.

Self-text The sum total of a person's (a "self's") knowledge, experiences, values, etc. that one brings to the act of interpreting a text.

Septuagint (abbreviated LXX) One of the Greek translations of the Hebrew Bible, which was initiated ca. 250 BCE. In addition to translating texts found in the Hebrew Bible, it translated other texts. The Septuagint, including its translation of texts in addition to the Hebrew Bible, was the Bible of the first Christians, leading many Christians to recognize these other texts as scripture alongside the texts of the Hebrew Bible. See DEUTEROCANONICALS.

Shiloh A town in the central hill country of Palestine that served as one of the the central shrines in ancient Israel. The Ark of the covenant was kept there before the Temple in Jerusalem was built.

Sicarii Jewish rebels of the first century CE, known to use small daggars (*sicae*) to assassinate opponents.

Social Text The text of culture; a way of referring under the rubric of Intertextuality to the social/cultural/historical environment of a Literary text.

Succoth A celebration commemorating the time when the Hebrews, en route from Egypt, lived in "booths" or "tabernacles."

Suzerain A nation or king that has power over another nation but allows it domestic independence.

Synagogue From the Greek word meaning "to gather together," it denotes Jewish places of worship and study.

Syncretism/syncretistic The practice of combining features of originally different beliefs or practices.

Synoptic Gospels Denotes the first three gospels of Matthew, Mark, and Luke; so named because they are so similar in content and structure. In a manner of speaking, they may be read with one (*syn*) eye (*optic*). See TWO-GOSPEL HYPOTHESIS; TWO-SOURCE HYPOTHESIS.

Syria Denotes that country just to the north of Palestine whose capital city was traditionally Damascus. It is a region of high mountains and is especially known for Mt. Hermon.

Tabernacle Designates the portable tentlike shrine that the Hebrews carried with them in the desert. It served as a meeting place for Moses and the deity.

Targum This is an Aramaic word that comes from the root *regam,* meaning "to translate," thus it is itself a translation. Targums were very likely produced in the context of scripture reading in the Synagogue as a means of making the Hebrew scripture understandable to the Aramaic speaking audience.

Testament A genre of literature well represented among the Pseudepigrapha and within the Bible that portrays a worthy figure of the past (often remote), who offers to followers or children a farewell discourse dealing with important issues pertaining to the time of the testament's composition.

Theocracy Designates a state that is ruled by God rather than an earthly king. The deity rules through his priests and their Temple rather than through political advisors and a royal court.

Theology/theological From the Greek words meaning "reason," "thought," or "talk" (*logos*) and "god" (*theos*). Hence, theology refers to what one thinks or says about god or divine/supernatural matters more generally.

Theophany/theophanic Designates the appearance of a god. As an adjective the term refers to specific physical events that accompany the appearance of a god.

Tiglath-Pileser King of Assyria from 745–727 BCE. Known in the Bible as Pul (2 Kgs 15:19). Responsible in large measure for the initial eighth-century military expansion of the Assyrian empire toward the Mediterranean region. He conquered the smaller states of the area.

Torah May be used in either of two ways: First, the term designates the first section of the Hebrew Bible; the Law (see PENTATEUCH); second, the term means "instruction," and usually designates a priestly instruction regarding cultic matters.

Two-Gospel Hypothesis A hypothesis held by a minority of New Testament scholars to explain the literary relationship between the Synoptic Gospels. It proposes that Matthew was the first gospel written. Matthew was used by Luke. Mark then used and condensed these two gospels in writing his.

Two-Source Hypothesis A hypothesis held by a majority of New Testament scholars to explain the literary relationship between the Synoptic Gospels. It proposes that Mark was the first gospel written. Matthew and Luke each used Mark, along with a now-lost second source, designated as "Q," to compose their gospels.

Typology/typological A method of interpretation wherein the literal and historical meaning of a text is taken seriously, but where the interpreter also attempts to find a more significant meaning that corresponds to his or her present situation. Compare ALLEGORY.

Urim and Thummim Designate some kind of objects that were used by priests to determine God's will. They were cast and, depending upon the particular nature of their physical orientation, they determined the answers to specific questions.

Vassal A nation or king who is subject or subserviant to another nation or king.

Wisdom literature Biblical writings devoted to an intellectual tradition that apparently thrived within ancient Israel. The biblical books include Proverbs, Job, and Ecclesiastes, and reflect a worldview that, though religious, attempts to conceive of the world in terms of human processes of intellection, reason, reflection, and poetic formulation.

Worldview Designates a comprehensive set of social, cultural, political, and theological assumptions that provides a particular society with values and beliefs of ultimate significance. Compare SOCIAL TEXT.

Yahweh The name of the Israelites' god as it has been vocalized through the addition of the vowels for the Hebrew word for "lord," *'adonay,* to the unvocalized Hebrew consonants YHWH, the deity's name. *YHWH* is represented in most English Bibles either as LORD or GOD.

Zadok The priest who had formerly served David alongside his colleague Abiathar. Abiathar was ousted by David's son Solomon. After the rise of Solomon, according to 1–2 Kings, the family of Zadok ruled the priesthood of the Temple (see 1 Kgs 2:26–27).

Zadokite Adjectival form of Zadok that describes families and priestly institutions and practices that are associated with the priestly family of Zadok.

Zealots Anti-Roman Jewish revolutionaries that formed one of the rebel factions of the revolt of 66–73 CE. Some scholars use the term more broadly to refer collectively to all first-century CE Jews who violently opposed Roman rule.

Index of Topics, Persons, and Biblical Books

Index of Biblical Texts Discussed

Index of Closer Look Boxes

Index of Maps